PETER COOKSON SMITH

THE URBAN DESIGN OF INTERVENTION

IMPOSED AND
ADAPTIVE PLACES
IN ASIAN CITIES

CONTENTS

FOREWORD

The term "Asia" is an evocative umbrella for what is, in practice, quite massive diversity in terms of cultural patterns, geographic spread, density and complexity of urban environments. Cities in large countries such as China, India, Indonesia, Japan, and the Philippines together with cities within IndoChina and the Straits Settlements, embody innate and distinctive regional, cultural and historical differences. Commonalities can be difficult to pinpoint within such a heterogeneous area that makes up 20 per cent of the planet's total area, and more than half of its population at a density three times the world average.

Asia, like the West, is now so urban in nature that we tend to take its context for granted. The first "urban system" made its appearance around 5,500 years ago in the Mesopotamian region. This was followed by civilisation in the Indus Valley around one thousand years later, and the cradle of civilization in China began around 1500 BC in the Chang'an-Xi'an region. The essential catalyst for this was that these latitudes and geographies were suitable for farming and irrigation from the great rivers. In the 1800s the rate of global urbanization was still only around 5 per cent. Even in 1950 only 18 per cent of people in Asia lived in cities. At the beginning of the third millennium this has multiplied ten-fold.

The notion of exploring Asian cities through their interventionist history follows a course plotted in two previous books: *The Urban Design of Impermanence* on Hong Kong, and *The Urban Design of Concession* on the growth and transformation of the Chinese Treaty Ports. Underlying this is the conjecture that much of the design and form of cities that we perceive today can be traced back to identifiable catalytic processes that go a long way towards explaining why cities have grown in the way they have and, to a great extent, look the way they do. In Asia the various galvanising forces with regard to urbanisation have been a burgeoning maritime economy from the fourteenth century; intra-Asian trends in immigration; and, from the late sixteenth century, colonisation stemming initially from the opening up of new trading routes with the West, military invasion and occupation. In the post-colonial situation globalisation has largely been the major force for physical and economic change.

Looking at a selection of Asian cities, through the lens of interventionist influences, tends to suggest an emphasis on historical studies relating to places and incidents. However an interpretation of urban design needs to go beyond that, through an ontological approach which maps out various aspects — economic, social and cultural in relation to "place". The urbanization process itself is a normative one and if critically examined, goes some way to explaining, or at least rationalizing, the resulting urban forms. In carrying out studies on cities, the general modes of inquiry are therefore a combination of three aspects: *descriptive* based on historical evidence relating to specific events and the related evolution of stylistic characteristics; *empirical*, through actual observation and experience that relate to physical attributes of cities as well as natural processes; and *theoretical* based on deductions made on the basis of knowledge and research. The book has been pieced together over a period of several years. Some of the city studies I was familiar with, others less so, and one or two not at all. The general direction and compilation process has therefore been to research each city from a historical and planning perspective up to a certain point, visit the city in question with a broad itinerary, wear out a lot of shoe leather, and talk with as many knowledgable people as possible. Even with cities we think we know well, exploration on foot is really the only way to truly understand them and assimilate their patterns of use. In so doing it is possible to highlight the complex interactions between people and their surroundings and the values that stem from this. A knowledge of how cities came about, how they are used, perceived and lived in, helps to bring together urban design theory and practice.

Visually representing intervention by means of sketches is a deliberately fragmented means of conveying character of a locale, but its meaning must relate to the wider spatial unit — the district, territory or street. In general this embodies its own organisational logic related to urban texture, neighbourhood place, and the wider vocabulary of settlement. Thus the prevalent morphology is in some cases expressed through figure ground plans while the city fabric and texture are presented through drawings which attempt to capture the prevalent sense of place.

The book is based on the premise that urban planning and design solutions to the massive programme of urbanisation in Asian cities require an understanding of historical, cultural and political dynamics that have created the physical condition of the modern city. Cities are grouped according to broad geographic areas that might be expected to display certain cultural and ethnic commonalities, where vernacular patterns of settlement and interventionist incident have become assimilated and intertwined. In practice however, cities are subject to the indeterminate interstices of growth, change and evolving relationships between neighbouring countries, which help to shape their urban design in unpremeditated ways.

PREFACE

The book examines a selection of Asian cities through the prism of urban design and its interwoven cultural values which have, in various combinations, contributed to existing city forms and settlement patterns. This brings together three abstract concepts — Asia, Intervention and Urban Design. The first is a somewhat broad geographic term that embraces some of the largest and most diverse concentrations of population in the world; the second relates to a series of events and forces to which Asian countries and cities have been subject over the centuries; and the third represents different spatial outcomes that have emerged and evolved as a result of these interactions.

Asia has no overall historical unity — it embraces large land masses and archipelagos divided by the Indian Ocean, the Andaman Sea, the South China Sea and the Pacific Ocean, and is bisected by massive riverine systems such as the Yangtze, Mekong, Irrawaddy, Ganges, Indus and Chao Phraya, around which capitals and port cities came into being. It is separated from Europe by the Ural Mountains and the Caspian Sea, but can be further defined by breaking it down into sub-regions which vary significantly, and which for many centuries were relatively isolated from each other. East and Central Asia includes China, Korea and Japan; South Asia includes India, Pakistan and Bangladesh; while Southeast Asia covers the Indo-Chinese states of Myanmar (Burma), Thailand, Vietnam, Cambodia and Laos, together with the Malaysian archipelago, Singapore, Indonesia, Brunei and the Philippines. These sub-regions embody topographical and climatic extremes, unique indigenous traditions, overlapping ethnic and linguistic patterns, and complex religious rituals and ideologies that are both embodied and expressed in the contemporary city. Asian cities include some of the largest conurbations in the world — Tokyo, Beijing, Shanghai, Jakarta, Mumbai (Bombay) and Kolkata (Calcutta). A number of Asian countries, including China, now house more than 50 per cent of their people in cities, and the extended Tokyo — Yokohama corridor accommodates around 30 per cent of the country's entire population. China is now planning to build 100 cities of more than one million people, and by 2025, 21 cities in Asia will have populations in excess of ten million.

The Asian city is in transition, from a situation where the slow stream of influences over the centuries has generated a precarious balance between flourishing but very different urban cultures and subcultures, with latterly a surge of commonalities generated through the dominant forces of globalisation. From a post-colonial situation where embedded traditions were insinuated in modernising interventions to meet rising aspirations, rapid economic development in recent years has produced a force field that continues to induce unprecedented disruption to long-standing development patterns. Commonalities can be difficult to pinpoint within such a heterogeneous geographic area that contains almost 60 per cent of the planet's population. The notion of orchestrated cityscape and imageability that characterise Western urban design is generally derived from a 'picturesque' ideal centred around compositional appreciation that posits the individual as an appreciative observer. However, the Asian city, despite long-standing Western influences, generally displays a more pragmatic and expressive vocabulary of sensory values related to the behavioural setting and the miscellany of use. In the process this creates a more socially expressive and economically responsive street environment. A variety of urban forms and textures reflects the simultaneous existence of complexity and pattern out of which emerges its underlying urban design framework.

Urban design is a somewhat open-ended term that can just as easily relate to a place marked by architectural heritage as to an established gathering space with strong but informal cultural connotations. It is in fact the public face of human settlement and spatial organisation, historically expressed through elusive narratives of myth, memory, power and aspiration, and is the means of articulating a conceptual physical vocabulary in relation to various long-term processes. This acts to emphasise a link between cultural form and the social organisation of urban space, which in turn contributes to urban identity. But the Asian city has, at the same time, been the historic repository of monumental religious edifices, palace citadels and fortifications, which in the past signified concentrations of power and elitism. Today it must interface with the wider values of urbanism with its integral but often ambiguous blend of historical and cultural factors, economic functions, social structures, political processes and other related urban interventions. The three-dimensional outcome is therefore an identifiable and occasionally symbolic result of inter-relationships and attributes which merge in the distinctive character of urban places — something that Sharon Zukin has described as 'the landscape of contemporary transformation'.[1]

Miscellaneous forces have left a residue of urban imprints on the Asian city, brought more recently into focus through the economic and spatial consequences of globalisation. Urban design in the modern age must therefore address the whole — how places look, how they work and what sustains them. It must also connect with the residential and working communities themselves which

[1] Zukin, S, *The Culture of Cities*, Blackwell, London, 1995

ultimately determine the success of the urban design process, and the involvement of stakeholders who are the mainstay of its workability. The values that result from this are key to understanding the urbanity of the Asian city and the ability to bring about its betterment.

While the fate of cities and their mother countries tend to run together, the urban design of intervention is about the former, albeit subject to the fortunes or otherwise of the latter. As city planning is directed increasingly to government's economic and management interests and the homogenizing effects of zoning to meet a common global agenda, an important aspect is not merely to retain traditional references, but to embrace adaptability and ensure a constantly changing mix of uses and ownerships — a "structured turbulence" that remains a strong characteristic of the traditional multi-layered urban neighbourhood. The shaping of urban design patterns in Asia, just as much as anywhere else, embodies a historical meaning. What might at first appear organic or informal in its present state, might just as easily be the result of early settlement imprints, regulatory regimes, land ownership structures or trading trajectories. Cultural expression in terms of urban form is not merely the natural outcome of these but the result of their collision with interventionist forces.

Amid the vast interventions on the contemporary urban landscape — the modernised fabric of commercial and residential quarters with their towering business districts and high rise estates contained by primary road corridors — there is a parallel universe of indigenous urban space. This might include the remaining Ming dynasty *hutongs* of Beijing, the *sichuyen* of Shanghai, the traditional gated *roji* of Tokyo, the *chowks* of Delhi, the *travessas* of

Macau or the *durbars* of Kathmandu, many of which help to establish spatial continuity and identity. In contrast, Hong Kong's traditional vertical urbanism operates through an intense three-dimensional matrix of mixed uses, each interfacing in a private and public juxtaposition dictated by compressed convenience and the ebbs and flows of the free market.

Saskia Sassen suggested in 'The Global City' that an increasingly globalised economy is creating new strategic functions: first as 'concentrated command points' of headquarter functions, second as specialised service and finance centres, and third as areas of innovative industrial production.[2] These continue to have a significant impact on changing urban form and ways in which the social and economic order of Asian cities are being restructured and reshaped through new forms of capital investment, overlapping divisions of labour and redirected spatial patterns. In addition cities have to continually upgrade their services to remain competitive. Sassen argues that it is precisely the territorial dispersal of certain types of activity, facilitated by new communication and information systems, that accounts for a continuation of high density centralised agglomerations of specialised services, such as that developing in Hong Kong in relation to the Pearl River Delta. This encourages increasingly innovative organisational systems relating to production, finance, management and advanced corporate and professional service industries that are transforming how activities are carried out, and can be readily observed in Asia through a continual shift of manufacturing industries to countries or cities with lower production costs. Asia's primate cities, in the throes of increasing competition for investment, are therefore fuelled by both local and foreign capital leading to large scale redevelopment

and regeneration which is transforming city space and establishing new cultural meaning to built environments. In this sense the process of globalisation is in some cases leading to increasingly homogenised city quarters, while in others it stimulates more transformative and heterogeneous qualities, further accentuated by large-scale migration of labour.

A typical "figure ground plan" of the dense Asian city core illustrates, in virtually every case, a duality of both fine and course grained urban space patterns that have emerged, not as part of a definitive master plan, but as a by-product of indeterminate development processes, diverse planning decisions and regulatory mechanisms, where inter-relationships and long-term impacts were rarely considered in rational urban design terms. Similarly the modulated disposition of contrived building composition and large urban spaces has never developed in the Asian city, unless through foreign intervention or as a form of political expression such as Beijing's Tienanmen Square. Instead incidental "pocket spaces" and gardens together with the residue of colonial military spaces — such as the *Maidan* and *Padang* — act as places of serene contrast to the busy streets of the compact Asian city, while informal and interconnected spaces and routes become places of encounter and transaction, marked by high user flows and crowded configurations.

It must also be acknowledged that the notion of architectural legitimacy is itself a Western preoccupation. Much of the indigenous city building in Asia up to the modern age was produced by artisans, craftsmen and self-builders who were both open and susceptible to a range of immediate influences and resources. Thus, design references in practice came from far and wide but nevertheless met the prevailing needs.

Examining a cross-section of Asian cities

2 Sassen, S, *The Global City*, New York, London, Tokyo, Princeton University Press, 2001

in terms of different realms of intervention provides an opportunity to identify both the historical and current drivers of growth and change. Implicit in this are the contemporary influences that include increased rates of immigration to cities from rural areas, and an accelerating process of urbanisation that introduces a significant impact on social, economic and physical development patterns. Urbanisation is a key driver of infrastructure planning, but poses severe challenges in terms of funding. The majority of this at present represents direct funding from governments, and it is almost inevitable that capital markets will be induced to play a greater role in urban development.

Interventions come in a variety of ways, and go some way to establishing not only why cities work in the way they do, but also how they are shaped and experienced. It is possible for example to acknowledge and appreciate older city building forms in various ways, while not altogether accepting some of the circumstances that produced them. This also gives some indication as to how resilient the inherent socio-cultural elements and traditions are to political and economic change, and how interdependencies and persistencies can be induced to both inform and mitigate the impacts of new development.

Section One examines aspects of intervention that have shaped some of Asia's largest cities, and continue to influence city form and urban traditions.

Chapter 1 sets out an introduction to the region and the city. The broad cultural and transformative processes, and realms of intervention are examined in relation to South, Southeast, East and Central Asia.

Chapter 2 discusses the contested identities associated with cultural heritage in terms of changing traditional value systems; cultural identity in terms of its association with tangible and intangible heritage; the equation of cultural and functional identity; patterns of land tenure and ownership; textual interpretation through place name connotations; and shophouse design typologies in their representation of Chinese trading and migration trajectories.

Chapter 3 discusses the colonial interventionist process in Asian cities in terms of the prolonged impact on urban design through imperial city-building ideologies; the representation of urban space; colonial planning and city building; the design paradoxes of ethnic segregation; and the political purpose behind urban design from the late nineteenth century.

Chapter 4 examines the spatial transformation resulting in the economic transition during the twentieth century to modern post-industrial and manufacturing economies which are shaping new morphologies. This encompasses the process of globalisation in restructuring the city region and the implications for urban design; the growth of primate cities as institutional foci of development; operational chains which extend into diverse city regions and give rise to expanding urban footprints; mega-urban regions and their impact on material welfare in the cities themselves; and the emerging geography of agglomeration in the Asian city.

Chapter 5 examines the design dimensions of the Asian street and public place realm, and interprets their various characteristics in relation to distinctive types and patterns of activity.

Section Two examines the roots of urban design through interventionist processes and phenomena in twenty Asian cities, and their spatial evolution up to the present time.

CHAPTER 1

INTRODUCTION

THE REGION AND THE CITY

Prior to the European arrival in Asia, there were two predominant urban settlement types that had flourished for many hundreds of years. The first was the "sacred" settlement which generally served as both a capital containing a seat of kingship, and as an organisational centre related to surrounding patterns of agricultural development, overland trade routes and economic administration. Cities such as Angkor, Ayutthaya, Luang Prabang, Borobudor and Majapahit, along with Xian in China, functioned as symbolic hubs of divine authority and bureaucratic government, where morphologies reflected both celestial intersections and religious imagery broadly related to Hinduism and Buddhism. The second settlement type was the port city that acted as an entrepôt in relation to strategic sea routes and long-established maritime relationships with other Asian cities. The status of cities such as Malacca, Macassar, Timor and Brunei came not from territorial gain, but from economic power arising from commercial alliances through a far-flung network of trading centres that Western interests were later able to plug into, and in many cases exploit. What is sometimes known as the 'Asian Corridor' broadly corresponded to the continental and maritime Silk Route, together with the 'Mongolian Corridor', along trajectories that were most propitious to the transport of merchandise. The discovery of the route from Europe to India by Vasco da Gama in 1497 gave rise to new port cities in the West such as Venice and Genoa, and the birth of world maritime empires: the Spanish, Portuguese, Dutch, French and English, which were to have a significant role in the emergence of new Asian townships and ocean cities. In the late nineteenth century many of these became hubs of railway traffic, opening up new inland cities which rapidly evolved through inter-city communications networks.

Early Asian cities were based on the ideological relationship of a ruling elite and its associated military and religious bureaucracy. The ritualised and ceremonial order created a cultural basis for urban layouts — for example Yogyakarta is focussed around the palace or *Kraton* of the Sultan, and neighbourhoods were symbolically structured through the relationship of land holdings to the palace, with a sense of grandeur reinforced through monuments and institutions. Bangok's Royal City, with its complex network of buildings, radiates a sacred presence and an associated public space, *Sanam Luang*, provides a site for public gatherings and a stage for ceremonies. The urban "centre" has therefore traditionally been conferred with special status in relation to an elite social or ruling hierarchy.

Urbanisation in Asia is not an alien phenomenon entirely associated with colonisation, although this in itself was a major urbanising force. Older cities were essentially market centres which created an urban culture through the amalgamation of cosmopolitan trading influences and extended associations with productive hinterlands. Cities such as Edo housed up to a million people in the seventeenth century, although most urban centres had populations of around 50,000. Major Asian cities of today all had pre-colonial origins, but the advent of European settlement brought about planned urbanisation, with cities linked to an increasingly extensive pattern of global trading routes. Almost all countries experienced colonial intervention, some

The Angkor complex in Northern Cambodia (left); Taxila – the urban product of Graeco Indian Culture from the fourth century BC (below)

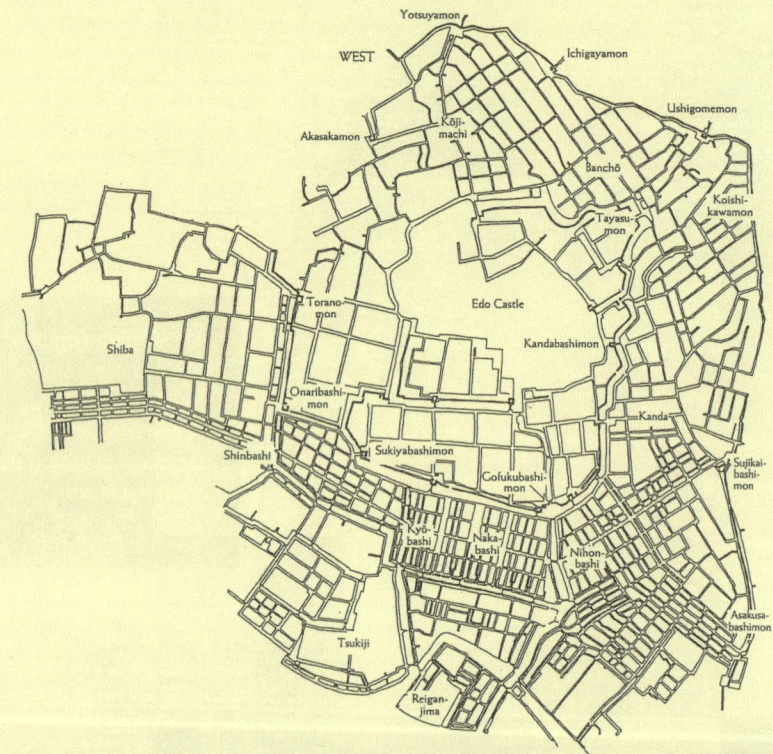

WEST

Yotsuyamon
Ichigayamon
Ushigomemon
Akasakamon
Kōji-machi
Banchō
Koishi-kawamon
Tayasu-mon
Torano-mon
Edo Castle
Shiba
Kandabashimon
Onaribashi-mon
Kanda
Shinbashi
Sukiyabashimon
Sujikai-bashi-mon
Cofukubashi-mon
Kyō-bashi
Naka-bashi
Nihon-bashi
Tsukiji
Asakusa-bashimon
Reigan-jima

Plan of Edo (ancient Tokyo), seventeenth century

several times over, which left a profound mark on political development, economic health and cultural continuity. With the growth of urban populations in colonial port cities, land took on value, usually associated with a planned hierarchy of spaces which developed as ethnic quarters, largely reflecting social, cultural and economic standing. These helped define both the spatial and architectural make-up of expanding cities.

Western trading and colonial invasion from the sixteenth century prompted a swift transition from early forms of commerce towards a more dynamic commercial order that still resonates in contemporary urbanisation. Redfield and Singer labelled this as representing a transition from an 'orthogenetic' or traditional and relatively feudal state, to a 'heterogenetic' state that generated new cultural and economic trajectories through a combination of influences, including forces of migration and

international acumen.[1] During the early period of Western intervention urban centres were developed in the coastal communities of Asia, founded by trading companies. Urbanisation grew rapidly during the mercantile era in response to a new ideology of material accumulation and industrialisation which saw the emergence of a new middle class. The wealthy merchant class, indigenous or otherwise, generally overcame artificially induced boundaries as colonial city economies developed to include government employment, specialist institutions, banks and shipping companies.

Western imperialism did not simply lay the foundations for some of the largest cities in Asia, it was responsible for major migration of labour, new ethnic configurations, and a new capitalist order. In the process it induced far-reaching patterns of international trade. Above all, it restructured and in most cases redirected the process of city building. Indigenous cultural institutions were absorbed rather than subordinated, but the result was a transformation of city form through urban planning.

From the turn of the twentieth century, primate cities began to massively outstrip second-tier cities in terms of both economic and demographic growth, largely through their development as centres of government and administration. However large-scale rural-urban migration was largely a phenomenon of post-independence situations that firstly tended to reflect political instability, and later a transfer of power to an urban elite which in most situations has sustained a capitalist outlook towards the economic challenges of industrialisation and globalisation. At the end of World War II only 17 per cent of

1   Redfield, R and Singer, M 'The Cultural Role of Cities', in *Economic Development and Cultural Change*, 3(1), 1954, p53-73

Asians lived in cities. By 2014 this exceeded 50 per cent, one of the chief influences being the pre-eminence of primate cities which in certain situations have evolved into mega-urban regions as a result of concentrated economic development and investment. A fundamental difference between Western and Asian city regions from the 1990s is that the latter situation includes densely populated rural enclaves on the peri-urban fringe which have been drawn into the city ambit through industrialisation while also embracing lingering rural characteristics.

The spatial consequence of unregulated urban development is a mix of dense but dispersed settlements, increasingly consolidated and integrated through primary road and service infrastructure, but which in some cases has led to environmental and ecological degradation and the relocation of productive agricultural land to areas further afield. On the positive side, spatial dispersion has brought about wider capital accumulation, increased job opportunities and housing choice provided by privately built townships. City cores have been regenerated through redevelopment at an accelerating rate, which technically provides for a relatively sustainable situation providing that a balance can be retained between economic momentum and urban growth. This is not always the case however. The Asian economic crisis in 1997 had crippling repercussions for some Asian cities (such as Bangkok and Jakarta), that reflected a speculative misreading of development demand and the dynamics of growth, and continues to underscore the need for both regional planning control and public investment in infrastructure.

Temporary structures along the railway alignment, Dharavi, Bombay

The growth of a significant middle class through urban-industrial growth and the rise of business interests has transformed many cities from centres of production to theatres of accumulation and consumption. This has created on one hand a requirement for mass housing at high densities, and on the other a responsive new architecture of retail, entertainment and cultural infrastructure geared to the changing economic profiles of users — both citizens and visitors. These multiple landscapes reflect a range of subcultures endowed with different needs and building requirements at a time when civil society is asserting changing social agendas and political reform movements in the wake of the centralised and authoritarian regimes of the immediate post-colonial period. However in most Asian countries the state assumes a major role in transforming urban space and delineating its symbolic qualities. Public investment has entailed the adoption of ever more complicated measures to control city design and layout, such as zoning, building regulations, planning ordinances and resumption mechanisms. The growth of motorised transport has facilitated new forms of agglomeration through suburban development and sub-centers, which have in recent years given rise to urban ribbon development and linear corridors which have merged hitherto separate settlements.

CULTURAL CHANGE

The Asian city represents substantial cultural shifts in its twenty-first century manifestation, with new and different values superimposed on long established patterns of urbanisation. Mega-urban regional growth patterns provide for different degrees of co-existence and overlap, and frequently reflect dual economic structures where both cutting-edge technologies and pre-industrial interconnected networks of small businesses operate virtually side by side. This leaves open the question of how urban design should respond to situations where cultural bonds with the past are being steadily eroded through the homogenising tendencies of globalisation, or sustained only artificially as tourist attractions. Because Asian cities have generally not inherited the formalist configuration of spaces and the highly defined public realm of most European cities, nor necessarily a systemic organisational framework that underpins the urban structure, the term 'Westernisation' in its current sense is more about the internationalisation of business, finance and technology than formalistic layouts. This might be said to represent a new and innovative type of post-colonialism, where cities are extended or manipulated on a similar vast scale to their colonial forebears but where economic rather than overriding political priorities tend to hold sway. This underscores David Harvey's assertion that urbanism should be viewed as 'the history of the system of cities within, between and around which surplus value circulates at any particular moment'.[2]

The majority of East Asian societies share Confucianist traditions that emphasise community ideals, manifested in cultural and social values. However the practice is far from uniform and is culturally indistinct. While Confucianism has been diluted by advancing materialistic influences associated with capitalism and globalisation, cultural differences shape the dimensions of change and urban transformation. The city has become the vehicle through which the forces of change are acted out. At the same time, as cities take on similar spatial signatures, there is a commensurate resurrection of cultural heritage to form beacons of city identity and foci of visitation.

Urban change is continuous — in some situations it is dramatic while in others it is more elusive. In some states, a longstanding noble or imperialist elite gave way to colonial dominance or socialist authoritarianism, establishing new political and economic hierarchies that controlled national resources. In others, urban change has evolved more gradually and less dramatically, and cities themselves have appropriated concentrations of power and economic organisation that have recast their physical form. Cultural variants are often the result of urban palimpsests whereby new forms are themselves influenced and shaped by the imprints and interactions of their predecessors. The catalytic impacts of these interfaces generate different urban redevelopment and regeneration patterns, but also introduce a variety of economic and social structures. Rapid change in these values, together with globalising forces, tend to result in a pragmatic sensitivity towards other contemporary priorities such as a sustainable environment. A realisation of this helps to guide the urban planning process itself, and reinforces the value of urban places. It also promotes the co-existence and interplay of cultural types that establish a particular urban chemistry and are arguably more important in the Asian city than its purely physical form. An attachment to place on the part of many urban communities breaks down at the point where localities no longer foster and facilitate mutation and adaptation, and where people are no longer engaged or participate actively in the process of growth and change. At worst the expedient process of redevelopment over regeneration obliterates the technically inefficient or uneconomic at the expense of heritage, or at best juxtaposes it with the evident prerequisites of modern cities — the traffic artery, the flyover and the superblock.

Cities that have evolved without the organisational discipline of an underlying growth strategy have come to represent a sequence of interventions overlaid on an indigenous fabric, with adaptations and superimpositions interfacing with natural characteristics that contribute to a localised blending of both the formal and informal. Urban space itself is never static in either its use or its component parts, and this in turn both facilitates and reflects changing cultural overlays, to be reconciled in turn with the conforming imperatives of modernisation. But historical persistencies and occasional cosmic influences still inject a considerable spatial presence in the form of sacred places and complicated realms of transaction. As these are confronted and challenged by the need to accommodate new and reshaped forms, densities and scales of building, the question arises as to the extent to which deeply embedded social customs and cultural beliefs

2 Harvey, D, *Social Justice and the City*, Edward Arnold, London, 1973

can continue to be insinuated as core values in developing cities.

The commodification of culture is an inevitable aspect of contemporary Asian urbanism. Cultural artifacts and heritage features, whether genuine or contrived, represent symbolic capital linked to lifestyle choices and amenities. This in turn influences the way in which cities are used and experienced. Rich and robust urban settings and sites for international gatherings or festivals have become the means to capture both business investment and a slice of the bourgeoning tourist market. Cities are increasingly refining cultural models, often grafted onto new development areas. In Singapore this is marked by a somewhat cosmetic upgrading of older ethnic quarters, while Hong Kong has invested in Disneyland as a means of attracting increased visitation from the Chinese mainland.

TRANSFORMATIVE PROCESSES

Urban design is about making cities, and the shaping of forms and patterns that in Asia, as much as anywhere else, embody an historical meaning. Asian cities as a whole, in their transition from feudalism to modernism, have oscillated over several centuries between centralised or imperial governmental structures, and decentralised or democratic ones. The city is also the space where local indigenous forces meet foreign or interventionist ones, establishing new political and economic hierarchies that control national resources. This has created, in various degrees, political, social and economic transformations, reflected by distinctive spatial patterns but also diverse development pressures and conflict over urban space.

Sense of dissonance in the Hong Kong street environment

The issue of an over-emphasis on urbanisation continues to be brought into focus as many parts of Asia extricate themselves from under-development. Some Asian countries project that their cities will contain 60 or even 70 per cent of their national populations by the mid-point of the twenty-first century. In the age of globalisation there is an obvious danger that cities will become less of an economic springboard for their populations, but rather a magnet for attractions or places of refuge as worldwide production processes become increasingly polarised. In the process, Asian cities are undergoing profound transformations with a blurring of urban boundaries and the traditional distinctions between city and periphery. This is accompanied by a mutation of the older cores as spiralling land costs lead to high-rise redevelopment and intensification, but also in some situations, to competition between 'centre' and 'sub-centre' employment hubs. At the same time city expansion is leading to patterns of urbanisation increasingly dominated by emerging development axes and hubs associated with international growth corridors.

As cities become more tangible and predictable they need to sustain the narratives of urbanism, and this implies a sense of dissonance common in the traditional Asian city — the chance of interaction and encounter, the unexpected, the complex and the indeterminate. But in the modern age, where renewal and regeneration procedures are increasingly institutionalized, the tendency is for city making, and therefore urban design, to become more absolutist and financially expedient, more restrictive and less porous. This is personified by two sets of economic operations which overlap and occasionally conflict: the growing commercial requirements of the service economy through its emphasis on impersonal transactions within virtually self-contained office environments; and the bazaar economy that has traditionally evolved around market places and mobile vendors, with specialised trades and products, and strong retail interfaces associated with active city streets, distinctive urban quarters and indigenous cultural institutions.

Most Asian cities have local persistencies that have been constantly adapted, creating patterns of use and ownership that cannot be neatly defined by either master planning or urban design, but which exert a considerable influence on community perception and the relationship of urban quarters to the city as a whole. This creates opportunities to retain or introduce ad-hoc aspects of place with distinctive forms of expression that relate to the underlying grain and help to break down uniformity.

In structuring an analysis of Asian urbanism while acknowledging the vast historical and cultural differences between cities, and with limited commonalities in the urban landscape, it is prudent to steer away from normative models. The utopian city, with its historicist references, is an unobtainable ideal quite simply because it is impossible to envision in the face of society's continual struggles to innovate, renew and modernise. There is also a paradox, in that deterministic urban renewal itself is largely an economic process, not necessarily responsive to cultural or even social ideals. Urban design methodologies should be about facilitating, balancing and invigorating the process — not a continual looking forward to the final product. By this token, planning and urban design must maintain a balance between past imperatives and future expectations so that the process of regeneration and growth relates simultaneously to physical fabric, social aspirations, economic conditions and environmental sustainability. This somewhat simplistic classification is not by any means the whole story — the process of growth and change together with the evolutionary overlap between broadly successive regimes

Trengganu Street – part of the "Chinatown" shophouse district of Singapore

and power structures produces many socio-spatial variations. In fact in almost every Asian city there is discernable evidence of a tangible co-existence between all qualitative characteristics.

Indigenous urban traditions are one of many constitutive layers that relate to post-modern Asian city building. Colonial practices generally reflected, at least in part, the need to ensure a stable social order, with a duality between traditional and informal production processes, and modern use of capital and

management. McGee noted that new divisions of labour were largely slow to emerge from the post-colonial city, but have accelerated in an extraordinary way since the 1980s. This was encouraged by funding from international agencies, which that has produced major sectoral shifts in national economies along with corresponding economic and class divisions.[3] Commensurate with this have been two related forces: first an ignited emphasis on transactional flows of capital, information, people and commodities, in association with increasing reliance on transportation and delivery systems which have become infrastructural and logistical drivers of a new urbanism; and second, spiralling consumption rates in relation to increasing wealth, expenditure and urban densification patterns, which perpetuates a realm of urban design built around lifestyle (shopping, food and entertainment uses), but also a massive growth of private housing estates and new towns through large-scale urban renewal and city expansion.

Rapid growth has transformed both social and spatial patterns within city enclaves. Cities and mega-urban regions (even within the same countries) compete for investment and visitation, along with the attractions to facilitate this — new airports, station 'gateways', science parks and convention centres — that are large enough to provide nodes of special but interlinked activities. As Asian city environments are re-fashioned, the traditional and authentic become marginalised or made more uniform, unless accommodated and reinvigorated through sensitive conservation and adaptive re-use.

Persistencies such as sacred places, gathering spaces, palace compounds,

[3] McGee, T. G., *Cultural Identity and Urban Change in Southeast Asia : Interpretive Essays*, Eds. Mark Askew and William S Logan, Deakin University Press, Geelong, 1994

speciality markets and bazaars together with indigenous mixed use quarters, also create 'locales of complexity' that characterise many older neighbourhoods. These remain intact, depending on their capacity to adjust to conditions within the new contested urbanism where different interest groups compete for priority and space, and where 'high' and 'low order' components often experience a less-than-stable relationship, usually existing together in informal allegiances through layering and overlap. In these situations, commercial transactions are fragmented yet are symbiotically connected, for example between street market operators and shops alongside. This juxtaposition of uses tends to be increasingly limited to older mixed use quarters, as more specialised zones of homogeneous land use such as central business districts, industrial estates and technology parks must meet increasingly high operational specifications. Similarly, labour-intensive "cottage" industries in wealthier cities are often restricted to certain older or ethnic quarters where zoning and adaptable lease conditions permit this type of use, or in poorer cities where there is little planning or environmental control.

The nature of socio-cultural change in Asia has varied considerably. Vietnam, Cambodia and Laos for example emerged from long periods of colonial domination to extremes of socialism and violent conflict, as did China from its periods of foreign domination and the ensuing Socialist Planned Economy under Mao. Beijing and Hanoi have therefore had to reconcile competitive forces for access to urban land uses — something that Phnom Penh and Yangon are now facing. In the process this is reconfiguring the relationship

Nakhon Pathom, Central Thailand

between society and the state, assisted by a commodification of exotic heritage and previously inaccessible monuments such as Angkor, Sukhothai, Burobudor, the Shwedagon and the Forbidden City. In the blossoming market economies, this new egalitarianism is reflected in people as opposed to political symbolism associated with urban space, but with commensurate development pressures on the still contested city landscape.

REALMS OF INTERVENTION
With the exception of ancient temple and palace complexes enfolded within the intricate cosmic symbolism governing

traditional cityspace, pre-industrial and agrarian communities in Asia mainly gave rise to spontaneous or relatively low-density settlements circumscribed only by natural geographic and climatic conditions. However at some stage over the past five hundred years, virtually all Asian societies became subject to significant interventionist forces through authoritarian control, military invasion, trading regimes, colonising ambitions or the proselytising zeal of imported religious beliefs. External intervention has arguably been a key factor in the physical layout and growth of most Asian cities. However it should be acknowledged that while cultural continuities have produced distinctive settings and rich variety, external forces have acted as galvanising elements in the evolution of urban land use patterns and spatial configurations. Their social and economic impacts produced periodic waves of immigration and emigration within Asia itself, importing or exporting building styles, and amalgamating these with prevailing development conditions to produce new or hybrid forms of urban design. These in turn determined future development patterns that became manifested in sequences of growth and change, influencing the predominant scale, form and architectural design of the urban settlements that we can perceive today, even as the regimented impact of contemporary globalising forces imparts an inevitable homogeneity to many city quarters.

There is some dispute as to who or what is the main generator of interventionist change in Asian cities — those who set public policy and promote development goals; those who underwrite the cost of necessary but transformative investment; those who hold political power and demonstrate cultural

The historic built heritage of Macau's old city is the result of over 400 years of cultural exchange between the Western world and Asia.

control; the strident emerging middle class who exert an enthusiastic materialist ideology; or the planners and designers who articulate the vision. In this sense the past inequalities of colonisation have been replaced by the unequal relationships and changes inherent in modernisation, made more complex by social and ethnic plurality. These are characterised by different customs and traditions that are emphasised and re-fashioned to meet contemporary needs and values which are themselves embedded in

new lifestyles. Possibly the most enduring characteristics shaped by this process are the design prototypes and adaptations that both symbolically and functionally relate architectural 'substructures' to climatic and environmental factors. Arguably the most ubiquitous example of this is the colonnaded street, as a consistent feature of the older Asian city.

Urban interventions represent direct change or interruption to social, economic, environmental and cultural conditions, or events. These tend to merge and overlap given the complex morphologies of Asian cities and the diversity of political and planning systems. However an overriding condition from the sixteenth century onwards has been that of Western intrusion. This initially represented exploratory and trading ambitions, but later extended to colonial regimes and political dependencies of varying persuasions up to the late-twentieth century, applied in particular to countries of South and Southeast Asia. Western religion in the form of Christianity, in its various strains, made tentative headroads in certain Asian countries, exemplified by the residue of ecclesiastical buildings, but in others was treated warily with bouts of antagonism and rejection. The perceptual barriers between East and West were generally tinged by conflict between the expansionist and 'civilising' regimes from the West which often disguised imperialist intentions, and the weight of tradition in Asia which emphasised philosophical religions and sacred strictures that are still deeply embedded in society, culture and ruling patterns.

In China the city historically represented an ordered state based on a social and moral protocol, the *Zhou-li*. Older urban forms

revolved around regularised concentrations of authority, and both geometric and geomantic design principles based on axiality and centrality. Until comparatively modern times, China represented an urban rural continuum, governed by highly regulated administrative regimes and a strong interdependence between the city and the natural order of the countryside, which created the pre-requisites for commercial activity. Cities that were occupied or strongly influenced by China in feudal times such as Seoul and Hanoi therefore took on centralised forms of concentration albeit with some spatial differentiation and strict regulations on lot sizes and buildings. While both Hanoi under the Mandarin monarchy and Edo under the Tokogawa Shogunate developed commoner cities in co-existence with royal citadels, the more severe application of Confucian principles and centralised bureaucracy in Beijing and Seoul discouraged forms of commercialisation until the nineteenth century.

Documenting the state of Asian cities suggests that in addition to examining their evolution, it is prudent to establish a rationale for their actual performance as a framework for understanding the tenuous links between past, present and future. The Asian city itself is a complex interaction of impositions and everyday choices that shape its physicality, increasingly governed by the economics of the marketplace at the expense of exclusiveness and overdevelopment. The involvement of small business is just as important an issue to the functioning and self-supporting city as larger global institutions, and these need to be kept in a dynamic balance. But the modernising Asian city is also a product of two

ST JAMES'S CHURCH lies to the east of the Kasmiri Gate within the old city of Delhi, built in 1836 by Colonel James Skinner. The church was built by army engineers in a neo-Classical style, with the dome sitting on an octagonal base. This and other British administration buildings were constructed on the site of seventeenth century mansions belonging to Shah Jahan's oldest son. Because of its proximity to the railway station the area became fashionable, and a centre for educational buildings.

other significant factors: a precipitate demand for improved and expanded accommodation, and an accompanying opportunity for innovation. Urban commentators have observed that a dynamic city mayor or equivalent, with powers to match and redolent of most developing cities in China, can make both prompt decisions and draw on the experiences, public initiatives and investment outcomes that have filtered through from elsewhere. The downside to this is the risk that opportunist administrative bodies can equally make questionable decisions to solve immediate rather than long-term problems, for the sake of political expediency. This can achieve the spirited uplifting of new waterfronts and upgraded heritage enclaves, but also the vertiginous battlements of new high-rise housing areas stretching behind them to the horizon.

In planning for the public good there must clearly be some degree of control and balance over private interests — in particular the social and economic rights associated with free market mechanisms to which most Asian societies now broadly subscribe. Western style democracy reflects the supposed rights of the individual, but the more nuanced version in Asia, with its varied history of strong and frequently inviolable government tenets, tends to prioritise protection of wider community interests and social organisation. The more the governing power is able to transmit legitimacy and inclusiveness, the more citizens accede to its rules. This in turn relates to the degree to which the community perceives that its well-being is a priority of government, and that private interests are made secondary to the public good.

It is estimated that cities in Asia will extend their population size by up to one billion new inhabitants by the mid-twenty-first century, and in China it is projected that in excess of 70 per cent of its population might be living in cities within the same time-frame. Cities must therefore renew and regenerate but also expand. As there is a continuing tendency in virtually every Asian country towards reduced household size, housing programmes must cater for increased numbers and sizes of dwellings to reflect growing urban wealth; more institutional and community buildings must reflect improved standards of urban care; and greater numbers of commercial structures will be needed to cater for the continued growth in service industries and global economic ties. Further issues to be resolved are how scarce road space can best cater for different modes of transport; how to prioritise public transport while achieving low levels of private car use; and how to extend patterns of pedestrian connectivity and public space.

The social organisation of urbanisation introduces a systemic problem with regard to both land use and availability. At the root of the problem is land management. In certain countries such as China and Vietnam, land is owned by the state, which should in theory provide ideal conditions for land management and urban design in the city. In practice, existing occupants of accessible land within urban pockets around the periphery must be compensated, but this does not always work well — land often being acquired through eminent domain at agricultural rates and sold on to private interests at a much higher price.

In other cities there is little or no sub-regional planning, and private land is often developed in a sporadic and wasteful way with poor or negligible road and service infrastructure. This then compromises future and more articulate forms of land-use structure. Land that is not preserved for properly planned expansion is effectively wasted. This even includes the highly demarcated planning and land use system in Hong Kong with its massive land values, where a lack of statutory control over supposedly rural land uses outside new town and country park areas, coupled with misguided policies over indigenous village housing rights, has led to a largely unplanned and despoiled hinterland.

INTERPRETING THE INTERVENTIONS

A historical view of Asian urbanism over the past four hundred years presents a dichotomy — that there has, until relatively recent times, been a Eurocentric conceptualisation of its values, possibly stemming from the industrialisation and secular processes that took shape in the eighteenth and nineteenth centuries. Asian states evolved different governmental structures within constantly changing political boundaries that evolved through conflict and internal divisions. By the time Western adventurers arrived in Asia in great numbers, many states were in disarray, either operating within feudal and warring factions, or divided by different religious beliefs. Only China and Japan had achieved a relatively stable and unified body politic, China even absorbing Ghenghis Kahn's Mongol forces and later Manchu invaders into a dynastic continuity. Western intervention in Asia denoted what is arguably its most fundamental cultural intrusion, introducing

Italianate-style villas form part of a group around Dante Plaza in Tianjin, China

a new international order through trading and political regimes, combined in some of its early stages with the forces of religious conviction and praxis.

Virtually all cities came into being as military concentrations, ports or market towns (rather than manufacturing centres), consolidated around the grand plans and priorities of changing regimes. These brought with them both the purposeful and organisational tools that, however crude the superimposition, established visionary physical frameworks on prevailing structures that in most cases had simply evolved to meet the continuing but casual needs of established society. In certain situations rationalisation of land use for 'new' city development — for example through the concession area administrations of China's port cities or through relatively benevolent occupying powers in other countries — left the older

city core intact so that urban development progressed as a duality of both informal and planned growth. In most situations urban design was, of necessity, highly interventionist and ideological, whether through enforced trading structures or military inducement. This has left a rich and complementary residue of contrasting urban forms and equally different versions of political economy.

At the heart of Asian urbanism is the maritime economy from the fourteenth century that linked together a vast geographical and geopolitical sphere, opening up layers of complex cultural and commercial realms that extended from the East and South China Seas to the Arabian Gulf. These same maritime forces and emerging sea routes were also the means by which European exploration, closely associated with its new naval powers, entered a diverse but sophisticated Asian maritime world, not unlike a new set of actors intervening on an already crowded stage. In this sense the intermingling of technologies, design and economic practices fashioned patterns of urbanisation based on cross-cultural pollination, where the driving forces of maritime trade and exploration were reflected primarily in the characteristics of port and primate cities.

The foreign political presence probably achieved its zenith in the late nineteenth century and while its secular attributes were appropriated in different degrees in various countries, this gave way to new waves of nationalism over the course of the twentieth century. In the period immediately following World War II, Western powers withdrew from most Asian countries either voluntarily or under siege. This was scarcely the end of Western influence however — the Cold War brought military intervention in Korea and Vietnam, and confrontation with Communist-led regimes that enveloped entire sub-regions in conflict. With the demise of the Soviet Union and a commensurate alignment with new globalising forces, Asian countries have, over the past twenty-five years, registered a powerful regional bloc, assertively focussed on economic growth and development. In many cases this continues to involve a superimposition of new development regimes on older urban fabric — a physical as well as economic intervention — with ample evidence of a comfortable co-existence between old and new. However imported modernisations, including those between Asian countries themselves, now threaten to overwhelm time-honoured routines and social customs, often reflecting the inability of prevailing planning systems to control the politically and economically inspired impetus of rapid growth and change that stems from the global marketplace.

The transformation of cities has not necessarily improved social space or prevented the erasure of established day-to-day practices. Nor has economic upgrading been matched in many cases by environmental improvement. Nihal Perera suggests four reasons for this: first that foreign intervention provided early models of "top-down" urban redevelopment practices rather than the "bottom-up" regeneration processes that are now followed in Western cities through refined planning practices; second that Western planning experience has been accepted as having universal truths and application, as opposed to the traditional culturally responsive Asian approach, because of its emphasis on deterministic form and layout; third that

Old tenements give way to more intensive developments along the narrow streets of Macau.

private investment and its ability to rapidly transform cities has been encouraged and adopted with too few controls and conditions; and finally that there are few knowledge-based sources to draw on when it comes to Asian development planning and the relationship between society and culture specific space.[4]

A further aspect is that in many post-colonial situations, the older planning and lands mechanisms have, with little

modification, been left broadly in place for dealing with the changing needs of the contemporary city. These have been applied to the accommodation of new and far-reaching development agendas that serve to meet different requirements and pressures, while maintaining political legitimacy. At the same time innovation in design has been primarily geared to incorporating new prototypes to achieve housing targets in a uniform and often standardized way, marginalizing the complicated qualities of symbolism and ritual associated with traditional urbanism. There is therefore, in many cities, an inadequate connection between modern-day planning, urban design, and the history of place. Richard Sennet has noted that the proliferation of zoning, together with the dissemination of regulatory mechanisms, actively disables local innovations and effectively acts to 'freeze' city development in time through segregated functions, establishing a closed system where aspects that don't fit are diminished in value.[5]

With accelerating urban growth, all urban space can be said to be contested. In general urban design intervention must seek to improve urban neighbourhoods as far as possible within their existing socio-economic frame. Providing there is an adequate supply of affordable accommodation, gentrification is beneficial — it begins to break down at the level where renewal starts to transform mixed communities into more sterile, deprived or elite ones.

In simple terms there might be said to be three distinct categories of urban quarter or enclave:

Self-regenerating quarters — which embody something of an equilibrium between

4 Perera, N, 'Transforming Asian City: Innovative Urban and Planning Practices in Asia', in *The Transforming Asian City*, Eds. Nihal Perera and Wing-Shing Tang, Hong Kong Baptist University, Hong Kong, 2007
5 Sennet, R, 'The Open City', in *The Endless City*, Eds. Ricky Burdett and Deyan Sudjic, Phaidon, London, 2010

resources and need, where environmental quality and neighbourhood services are sufficient to attract continued investment, and stimulate frequent incremental change and upgrading as part of the urban economic process. These areas are generally in private ownership with heritage features built into the community structure, and play a prominent and stable role in city growth.

Transitional quarters — which represent buoyant communities in older established and accessible cores and contain a mix of commercial, retail and residential uses. These lower-end low density areas embody a capacity for environmental improvement, but because of their locational advantages are vulnerable to incremental redevelopment for higher-end high density uses, and are likely to display a combination of new and run-down properties as a result of economic change and speculation.

Threatened quarters — which frequently represent areas of dilapidated fabric or buildings with complicated tenure systems that disincentivise upgrading, and where the costs of improvement are beyond the means of owners. These areas are likely to suffer from deprivation of services and public facilities, but often represent essential rental accommodation for low-paid workers or recent immigrants. They are, nevertheless, an obvious target for institutionally orchestrated redevelopment that generally involves major changes in use, layout and socio-economic fundamentals.

There is in fact no single and technically appropriate way of city building that can be derived from the older Asian city. Defining the nature of good urban environment is more about soul than science. The notion of the town or city as simply a larger version of the village has long disappeared in Asia, as growing conurbations strive to balance fragile built infrastructure with new growth trajectories.

In examining the conflicts and co-ordinates of heritage, the paradoxes of colonialism and the spatial transition that Asian cities are undergoing, several aspects must be acknowledged: first, urban transformations have largely been the result of external forces reflected in new socio-economic penetration and/or exploitation; second, cultural exchange through intervention within and between Asian societies has not created single beliefs or ideals but has led to significant differences; third, intervention has produced no totalising urban design or overall vision, but multiple landscapes open to both assimilation and restructuring in terms of new development paths; and lastly, new global economic interactions will increasingly impact on the use of space, its cultural symbolism and the interplay between the city and social change.

In an 'Afterword' to his book *Edo, the City that Became Tokyo*, Akiro Naito sums up what is at the heart of urban design:

"This history of human development, exemplified by the history of Edo, shows that we are not gods, and that we cannot live in or feel joy in a heaven of perfection. Instead, we need urban spaces that also countenance — insofar as they do not cause outright suffering — the dirty, the ugly, and the antiheroic; these too are part of the human make-up. We need cities that reflect the complexity of the human spirit".[6]

The following chapters seek to address and further explain these issues in the context of Asian urbanism.

[6] Nailo, A and Hozumi, K, *Edo, the City that Became Tokyo*, Kodansha International, Tokyo, 1982

Delhi Gate Bazaar in Lahore undergoing renovation as part of the Conservation Plan for the Walled City.

CHAPTER 2

Conflicts and Co-ordinates of Heritage

TRADITIONS IN TRANSITION

Asian cities are in transition, from a situation where the steady stream of influences over the centuries has generated a precarious balance between flourishing urban cultures and subcultures which are experiencing slow growth and change, to a surge of commonalities resulting from the dominant forces of globalisation. From an immediate post-colonial period when embedded traditions were insinuated in modernising interventions to meet rising aspirations, recent rapid economic development has produced a force field that continues to disrupt long-standing development patterns. Value systems also change and evolve. The International Council of Monuments and Sites (ICOMOS) now accepts "intangible heritage" in Asia as having an equal and possibly an even greater cultural relevance than physical traces in transmitting authentic value.

UNESCO World Heritage extended its conservation and preservation activities to cities in Asia in the 1970s, at almost precisely the same time that many of them were undergoing substantial advances in economic production and modernisation. Reconciliation between these different forces, sometimes overly contrived, continues to preoccupy urban design approaches. Nevertheless the soul of a city, however elusive this might be, needs tangible and even symbolic forms of expression related to community identity, memory and continuity. This in itself throws up something of a dilemma — should a city obliterate traces of alien and possibly despised colonial intervention, no matter the quality of its architectural residue, or retain and preserve it as a tangible part of its history that acts as a legitimate tourism resource. Hong Kong, one of the last of Britain's colonies until 1997, has all but obliterated its enormous reserve of nineteenth century urban buildings, sacrificed to the demands of development intensification and prolonged but questionable adherence to free market principles. Conversely Singapore — an independent state since 1965 — has retained and preserved buildings redolent of its colonial past, and presents them as an effective tourism resource and attraction that underscores its historical identity.

Japan's occupation of several Asian countries during World War II, as part of its colonizing agenda, saw the large-scale demolition or modification of structures identified with previous regimes. During the occupation of Seoul it is said that a new Japanese building in front of Gyeongbokgung Palace deliberately destroyed the city's spiritual axis and its *feng shui*. Its restoration after independence, by dismantling the building as part of a modernisation programme, was a crucial step towards re-establishing a new urban identity. In some urban situations such as the old International Settlement and French Concession areas in Shanghai, Western styles of architecture and urban design, redolent of foreign occupation, has such a tangible place in both the city's development history and awkward drive towards nationalism, that it underscores the essential image of the city. No less a personage than Zhou En-Lai is said to have saved the unique collection of buildings along the Bund from damage during the Cultural Revolution. However this has not been extended to the Old City which survives only in isolated remnants and tourist-oriented pastiche, calling into question city priorities where intervention is subject to constantly changing fashions and enthusiasms. One politically inspired initiative in Shanghai after 1949, was to change the British and French street names to form a more neutral encoding of the urban landscape, east-west roads being named after Chinese cities, and north-south roads after provinces.

Precisely what constitutes the concept of cultural heritage can present a conundrum, and appears to have put even World Heritage Listing applications into a problematic position. The fundamental issue is the cultural value and understanding that might be applied to places of historic character by local populations, as opposed to Western conservation criteria that could be geared to reconstituting a largely imaginary past. This may however represent a "chicken or egg" position, particularly in situations where large segments of the population live in seriously deprived conditions and have little knowledge or education that would help to inculcate a sense of recognition and cultural value in the built environment. Progress in city building should not mean that heritage initiatives become swamped in confused consultations, but more that pro-active collaboration with local communities on conservation issues should go hand-in-hand with socio-economic consolidation. Such considerations raise questions about the identity of elitist architecture in relation to vernacular development. It also introduces a situation whereby the forces of international tourism — possibly attracted by a heritage listing as something of a "commodifier" that brings new identity and attraction to a location — might introduce forces that threaten the prevailing sense of place and sustainability.

World Heritage status brings to Asia

THE AYER HITAM, constructed between 1893 and 1905 in Penang, is the largest temple complex in Southeast Asia. It is said that the surrounding hill forms resemble a crane — the Buddhist Symbol of immortality. It was supported by the Manchu Emperor Kuang Hsi, who gifted to the temple 70,000 volumes of the Imperial Edition of the Buddhist Sutras.

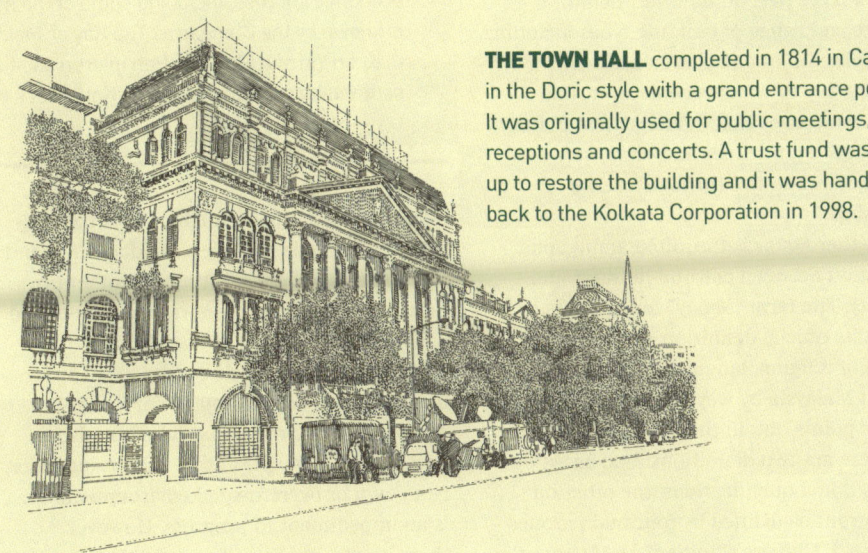

THE TOWN HALL completed in 1814 in Calcutta in the Doric style with a grand entrance portico. It was originally used for public meetings, receptions and concerts. A trust fund was set up to restore the building and it was handed back to the Kolkata Corporation in 1998.

certain responsibilities such as UNECSO-endorsed height limits for new development. Unsupervised restoration can strip away heritage character, but enforcement can make restored areas almost too precious. Conservation is also subject to competing visions — gentrification exchanges older tenants and traditional trades for upmarket commercial outlets. This invariably removes the mellow patina of older fabric which is impossible to duplicate without superficiality. While sensitive restoration adds value to heritage properties, revitalisation must be both socially and economically relevant to the local population and to artisans themselves, in order to preserve a sense of belonging. This calls for complementary intervention, particularly measures to control vehicular intrusion within the older street framework. The historic streetscapes of Georgetown, Malacca, Yangon and Macau for example, rely to a large part on their multicultural heritage and range of building types including ancestral temples and clan houses. This holds the key to wider regeneration, one that encompasses clear management plans, conservation guidelines and empowerment of local communities through a sense of ownership.

A further factor is the, often ambiguous, correlation between cultural heritage and ethnicity. The term "Malay" for example, at least in its official definition, encompasses criteria of religion, language, custom and roots in Malaysia by way of birth. Gwynn Jenkins points out, in the context of Penang, that there are two definitions: one based on constitutional qualifications, the other on ethnic grounds defined by four main groups — "Malay", "Chinese", "Indian" and "Others",

CHINA STREET IN GEORGE TOWN, Penang, lies on an axis from the waterfront to the Goddess of Mercy Temple on Pitt Street. It is now associated with Penang's earliest Chinese settlers, and was laid out by Francis Light and Koh Lay Huan — the patriarch of a large family from Kedah who settled in Penang along with several hundred Chinese followers. His descendants continued to contribute to the commercial development of the area and its economic success, including some of the most ornately decorated shophouses in the city. It is known by the Chinese as Tua Kay or Main Street. The Goddess of Mercy Temple, dedicated to Kuan Yin and Ma Chor Poh (patron saint of seafarers), was the first to be built by Chinese settlers. Its original name was Kong Hock Keong (Canton – Hokkien Temple).

and even these can be further broken down into, for example, Hokkien, Hakka, Tamil and Sindhi.[1] Precise identification of authentic heritage is therefore often rather open-ended.

It is occasionally said that Asian communities show little sentiment to built heritage, both because many surviving remnants are colonial in origin, but also because of a perception that preserving older, run-down or overcrowded environments is an impediment to progress. However there is evidence from around Asia that this

is changing — the 'memory' of cities and their historical associations are becoming increasingly important as urban populations become more affluent and concerned about cultural perception of the city in today's competitive economic climate.

Taking all these factors into account, the declaration of "heritage" as something inviolable is in itself an intervention in the workings of the city building process. It acts as a constraint to unconscionable development forces and exerts a beneficial influence on the

[1]   Jenkins, G, *Contested Space : Cultural Heritage and Identity Reconstructions*, Transaction Publishers, Rutgers University, New Jersey, 2008

perception of policy makers, but it is essential that this does not exclude interdependent factors that contribute to actual community betterment.

CONSERVING CULTURAL IDENTITY

Distinctive traits of Asian urbanism, including significant parts of its physical heritage, have been lost or compromised over the past forty years. Historical and informal urban tissue is progressively dismembered through expedient redevelopment approaches often led or orchestrated through government or quasi-government bodies. These provide few opportunities to reconcile new formal and single-use development with complex and intuitive urban forms that reflect more established and different values. In practice this can be broken down into tangible heritage that represents physical building enclaves, and intangible heritage associated with complex and even random urban activities that nevertheless mark a genuine *genius loci* through strong cultural and social ties. In the main, traditions that continue to thrive in Asian cities — outside clearly demarcated precincts such as temple compounds — relate more to patterns of activity than to specific physical fabric. This is focused on urban spaces and streets as places for social rituals, ceremonial activities, festivals, markets and other communal uses.

The more complex an area in terms of its ethnic properties and representations of interstitial space, the more informal overlaps and interfaces produce expressive urbanism that is not readily discernible. In practice however this is often the very characteristic that frames points of local activity and community identity. Such

Ex-offices of the International Credit en Handels Vereniging Rotterdam on Jalan Kali Besar Timur built in 1913 in Jakarta and designed by EHG Cuypers.

features are generally far removed from the chaotic first impressions, and raise issues that cannot be easily resolved other than through carefully orchestrated forms of participatory planning. An urban landscape of culturally and functionally identifiable forms can be assessed at different levels: first as architectural representations of tradition and invention, where intervention might impact on physical integrity; and second as functioning components of a particular community, imbued with memory, and the spiritual associations of use. Both of these need to be assimilated, not so much in terms of a cosmetic or 'reproduced' identity, but as a necessary acknowledgement of the intuitive values of 'place' that is somehow

expressive and integral to the language of the whole. An underlying problem is the realm of uncertainty brought about through a combination of indeterminate policies and conflicting priorities, for example a blurring of objectives relating to conservation, maximisation of land value and heritage tourism. As the context changes so does the community's sense of identity with the tangible heritage of the past. This implies that the term 'conservation should not necessarily mean merely the retention of physical structures, but a moderation of the rate of economic change to accommodate a continuing and evolving system of activities.

Urban development, particularly in terms of its relationship with older fabric, is associated with a number of time–bound factors that can be acknowledged in different ways according to context. Peter Rowe suggests that the 'past-present-future' balance can be manipulated by analysing the 'past' in terms of preservation; the 'past-present' in terms of conservation, and the 'present-future' representing a fundamental contrast with the past, even as it conserves and connects with it.[2]

The notion of "cultural identity" is, in practice, highly sensitive in situations of multi-ethnic quarters, where cultural tourism can be a catalyst to fragmentation as well as unification. This is something that might be perceived in Asia's distinctively demarcated and commercially orchestrated ethnic enclaves, such as in Singapore. Perceptions of cultural identity are elusive in that the interpretation of "historic" city fabric and sense of place must also reflect constant changes, ambiguities and dichotomies. Major tourist infrastructure can create physical conflict with historic areas themselves,

2   Rowe, P.G., *Emergent Architectural Territories in East Asian Cities*, Birkäuser, Basel, 2011, p163

P'ojang mach'a (mobile food carts) form activity foci along the narrow shopping streets of Namdei-mun Sijang, Seoul.

detracting from the very elements that make them distinctive while leading to an over-dependence on tourism as an economic base, vulnerable to economic downturns. A viable means of safeguarding authenticity without incongruity is to upgrade the public realm and enrich the memory of place through regeneration programmes. By extending cultural heritage to include traditional events, celebrations, religious festivals and heritage trails, development pressures can be counteracted by business collaborations between different neighbourhoods which further the evolution of localised identity.

Successful areas of historic conservation have in common an evolving cultural, social and economic framework that underlies the dynamics of change. The urban representations for which these areas are often most appreciated are embedded in a range of intangible influences and eclectic interpretations outside any precisely articulated planning framework. The inadequacies of modern planning mechanisms in the face of policy "silos" associated with big governments has detracted from the potential of cities to assimilate holistic approaches to conservation-oriented city development, given the importance of tourism to the economic health of Asian cities. The active promotion of tourism brings with it the need to foster stewardship of cultural heritage in order to ensure authenticity. If traditional culture is appropriated for visitor consumption in a commodified way, every means must be made not to devalue or misappropriate the cultural assets themselves. At the same time this should create an economic momentum towards restoring older structures as urban assets, embracing both tangible and intangible characteristics. This tends to succeed when there is a strong cultural identity either as a whole, or in minority ethnic neighbourhoods, and in situations bound closely with religious beliefs that impact on lifestyle in a fundamental way. Active ceremonies and festivals associated with temple, mosque and church are not incompatible with the integration of new uses that cement modern urban lifestyles.

A further factor is diversity of residential and commercial tenure, and the flexibility of building fabric to adapt through sub-division. In old established Asian communities such as Penang, the cultural and economic orchestration associated with ethnic groups range from extended family arrangements to the use of shophouses for cottage industry, or the administration of endowment properties located around mosques for Muslim families. These create informal activity frameworks that inject an essential authenticity on urban design directly associated with its spatial representation. The street rhythm must accommodate the requirements of religious festivals and processions often associated with just one urban enclave. For example in Penang's Little India, part of the daily cultural ritual is the mix of turmeric and sandalwood strewn on the space between the public street and the private building edge, often accompanied by decorative *Kolam* artwork, corresponding with building entrances, and the burning of camphor.[3] In Hong Kong,

3   Jenkins, 2008, op. cit.

INTERFACING STREET FABRIC ALONG JALAN LEBUH AMPANG injects contrasts in age, style and use, forming a backdrop to the pressure of traffic flow in Kuala Lumpur. The corner block of three-storey buildings on Lebuh Ampang and Jalan Tun Perak was constructed in 1909. They were built by different owners in a range of styles but with a common roofline, and designs that blend English, Dutch and Islamic influences. The corner building was occupied by the Gian Singh textile store from the 1920s.

City hall and cathedral, Ho Chi Min City

certain festivals involve the burning of "paper money" and incense along the street edge.

The urban design of indigenous societies sustains a communal way of life that is strongly influenced by spiritual heritage, and necessitates reciprocity between different interests and customs, which establishes a workable order out of apparent diversity. This creates a constant tension between intuitive and behavioural traditions, particularly where different ethnic cultures share the same environment, and bureaucratic demands for ordered urban management and rationalisation exist. The enigmatic influences of *feng shui, vaashtu shastra,* or even the association of certain types of vegetation within the precincts of temples and mosques, establishes an ambiguous but symbolic identity, and requires wide community participation in any new planning initiatives.

Many historic buildings have colonial associations, therefore emerging economies frequently have to battle elitist perceptions associated with conservation. It is not merely the most prominent buildings that are at risk, but the intangible cultural heritage connected with urban places. The clearing of older quarters and commensurate dislocation of communities in response to rising land values brings with it the disappearance of cultural meaning, local traditions and uses. To be sustainable and ensure continued economic health, government must work towards an effective balance between private and public sector interests, and must activate co-ordinated housing, institutional and business area programmes.

CONTESTED SPACE

Public space is part of what defines a city. When urban open space is analysed according to dominant function, there are seven types: civic, community, corporate, domestic, consumption, service and transit. Asian cities that evolved without a fully orchestrated programme of urban formation and civic set-pieces as unified physical foci for public life and activities, rely on spaces at the extreme — a large area of urban parkland such as a central Padang or Maidan for relaxation, and the local precinct and street system for encounter. Between these is a realm of incursion and overlap of uses that extracts value from what are often fragmented or utilitarian spaces. Small trading spaces for example are often formalised only through pre-determined pitches and product specialisation, and therefore have a heightened significance and value. However the awkward relationship marking social and economic space in the contemporary city underscores the tension between different agendas of urban design in the public realm and the gradual commodification of public space that tends to encroach on the diversity of uses which sustain urban society.

STREET SPACE

Open spaces in Asian cities have traditionally functioned, to a significant extent, as relatively organic activity systems, often operating in an informal way as layered networks, outside what is officially planned. Spaces — including street edges — create opportunities for an unofficial system of economic transaction and exchange that might cater for a mix of merchants, investors, brokers and consumers. Cities embrace or control this phenomenon in different ways. In Hong Kong street markets are occupied by licensed hawkers and patrolled by uniformed officers, but with a loose fringe of mobile traders and cooked

Elevated pedestrian movement systems follow the street alignments in the Central District of Hong Kong

food operators. Most Asian cities have a high degree of tolerance to street vendors who have traditionally operated along certain avenues without a license. Traders are generally separated into broad categories according to a range of products — clothing, food, toys and electric goods etc. Conglomerations also occur next to major retail attractions such as indoor markets, shopping centres, and around public transport nodes, so there is a high degree of symbiosis. The informal sector and the varied entrepreneurial skills associated with it, form part of a labour market that is necessary

for economic survival and is often closely connected with an informal housing or 'self constructed' situation.

As the Asian city undergoes both physical expansion and changes in economic direction, the informal sector is likely to grow in parallel. Places and spaces need to be designed to cater for this situation, which means accepting the unpredictable and the indeterminate. Reclaiming public space means forcible eviction, whereas an acceptance of the informal retail sector requires recognition of its economic contribution to the social life of the city, and its impact on local character. Older city quarters attract investment in property fronting these areas because of the authenticity of their identity and the range of potential customers they represent.

In Singapore, Bangkok, Kuala Lumpur, Penang, Taipei and Hanoi, specially demarcated outdoor areas are set aside for cooked food vendors to operate in hygienic conditions, reflecting an understanding of the underlying dynamics and interfaces affecting both the provider and the consumer. In Singapore outdoor cooked food areas are imaginatively designed and well integrated. In Malaysian cities the *pasar malam* form a traditional means of equating temporary food stalls with local employment and social interaction, so that street vendors occupy space at a specifically agreed time. The *pojang-macha* in Seoul operate in a similar way. In Hong Kong the traditional *dai bai dongs* or "street cafes" have become progressively limited, inadvertently redirecting customers to patronize fast food outlets.

As cities are gradually regenerated through gentrification and new vehicular movement patterns, the shift in terms of street scale and retail emphasis is introducing a greater refinement and consequent rationalisation of socio-economic conditions. This is tending to restrict the informal market sector to specific areas, therefore planning has become more about managing its impact in order to ensure that sufficient space is maintained for pedestrian or vehicular circulation.

COMMUNITY SPACE

Public space intervention must meet an overall civic vision while reflecting social needs. Integrative elements should be based on both connection and continuity, as well as the creation of adaptable space to encourage diverse uses including local festivals, economic exchange and local consumption. The Asian city has traditionally provided opportunities for open space and local amenities such as markets, sacred places and such things as bathhouses that provide for and generate interaction. The history of cities as a coalescence of different urban quarters is often characterised by different ethnic or religious spaces that signify identity and nurture community life. In general, fragmentation of these spaces through activity segregation and appropriation by particular interest groups, is often accompanied by conflict.

An important factor is to evolve a viable and community oriented mix of uses in relation to neighbourhood fabric, one that ensures a maximum of amenity and a minimum of conflict. Problems are most likely to arise in relation to the design and use of space in conjunction with urban gentrification and the requirements of different stakeholders, for instance where the desires of residents for privacy and quiet

relaxation conflict with the desire of the wider community for multi-use and animation. In practice it is the drive towards urban regeneration and higher built densities that make new spaces viable and deliverable. However this tends to best succeed in cities with a high degree of urban management, where genuine public gain can be derived from private investment, and where change is rooted in tradition and the history of a locality to avoid built heritage being increasingly dwarfed by building intensification. In these situations public space both supports the wider urban environment and is supported by it, whether the main emphasis is commercial, cultural or residential.

In general, urban space in Asian cities is self-policed by the community, and in most cases congestion and even conflicting uses are accommodated without spaces becoming unnecessarily degraded. How public space is shaped and reshaped is due less to the sensibilities of designers or those with regulating responsibilities, and more with the aspiration and resources of the community. Citizens enjoy the benefits, market flexibility, and diversity of functions, all of which normally overwhelm aesthetic pretentions. Therefore while urban space, including residual space, might be dilapidated this rarely leads to severe levels of blight or abandonment, primarily because it is

PLAZA MIRANDA IN FRONT OF QUIAPO CHURCH IN MANILA became a post-war centre for political demonstrations. It was after an assassination at a congressional rally in the square, followed by insurgency, that martial law was introduced in 1972. It forms the focus of market streets, creating flows of pilgrims, worshippers and traders, including lines of incense sellers.

subject to a range of uses at different times of day. "In-between" space serves a special purpose in relation to a fine grained system of incidental spaces, narrow connecting streets, and new public sites carved out of older institutional ones — such as internalised courtyards — that are then able to form part of a larger and more continuous public realm and activity matrix. At the same time ad hoc spaces are open to change with both loss of function and reinvention as circumstances dictate, and are often hidden within older urban quarters which house the most likely constituency of users. This tends to support the case that simple spaces frequently have the greatest social impact.

PUBLIC SPACE VERSUS CONSUMER SPACE

Increasing affluence has created a considerable impetus to retail environments within large Asian cities, matched by enormous catchments from both city populations and visitors, together with their evolving consumer habits. Retail has therefore become an important part of city economies, at both ends of the market spectrum. The urban shopping mall has become a mainstay of main street frontage, while in high density and high land-cost situations the internalised environment forms part of transit nodes with multi-use realms of retail, commercial, residential and recreational space. This tends to divide space into public, semi-public and private zones, but also raises concerns about 'placelessness' and an exclusionary re-ordering of many historic functions in the urban realm. Global chain stores have created a replicated and formulaic brand of urbanism operating across national boundaries, which

THE DUALITY OF TALL AND MODERN STREET

frontages with a maze of narrow streets and adaptable premises behind, generates a framework of vitality, change and indeterminacy in Tokyo. This, establishes a tension between rationalised urbanism and liberating expression — new and old are inextricably interlinked, and vernacular elements still permeate the post-industrial fabric as an urban mosaic, with no systematic street vocabulary or symbolic centre. Hidenobu Jinnai states that the city is comparable with the board game sugoroku made up of autonomous neighbourhoods with little subordination to the whole.

drives outlets into progressively upmarket commercial concentrations.

Corporatized 'destination spaces' are highly choreographed within the process of manufacturing space to shape market interests, creating an uneasy correlation between the homogenised space associated with the global city, increased private management and a marginalisation of the public realm. However in some situations such as Hong Kong, Singapore and Tokyo, this forms elevated connections between commercial and community uses and urban transit nodes, generating spaces that integrate

circulation and retail structures within a wider pedestrian movement framework on several levels, and accessible on a 24-hour basis. Another variation of this can be termed 'dedicated' space, for use by the public but technically managed by a corporation or other private interest. This type of 'public gain' might be negotiated with a developer as part of the planning permission process, or in return for a 'bonus' of plot ratio value. In this situation the public is presumed to benefit through the provision of open space as an integral part of large-scale development at no actual cost to the Government, while developers maintain full control over its design. A growing corporate landscape of towers and 'groundscrapers' brought about by international investment in Asian cities has tended to result in a concentration of new and often ambiguous spaces and plazas of low authenticity and related primarily to commercial undertakings. Central to this is the nature of the street itself — the essential public stage for social interaction, cultural exchange and informal activity, outside the internationalisation of standard development forms and spaces. As Asian society becomes increasingly stratified according to wealth, education and opportunity, and as cities compete for investment, quality of space becomes associated with specific purposes, while enhancement of the public realm is often no more than beautification.

The trend to physically "gate" affluent communities — segregated through both fear of crime and an overall sense of exclusivity — is a further factor in community division, and at least in part, a wilful withdrawal from active engagement with civil society. However to some extent this also reflects the fact that many social and civic functions that were historically conducted in the public realm can now, through modern communication devices, be undertaken from private space, including the "third places" of face-to-face communication — work spaces, coffee shops, cafés and leisure spaces that support social interaction.

INVADED SPACE

Over the past thirty years Asian cities have become subject to what might be termed 'invaded space', the most pervasive of which is the impact of private vehicles. Without a

Street market — Canton Road, Hong Kong

controlled hierarchy of use, traffic tends to seep into the fine-grained street systems and usurp both pedestrian space and comfort. This often impoverishes precisely the older area quarters that should present a distinctive historical identity. In general the social function of open space is compromised rather than lost completely, but it has the effect of limiting the area dedicated to pedestrian functions and tends to result in a series of fragmented enclaves, where some parts remain as vehicle-reliant environments. In addition street parking encourages congestion and reduces opportunities for informal activities and exchange.

New traffic arteries effectively sub-divide the urban realm into fragmented parts, frequently disassociating spaces from their potential and even existing catchments. Reclaiming space from traffic is most likely to be successful in achieving a balance between motorised traffic and a connective realm of other forms of movement. This has the added incentive of generating positive economic, social and health benefits. In some countries such as Indonesia and Malaysia, cheap fuel exacerbates the attraction of private cars, and rising affluence introduces more first-time owners at a time when many Western cities have introduced measures to curb car use through traffic management, congestion charge zones and park-and-ride schemes.

CULTURAL AND FUNCTIONAL IDENTITY

An equation of cultural and functional identity is an underlying issue in Asian urban design. As indigenous forms disappear and heritage increasingly takes on contrived and commodified characteristics, ethnic cultures imperceptibly merge. At the heart of this is the question of cultural and stylistic references that exemplify a particular city or locality as being uniquely "Thai", "Vietnamese" or "Chinese", when each has inherited strong historical injections of building and architectural style from the others. There are however several ways in which this can be legitimately approached in terms of urban design. First, prioritising patterns of distinctive urban streets and places based on a variety of factors such as existing morphologies, climate and topography, rather than zoning for dominant land uses; second, engendering a dynamic contrast between old and new, through sophisticated technical application, elegant detailing and permeable connections to offset the retained and reconnected forms of a different era; third, sympathetic regeneration of older urban quarters, including 'native' or ethnic neighbourhoods dispersed throughout the city, through a combination of incremental upgrading, conservation and new inserts within the older fabric, allowing these areas to retain their essential characteristics; and lastly, upgrading and landscape restoration of older urban ecologies such as canals, river courses and stream beds, as recreational and connective elements.

An underlying conundrum is that as cultural, social and economic differences between societies in Asian and Western cities diminish, 'globalisation' or 'internationalism' is equated by many Asian governments, institutions and developers, with Western industrialised city precedents. This means that planning and infrastructural elements are taken to relate almost exclusively to axial boulevards, large civic spaces, undifferentiated areas of open parkland, and a monumental emphasis on large public buildings. In established Western cities such elements have been introduced as formal interventions in the older city fabric over several centuries, modified in response to surface traffic, and mellowed through both time and the machinations of different planning and urban design emphases — for example a city such as New York has over 4,000 listed historic buildings. In these cities, both social and economic planning is about incrementalism and regeneration of, for example, old and

Raohe Street night market in Taipei

despoiled waterfronts. This is not to condemn the current globalising ideology of Asian primate cities, but direct it along appropriate and responsive channels. This should ensure that the accelerating process of growth and change in both new and existing city quarters will add up to more than the sum of the parts, and enhance the stability of the community as a whole by satisfying the needs of all stakeholders. With a high percentage of Asian populations now living in cities it is also incumbent to ensure their sustainability far into the future, possibly planning for periods of retraction as well as growth.

In many ways the Asian city has evolved towards an urbanism of high contrast and disjointed image. This stems from post-modernism, which has generated a highly functional 'international style' of tall and highly rationalised commercial and residential environments. These are laid out to contemporary standards of road and service provision, often in the form of self-contained enclaves, in juxtaposition with older patterns of development that represent almost precisely the opposite, with the minimum of overlap.

This fails to reflect the frequent co-existence of different economic and social systems and the perceptions associated with them — a duality of rich and poor; modernity and tradition; global and local; progressive and hidebound. Modern development responds to demands from new financial and service industries and these have transformed cities both economically and culturally. In this context of unrelenting change, older street environments can easily be perceived as outliving their usefulness, having been largely superseded or made irrelevant by new economic trends and because older fabric is often deemed bad for a progressive city image.

If this position becomes sufficiently entrenched in government municipal policy, the city growth model itself comes into question. In such situations, decisions are made between heritage conservation and extraction of value in the face of rising urban land costs and development expectations, often in the absence of an alternative lobby. In Singapore, the Urban Renewal Authority made a quantum leap in terms of protecting and refurbishing older enclaves. In Kuala Lumpur it was a coalition of professionals who began to act in the wake of wanton destruction of important older buildings in the 1980s, that helped turn the development tide towards conservation. In Yangon it is the architectural institute leading the call for adaptive re-use of many old colonial structures. In other situations it has come about through public programmes of gentrification as an adjunct to urban upgrading initiatives and tourism programmes.

There is, in general, inadequate analysis of the long term costs and benefits of encouraging and reinforcing the inherent flexibility associated with older building blocks in multi-ownership and in the adaptive re-use of redundant buildings in public ownership. In many situations these can be used to meet the demands of small business growth and change, and develop relationships with the underlying colour and dynamism of older city quarters. Three current projects in Hong Kong suggest that such initiatives are gaining momentum, these being the conservation and conversion of the Central Police Station and Victoria Prison complex to new community, commercial and cultural uses; the transformation of old Government Married Quarters into a Centre for Creative Industries; and the conversion of an old Magistracy to an Art and Design College.

COMMUNITY ENGAGEMENT: FROM TOP-DOWN TO BOTTOM-UP

In many Asian countries both traditional cultural and philosophical precepts, combined (over many generations) with political prudence and ethnic loyalties, have encouraged a consensus-driven rather than an individualistic approach to civic matters.

ONE OF THE OLDEST ADMINISTRATIVE BUILDINGS IN YANGON was constructed in 1877 for Burma Railways. They leased the railway system from the government and facilitated the opening up of Myanmar. The building on Bogyoke Aung San Road with its distinctive filigreed awnings has been derelict since 1994, but has been selected to undergo renovation and conversion.

There are of course more ambiguous traits such as the Confucian promotion of harmony and respect for authority. This is reflected in the relatively compliant characteristics of Chinese society and the hierarchical structure of religious and extended family groups, therefore individual expression on public issues is purposely and conveniently suppressed. Likewise, this inspires both respect and acceptance of 'strong' leadership, which often expresses itself in systems of political authoritarianism and 'one-party rule', and in the most extreme situations broaches nil or only token opposition. This does not necessarily mean that central and municipal systems of government operate in isolation, or that for the most part they are not responsive to public need, but that they work on behalf of the community rather than with them.

Top-down systems make policy and implementation mechanisms difficult to change, as they are underscored by a bureaucratic hierarchy with a solid interest in perpetuating the prevailing system with little consideration being given to the views of other stakeholders. What are often construed as planning decisions are in fact more related to imposed political and financial policy which makes co-ordinated urban design difficult to achieve. Zoning tends to be a favoured planning tool because it presents an efficient and deterministic land management instrument rather than an urban design mechanism. In spite of this, political regimes in growing economies, including fledgling democracies, have achieved impressive results in terms of housing, social and environmental initiatives. At the same time they have mostly been preoccupied in steering a balance between economic prosperity and a new

development culture that reflects the speed of urbanization and industrialization.

However, centralised authority also bequeaths bureaucracy and inefficiency, such as extensive but futile public consultations over planning matters, which solicits comments but ultimately fails to properly heed or reconcile them. Urban renewal processes are therefore carried out through a conciliatory process that prioritises the requirements of those with vested interests, including those of governments, rather than properly orchestrated public participation. A further factor is the Government's frequent acquiescence to the private pro-development lobby, making redevelopment a more favourable and expedient option than sensitive regeneration.

THE IMPACT OF LAND OWNERSHIP AND SPECULATION

The issue of land tenure and ownership is fundamental to both the socio-economic and spatial dimensions of urban design, and is an important aspect of urban planning procedures. It is also a contested one. Access to urban land is through social or family relations, squatting, administrative means such as public housing, and through the real estate market. The concept of private property and urbanisation are inextricably linked. There are few detailed studies of this in Asian cities, although the processes of land assembly and sub-division are relatively consistent. Land holdings are likely to be more fragmented in urban situations than in surrounding or rural areas, as rising land values act to propel the sub-division process. However when land is in short supply, for example in Hong Kong, the situation can

be reversed, with individual agricultural lots being bought and sold for investment purposes, creating a clear momentum towards segregation. With urban growth, the ownership of urban land in itself establishes a causal relationship between the evolving framework of urban social structures and class relations. In most cases within cities, this also reflects the link between government administration and commercial investment in building stock as part of the economic development process.

Both private and institutional land speculation inevitably leads to significant appreciation in land value. The greatest impacts of this are on housing availability and affordability to various income groups and unless public housing is provided, a large proportion of poorer household income is spent on rent. While the concentration of land ownership leads to high population densities in central urban situations, in many cases rapid urban growth and accompanying land pressures extend to suburban and rural areas where lots are amalgamated to form large housing compounds, industrial estates and shopping centres.

While the process of land speculation and urban land ownership is clearly not identical in all situations, a surprisingly consistent pattern emerges in rapidly growing Asian cities. As described by Evers and Korff — a first wave of speculation in the inner fringe areas, through the development of private middle-class housing, is followed by a second wave of densification within and around the central business district with resulting population redistribution.[4] Former low-income and inner city inhabitants tend to either become urban tenants in overcrowded

4   Evers, H.D. and Korff, R, *Southeast Asian Urbanism: The Meaning and Power of Social Space*, St Martin's Press, New York, 2000, p169

older buildings through sub-letting, move to temporary settlements or to the urban fringe where they compete with both suburban developers and rural-urban migrants, thereby intensifying the competition for building land. In the process this fuels a change from agricultural to urban land use with many former low-income owners of rural land becoming tenants, and with agricultural intensification for production of cash crops. A growing urban elite is then concentrated in new high-rise enclaves within the city and in low-to-medium density suburban estates, with a high percentage of surrounding rural land owned by absentee landlords and under rent or sharecropping.

The Government itself is generally a significant land owner, and in most cases the predominant one, enabling land to be sold for profit on a leasehold basis. In Hong Kong and Singapore large public housing programmes, on urban land and under controlled conditions, have been constructed for rental or sale to low-income groups. In situations where land is particularly valuable, new land has been created through reclamation at strategic locations along the shoreline. In the case of Hong Kong this goes back to the 1870s, with significant income derived from sales and rents, and with lots throughout the city classified into *marine, town and suburban*. The new town programme that commenced in 1972 was reliant on large-scale formation of new land from shallow estuaries and bays around the coast of the New Territories in order to skirt around the problems of private land resumption. In Singapore approximately one quarter of the entire land area has been created through reclamation.

A direct result of colonial intervention in

the urbanisation process was the registration of land, reflecting the simplistic notion of individual property rights in the city and native land rights in rural situations.[5] Colonial policies instigated conflict between the systems through regularising this distinction, but in later periods of rapid economic development those customary land rights have frequently been overwhelmed by a recalibration of land tenure at the urban fringe, often with little legal basis. In countries such as Indonesia and Malaysia where urban populations are made up of different ethnic groups, disparities in access to business opportunities and urban production through ownership of centrally located land sub-divisions are apparent. This imbalance has been a cause for concern in, for example, Jakarta and Kuala Lumpur. Social relations and neighbourhood organisations in low-income communities offer some means to resist the forces of demolition and eviction associated with the impetus of economic change. Certain types of established communities such as the Indonesian or Malaysian *kampungs* are based on cohesive social and family ties. That compatibility creates patterns of conformity and co-operation, with close neighbour relations, but not necessarily any sense of formal spatial organization.

In Bangkok the pattern of land ownership is somewhat fragmented as a result of early royal land allocation to a noble elite, making public agencies and high ranking officials the biggest land owners. Various ethnic quarters could be identified until the early twentieth century — the Western trading quarter along the Chao Phraya River, the Sampheng and Yaonarat Chinese quarter, the Indian

neighbourhood along Phahurat Road and the Malay quarter at Phya Thai. The matrix of canals which crossed the city was largely reclaimed in the mid-twentieth century to form streets, which acted as a catalyst to the transformation of older settlement patterns to create "ribbons" of new commercial and shophouse avenues, such as Sukhumvit Road, with residential development behind. As land values rose, these urban corridors were redeveloped into high-rise alignments of offices, hotels and apartment blocks, with smaller lanes connecting a more fine-grained amalgam of residential lots set back from the main street network, and often low-lying with a high watertable. As this variable pattern is extended through new development, the land use pattern becomes increasingly complicated and the connecting network more congested.

THE TEMPORARY SETTLEMENT PHENOMENON

The problem of squatter settlements became acute in most Asian cities during the post-war industrialisation process and was only resolved in the more economically advanced cities in the 1980s and 1990s through major public housing and new town programmes. However large squatter areas are still a characteristic of Manila, Jakarta, Bombay, Bangkok, and the fringes of large cities in China. With rising rates of urbanisation, the only long-term solution is new low-cost housing.

Within slum or squatter areas, social networks and local associations develop over time. Kinship plays an important part in providing initial access to a building lot and assistance with construction, with reciprocal ties and co-operation based on traditional cultural values but also on common economic

5 Evers and Korff, 2000, op. cit., p165

The old Customs House built in 1900 in a neo-Classical style on the Chao Phraya River in Bangkok is now a police station.

situations which generate overlapping networks of interdependencies. This makes communal action relatively easy to organise, and creates the means of community representation and leadership in dealings with authorities. It also facilitates the swift flow of information and potential mobilisation of the community in the face of eviction, sanctions or threat.

The growth of large temporary settlements around the periphery of many rapidly growing cities reflects the informal means by which low-income workers, including new migrant populations, are integrated into the urban labour market. This includes both occupation of public land, or rental of lots on private land, making tenants vulnerable to eviction with rising land values (although long-term leases can be negotiated under public auspices). In the Klong Thoey area of Bangkok, rising demand for land leads to tenure contracts

being purchased by middle-income groups. This establishes a form of gentrification which gradually transforms the slums through upgrading, albeit in a fragmented way, while those who sell their leases move to other slum areas.[6]

While squatter areas are characterised by temporary buildings and a general lack of proper service infrastructure, a further lingering problem is that of substandard tenement accommodation through subdivision. In Hong Kong, the inner city neighbourhoods make up around three million people, with extreme densities in older districts — such as Yau Tsim Mong, Kowloon City and Sham Shui Po — of up to 6,000 persons per hectare. A recent study showed that about 72,000 households or 170,000 people are deemed to be poorly housed with a further 29,000 households living in other substandard forms of accommodation such as

cocklofts and unsheltered rooms attached to private quarters. Of those in "poor condition", households living in single rooms or cubicles are the most common problem, with a high proportion of poorly housed people being elderly and single. While new immigrant families make up 8 per cent of Hong Kong's population, 26 per cent of this category are living in poor housing.[7]

THE CITY AS TEXT

Textual interpretation of cities — through nomenclature and iconography — is a means of signifying cultural change. In the post-colonial world, place name connotations of streets, parks and highways, which include the names of European royalty as part of the colonial lexicon, might justifiably be considered outmodish but might also personify a sense of history. They also provide cues to social mapping and ethnic groupings, and establish an elusive engagement with the signification of place.

In the Chinese treaty port concession areas, street names redolent of the "unequal treaties" were quickly erased after 1949. In Shanghai, streets in the French Concession named after French revolutionary heroes and Paris boulevards (such as Avenue Foch, Rue Lafayette, and Quai de France) were politely changed to more neutral nomenclature, as was the wide road between the International and the French Concession — Avenue Edward VII. But street names in the old city named after guild activities, such as Woodworkers Street or Pickled Melon Street were also phased out in more contemporary times.

In the reconstituted treaty ports new names generally accorded with cities and provinces. In Harbin, Russian street names quickly lost

6   Evers and Korff, 2000, op. cit., p204
7   Business and Professionals Federation of Hong Kong, *Poor Housing Conditions in Hong Kong: Extent, Distribution and People Affected*, 2007

Street texts in Shinjuku, Tokyo, establish an architecture of communication and surface change.

neutral in connotation with few overtones. In Singapore non-Malay residents found Malay vocabulary difficult to pronounce, and so re-naming was mainly restricted to single types of flora and fauna, while conversely certain Malay place names were rechristened e.g. "Sentosa" meaning tranquility, replacing *Pulau Blakang Mati* for the new resort island. In turn Chinese street names were simplified to avoid confusing transliterations. In the Jurong Industrial Estate, permutations of words suggesting "industry" such as *Jalan Pesawat* added to a linguistic realm that excluded ethnic associations.[8] Bridges also represent dominant public objects on which political instigators can append their names, for example the Cavenagh and Ord Bridges in Singapore are named after Governors, and the Elgin Bridge paid colonial homage to the then Governor General of India.

The symbolic iconography of a borrowed regime is frequently used for marketing purposes, promoting a desirable image or geographic identity which seems to invoke the illusion of attainment, and suggest a sophisticated lifestyle. This perhaps intentionally plays on the global city reference, but lacks any consistent link between image and actuality, with social identity stylishly manufactured as a virtual reality.

In Penang, street names not only reflect the far reaches of the British Empire such as Victoria Street and King Street, but also embody references to different ethnic groups and places of origin, such as Malay Street, Kampong Java, Bangkok Lane, Burmah Road, Chulia Street and Armenian Street. These make up a series of urban villages comprising an assimilation of different communities, also reflecting a fusion of indigenous forms and

favour after 1946, so that Kitaiskaia Street, the central spine of hotels, department stores and restaurants, became Zhong Yang Street — now refurbished as a "museum" street of old Russian buildings. Hong Kong retains the names of former colonial governors and senior administrators in its street names and even country park trails, with the ubiquitous "Victoria" (associated with road, park, memorial and peak), having survived the political transition intact. In Yangon it is said that Lord Dalhousie, Governor-General of India, accorded street names to British officers and Commissioners, which happened to include Dalhousie Street. After independence in 1948, names were changed to leaders of the independence struggle and army generals. Fraser Street was changed to Anawrahta Road after the ancient founder of Pagan, while Fytche Square was changed to Mahabandoola Garden after the general who resisted the British during the first Anglo-Burmese War. In Malaysia, many anglicized street names have been assigned indigenous equivalents, while in Singapore changes in street-naming policies were intended to assert independence from its colonial identity.

In all cases, new names are suitably

8   Kong, L and Yeoh, B.S.A., *The Politics of Landscapes in Singapore*, Syracuse University Press, New York, 2003

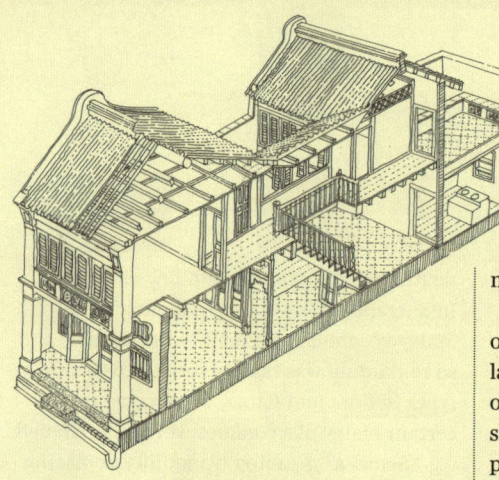

cultures that keep traditions alive. In Penang's Little India for example, the street names connect with past occupations within the area. The Tamil name for King Street is *Padarukara Tharuva* or the Street of Boatmen; while *Kitengi Teru* along the quayside is known as the Street of Company Godowns.

THE SHOPHOUSE DESIGN AND STREET MAKING TRADITION

The degree to which urbanisation is unified by commercial values requires a sympathetic and responsive homogenising force to translate these into new cultural models, with at least some affinity with traditional values. Shophouses in Guangzhou, Hong Kong, Singapore, Penang and Malacca illustrate a social as well as an economic dimension, representing a situation that is still predominant, where family and business life are closely related. The shophouse — as a fundamental component of street formation in the growth of port cities from Macau and southern China, to Malaysia, Bangkok and Vietnam — was developed in ways that varied in terms of architectural style, volume and climatic features. While the colder northern climate produced variants with a narrow frontage and generally short depth, the southern version tends to integrate a deeper plan form with an open courtyard to assist ventilation, and generally subscribes to a

north-south orientation.

The shophouse, as a generic type, originated in Southern China and from the late eighteenth century was a basic component of city growth in Penang and Singapore with a simple form of one or two storeys. Lee Ho Yin provides a historical account of the Chinese exodus to southern destinations bringing with them building traditions dating back to the Song dynasty.[9] More formal relations were established in the fifteenth century when members of a Ming court retinue to Malacca intermarried with local Malays to create the beginning of a "Straits-born Chinese" culture. With the Portuguese arrival in Malacca in 1511, and their new trading links with China, many thousands of Chinese moved to the growing city over the next two hundred and fifty years of Portuguese and Dutch rule. However dwindling trade trajectories were reflected in a declining Chinese population. It was not until 1786 when the British East India Company took possession of Penang, and again after 1842 following the foreign concessions within the Chinese treaty ports, that trading ties were reinforced. The many internal upheavals in China were catalysts for the Chinese to emigrate in large numbers to escape their economic predicament and take up business opportunities in the new Asian colonial settlements.

Between 1840 and 1900 the shophouse style evolved to incorporate a more decorated façade with carved doorways, distinctive gable ends and terracotta roof tiles. In response to the tropical climate, louvred shutters were used to protect openings on the upper storeys, with air-wells introduced for ventilation. Later, and more eclectic, models were influenced by Western styles and decorative devices reflected

British colonial influences with full-length upper storey windows. The upper storey was designed to project over the pavement, supported by pillars, creating a colonnaded public circulation space at ground level, and separated from the adjoining roadway by a granite step. "Late Straits" period shophouses were often highly decorated with projecting columns, arches, plaster relief, embossed tiles and ceramic air-vents. An Art Deco style followed the European design trend in the 1930s with geometrically designed façades and plaster wall finishes replacing the

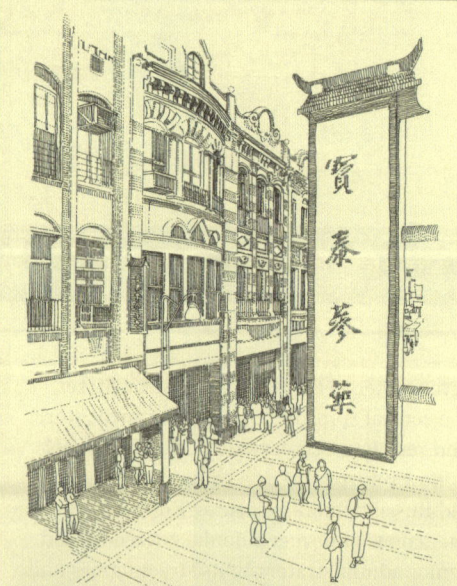

Dinhua Street is representative of one of the oldest districts in Taipei dating from the Ching dynasty. A programme of regeneration has upgraded most of the older structures.

9   Lee, H.Y., 'The Singapore Shophouse: An Anglo-Chinese Urban Vernacular', in *Asia's Old Dwellings: Tradition, Resilience and Change*, Ed. Ronald G. Knapp, Oxford University Press, Oxford, 2003

earlier decoration. Designs were even further simplified from the 1950s, reflecting Modernist influences together with the availability of new building materials and construction techniques. As shophouses were constructed mainly by Chinese builders and craftsmen in so many parts of Asia, they can be regarded as a predominantly Chinese building type with a common heritage, yet adapted to suit local environmental and economic conditions.

Cultural diversity tended to reflect a combination of varied neighbourhoods with long-standing social heterogeneity, distinctive urban design characteristics, spacious layouts for Western residents under colonial regimes, and dense concentrations of urban terraces. These came to represent the dominant older typologies and characteristic heritage quarters as the post-industrial city changed its economic emphasis. In certain locations, notably in Indonesian cities and the Straits settlements, the outer semi-rural fringe would be characterised by *kampongs* that became subsumed into expanding city forms through consolidation and redevelopment.

Migrant settlers tended to bring with them both design and building traditions, modified to fit climatic and contextual situations, but also responsive to prevailing foreign influences and available materials. In tropical situations, colonnaded structures and verandahs functioned as transitional spaces which regulated the relationship between internal and external space. The grid layouts allowed for shophouse depths of several times the width, with internal airwells and service lanes at the rear. Each floor could be sub-divided into semi-private compartments through partitions to increase the capacity to sub-let spaces to new immigrants.

Singapore's five-foot ways act as both protected circulation and display areas, forming a physical transition between the public and private realms.

Low-rise Chinese tenement structures in Hong Kong constructed after 1842 were known as *t'ang-lou* where the internal walls were separated from the structural fabric to allow for flexible sub-division. This allowed Chinese city quarters to absorb high population densities and intense patterns of economic activity. The open arcade was a southern European design feature probably introduced by the Portuguese in Penang,

Malacca and Macau, and later transferred to shophouse street designs in Hong Kong and the Chinese Treaty Ports, such as Canton, Swatow and Amoy. Its most widespread use was in Singapore during the early twentieth century, where the 'five-foot way' — a generic feature formed by an overhanging upper storey — characterised large parts of the city, acting as both a social and commercial threshold, and offering untold opportunities for hawker activities.

What makes the shophouse stand out from other indigenous Asian residential types is its relationship to the process of city-making through a consistency of form but with a variety of interpretations, including aesthetic treatment. The redevelopment of Singapore's Orchard Road, from a shophouse avenue made up of small lots to a high-rise commercial and hotel spine in the 1970s, creates a contrasting template to the older row houses and narrow roadways of Emerald Hill, and the inter-linked shophouses that have been converted into cafes and bars.

The Singapore shophouse, while technically reflecting a Chinese typology that developed virtually simultaneously in various port cities, evolved in both stylistic and ornate terms to embody an almost unique combination of Chinese details and European neo-Classical references. There were several reasons for this, the primary one being the rapidly developing coastal settlements in the eighteenth and nineteenth centuries as competing Western nations developed Asian trading routes that became bases for trade in and around the South China Sea. As territorial 'possessions' changed hands, the British became a prevalent force in nineteenth century trade, opening up the Chinese treaty ports, the Malay peninsula,

the Straits settlements, and the Indian sub-continent. European settlers introduced aspects of 'grand design' that were prevalent in Western cities — including classical orders, Palladian motifs, baroque, neo-Classical, and later Art Deco elements — and combined them to create a new architectural realm. Through the involvement of builders, carpenters and compradors, these details were passed across strict typological boundaries (and also across regional borders), to insinuate themselves by adaptive integration within the most prevalent of building prototypes — the new Chinese commercial enclaves. Associated with the

continued development of trading links was the migration of traders from southern China, in particular Amoy, Foochow and Canton. They brought new stylistic innovations to such outposts as Singapore and the Philippines, which then intermingled with local carpentry and masonry skills to evolve new typologies and decorative additions. In some cases these typologies were then brought back to China by returnees, for example to the streets of Amoy (Xiamen) and its villas on Gulangyu island.

The "bamboo barrel houses" in Canton and Hanoi were designed with a long plan form and narrow frontage, the frontal part serving

as the shop and the rear part residential, while the upper storey could be either for residential or storage use. A narrow lane divided units, which were largely laid out in parallel street blocks, so that servicing could be carried out from the rear. A similar type can be found in the old city of Hanoi where they are known as 'tube' houses. In this case, the long plan form might extend to 60 metres and is divided by courtyards to introduce light and ventilation. In late nineteenth century Canton, certain shophouse streets faced the waterways that permeated the Liwan area of the city. The transport of mineral ores and jade depended on the waterways and the orientation of shophouses facilitated and enhanced both the delivery and business systems. These later became centres of visitor interest, including the Yuan Sheung and Hua Lin jade markets, and as water channels became filled in for road formation strong retail edges were established alongside new transport corridors.

In Malaysia and Indonesia the relationship between built and social characteristics also draws on climatic traditions of the village or *kampong*. These relate to the informal clustering of dwellings that allow cooling breezes to penetrate the spaces between them, while roof overhangs provide shade and protection from tropical rain downpours. They not only act as an ecological response to climate, but also reflect interrelationships between extended family structures and shared land use patterns, where communal space is more of a focus than private space. This sense of openness is transferred to modern villa design that maximises external wall surface exposure and window openings to facilitate air movement.

Shophouse streets and clusters still

maintain a low-density and predominantly 'green' presence in many rapidly regenerating cities. As city cores change their identity and mass through new business structures, fragmented older quarters take on what has been described as a 'bazaar economy'. Commercial transactions relate to the street framework of shops and mobile vendors, including street markets, which embody a colourful character, independent of the centre. These older and more flexible quarters have strong social and cultural ties, as well as persistent but relatively informal trading patterns. They are responsive to facets of change, but vulnerable to officially sanctioned renewal policies on the often questionable grounds of improving conditions and imposing high urban densities commensurate with increased urban land values.

The conservation methods adopted in some shophouse street blocks has sometimes attracted criticism as to its authenticity, particularly in Singapore, where the process has often entailed restoring the façades and rebuilding within the existing party walls. This raises questions, not only about the inherent architectural qualities of older buildings in the preservation process, but the lack of reference to traditional activities which contributed to the spirit of place. Bereft of their former intangible qualities of use and diversity, this approach to conservation can distort rather than reflect cultural memory. Parallel to this is the creation of a simulacrum — the replacement of something that was intrinsic to the economic and social activities and traditions of an area, with a representation that relegates its cultural value to the commodified realm of the tourist market.

Macau's old city core was granted World Heritage status by UNESCO in 2005.

48-52 HANG NGANG STREET within the Thirty-Six Streets Quarter in Hanoi. There is a strong interface between domestic and public activities, some of which share the same space. In most recent infill construction, roof terraces with canopies or lattices provide additional private space, used for practical purposes such as clothes drying during the day, and for sitting out in the evenings.

COLONISING
PARADOXES

Civilising
Ideologies and
Transformative
Filters

THE COLONIAL INTERVENTIONIST PROCESS IN ASIA

Colonialism refers to the establishment and maintenance of rule, by coercion or conquest, over an indigenous people who then become subordinate to the ruling power and in the process experience some degree of cultural transformation. Colonial settlements tend to sanctify this process in physical form through civil divisions and superimpositions. In older colonial situations such as India, patterns of settlement were commonly referred to as the Civil Lines or Military Cantonments. In Asia, the main colonising regimes have been the Spanish, Portuguese, Dutch, British and French, and in terms of the motivation and priorities attached to the process itself, a division can be drawn. In the sixteenth and seventeenth centuries the Spanish in the Philippines, and Portuguese in Goa and Malacca, were motivated not merely by financial gain but religious ideology. Spatial planning and the extravagant disposition of church property was related to forms of social control, and the cultural assimilation of the indigenous populations into new urban communities. The British, Dutch and French on the other hand were drawn to Asia primarily for trading benefit but with strong religious undertones and backed up by military force where necessary. With the opening of the Suez Canal in 1869, much of Asia became subject to Western imperialism through partition by the British, French and Dutch.

More than 70 per cent of Western territory in Asia was acquired between 1860 and 1914, often involving military conquests. The process largely came about through a combination of technological advance and commercial ambition, coupled with a strong moral fervour. Diplomatic rivalry among European powers was a main factor in this process, along with the need to establish trade routes to feed the needs of the industrial revolution and to protect the flanks of existing possessions. This unleashed forces of modernisation and urbanisation, that in the dying years of colonial regimes created the first seeds of nationalism. A significant factor in this was that while the infusion of Western capital and technological knowhow did not in general raise local economic well-being, Western education and training together with knowledge of the tumultuous social movements happening in Europe, acted to raise expectations and ambitions.[1]

The colonial city has been termed 'parasitic' in the sense that it inhibited economic progress in relation to natural growth and need, with a commensurate exploitation of natural resources and a redirection of the domestic economy. Income differentials within the poorer economies made immigration to the cities from rural areas essential for survival, creating a cheap labour supply for marginal occupations in urban industries. From the mid-nineteenth century until the 1930s, two-thirds of British exports went to its colonised territories or dominions, which in turn satisfied almost half of Britain's imports during the same period. Urban industrial processes in Britain were reliant on raw materials from its colonies while at the same time colonial cities were dependant on British capital and administrative expertise in city management. It was from these cities as ports, commercial entrepôts and centres for accumulation and consumption with new and expressive identities, that many of Asia's

[1] SarDesai, D.R., *Southeast Asia: Past and Present*, Westview Press, Colorado, 2010

modern 'global' cities developed. In India the incorporation of indigenous elites as part of the imperial system provided some continuity of the pre-colonial social hierarchy and cultural divide, while engendering support for the new institutions of governance. New infrastructure and transport systems extended lines of authority well beyond the cities, facilitating new patterns of urbanisation as well as exploitation of rural resources.

The interdependent nature of this process in the capitalist world-economy is equally demonstrated through the commensurate urban and industrial growth process in the colonising countries themselves through expansion of different modes of production. The urban form associated with colonial settlements can therefore be viewed as part of an interventionist system, unified by its built environment and largely determined by its modes of social formation, production and control of surplus.

Colonialism together with the import of market capitalism and *laissez-faire* ideology also had a striking impact on land values and the urban landscape. By creating an impetus to urban growth and manipulating land availability in cities such Hong Kong, a process of almost constant redevelopment was instigated, at the same time inducing a vertical urbanism, and increased government activity in aspects of city-building such as public housing and new town development.

Anthony King has argued that colonial planning was the vehicle by which a Western ideological style of master planning was exported to various types of settlement including both cities and military quarters. This was backed up by regulatory ordinances geared mainly to health and safety for

SIR STANFORD RAFFLES introduced Freemasonry to Singapore although the Masonic Lodge was only inaugurated in 1879, to a neo-Classical design by Thomas Cargill, the Municipal Engineer. Incorporated into the façade are the traditional Masonic symbols. The lodge overlooks Coleman Street, with a public dining room acting as a bridge between the public and the markedly ceremonial realms.

Statues on the Main Building frontage of the University of Santo Tomas in Manila were designed by the Italian sculptor, Francesco Monti to symbolise Hope, Faith and Charity.

THE FORMER SECRETARIAT, built after the British annexation of Upper Burma between 1889 and 1905, is the largest colonial-era building in Yangon, designed by Henry Hoyne-Fox from the Public Works Department. It was in the south-west wing that General Aung San and six ministerial colleagues were assassinated in 1947, and where independence was marked in January 1948. The building was left empty in 2005 after the government moved to Nay Pyi Taw, and it is now scheduled for renovation. The surrounding roads are lined with colonial-era structures.

the public good, and control of land that aided the expedient process of urban management. While the modus operandi of colonial interventionist and transformative processes was essentially economic, King sets out seven categories of features that characterise the colonial city and are intrinsic to the interventionist process of colonialism: geopolitical, functional, political/economic, political, social/cultural, racial/ethnic and physical/spatial.[2] Urban design therefore emerged from a symbiotic inter-relationship and dialogue between these aspects. McGee suggests three fundamental forms of urban settlement: firstly pre-industrial cities such as Yangon (Rangoon) or Hanoi onto which Western forms were grafted; secondly planned cities such as Singapore and Batavia (Jakarta), which grew independently of pre-industrial forms, with a Western imposed planning framework; and thirdly indigenous or royal settlements such as Yogyakarta which retained their essential character during periods of colonial rule.[3]

Port settlements, established primarily for trade, were often constructed to meet quite basic requirements, essentially the need for a protected anchorage with capacity for residential and godown areas. Under these regimes cultural and ethnic divisions were often institutionalised. The evolution of early port settlements into primate cities was a nineteenth century phenomenon. This stemmed from new governmental and administrative systems as they moved away from trading and military pre-occupations,

2   King, A.D., *Colonial Urban Development: Culture, Social Power and Environment*, Routledge & Kegan Paul, London, 1976
3   McGee, T.G., *The South East Asian City*, G Bell and Sons Ltd, London, 1967

and varied according to the degree to which the indigenous society was represented in this process. In certain situation, such as Singapore where there was a wide social composition, the natural formation of separate ethnic immigrant groups such as Indians, Malays and Chinese helped to reinforce extended patterns of kinship and local welfare.

Colonial urban design can be largely considered as an exported practice, shaped by expatriates and officials in the service of a governing body. The urban design of New Delhi between 1911 and 1940 was almost entirely given over to administrative and governmental functions. Local populations were therefore seen to have a supporting rather than an inclusive role, often reflected in stratified housing policies, municipal controls and statutory legislation that regulated both the urban environment and behavioural patterns, even though the same buildings came to house the national government after 1947. In many cases this unwittingly created the ingredients for a contested urban landscape as ideas and practices shifted and evolved from one imperial location to another. In urban design terms the institutional functions of government, law, religion and economy translated into the first public buildings — the fortifications, barracks, court houses, police stations and prisons, some of which have been converted to new uses. This includes a fine group of buildings in Hong Kong dating back to the mid-nineteenth century — the Central Police Station, Victoria Prison and Magistrates Court and Married Quarters that are currently being rehabilitated for cultural and commercial purposes. In Singapore the City Hall built in 1929 is now the National Art Gallery, and Fort Canning

Regeneration of nineteenth century police and prison structures in Hong Kong

has been converted into a War Museum.

Later, institutions leaned towards necessary services such as hospitals, schools, and cultural buildings which symbolically reinforced the prevailing colonial culture. At the same time private investment developed more commercial components — the trading houses, banks, shops, clubs and hotels. Building controls, together with a land market orchestrated by colonial bodies and the provision of roads, transport systems and utility infrastructure, also had implications for both spatial organisation, ethnic segregation and social stratification. A degree of spatial segregation between ethnic groups in some of the early settlements was generally expressive of inherent practices within some indigenous communities. This tended to change and fluctuate over time through economic and social advancement.

The prolonged effects of colonial urbanisation as part of a political, cultural and economic process are somewhat open-ended — on the one hand the colonising power incorporated the subject state or city into a capitalist urban system, but in the process introduced the benefits of urban experience along with administrative techniques and ideologies that bequeathed to colonial cities a certain commonality and established the basis for future economic transformation. McGee describes the colonial city as a "cultural filter" through which elements of Westernisation entered the structure of society, so that prominent local figures participated in city administration and began to form an "elite nationalism".[4] However there is an essential difference, which extended into the post-colonial situation; while industrialisation was related directly to urbanisation in terms of expanding production and new development in advanced colonising societies, this led to what Castells has termed 'dependent urbanisation' whereby colonial cities tended to develop as entrepôt economies reflecting an interdependence between production, import and export.[5] To a large extent therefore, patterns of urbanisation in colonial cities, in concert with the political system, acted to ensure stability and continuity of the prevailing institutions.

Colonial dominance was also exerted

4   McGee, 1967, op. cit.
5   Castells, M, *The Urban Question*, Edward Arnold, London, 1977

through professional and technological knowledge in relation to emerging planning ideologies during the inter-war period, and the transfer of this to local populations through an expanding area of professional work in architecture, planning and military engineering. New urbanisation was generally articulated through urban design forms expressive of those in the industrialised 'home' environments, but adapted to meet local climatic and cultural situations. Architectural development therefore ran the full gamut of forms from Neo-Classicism and high imperialist Victoriana, to the blossoming international modernism of the 1930s.

In the post-colonial situation, the advantages of industrial urbanism have steadily diminished along with a revision of Eurocentric ideas. In this situation, changing modes of production, knowledge-based patterns of transactional service industries, and new realms of spatial structures and infrastructure aimed at optimising market processes, have been largely easier to accommodate in Asian primate cities than in the tightly controlled and conserved post-industrial urban cores of the West. This has in turn accelerated the trend in primate cities towards new urban forms and massive programmes of city expansion which in many cases is problematic in terms of urban design.

IMPERIAL TRAJECTORIES

The formation of cities was arguably the most lasting legacy of imperialism. The first colonial cities in Asia were Goa, established by the Portuguese in 1510, and Manila, a Spanish settlement on the Pasig River in the Philippines dating back to 1571.

Portugal and Spain had several things in common. First a background of adventurism and conquest in the Americas which introduced the galleon trade between Europe and South America. The Spanish *conquistadores* had honed imperial ambitions through territorial expansion, and were able to draw on considerable city-building experience in the New World, which functioned through seats of administrative and commercial power, facilitating hierarchical formations of metropolitan, regional and provincial centres. The first Spanish expedition to the Philippines was in fact not from Europe but from Mexico.

A second commonality was the intensely purposeful and proselytising force of Catholicism which brought about economic exploitation and cultural transformation as part of the expanding empires. Religious conversion was therefore a keystone of early colonial ambition, and urbanisation was seen as an integral aspect of this "civilising mission". The colonial primate cities were designated *ciudades de españoles* or 'Spanish cities', while Catholic missionaries in outlying *cabeceras* acted as orchestrators of Hispanisation, whereby mission centres were gradually transformed into substantial towns. This systematic process was imposed in the Philippines, bringing about a practical transition from scattered coastal settlement patterns to compact townships of which Manila was developed as the capital.

Portugal's subjugation to Spain in the late sixteenth century led to its slow decline in Europe and the Americas. This led to a gradual loss of influence over its initial 'possessions' in Asia (notably Goa and Malacca), although the Portuguese remained active in China and eventually consolidated their Asian trading ambitions in Macau.

Spain's colonial city building parameters were embodied in the *Ordinanzas* — a detailed collection of statutes and guidelines issued by Philip II in 1573 and later incorporated in the Laws of the Indies. The physical form and strategic impact of this revolved around the role of the Hispanic city as an instrument of colonial rule and domination. The *Ordinanzas* represented an attempt to equate uniform urban design parameters with administrative and legislative controls for both coastal and inland cities, therefore practical knowledge was effectively

Marble Palace, Kolkata

codified as part of the planning process. A further administrative measure, again reflecting colonial experience in the Americas, was the *Audiencia* — a legal tribunal which acted to counterbalance the authoritarian power of the prevailing Governor-general and shape future colonial direction as the nucleus of the first Western colonial empire.

The link between colonialism and internationalism is embedded in imperial ideology and can be traced back to the eighteenth century economic models of Adam Smith.[6] Colonialism brought with it modernisation as an economic concept — the shift from production based on local markets and self-sufficiency, to an export market of resources and an import market for foreign goods. This change brought with it colossal shifts in infrastructure — roads and rail systems, plantations, industrial concerns,

banking and finance, all assimilated within new patterns of land use.

A further stage in the historical interventionist process took place in a series of port cities where European East India companies established trading posts, beginning in 1602 with the Dutch in India and Batavia. This type of body had no previous equivalent in Asia and was therefore a significant catalyst for geopolitical change. Haneda Masashi extracted various points of cross-cultural relevance, all with interventionist connotations relating to the location and urban design of fort and factory settlements of the Dutch and English East India Companies, also noting their significance in terms of local planning strategies, ethnic separation, fusion of architectural styles, land and property ownership, and aspects of local law.[7] However the cautious absorption of historical narrative

as part of post-colonial nationalism (with its new political and cultural ambitions, achieved within a relatively short time-frame), could be argued to have been abruptly recalibrated in primate cities through a rapidly evolving commercial globalisation spurred on by economic competition. Asian cities that perhaps only embraced manufacturing industry in the 1950s or 1960s, have experienced rapid transformation in the post-industrial age, as societal and cultural modes of expression extend from national to global, and interactive engagement between the two acts to personify their emerging identity.

In much of Asia, the impact and dependencies generated by colonial occupation almost inevitably created an urban settlement dominated by a first rank of cities. Population growth from the late eighteenth to mid-twentieth centuries therefore encouraged migration of certain ethnic groups, particularly those from India and China, from one part of Asia to another. Burgeoning relationships structured new commercial areas and functional entities, for example administrative and service centres, military establishments and ports. Cultural interaction and mutual trading advantages have in some cases generated urban commonalities, reinforced in recent times through mega-urban growth trajectories. While regional and cross-border integrative forces have gained solid momentum, the fragmented nature of regional growth is made more complex by the international growth of service-led and knowledge-based development, and the rapidity of information transfer. A further aspect has been the longstanding position of private investors as main agents of development. These

6   Ferguson, N, *The Ascent of Money*, Penguin Books, London and New York, 2009
7   This is the basis on which Haneda Masashi and others based historical studies, see *Asian Port Cities 1600-1800 – Local and Foreign Cultural Interactions*, NUS Press in association with Kyoto University Press, Singapore and Kyoto, 2009

MANILA CATHEDRAL has been rebuilt eight times since the first structure of nipa and bamboo, built by a Royal Decree in 1579 in Manila. A series of stone buildings commenced in 1597 and suffered various degrees of damage by earthquakes. The 1879 design by Vicente Serrano followed the seventeenth century plan by Juan de Uguccioni with a mix of Byzantine, Romanesque, Baroque, and Gothic details, together with the addition of side chapels. The building was then reduced in height and survived until 1945 when it was badly damaged during the American bombardment. The present version reconstructed in 1958 with help from the Vatican retained the façade but with a

tall bell tower that acts as a local landmark. The centre of the cross on the dome is a reference point for the astronomical longitudes of the Philippine Archipelago. The bronze main door, cast in Italy, depicts scenes from the cathedral's history. The Plaza Roma adjoining Manila Cathedral, the original Plaza Mayor, was converted into a pack in 1797, and renamed Plaza McKinley in 1901. It was named Plaza Roma in 1961 to honour the Sacred College of Cardinals in Rome. The bronze monument to Carlos IV of Spain was erected in 1824 to commemorate the introduction of smallpox vaccine to the Philippines. It is managed by the Intramuros Administration as a historic landmark.

factors combine as interventionist forces to configure the emerging morphology and spatial structure of the mega-urban region. The challenges therefore relate to the central issue of ensuring workability and sustainability through adequate housing, transport, and environmental infrastructure within an organising framework of administrative responsibility that represents a reasonably co-ordinated polycentric structure. A necessary measure is to exert a greater level of strategic planning at the level of the city region, and where necessary to engender cross-border co-operation between cities to achieve more resilient, sustainable and equitable development patterns.

PLACE AND SPACE IN COLONIAL PLANNING

Urban space often framed ethnic or cultural divisions, as was frequently reflected in residential neighbourhood disposition, where a sense of belonging was articulated and underscored through a separate spatial identity. This extended to the appropriation of specific uses such as clubs or schools that reinforced a sense of community, sometimes physically demarcated by a *cordon sanitaire*. In post-independence contexts, ethnic-spatial divisions gradually gave way to social and economic ones. In some situations, for example Jakarta, residential patterns represented different urban ecologies.

Modernised quarters for the emerging middle-class elite of civil servants, professionals and military were built on Western suburban models, while poorer immigrant and kampong residents formed more complex and informal patterns.

In Spanish and Portuguese colonial cities great emphasis was placed on community space in the form of a *plaza mayor* defined by a church or cathedral. Stately government or institutional buildings were constructed in proportion to the dimensions and positioning of the space as well as its functions, which included religious pageantry, political ceremonies and military parades. Sites were allocated for monasteries, hospitals, churches

Frontispiece for Chart Atlas, 1710

THE PLAZA ESPANA in Manila with its statue of Philip II of Spain was the site of the Santo Domingo Church and Convent of the Dominican Order. It was destroyed and rebuilt several times before the bombardment of 1945. From 1593 it housed the Nuestra Senora de Santisimo Rosario, honoured for her divine intervention in the Spanish victory against the Dutch. The neo-Classical Aduana or Customs House, completed in 1829, was designed by Tomás Cortes to attract merchant activity within the city and served for a time as the Central Bank and Treasury of the Philippines.

and chapels, which emphasised long-term political intentions. Design guidelines also laid down considerations to be given to environmental and climatic factors, including the location of polluting industries.

Ashcroft points out that the concept of 'place' in colonisation has much to do with the ways in which spatiality was conceived in the West through the development of modern mapping, the discovery of longitude and the establishment of Greenwich Mean Time. When this is linked with 'knowledge' and 'reason', together with the 'vision' embodied in the European Enlightenment, the dominance of space in the colonised city becomes apparent.[8] Maps from the sixteenth century — the results of Western voyages of discovery — placed Europe ideologically in the centre of the world, while the refinement of ship building techniques and the conquering of oceans, made the furthest parts of the world increasingly accessible. Thus the map took on ideological significance, textualising spatial settings by re-inscribing place names and overlaying surfaces with predominantly European forms, and physically annexing local place values.

Cadastral mapping by European land surveyors was a further instrument for intervention, as the delineation of land was a means of imposing a new administrative and economic order on a colonised territory, together with a demarcation of ownership. In India, British surveyors mapped the entire sub-continent in a Trigonometric Survey and in the process British proprietary rights of land ownership replaced the Mughal system of land tenure.[9] British surveyors from India surveyed Hong Kong's New Territories in the nineteenth century, naming local streams after the great Indian rivers — the Sutlej and Indus. Land registration procedures required a compass bearing on all roads, which necessitated the adoption of straight rather than curvilinear alignments, many of which were laid out by military engineers to somewhat standard patterns. This included specialised building forms for new

8 Ashcroft, B, *On Post-Colonial Futures: Transformation of Colonial Culture*, Continuum, London, New York, 2001
9 Edney, M, 'Mapping and Empire: Trigonometric Surveys in India and the European Concept of Systematic Survey', in *Of Planting and Planning – The Making of British Colonial Cities*, Ed. Robert Home, E and FN Spon, London, 1997, p39

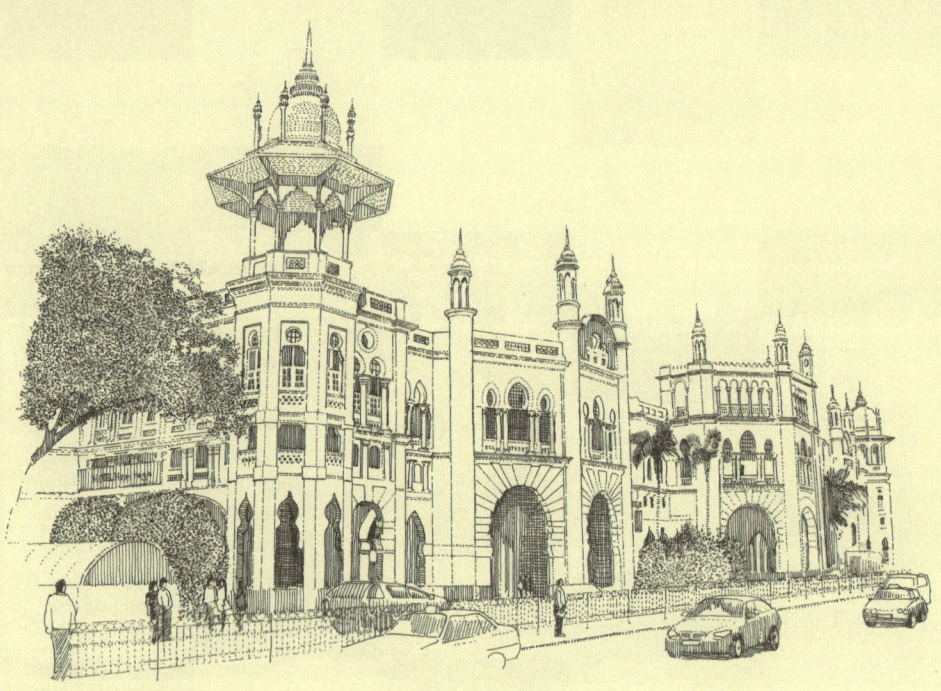

THE OLD KUALA LUMPUR RAILWAY STATION (Bangunan Stesen Kereta Api) was built in 1892, replacing an earlier building. Designed by A B Hubbock it is similar to the Sultan Abdul Samad building by the Public Works architect A C Norman, and its domed towers, minarets and Moorish fenestration is in part credited with establishing a Malaysian architectural style with which it is still identified, some way removed from its indigenous roots. Major renovation was carried out in 1986, and it now houses a miscellaneous collection of restaurants, and the station hotel.

institutions, such as barracks, prisons and even clock towers.

Nineteenth century colonial power was also expressed in symbolic representations associated with space. Statues in prominent positions were invariably images of imposing officers related to the European hegemony — rulers, military figures and local dignitaries. These were in some cases eventually replaced by statues of independence leaders. Urban space also reflected cultural traits and in certain situations framed contested power struggles over its use and appropriation.[10]

At the same time the development of perspective for artistic representation of space, allowed it to be appropriated for idealised or utopian city forms — a means of perceiving and conceptualising urbanisation through objectification and absoluteness.[11] In this sense the physical assertion of a new transforming identity became the embodiment of power. Architectural representation in, for example, colonial India and Malaysia, began to reflect a dialogue between Western interpretation of Saracenic forms for major civic buildings that remain as ambivalent nationalist icons, embedded in the experience of place and blurring the edges between different regimes. Post-colonial cities have therefore become urban palimpsests where both inscriptive trace elements and erasures underscore complex historical associations, but also the contemporary experience of place with its reconstituted edges and boundaries.

BRITISH COLONIAL CITY BUILDING IN ASIA

The legitimacy of British colonial rule was based on 'moral and material progress' — a tool to introduce modernity to subject peoples.[12] However its practical basis lay in the slave trade, which Britain dominated in the sixteenth and seventeenth centuries. The transport of millions of Africans to Spanish territories in the Indies transformed Britain's economy through the resulting import trade, which in turn built up a money market and created a new commercial and political class. The vague principles of colonization, later applied to various parts of Asia, were honed in the Caribbean, North America and the New World. Its later stage from the mid-eighteenth century effectively stemmed from the institutionalisation of the European Enlightenment, which was seen as releasing entire populations from subjugation under the prevailing regimes of oppression. This can in some ways also be considered an evangelical mission that emanated from benevolent reformist ideologies experienced in eighteenth century Britain and other European countries, and coincided with avenues of trade or conquest. Urban development, new engineering infrastructure, and educational initiatives were part of a modernising programme that tended to downplay or compromise local cultural heritage, traditions and values within colonial constructions. Modernisation and "betterment" therefore accorded with Western

10 Yeoh, B.S.A., *Contesting Urban Space: Power Relations and the Urban Built Environment in Colonial Singapore*, Oxford University Press, Oxford, 1996
11 Ashcroft, 2001, op. cit.
12 Fischer–Tiné, H and Mann, M, *Colonialism as Civilizing Mission – Cultural Ideology in British India*, Anthem Press, London, 2004

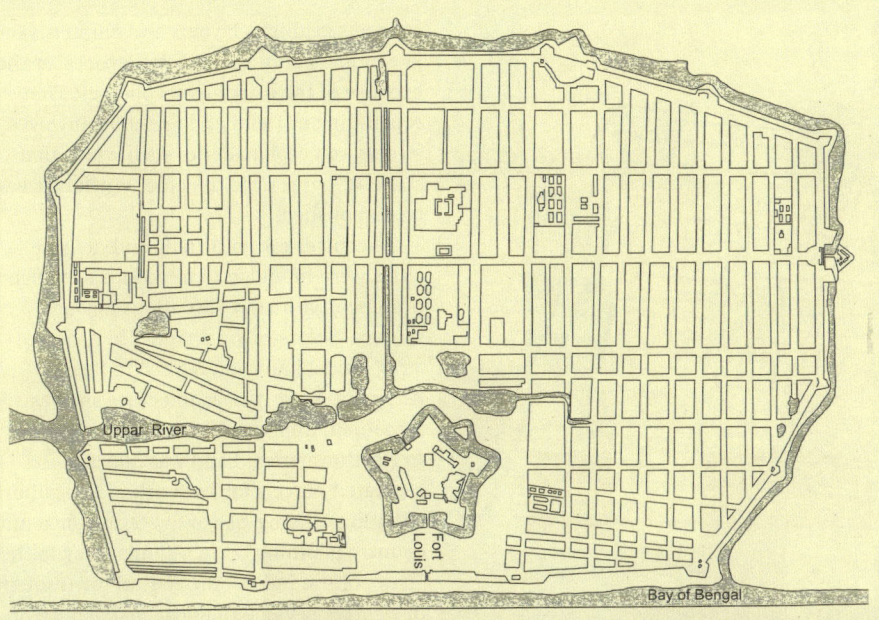

French plan of Pondicherry around Fort Louis, 1755, showing grid-iron layout of streets, that came to be associated with both local trades and cultural groups.

notions of administration and organisation, which included the consideration of land as an economic commodity. Reform was associated largely with recalibrating the relationship between the individual, government and society.[13] This combination of "Christianity, Commerce and Civilization" created, almost accidentally, the drive towards Empire.

Arguably the turning point came with the Battle of Plassey in 1757 and the resulting Treaty of Paris which redirected Britain's trading role in Asia at almost precisely the same time as its American 'possessions' were seizing independence. With the defeat of Napoleon in 1815 together with the revolutionary quagmire in much of Europe, Britain's merchants were virtually free to explore all available markets, driven by control of international sea channels. The East India Company ended up raising its own military forces to translate trading operations into a wider drive to political power.

If planning can be said to represent control of the built environment, then colonial planning often embodied coercive control over populations through an amalgam of defensive and military installations, resettlement programmes, and even the design and distribution of public open space. While the Enlightenment period technically strengthened the 'rights of man' in Europe, the nineteenth century period of Empire and military activity was also a time of prison building, asylums, cantonments and transport of inconvenient social groups such as convicted criminals, debtors, and religious dissenters to far-flung colonies, which sometimes transformed new urban environments into forced labour camps. The first concentration camps were built by General Kitchener during Britain's military campaign against the Afrikaner Boers. In post-war Malaya, in order to combat the Communist insurgency during the 'Emergency' of 1948-56, and to protect Britain's investment in rubber estates, more than half a million Chinese were forcibly 'resettled' in village camps surrounded by double barbed wire fences laid out by the Town Planning Department. Temporary camps built along not dissimilar lines were set up in Hong Kong in the 1980s to cater for Vietnamese refugee 'boatpeople'.

Robert Home pointed out that the predecessor of Britain's eighteenth century Colonial Office was called the Board of Plantations, as a means of settling or re-settling people. He identifies three ideological positions with regard to programmes of colonial urbanisation: first, expression of political authority through a symbolic representation of physical form using the vocabulary of urban design; second, the accumulation of wealth from trade, extraction and production, which in certain circumstances combined private enterprise with political control; and third,

13 Fischer–Tiné and Mann, 2004, op. cit., p32

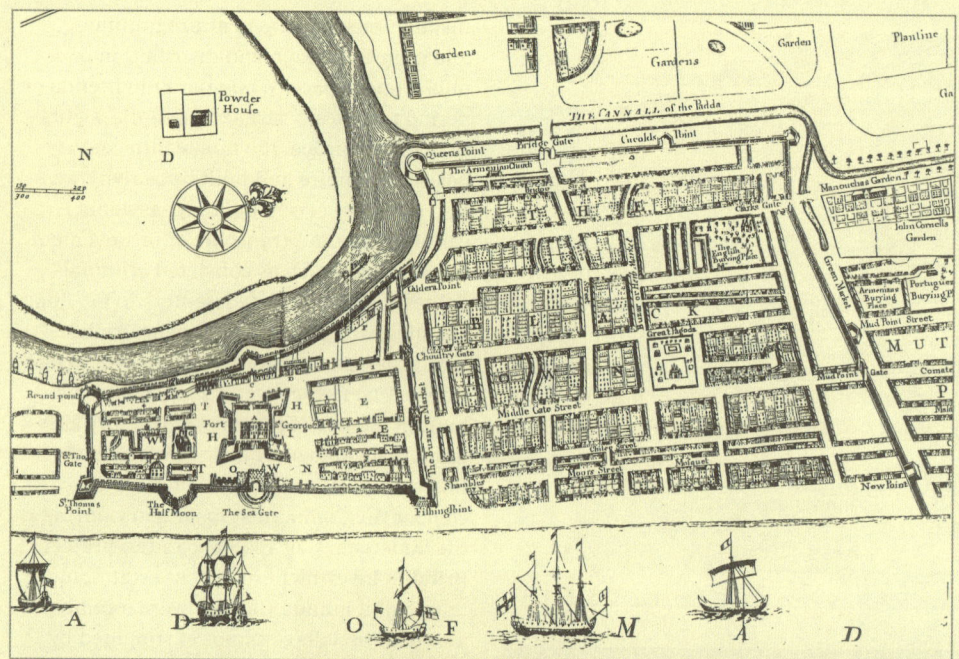

Map of Madras 1710. Major clearances to facilitate defensible space around Fort St George was instigated by the French and continued by the British after 1749.

a "utopian" potential to experiment with forms of social organisation.[14]

In most cases of colonial settlement, the number of foreign settlers was comparatively small in relation to the indigenous population. The nature of occupation was imperialism, embedded by new administrative and cultural institutions, and cemented through its language and social customs. English constitutional history was seen as a benign process that had undergone lengthy refinement as a result of the European 'Enlightenment', and this tended to generate

a sense of inevitability to imperial expansion, which made it easy to obtain political endorsement.

The Spanish and Portuguese modes of urbanisation within their empires formed a preliminary model for British colonial city planning from the late seventeenth century, although the general lack of a religious agenda under British regimes focussed the exercise particularly on trade and associated port development. For the next 250 years this was modified and elaborated in terms of reconciling political and social forces through

spacious grid-iron layouts and emphasis on key public buildings and civic spaces, at the expense of the existing morphology. The replanning of Delhi and Lucknow involved streets and esplanades of such width that some 40 per cent of the older city fabric had to be demolished.

As centres for both trade and defence, cities were intended to introduce a civilising presence, with land allocations for new settlers. Before being directed to Asia, the 'grid' model had been refined in South Australia, West Africa, and cities such as Savannah, Charleston, and Philadelphia in North America. Land was allocated in regulated parcels for both urban and suburban situations, giving rise to the term "town and country planning".[15] In a similar way to the "Laws of the Indies", the central town square or *padang* became the principal feature of planned development as places for meetings, military training, public statuary, landscape and recreation, with their urban design based on forms of Renaissance planning that had been widely adopted elsewhere, for example in seventeenth century London estates. In Bombay and Calcutta the *Maidan* — a wide space demarcating the theoretical line of fire from fortifications — was used as an esplanade for flaneurs at certain fixed times.

A paradox of nineteenth century colonial planning was the notion that minimal government interference in British's free trade situation depended on much higher degrees of regulation in colonial situations.[16] This tended to automatically translate into clearly demarcated neighbourhood sectors and 'grand designs', which secured political hegemony with little consideration for indigenous urban traditions or previous types of municipal

[14] Home, R, *Of Planting and Planning – The Making of British Colonial Cities*, E and FN Spon, London, 1997
[15] Home, 1997, op. cit.
[16] Home, 1997, op. cit.

MUMBAI'S MAIDANS were created by the British in the nineteenth century as a 'free field of fire' between the walled fort and the native city in order to ward off attack. As these tracts of land were kept free of structures, they developed as recreationally oriented public parkland, together with an esplanade that stretched from the fort to the western shoreline. Wide avenues bisect the esplanade creating the Oval Maidan, Cross Maidan and Azad Maidan, which act to relieve the high physical density of the city and provide simultaneous opportunities for sport and

relaxation, but also for political rallies. One of the largest is the Shiraji Maidan located in the western waterfront, and surrounded by a boardwalk. The Oval Maidan in the foreground is used for cricket, defined by the backdrop of Mumbai's High Court. In the background is the old Secretariat, designed by the Public Works Department. Its completion in 1874 set a standard for subsequent civic projects, and its long façade creates a compositional urban design with the adjacent High Court and University.

organisation. Lord Wellesley, who arrived as Governor-General of Calcutta in 1798, even demolished previous colonial institutional and private buildings in the city, and replaced them with an imposing new Government House which continues to symbolise the core area. A number of public building types were expressly representative of Western cultural symbolism. These ranged from government offices, educational institutions and post offices, to railway stations and even opera houses, such as that built by the French in Hanoi. Iconic buildings and urban designs

were not only seen as imparting specific Western cultural values, but were intended to be imposing.

Port cities became the most important urban and economic entities in the development of both colonial and post-colonial systems, opening up vast Asian markets for European trade. The Dutch East India Company has been described by Neil Ferguson as the world's first joint-stock company.[17] Britain's port development programme in Asia began with the British East India Company which acquired Madras

A bronze statue of Queen Victoria by Sir George Frampton gazes down to the northern drive of Government House in Kolkata. The throne is decorated with representations of Art, Literature and Justice, the Lion of Britain and the Tiger of India.

[17] Ferguson, N, The Ascent of Money. Broadcast video.

in 1639, Bombay in 1665 and Calcutta in 1690. They were known collectively as the Imperial Presidency towns, and used as stepping stones to push further into East Asia while extending sea routes. Ports were progressively linked to an expanding system of land transport and rail lines that opened up the hinterland of cities to further economic development through plantation agriculture and mineral exploitation. During the second half of the nineteenth century Britain controlled virtually all major ports between Europe and Asia, from Port Said, Aden, and Bombay to Singapore, Hong Kong and the major Chinese treaty ports. In China the Inspectorate of Imperial Customs was established in 1881, run by 700 foreign commissioners under Sir Robert Hart, and apart from collecting import and export taxes also carried out coastal surveys, drew up navigation and hydrographic charts and managed the ports. This was generally mirrored across all British controlled ports, through a sequence of harbour-masters, shipwrights and local navigation aids.

With shipping and the rapid expansion of export industries increasing the pressure on ports, harbours had to be extended, dredged, and in some cases relocated with new docking facilities to accommodate larger vessels, reflecting the increased commercial interaction between port cities. Bombay and Calcutta, with populations in excess of 800,000 had, by the second half of the nineteenth century, superficially adopted many of the characteristics of British Victorian cities with municipal authorities elected to carry out city improvement works and sanitary measures. Rapid urban growth resulted in extensive slum areas, which created a receptive environment for the

Baroque-style buildings in Zhongyang Street, Harbin, heavily influenced by the city's role as a Russian enclave

spread of disease. Environmental engineering works were subject to negotiation between the authorities and local communities, but were essentially utilitarian, generally based on what was expedient and easy to manage. This type of intervention, itself necessitated by uncontrolled urbanisation and deprivation, frequently provoked discontent among local populations at the imposition of slum clearance and ventilation programmes which involved demolition and redevelopment. Bombay was almost entirely regenerated

using British planning theory and techniques, including low-cost housing areas for industrial workers. By the turn of the twentieth century it was the busiest port in Asia, with two-thirds of India's cotton mills producing yarn for export. Its gradual transition to a financial centre was accompanied by the constant remodelling of its urban framework to include new symbols of imperial status — the institutional, banking and commercial buildings.

In order to carry out remodelling of cities, "Improvement Trusts" were set up, as separate mechanisms from those concerned with port works. This acted to institutionalise urban redevelopment and was based on British planning legislation. The first of these in Bombay in 1898, concerned itself with public health measures, development control, demolition, street widening and reclamation to create additional land. This was followed by similar trusts in Calcutta, Rangoon and Singapore in the early twentieth century. These encountered some local opposition, particularly if proposed changes embodied social or cultural repercussions that stirred up tensions and hostility between castes or those of different religious persuasions. The objectives for Calcutta were "to make provision for the improvement and expansion of the city by opening up congested areas, laying-out and altering of streets, providing open spaces for purposes of ventilation or recreation, demolishing or constructing buildings, acquiring land for the said purposes and for the rehousing of persons of the poorer and working classes displaced by the execution of improvement schemes".[18] In general the programmes acted to remove slum and squatter accommodation, and included

[18] Home, 1997, op. cit., p171

the re-planning of the inner city together with new highways, but generally failed to resolve the prevailing low-cost housing problems. Trusts were later established in other cities, although arguably the greatest success was in Lucknow, where the city authorities were advised by Patrick Geddes who succeeded in minimising demolition and helped to establish an effective low-cost housing programme. Delhi had to wait until 1937 for a transfer of municipal powers to a Trust after mass protests over living conditions.

The Singapore Improvement Trust was created in 1927, and responded to the unsanitary conditions in older housing areas by creating service lanes at the rear of street terraces. Separate authorities for housing, new towns and urban redevelopment remained as features of government organisation in both Singapore and Hong Kong. On the whole, action within the Trusts was insufficiently concerted or comprehensive enough to resolve problems of urban overcrowding, shortage of proper housing, or convey sympathy for older urban traditions.

DESIGN PARADOXES OF SEGREGATION

The extent to which racial or ethnic segregation played a part in British colonial urban design through spatial separation — as a means of maintaining cultural differences and imposing political and social order — has long been discreetly acknowledged. However the notion of segregated quarters went beyond colonial ideologies, reflecting the allocation of separate European trading establishments in a number of eighteenth century Asian cities. In Japanese cities during the Edo period Portuguese, Dutch and Chinese settlements were spatially separated

from Japanese in special areas or *dejimas*, and in order to tighten the prohibition against Christianity, every person had to be registered as a practicing parishioner of a temple. In Nagasaki, Dutch and Chinese were both restricted to separate parts of the city, and relations strictly circumscribed, for instance forbidding foreigners from learning the language — a measure later followed by eighteenth century Chinese law. It might also be said to include the Concession Areas granted to foreign powers in the treaty ports of China in the late nineteenth century.

As a generally deliberate intervention in

the planning process, the discriminatory overtones of segregation are somewhat ambiguous, because this was neither officially nor legally sanctioned in Asian cities. In some situations segregation was introduced into the urban morphology through the very act of city making itself. Even pre-existing and loosely differentiated ethnic divisions became physically circumscribed, often articulated in terms of distinctive urban design elements, and sometimes architecturally elaborated to emphasise differences. In part this reflected the clearly suspect notion of cultural superiority displayed by the paternalistic

THE "MUTINY" or Fatehgarch Memorial in Delhi was constructed on the site of Taylor's Battery to honour British soldiers who were killed during the siege of Delhi in 1857. It is built in the shape of an octagonal tower of red sandstone on a two-tiered platform. It was later rededicated by the Government of Delhi to the soldiers who fought the British during the Mutiny and the names of all British and Indian casualties are inscribed on slabs around the tower.

powers who orchestrated the planning and municipal control systems. A high standard of living and comfortable conditions for early foreign residents preserved social and cultural differences, which hindered urban assimilation, but in the process this possibly helped indirectly to preserve long standing cultural traditions. However in spite of this there remained strong social links and cultural bridges between high-ranking foreign merchants, their local counterparts and the aristocracy, leading to increased intellectual exchange.

In some asian cities segregation polices might arguably be said to have helped perpetuate heterogeneous societies. The plan for Singapore to a large extent framed and consolidated existing ethnic groupings of Chinese, Malay, Indian and Bugis, as well as Europeans. This was at a time of massive trading growth and commensurately high rates of immigration, so segregation was used as a means of reconciling diverse cultures with British customs and administration. Areas were zoned for a 'European Town' with building lots set out for prominent trading houses, Government uses, ethnic reservations and kampongs. The Chinese quarter was informally sub-divided into different provincial groupings based on places of origin e.g. Fukienese and Cantonese. Permanent heads of each ethnic neighbourhood were appointed, possibly emanating from the experience of Stanford Raffles in Java where this was an intelligible procedure within native communities, establishing a basis for local administration. In Singapore the early Planning Committee also allocated street and place names associated with different groups.[19]

In India the segregated cantonments or garrison camps which originated in Poona were built in the mid-nineteenth century and located several kilometres outside the native city. A pertinent consideration in the cantonment system was public health and protection from the periodic epidemics that beset the subcontinent. In response to a Royal Commission in India, the Military Cantonments Act of 1864 became the first piece of legislation in India concerned with measures to improve public health, which included a *cordon sanitaire* between the cantonment and the native city, and limited extension of more spacious layout principles to the wider city framework.

In practice the cantonments operated as virtually self-sufficient and self-governing township enclaves, laid out with residential and community facilities that reinforced the sense of isolation, privilege, and social exclusiveness. Spatial demarcation, better ventilation through building-free zones, and proper service infrastructure clearly reduced the spread of disease in the better off and mainly foreign occupied areas. This generally translated into a segregated system, so that prejudiced reports of dubious health practices in native quarters often turned out to be self-fulfilling prophecies. As British civilian populations within the cantonments increased during the traumatic period following the Indian Mutiny, the sense of separateness and insecurity was perpetuated. This led to the systematic destruction of parts of old Delhi, built by Shah Jahan, at least in part because the intricate morphology of the older areas made them conducive to urban unrest, and difficult to police. Reconstruction was subsequently based on wide streets, transport routes and esplanades through the most built-up part of the cities, sometimes destroying both their urban integrity and religious buildings, and replacing the older morphology with an entirely different urbanism which embodied alien values. A not dissimilar process, entailing dismantling walls and widening of city gates, was carried out in Lahore's Old City. In order to meet the needs of ongoing modernisations, the cantonment enclaves that evolved as 'new' cities, have survived in the post-independence period under new regulatory and urban conditions.

URBAN DESIGN AS POLITICAL PURPOSE

Urban development in British colonial possessions was closely interlinked with industrialisation in the homeland, thus colonisation became the vehicle by which the culture of modern capitalism became inextricably integrated within a single urban system.[20] The late nineteenth century was a time of new planning theories emanating in the West, and strongly influenced Britain in response to the environmental and social ills arising from nineteenth century urban industrialisation. These theories included the Arts and Crafts movement of William Morris and the 'Garden City' movement of Ebenezer Howard, which became tentatively introduced into colonial and concession areas in parallel with the commodification of land. City building therefore took on the characteristics of an urban design laboratory where surplus wealth could be translated into new consumption-oriented city forms reflecting evolving social and economic relations. At the same time certain developing colonial economies had direct links to industrial urbanisation in Europe, so that urban design

[19] Home, 1997, op. cit., p120-121
[20] King, 1976, op. cit., p39

knowledge and development (both theory and practice), were to an extent, symbiotic. India for example supplied cotton to the Lancashire mills, while the Burmese delta area became the chief supplier of rice for milling in London.

Interventionist plans for Western quarters of colonial cities reveal a preoccupation with an "ideal" morphology which evoked the expansive boulevards, gridded avenues and placement of spaces and monuments redolent of a European background. These were deemed appropriate to the new political authority and imposed social hierarchy. Urban design formed a highly evocative and compelling part of this strategy in terms of image, bringing into focus the broad "civilising mission" while reiterating a benevolent spirit of accomplishment amidst the exotic native surrounds. The context for colonial intervention reveals a narrative of events which reflected the rapidly changing geopolitics, industrialising imperatives and religious movements in Europe from the seventeenth century onwards, at a time when new trading trajectories began to fuel political ambitions.

The physical ramifications of urban design represent a multiplicity of contending forces as well as the preoccupations of new city builders. These were partly stylistic impositions through new governmental initiatives and imported professional advisers, but also the results of objective efforts to contextualise physical and economic development with cultural continuity and complex political agendas — a fine balance that was continually shifting. Beyond aesthetic considerations, attempts from foreign interventions to merge Western designs with indigenous forms, motifs and materials, denoted a somewhat paternalistic position, as well as offering certain architectural challenges. Although there were no universal rules, architects and planners such as Patrick Geddes, Edwin Lutyens, Patrick Abercrombie and Ernest Hébrard were largely dependent on specific political intent in determining their principles of urban design, and were aware of the implications of political decisions on both physical form and social conventions.

The decision to move the Indian capital from Calcutta to New Delhi represented a symbolic and deterministic act and was based on the model of the cantonment "Code of Government" — as a highly stratified system of administration which translated itself into an urban design code, and underscored the hierarchical status of the imperial system.

It is arguable that the emergence of town planning as a mainstream profession in Britain in the early twentieth century was as much the result of nineteenth century colonial city building — particularly in India which involved the practical exploration of new ideas — as it was with a growing sense of social purpose and far-reaching ideas in Britain itself (such as the Garden City movement). London in the mid-nineteenth century began to take on the trappings of an imperial capital, through buildings such as the Colonial Office and India Office with their elaborate sculptural references to British overseas power.[21]

Planners who had been active in colonial urban development had a strong influence over new urban design theory. Underlying this was a strong but perhaps exaggerated sense that planning and design had a higher political purpose as being symbolic of the endurance of Empire. Thus the Janpath in the Indian capital of New Delhi virtually coincided with the construction of the Mall in London — both intended to be grandiose in scale, and to emphasise formal processional routes equating with symbolic landmarks. New Delhi, the result of a planning committee chaired by GSC Swinton and including Edwin Lutyens, represented an almost unprecedented scale of urban intervention to the south of the old city. Its system of radiating avenues provided a Beaux Arts setting for a stylised combination of High Victorian classicism and Mughal references that conveyed grand design ideals rather than an integral framework bringing together new and old. Its completion in 1931 was not so much an assertive definition of a secure Empire, but a faltering confidence as to its future.

The involvement in Indian planning by Patrick Geddes began in Madras in 1915. He is credited with an inspired educational role and sensitive approach to urban regeneration, which changed the focus of wholesale demolition and redevelopment undertaken up to this point under the British administration. A theoretician as well as a practitioner, Geddes's work in India occurred in remarkable contrast to much of the grand urban planning gestures of the day. It was concerned with a more surgical process of repair and recovery, protecting indigenous elements in the face of large-scale urban interventions. A comprehension of the dualism inherent in the Asian city, acknowledgement of customs and traditions, and a desire to engage residents in planning operations, set his work apart from the more monumental engineered master plans of the time. He described the process of urban improvement as an evolutionary

21 Paxman, J, *Empire: What Ruling the World Did to the British*, Penguin Group, London and New York, 2011

cycle in which individual activities related to the "highest deeds in the city", and equated the shaping of the environment with social imperatives. His more incremental approach to renewal, conservation and upgrading to meet established community needs and social practices, was very much in line with contemporary planning, including the retention of customs and traditions. Geddes, together with H.V. Lanchester, carried out more than fifty consultancy assessments in various princely states and company towns for clients who were happy to deploy new urban design ideas for city quarters and garden suburbs. Other new settlements included more than thirty 'railway towns' associated with new British-built transport routes. However, he was attempting to revitalise older cultural forms, just at a time when a new generation of Indian leaders were intent on European-style modernisations to reflect new aspirations and ideals.

Town planning legislation in the early twentieth century was geared mainly to both city expansion and urban renewal. The Bombay Town Planning Act of 1915 drew on colonial planning experience elsewhere to facilitate urban upgrading through cooperative amalgamation of private agricultural holdings. This provided new areas of development land, with roads and transport routes paid for through a district rating system. In essence these were land management plans backed up by regulatory standards. The act also empowered municipalities to prepare planning layouts based on comprehensive improvement schemes, road and infrastructure reservations, open space and heritage preservation. The Madras Town Planning Act several years later attempted

to improve on this by facilitating a more sensitive upgrading approach, particularly to poor housing areas.

The 1932 Town and Country Planning Act in Britain established comprehensive planning and land-use control, creating a timely model for use in rapidly growing colonial cities such as Hong Kong and Singapore which were beginning to concern themselves with public welfare issues. This formed the basis of further legislation applied to specific territories, although adequate resources were not always forthcoming at a time when Britain needed support from its colonial 'possessions' during World War II.

In 1946 the Hong Kong government requested a development planner from London who "should be a person of standing in order to counter the strong vested interests in Hong Kong". Patrick Abercrombie was appointed the following year when the first Town Planning Office was inaugurated. Abercrombie's plan proposed to cover the City of Victoria and Kowloon, and was considered a "Plan of Development, using the word in its strict sense and of allowing for revision from time to time in the light of changing requirements and technical accomplishments".[22] This was intended to act as a statement of policy and guide both the government and private developers in properly orchestrated urban renewal. The result was that the government tended to place emphasis on new development areas such as reclamations, which were problem-free. By 1953 the urban area had been divided into thirty-two planning districts and three more added in 1956, all of which were subject to the production of outline development plans.

In the post-war period, economic policies

varied between Asian countries, but with one commonality — the requirement to steer a more balanced policy of economic development than during the colonial period. However this has been dependent on both political stability and sources of investment. These circumstances have had a dual impact on patterns of urbanisation through emergence of new industrial centres around sources of raw material and power supply, with economic diversification of existing cities leading to new urban growth cycles. Independent seaports were essential to this process of growth and diversification in the 1950s and 1960s. The initial beneficiaries that fulfilled all these criteria were the "Little Dragon" economies of Hong Kong, Singapore, Taiwan and South Korea. Continued immigration was a key factor in this — for example, the flood of arrivals from Southern China into Hong Kong in the 1960s and 70s provided a source of employment in industry, in a similar way to economic migrants from rural areas to China's expanding cities in the 1990s and early twenty-first century. Today, wealthier cities continue to import certain types of contract labour from the poorer parts of Asia. In this context, an important role of city government is therefore to further national integration, identity and nationhood through its cultural and administrative institutions, and specialised services. In general, economic growth and high employment rates have provided a tenuous equilibrium to most Asian societies despite the frequently substantial wealth gap between the elite who occupy positions in government and the commercial world, and unskilled labourers and service providers.

Planning in former colonial Asian cities

22 Sir Abercrombie, P, *Hong Kong: Preliminary Planning Report*, Hong Kong Government Printer, Hong Kong, 1949

has continued to focus on programmes of mass housing in response to rapid population growth and rural–urban immigration trends. In most cases this has been informed by Western planning models. In both Singapore and Hong Kong, large-scale immigration and refugees from conflict in China saw the formation of squatter settlements followed by intensive concentration on public housing programmes. In Singapore the Housing and Development Board constructed half a million housing units in fifteen new towns so that 86 per cent of the population live in public sector accommodation, albeit a high proportion in home ownership. In Malaysia, following the establishment of the new Federation in 1957 and the later creation of an Urban Development Authority, new towns such as Petaling Jaya outside Kuala Lumpur, and Shah Alam with urban settlements for indigenous Malays, were built in part to deflect growth to constituent states.

In Hong Kong, Abercrombie's 1949 plan became outdated because of massive urban area population build up. After a disastrous 'fire' in a Shek Kip Mei squatter settlement in 1953, basic resettlement estates were constructed within the city. However it was not until 1972 that a public housing programme was initiated with the majority of new housing allocated to ten new towns, which were developed in the New Territories over the next forty years. In both Singapore and Hong Kong low-cost housing policy involved a significant proportion of total government expenditure, and was an important factor in the integration of immigrant labour, but also of maintaining low labour costs at a time of massive industrialisation and economic growth.

PUNJAB UNIVERSITY was established in 1882 in Lahore, and the University Hall was designed by Bhai Ram Singh twenty years after the nearby Museum site in a similar and complementary Anglo-Mughal style. The two-storey building, now known as Woolner Hall, houses the Fine Arts Department. It incorporates arcaded verandahs in bays along its frontage facing the Upper Mall, domed corner towers and a high central clock tower. Each bay is defined by columns which extend above the parapet, where the cupolas form a distinctive skyline.

Decentralisation saw half of Hong Kong's population move to the new towns by 2000.

Partition in India similarly led to large-scale population movement and the construction of 118 new towns between 1949 and 1981, some to house refugees and others to house workers for new large-scale industrial complexes. Chandigarh, founded in 1951, was created as a new capital city for the new Punjab after the transfer of Lahore to Pakistan. Planned initially by American consultants it came into the autocratic architectural hands of Le Corbusier whose radical urban design ideas of segregated neighbourhoods and superblocks was geared more to high expressionism than social traditions or climatic sensibilities.

The colonial city was both shaped and continuously transformed by many forces and processes, including those of conflict and compromise, so there was a constant re-shaping of identity. British colonial planning in particular had certain consequences for urban design in the homeland, being influential in the promotion of garden city layouts and low-density suburbs. There was also a certain symbiosis, in that new planning theories and approaches such as land-use zoning, urban renewal, compulsory land acquisition and compensation could be tested in different contextual situations, such as Model Town in Lahore. Likewise certain building types incubated in India were successfully imported to Britain such as bungalow development. This was reinforced by many returnees from colonial service, together with planning devices such as green belts. At an administrative level, experimentation with forms of management and land use control through special boards and corporations in colonial cities, found a new context in urban development, regeneration, and new town bodies in the United Kingdom.

In post-colonial Asia, what was once the "Western" space of the colonial city has become the preferred quarter for the indigenous elite, some of whom acquired the cultural capital of imperialism.[23] It can therefore be argued that a key urban characteristic of many Asian cities is the lingering reinforcement rather than abandonment of social and spatial divisions that characterised earlier colonial urban layouts. At the same time the symbolic significance of major colonial building constructs have all but lost their initial symbolic connotation, and have generally been replaced by a belated acknowledgement of their cultural heritage value. Western urban design and its often monumental

undertakings continue to convey their colonial relationship in the post-colonial era, often defining the footprint of modern cities even as they are informed by new urban design expression.

Freedom from colonial authority has by no means coincided with democratic rule. Military or other forms of authoritarian rule have dominated certain governments while others have effectively established one-party rule. A central issue has been one of ethnic minorities, some of whom have asserted

special rights and calls for autonomy. This has occurred in Myanmar, Southern Thailand, parts of Indonesia and in the Philippines. In some situations, lingering discriminatory policies have helped maintain disparities in financial and professional standing compared with indigenous populations, although in general the plural character of society helps to build bridges between communities, celebrating the differences and contributing to the cosmopolitan character of Asian cities.

The High Court building in Kolkata designed by Walter Granville in a Gothic style, is an adaptation of the thirteenth century Cloth Hall at Ypres, Belgium, but modified because of poor soil conditions.

23 King, A.D., *Spaces of Global Cultures*, Routledge, London and New York, 2004

A RESIDENCE FOR THE BRITISH VICEROY OF INDIA IN NEW DELHI was designed by Edwin Lutyens after the decision to move the capital from Calcutta in 1911. Around 1600 hectares were acquired for construction of the house and the adjacent Central Secretariat between 1911 and 1916, necessitating the removal of two villages under the 1894 Land Acquisition Act.

Lutyen's refined neo-Classical design introduces architectural details drawn from Indo-Saracenic references, although the overall politically charged intention behind the design was to emphasise imperial authority. It is said that the central dome was inspired by the Pantheon in Rome. The original plan was to site the building on top of Raisina Hill, situated at a higher level than the two adjacent Secretariat blocks, but a later decision to move it 400 metres further back somewhat diluted its visual prominence from the main approach.

The Viceroy's House was officially inaugurated in 1931. After independence in 1947 it became the residence of the Governor-General, and when India later became a republic it became the Presidential Residence or "Rastrapati Bhavan". The Guest Wing is used by visiting Heads of State.

The 47-metre high Jaipur Column, a gift from the Maharaja of Jaipur and designed by Lutyens, stands in the centre of the main access road, as a strong focal point. A map of New Delhi is incised on its eastern side, and carries an inscriptions, "In thought faith, in word wisdom, in deed courage, in life service, so may India be great". The symbolic "Star of India" at the top of the column is also echoed in motifs within the residence. The bas-reliefs around its base were designed by the British sculptor, Charles Sargeant Jagger.

4

DINOSAURS &
DISJUNCTORS

The Asian City in Transition

The spatial transformation in Asian cities over the past century can be seen as a transition — from pre-industrial centres to manufacturing hubs, and finally in recent years a rapid momentum towards post-industrial business and service economies. Cities that traditionally acted as gateways for product delivery and export, are now 'virtual' portals for global influences and ideologies. Cultural dimensions are no longer discernible merely in terms of historic fabric. Increasingly the 'sense' of the city as a series of varied and ephemeral experiences associated with urban places has become more abstract, giving way to high density residential estates and business parks with significant disjunctions of scale. Older and more informal land uses reflecting social and economic patterns that encapsulate aspects of both specialisation and choice, and which are sufficiently durable to persist in relatively independent enclaves, now exist alongside self-contained, high-rise quarters which shape a completely different morphology.

A heterogeneous collection of development types, consolidated through international corporate investment and moulded by largely unregulated local forces, is re-formatting the Asian region through new forms of capital growth and distinctive spatial patterns. Friedman has noted that transnational capital creates its own requirements for these new types of urban spaces — world finance centres, exhibition and convention centres, logistics centres, and export-processing zones, together with the need for a world-class transport infrastructure.[1] In turn this is establishing concentrations of outward processing and techno-commercial services that continue to have a significant impact on existing cities in terms of physical restructuring, employment, housing, transportation and tourism. New development trajectories are accompanied by structural adjustments to the economy, which in turn necessitates an almost constant review and evaluation of development needs, planning programmes, urban management and community facilities. In this sense the Asian city is not immune to some of the characteristics of Western cities — the insulated citadels and exclusive enclaves of the elite, the middle-class suburbs and the ghettos of exclusion. But the emergence of mega-urban regions has also led to a situation where people can choose to live in the city for its social, cultural and recreational attractions, and commute to jobs outside it. This fuels the momentum to preserve characteristic older parts of the city and its heritage monuments, in turn perpetuating a process that culminates in "consumer cities" in which residents are willing to pay a premium to live.[2] There is in fact a broad correlation between urbanisation and prosperity — per capita incomes are generally around four times higher in countries where a majority of the population live in cities.[3]

The change in urbanisation patterns within Asian city regions are both far-reaching and, to a great extent, unpredictable. City populations often vary considerably from official figures, partly through the difficulty in classifying temporary workforces, and because smaller towns within an urbanising region surrounding a primate city, are positioned beyond administrative boundaries. This is not simply an urbanisation of suburbia, but a complex and ongoing recalibration of polycentric networks. These are constantly being reconfigured through the disengagement

1 Friedmann, J, *Life Space and Economic Space*, Transaction Books, New Brunswick, New Jersey,1988
2 Florida, R, *Cities and the Creative Class*, Routledge, London and New York, 2005
3 Glaeser, E, *Triumph of the City*, Macmillan, London, 2011

of firms from metropolitan areas and the emergence of new community concentrations around centres of clean industry and business park development. The Metropolitan Base Region must therefore be considered in relation to metro and non-metro zones, and their economic, social and environmental linkages. Such urban phenomena are helping to redefine territorial boundaries through these significant inter-relationships between industry, specialised services and high value-added production processes.

Cities can be broadly distinguished by the extent to which their surrounding region is fragmented from the city boundary itself. In the case of major conurbations, urbanisation has extended beyond established city boundaries to consolidate within expanding growth corridors, meaning that increasing numbers of people live in surrounding jurisdictions, which makes co-ordinated intervention difficult. This does not necessarily mean that there is an explicit regional development framework, but more that the economic operations of the city region might relate only partially to the city itself. Conversely, fragmented municipalities with different power structures can massively constrain the region's ability to frame and control development, and provide requisite infrastructure for co-ordinated growth. Business exchange still personifies the city's essential purpose, but the means and dimensions of this are becoming part of a more complex process that affects the concept of place, living and work cultures. An array of ethnic communities from all parts of Asia, and therefore culturally diverse, are becoming re-aligned and re-territorialised as part of a floating labour market, but also forming new

claims for legitimate rights as stakeholders and a commensurate loosening of ties to nation or place. We can therefore observe at one end of the spectrum the relentless urban footprint of global capital, and at the other the migrant workers — the lifeblood of city growth that at any one time in Chinese cities might amount to 150 million people. Land speculation within metropolitan regions has led to removal or relocation of squatter settlements at almost precisely the same time as rural-urban migrants were arriving in cities to assist with their reconstruction. The provision of adequate housing to cater for both expanding and upwardly mobile populations is therefore arguably the greatest challenge facing Asian cities.

The term "desakota" was coined by Terence McGee to explain the development conditions pertaining to the expanding metropolitan areas of Asian cities, in contrast with the more rigid distinction between 'rural' and 'urban' as part of an ongoing urbanisation process. McGee argued that patterns of urbanisation in many Asian cities, including the present growth of mega-urban concentrations, reflect a process of settlement transition, broken down into the Bahasa terms — desa for a village settlement along with tanah desa for its immediate physical environs, and kota for town or city.[4] Spatial configurations within regional growth patterns conforming to this process tend to incorporate large urban cores and peri-urban zones separated by densely settled mixed rural-urban land uses and economic activities. While the precise nature of the space-economy varies considerably between cities and countries, mega-urban regions in Asia illustrate several different desakota types: those such as the Tokyo

Metropolitan Area with persistent patterns of agricultural land use even in the face of a shift to more intense urbanisation; those with declining agricultural land use in the face of gradual industrialisation but where more intense forms of 'agribusiness' are carried out, such as the Bangkok Metropolitan Region, the Pearl River and Shanghai Delta areas; and regions that still retain relatively large agricultural areas but are experiencing steady growth in small manufacturing industry such as the Manila extended region. This broad breakdown is in a constant state of change due to economic investment in mega-urban regions, urban land use intensification and fluctuating patterns of population mobility and immigration to both urban and peri-urban areas. Planning must therefore be able to resolve conflicts between incompatible and potentially environmentally despoiling uses, while retaining the social and economic momentum of use mix.

RESTRUCTURING THE CITY REGIONS: THE INTERFACE WITH URBAN DESIGN

The social organisation of space and capital, together with other spheres of cultural production, contribute to urban identity and the symbolic forms of urban design in relation to this. Transformation of space through redevelopment introduces a parallel narrative of demolition, disappearance and replacement, therefore it is necessary to ensure that new and old cultural forms can co-exist and overlap. Anthony King has suggested that in this sense, the process of globalisation can lead either to increasingly homogenised environments or to a more transformative and therefore a more heterogeneous urbanism.[5] Either way, internationalisation of the

4   McGee, T.G., 'The Emergence of Desakota Regions in Asia: Expanding a Hypothesis', in *The Extended Metropolis*, Eds. Norton Sydney Ginsburg, Bruce Koppel Ginsburg and T.G. McGee, University of Hawaii Press, Honolulu, 1991, p7
5   King, A.D., 'World Cities: Global? Post colonial? Post imperial? Or Just the Result of Happenstance? Some Cultural Comments', in *The Global Cities*, Eds. Neil Brenner and Roger Keil, Routledge, London and New York, 2006

economy has brought about a marked degree of de-territorialisation. This can be readily observed in Asia through the continual locational shift of manufacturing industries to countries or cities with lower production costs — a trend that is both reflected in and accentuated by large-scale migration of labour. The replacement of low-end manufacturing with post-industrial service, trading and financial functions, supported by new educational and research organisations, is creating a web of cities that control global systems of production and are inevitably shaped by globally generated ideologies. The role of Asian cities is therefore being constantly repositioned, with new spatial configurations that are place-bound but some distance removed from their capital underpinnings.

In East Asia, cities such as Tokyo, Hong Kong, Taipei and Seoul have adopted interventionist stances to stimulate economic growth through the relocation of labour-intensive manufacturing production, from high-cost environments to lower-cost locations in collaboration with transnational organisations. This process has gained pace to the extent that new production locations have to be periodically moved to more economic territories.

Density is the key component of a city's environmental footprint. Relatively short commuting distances generally translate into low per capita energy consumption, low overall carbon emissions and high levels of public transport use. However this must also be equated with compatible planning of the urban hinterland. As the structure of business and employment patterns change, new values emerge through escalating land prices. These

economic forces exert a polarising impact on the traditional mix of activities. Such trends are apparent in virtually all Asian cities experiencing a continued rise in globalised competition. Older inner areas are subject to large-scale renewal, often constrained by complicated land ownership patterns, hence encouraging new medium and high density cores on the urban fringe.

Asian cities have, for centuries, undergone a continuing process of transformation and change. While their existing forms might give the impression of relatively organic growth, their fragmented texture is generally the product of innumerable decisions made over long periods of time for separate purposes, and reflects contrasting but mutually supportable economic structures. In many cases formalist building configurations and a highly active public realm exist side-by-side with informal spatial patterns and incidental activity. Traditional urbanism for the most part contains a mix of permanent and impermanent fabric that establishes a 'locus' of collective memory. This insinuates its way informally into the functional workings of the urban structure over time, and contributes to a resource base from which to establish planning, urban design and social programmes. These can be framed within the spirit and culture of the city where spaces have evolved or been designed to engage both specific and incidental activities.

In some situations the cultural residue of physical fabric can only be perceived through activity traces that allude to previous uses. Redundant premises scarcely ever translate into dereliction but spell opportunities for adaptive transition to more gainful activities. It is therefore necessary to assimilate and

reinterpret the city language and what is characteristically embodied in the local morphology — essential values of the street, city block, sacred place and monument — and how these can be translated into typologies that relate to the culture and configuration of urban districts. New development must form a balanced co-existence with the physical, social and economic characteristics of older urban streets and places, but in ways that satisfy changing community ambitions and that extend cultural definition to urban form. The gentrification of older mixed use areas into thriving sub-centres based on vigorous commercial investment and tourism can generate its own demand and supply vehicles for goods and services, establishing in the process a more cosmopolitan urban regime.

At the heart of contemporary planning in Asian cities is a paradox — that while there is in some cases colossal investment in the city and a deep respect for traditional cultural institutions, available planning mechanisms, even advanced ones, are rarely used with vision and creativity. What should be a sensitive process of incrementalism and adjustment to effectively regenerate the city by modernising its infrastructure and opening up possibilities for urban expansion while retaining both cultural and intangible heritage, has been overtaken by an overly-deterministic process of zoning. This has been geared to expedient land management and is reflected in a bureaucratic accentuation of order and homogeneity manipulated by an elite combination of government and large development organisations. Urban redevelopment and renewal on the basis of capital accumulation and exploitation of land value is an increasing driver of change in the

Asian city, and has become more robust as a result of global market forces. Single-minded exploitation of land values tends to skew urban renewal policies towards perpetual redevelopment and impermanence, resulting in undifferentiated urban quarters with an emphasis on efficiency and expediency rather than regenerative values.

Rapid development has become an ideology in itself. Won Bae Kim has stated that the obsession with economic growth takes both visible and more elusive forms, leading to 'bubble cities' with escalating values stemming from industrial and financial capital.[6] This results in different degrees of environmental deterioration and social disintegration, with a jolting departure from enduring traditions where family and kinship play an important role in society. A fundamental question is therefore "what do we want to sustain"? Primary concerns vary from ecological and environmental issues, to social justice, and resolution of poverty.

PLANNING AND THE SOCIAL CONTRACT

The role of the state is pervasive, either through direct market intervention or indirect manipulation. In the face of global pressure, virtually all Asian countries with the exception of North Korea have come to adopt market principles, albeit with socialist overtones in some cases. Tokyo, Singapore, Taipei and Seoul have adopted systems of centralised planning alongside benevolent social policies focussed on global city status. Beijing and other major Chinese cities have been propelled to the forefront of globalisation through top-down policy accompanied by an aggressive urbanisation strategy, albeit one made viable by its responsiveness to the unified traditions

of Chinese society. At the other end of the spectrum are Jakarta and Manila with less than effective municipal government and planning coordination.

As cities encapsulate and articulate the dominant forms of social and economic organisation, they also become more complex, incorporating increasingly specialised elements to acquire an urban design of deeply symbolic content. The ideology of market capitalism in the context of the globalised economy is still, in some Asian countries, at odds with deeply-rooted cultural philosophies. In Korea and Japan, and to a lesser extent China, a single underlying factor historically circumscribed the growth of cities in terms of their urban footprint — the supply of agricultural food from their hinterlands.[7] The gravitational pull exerted by advanced market economies, with the accompanying lure of consumerism, now puts inevitable strain on the process and priorities of urbanisation. Hedonistic consumption not only conflicts with sustainable planning objectives but also with Buddhist and Taoist precepts practised in many Asian cities. These underpin a spirituality built around the impermanent and ephemeral, reflecting a natural and unified order. There is also Confucianism, which places an equal emphasis on social ethics and priorities of the community above those of the individual. In terms of territorial organisation, these key factors might influence the place-making interface between physical and social environments as it reflects civil society.

As transnational capital is attracted to these cities and urbanisation intensifies, so a social contract develops between people and government, which facilitates change through economic inducements. Eventually

the emerging middle class demands greater participation in city affairs and expresses a widening concern for the public realm, creating tension between top-down provision and regulation, and calls for greater public participation in local planning.

The delicate tools developed in Western cities for community planning through grassroots coalitions, workshops and charrettes help to sustain the dialogue between past and present, but these have yet to find a grounding in Asian cities. This is partly due to more restrictive or controlling political regimes, and to the conciliatory temperament of their populations. Inevitably this translates into an overly top-down level of decision-making, however good the intentions, and a lack of local empowerment. The traditional process of growth and change that accompanies both economic and social development (while retaining underlying urban values), is replaced by regimes of control and efficiency, with an economic commitment that segregates functions and freezes development in time. This poses serious questions over the capacity for change in new-built environments, except through replacement. Things that 'don't fit' or that do not fulfil their full site development potential have no place in this system.

URBAN DESIGN VERSUS ZONING

More than anything, the deterministic master zoning plan overrides cohesive urban design and generally eliminates the fundamentals that generate mixed use environments. It also tends to facilitate an indeterminate process of land disposal based largely on income returns to government from land sales. In Hong Kong's metro area for example, every

6   Kim, W.B., 'From a Bubble City to a Sustainable City: How to Tame a Greedy City', in *Compact City: A Sustainable Urban Model for Seoul*, Seoul Metropolitan Fora Conference Proceedings, 2002
7   Kim, W.B., 'Culture, History and the City in East Asia', in *Culture and the City in East Asia*, Clarendon Press, Oxford, 1997, p25

urban site forms part of an Outline Zoning Plan. This, in concert with Building (Planning) Regulations, establishes an existing or potential development value that incentivises redevelopment and undermines any coherent approach to conservation. Subsequently, urban renewal increasingly transforms neighbourhoods into fragmented residential or commercial locales, which satisfies highly specific requirements and maximises private space at the expense of an interactive public realm. In a situation where the land market is effectively controlled by government, and where the participating forces of social planning and urban design are insufficiently integrated, land becomes a mechanism for power relations, and the city is treated as a chessboard of opportunity to which the fabric must continually respond.

Such processes raises important choices — do we document and plan the city according to acknowledged standards of use mix and diversity, entailing an emphasis on preservation of fabric and authenticity; or do we subscribe to new and emerging development imperatives based on expedient notions of competitive economic performance? In cities as diverse as Hong Kong or New Delhi, the on-going planning response to the colonial 'designed' city — with its axial avenues, prominent public building and defined vistas — represents a quirky juxtaposition of massively scaled intervention with street-scaled ad hoc and reflects the post-colonial city transforming itself into the commodified city.

This implies that urban design strategies should systematically promote diversity, using essential differences in urban culture and content positively, to nurture local identity and attraction. However this approach would require concepts of change and adaptability to be integrated within the planning process. In this regard, urban design becomes a means of articulating a conceptual vocabulary in relation to long-term social, economic and political processes, and eventually a way to forge a link between cultural form and the organisation of urban space, proactively directed towards city betterment. The process must be intentionally open-ended, involving a raft of initiatives, and must reflect measures of varying degrees and scales to resolve a range of problems in the urban domain. This requires both a comprehensive and integrated vision.

The underlying morphology of much urban fabric is partly the result of formative foreign intervention in the city development process. This varies, from the international settlement of Shanghai and other old treaty port concessions in China; the colonial inspired monumentality of Indian cities such as New Delhi, Calcutta and Bombay; the mellowed French-style boulevards of Hanoi; the public spaces and cultural buildings of Singapore; the disjointed growth pattern of Jakarta; and the tight urban massing and street culture of Hong Kong and Tokyo. While their urban patterns and consistency of street fabric are surprisingly resilient, the Asian city is far from restful. The accelerated rates of post-colonial growth and change are largely the result of population pressures, therefore new development is often pragmatically distributed or superimposed on older fabric. This creates an interweaving of uses and a duality of social and economic processes that co-exist as mutually reinforcing drivers of the urban structure. As redevelopment induces higher population densities, this generates an intensity of use and a typological complexity that cuts across cultural boundaries. The informal intermingling of modernity and tradition produces a contemporary form of development that contrasts yet co-exists with remaining established places and activity centres.

It can be argued that the architecturally expressive historic street environments, conserved and integrated within the older urban texture of Asian cities, are unlikely to be repeated in cities today, simply because development conditions and contexts have changed so dramatically. Land economics, ownership patterns, commercial and servicing requirements now determine the course-grained structure of emerging city layouts. This is precisely why older and more fine-grained environments in multi-ownership need to be protected and reinforced, as they imbue the city with contrast and community through an innate ability to adjust their ownership and use mix.

With this approach the issue of regeneration, by means of a "bottom-up" process, takes on a special significance in terms of stitching together an amalgam of incremental projects and measures to help resolve existing problems and provide the best conditions for urban upgrading while perpetuating a sense of local identity. This requires an integrative urbanism which seeks to bring about lasting improvement, and must therefore be carried out in an adaptive way, providing continuity of urban character and sense of community. Regeneration needs to be recognised as a more complicated process than an almost purely economic one of physical renewal, and must represent all stakeholders with a legitimate interest in this.

PREDOMINANCE OF THE PRIMATES: CONCENTRATIONS AND MONOPOLIES

In the post-war period the predominance of the primate city in all Asian countries, apart from the very largest — China and India — has dominated national development programmes. For historical reasons if we include the "city state" of Singapore, and Hong Kong — now a "Special Administrative Region" of China — within this category, the primate city has continued to grow as an overwhelming institutional focus of development. Many coastal cities that developed as trading centres in colonial times, now serve as production and management centres for world markets. These have therefore become not merely power bases but cultural and investment hubs built around a sense of history, tradition and rulership, while symbolising national unity, identity and forging an international modernising image.

There is a long tradition of urbanisation in Asia, however the massive growth of primate cities is a comparatively recent phenomenon. Major cities began life as small trading settlements, sacred places or palace compounds, so ties between city and country were commercial rather than cultural. The first major colonial city, Manila, was founded by the Spanish in 1571; Batavia (present-day Jakarta), by the Dutch in 1750; Bangkok by Rama I in 1782; Singapore by the British in 1819; Hong Kong granted to Britain under the Treaty of Nanking in 1842; and French Indo-Chinese cities from 1861. Furthermore, early city formation attracted large numbers of ethnic groups from other parts of Asia, some even orchestrated by the colonising powers themselves.

Concentration of power within the primate city creates a tenuous link between global trends in urbanisation, and the priorities of centralised power structures. Emerging nationalism continues to exert an expressive impact on patterns of urban form, often through the design of spaces and monuments, and this in turn reinforces identity and dominance. The ultimate symbol of modernisation is the tall building — the 'gateway' International Finance Centre and World Finance Centre towers in Hong Kong, the Jin Mae tower in Shanghai, the Petronas towers in Kuala Lumpur, and Taipei 101 — that assumes a purposeful prominence in emerging business districts as inventive but enigmatic cathedrals of commerce. However none contribute to the overall urban design with anything more than an imposing and monumental presence.

The hierarchical model evolved through the growth of entrepôt cities as nodes relating to trading routes. Inland provincial cities formed interdependent parts of this network, occasionally leading to conflict over patterns of trade, access to resources, and territorial control in relation to the process of state formation. Until the priorities of colonial powers changed from control of trade to control of production and cultivation of commercial crops, most island states and cities remained relatively independent. Production of such things as spices and coffee in Java, tea in Ceylon, cotton in India, timber in Burma and rubber in Malaysia created colonial plantation economies, creating a dual structure of colonial administration and commercial control that was reflected in new and consolidating patterns of urbanism.[8]

Primate cities in Asia contain by far the largest concentrations of temporary settlements and informal economic sectors.

Past growth was fuelled to a large extent by low-wage manufacturing, but recently that fuel has been increasingly substituted by high technology. Social surplus brings with it new industries built around services, communications, consumption and cultural production. As agglomeration economies continue to grow in size, the influence on spatial planning becomes considerable with intensified dependence on central locations for administrative and professional services, entertainment and cultural uses. Meanwhile, low-end manufacturing can be decentralised, hence disparities in GDP between primate cities and secondary or remoter settlements continues to increase.

In their current state most primate cities are also capitals, far exceeding other national cities in terms of population and commanding prime locations for national administration, business investment, industrial production and port development, with economic control over a large hinterland. The Bangkok Metropolitan Region, which encompasses five contiguous provinces, represents 20 per cent of Thailand's population and generates more than 60 per cent of its GDP. Calcutta, with a hinterland of 220 million people, has an urban population ten times the second city in Bengal — Patna. Manila is similar to Bangkok in effectively dominating its national administrative, industrial and commercial sector, with an urban region that includes six provinces surrounding Metro Manila and 25 per cent of the Philippine population, accounting for 35 per cent of national GDP.[9] The inner zone comprises a number of townships and municipalities which spread out from the core to the northwest, east and southeast. Its population of twelve million is

8   Evers, H.D. and Korff, R, *Southeast Asian Urbanism: The Meaning and Power of Social Space*, St Martin's Press, New York, 2000, p31
9   Rimmer, P.J. and Dick, H, *The City in Southeast Asia: Patterns, Processes and Policy*, University of Hawaii Press, Honolulu, 2009

ten times the size of the next cities — Cebu and Davao.

For newly independent states, primate cities with their monopoly of modern institutions have formed the key economic and administrative apparatus to support the necessary nation building processes. They are places where local forces meet those of national integration and globalisation, fuelled by both local and foreign capital and increasingly competing for investment, leading to the transformation of city space. Simultaneously, the city's material reality and spatial expression are establishing new cultural meaning to built environments and social organisation, but this needs to be balanced with the social and spatial divisions of labour. It makes for a contrasting but not necessarily integrative urbanism. On one hand, there are the spatial imprints of transnationalism which creates a corporatised link between cities and on the other, established local economic networks propelled by the constant transfer of labour in the form of streams of immigrants with diverse sub-cultures. However virtually all primate cities pay a price for this through social polarisation, wealth differentiation and areas of physical segregation.

The spatial and social construction of the Asian primate city is the result of various processes — demographic, cultural, segregational, political and economic. Underscoring this is the constant issue of conflict between dominating forces and stakeholder priorities, and between the permanent and the impermanent. Flows of information, goods and capital that previously found form and meaning in specific locales are giving way to a more abstract and undifferentiated definition of place.

A predominance of elite establishments puts progressively greater pressure on the city, but in turn inhibits the development of any potential competition, thus the primate role is gradually reinforced. At the same time this accelerates the modernisation process whereby entrance to the global marketplace requires increasingly intensified land use. Low-income workers build up communities in older and overcrowded urban quarters that are under constant threat from urban redevelopment, or they are eventually relocated to public housing in secondary locations. As central urban land becomes progressively valuable, new employment opportunities are created and urban populations re-distributed. Higher-income households occupy new accommodation within the redeveloped core, and low-to-medium density enclaves at the urban fringe or in new towns. The need to reside close to places of urban employment, coupled with the workings of market-driven economies, have clear repercussions on both density levels and city form. Hong Kong for example accommodates around two-thirds of its population within a 10-kilometre radius of its urban core, linked by highways and high-speed rail systems.

Redevelopment at higher densities brings with it similarities in spatial disposition and morphology, and an urban design of sameness. To counteract this, unique heritage buildings such as temples, palaces, and other monuments are showcased for tourism, articulating a necessary but commodified role as the containers of city history. Accordingly primate cities can only be measured from a relativist standpoint, taking into account the distinct imperatives and cultural conditions that make them diverse, and the extent to which their modes of production form an integral and transformative part of the global economy.

OPERATIONAL CHAINS AND DIVERSE CIRCUITS

Cities rather than countries must compete for specialised markets to meet growth and investment targets. Shanghai, Hong Kong, Tokyo, Singapore and Mumbai form established economic interdependencies through trade and financial markets, while temporary circuits based on cultural transactions such as those associated with Beijing, Tokyo and Seoul as Olympic Cities, or Shanghai as an International Expo City, have helped create new intercity networks. Major cities must sustain both the number and diversity of circuits, and expand these where possible to provide city wealth and employment among various sectors. Interdependence goes well beyond commerce and trade, and innovations need to be extended and shared. Cities that cannot compete, or are excluded from these processes because they have lost their primary function, must develop specialised services such as tourism which might then form part of an intra-national circuit but with less rigid social and spatial segmentation.

In some situations — such as the Pearl River Delta in relation to Hong Kong and Guangzhou, the Beijing-Tianjin corridor, and the Seoul-Busan-Taelon region — trans-regional operational chains extend the city dynamic through opportunities for agglomeration of headquarter functions and dispersal of service back-up and manufacturing operations. This can however be an uneasy co-existence, with shifting economic priorities possibly de-stabilising or accelerating growth around various sub-centres.

A mix of specialised functions provides the underlying logic for agglomeration and allows certain cities to develop as strategic knowledge economies. Globalisation is undoubtedly interventionist but this does not necessarily lead to sameness. Saskia Sassen makes the point that similar urban landscapes do not necessarily correspond with similar economies; cities have different economic and cultural demands that insinuate themselves within the sub-regional fabric, and provide a counterpoint to the increasing similarity of Asian state-of-the-art city infrastructure.[10]

Traffic and transport service interventions are the new expressive agents of change, driven by a need to order the city through its underlying structural elements, but also to competitively market and "brand" the city for business visitors and tourists. There is a marked emphasis on the multi-dimensional elements associated with high-speed movement corridors. In-town rail termini with rapid connections to airports, passenger ferry and cruise terminals, all contribute to a new and enterprising phenomena — the re-creation of the nineteenth century European city railway gateway as a commercial and cultural activator. "Airport City" conglomerations now integrate shopping cores, conference centres and entertainment venues, where "star" architectural designers add a strong dose of finesse and invention in order to promote city landmark status. Urban movement systems create a lattice work of connections which indirectly structure new layout forms, such as the high-rise residential and commercial nodes that sit atop Hong Kong's MTR stations with their multiple connections and interfaces. These also go some way in subsidising railway construction costs.

Over the past two decades the majority of Asian cities have experienced a growing demand for corporate and professional services. In this respect, corporate capital is defining emerging spatial patterns at a time when manufacturing industry frequently relocates to whatever country or region offers the best production economies and skill sets. Depending on the controlling nature of planning and the relative sophistication of land management, this process is steadily changing the spatial organisation of cities, with both gentrified older areas and new development areas lying almost side-by-side with older street trading activities, some of which are uncompromisingly focussed on the tourist market. This varies considerably — Shanghai has transformed its downtown area through massive investment while also developing Pudong as a business hub, other megacities such as Guangzhou, Delhi and Mumbai have demarcated sites for new financial centres. A common characteristic however is the ad hoc redevelopment of sites so that commercial functions with large building footprints co-exist in juxtaposition amongst older and more fine grained urban cores. These developments in themselves put clear constraints on integration within the wider economy as a whole, despite the economic and social diversity of the cities themselves.

The expanding urban footprint nurtures a symbiotic relationship with its central place, which in turn perpetuates a vast web of connectivity. By the same token primate cities are fused to each other by global communication systems, with satellite cities attaching onto their circuits according to the geographies of specialisation. Density is no longer the necessary marker of centrality — city regions are being assembled from state of the art 'edge' environments for residential development, commerce, science and education in multiple realms of physical concentration and dispersal.

In general it is the most specialised functions of global companies — with internationalisation of capital — that are subject to the highest levels of agglomeration. The physicality of these functions appears to be increasingly detached from the national economies to which they belong. Sassen describes this utilisation of the city by global capital as an 'organisational commodity', with a commensurate loosening of place identities.[11] At the same time the demand for feeder services in Asian conurbations is satisfied by the changing economy of secondary cities or regional centres.

The economic histories and degree of specialisation of cities are other significant factors in the global company's ability to adapt and reposition in response to economic change. Hong Kong's rapid transition from a trading and manufacturing economy to a knowledge economy servicing the wider Pearl River Delta, reflects a re-calibration of existing capabilities rather than a replacement, and has therefore imperceptibly facilitated entry to a global economic network. Growth in the high-income strata of the population has labour intensive ramifications due to increasing demand for goods and skilled services. However because of massively escalating land values

10 Sassen, S, 'Seeing like a City', in *The Endless City*, Eds. Ricky Burdett and Deyan Sudjic, Phaidon, London, 2010
11 Sassen, 2010, op. cit., p283

this inevitably displaces or marginalises the myriad of small-scale creative industries and the informal economy of street-related activities. This in turn creates a strategic infrastructure to which other supporting networks, including production processes, can plug in rather like a neural framework, but the growth of multiple economies gives rise to the valorisation of many subsidiary activities.[12] Economic polarisation means that the low-wage work force must continue to be subsidised through public housing. East Asia in particular is absorbing a large share of 'transnational' migration, which includes a more informal but low-income supporting realm of migrant 'temporary' workers from less developed economies. These workers carry out manual and household tasks in the more advanced service-based cities, maximising the ability of high-skilled workers to function effectively in the labour market. In the process this is breaking down longstanding cultural homogeneity. Cities such as Hong Kong and Singapore rely on low-paid domestic workers from the Philippines and Indonesia, while Shanghai and Bombay are supported by migrant workers from within their countries leading to highly visible inequalities, evidenced by areas of overcrowded accommodation and temporary housing. In this sense these intra-national economic networks are integral to the functioning of the Asian economy as a whole, and their commensurate requirements and diverse cultural environments need to be understood.

REGIONAL RECONFIGURATION: THE EXPANDING URBAN FOOTPRINT

The term 'mega-urban region' can be applied to a number of similar situations but it can also cover significant variations in urban agglomeration, where cities have extended beyond their political boundaries, or where these boundaries have been re-drawn to include previously rural enclaves. Around 60 per cent of national GDP in Asia is produced through these regions, which have a tendency to double their populations every 15 to 20 years.

In exploring the morphology of mega-urban regions, Mike Douglas and Gavin Jones correlate this with an intensifying process of globalisation within and between urban economies in terms of circuits of capital. From colonial times these are identified chronologically as firstly, primary commodity production and resource extractions; secondly labour–intensive export-oriented industrialisation; thirdly global retail consumption; and fourthly global finance capital.[13] This has transformed the scale and form of development patterns within these continually reconstructed landscapes, and is reflected in the transition to smaller household sizes. Basic services, environmental infrastructure, and such things as the embedded cultural permanences of sacred places — resulting from government investment — become the main features that distinguish the character of these regions.

The actual dynamics of change over thirty years correlates in most cases with rapid economic transition from dense agricultural hinterland around large villages and small townships, to unstructured spatial expansion within mega-urban regions, although this differs widely commensurate with the deceleration of rural population growth. At the same time, core city populations in most primate cities continue to be accommodated at increased densities, but with rising land values leading to a polarisation of living conditions between rich and poor.

During the 1970s and 1980s South Korea, Taiwan, Japan and Hong Kong deployed production to low-wage economies. Thailand, Indonesia, the Philippines and Malaysia followed suit as secondary centres of labour-intensive manufacturing. China and Vietnam later established special export-processing zones which acted as catalysts to economic shifts in surrounding areas. This shift from agricultural to urban-industrial based economies consolidated growth in the mega-urban regions and led to urban restructuring on a large scale in the 1990s. The Asian financial crisis stiffened competition for global investment. This coincided with government backing for mega-projects and a further transition from manufacturing to high-end business and hi-tech developments along with huge transportation infrastructure to promote emerging international cooperation. The spatial result of this is a multi-centred pattern of regional development around a metropolitan core.

Development corridors are expanding beyond metropolitan boundaries, emphasising the regional or mega-city dimensions of the urbanisation process whose parts are interdependent but still evolving. The largest of these are: the Pearl River Delta comprising an urban population of over 40 million within the integral cities of Hong Kong, Shenzhen, Zhuhai and Macau; the Shanghai, Nanjing, Hangzhou region configuration with 50 million; the Beijing, Tianjin, Tangshan corridor of 36 million; and the Tokyo-Yokohama region of 55 million people which makes up around 30 per cent of

[12] Sassen, S, 'Analytic Borderlands: Economy and Culture in the Global City', in *A Companion to the City*, Eds. Bridge Gary and Watson Sophie, Blackwell, 2000
[13] Jones, G.W. and Douglas, M, *Mega-Urban Regions in Pacific Asia: Urban Dynamics in a Global Era*, NUS Press, Singapore, 2008

the total Japanese population. Extended and reconfigured forms of urbanisation include: the Zhangjiagang delta east of Nanjing in China; the Seoul-Pusan-Taejon region which has grown through the transnationalisation of large Korean corporations to 44 million; the Fukuoka-Hiroshina-Kitakyusho corridor of 20 million; the Greater Taipei-Kaoshiung corridor of 17 million people in Taiwan; the Chiang Mai region in northern Thailand; Cebu City in the Philippines; and Bandong in Indonesia. In addition to this, on the Indian sub-continent alone, there are the city regions of Bombay (Mumbai) and Delhi with 20 million each, Calcutta (Kolkata) with 15.6 million, Karachi in Pakistan with 14.3 million, and Dhaka in Bangladesh with 13.2 million.[14]

Historical patterns of intensive agricultural production and ecological conditions have created significant rural population concentrations in large villages, many of which have expanded to become townships. With improved transportation links through the urban-rural continuum, this provides large pools of labour and attracts migrant workers to industrial zones on the urbanising periphery. In turn this reduces the clear demarcation between urban and rural activities within an extended metro area. This is assisted, in wealthier regions, by new highway and transit corridors, and in poorer ones by forms of cheap, low-technology transport such as two-stroke motorcycles which facilitate the rapid movement of both people and commodities. Therefore over the past twenty years, bands of peripheral development have been expanding at faster rates than redevelopment of city cores, and reaching similar population densities. The stimulus that creates such agglomerations stems from the requirements of economic development, but also drives changes in industrial emphasis from low-end manufacturing to high technology. Investment in hi-tech industrial estates, educational campuses and government complexes continue to extend the density and range of interdependencies.

McGee has identified a number of priorities for planning and policy directions in ASEAN countries — using the generic term 'Metrofitting' — suggesting comprehensive rehabilitation, planned infill and co-ordinated infrastructural development.[15] These include policy priorities for governments to develop an integrated management approach to urban regions, improvement of access and arterial routes, and the means to minimise environmental problems and land-use conflict. Existing communities that become absorbed within the fabric of regional development corridors have become dynamic employment centres, but with unsynchronised layouts and unregulated redevelopment densities which require enhanced local services and public facilities. A further aspect of these changes is the spillover of slum areas which reflects the rate of immigration to urban regions, but also rising urban poverty as city growth requires cheap labour but cannot easily house it. Many cities are therefore experiencing a 'dualism' or polarity created by a growing wealth gap. This is personified by gated communities, gentrified cores and suburban neighbourhoods on one hand, and on the other, overcrowded tenements and squatter areas which in some situations house up to two-thirds of the urban population. In large Asian cities that have a low per capita income and a large informal work force, such as Manila, Bangkok and Jakarta, it is evident that urban subsistence production is an important economic sector, both for local market consumption and for the producer. Foodstuffs emanate from small urban agricultural holdings or fishponds. Similarly waste materials are recycled for housing and furnishing to satisfy basic needs.[16]

In the densest cities (such as Tokyo and Hong Kong), the high cost of urban land precludes extensive urban decay, but nevertheless induces changes in resident populations. These have steadily declined in core 'downtown' areas to make way for commercial, entertainment and creative industries. Commensurate with this are the increasingly dense inner urban fringe and high density new towns linked to the city by high-speed rail systems. If planned strategically, dispersal of population and economic activity from the heavily urbanised core into secondary locations or subcentres can assist the process of regeneration. It could also establish a polycentric and heterogeneous spatial structure at regional level along with a supporting range of community services and facilities.

Polycentric networks tend to have few set boundaries. They generally comprise the older city as either a central core from which development spreads outwards, or a pole point at one end of a broad transportation corridor creating new 'edge' cities on former semi-rural fringes. These networks have been described as 'sets of interacting and overlapping localised subsystems', and represent complex realms of urban and rural interaction.[17] Because this interaction does not necessarily fit within any recognised overall administration, there is a general lack of responsibility for overall strategic

14 Soja, E and Kanai, M, 'the Urbanisation of the World', in *The Endless City*, Eds. Ricky Burdett and Deyan Sudjic, Phaidon, London, 2010, p54
15 McGee, T.G., 'Metrofitting the Emerging Mega-Urban Regions of ASEAN: An Overview', in *The Mega-Urban Regions of Southeast Asia*, Eds. T.G. McGee and Robinson Ira M, University of British Columbia Press, Vancouver, 1995
16 Evers and Korff, 2002, op. cit.
17 Webster, D, 'Mega-Urbanisation in ASEAN: New Phenomenon or Transitional Phase to the Los-Angeles World City', in *The Mega-Urban Regions of Southeast Asia*, Eds. T.G. McGee and Robinson Ira M, University of British Columbia Press, Vancouver, 1995

planning. The spatial development process might therefore envelop and integrate outer satellite communities and jurisdictions, urbanising townships and villages with thriving enterprises, and associated pockets of agricultural land. This forms a loose regional network of not always compatible uses, but collectively fuelled by rapid economic growth.

Some analysts are recognising emerging supranational development corridors within the ASEAN region — for example between Seoul, Taipei and Hong Kong.[18] Transborder city regions also occasionally harbour ethnic and cultural differences, induced over long periods, which occasionally give rise to tensions although international boundaries between states help to maintain social and political stability in the face of economic and employment differences. The notion of a metropolitan region tends to imply an extension of previous limits whether these are socio-economic, administrative or ecological. Several patterns of metropolitan growth can be identified: first those associated with the medium-to-high-density regional growth corridors including Shanghai, the Pearl River Delta, Tokyo, Jakarta and Bangkok, where high proportions of the population reside outside the city cores; second, polynucleated regions such as Malaysia's Klang Valley conurbation, which are assisted by controlled growth models with planned low to medium new town and suburban development along main arterial routes; and third, the city state model such as Singapore with a high density core area including a CBD, but a surrounding growth region that extends into the neighbouring Indonesian Riao archipelago and Johor State in Malaysia.[19]

There is likely to be an upper limit to net urban migration with rates of growth in extended urban regions possibly stabilising or even falling over the next two decades. In physical terms, urban regions will continue to transform themselves through the addition of new high-order functions within urban structures dominated by regenerated townships and expanded urban 'villages'. In growth corridors such as the Pearl River Delta, extended family connections and strong neighbourhood institutions consolidate identification with the core communities. In physical terms this is, in some locations, producing realms of self-sustaining integration through intricate patterns of interconnection, both systemic and informal.

In some cases, tying a city region into the global economy has had a downside. The Bangkok Metropolitan Administrative Area covers around 1,500 square kilometres and was created in 1972 from several *changwats*. However the extended Bangkok Metropolitan mega-urban region covers 7,700 square kilometres and includes at least six cities within a 100 kilometre radius of Bangkok, including the ancient capital Ayuthaya, and is the recipient of all state and local government investment in Thailand. The city has experienced severe environmental deterioration in areas often outside the municipal jurisdiction. Inadequate land use control and regulatory intervention has contributed to ribbon development following highway alignments, while agricultural land has been converted to housing, commercial uses, major smelting and chemical plants, contributing to the degradation of waterways that threaten the freshwater aquifers which feed Bangkok. Private land-use conflicts exacerbate problems of slum and squatter

areas around the city itself as land is cleared by owners and poorer people are displaced. New patterns of urbanisation, in many cases more than 30 kilometres from the city centre, have simply outgrown the ability of any one authority to co-ordinate development activities.

In Jakarta, the core of the metropolitan area has the highest density at around 13,000 people per square kilometre, but the proportion of people living in urban areas within the mega-region (i.e. in core, inner and outer zones), is in excess of 85 per cent. In recent years urban expansion and agricultural intensification has taken place predominantly on the higher land rising from the southern coastal plain from Tangerang to Bekasi. Typically a lack of planning control in the inner zone has led to chaotic and wasteful patterns of land use, with incompatible adjoining uses and little provision of low-income housing, while the core area has evolved from a predominantly low-rise market centre to a global business centre. Excessive groundwater extraction compounded by reclamation of wetland areas for development has resulted in subsidence, and annual floods submerge up to 40 per cent of the city.

In Manila, the National Capital Region was constituted in 1975 bringing together the city of Manila and 16 other cities and municipalities (which now occupy 617 square kilometres), under the administration of a Metropolitan Development Authority.[20] As a result, land for housing is in short supply, and low-cost projects along with squatter settlements are located on the urban fringe or in the wider urban region in Laguna, Cavite and Rizal. An industrial dispersal policy has been implemented to encourage firms to locate outside Metro Manila within regional

[18] Rimer, P.J., 'Moving Goods, People and Information: Putting the ASEAN Mega-Urban Regions in Context', in *The Mega-Urban Regions of Southeast Asia*, Eds. T.G. McGee and Robinson Ira M, University of British Columbia Press, Vancouver, 1995

[19] McGee, 1995, op. cit.

[20] Racelis, R.H. and Collado, P.M.G., 'The Manila MUD: Continuing Magnet for Migrants', in *Mega-Urban Regions in Pacific Asia: Urban Dynamics in a Global Era*, Eds. Gavin W. Jones and Mike Douglass Jones, NUS Press, Singapore, 2008

industrial centres and in close proximity to major transport routes.

Demands for commercial space, caused by the burgeoning service sector and housing needs of employees, has elevated the real-estate industry as a significant economic driver of the mega-region, with property becoming not merely an essential means of occupation but an investment vehicle. Arguably the most difficult task in terms of integrated planning and urban design is the reconciliation of private capital investment with the means to overcome the potential environmental problems stemming from this. The concept of "metrofitting" is currently being applied to the Guangdong — Hong Kong (Pearl River Delta) PRD region, which has long been commonly known as a "front shop, back factory" model. Its evolution was based on the marriage of low production costs and a multinational–dominated international market and supply chain. While all production materials are made in the PRD, Hong Kong acts as a service provider, engaged in logistics, and freight forwarding. Under the twelfth Five-Year Programme endorsed in 2011, the goal is to accelerate the implementation of a resource saving and eco-friendly framework with new express rail connections. The main component cities of Shenzhen, Guangzhou, Foshan and Dongguan have high levels of industrial activities with dense population cores, and the provincial government plans to invest in environmental infrastructural projects up to 2020.

TRENDS IN MEGA-URBAN REGION DEVELOPMENT

The mega-urban region continues to be driven by global competition, fomenting concentrated fields of interaction that transcend former city or metropolitan boundaries. This poses a fundamental question over urban design, liveability and material welfare in the cities themselves in the face of more regional growth trajectories, allocation of services and the associated depletion of natural resources. This situation inevitably leads to elusive trade-offs between economic growth, quality of life, and the dimensions of urban habitat, all of which are discussed in other chapters.

Mike Douglas et al propose three interconnected components of liveability.[21] The first is the existence of urban 'lifeworlds' in the form of responsive planning (rather than speculative and sporadic development), with a strong public realm that promotes community values and co-existence of local activities and social encounters, rather than overly commodified environments. This extends to the relationship between civic space and sacred place that in Asia establishes a social link between community and spiritual life while adding vitality to the urban setting. The second is personal well-being in terms of livelihood, health, education and security, in situations where urban poverty in the outer realm of expanding regions continues to have a high impact on agricultural and immigrant workers, with substandard housing, inadequate access to health care, and concerns over safety including child labour. The third is environmental well-being, in situations where intensive urbanisation has led to increasing air, land and water pollution, inadequate access to water supply and seasonal flooding as a result of deforestation, erosion and reclamation.

While sustainable natural environments have become an issue of great concern, a fundamental objective is to ensure inclusion and a considered approach to equality as a social goal. It is therefore a central role of government intervention to ensure as far as possible that public good prevails over private interest and to manage potential conflicts in the best public interest. This requires a conceptual shift from intervention in "space" to identification with "place".

Governance is a key factor in liveability and varies from country to country, and between developing regions. In general this is best achieved by a balance of state power and local autonomy, together with fiscal decentralisation programmes that can, in ideal circumstances, lead to community participation and involvement in development policy. Local government bodies are often not allocated sufficient budgets to properly orchestrate the hyper-growth rate of emerging mega-regions, although in certain countries capital city regions are relatively autonomous, reflecting their role as the economic engines of national growth.

The phases of growth within these extended urban regions (albeit with key variations), stem from the accelerated industrial development and rural-urban migration experienced in many Asian countries following national independence from colonial governments. Commensurate with this, mechanised farming techniques have facilitated large population movement to cities, with industry focussed in the urban core, together with the growth of large urban slums. This process broadly continued through the 1980s when a shift to new service economies and the influence of global economic forces began to complement labour-intensive industrialisation, such as large-scale

21 Jones and Douglas, 2008, op. cit.

assembly and manufacturing processes. This led to slower rates of growth within the mega-urban regions reflecting demographic transitions as well as new consumer trends. Continued migration from rural areas to primate cities has also generally been accompanied by large-scale redevelopment of obsolete core areas such as military bases, old port works, and redundant industrial uses, but at a slower rate.

In the current growth stage, urban populations in most Asian countries have topped 50 per cent, with manufacturing shifting to low-wage economies and increased inter-city migration of skilled labour, including labour movement across national boundaries. Urban agglomerations therefore continue to absorb an increasing percentage of national populations, and are becoming more spatially complex with multiple interactions, new central business development for regional headquarter functions, and previous core functions moving to outer locations.

THE IMPACT OF GLOBALISATION

"World City" ranking is based upon a city's level of advanced producer services, but this raises questions regarding the effect that the globalisation process itself is having on Asian cities and how this is being spatially characterised. Arguably the network of "global" cities has expanded from the 1980s with the leap in information and transportation technology, more dynamic economic relationships with the west, and greater cross-border integration and investment. However there are clearly other forces at play. The concept of the quartered city set out by Peter Marcuse, elaborates distinct but not rigid residential and economic patterns with distinguishing but overlapping characteristics that reflect physical, social and economic conditions.[22] These in turn suggest parallel divisions, from gentrified areas to tenements, and from advanced services to informal manufacturing. Such divisions inevitably assume similar urban design characteristics, from protected residential and business citadels to old established neighbourhoods, ethnic enclaves, edge configurations, airports and transit nodes. Within these sub-division are "soft" locations that might represent "brown field" areas such as defunct industrial sites, waterfronts opened up through old port closures, entertainment areas, and historic quarters. In this situation post-colonial dynamics have necessitated that state-directed institutions encourage outward investment processes. The Singapore Urban Redevelopment Authority for example is answerable to the Ministry of National Development so that all urban planning policies, programmes and projects subscribe to the politics of nation-building. In practice there is no "model" for global city formation.

Globalisation has implications at the city as well as national level. It can also instigate various processes combining new technology, capital intensive means of production, concentration of economic development areas, growth in service industry and migration of people. In the process, spatially contained neighbourhoods, while important in terms of community and urban diversity, are becoming less relevant to the economy as a whole. The impact is one of spatial disconnection and gradual socio-economic polarisation. Coupled with this, there are changing patterns of individual choice emancipation, and flexible working opportunities. These tend to physically consolidate in the form of 'quartered' cities, each with special social and economic characteristics, but subject to changing societal forces.[23]

THE GEOGRAPHY OF AGGLOMERATION: CONNECTING THE LOCAL WITH THE GLOBAL

Business networks benefit from the economies of agglomeration. Consequently the modern Asian city, plugged into a global communication network, is seeing a concentration of head office 'central' functions as "concentrated command points", and the increasing dispersal of secondary or back-up office functions. The geography of centrality set out by Saskia Sassen relates to the top echelon of internationalised service industry — legal, accounting, insurance, managerial, co-ordinating and executive functions that control business organisations in surrounding regions or across national boundaries, as a function of cross-border networks.[24] These specialist agglomerations encourage the creation of increasingly innovative organisational systems which are continually transforming ways in which these activities are carried out. They are located in cities with highly developed services, and which form part of an expanding network of international centres. Such concentrations function virtually independently of national economies, and are increasingly oriented to the global marketplace. This is in turn fuelling the growth of strategic sub-centres of production or secondary services with their own back-up infrastructure linked to a limited number of economic circuits.

Thus Asian financial centres now fulfil gateway functions, establishing a nexus

[22] Marcuse, P, 'Space in the Globalising City', in *The Global Cities*, Eds. Neil Brenner and Roger Keil, Routledge, London and New York, 2006
[23] Marcuse, P and van Kempen, R, *Globalising Cities – A New Spatial Order*, Blackwell, London, 2000, p12
[24] Sassen, S, 'The Formation of Intercity Geographies of Centrality', in *Architecture and Urbanism for Modern Cities*, Eds. Seng Kuan, and Peter G. Rowe, Prestel, Munich, New York and London, 2004

between the city's resources and the global marketplace, and between foreign investors and available opportunities. This requires social as well as technical connectivity, and is leading to strategic alliances between organisations that essentially provide the same global service, whether in telecommunications, power supply, finance or law. In turn, an expanding transactional economy between major cities is establishing a connective structure of business districts, cross-border hierarchies, and special economic zones. These are transforming patterns of urbanisation as a result of programmes of investment that produce the multiple economic, social and spatial dynamics of mega-urban regions, loosely structured through well-connected primary centres and sub-districts.[25]

In assessing the implications of the trend towards the dominating city region in Asia and its continuing influence on the growth and direction of agglomeration economies, it is possible to make two main observations. The first is the clear correlation between concentrated areas of economic activity (often supported by policy and regulatory intervention), increase in GDP, and wealth transfer between urban and rural areas. In the main, the number of sub-centres tends to have an equalising effect, establishing not only employment opportunities but options which are made viable through ease of mobility and condensed industrial patterns. The second is the increasing significance of ecological carrying capacity in relation to the city region, with the potential side effects of less than efficient regional settlement and increasing consumption patterns. Where strategic land-use planning systems are weak or only able to focus on key areas of leverage

in order to manage regional development rather than plan for it, the most important driver of growth must be the installation of water, sewerage and waste disposal systems. Efficient and cost-effective transportation infrastructure represents the key to both shaping and servicing these urban regions, and will vary according to either their decentralised or consolidated structure.

In the past, regulatory policies in the majority of Asian cities have been poor, although most cities have increased the capacity of light rail and mass transit systems. Future growth presents a challenge in matching efficiency of urban organisation with maintaining relative self-sufficiency of food production and other resources. This equilibrium needs to be closely monitored through deliberately explicit government policies and integrated management approaches to such things as agriculture and low carbon energy sources according to regional priorities. These issues spark some pertinent questions with regard to planning direction — whether to be highly regulatory through zoning or, if this is already applied, upzoning in relation to use definition, development ratio and coverage with its highly prescriptive implications; and whether to focus on development control with its more subjective means of evaluating the form and nature of city growth and regeneration.

The underlying factors might be said to reflect two interrelated processes. The first of these are 'transactional' activities which relate to people, commodities, capital and information that act together to forge compact urban configurations, with extended growth trajectories that link together existing urban cores. In the process these create

discontinuous land use patterns characterised by rapidly evolving changes in economic activity and land costs. Explicit policies aimed at rationalising or restructuring city cores, along with local geographic, land use conditions, layouts and open space standards, all act together to express scale and form. To reinforce the attractiveness of established cities to investors and business visitors, as well as tourists, there is an implicit incentive to renew or regenerate the existing city environment, and to broadcast its cultural attributes and points of identity.

The second process involves forces which operate at both a national and urban level, namely advances in communication, production technology and logistics. These have developed a strong momentum in Asia since the mid-1980s and have facilitated the large-scale transfer of manufacturing to areas where labour costs are low, and real or potential skills are high. However Soja and Kanai state that what is changing from past trade and financial flows is the global geography of industrial capital involved in the production of goods, services and information through new technology.[26] This in turn reinforces the incentives for economic investment to focus on mega-urban regions, with their primary city nodes becoming pumped up centres for capital, transportation hubs and service provision, with a strong international outlook. The outcome is a multi-layered network of global corporations interacting with smaller and more localised production and distribution systems. Intervention therefore facilitates a hierarchical pattern of land values and the necessity to make considerable investment in infrastructure and new commercial operations.

25 Marcuse and van Kempen, 2000, op. cit.
26 Soja and Kanai, 2010, op. cit.

5

URBAN
NARRATIVES

Interpreting
the Public
Realm

Asian cities as we have seen, have been shaped by a narrative of expressive features, much of this generated through intervention in the city building process. Contested urban environments present a fundamental problem for urban planning, in reconciling political, economic, social and environmental objectives with physical design. Even if we put to one side far-reaching but ambiguous issues that are arguably crucial to the future of cities, such as social justice, the resolution of poverty and the need for colossal investment in housing, infrastructure and urban services, we are still left with elusive questions. These include: how cities can shape our lives for the better, how attuned they are to satisfying human needs and the degree to which they can be more sustainable. The obstacles are in many ways obvious but the solutions are less so, apart from those that are more general: better city governance and management, more sympathetic urban renewal and increased investment in urban infrastructure.

There is a need to respect land economics, ownership patterns, and increased servicing requirements. However, it is necessary to ensure that the almost constant process of redevelopment does not dictate a course-grained structure of new urban layouts across different city morphologies that result in massive displacement and undifferentiated urban quarters. Instead, it is important to effectively regenerate cities through incrementalism and adjustment, opening up development and expansion possibilities while retaining cultural and intangible heritage. At the same time, the focus should be on protection and reinforcement of the older fine-grained environments in multi-ownership, in order to produce an integrative urbanism. City

planning processes, management mechanisms, sophisticated regulatory controls and land use zoning, geared to making cities increasingly efficient and functional, must be used flexibly with vision and creativity.

While Asian cities differ from each other in all kinds of ways, there are many commonalities and inherent urban strengths where urban form can avoid normative models and better reflect cultural expression and successful precedent. Great cities must be rooted in ideology, and successful urbanism can no more be left entirely to government than to market forces or the community at large. A fundamental objective of good city planning is to ensure inclusion and a considered approach to equality as a social goal. It should therefore be a central role of government to ensure, as far as possible, that public good prevails over private interest and to manage potential conflicts. This implies a need to assimilate what is characteristically embodied in the local morphology — the essential values of the street, the city block, and other spatial configurations. These can be reflected within sympathetic typologies that acknowledge and accommodate changing community structures and ambitions, and that extend cultural definition to cosmopolitan types of urban design.

THE STREET AS A CENTRAL TENET OF URBANISM

The street is the organising mainstay of Asian urbanism where constant re-invention and adaptation takes place in co-existence with more static components, and where changing sequences of use can be interjected, superimposed or layered within the existing fabric. Asian cities do not necessarily have

THE FABRIC cannot be disassociated from the constantly changing nature of society — a diaspora that absorbed different communities within different quarters of the city, with assorted trades, craft guilds, producers of foodstuffs and specialised professions. The separate bazaar characteristics have survived throughout more than three centuries of physical change and adjustments within a complicated network of associations, framed within a hierarchy of narrow lanes and local access routes in Delhi.

the formalist configuration of spaces and the highly defined public realm bequeathed to most Western cities. Where the typical European street has a typological uniformity that asserts a collective definition, the Asian street is more likely to reflect a heterogeneous assembly of types that vary in terms of form, scale, and the degree of informality. This allows it to integrate a range of complex interactions including social rituals, ceremonial uses, market trading, and economic transactions that relate more to patterns of activity than conceived physical form. The Asian street therefore functions in several dimensions, generally responsive to free-wheeling imperatives that intensify levels of use. In its twenty-first century manifestation, it represents substantial cultural shifts with new and different values superimposed on long established patterns of urbanisation, reflecting the co-existence of different economic and social systems.

Dunlop Street forms part of the low-rise shophouses matrix within "Little India" in Singapore, creating a contrast of styles within a controlled pattern of display and signage.

Jonker Street, Malacca

CAMPBELL STREET IN GEORGE TOWN, PENANG, was created in the mid-nineteenth century and is known in Malay as Jalan Macau because of Cantonese emigration from Macau, including courtesans — hence the term Jalan Nona Baru or "street of new maidens". Today Campbell Street houses the landmark municipal market on land purchased from the original grant to the Kapitan Kling Mosque. Related market activities tend to extend alongside the street frontage, accentuating the function of this heritage feature.

JOINED-UP TYPOLOGIES

The relationship of 'joined-together' buildings to the process of street and city-making is fundamental, enabling the absorption of high population densities, intense patterns of economic activity and formulating a distinctive urban identity. The flexible t'ang lau or shophouse tenement that can be sub-divided and constantly re-fitted to encompass different uses is a cultural and social model with an important economic dimension. It represents a historically dominant street typology that is consistent in form yet modifiable to fit climatic and contextual situations, yet there are varied interpretations in style, plan form and fenestration features. In essence, it signifies a sense of likeness and consistency tempered with difference.

Shophouse streets form a 'rhyming' urbanism where there is an affinity between elements within the overall street block, rather than repetition of identical characteristics. In this way a complex organisation of profiles and textures can procure a state of balance. The result presents contrast within a highly intelligible pattern, where older street buildings accommodate a diverse range of uses behind façades that have changed very little. The cultural dimensions of the street are therefore intrinsically interwoven with a sense of immediacy, economic change and fragmented incident embedded in a sense of dissonance — the chance of interaction and encounter, the unexpected, the complex and the indeterminate.

COMPLEXITY AND CORRESPONDENCE

A successful public realm exists through interactions between complexity and order, novelty and familiarity. Urban configurations are shaped by early settlement imprints, imposed regulatory regimes, land ownership structures, market imperatives and trading trajectories that often reflect intangible processes. These help to strengthen the perceived boundaries of urban space through a contextual juxtaposition that emphasises variety over harmonious form, but one which establishes an effective dialogue between uses. Thus Asian streets and urban places represent an urbanism of high adaptability but disjointed image. 'Places' tend to be defined by types of activity, independent of compositional elements. They are expressed through asymmetrical forms to which the parts subscribe in accordance with practicality, patterns of movement, change and flexibility. This tends to represent an architecture of parts rather than standardised assemblies, where values can be translated into typologies that satisfy community objectives and ambitions. In this situation memory is embedded less in the solid fabric of the city and more in its ephemeral responsiveness to change and regeneration, and the expressive aspects of urban texture.

This lends symbolic meaning to a locality, where a sense of place is marked by strong cultural and social associations. It also creates an elusive relationship between what is known and what is seen. Likeness and repetition are alleviated by a multitude of irregularities and layered uses, and unified through patterns of correspondence and self-organisation. Realms of ad hoc activity evoke long traditions of inventive and expressive bricolage that dramatise the street frontage and establish a dialectic between internal and external space, embedded in the complex framework of everyday life.

Shibuya, Tokyo (left); The Plaza Santa Cruz represents the centre of the commercial district of Binondo in Manila, north of McArthur Bridge (right)

STREET-BASED COOKED FOOD AREAS, such as this on Jalan Alor in Kuala Lumpur, extend across pavements and establish informal meeting and gathering points from early morning to late evening. Simple street furniture allows for easy use and storage. They are patronised by all sectors of the population and form an integral part of urban life. The pasar malam is a travelling night market, synonymous with Malaysian and other Southeast Asian cities. Held once a week, in different localities, the market sells food, clothes and electronics and often interfaces with open-front cafes. During this period the street is closed to traffic. Other examples are the one-day market or pekan sehari and the pasar tani or farmer's market.

TEMPORAL TRANSITIONS

Temporal transitions in the Asian city reflect the relationship between the passage of time and the programmatic change of uses throughout the day and evening. This generally involves different sets of users who inhabit street space at different times for different purposes, sometimes with a high degree of overlap. Locations are shared on a time basis rather than being used intensively but intermittently by one particular interest group. Change through time is therefore a function of the availability of street space in relation to specific interest groups that have easy access to it. The transition from day-time to night-time uses allows users to become participants in a series of unfolding events. This daily metamorphosis, often associated with the construction of stands for night markets and food stalls, are expressions of public ritual that convolute the normal experience of urban space, and both absorb and promote constantly evolving patterns of activity.

ARTICULATED MARGINS AND THRESHOLD SPACES

The street margin represents a public or semi-public space between the street and the building edge. In many Asian streets this tends to be treated as a transitional 'threshold' rather than a rigid demarcation. This therefore acts as a functional space in its own right with a strong expressive quality where the informal street rhythm involves a daily reciprocity between different interests and rituals. Colonnaded walkways are still a feature of older urban districts, articulating their edges in a consistent and unifying way,

Colonnaded frontages around Senate Square in Macau

providing climatic shelter, and creating space for adjustable display areas. The interface between 'private' and 'public' is thereby enlivened and animated by edge activities that percolate into the street itself and engage passers-by through overlays of use and display.

Until the mid-nineteenth century, buildings in the old city of Hanoi had to adhere to the royal 'Annamite Code' which forbade consumers from erecting buildings in a solid construction of over one storey, and also prohibited excessive decoration.[1]

AMEYA YOKOCHO lies between Ueno station and Ueno Okachimachi station in Tokyo. It is known as Ameyoko ('Confectioners Alley') and began life as a thriving black market area for American goods during the Korean War. The market incorporates the lanes on both sides of the elevated tracks of the Yamanote/Keihin Tohuku Line, together with all areas below the tracks, forming long and narrow internal malls.

Contrast and complexity in Hong Kong

MUTATION AND REINVENTION

A central tenet of the Asian public realm is its versatility. The spirit of place is defined by constant insertions, adjustments and localised improvisation that invoke different qualities of use, and stems from discernible values that transcend time and place. Older street buildings are sporadically transformed by their occupiers in a fluid way through personalised building extensions and functional appendages to façades and roofs, generally on the basis of practicality and immediacy rather than design considerations or strict adherence to regulations. Constant subdivision of land in older city quarters establishes a hierarchy of main "front" streets and tight "back" streets that preserve an urban duality of different but complementary uses. Where there is positive utilisation of surplus space, voids become positively charged with temporary uses and rapidly establish a sense of 'fit' responding in an empirical way to the active street pattern.

Temporary colonisation of space under elevated connectors, such as highway and railway alignments, evolve into an often permanent and additive texture of parts, effectively insulated from overhead transit activities.

1 Logan, W.S., 'Hanoi Townscape: Symbolic Imagery in Vietnam's Capital', in *Cultural Identity and Urban Change in Southeast Asia: Interpretative Essays*, Eds. Marc Askew & William S. Logan, Deakin University Press, Geelong, 1994

PERSISTENCIES AND PALIMPSESTS

The evolving framework of land values and ownership patterns, leads to an accretion of historical trace elements, both physical and metaphysical. Historical persistencies and cultural overlays inject an influential presence in the form of festival grounds, ceremonial spaces and speciality markets, forming an urban continuum that brings the past into the present, and relates to time as well as use. Shop-lined street markets may have evolved in some cases from, for example from temple approaches, traditionally made up of stalls which sold offerings. Place identity is reinforced through adaptable fabric that can accommodate acceptable degrees of change, while retaining physical 'permanences' which have strong local associations.

Walled City, Lahore

ASAKUSA, the area around the Senso-ji Temple in Tokyo, continues to accommodate the older shop-lined street that used to flourish along the temple gate avenue. The temple itself represents a spiritual focus for Tokyo and a link with the old Tokugawa capital. The Kaminari-mon gate and the Hozo-mon gates are positioned at certain stages in the approach to the Asakusa Kannon, emphasising the spatial transition. The temple approach has traditionally been made up of stalls selling temple offerings, but which now mostly sell gifts. These frame the walkway to the Kannon Hall. To the side, narrow streets present a more casual collection of residences, bars and shops, together with covered shopping arcades linked to the wider street matrix within the locality.

HINDU TEMPLE on Shobhabazar Street, Kolkata. Hinduism evolved through a multiplicity of beliefs, finding a focus in Brahma — the Creator, and twin manifestations — Vishnu — the Preserver, and Shiva — the Destroyer. Temples reflect a prolific literature of epic stories, embedded in both religion and culture.

Marriage ceremony, Meiji Jingu, Tokyo (top); roadside shrine, George Town, Penang (below)

SPIRITUAL HERITAGE AND SACRED PLACE

The sacred place, in terms of its physical form and urban 'fit', is the antithesis of the absolutist position. In many situations the location of temples, shrines, pagodas and other ceremonial features are identified through geomantic diagnosis in relation to natural features. This produces a sense of harmony between perceived divine forces on one hand, and the more transient material expressions of life on the other — an intuitive balance between opposing but complementary forces. Instead of dominating its surroundings, the temple establishes a low-key but purposeful presence which heightens its relatively informal relationship with the public realm. It also generates a powerful identity in relation to many small trading establishments and stall holdings selling offerings and gifts. The juxtaposition of the spiritual and the urban achieves a relaxed co-existence through a combination of ceremonial and social gathering spaces. This fosters an intimate relationship with the community, which in many cases reflects the non-proselytising traditions of the predominant Asian religions — Buddhism, Shintoism, Hinduism and Islam. Building forms relate to the cosmos because they symbolise the relationship of man to the universe, endemic of change, transition and transformation, and reflecting the fundamental laws of nature.

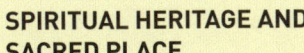

TRANSACTIONAL REGIMES

Small-scale and diverse points of transaction in off-street situations create vibrant places that focus on special types of self-organising retail activity, offering the potential for interaction and ad hoc improvisation. These are shaped and animated by a wide range of users with their accompanying array of small kiosks, food stands, push carts and cycle carts. A high tolerance towards mobile street vendors and cooked food operators, reflects the informal trading sector's contribution to the social life of communities, and forms a traditional means of matching affordable needs with local employment capacity.

STREET HAWKERS are a feature of street life, generally peddling food and herbal medicines from painted carts or kaki lima, through the day and evening. Book sellers occupy the pavement in Jakarta.

Food carts, Yangon (above); A distinctive backdrop of shophouses against a street market on Sule Pagoda Road, Yangon (below)

CONCENTRATION OF VENDORS along street edges and pak soi in Bangkok represent specialised outdoor market areas for cooked food, clothes and flowers that have established long-standing trading patterns for low income groups as part of a burgeoning informal economy.

URBAN DELINEATIONS

Markers traditionally delineate points of spatial transition along important routes. In certain cities, "gateways" assist in orientation and legibility acting as urban signifiers, point references and physical landmarks, known in China as *pāilou,* and in Japan as *torri*. Towered decorative gateways to sacred places can be marked by a narrative of tiered niches and statues and a sequence of stepped approaches, establishing an elusive link between spirituality and 'place'. The use of banners, flags, signage displays or lanterns create peripheral characteristics and atmospheric emphasis where animation overwhelms the actual setting. Processional routes to sacred shrines are delineated by physical elements such as gateways, spirit shrines and stone lanterns that emphasise transition rather than spatial demarcation in a compositional sense. More secular landmarks typically relate to the physical identity of places of convergence and intensive foci. The more complex the street matrix — through its represention of interstitial space — the more its intersections and interfaces produce opportunities for markers to fix an identity through a spatial emphasis that is expressive of durable city values.

A pailou demarcates entrance to residential area, Beijing

THE APPROACH TO THE ZOJO-JI TEMPLE (left), situated close to Roppongi Hills in Tokyo, is marked with a large torri-gate along the main avenue, indicating its historical role as a way-station for pilgrims. The temple was founded in 1393 and was later chosen by the Tokugawa Shogunate as their ancestral temple in order to protect Edo from disaster. The red-lacquered Sanmon Gate dates back to 1612 and the Main Hall contains ancient sacred objects. Many of the old temple buildings that were destroyed by fire have been re-built. The Meiji government later turned the extensive temple grounds into the Shiba Park.

MARKET QUARTERS

comprising both open-air stalls and narrow arcades with makeshift roofs, are installed above the street system in parts of Seoul. This includes speciality arcades or tonam-dong for clothes, shoes and cooked food and sul-jip or small café-bars associated with the Gwanjang and Tongdae-mum markets that parallel the mid-section of the Cheonggyecheon River.

COMMODIFIED CONNECTIONS

The condensed nature of business districts increasingly incorporates contrasting interventions at different scales. Vertical people movers and elevated skywalks cut through buildings and across street corridors. These support a three-dimensional matrix of uses that demand a high level of access and connection, and where routes between uses work just as effectively in three dimensions as in two. Elevated and vertical connections introduce an extra dimension of urban movement that heightens the user's encounter with layered commercial patterns. An intensive mix of spatial situations accentuates different patterns of use and promotes constantly evolving patterns of activity along their path, re-shaping edge spaces.

The ambiguous transition from the public realm to the privately managed commodified sphere introduces a complex secondary typology of circulation channels made up of footbridges, escalator links, malls and atria where users are induced to interface with products. Continuity of space provides an intricate and episodic movement experience interwoven with retail distribution systems that stimulate consumption. The availability of public connections with transit nodes and commercial blocks at various levels create three-dimensional permeable alternatives to the ground level street pattern, recasting the way in which increasingly dense urban environments are experienced.

INTERCONNECTED PEDESTRIAN SYSTEMS

The biggest challenge to the public life associated with street space comes first, from situations where traffic has usurped other urban uses, and second from the advent of the 'superblock', divorced from the established urban fabric. This creates a need to reduce conflict between pedestrians and vehicles, through hierarchies of pedestrian connectivity via street closures and connected open space systems at various levels.

A programme of interconnected pathways and spaces builds up a cellular structure of functioning arteries that tie together urban neighbourhoods. This requires new or upgraded connective tissue to join existing pedestrian channels and recreational elements. In this way traversing of city quarters becomes more legible and exploratory, designed to accommodate a multiplicity of experiences through contrasts in scale, use and density of activity.

Vertical gateway to Times Square Shopping Centre, Hong Kong

ICONOGRAPHY OF CONSUMPTION

The post-industrial Asian city represents a fundamental shift in the values of consumption over production, and the street is subject to a constant process of urban adaptation reflecting these values in relation to social space. The vocabulary of consumption embodies a representation of script, be it Chinese, Japanese or Islamic, that can be read as a texture of parts in both a pictorial and descriptive sense, and can be added to or subtracted to reflect changing situations. This contributes to an elaborate imagery that is both unpredictable and self-organising, and asserts a symbolic identity through its confrontational dominance.

THE TSUKIJI IN SHITAMACHI (right), the old nineteenth century foreigner's compound is known as Tokyo no daidokoro — home of the vast centralised fish market full of small family-run operations serving 14,000 restaurants and sushi parlours in the city.

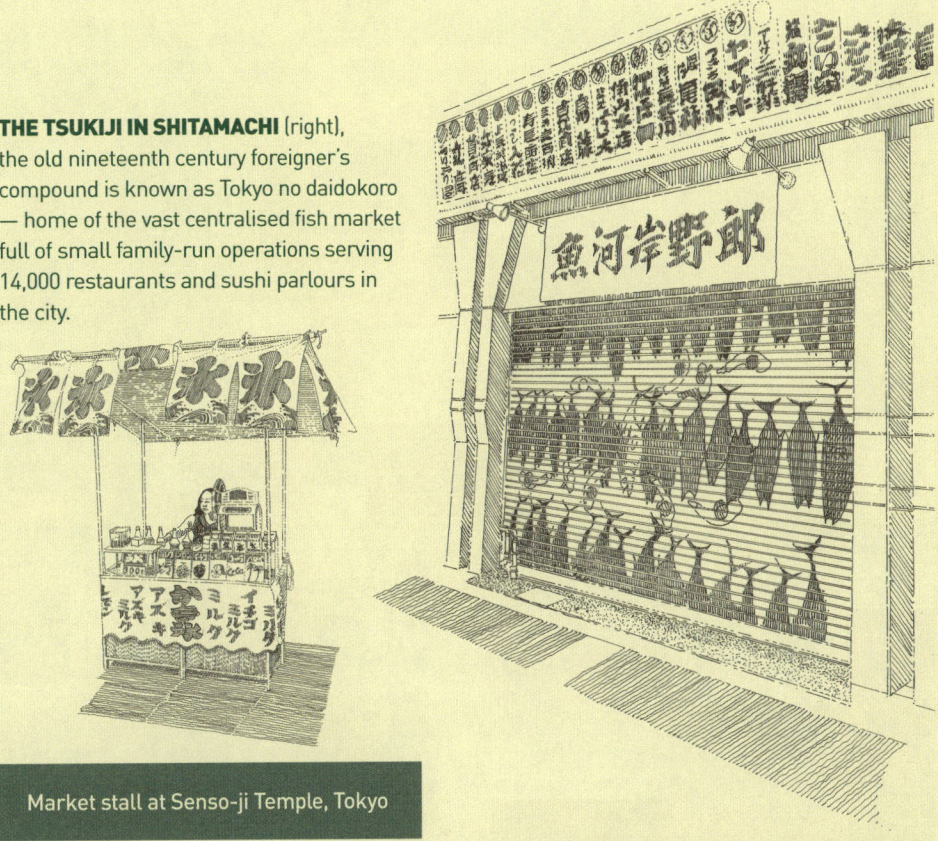

Tenement façades tempered by building additions on street frontage in To Kwa Wan, Hong Kong

Market stall at Senso-ji Temple, Tokyo

REQUISITIONED FAÇADES

Continuous channels of information displays assert an overriding street syntax which animates the public realm and effectively neutralises the architectural streetscape. The urban foreground of building planes and resonating surfaces becomes dematerialised from its surroundings through a multi-layered collage of temporary elements that distort established notions of intelligible form and aesthetics and convolute the normal experience of space.

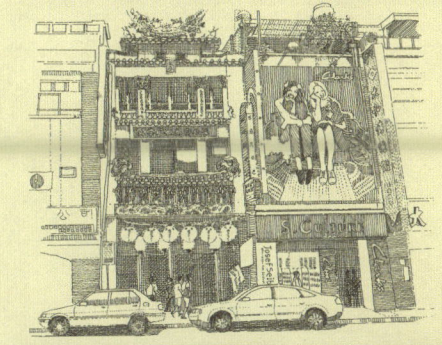

Advertising display overwhelms its shophouse context in Taipei

Lahore

The effects of geography, the impact of foreign intervention and migratory trends have, in combination, formed the directional patterns of urbanization in South Asian countries. The overwhelming majority of settlements have been associated with coastlines, rivers, estuarine and delta lands — as around two-thirds of South Asia's land masses are too mountainous, dry and infertile for self-sustaining habitation. The sub-continent is made up of mountainous terrain between the Bay of Bengal and the Persian Gulf together with the course of the three main rivers — the Indus, Ganges and Brahmaputra — and their tributaries, which have divided civilizations, demarcated national boundaries and fostered empires based on ancient Aryan and Muslim cultures. The rich cultural heritage of South Asia has been shaped by historical events and more recent regimes of foreign intervention and imperial ambition. This has given rise, in the late twentieth century, to a strident and competitive nationalism, as newly independent economies continue attempts to gain a foothold in the international marketplace.

From 500 BC, Indic civilisation in South Asia was centred around Hinduism — a polytheistic religion that established a strong moral code and rigid societal structure. Other faiths developed almost in parallel and to some extent overlapped, in particular Buddhism which spread to many parts of Asia. Much of its evolving culture embraced a philosophical sense of purpose and ethical precepts, reflected in pictorial art, architecture and literature. Islam was introduced in the twelfth century from Afghanistan, its leaders unifying the fragmented states of northern India by force and establishing a new Turkish Sultanate based in Delhi.

In 1526 following the earlier pillage of Delhi by Tamerlane, the Mughal Empire was established, headed by descendants of Genghis Khan. This resulted in a consolidation of what had been relatively autonomous states in northern and central India, winning Rajput loyalty and creating a political precedent for the British ruling strategy some three hundred years later. New capitals were built, first at Agra and then at Fatephur Sikri. Through the reigns of Shah Akbar and his grandson Sha Jahan, the country experienced a flowering of culture and city building. A narrative of European intervention in South Asia during the eighteenth century needs to acknowledge the decline of the Mughal Empire and the radical changes and re-alignment of commercial relationships that occurred in the constellation of cities and trade centres. The rise in Maratha power opened up new trade and communication routes together with new administrative centres and market towns that evolved into major settlements with significant agricultural catchments. The major cities themselves, through the accumulation of capital, began to function as government and commercial business hubs.

With new trading routes the port cities began to assume a growing importance exporting spices and other commodities. It was this that attracted the first European adventurers.

THE IMPACT OF FOREIGN INTERVENTION

The colonial impact on urbanisation in South Asia during the British Raj needs to be examined through its associated innovations in transport and technology, which in turn influenced urban design. It is estimated that only 11 per cent of South Asia's population of 160 million lived in cities at the turn of the nineteenth century. This changed largely through the growth of three powerful cities — Madras, Bombay (Mumbai) and Calcutta (Kolkata) — co-ordinated under the auspices of the English East India Company. City expansion occurred intensely in the primate coastal cities most associated with imperial

SOUTH ASIA

policy, which indirectly suppressed the growth of secondary cities. However due to the dispersed organisation of market and administrative centres, an organisational network of manufacturing, collection and trans-shipment centres was maintained virtually throughout the nineteenth century. Cities became the administrative trading and commercial nodes, while the emerging transportation routes became the distribution and connecting channels for movement of people and goods. This enabled the colonial system to be viable and facilitated the modernising transition through its evolution from a mercantile community to a militarised bureaucracy. It was personified in the design of public space, and buildings that reflected a contrast between the native city, and the civil and military stations.

As the last remnants of Mughal rule disappeared, sovereign authority over India was officially transferred from the English East India Company to the Crown in November 1858. This strategy became the keystone to political and economic intervention in other parts of Asia and transformative in terms of the agenda of modernisation. The early Viceroys presided over India from the colonial capital in Calcutta. Under the Viceroy was an Executive Council of members appointed by the Crown, and a Legislative Council, while provinces and cities were ruled by governors and commissioners. Urbanisation thus followed British planning protocols and Victorian styles of architecture, tempered by Mughal embellishments and flourishes. New universities were built in Calcutta, Madras and Bombay as a force for both advanced education and Westernisation. The need for new government and institutional uses together with British investments in industry and commercial activities, facilitated the introduction of new realms of city development, made even more necessary by the opening of the Suez Canal in 1865, which provided rapid transport between India and Europe. By the turn of the twentieth century, there were more than two and a half million Indians spread throughout the British Empire including large settlements of both Hindus and Muslims in other parts of Asia, notably Malayasia, Singapore, Burma, Penang and Sri Lanka.

However outside intervention could also be divisive. Reforms and modernisations continued to impact on long-held social and economic patterns within older cultures as improvements in education and working conditions undermined traditional customs, intensifying calls for separation. Pakistan was split into eastern and western sectors through partition of British India, and a constituent assembly convened by the governor-general declared the country an Islamic Republic nine years later. In 1958 the capital was moved from Karachi to Islamabad — a new city.

In 1971 secessionist Bengali forces in East Pakistan, supported by India, declared independence and a new state, Bangladesh, was formed. Through considerable political changes and periods of martial law, an underlying problem remains — that of over-population and the vulnerability of the predominantly agrarian economy to flooding and cyclones.

At the heart of urban design in the modern South Asian city is the equation between post-colonial economic development and the confounding legacy of imperialism. Interwoven with historical settlements and contemporary fabric is the architecture of empire. It borrowed from and transformed established cultural forms to fit the new power structure of the Raj, expressed and made visible in spatial terms through its public monuments. Those statement pieces were the result of prolonged debate over the most appropriate stylistic mode of representation, and framed within an urban design that reflected an assertion of control and order. However the architecture of empire was also embedded in a fixation with the "mystique" of the Orient, and that cultural and societal expression informed the physical representation of the colonial city. The result encompasses an urbanism of constant re-interpretation as cities seek to accommodate massive population growth and economic investment.

THE INDIAN SUBCONTINENT

The Indian subcontinent occupies the largest landmass in South Asia, accommodating seven countries: India, Pakistan, Bangladesh, Sri Lanka, Nepal, Bhutan and the Maldives. Prior to 1947, the countries of India, Pakistan and Bangladesh constituted British India. It covers around 4.4 million square kilometres, and is delineated by the Himalayas in the north, the Arekanese in the east, and the Hindu Kush in the west. It is defined to the south by the Indian Ocean, to the southeast by the Bay of Bengal, and to the southwest by the Arabian Sea.

India is essentially a rural country with 70 per cent of its population living in half a million villages. Urban India consists of around 3,800 towns or cities, of which Maharashtra is the most urbanised state with 39 per cent of people living in cities, followed by Gujarat at 35 per cent, Punjab at 30 per cent and West Bengal at 28 per cent.[1] The four largest cities today are Mumbai (Bombay); Delhi, Kolkata (Calcutta) and Chennai (Madras), but before the arrival of the British only Delhi and Hyderabad existed as major urban entities. In all of these, slum and squatter settlements indicate something of a mismatch between population growth, planning and investment programmes, economic development and city management. Today Bombay with 26 million, Kolkata with 17.3 million and Dehli with 16.8 million inhabitants are the ten largest urban agglomerations in the world. All have virtually doubled their populations since 1991.

Pakistan was home to a number of ancient cultures, and was ruled at different times by a number of empires and dynasties. It was created in 1947 as a Muslim nation, and became an Islamic Republic in 1956. A civil war between east and west, resulted in the secession of East Pakistan to form Bangladesh in 1971. The country is made up four provinces: Punjab, Sindh, Baluchistan, and Khyber Pakhtunkhwa as well as the Islamabad Capital Territory and the Administrated Tribal Areas. Its population is around 180 million people with around one-third living in cities, making it the most urbanised country in South Asia. Lahore is the second largest city after Karachi, with a population of some 6.6 million people.

Urbanisation on the Indian subcontinent dates back many centuries. During the Muslim Mughal period urban development extended from Srinagar in the north to Madurai in the south, regenerating many of the older cities through the building of mosques, forts and palaces. Cities and market towns assumed a new significance through new trading routes. The scattered impact of Europeans began in 1498 when Vasco da Gama who reached the Malabar coast in 1498, and two years later returned to found a trading post at Cochin, south of Calcutta. In 1510 Affonso de Alburquerque, the second viceroy to be appointed by the Portuguese government secured control of Goa which became the Asian centre for Portuguese political, commercial and religious expansion for the following century. Portuguese explorations were said to be inspired by 'gospel, gold and glory against the enemies of Christianity'. Trade and religion were therefore interconnected. Alburquerque obtained port facilities around the Mandovi and Zuari rivers, at the point where they entered the Arabian Sea. Their estuaries formed both a protected harbour and an ideal location for defensive fortifications. By 1524 the Portuguese had extended their territorial gain to Bardez in the north and Salcette in the south, and went on to introduce European architecture and the first artistic representations of Renaissance culture. By the late sixteenth century, Old Goa had a large shipyard and arsenal, and within the fort a customs house, warehouses, the Palace of the Viceroys and the grand bazaar. At the centre

1 Eds. Misra, R.P. and Misra, K, *Million Cities of India*, Sustainable Development Foundation, Delhi, 1998

of the city was the square of the Holy House of Mercy. The walled city had a circumference of around seven kilometres, and as in other Portuguese cities the overall framework was influenced by Renaissance planning with an orthogonal street network and strategic siting of important public buildings where they would have the most urban impact. City quarters were distinguished by prominent trades or guilds, and churches tended to dominate Old Goa, both socially and physically. The largest of these was the Cathedral of Santa Caterina — one of six cathedrals that dominated the skyline. However efforts to convert the population to Christianity were accompanied by equally determined steps to eliminate existing temples.

The decline of Old Goa occurred largely through Portuguese distraction in countering interference in the wider region from Dutch and English competitors who were less inclined to proselytise, and more concerned with commerce and trade. They were also funded not by Crown undertakings but by joint-stock investors. Commodities that could be traded were therefore considered, at least in the first instance, more important than territorial gains. However this in itself created questionable tactics including military–backed protection of trading interests and sources of raw materials and production. The first East India Companies were able to interact with local merchants and in the process enter the market of intra–Asian trade.

In examining the historical forces of intervention, a clear starting point is the series of port cities where European East India Companies, beginning in the early seventeenth century, established trading posts that took the form of financial organisations, based on acquiring a trading monopoly and maximising profits from commerce. This type of body had no comparison in Asia, and was therefore a significant catalyst for geopolitical change.

In 1602 the Dutch East India Company

was established by charter, and began to develop new trading and commercial ventures in India and Ceylon (Sri Lanka). The Dutch negotiated a port anchorage from the Golkunda Sultinate at Masulipatnam which became one of the leading trade settlements on the Coromandel coast, and later established bases at Surat and Cochin. In 1613 the Mughal Emperor Shah Jahan granted permission for English "factories" at various points along the coast. Shortly after this in 1616 a Danish East India Company was set up at Tranquebar and a French version during the reign of Louis XIV, with the establishment of a trading port at Surat near Bombay, and later the port of Pondicherry and a protectorate over the Indian state of Hyderabad. At the time goods from eastern India were traded in Sri Lanka, Sumatra and Java, and the Portuguese, Dutch, French and English vied with each other to establish new and defensible bases, and to eliminate the monopolies of their rivals through incursions, while also controlling indigenous forces.

The English profited at various times from the over-exertions of the Portuguese in the face of their declining fortunes in Europe, the over-ambitions of the Dutch, and the timing of the French Revolution. It was the English, through the London East India Company, which evolved from its initial trading mission to facilitate rule over a populous subcontinent with altogether different traditions and social structures. Arriving ten years after the Dutch, the Company established the first English trading post at Surat, and in 1639 were ceded a site in Madras on which they built Fort St. George. In 1660 the company acquired the port of Bombay under curious circumstances, as it formed part of the dowry from the Portuguese wife of Charles II. In 1691 they established Fort William near Calcutta so that by the beginning of the eighteenth century the Company had established three strategic settlements and consolidated east coast operations through a 'Presidency' controlled through London by its directors.

2   Heitzman, *The City in South Asia*, Routledge, London and New York, 2008

By the end of seventeenth century, the British 'Presidency' cities had established a commanding pattern of trade on the periphery of the Mughal Empire, and the British East India Company had grown to be a major force. Warren Hastings who became Governor General of India in 1774 realised that opportunities for political intervention could be exercised through a thorough cultural re-interpretation which went on to underpin colonial rule. Even the two foremost languages of Hindu and Urdu were combined to form Hindustani — the language of Government.

The French East India Company, backed by the State, commenced operations at Surat in 1668, six years later at Pondicherry and in 1690 in Chandranagar. This was conquered by the Dutch in 1693 who planned the city around Fort Louis which overlooked the Bay of Bengal. When the city again reverted to the French Company as part of a peace accord, they implemented the plan so that by 1740 the city housed 130,000 people. The orthogonal plan which established a formal layout within the bastioned fortifications gives an insight not just to street block form and the placement of prominent buildings, but to the ethnic street assignments given over to Chetis, Chuliyas or Malabars reflecting their commercial prominence, and the artisan and trade quarters which included goods and services such as blacksmiths, tile makers, weavers, goldsmiths and coral-workers. The city was partly demolished by the British and both the Seven Years War and continuing hostilities between the two trading regimes, interspersed with periods of restoration and reconstruction, led to the city's eventual decline. The old established street pattern however lies at the heart of the modern city. The decisive defeat of the French at Plessey in 1759, allowed the English to take over direct rule in Bengal and establish rights over various wealthy provinces. In 1773 the British Parliament passed the Regulating Act

Allegorical figure of Urbs Prima in India, holding a ship

which provided for Government supervision of the Company. This was followed by further restrictions on its activities through the India Act of 1784, and twenty years later its trading monopoly was abolished altogether.

The colonial period after 1818 that brought British ascendancy over France was characterised by a strategy of urbanisation in primary cities, technical innovation and organisational dexterity. In common with other interventionist regimes, this presence was marked by different but predominantly urban elements - fortifications expressive of defense, and government buildings expressive of occupation. This was personified in terms of administration, transport, construction, communication, education and social mobility that signalled a new order of imperialism. Expansion of the major coastal cities of Calcutta, Madras and Bombay through the

intersection of steamship and rail terminals was so great that it suppressed secondary city growth.[2] As colonial interests began to exceed trading ones, fort ramparts sheltered the new institutions of the colonial elite — administrative, religious, mercantile and residential as well as the garrison itself. British investment through management agencies specialised in shipping, railroads and plantation agriculture, and later moved into commodities, mining and power generation, and this in turn established a concentration of new professional firms, headquartered in the primary cities.

Madras, the first major English colonial settlement in India developed around the nucleus of Fort St George. In a similar way to Pondicherry it developed as a grid, and was loosely divided into a "white town" characterised by spacious streets, and a "black town" for native traders who helped to service the Company. It was captured by the French in 1746, but reverted again to the British, thanks to the peace treaty following the War of the Austrian Succession. Threats from the French and Mysore armies led to a remodelling of the fort surrounded by a fire-free esplanade that formed the model for future *maidan* spaces in both Bombay and Calcutta. The defining characteristic of the city was the incorporation of "urban village" neighbourhoods designated for various trades. The city was gradually extended through absorbing existing townships, each with a strong historical identity. The destruction of military capabilities in Mysore and the occupation of Delhi in 1803, together with the final victory over the Marathas in 1818, effectively created a dominant foundation on which the colonial model of urban development and Presidency city-states could be imposed.

The British consolidated power through boosting urbanisation on a large scale, adding cantonments to the cities, and constructing a network of railways linking interior

3 Heitzman, 2008, op. cit.
4 Koch, E, *Mughal Architecture – An Outline of its History and Development*, Prestel, Munich, New York and London, 1991

mining towns and cotton-producing areas to the ports. In return for recognising the superiority of the British under "perpetual friendship" agreements, the Maharajas were allowed to retain their principalities and some built replicas of European chateaus, such as the Noor Mahal in the hot desert climate of the Punjab. With a reduction in aggression, fortified cities gave way to new amenities which better suited westernised habits. The design of urban space was intended for political effect and reflected the importance of processional movement and pageantry. In many cases major public buildings were designed by military engineers and architects, with standardised models for buildings of lesser importance. To meet the needs of public works, Government established schools of engineering to supply technicians who could instruct and supervise workers. It was not until the late nineteenth century that Schools of Industrial Arts and Design were established, first in Bombay and then Lahore. In 1901 there was however only one city with a million people — Calcutta, then the capital of the Raj. The colonial pattern of urbanisation according to Heitzman, involved three features — the 'old city' generally inhabited by the indigenous population, the native bazaar catering to the needs of colonial personnel, and the civil and military station within a cantonment.[3] Spatial organisation therefore reflected a hierarchy of social exclusivity and ethnic separation.

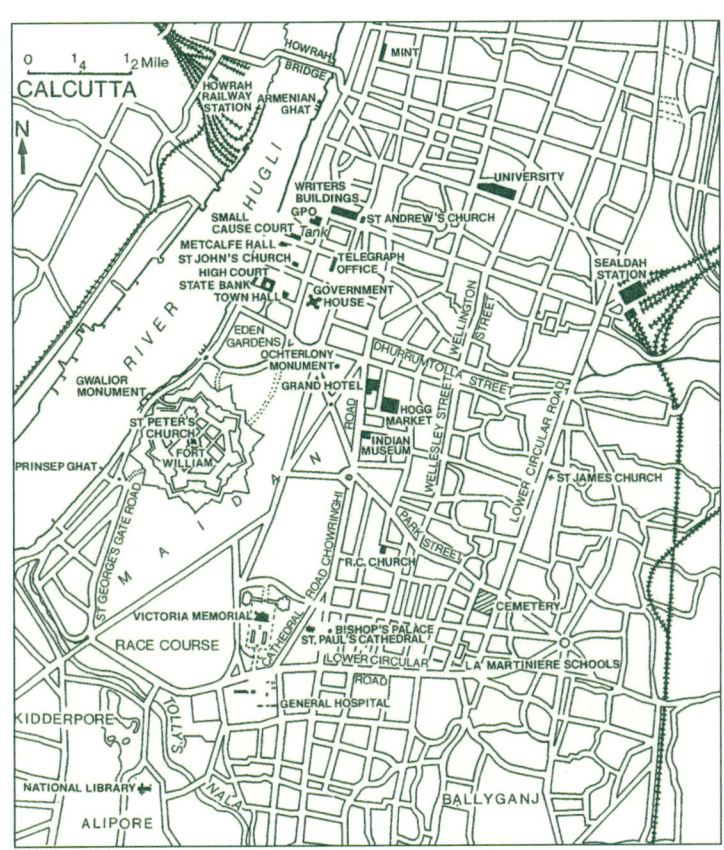

Early plan of colonial Calcutta

THE SARACENIC URBAN DESIGN CONNECTION

Much of the urban design legacy of the Indian subcontinent, in terms of its religious and secular building, comes from the Indo-Islamic architecture of the Mughal dynasties. While Akbar, who ruled until 1605, was noted as both an enlightened administrator and liberal thinker, it was his son Jahangir and grandson Sha Jahan who achieved the greatest level of stability and founded new cities as patrons of architecture and urban planning. Stylistic innovations in Mughal design were introduced by synthesizing various heterogeneous elements from Timurid, Indian, Persian and even European references within a new vocabulary of architectural forms offset by elegant decoration.[4]

Urban design was generally based on axial planning with symmetrical features and uniformity, achieved by a reduced architectural vocabulary. An overriding aspect of layouts was a defining central axis, such as the great bazaar at the Red Fort.

The expansion of government under the British entailed a range of public buildings designed after 1845 by the Public Works Department through pattern books that reflected European neo-Classical and high-Victorian gothic revival buildings. These came to dominate public architecture, particularly in Bombay. The later Indo-Saracenic style reflected a fascinating but architecturally questionable attempt to resurrect traditional Mughal features including the projecting balcony-*jharoka*; the canopied roof turret-*chattris*; the pierced stone lattice screen-*jaalis*; and the wide projecting cornice-*chajja*.

Saracenic architecture had its origins in the Islamic legacy of structures from AD 1200, regarded by some historians as an architectural "bridge" between East and West. In practice Muslim builders used the skills of Hindu artisans, frequently exhibiting a rhyming fusion of elegant structure and overriding architectural elements of arch and dome, offset by a delicate ornamentation. The dome, a predominant feature of Mughal architecture, also reflected a similar tradition in Europe from the Pantheon to Renaissance cathedrals and St Pauls. The emperor Akbar's hilltop city of Fatehpur Sikri in Rajasthan and Shah Jahan's Taj Mahal represented refined and exemplary ideals, with a symbolic identity that could be levered from their historical context and matched with political objectives.

While the strong cultural history of Indian civilization together with its traditions and interactions was conceded by early Western scholars, they found it difficult to reconcile this with the underlying notions of a new society emanating from the European Enlightenment, and justified through a high-minded Victorian self-righteousness. James Fergusson for example commented in his *History of Indian and Eastern Architecture* of 1876, that "... it cannot of course be for one moment contended that India ever reached the intellectual supremacy of Greece, or the moral greatness of Rome". Fergusson largely acknowledged only Hindu and Muslim (Saracenic) distinctions and largely ignored the hybrid architecture of non-religious buildings, even though he acknowledged a divergence of cultural ideals. As British cities in the throes of the industrial revolution were being substantially underpinned through an assertive array of neo-Gothic, neo-Classical and Baroque buildings, this concept of progress tended to shape any discourse on urban design. Ultimately it brought about an unlikely but ambitious combination of architectural cultures that continues to characterise the urban heritage of the Indian city — a combination of the "Indo-Saracenic", derived from values that infused ancient Hindu and Buddhist monuments,

THE VAULTED ROOFED STREET leading from the Lahori Gate to the inner part of Delhi Fort is known as Chhatta-Chowk or Meena Bazaar, and was built as the main market place within the Palace, shielded from the summer heat. Each side contains 32 arched cells at first and ground floor levels with shops that originally specialised in luxury household goods, silk, silverware and jewelry. The market is divided into two sections by an octagonal court, the Chhattar-Manzil, and was originally covered with inscriptions from the Quran.

and the imported European classicist, gothic revival and baroque styles that formed the cornerstone of eighteenth and nineteenth century city building. Indian cities became associated with certain imported stylistic influences that were covertly termed "Madras Classical", "Bombay Gothic", "Calcutta Corinthian", and "Bengal Baroque".

After the abolition of the East India Company and the imposition of direct Crown rule in 1858, a new ideological order was applied to the cities, geared to the assumed legitimacy of imperial power, that had strong urban design connotations. This reflected an exploratory means of equating the concept of empire with an indigenous quality through the purposeful incorporation of Indian architectural features into the urban repertoire. From the beginning the process was subject to fits and starts, but arguably commenced with the appointment of Robert Fellowes Chisholm as architect to the government in Madras at virtually the same

time as Lord Napier was appointed governor in 1866. Napier advocated the use of "native art" in building, and Chisholm's first building in this style was designed for the Revenue Board offices in Madras — a flamboyant two-storey concoction of Mughal arches, domed spires and an elaborate onion-domed tower.[5] Chisholm stated that "for an imported architecture to be accepted it must be adapted to the climate and to the requirements of the people; capable of expression in local materials; and present surfaces and forms for elaboration, which the people have been in the habit of rendering ornate in other words through modification of traditional usage".[6] Chisholm drew on Ruskin's arts and craft's views and the native Malabar Coast architecture in his designs. After he became Head of the Madras School of Arts, Chisholm moved more cautiously and acknowledged a range of stylistic influences, including the Byzantine, that more closely equated with a European conception of appropriateness

5 Metcalf, T.R., *An Imperial vision – Indian Architecture and Britain's Raj*, University of California Press, Berkeley, 1989

6 Walker, P, 'Institutional Audiences and Architectural Style', in *Colonial Modernities*, Eds. Peter Scriver and Vikramaditya Prakash, Routledge, London and New York, 2007

THE CHARING CROSS AREA OF LAHORE forms a comprehensive urban design composition at the junction of the Upper Mall with Ferozpur Road, designed by Basil M Sullivan, consulting architect to the Punjab Government. It is flanked by the Masonic Lodge and Sha Din Buildings to the south, and the Punjab Assembly building to the north. The junction focuses on the Marble Pavilion as a centrepiece within a public square. It represents an Anglo-Mughal design in white marble with a crowning canopy, and was built to house a statue of Queen Victoria. After independence the statue was moved to the Lahore Museum, and replaced in the Pavilion by a Holy Quran encased in glass. The Masonic Lodge reflects Lahore's role as the centre of freemasonry in the Punjab.

for certain types of public building. With the Madras Post and Telegraph Office, the Indo-Saracenic architecture took on a more refined and proportional form with high pitched roofs rather than domes.

Other architects, with necessary patronage, began to elaborate on the Indo-Saracenic style. However in both architectural and political circles the manipulation and melding together of design references, stylistic principles, and the priority given to "borrowed" Hindu and Mohamedan appendages such as open cupolas, canopied balconies, turreted parapets, and the use of both plain and cusped arches, were debated at length. A key factor in this was the role of the princes, who represented the ancient Indian dynasties and had much to gain from both an acceptance of the new ruling system and from

a personified link with an enduring tradition. Two museums that took on the early Saracenic style were the Prince of Wales Museum by George Wittet in Bombay which incorporated Gujerati detailing, and the Victoria Memorial Hall by H.C. Irwin in Madras which embodied a stylised concentration of Mughul features constructed in red sandstone.

The natural consequence of an increasing familiarisation with Indian forms was the production of reference guides, together with publications of the Archaeological Survey of India which catalogued architectural monuments from antiquity. George Campbell's *Vitruvius Britannicus* and Swinton Jacob's six-volume publication *Jeypore Portfolio* illustrating architectural measured drawings of Jaipur, were arranged to enable designers to choose and mix Indic details, often producing

an indiscriminate eclecticism applied to programmatically unrelated building types.

The link between materiality and representation that underlies an examination of urban design is particularly well directed at colonial urbanism with its injected alchemy of cultural dominance and exclusion. The flamboyant Indo-Saracenic style can possibly be attributed to three elusive influences: first the Renaissance revival architecture of Victorian Britain embedded in the 'cult of the picturesque', that established an architectural precedent for the adoption of a hybrid interpretation of past styles in a new and provocative context; second as a means of articulating a metaphorical cultural assimilation of Britain and India through Indic stylisation and ornamentation on modernist public building types, many of them carried out by the Public Works Department; and third as a result of seminal works of scholarship by architectural historians such as James Fergusson and Swinton Jacob, who researched and laid down volumes of indigenous details. Jacob, a military engineer by training, criticised the 'stereotyped conventionalities of public works design, and in 1890 produced details orthographically, that enabled their practical reproduction and repetition by trained artisans. However the architectural language of a "pattern book" gives little insight into the urban design of social space and the relationship between the power structure and the artifice of its built fabric. It also does not account for the later innovations of Lutyens which intellectually reflected the more refined political economy of the times.

The pattern book approach found an application in Bombay as a thriving port city with anglicised Parsee patrons looking to cement ties with Europe. Traditional forms could be grafted onto the imported Victorian Gothic style, an early example being the vast Victoria Terminus in Bombay by F.W. Stevens. Buildings were in fact sometimes designed

Pachaiyappa's College, Madras 1850, based on the Athenium Temple of Theseus.

Gateway of India, Mumbai

by the same well-known architects as their London forebears, — for example George Gilbert Scott's University Hall in Bombay. Other notable Indic-Saracenic buildings in Bombay, were John Begg's central post office, and George Wittet's Gateway of India arch. A Gothic style was also generally used for Indian church and cathedral architecture which still sought to present its physical manifestation in a conservative Western European style.

The most prominent engineer architects, inspired by local temples and forts, and incorporating appropriate design elements from these, constructed new palaces for the wealthy princes of India, probably the most unified and successful being the Lallgarh Palace in Bikaner by Swinton Jacob, with a strong reference to the red sandstone forts of Rajasthan. Jacob also supervised many of the public works projects for the Maharaja of Jaipur, the centrepiece of which was the Albert Hall Museum in honour of the Prince of Wales — generally accepted as one of the most successful applications of the style to a public building. In some cases such as Lakshmi Vilas Palace by R F Chisholm, assembled components were ordered in such a stratified way that the elevation could almost have been lifted from a Venetian waterfront tableaux. However Tillotson's view is that historicism should be distinguished from the continuity of tradition, and that Indic-Saracenic design mimicked the style rather than the material substance of traditional materials and craftsmanship — "presenting a lexicon of Indian architecture but without the grammar" - so that there is no real synthesis between the two traditions.[7]

The Great Exhibition at Crystal Palace in 1851 brought together a collection of Indian artwork and crafts assembled by the East India Company. This and other international exhibitions which contained replicas of ancient Indian buildings, brought into vivid focus the "exotic orientalism" of the sub-continent that possibly represented

7 Tillotson, G.H.R., *The Tradition of Indian Architecture : Continuity, Controversy and Change since 1850*, Yale University Press, New Haven and London, 1989

8 Metcalf, 1989, op. cit.

an enthusiasm on the part of Victorian Britain, which was caught up in the urban consequences of the industrial revolution, for a pre-industrial society. The way in which the Crystal Palace challenged industrial ingenuity generated a reform of art education with an emphasis on industrial design. This was furthered by the development of photography after 1850 which fuelled even greater interest and knowledge.

Architectural inspiration was equalled by indigenous building skills and craftsmanship, but increasingly the disintegration of traditional building put these skills under threat. Thomas Metcalf suggests that the English Arts and Crafts Movement, articulated by John Ruskin and William Morris whose textile designs drew inspiration from the Orient, helped to reinforce a justification for preserving medieval ideals in India through an architecture and arts approach reflected in craft production, in order to establish a contrast with the commercialisation brought about through colonial interests.[8] Older buildings such as the palaces, temples and mosques of Rajasthan, which embodied superb craftsmanship, were particularly admired. Art schools began to teach the traditional crafts of native buildings or *mistri*, and Indian motifs began to be incorporated into buildings that had an every-day use. Integration of artwork occasionally depicted scenes of Indian life. John Lockwood Kipling, professor of architectural sculpture at Bombay, designed bas reliefs for Crawford Market, along with a decorated fountain in its centre. There was however an anomaly in this, in that new projects were generally circumscribed to meet colonial demands which required an overarching European design so that traditional practices tended to have to work within a reconstructed approach to decorative arts and architectural stateliness that reflected the British mission in India. However Kipling's work, which was to train Indian sculptors to execute the decoration of Bombay's public

The Flora Fountain surmounted by the Goddess of Flowers.

buildings, is also credited as a major step in reviving Indian crafts and resuscitating architectural education. In this he was supported by E.B. Hawell, Superintendent of the School of Art in Calcutta. The Mayo School of Industrial Arts, established in Lahore in 1875 under Kipling, and later under Bhai Ram Singh, enunciated a practical type of design training through an atelier approach involving staff and students in furniture, interior and practical architectural projects.

CROSS-CULTURAL DISTILLATIONS

At the heart of urban design in modern Indian cities is the uneasy equation of post-colonial economic development with the confounding legacy of imperialism.

Interwoven with historical settlements and contemporary fabric is the architecture of empire, which borrowed from and transformed established cultural forms to fit the new power structure of the Raj, expressed and made visible in spatial terms by its public monuments. This was in itself the result of prolongued debate over the most appropriate stylistic mode of representation, framed within an urban design that reflected an assertion of control and order but which was also embedded in a fixation with the "mystique" of the Orient, and its cultural and societal expression that informed the physical representation of the colonial city.

The residue of the colonial city has evinced a pluralism of spaces, whether social, economic or cultural, where planning has established realms of separation in order to maximise control and minimise conflict. Mass migration and the latter-day impacts of the post-industrial economy have brought these realms together within the expanding city. Rahul Mehrotra argues that this has introduced two issues that underscore contemporary urbanism: the Static City based on physical permanence and focussed on elite domains of production; and the Kinetic City related to motion and temporary use.[9] Thus the former type relates to object-centred constructs framed and encoded through architectural design, while the latter is perceived through the use of space and patterns of occupation that frame a language of change and adaptation open to constant re-interpretation. Given this distinction, cultural significance through the urban enactment of festivals and the resilient bazaar economy fall predominantly inside the 'kinetic' category, rich in meaning and community acknowledgement, which forms the greater part of Asian city reality. Mehrotra cites as an example the *dabbawalas* or 'tiffin men' of Bombay who deliver hundreds of thousands of lunch boxes every day throughout the city via a complex network that involves an exchange up to five times between pick-up and return. This and other informal services leverage different sets of informal relationships and resource recycling, facilitating both productivity and competitiveness.

In the contemporary city the search for a regionally identifiable urban design, responsive to local space conventions and established cultural needs, continues to flirt with the relevance of tradition in style and motifs that are genuinely derivative rather than imitative. Urban design, at a time of returning Western influence through globalisation, must recover enduring values that derive, first and foremost, from vernacular properties related to form,

spatial organisation and decorative devices, but with a contemporary vocabulary that echoes traditional design without evoking it literally. An imposed urban design can come to assume its own authentic credentials over time, both through the planning of prominent monuments and the creation of new urban identities. Whether colonial design abstractedly absorbed or ignored vernacular traditions in India, it established symbolic frames of reference that resonate through contemporary urbanism.

The Dabbawalas or 'tiffin men' deliver around 200,000 lunch boxes every day using Mumbai's train network, establishing a link between the formal and informal economic sectors.

9 Mehrotra, R, 'Kinetic City – Issues for Urban Design in South Asia', in *Reclaiming (the Urbanism of) Mumbai*, Eds. Kelly Shannon and Janina Gosseye, Sun Academia, Amsterdam, 2009

The east front of the Secretariat blocks in New Delhi

THE EXISTING TOWNSHIPS OF MARGÃO AND PANAJI retain many design characteristics of the early Portuguese settlements, including the prominent location of churches designed in Baroque and Rococo styles. These were fronted by an ordered public realm of town squares traditionally used for a variety of functions. Later architectural styles combined both Portuguese and Hindu elements. The two-storey townscape of Margão is defined by a cacophony of traditional elements — colonnaded frontages, open balconies, elaborate window openings, tiled roofs and elaborate entranceways.

[1] Malgonkar, M, *Inside Goa*, Architecture Autonomous, Goa, 1982

IT IS SAID THAT GOA, or Govapuri, was first peopled by Sarawak Brahmins who arrived to perform ceremonial rites and stayed to cultivate the fertile coastal strip, at the same time serving as priests in family temples. The name itself was first given to the town, but under the Portuguese came to be applied to the wider region encompassing four islands which represented their various acquisitions on the West coast of India. By the eleventh century Goa had become a flourishing centre of trade with Arabia on the Zuari River, but was later relocated to a new capital city on the Mandori river after its destruction by the Sultan of Delhi. It gradually became a major transit point for Muslim traffic between India and Mecca, and in 1472 Goa fell under Muslim rule.

The wealth and importance of Goa in relation to trading routes with Arabia, China and Java attracted Vasco da Gama, who in 1497 opened up the passage from Europe to India, landing in Calicut and occupying Goa with little opposition. A plan was conceived in Portugal to monopolise trade between Asia and Europe, and in the process embark on a Christian crusade against Islam. This quest was enthusiastically supported by Pope Alexander VI who conferred upon King Manuel the title "Lord of Navigation, Conquest and Commerce, of Ethiopia, Arabia, Persia and India".[1] In 1502 da Gama made a second visit to the Malabar coast, which paved the way for an armada led by Affonso de Albuquerque in March 1510. He took four years to reach Goa, but secured the city region for Portugal ... twice ... the first quite peaceably, the second six months later against an army sent by the Sultan of Bijapur. However Cochin continued to be the main Portuguese settlement until 1530.

The victory is commemorated by two existing churches: the first situated on the square of the ancient but abandoned capital, Velha Goa: and the second, the Lady of the Mount, recently refurbished by the *Fundacao*

The Idalcaon Palace in Panaji built by Yusef Adil Shah in the fifteenth century was slowly transformed though constant modifications up to 1900, symbolising changing Portuguese stylistic influences including Iberian window treatment. It is now the Government Secretariat building.

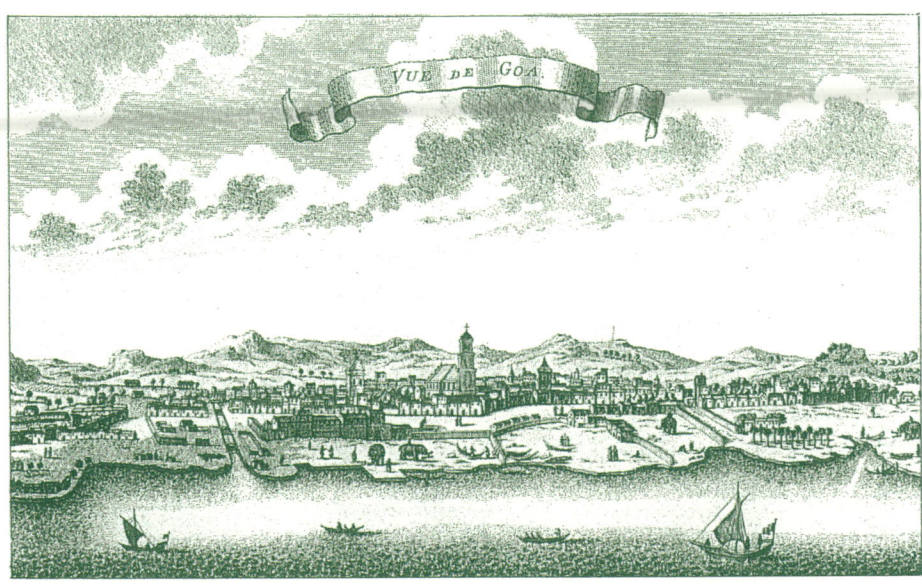

2 Pandit, H and Mascarenhas, A, *Houses of Goa*, Architecture Autonomous, Goa, 1999

THE PIAZZA CROSS fronting the Espirito Santo Holy Spirit Church at Margao indicates the imaginative siting, scale and design composition of Portuguese layout planning. The piazza crosses represented a Goan adaptation of the Syrian crosses to the south of Goa in Kerala. The artisans who formed these from stucco moulding, based them on a combination of Rococo church interior decorations and Hindu temple architecture. They contain niches for lamps and are generally located in front of churches, and represent elaborate shrines for private worship.

Oriente (based in Lisbon) which has restored a number of old Portuguese buildings in Goa and Macau. Alburquerque went on to capture Malacca, and over the next fifty years consolidated Portuguese territory in Goa by gaining the districts of Bardez and Salcette in exchange for providing weaponry to the local Sultans. The Portuguese went on to establish a chain of coastal strongholds including Bombay and Cochin.

There followed a new regime of land acquisition and city building. Dominican priests arrived with orders to grant land for new religious buildings and Portuguese institutions, and for the next 260 years those converting to Catholicism were favoured with official positions. Hindu festivals were prohibited and properties confiscated. Those Hindus who converted to Christianity acquired the freedom and privileges of Portuguese society. Others, such as the guild of goldsmiths, the *sonars*, retained their ethnic status merely because of their value to the economy. In 1560 the Portuguese Tribunal of the Inquisition was introduced, and Goa was made an Episcopal See with jurisdiction over Malacca.[2]

In terms of city building, a combination of new traders and settlers created a collision of cultures — the Luso-Indian fusion that came to mould the identity of Goa. With a population in the sixteenth century of around a million people, Jesuits and missionaries were the energisers of new building programmes, while Brahmin Hindus practiced a more private and subdued faith in a constant climate of persecution. The cultural fabric of Catholicism, led in the early sixteenth century by Francis Xavier, insinuated itself in society just as Portuguese stylistic influences became slowly admitted to the architectural pantheon of Goan urban design. Xavier spent comparatively little time in Goa but travelled widely in Asia. After his death some ten years later, he was buried in the Cathedral of Bom Jesus in the central square of Velha Goa, which has since become a centre for pilgrimage.

THE ESSENTIAL CHARACTERISTIC OF GOA encompasses an urban residue of both architectural imposition and tolerant assimilation, resulting from military and religious intervention within a well-defined geographic, defensible and culturally distinct region. Hindu temples gradually acquired characteristics of Portuguese ecclesiastical architecture including church towers, prominent domes and pillared porches. Effective isolation from the Indian mainland, which endured centuries of internal convulsions and colonial conquest, had little impact on development in Goa. Mughal and Maratha references subtly interwoven with Hindu and Christian values created a composite layering of cultures where the effect of the whole seems greater than the parts — evident in the Temple de Manguexa complex at Pondá. This is almost precisely because inherited traits together with social and religious compromises have survived and become synchronised over several centuries. In the process they have established a unified identity of monuments and relics that seep into the city fabric, and therefore into the urban consciousness. An interwoven mix of uses is balanced by a formal axial positioning of church and public space, while the temple provides a more discreet and serial accumulation of buildings, with church festivals and Hindu jatras offering a commonality of celebration.

The Graeco-Roman façade of St Cajetan Church in Velha Goa, with its ribbed dome styled after St Peter's Basilica in Rome.

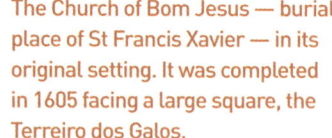

The Church of Bom Jesus — burial place of St Francis Xavier — in its original setting. It was completed in 1605 facing a large square, the Terreiro dos Galos.

3 Issar, T. P., *Goa Dourada: The Indo-Portuguese Bouquet*, TP Issar, 1997

NON-ECCLESIASTICAL BUILDINGS avoided the distinctive white colour reserved for churches, although wall decorations, that now take on a commodified form in painted wall signs, were originally inspired by church frescos and stencil designs. Most Goan buildings were plastered with lime, and lime washed in colours derived from natural or vegetable dyes such as yellow ochre, red oxide and indigo. These were later extended to a range of pastel colours — pale blue, green and brown offset by white mouldings. The effect lent itself to superimposed treatment, either through patterned tiles and painting of decorative motifs, or 'marbelling'. Decorated gateways embody both Hindu and Portuguese features including curved 'scrolls' and carved finials. Gate-houses endured longer than fortified walls. The last remaining towered gate-house in Goa is in Pernem, which shows evidence of both European and Hindu influences. This is carried through to the modern villa design with its flamboyant tiling arrangement and wrought iron gate.

By the seventeenth century, Goa was noted for its pageantry with the principal roads lined with stately buildings, banks and trading houses representing merchants' businesses from as far away as Venice. The Palace of the Viceroys faced the Terreiro do Paço square, outlined by elegant residences. Increasing wealth was derived from a flourishing slave trade, which was carried out until 1865 — slaves were brought from other parts of India, Ceylon and Malaysia and exhibited in the central square.[3]

Village assembly halls were an integral part of the community before the Portuguese arrival. This was where the local deity was installed and the local council of elders or *Dhajan* met. The hall was therefore partly a temple and partly a presidium and a court which resolved disputes, and formed the focus of Hindu festivals. This system was broadly sustained under the Portuguese administration as a form of local self-regulation, although the systematic resumption and redistribution of land became part of prolonged religious persecution. Catholic converts were allocated land and other privileges, while the introduction of efficient farming techniques was used to generate income for foreign missions. By the end of the seventeenth century, land parcels were being consolidated into larger holdings, and proprietary rights of land were vested with the Crown, and leased to farmers. The role of *gaunkari* or co-operatives of landowners was replaced by a body charged with the conveyance of land, and during the inquisition many Hindu owners were made to relinquish their holdings to Goan Catholic converts.

Land became a means of accumulating both power and prestige. Wealthier local families adopted Portuguese architectural and urban designs as well as Portuguese social conventions. Building design was increasingly adapted to cope with high temperatures, heavy summer rainfall, humidity and solar radiation. Certain features contributed to the characteristic forms — the construction of houses on high plinths to protect from rising damp, roof overhangs, and verandahs to offer shade and protection from monsoon rain. Also common was the predominant practice of east-west orientation following the direction of the sun, first used for temple layouts, but adopted for both Hindu and Catholic houses — amalgamating the Indian tradition of the house as a reflection of the cosmos, and the European notion of a divine universe. The result was an embrace of new architectural influences and decorative elements from Europe and Africa, with more than a touch of Baroque stylistic embellishments.

In exploring the evolution of house form, Pandit and Mascarenhas make a distinction between the traditional Hindu residence

The Portuguese architectural influence extended to the design of individual houses in semi rural areas.

A LASTING LEGACY from those times are the Portuguese style villas and row house developments which extended into the city suburbs with mansions surrounded by pleasure gardens and plantations. These embody features that still personify the traditional urban design of Goa that evolved from the early religious buildings — long verandahs supported by stone corbels and wooden or stone columns supporting an overhanging roof, which runs the entire length of the dwelling. The structure itself was generally built of stone and mortar, finished with tiles or lime rendering obtained from seashells. The most intricate design features are the elaborate carved railings that embellish the long verandahs, integrating various bas-relief motifs including traditional Portuguese floral patterns or those copied from Hindu temples. Early railings were in carved laterite or wood, but cast iron and wrought iron railings and balusters were introduced in the mid-eighteenth century from British-India and painted in bright colours. The covered verandah extending along the entire front façade possibly evolved from the balcão — a Portuguese entrance porch with built-in seats that served as a semi-private threshold space where visitors could be entertained. In many houses the balcão and verandah are linked, and act as an external addition to the interior reception room or sala — the grandest room in the residence. The house shown here is the Carsa de Cristâo em Loubulin at Salcete.

with flexible space and little concept of privacy, which largely outlived the more carefully demarcated socio-cultural features introduced by the Portuguese. However Portuguese influence over Catholic residences was considerable, with a much more formal allocation of space, and ostentatious design embellishments imposed on the more traditional concept. In part this reflected the contributions of the same carpenters and masons in the evolving Goan design form, whether Hindu or Catholic, so that certain derivative elements subscribed to the overall design. Internal spaces, courtyards and verandah spaces were used in different ways, expressive of Goan ethnic identity. The traditional *devghor* or altar was an established feature in Hindu households, with niches to display religious artefacts — something that was adopted in the arrangement of Catholic altars, designed to face west. The centrepiece of the Portuguese church was a flamboyant Baroque altarpiece, integrating carved figures and flower designs, covered with gold-leaf and illuminated by shafts of light admitted through strategically located high windows. The walls were adorned with elaborate mouldings and frescos, with screens, lectures and pews featuring the finest Indo-Portuguese woodcarving.

A representative local feature is the decoratively carved eaves and gable ends that define roof overhangs. These date back to early Portuguese influences, and are generally curvilinear in design pierced with a variety of geometric shapes, which match the equally decorative balustrades. These can also symbolise Hindu religious motifs. Their main value is aesthetic, but they additionally help reduce solar glare and mask the line of rafters behind. In the process they produce distinctive contrasts of light and shadow. Decorated cornices and pilasters form additional features moulded in stone and plastered over, while columns and pillars take on a variety of qualities — circular, tapering or fluted shafts in masonry or wood, and with ornamented capitals based loosely on classical designs that are known locally as Indian Tuscan.

By the late seventeenth century Goa's capital was under increasing threat from the Marathas and the Dutch. The Court in Lisbon supported a scheme to shift the capital to Mormugão, and to demolish public buildings so that materials could be salvaged for use in the new city. While this scheme was later abandoned, buildings in the old city fell into disrepair, the only ones left standing being churches, the Fortress Palace and a handful of public buildings. Rebuilding was axed through lack of funding. Meanwhile Portugal extended its territories to the north, which became collectively known as the *Novas Conquistas* or New Conquests.

It is said that with a virtual monopoly of trade, up to 300 ships sailed between Portugal and Goa every year, bringing such riches to the motherland that they roused the attention of other sea-going powers — Britain, France and the Netherlands. The walled port city of Velha Goa was known as the "Rome of the Orient" with squares and streets lined with magnificent buildings, parks and ornate fountains, made holy by interspersed churches, the Royal Hospital, seminaries, nunneries and other religious institutions, conveniently protected by military fortifications. These edifices broadcast a spatial message of supremacy but also conveyed a grand display of architectural imagination.

The European Baroque style evolved out of a new arts, crafts and architecture movement in Europe, of which the most famous exponent was the Italian architect Bernini. The style was exported to India by the Portuguese in the early seventeenth century, and adopted as a "Counter-Reformist" style by the Catholic Church, with richly carved and frescoed details developed in response to the austere styles of the more ascetic Protestant Church. The responsive architectural inter-relationship was based on similar cultural and aesthetic values.

Perhaps the same buccaneering sense of glory and righteousness that brought prosperity to sixteenth century Portugal paved the way for the disastrous battle of Alcazar in Morocco. This was followed by the Portuguese subjugation to Spain that led to a decline over sixty years and an inability to sustain manpower and investment in Goa. Over the following two centuries it was besieged by assault from Mughal and

The Goan street market

The central Baroque-Rococo altarpiece from the Church of St Cajetan at Velha Goa.

ORNATE WINDOW AND DOOR OPENINGS

together with elaborate mouldings, establish both decorative character, individuality and symmetry as in the Braganza House at Chador. Window frames were traditionally carved by local craftsmen who were often inspired by designs from church and temple architecture. One of these features is the arch, constructed in various forms — semi-circular, segmental, tre-foil and cinque-foil. Lancet arches reflected the strong Catholic influences on urban residential architecture. Functionally the large apertures admit light to quite dark interiors, but also express an animated relationship to the public frontage. Patterned or louvred shutters filter the strong Goan light and are generally opened daily for social interaction with the street. The use of columns, pilasters and arched fan lights to emphasise the central entrance door is frequently matched by ornamentation such as decorated moulding, carvings and inscriptions, with intricately carved shutters. The Braganza House characterises all the features common to the Goan House, including Baroque pediments, arched openings and a long verandah.

"Hole in the Wall" interventions in the street fabric of Margão.

Maratha forces, losing certain cities but also making territorial gains through new treaties and military acquisitions. In 1788 with the cession of Pernem, the *Novas Conquistas* reached its zenith. The decline of Portuguese influence led to the British occupation of Goa as part of a military strategy to combat French influence in India, although Goa stubbornly remained under Portuguese rule. In 1845 Goa was allowed representation in Portugal's new parliament, and for several years in the early twentieth century Goa had a largely elected legislative council. The Portuguese government prepared a register of land ownership through comprehensive surveys, and concluded that 60 per cent of land belonged to the *communidades* and the remainder was either in private hands or those of a religious body. In 1961 Goa was peacefully absorbed within India following the fall of the Raj. This then led to an increasing development emphasis on Bombay rather than Goa, and migration of many people to other Indian cities.

Today the towns of Margao and Panaji retain many of the characteristics of the early settlements — the prominent location of churches, the strong public realm of squares and streets, and the decorative architectural elements derived from both Hindu and Portuguese designs. The old city of Velha Goa is dominated by the Se Cathedral, the Churches of Bom Jesus and St Francis of Assisi, and St Monica's Convent. Its voids, which include the two-dimensional silhouette of the ancient College of St Paul, suggest as much urban design history as its three-dimensional anatomy, in an intangible interplay of 'figure' and 'ground'. Its most remarkable religious buildings are the Se Cathedral completed in 1652 and the Basilica of Bom Jesus. The decline of Velha Goa began with Portugal's loss of its trading monopoly, but also because it was disease-prone. It retained its importance as a port until the nineteenth century, and remains as an elusive template to the urban design of Old Goa, devoid of its urban context, with its remaining buildings standing as haunted sentinels to a formidable but ambiguous Christian obsession.

STREET TERRACE IN MARGÃO. Early Portuguese architecture was heavily influenced by a simple Mannerist design, but in its later eighteenth century secular structures displayed a more lyrical Baroque and Rococo embellishment, particularly on the upper storey of the front façade, with elaborate window openings and strong vertical divisions defined by mouldings and pilasters. This formed proportional bays giving an overall rhythm to the façade, and reflected the use of the upper floor for official or family use, with the ground floor for services. In later nineteenth century buildings, particularly the Goan house, Maratha and Mughal features were introduced to form an eclectic combination with Baroque entrance steps, including an elaborate colonnaded porch entranceway.

Street traders

Makeshift temple in Panaji surrounded by a multitude of offerings

INDIA

Kolkata

IN THE EARLY NINETEENTH CENTURY, grand houses occupied most of the sites along Shobhabazar Street. Even in their present deteriorated state they act as permanent markers of imperial intervention that frame a realm of neo-Classical buildings and monuments in Kolkata. These now help to underscore the inherited diversity of the city's urban design and its associated identification with the cultural wealth of modern institutions including educational and arts establishments.

1   Banerjee, H, Gupta, N, and
    Mckberjee, S, *Calcutta Mosaic*,
    Anthem Press, London,
    New York and Delhi, 2009
2   Dutta, K, *Calcutta – A Cultural
    and Literary History*, Interlink
    Books, Massachusetts, 2003

CALCUTTA embodies what might be called a "cultural landscape" made up of many urban components — historical government buildings, neo-Classical and baroque palaces, vernacular appurtenances, temples, churches, and industrial and warehouse archaeology. These combine a mix of Western and local characteristics that insinuate themselves within the street setting. As the capital of British India until 1911 the city was at the centre of a renaissance of public building and educational establishments.

Urban design in Calcutta has partly been influenced by its cosmopolitan migrant community of Armenians, Chinese, Parsis and Iraqi Jews, originally from Baghdad and Alleppo, as well as communities from various parts of the Indian subcontinent such as the Marwaris, who shaped the city culture. Traditionally the city has facilitated interaction and an intellectual temper, inextricably intertwined with Western influences. By the early eighteenth century the city had well-defined European neighbourhoods, and the native quarters had spread over Sutanuti, Chitpur and Gobwindapur.[1] Immigration led to the development of synagogues as well as churches, mosques, masjids and temples. The Anglo-Indian community dates back to the sixteenth century and forms a continuum through to the modern city. Mapping the spaces of minorities is therefore an indication of ethnic as well as historic design characteristics. The Chinese community made up largely of Cantonese and Hakka, concentrate around the Bow Bazaar, Lower Chitpur Road and Bentwick Street through occupational associations with other groups, while the Marwari trading community is associated with large land holdings around the Burra Bazar. The Amenian community developed large parts of the city, and some of the hotels and residential mansions in Central and South Calcutta remain as excellent specimens of period architecture. The Maghen

THE KALIGHAT TEMPLE is the oldest in Kolkata, completed in 1809 on the site of a medieval temple. The goddess is reputed to have given the city its name, and it is the site of one of the popular festivals — Kali Puja. As a site of veneration, officials from the British East India Company made offerings to Kali in the eighteenth century. The spaces around the temple and those attached to its outer walls are filled with stalls selling temple offerings and stylised images of Hindu gods and goddesses.

David synagogue is the largest in Asia, and was reproduced from plans of the Florentine synagogue. Hindus constitute the majority among religious groups in most wards, but Bengali–Muslims make up a considerable presence in all wards.

There is some dispute about the origin of Calcutta, or its Bengali pronunciation — Kolkata. However the most popular view links it with the goddess Kali, the consort of Shiva, and the city patron deity.[2] The temple to Kali on the banks of the Hooghly River is a sacred focus for Hindus — the purveyor of a primal force with powers of both creation and

destruction, she is an appropriate metaphor for the city.

The first European trading post in Bengal was established in 1535 by the Portuguese, followed by the Dutch in 1636, the French in 1673 and the British through the East India Company in 1690. The first British settlement was situated on land purchased by the East India Company from landlords of three fishing villages — Sutanuti, Govindpore, and Dihi Kolkata in 1698. The company gradually absorbed additional land comprising thirty-eight villages in 1716. Despite the swampy and generally unhealthy conditions, it came under periodic threat of invasion from Maratha forces and a circular protective trench — the Maratha Ditch — was dug around the southeast part of the city in 1742, but later filled in as a thoroughfare marking the city boundary and known as Circular Road.

Bengal was one of the most productive parts of the Mughal empire in the seventeenth century, with an extensive agricultural base, a flourishing trading network, and an integrated market and financial structure with major areas of settlement. Its very success attracted European trading companies who worked in a complementary way with local trading communities operating from a cluster of islands in the delta until the Battle of Plassey in 1757. Calcutta did not develop from scratch as a British city, and the urban markers that came to symbolise the city from an imperial viewpoint belie the dual narratives of complex cultural interfaces and settlement patterns. As a result of the Permanent Settlement Act of 1793, wealthy landowners — *zaminder* — moved to the city, established businesses and built large residences. The latter often featured classical details including Corinthian, Ionic or Tuscan colonnades that reflected the colonial architectural style with an abundance of stucco work and balustrades, and complete with theatrical and musical salons, so that they become patrons of literature, music and dance.

The "White Town" gradually took on the characteristics of an administrative and business district along with spacious residential streets. Meanwhile, wealthy Bengali traders and Hindu money-lenders subscribed to city building and commercial development in the "Black Town", investing in land, warehouses and bazaars, introducing communities of artisans, and in the process creating a dynamic tension between different ethnic cultures. In fact both communities were represented by common configurations of 'separateness' based on class (caste),

Nakhoda Mosque from Zakaria Street

occupation, and ethnicity. It was however common in the eighteenth century, just as it is today in north Calcutta, to have substantial houses interposed with simple dwellings built along narrow alleys.

By the mid eighteenth century the occupied lands of the "White Town" were around five kilometres in length adjacent to the fort. The more extensive "Black Town" to the north had an ambiguous boundary, which established somewhat arbitrary neighbourhood demarcations. The initial city structure therefore developed around an open core, with the high-income and largely expatriate area to the south laid out to Western standards, and the native town to the north in unplanned and poorly serviced areas whose residents either worked as traders,

administrative clerks or as servants.

The unfortunate but exaggerated incident of the infamous "Black Hole", and the capture of the rudimentary fort, almost inadvertently marked the beginning of British rule in India as Robert Clive from the English East India Company went on to defeat the French and win victory over the Mughal army in 1757 at the battle of Plessey. Amongst other loot, Clive annexed nine hundred square miles of land south of Calcutta. The city's reputation as a "city of palaces" arose from the mansions built by company personnel, some of which still exist along Russell Street and Sudder Street.

The original fort was virtually destroyed during the siege of Calcutta in 1756. The new fort, Fort William, was built in Govindpore to the south and completed in 1773 using

3 Chakraborty, S, 'From Colonial City to Global City? The Far-From-Complete Spatial Transformation of Calcutt', in *The Urban Geography Reader*, Eds. Nicholas Fyfe and Judith T. Kenny, Routledge, London and New York, 2005, p84-92

A view of the eastern Esplanade in 1859

forced labour. Its overall shape and disposition generated a new urban design framework related to a vast open esplanade or *maidan* which protected the supposed line of fire and served as a gathering place for imperial display up to the line of Chowringhee Road to the east, which became lined with mansions. Wealth was displayed through building opulence. The fort's irregular octagonal fortifications created a walled city, with three sides facing the Hooghly River and five facing the Maidan. Permission was granted to all British inhabitants of the city to construct houses within its walls, and company clerks were required to live there. The surrounding defensive moat could be filled through a sluice gate, although the fort itself never came under attack during its long history. It was used for some time as a granary, and later as a prison and army museum commemorating past British military victories on the Indian sub-continent. St Peter's Church and St Patrick's Church lie within its walls.

In 1773 the supremacy of Calcutta was recognised over Bombay and Madras, and even at this time Calcutta came to be described as a city of palaces and hovels. With the expansion of city limits, investment in landed property by wealthy Indian traders and Europeans increased to the north and east, and extensive

docks were constructed. As in Bombay, the surveying and mapping of land was necessary so that the colonial government could produce a registry and assess revenues, reflecting the link between land as a commodity, and political control over local territory when fixing boundaries.[3] A sequence of cartographic representations illustrated the emerging morphology. Upjohn's survey map of 1792 shows a surprisingly advanced plan form, with ribbon development along the main arteries, particularly the major north-south spine along Chitpur Road, and east-west commercial avenues — Bow Bazaar and Dhurumtula Streets. The latter linked the stepped cargo landings or *ghats* on the Hooghly River with warehousing facilities and administrative support, and the network of bazaar trading areas in the east. This created a mutually supportive framework of wholesale and retail uses linked by efficient transport corridors.

A Town Improvement Committee was set up in 1803 under the governorship of Lord Wellesley to formulate planning layouts, which continued under a Lottery Committee until 1836. During its tenure, various public works were carried out including the Beliaghata Canal, Strand Road, and a series of north-south streets. However, despite plans for basic infrastructure, water and sanitation under a

Municipal Improvement Committee, no overall plan was prepared for city growth. Inhibiting factors were the poor ground conditions which caused subsidence, and the annual monsoon which required periodic replacement of wooden elements.

In 1873 the East India Company was formally disbanded in the wake of the imposition of direct rule by Britain, with the governor-general appointed as Viceroy. It came at a time of new urban awareness and city-building which reflected both the obligations and agendas of Victorian society and the growing number of Western–educated Indians with conflicting loyalties. Rapid commercial expansion was not accompanied by effective planning, as industrialisation and infrastructure quickly transformed the urban landscape. The city itself was pervaded by a strong underlying culture of Sanskrit aesthetics, art and architecture that embodied a resistance to the British policy of extortion — indigenous cultural practices included drama and newspapers in Bengali, that provoked moves towards an Indian National Congress, even as it was acknowledged that British connections were beneficial.

Even without a full city plan the central business district of Calcutta in the late nineteenth century spatially manifested the

4 Chakraborty, 2005, op. cit.

MARBLE PALACE situated at 46 Muktaram Babu Street is a residence and museum built in 1855 by the Raja Rajendra Mullick, and one of the must richly decorated palaces in Kolkata. While its design is neo-Classical, it is planned around a traditional courtyard. Its name is derived from ninety varieties of patterned marble, and the elaborate pediment above the portico is supported by six Tuscan columns. On each side are French wrought iron canopies reflecting the eclectic taste of its French architect. In the middle of the garden is a fountain with Greek figures.

dominance of the Raj with an imperial array of state offices. The prominent Memorial Museum to Queen Victoria represented a powerful monument to imperial aloofness, but at the same time the educational neighbourhood of College Street produced a cross-cultural forum for architecture, music and literature. The administrative district itself was centred around Government House, the Council House and the Customs House together with the East India Company's Writers Building. At the centre of the area was Tank Square. Proximity to the river and port attracted European businesses, auction houses and places of entertainment along the wide streets. Almost a century later, a map of 1894 by Ramanath Das illustrates the growth of the bazaar area and its specialised nature, together with main commercial streets and

markets within a city that had tripled in size. Many migrants settled in the vicinity of the Kalighat temple and became folk painters, documenting vivid scenes within the bazaars.

From the early nineteenth century, the need for orderly planning, sanitation and beautification were recognised. A Town Improvement Committee was set up in 1803 and a series of public lotteries held to raise funds for municipal improvement. This was directed at infrastructure improvement and road construction through the denser parts of the indigenous town, but also at the orderly urban design of major street frontages and grand buildings. It resulted in a hierarchical grid of streets that incentivised redevelopment of the most impoverished areas, but largely retained the small business networks — the Bengali system of broad

territorial divisions and localities: *paras*, *tolas* and *tulis*.[4] The eighteen *paras* in nineteenth century Calcutta tended to derive an essential identity from physical landmarks, but were encompassed by larger city wards for administrative purposes. The Ramaneth Das map conveyed urban design information by overlaying a grid over the *paras*, allowing a layering of information and a means to locate particular places — a process now used on all international city street guides.

The *paras* north of the Lal Bazaar formed a dense system of multi-functional neighbourhoods with commercial, residential and market components establishing a strong physical and social identity, where activities, gatherings and religious festivals were centred on public places. North of the bazaar, localities were named after trades and markets.

BURRA BAZAR IN THE NORTH OF CALCUTTA was traditionally peopled by the Marwari community from Rajasthan, who were money lenders, similar to the Chettier. After 1911 many wealthy Marwaris later moved to mansions on Zakaria Street and Chittaranjan Avenue on land cleared from the original Muslim settlers. This indirectly lead to riots against Marwari and civic property several years later. The bazaar was utilised as a market for jute and textiles under the British, but with the advent of new rail infrastructure it grew into the biggest wholesale market in India extending almost 10 square kilometres. Like many large market operations the labyrinth of informal trading is overlaid with a strong sense of organisation with trading desks and showrooms. It forms a counterpart to the network of commercial streets around the Writer's Building lined with offices, extending to Dalhousie Square, Park Street and Camac Street with its shopping arcades and restaurants.

ST JOHN'S CHURCH in the heart of the business district was the original Parish Church of Bengal designed by James Agg and built on the site of an old burial ground in 1787. It became the principal Cathedral of Calcutta in 1815 and remained so until the consecration of St Paul's in 1817. It was originally the property of Maharaja Nabakrishna Deb who was persuaded to sell it by Warren Hastings.

The highly decorative entrance to Butto Kristo Paul Medicine House on Shobhabazar Street

In response to a serious outbreak of bubonic plague, a special commission was appointed in 1886 to investigate the best means of opening out the older tightly packed areas, and this culminated in the Calcutta Improvement Act of 1911 which was based almost entirely on the English Housing of the Working Classes Act of 1890. The object was to provide for the improvement and expansion of the city in an orderly manner. Over the next forty years the Improvement Trust carried out road improvement schemes, rehousing and open space projects. New arterial roads provided some means of co-ordinating urban expansion.

In the mid-nineteenth century, Calcutta became the production centre of a jute industry set up by merchants from Dundee, and by 1927 this represented 26 per cent of all exports. The jute mill settlements along the Hooghly River became satellite cores around which the city suburbs expanded. Basic housing was provided for the expanding workforce, which attracted non-Bengali migrant labour. However after Partition the city lost most of its jute producing hinterland on the western side of the Hooghly River, with the city itself lying to the east. These spatial divisions generally persisted after 1947, but large-scale resettlement after Partition reinforced both spatial and class divisions in the city, which also extended outwards with upper income groups occupying much of the old core area. The congested Burra Bazar area adjacent to the central business district, and the Chowrangee area, declined in terms of infrastructure and amenities. Meanwhile, the majority of overcrowded slum areas formed an outer ring to the east of the Hooghly, often on public land along railway tracks and drainage alignments, with smaller squatter areas and pavement dwellers scattered with the high income areas.

By this time Fort William and the extensive *maidan* occupied a considerable part of the southern city, with main road connections between Government House, new administration and commercial buildings on large sites amalgamated from previous small lots, and large residences around Tank Square (later named Dalhousie Square). Buildings on the main axes were designed in a neo-gothic style underscoring the focus of imperial power and the prestige of the commercial and administrative centre. The *maidan* itself provided a space for ceremonial grandeur but also for leisurely promenades, drives and walks. These activities were made a European preserve at certain times of day, reinforcing a symbolic urban framework of division and separation. This extended to elaborate elements of exclusion — gateways, railings and walls used as territorial markers, and creating anomalous counterparts to the overall heterogeneity of the city.

A TEMPORARY MARKET

forms the foreground to the Ochterlony Monument. This fluted column of brickwork was erected through public subscription in 1828 in memory of Major General David Ochterlony. It is a rare combination of three distinct styles of architecture — the base is Egyptian, the column Syrian and the dome and its metal empola is Turkish. It is now known as the Martyr's Memorial or Shaheed Minar.

5   Cattopadhyay, S, *Representing Calcutta: Modernity, Nationalism and the Colonial Uncanny*, Routledge, London and New York, 2005
6   Cattopadhyay, 2005, op. cit.

Swati Cattopadhyay, a professor of architecture at the University of California, has examined plans of nineteenth century colonial houses in Calcutta, which illustrate their genealogy in terms of subdivisions and multiple purposes — for lodging, offices, shops and godowns — maximising the relationship to the public realm and central space.[5] Kitchens and servants' spaces in the "White Town" were not designed as an integral part of the house, as preparation of food and cooking took place outdoors. In the urban context this translated into accommodation for servants alongside the outer boundaries, creating solid divisions between neighbouring sites and outer street edges. Much of the neo-Classical architecture was stylistically hybrid with Hindu and Islamic influences. Within the *paras* they were locally "authenticated" with appendages and decorations, creating a streetscape of ambivalence sustained by diverse uses and practises.

According to Chattopadhyay, the chief difference between inner districts in the early nineteenth century was density of the urban fabric — a spacious but ordered pattern of development with some detached dwellings on Chowringhee Road, Park Street and around Tank Square which was regarded as the fashionable centre; and a higher density in Black Town. However at no time did White Town form a homogenous space for Europeans only.[6] Colonial Calcutta consisted of overlapping spaces and geographies — the result of constant territorial negotiations.

Calcutta inherited a formality in its urban design adoption of British city-building experience, demonstrated by a civic vocabulary of streets, squares and open spaces such as Eden Gardens and Horticultural Gardens, along with the major central open space — the *maidan*. The axial organisation of streets was frequently focussed on fountains, sculpture and prominent building façades. Government House itself was placed

KOLKATA'S OLDEST SQUARE, originally called Tank Square, was derived from the Lal Dighi water tank that was one of the sources of the city's drinking water. Now renamed BBD Bagh, it is the location of some of Kolkata's most prominent colonial buildings. The decorative roof profile of the Writer's Building, which provided accommodation to the East Indian Company's junior servants or clerks, is on the left. In 1880 the Colonial government shifted the offices of the Bengal State Secretariat to the building, and in 1882 a new Corinthian order was added and Baroque statuary introduced at roof level representing Justice, Commerce and Science. To the right is St Andrew's Church, based on St Martin-in-the-Fields in London which was published in a source book on architecture in 1778. It thereafter served as a model for church designers in colonial India.

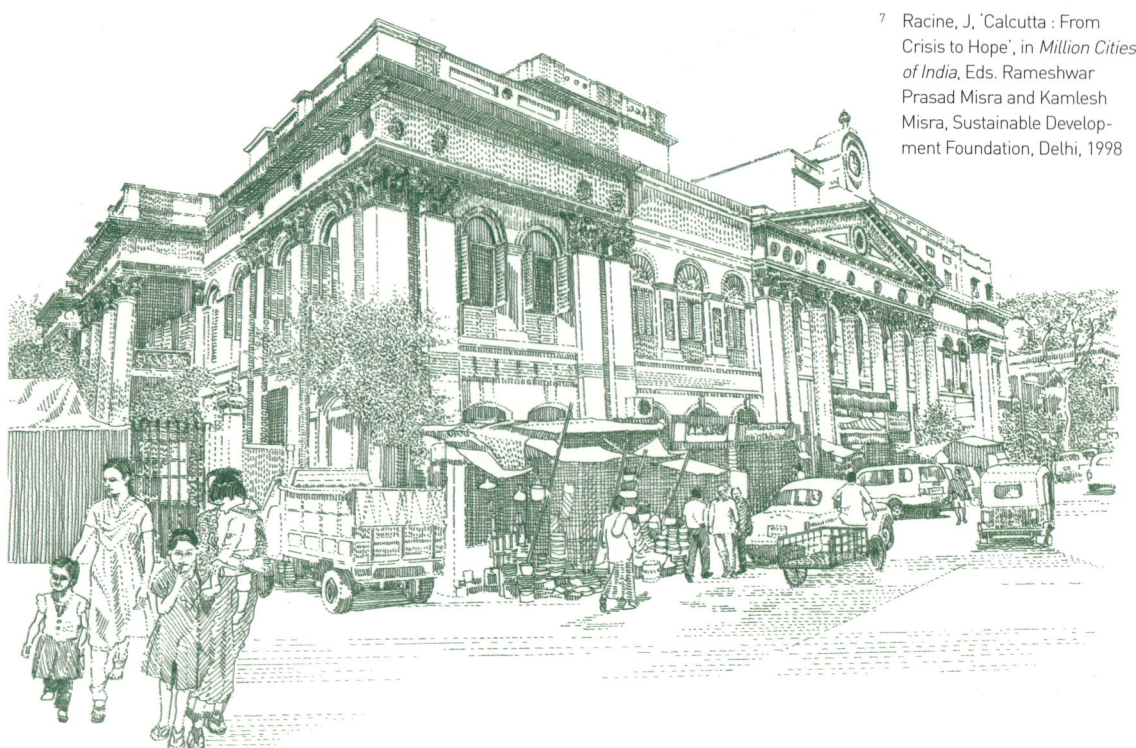

7 Racine, J, 'Calcutta : From Crisis to Hope', in *Million Cities of India*, Eds. Rameshwar Prasad Misra and Kamlesh Misra, Sustainable Development Foundation, Delhi, 1998

A grand mansion facing the neo-Classical façade of the Lohia Matri Serua Sadan Hospital, informally extended by temporary interventions along Chitpore Road, now renamed Rabindra Sarani.

on the axis of Dalhousie Square. Streets radiating from the square encompassed both government and commercial buildings. The Calcutta Improvement Trust created in 1911 carried out large-scale works, including new roads and service infrastructure, but cleared much historic fabric in the process.

The confrontation between the business of a colonial state and a socio-cultural sphere dominated by the indigenous Hindu Bengali elite, gave the organisation of urban space a certain tension. In terms of urban design the colonising body signified a hierarchical distinction, while the workings of Bengali society itself tended to erase such signification. Superimposed on this was a parasitic attachment to native landholdings, continually reinforced by middle and poorer class professionals or *madhyabitta,* connected through kinship patterns.

The city morphology reflects historical interventions and settlement patterns. The area around Burra Bazar, where merchant traders settled, is still the hub of the city. The Maidan around Fort William is the major open space, while the central business district is concentrated between the two. East of the Maidan, the prominent areas are

Chowringhee, Park Street and Shakespeare Sarani which house established structures from the colonial era. To the south, Bhowanipore, Ballygunge and Tollygunge are prime residential areas. The eastern part of the city is given over to low-cost housing, factories and railway yards. Along the Ganges delta and the Hooghly River are the old trading posts of Hooghly (Portuguese), Serampoe (Danish), Chandwerwagore (French), and Chinsurah (Dutch).[7]

THE BLACK TOWN

In spatial terms, the "Black Town" or native city, was a complete contrast to the Chowringhee district, with narrow crowded streets, simple two-storey buildings, and an intermingling of housing, commercial and manufacturing establishments.

The materiality of public space in the native city involved an elusive sphere of power structures. At its apex was the landed elite who possessed recourse to social power and status within the colonial order through political advantage. Owners of large properties rented out land, which resulted in a closely packed mass of both permanent and temporary buildings. At the same time

they philanthropically controlled many of the voluntary and religious organisations representing community interests and these were frequently in conflict with the colonial administration. Middle-class interaction was more intangible, being mediated through education, literature and other cultural channels. Bengali literature in particular expresses affectionate concerns about the beauty of the city and the pleasurable communality of its spaces. This fashioned a sense of sociability and discussion or *adda* — talking shops where groups partake in verbal jousting for an exchange of views, the telling of anecdotes and a conduit for raconteurs to hold court.

The Bengali language is alliterative, lyrical, and steeped in metaphor. This seems to metaphysically seep through the flourishes and flounces of the written word and the rich fusion of word and musical rhythm in the work of the poet and composer Tagore. An integral part of the city is its theatrical tradition. The city's first Western-style theatre was built in 1753, and by the late nineteenth century both English and Bengali theatre flourished in both the Babu and Sahib communities, divided by language.

BLACK TOWN developed along a series of streets to the north of Dalhousie Square (BBD Bagh) and contained the mansions of Bengal's wealthiest merchants who were linked to the East India Company. These form extensive frontages along Shobhabazar, Bagbazar and Jorasanko, co-existing with bazaars, street cafes and temples. Some mansions have been converted into public institutions while others have been colonised as offices and apartments. The most opulent formed street façades of Corinthian columns and elaborate pediments with large courtyards behind. Classical architectural forms were adapted from the early neo-Classical European buildings, showcasing Italian marble, Venetian shutters, Belgian chandeliers and Greek sculptures.

8 Dutta, 2003, op. cit.

Many affluent personages added a performance space to their mansions. The Minerva Theatre built in 1893 put on classic English plays to Bengali social and political theatrical commentaries in the 1960s.

At an elevated level there was much social interaction and the Bengali compradors or *babus* — a Persian honorific originally conferred by Mughal rulers — achieved highly influential positions as political intermediaries. One of them — Nabakrishna Dep — an orthodox Hindu, donated land for St John's Church in 1784. Almost all the *paras* had a renowned and wealthy *babu* who owned a mansion sitting among the ordinary alleys of the Black Town. Some of the most successful such as Dwarkanath Tagore pioneered independent banking, tea-growing, railway enterprises and shipping companies. Hindu College (now Presidency College), founded in 1817, was the first higher education institute in India and was dedicated entirely to the study of European philosophy and literature. Many of its alumni became public figures and well-known writers, establishing a Bengali literary tradition that extends to the famous annual book fair held on the Maidan.[8]

The collection of cultural and religious nineteenth century buildings on College Square reflects the multi-dimensional heritage of the city. Sanskrit College, Hindu School, the Bengal Theosophical Society, University Institute Hall and the Jalan Khan Mosque, are articulated in a variety of forms, from the Neo-Gothic to the Indo-Saracenic. V.S. Naipaul describes the style, somewhat caustically, as "Calcutta Corinthian".

The present day street fabric is sufficiently flexible to incorporate a wide variety of outlets, reflecting different ethnic groups, such as the Muslim stores around the Nakhoda Mosque, Hindu cafes, and the residue of a Chinese community centred around the See Ip temple. Chitpore Road (Rabindra Sarani) is one of the great Bengali streets of Calcutta, integrating the traditional

DURGA is the primordial mother image of Kolkata whose annual 'homecoming' is celebrated by the Durga Puja festival initiated to mark the victory of the British over the French at Plassey in 1757. Kumartuli is a north Kolkata neighbourhood alongside the Hooghly River where artisans specialise in making and painting elaborate clay images of Hindu deities for the festival. It is one of the oldest artisan collectives in the old Black Town, where potters assemble from surrounding districts. It is said that they began in the eighteenth century, being inspired by classical figures of Western

art. Mud is brought from the Hooghly River. Images are pre-ordered by Hindu communities throughout the world, and used for important festivals. One of the most revered figures is Saraswati — the goddess of learning — indicating the Bengali fountain of knowledge.

Deities are transported from workshops to temples and private houses, and are then carried through the streets to the River Hooghly where they are immersed by boatmen and return to the river clay from where they came — a symbolic act of the creative and destructive cycle.

"babu" culture with the modern. It was originally developed in the seventeenth century to connect the Chitteswari temple in the north with the Kalighat temple in the south. As the Bengali community gradually moved to the north, development was consolidated along the spine and adjoining lanes. A number of eighteenth century neo-baroque mansions are still standing — some have become museums. In 1879 a tramway was built and still exists alongside buses, rickshaws, and bullock carts.

THE WHITE TOWN

Trade through the East India Company had, by the end of the eighteenth century, made Bengal a wealthy province. Buckingham House to the west of Chowringhee was the residence of the first four governor generals and rented from the Nawab of Chitpur. The Council House and adjoining mansions were later resumed to create the site for a grandiose Government House, which conformed to a neo-Classical design with the aim of projecting imperial authority. It was completed in 1803 and designed by Charles Wyatt who copied the plan from Kedleston Hall in Derbyshire by James Paine, while making essential modifications to interior

spaces based on different social functions. The design set a style for other colonial buildings. It is said that when, almost a century later, Lord Curzon, the owner of Kedleston Hall became Viceroy and resident of Government House in 1899, he made further modifications to make it look almost identical to the original. It is now named Rajyapal Bhavan, and houses the governor of West Bengal.

Lord Curzon not only personally supervised the preservation of Indian monuments at Agra and Fatehpur Sikri, but pursued the initiation of an Imperial Library. Arguably his greatest contribution to Calcutta urban design was the Victoria Memorial Hall. Curzon took up the challenge with the words: "Let us, therefore, have a building, stately, spacious, monumental and grand, to which every newcomer in Calcutta will turn, to which all the resident population, European and Native, will flock, where all classes will learn the lessons of history, and see revived before their eyes the marvels of the past".

In fact, common to the colonial period in India, architectural intervention seemed to follow a borrowed style from older European models. The design of the Eastern Railway Building of 1863 was based on Michelangelo's Farnese Palace in Rome; St Paul's Cathedral

VICTORIA MEMORIAL was built by Lord Curzon but largely funded by Indian princes. It was completed twenty years after the death of Queen Victoria in 1921 and was constructed of marble from the same quarry in Rajasthan that supplied Shah Jahan, which supposedly lends it resemblance to the Taj Mahal. Its central dome is crowned by a five-metre tall revolving "Angel of Victory" crafted in Italy. The principal architect was William Emerson, president of the RIBA, assisted by Vincent Esch, architect of the Bengal Club. Possibly to balance the evolving interplay between cultures, the design is a forceful mix of European Baroque and Indo-Saracenic with Mughal corner turrets. The staid classicism is relieved by restrained Hindu and Islamic details. It is quietly described in some quarters as the "Taj of the Raj" but now tends to serve as the dominant icon of the city. Its internal galleries document the history of the British in India, and a Calcutta gallery illustrating the growth and development of the city. Set around the building are statues of political and military figures associated with the British Empire.

9 Halder, S and Halder, M,
   *Colonial Architecture at
   Calcutta*, Abhishek Halder,
   Howrah, 1999
10 Chakraborty, 2005, op. cit.

Book stalls define the pavement edge along College Street and Surya Sen Street reflecting Kolkata's traditional reputation as a centre for education. College Street is a book district, and a centre for Bengali publishing, indicating the location of the first university in India founded in the area in 1857.

designed by William N Forbes is said to be derived from Norwich Cathedral with the present tower based on the bell tower of Canterbury Cathedral; and the Writer's Building of 1780 has a strong resemblance to Somerset House, which was built at precisely the same time in London.[9]

Both education and religion were forces for propagating Western cultural standards. Fort William College was founded in 1800 to educate East India Company recruits in administrative and colonial policy, but discouraged "Orientalist" teaching of any aspect of indigenous culture. Christian missionaries constantly attempted to redeem the population from "barbaric" Hindu practices, even translating Christian scriptures into Bengali. Educational books were produced by the Calcutta School Book Society founded in 1817. The Mission Press printed evangelical texts and theological colleges were established. Christian missionaries also introduced mass education in Bengal, teaching in Bengali and other vernacular languages. However there were curtailments on access to employment opportunities under colonial authority, which in some cases led to blatant discrimination.

Belvedere and Alipur, to the south of the Maidan, still represent exclusive areas of private colonial villas, occupied by wealthy Bengalis, Marwaris and Punjabis. Belvedere House, currently the National Library, stands on the site of a property that was gifted to Warren Hastings after the battle of Plessey. It was later subject to periodic remodelling and became the official residence of the lieutenant — governor of Bengal. It is surrounded by gardens of the Agri-Horticultural Society and the Zoological Gardens inaugurated by the Prince of Wales in 1876.

THE MODERN CITY

After the transfer of the capital to New Delhi in 1911, Calcutta remained for a time as the financial capital of India, and a leading port. The post-colonial economic emphasis was directed towards both key industrial infrastructure, and a more administrative and service-oriented role. However the benefits of industrial growth failed to ignite city development, due partly to high population and deteriorating infrastructure, together with barriers to foreign capital and investment. The demise of its traditional textile industry in favour of cloth manufactured in England exacerbated the situation, but the cultivation of tropical products such as tea and indigo acted to slowly expand the local economy and attracted massive urban migration from Bengal, Bihar and Orissa.

An economic, social and cultural process related to city development is based on enlightened and sympathetic decision-making with clear priorities as to the investment necessary for the steady progression of society. This can be expressed in an encapsulation of form but needs to be progressive rather than exploitive — stressing achievement rather than display. The unfulfilled promise of modernisation built on the colonial model, failed largely through lack of commitment in balancing economic promise with the crafting of city development to meet evolving needs. Colonisation for all its "civilising constructs" ultimately fails unless it unites, and economic exploitation in the colonial city, even in a relatively benevolent situation, is nevertheless repressive. Commitment must be equated with benevolence. By the late nineteenth century the popular European ideal of the 'rights of man' gave way to chauvinism in relation to the colonial city. Planning and development in many cases translated into an imposition as much as an intervention, and urban design became a matrix within which parts of the city were constantly reconfigured and realigned. The physical landscape of Calcutta is not merely one of cultural relativism, but the product of mixed priorities. Calcutta has

The General Post Office on BBD Bagh West Road designed by Walter Granville was completed in 1868 on the site of the Old Fort. Its dome is supported by an octagonal base and twenty-eight Corinthian pillars.

long experienced annual monsoon floods, periodic famine and religious upheavals, which have contributed to an urban design of transition and adaptation.

Post-colonial Calcutta was an acute victim of partition and became wracked by infighting and religious stubbornness. The biggest migration consisted of Hindu refugees from East Bengal after 1947 putting a massive strain on the city's resources, in particular housing. This led to a multiplicity of squatter areas throughout the city — forty in the southeast of the city and more than sixty in the north, together with overcrowding in the street tenements, which nevertheless formed the basis of strong communities. Still more refugees arrived 1951, and later in 1971 during the gestation of Bangladesh, with scenes echoing Kipling's "City of Dreadful Night". The depiction of human turmoil by the city's intelligentsia — writers, artists and film makers — have striven to both signal a sense of perspective, and stirred the political waters well to the left, supported by a large

peasant membership. While urban problems are acute, urban governance and investment are still wanting as the wealth gap widens to a chasm. Chakravorty observes the patterns of spatial separation — the non-Bengali business elite that occupies the centre; the Rajasthan Marwaris who occupy enclaves in the Burra Bazar; and professional Bengalis in the south.[10] Calcutta has also long been subject to foreign arrivals, following two centuries of British, Armenian, Chinese and Jewish immigrants from Baghdad that have added to the complex culture of the city. Chinese first came to work on the sugar plantations set up by Warren Hastings, and were later joined by artisans and refugees from the Chinese Communist regime after 1949. The Park Street area of Tangra is now the Chinese city quarter, and only the See Ip Temple in Chhatawalla Goli remains of the original Chinatown area in Chitpur.

While West Bengal lags behind other states, there has been significant investment in the inner city service sector, manufacturing

The Metropolitan Building on Chowinghee Avenue originally housed one of the early department stores – Whiteway, Laidlaw and Co. It is now a cottage industries emporium.

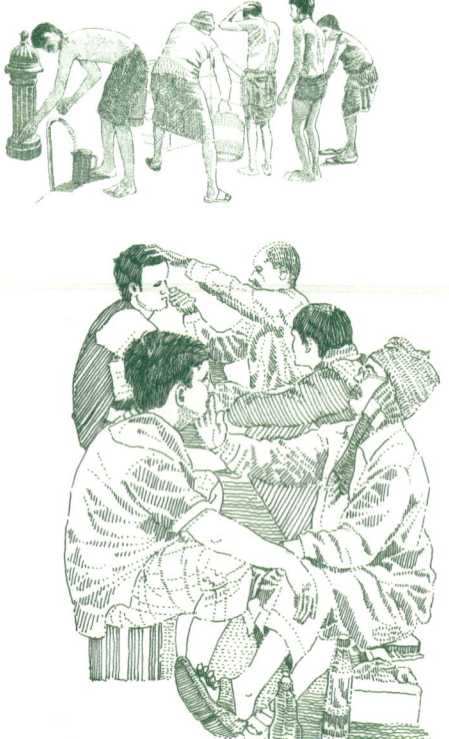

Street scenes

in the industrial suburbs and new port development at Kulpi. The Calcutta Metropolitan Development Authority is also implementing the "Mega City Programme". Furthermore a new town "East Calcutta" is under development on the inner eastern fringe to attract high-tech electronics and software industry, together with Salt Lake which has attracted the relocation of many state government offices.

In 1961 the Calcutta Metropolitan Planning Organisation was established, and in 1966 produced a twenty-year development plan for a single planning region. This was focussed on Calcutta-Howrah in the south and the new township of Kalyani in order to best absorb growth and arrest further deterioration of the older building fabric. It was superseded by the creation of the Calcutta Metropolitan Development Authority who produced a fresh development plan in 1976, which focussed attention on the development of economic and service infrastructure and environmental improvement with World Bank loans. An American planner, Allan B Jacobs formulated

a comprehensive Structure Plan for the Metropolitan District under the guidance of the Ford Foundations in 1965. This called for a linear pattern of development reinforcing the historical axis along both sides of the Hooghly River, connected by bridge crossings and served by new rail and road alignments that would link with suburban development. A further successful development initiative is investment in heavy industry in Haldia to the north. Planned and largely self-contained residential and industrial enclaves are likely to reintroduce the city to the globalised model, but also exacerbate the gulf between the planned and informal sectors. In the eastern fringe of the city is an entirely new development located on the reclaimed salt lakes, laid out in spacious sectors for residential, recreation, commercial and industrial development. The area is fast developing with new industries.

While prominent colonial buildings are lasting markers of imperial intervention they can also be viewed as monumental landmarks rather than integral components of the urban fabric. In practice there was a substantial blurring of ideological boundaries, that furnished more of a composite rather than a contested urbanism, and it is this that frames the realm of urban design in the colonial Indian city. In 1970 the Calcutta Metropolitan Development Authority was established with World Bank support for a programme of environmental improvements and renovation projects. This was taken further in 1979 with legislation providing for conservation of historic buildings in the face of urban redevelopment pressure. A number of initiatives by preservation societies have since focussed on heritage protection, including exhibitions during Calcutta's tercentenary events in 1990. In 1995 the Calcutta Environmental Management Strategy and Action Plan set out further powers for protection of historic monuments, and a State Heritage Commission was set up in 2001 by

[11] Ghosh, S, 'Calcutta : Heritage and Government Priorities' in *The Disappearing Asian City*, Ed. William S Logan, Oxford University Press, Oxford, 2002, p121

[12] Chakraborty, 2005, op. cit.

the Government of West Bengal.[11] This calls for a reinvigoration of older parts of the city for adaptive re-use, in order to elaborate the diversity of its literacy, arts and educational activities. These underscore the inherited cultural wealth of the city, blending new infill development within the older street pattern.

The fact that the cultural attributes of the "native" city have endured longer than many of the monuments to modernism and pictorial landscapes, suggests that the colonial rhetoric of superiority was itself contradictory, faced with a certain ambivalence. Imposed institutions such as the colonial bureaucracy and army were directly linked to the maintenance of administrative control and the capitalist process of consolidation and extraction. However, many modern cultural institutions were initiated and promulgated by local elites and voluntary associations through longstanding identification with sacred places and public spaces, which included schools, colleges, cafes and bookshops. There is now a strong momentum towards conservation of the city's historical buildings and monuments, and a large number have been listed for preservation.

Calcutta, now the capital of West Bengal, represents an Asian "Third World" geography of colonial urbanisation and extraction, alongside an elusive integration with the global marketplace. This has not materialised due to the transition from deindustrialisation as in the West, but through an urban industrial and capital intensive reform economy, which must necessarily, embrace a large "informal" sector comprising up to 40 per cent of the labour force.[12] Many problems still exist, but the city's plethora of architectural monuments and a street matrix of fascinating complexity, remains one of dynamic contrast, frenzied activity and urban exhilaration, redolent of its deep-rooted culture.

Mumbai

INDIA

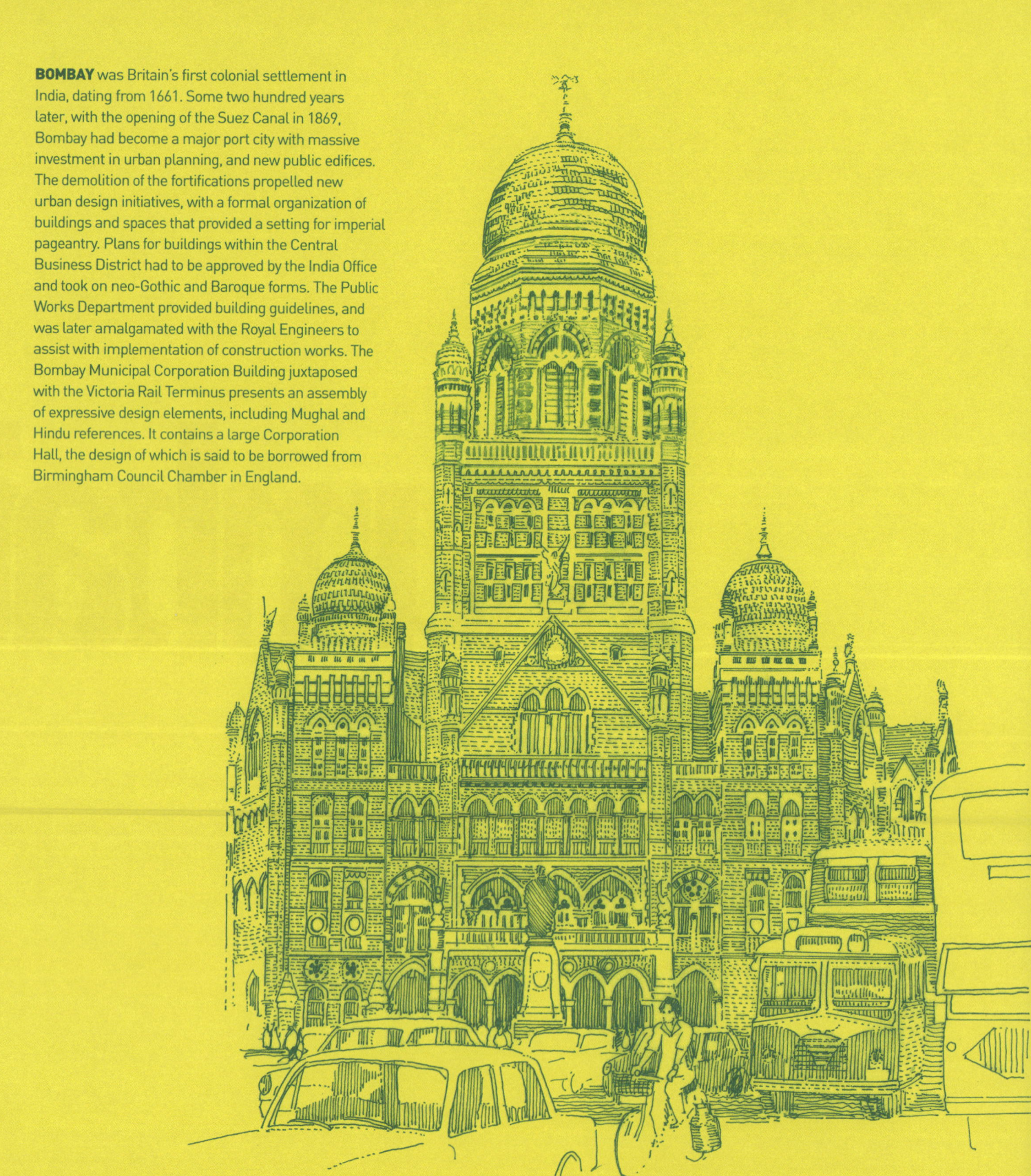

BOMBAY was Britain's first colonial settlement in India, dating from 1661. Some two hundred years later, with the opening of the Suez Canal in 1869, Bombay had become a major port city with massive investment in urban planning, and new public edifices. The demolition of the fortifications propelled new urban design initiatives, with a formal organization of buildings and spaces that provided a setting for imperial pageantry. Plans for buildings within the Central Business District had to be approved by the India Office and took on neo-Gothic and Baroque forms. The Public Works Department provided building guidelines, and was later amalgamated with the Royal Engineers to assist with implementation of construction works. The Bombay Municipal Corporation Building juxtaposed with the Victoria Rail Terminus presents an assembly of expressive design elements, including Mughal and Hindu references. It contains a large Corporation Hall, the design of which is said to be borrowed from Birmingham Council Chamber in England.

[1] Heitzman, J, *The City in South Asia*, Routledge, London and New York, 2008, p11
[2] Heitzman, 2008, op. cit., p154

BOMBAY, NOW MUMBAI, was originally a cluster of seven islands separated by tidal mud flats. It was made a capital in 1292 but its modern history dates from the role of the Portuguese in the mid-sixteenth century. Salsette was the largest land mass, separated from the Mainland by river courses with a group of small islands to the west and south, of which the southernmost were Bombay and Colaba. Portugal assumed control of the archipelago in 1534 and divided the territory into fiefdoms of which the largest were granted to the religious orders of Franciscans and Jesuits. They became known collectively as Bombay or 'Good Harbour', but a century later they passed into British hands in 1661 as part of the dowry of Catherine Braganza to Charles II. Bombay thus became Britain's first Crown colony in India, approached by sea through wooded islands and promontories. It was ceded to the English East India Company in perpetuity in 1667, which then shifted its centre of operation from Surat to the city. Jesuit estates were forfeited, but certain trading concessions were given to the Portuguese.

During the late seventeenth century the Mughal and Maratha empires were at war over land possession. Traders and artisans flocked to the city to pursue new business opportunities, setting a tone for cosmopolitan traditions and religious toleration. The English East India Company masterminded Bombay's development, which was characterised by the motto that came to represent the city — *Urbs Primus in Indus* — and adopted by the Bombay Municipal Corporation. In 1715 work commenced on reclaiming the marshy off-shore areas using fill from the hillsides, and enabling the city to extend northwards thereby transforming its early morphology. Between 1716 and 1725 the city defences were reinforced by trapezoid-shaped fortifications to counter attacks from both land and sea and major dockyards were set up. The settlement was

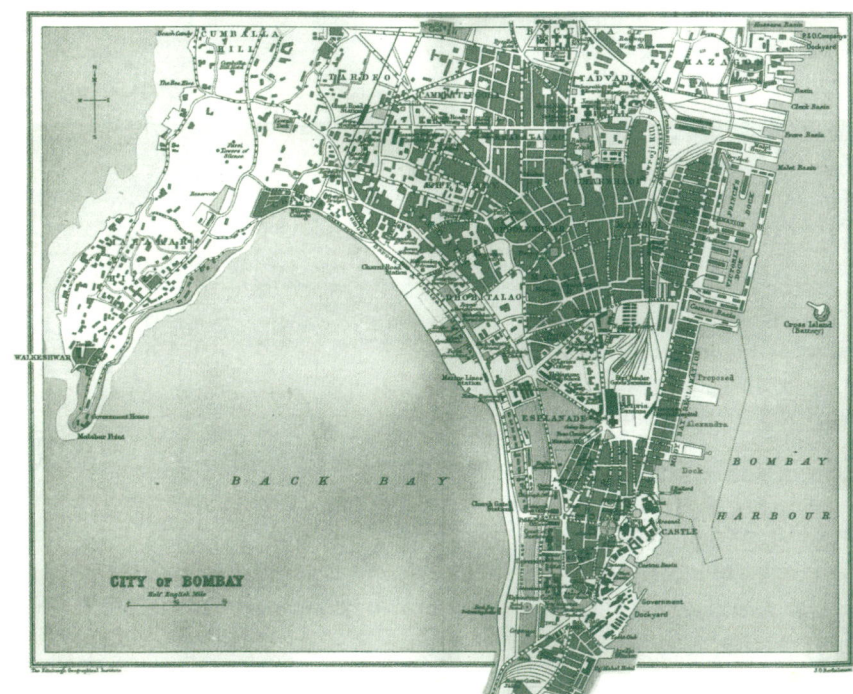

Plan of Bombay, 1909

accessible from three main gates: Apollo Gate facing the harbour, Bazaar Gate to the north, and Church Gate to the west. A moat was completed in 1713 — referred to as "the Maratha Ditch" — and all ground cleared around the walls to provide for cannon fire. In practice this was used largely as an esplanade and later widened to 1,000 metres. The work involved razing older buildings but created an opportunity for later commercial and population expansion outside the port after the acquisition of Salsette. The southern section evolved into the business district housing European firms, shopping companies and banks, while the northern area later became a residential quarter for native merchants. This extended to the bazaar area fronted by docks, which became known as the Old Town.[1] The shipyards become the linchpin of British expansion in the Far East, and were responsible for the construction of the opium clippers that were later to open up the Treaty Ports and China trade.

According to Heitzman, while the city attracted immigrants at an early stage of development, the Chettiar merchants from Gujarat were the most successful in establishing shipping financial and real estate enterprises, and maintained extensive properties in the fort.[2]

The native city had different neighbourhood identities based broadly on caste, religion, sect, and trade specialisation. Adjacent to the esplanade, buildings were constructed up to six storeys with ground level shops and two to three floors of accommodation above. These overhanging storeys were marked by carved screens and

3   Dossal, M, 'Bombay and the Famine of 1803-6: the Food Supply and Public Order of a Colonial Port City', in *Gateways of Asia: Port Cities of Asia in the 13th-20th Centuries*, Ed. Frank Broeze, Kegan Paul International, London, 1997

built around a central courtyard housing extended family groups. Building certificates had to be obtained to build on company land, and control over development and construction material extended to the demolition of properties that impeded planned uses. The reclamation of 1,700 hectares for the Breach Water Estates was carried out by established property interests. The government derived income for this largely from taxation and ground rent.

By the 1780s Bombay possessed a large natural harbour and commercial dockyards but much land remained contested and held under complicated tenure arrangements. A Building Committee was set up in 1787 to regulate construction activity and to establish clear regulations over the width of streets, building heights, and the installation of drainage to provide for run-off. To overcome this, many houses were built with narrow frontages.

In 1803 a disastrous fire in the fort provided the catalyst for a Town Committee to rationalise development further, reserving sites within the fort for government uses and well-connected merchants, while allocating a new settlement area to the north for native inhabitants, and 'dangerous trades'. The stability of the port and the means to support territorial growth depended on sources for export products and the provision of essential food supplies, but the dual function of Bombay ensured the prioritisation of scarce food resources.[3] The Portuguese authorities had previously prevented the sea transport of essential commodities to Bombay in response to the ceding of the island to Britain, and the British were aware that food supply lines were essential to the continued development of the city. However in 1803 the failure of the monsoon brought famine, which caused immense suffering. This re-occurred sporadically until 1812 when the government effectively adopted a laissez-faire approach to trade that had far-reaching ramifications for

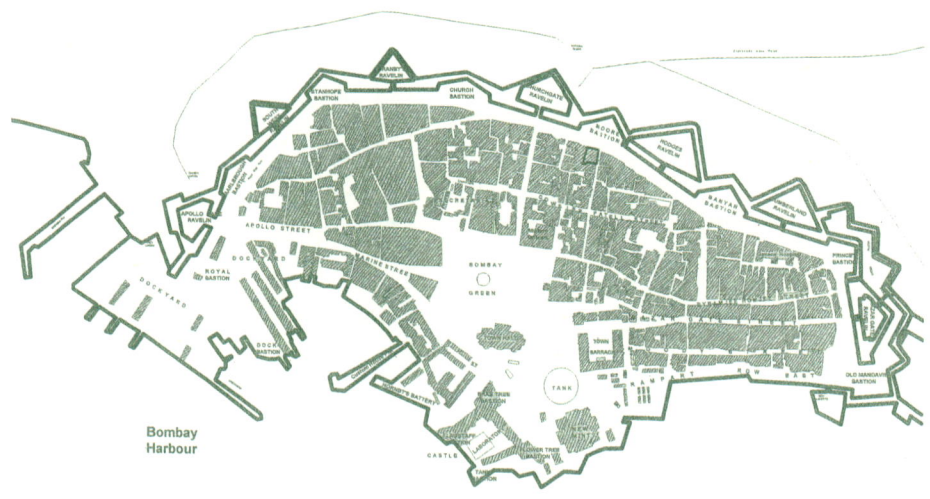

Plan of Bombay Fort

land transactions and urban development.

Subsequently, a comprehensive survey was initiated to delineate the boundaries of different land use and tenure categories, as a means of further regularising land transactions. The Land Registry Act of 1843 served a direct political purpose — surveyed lands were claimed by the Company. The "Black Town" developed to the north of Bazaar Gate, which encouraged a linear pattern of development. At the same time, large-scale reclamation transformed the island group into a coherent land mass with a deep natural harbour, completed in 1838 and known as the 'Hornby Vellard'.

Surat, which was a much larger settlement than Bombay in the eighteenth century, declined with the Mughal collapse. Traders, including many Parsee businessmen, gradually relocated to Bombay, which stimulated business growth encouraged by the city's role as an exporter of Gujarati cotton to China. The northern part of the re-planned fort became crowded with Indian commercial establishments belonging mainly to the Parsee and Borah communities,

centred around Borah Bazaar. The blockade of Confederate ports during the American Civil War had the immediate effect of creating a monopoly of the cotton trade in Bombay. The establishment of factories for cotton spinning and weaving between 1854 and 1874 represented a shift from the export of commodities to textile-based manufacturing, which lasted until 1920. The workforce were housed in rows of small apartments or *chawls* on several storeys, accessed by verandahs with shared facilities — not dissimilar to the first Mark 1 and 2 emergency housing estates in Hong Kong that also housed workers for the burgeoning textile industry some one hundred years later. These formed high-density neighbourhoods adjoining the factories. The Bombay Improvement Trust constructed similar *chawls* for municipal employees. At the centre of these areas were open plazas for religious gatherings and politically charged union meetings.

In 1854 the government imposed the right to resume land for public purposes. This facilitated the construction of rail lines and associated depots, workshops and

termini. An arbitration panel was set up to adjudicate land purchases and the requisition of buildings necessary for infrastructure and underground drainage works. The 1860s was a time of intense development activity, the most ambitious being the work of private reclamation companies following the development of accurate land surveys. Most of the reclamation work along the eastern and western foreshores was undertaken using fill material from the eastern ridgeline, enabling settlement of outlying areas. Both the Great Indian Peninsula Railway and the Bombay, Baroda and Central India Railway commenced operations at this time, symbolising European engineering prowess. They connected Bombay with the important cotton producing areas in Gujarat — the former extending to Calcutta and Madras, and the latter to Karachi.

The linear high density structure of the city evolved along the rail routes and around the stations. The first municipal piped water supply, and extension of the harbour and dock facilities, together with increased land supply, created a market for major development projects and changes in land use patterns. As the Vihar and Powai Lakes were created, all but two of the city's older 'tanks', which were important social landmarks, were filled in.

The supply of Indian cotton to replace that from America, and the opening of the Suez Canal in 1869, propelled Bombay's growth as a port city, with new enclaves developing along ethnic and religious lines. Public-private partnerships formed the base

THE BANGANGA TANK located in the Malabar Hill area is one of only two such man-made water bodies in Mumbai that have served a ceremonial and religious role. Fed by freshwater springs, they form places of ritual, bathing, and social gathering. India's tanks date back to the sixth century as a means of securing access to groundwater — a scarce resource. This also symbolically linked them to sacred places of pilgrimage or tirthasthana,

as part of a traditional spatial narrative. Banganga dates from the twelfth century. As a place of pilgrimage it became surrounded by memorials and temples, including the Hindu Walkeshwar Temple, which was destroyed by the Portuguese and re-built under the British in the seventeenth century. After the construction of the causeway that joined the island group, accessibility to the tank increased visitation until the early twentieth century when the area became a focus for houses and apartment blocks. However the diversity of uses, overlapping local spaces and the continuation of the barsalt steps or ghats around the tank into the steep and narrow fabric of the adjoining streets, creates a ceremonial sequence that links the present with the past. In 1995 the complex was declared a heritage precinct and a protected monument.

PAST STYLES in a new context — the Victoria Rail Terminus, now known as the Chhatvapati Shiraji Terminus designed by Frederick William Stevens. It is the most monumental of the neo-Gothic Victorian buildings in the city, featuring an exuberant combination of domes, spires, turrets, flying buttresses and allegorical friezes constructed on reclaimed land along the eastern side of the peninsula. Detailed sculptural elements of Indian animals, birds and foliage were built into the design and decorated the tympanums, capitals and gables. The terminus is said to be partly inspired by St Pancras Station in London.

THE "GATEWAY OF INDIA" arch with its amalgamation of Victorian neo-Gothic and Indian styles, intended to convey the ties between Britain and India. It was designed by George Wittet and built to commemorate the visit of King George V at Apollo Bunder in 1911. Construction was completed in 1924, and thereafter it became the ceremonial entrance to India for new Viceroys.

of various reclamation schemes during the 1860s to provide additional land for both development and infrastructure, levelling hills and realigning water courses in the process. The obsolete fortifications were removed, and infrastructure was constructed under the new British administration. Increasing wealth led to massive investment in city building, including prominent new pubic edifices such as Bombay University designed by George Gilbert Scott in 1857, and a school of art whose graduates went on to decorate some of the city's notable public buildings.

Reclamation encompassed 276 acres on the eastern side of the peninsula, providing land for the Victoria Terminus of the Great Indian Peninsula Railway. Railway development was not just necessary to transport raw materials and finished goods, but to satisfy the growing needs of commuters. Fill from the excavated Alexandra Docks was used to reclaim new

land for commercial development, which became known as the "new town", and developed through an amalgamation of settlements with a gradual extension of the administrative area. The parallel hill ridges terminate at Malabar Hill and Colaba so that Malabar and Cumbala Hills developed as prime residential areas, with a low lying area in between. This resulted in north-south alignments of transport and rail routes along which slum areas gradually developed.

The booming business economy influenced a re-ordering of the central core and the demolition of the fort walls in 1864, which made possible new urban design initiatives. Esplanade Road and Rampart Row physically, and as nomenclatures, echoed the line of the old fortifications. Elphinstone Circle, and a range of monumental public buildings followed the line of the esplanade — the High Court, University Library and the Secretariat,

with Victoria Rail Terminus to the north, and later the Gateway of India to the south. This formal organisation of open space provided a setting for imperial pageantry and processions.

The nucleus of the old city developed in the far south around commercial and manufacturing associated with the cotton textile industry. The administrative and commercial centre itself developed around the port while higher density residential development occurred in the western area. Suburban railway alignments formed the initial settlements with industrial concentrations, while the western areas initially evolved as dormitory suburbs. Gradually the areas became filled in, separating work place from residential areas, and leading to long-range commuting.

The Governor of Bombay between 1862 and 1867 was Sir Bartle Frere, and his term of office reflected a reformist dedication to both planning and empire building. He called for an invigorated city fabric "appealing in its complexity". This coincided with the demolition of the Fort and he produced a master plan that combined necessary development and service infrastructure with civic improvement. He also compiled a list of buildings to meet the requirements of civil and military administration. To implement this ambitious undertaking, Frere orchestrated large grants of money through the Bombay Special Fund. In order to provide building guidelines and implement construction works, the Public Works Department was amalgamated with the Royal Engineers. Under the direction of James Trubshawe a number of prominent British architects, who had honed their skills during the massive city building period in High Victorian England, became involved in a dynamic phase of Bombay development. This necessitated the tempering of British Gothic Revival forms to address local climatic requirements, which created a

CRAWFORD MARKET, completed in 1865 was named after the municipal commissioner who prescribed planning and zoning laws for the city. The market was the result of a competition won by William Emerson, and located at a downtown intersection. A 40-metre high clock tower made it a local landmark and on the tympanums above three of the seven arched openings are sculptural reliefs by John Lockwood Kipling — part of an arts and crafts approach advocated by a new school of industrial arts.

uniquely distinct urban design. The use of Indian craftsmen and local materials also introduced a complex array of sculptured features. These details harmonised with the flamboyant prevailing neo-Gothic architectural style, providing distinction and occasionally idiosyncratic solutions to both design and utilitarian needs. The eclectic range of architectural styles and decorative devices were derived from broadly neo-Gothic imagery, strongly related to Edwardian Baroque in its early twentieth century manifestation, and occasionally absorbing Indo-Saracenic design sources.

The development of 'Frere Town' — the term used for the range of civic buildings within and around the old fort precinct in the 1860s — served both commercial and political needs. The walls and ramparts of the fort were dismantled, and new commercial and public buildings constructed along the esplanade. Buildings within the new precinct had to conform with design parameters relating to height, street width and continuity of frontage, and all works had to be completed within three years from the date of sale to ensure a coherent assemblage. Plans for the Central Business District were approved by the India Office for a variety of neo-Gothic and neo-Classical forms, and construction specifications were set out, to which all building owners had to conform. Sample elevations were prepared as guidelines to ensure 'a certain extent of uniformity'. One of the must durable buildings was the Esplanade Hotel with its multi-storey prefabricated cast-iron frame, which underlined the experimental nature of colonial building. It was designed by a British engineer, Rowland Mason Ordish, as a set of prefabricated parts based on ideas from London's Crystal Palace. It was tied together with wrought iron girders, and windows were covered by Venetian louvres.

It still stands today as Mahendra Mansion. Other major buildings designed towards the end of the nineteenth century were the Bombay Municipal Corporation Building, the first Stock Exchange, the Victoria Terminus, the Central India Railway Headquarter, the High Court and the Standard Chartered Bank Building. Together they continue to present an assembly of some of the most advanced architectural design of their time in terms of craftsmanship, external expression and collective cityscape.

Until the mid-nineteenth century the land tenure system that dated back to ancient dynasties, and the feudal Portuguese system of land administration, inferred customary rights that made coherent land organisation difficult. In order to impose land use control the British administration had to undertake detailed land surveys, which in many cases necessitated political intervention over established interests and practices. Cadastral

4   Dossal, M, *Mumbai: 1660 to Present Times*, Oxford University Press, Oxford, 2010

5   Evenson, N, *The Indian Metropolis – A View Toward the West*, Yale University Press, London and New Haven, 1989

The Edwardian Baroque style was associated with many Bombay buildings after 1900, including the Orient Club on the Chowpatty Seaface built in 1910.

localities through better urban planning. Their aims were: decongestion of the worst areas, improved ventilation, and provision of additional housing for the urban poor. It was the first organisation in the city to carry out reclamation and control land development through neighbourhood design and new road construction. These measures opened up new spatial corridors, including the north-south Sydenham Road, and the east-west Princess Street and Sandhurst Road that linked suburban residential estates with the central business district. During its 35-year existence it reclaimed some 539 hectares on the western edge of the city and set out by-laws to regulate urban design.

Low cost housing was characterised by the *chawl* or multi-storey building of five to seven storeys, which were often added to illegally. The best chawls were built in brick or concrete under the auspices of the City Improvement Trust. A typical dwelling would be around ten square metres, with an enclosed verandah for bathing.[5] By 1938, the trust had built around 2,600 permanent buildings, contributing to the dense urban fabric of the city which was embodied in its street design. With greater land use intensity it became evident that a planning authority was essential to co-ordinate new and long-term infrastructure, port and industrial developments in order to prevent the more haphazard organisation of land uses. An important part of the development strategy, which was linked to the improved rail network, was to extend development to the north. Proposals in 1908 from the then Governor for the development of "New Bombay", included the Back Bay reclamation and Salsette Island, controlled by the East India Company.

The development of the northern suburbs in the early twentieth century took place among separate municipal administrations and was connected to the southern business district and industrial sites by rail. This led

surveys were carried out between 1811 and 1918, and reveal a difficult transformation of customary rights into a more rational land market, but one that underscores the patchwork quality of early development patterns.[4] Shortage of land and inefficiencies of use are a thread that runs through the history of urban design in the city, leading to both urban sprawl and incompatible juxtapositions. The Bombay Trust was founded in 1873 and commenced a process of wet and dry dock construction (including the Sassoon Dock), encouraging ancillary uses

such as manufacturing and godowns.

Workers in the cotton mills and docks lived in deplorable conditions with little drainage or sewerage, making the city vulnerable to the bubonic plague that arrived in 1896. Compulsory segregation of the afflicted created panic and led to a population exodus. Resistance to medical measures and civic neglect also led to urban violence, and eventually to the establishment of the Bombay City Improvement Trust in 1898, which was charged with opening up the congested and insanitary labyrinthine

The Chowpatti Waterfront

to the designation of Greater Bombay, which now occupies some 4,335 square kilometres, including the island, Trombay to the west and the southern part of Salsette to the north of Mahim Bay.

The Back Bay Reclamation Company was established in the 1860s with the intention of reclaiming the entire bay from Malabar Hill to the end of Colaba. This was finally completed around a hundred years later by the Bombay Development Department. It was set up in 1920 to implement plans to co-ordinate transport, tenement housing and open space, and extend commercial development in an arc facing the Malabar Hills. The legacies of this are Nariman Point, Cuffe Parade and the new Marine Drive. The latter was not completed until 1940 in a much modified form as a corniche, bounded by a consistent line of residential blocks forming an identifiable feature overlooking the bays — these later became eclipsed by commercial skyscrapers.

After 1900 the combination of neo-Gothic, Edwardian Baroque and Renaissance Revival styles for civic buildings began to decline. Urban design thereafter began to assume

a greater political significance with the growth of new nationalist movements. A new architectural sensibility was required, and there were calls for civic reform, harmonious and 'green' design of city quarters, and landmark public buildings — views widely promoted at the time by luminaries such as Patrick Geddes and Ebenezer Howard. A design renaissance to promote Indian architectural styles was supported by the new Indian Institute of Architects, set up in Bombay in 1929.

The notion of an overall master plan for the city, based on land use zoning sensitive to the topography, was first put forward by P.P. Kapadia in 1939, with the western foreshore earmarked for predominantly residential development, and the eastern shore for docks and industry. Between these areas, sites would be allocated for bazaars, markets and workshop industry. At this time the population was 1.4 million, and on the eve of Independence conditions became more acute as Partition refugees flocked into the city, putting an even greater strain on services and utilities, and also inflating land prices. The objective of the 1948 Master Plan for the

city was to relieve congestion by co-ordinated expansion incorporating new satellite towns, and limiting urban densities while shifting industry, together with noxious trades, to new areas.

THE MODERN CITY

Over the past two centuries, the natural geographies of the mountainous Borivali National Park and extensive areas of marshland and water have dictated the pattern of urbanisation, which has spread along development corridors within Maharashtra State. This formed a triangle of growth between the cities of Nasik, Pune and Mumbai. The Greater Metropolitan Region of Mumbai is centred around Salsette Island and extends to Thane in the north-east, Navi Mumbai in the east and the new Jawaharlal Nehru Port in the south.

Post-independence Bombay was primed for planned expansion to cater for a massive increase in population and to counteract the lack of development control. The 1948 Master Plan proposed the expansion of Greater Bombay to incorporate the northern suburbs, forging a more balanced distribution

⁶ Dossal, 2010, op. cit., p216

Continuity of tradition — an older townhouse in the Malabar Hills projects an articulate assembly of different fenestration elements brought together through indigenous building skills.

affordable housing for workers and nodes of development along mass transit routes. It included the deep-draught Jawaharlal Nehru Port with extended warehousing and oil storage facilities. Overall however, the notion of a "new" Bombay has experienced difficulties competing with the 'old', which continues to generate more employment opportunities, as populations densities have continued to rise. Realisation of planning initiatives has been slow, and subject to the critical issues of housing need and a fluctuating economic base. The shifting influences of urban growth and stagnation have themselves contributed to a dilemma of intensive overcrowding on one hand and underutilisation on the other. 50 per cent of the population live on only 8 per cent of the land. This perennially contested urbanism can be attributed to a variety of factors — from post-colonial attempts to re-align the city's economic base in the wake of global competition, to the incrementalism built into its reclamation and regeneration agenda in the face of continued population growth.

The shifting ecologies of Mumbai lie at the heart of its patterns of urbanisation. Historically, the role of water in the city was part of its culture, and its mobility. It also underscored its urbanisation. Water management remains a key issue, and the shortage of potable water is problematic.

Today, certain critical issues continue to confront the dual objective of meeting need, particularly housing, and coherent urban design. Of almost 1,400 hectares of land identified for low-income housing, only 213 hectares has been acquired, but then not used for public purposes. This can partly be ascribed to the Urban Land Ceiling Regulation Act, passed in 1976 to help ensure a more equitable distribution of land in the urban areas.⁶ Its repeal in 2007 did little to make additional land available for low and medium income families, and land prices have increased exponentially with multi-

of population, industry and employment opportunities commensurate with new rail corridors. However urban regeneration continued to be piecemeal, hampered by an inequitable distribution of land.

Bombay's urban design has a quixotic materialism based on its concentration of wealth juxtaposed with pockets of extreme poverty. The city's physical form under the Raj has changed little since Independence, as the old property laws have effectively limited opportunities for urban regeneration. Victorian Bombay lives on in the Gothic Revival and Indo-Saracenic eccentricity of its institutional buildings and its downtown commercial hub built around the defunct foundations of Fort George.

The idea of a 'Greater Bombay' was conceived in the 1960s with the advent of 'Navi' or new Bombay, primarily as a response to overcrowding of the old city. The new city was designed by a team led by Charles Correa, for a population of two million people, and required extensive reclamation of Thane Creek. It was planned to accommodate new commercial and industrial development with

7 Sita, K, 'Mumbai : A Global City in Making', in *Million Cities of India*, Eds. Rameshwar Prasad Misra and Kamlesh Misra, Sustainable Development Foundation, Delhi, 1998

Different levels of use are reflected in a stacked vocabulary of design components.

national investment. These problems have been compounded by factory closures, firstly the decline of cotton textile production, followed in the 1980s by wider manufacturing industry with its unique working institutions. The sale and redevelopment of mill sites in the face of efforts to reclaim these lands for public use have similarly led to further marginalisation of the poor and unemployed. The dismantling of the older industrial buildings — which have high heritage value embedded within the collective memory of the city — has partly resulted in legal battles between stakeholders, and redevelopment for high-end uses. The decline of the older docklands and the relocation of facilities to the Nhava-Sheva islands has technically made available a large amount of land along the eastern seaboard, including the Prince's and Victoria Docks which are in a state of decay. Urban design plans have been put forward that could rejuvenate and re-orient the city waterfront, just as has happened in other cities that have experienced dock closures. A further opportunity is the expiration of salt pan leases in the eastern suburbs that could potentially provide land for both public housing and open space to relieve city shortfalls.

While there is a large amount of under-utilised railway infrastructure, the suburban railway carries around 6.3 million passengers daily in 2046 trains. The Mumbai Urban Transport Project is partly funded by the World Bank as a means of integrating rail and road initiatives, increasing capacity and improving the environment. At the same time the city is activating a scheme to move major city functions from South Mumbai to Navi Mumbai.

The city core incorporates the nucleus of the colonial settlement including the fort area, which forms the administrative and commercial centre. Commercial development is clustered around the dockland areas while high-density residential development characterises the old inner areas of Girguan, Khetwadi and Dhobi Talao.[7] In general, commercial development has encroached on other land uses in the core business district creating an agglomeration of business uses extending south to Nariman Point. North of the business district, the bazaar area in the old native quarters of Girguan and Masjid

While a "pattern book" approach based on a cross-cultural design language was established at an intellectual level by architectural historians, the street fabric of downtown Bombay contains a more casual mix of stylistic and decorative references, assembled informally.

is characterised by a mix of high density shopping and residential areas together with small-scale manufacturing and engineering establishments. Markets are concentrated in specialised districts such as Lohar (tinkers') Bazaar, Zaveri (goldsmiths') Bazaar, or Chor Bazaar (thieves market).

Major concentrations of population and economic activities have given rise to problems of congestion with severe strains on transport and infrastructure — flows of people and goods are channelled through a restricted number of traffic arteries. As city boundaries were periodically extended, decentralisation has become a central platform of planning policy with new concentrated zones for heavy industry, dispersed processing zones, industrial estates and technology parks. The emphasis is on establishing an east-west axis of development and a new bridge link across Thane Creek to link Trombay with "New

Mumbai" on the mainland.

The Metropolitan Plan of 1973 divided the region into four zones for industrial development, although these were later modified. These programmes have produced a broadly poly-nucleated structure within the metropolitan area through new and expanded urban centres, although the operational area of the core city has also expanded. The resulting urban sprawl and fragmentation of activity limits the degree to which the expanding city can be knitted together through planned development, and has deflected urban-industrial and business growth into sub-regional centres, which act as counter magnets.

Areas of disused or redundant uses technically provide an opportunity to recalibrate both the structure of the city and its urban landscape. This could be achieved through new transport infrastructure linked

to development spines while creating green corridors that contain flood protection measures, water purification reservoirs and ecological rehabilitation of wetlands. Until 1990, around 243 hectares of factory space was dedicated to textile manufacture, mainly in the Girangoon area. However with a downturn in demand for textile yarn and a commensurate increase in land price, the government of Maharastra announced that redevelopment of factory areas would be permitted subject to certain conditions. The latter were related to public gain, with an emphasis on integrated development, new housing and employment opportunities for workers. However a drastic paring down of development conditions led to prolonged litigation and a Supreme Court ruling that effectively negated the validity of pubic interest, and acted to promote rampant real estate development and land speculation.

HORNIMAN CIRCLE was designed by James Scott and constructed in 1864 within the renovated fort. Prior to independence it was called Elphinstone Circle, and named after Lord Elphinstone, Governor of Bombay between 1853 and 1860. It was built around a circular park in a similar form to the eighteenth century urban design of certain British cities. It provided a covered arcade — a climatically sensible device, which came to characterise the commercial centre.

A significant amount of Mumbai's old industrial architecture has therefore been demolished, and only eleven out of fifty-eight old mill areas remain in operation, set within a profusion of poorly integrated private development projects. It is a painful reminder that the urban shift to a service economy inevitably reinforces wide disparities within the population and a displacement of its poorest class. This continues to take a highly physical and visual form in Mumbai.

Decommissioned 'brownfield' industrial sites, railway yards and docklands represent contested voids in an otherwise dense urban framework, but embedded in the social and economic history of the city. These elements, given their strategic locations, have the potential to regenerate the urban landscape. Contested urban space continues to form the focus of professional action groups and citizen initiatives. In addition to need, environmental

issues remain a threat. Indiscriminate land reclamation of low-lying areas, filling in of salt pans and ad hoc construction in vulnerable areas limit monsoon storm run-off and cause periodic flooding. Bombay remains an example of the need for firm regulatory and enforcement provisions as an essential corollary to urban design. Inter-tidal wetlands, which absorb the force of tidal flows and provide natural habitats, continue to be reclaimed in spite of 1991 regulations intended to selectively limit development activities in coastal areas within 500 metres of the high tide line. Private operators tap into groundwater supply resulting in irreparable damage to the water table and an increased salinity of wells.

Since the early 1990s vertical growth of the city has taken place largely in relation to a steady increase in the Floor Space Index, which equates site coverage with plot ratio

but not necessarily civic infrastructure — a common cause of concern in Asia's fast redeveloping cities. Initiatives to increase housing stock have included: integration of 'affordable housing' as a means of achieving greater density; and joint ventures to redevelop older housing blocks with a building mix and greater amenities. However supply-side constraints and ambiguous land ownership issues have created a model for ever-increasing values. The city is rich in history but its urban design is closely meshed with continued marginalisation of the poor and unemployed. Its transformation from a small colonial port city to a megacity has left a legacy of distinctive localised environments and places. Reconciling long-standing problems is a difficult but necessary part of city growth and rejuvenation through strong urban management. Mumbai remains a city of urban resilience, civic monument and

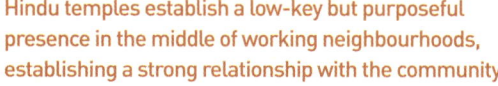
Hindu temples establish a low-key but purposeful presence in the middle of working neighbourhoods, establishing a strong relationship with the community.

considerable awareness of heritage, but also perennial challenge.

SLUM COMMUNITIES AND THE CASE OF DHARAVI

In 1995 a Slum Redevelopment Scheme was announced by the government involving the private sector under a 'land sharing' model — eligible slum dwellers would be re-housed in new tenements, and apartments built on cleared land for higher-income groups. However mobilisation of different resident and ethnic factions, coupled with community politics centred around inclusion and exclusion, have led to an atmosphere of socio-political uncertainty and caution. Inadequate resident records and physical surveys of actual plots have also made cooperation difficult. However the main factor is lack of a credible public policy. This has complicated the fundamental objective of improving living conditions for the poorest members of the

population, which is necessary to transform Mumbai into a world-class city. Today around 60 per cent of Mumbai's population of 16 million live in squatter colonies.

The largest slum settlement, Dharavi, began life as a fishing village on Bombay Island. It became the location of leather tanneries and its population grew through migration of low-caste workers who could only afford makeshift housing. In the 1960s the ghetto had grown to 175 hectares, occupying a central location, including land along the railway lines and around the older village cores and *chawls*. Dharavi is noted for its mix of independent Hindu and Muslim communities, with contiguous quarters that reflect different ethnic communities and languages. It also houses both residential and industrial space, including leather production, food preparation and waste recycling, and a potters' colony — the Kumbharwada.

Investment in infrastructure over the years has been negligible. Planning interventions in the 1960s focussed on solutions to the problems of overcrowding and the massive numbers of rail commuters, by moving industry into the northern suburbs and satellite towns. The result was the institutional planning of the metropolitan region and a tendency towards ambitious large-scale projects such as Navi Bombay, which proposed relocating state government offices through a new Development Corporation. The plan followed a linear form incorporating new residential townships, but a steep escalation in land prices allowed market forces to dictate the pace of change, therefore the ambitions were realised only as variegated parts. In the 1990s, industrial reorganisation contributed to the decline of large-scale manufacturing, with labour redirected to a reinvigorated informal workshop sector within the dense urban

Complementary forces — the spiritual collides with secular street frontage

neighbourhoods. Because of surrounding high land values, the area adjoining Dharavi became defined by high-rise blocks creating something of an urban anomaly.

In 2006 plans were put forward by the government of Maharashtra to redevelop Dharavi, which by this time contained more than 57,000 makeshift dwellings spread over 223 hectares — accounting for only eight per cent of the slum areas of Mumbai. The intention was to divide the area into five distinct neighbourhoods, each provided with municipal services. To attract financial support, the government offered developers a plot ratio of four times the individual plot size. However comprehensive regeneration required 70 per cent resident approval and came into conflict with the residents' wishes to retain the mixed land-use, economic patterns and livelihoods within the area. Therefore only pockets of development and utility infrastructure have been carried out.

Mumbai's open-air Dhobi Ghat — the traditional laundry of the city covers ten hectares. Clothes are delivered to the Ghat through narrow lanes by handcart. Dhobiwallahs soak each item in rows of tanks, beat them on flat stones and dry them on bridges.

INDIA Delhi

IN THE NINETEENTH AND EARLY TWENTIETH CENTURIES a classical revival in Europe was adopted in many colonial cities in Asia, and emphasised in major public building programmes. The new capital of India — New Delhi — created an unprecedented opportunity for an imperial vision of grand-scale urban design. It was designed by Edwin Lutyens and Herbert Baker to encapsulate an "eternal" concept of British sovereignty. The new imperial city was inaugurated in 1931 at which time British rule over India was nearing its inevitable end. It was five times as large as the old city, with main government buildings positioned on axial vistas, and a spatial order focused on Government House (now Parliament House) designed by Lutyens, symmetrically lined by the Secretarial buildings designed by Baker.

This drawing shows the Asokan columns in Government Court between the two Secretariats, each adorned with the emblems of a Dominion. Behind is the Dome of the South Block.

CANADA

INDIA

MCMXXX

DELHI REPRESENTS THE SOMEWHAT SCHIZOPHRENIC RESIDUE of almost constant intervention and physical reinterpretation over a thousand years. The first Sultan of Delhi, Qutbuddin Aibak in 1192, commenced a building regime that continued through several dynasties, giving rise to forts, palaces, mosques and tombs, many of which are still marked by scattered historical traces.

Over five hundred years two powers have largely contributed to its physical form and even its mode of operation, prior to Indian independence in 1947. The first of these was the Mughal Dynasty beginning in 1526, reaching its zenith with the construction of Shahjahanabad by Shah Jahan in 1638, which included the Red Fort, Jami Masjid and Fatehpuri Masjid. The second was the British colonial intervention and occupation beginning with the installation of the British Resident in Delhi in 1803 and virtually ending with the inauguration of New Delhi as the nation's capital. Because of early Muslim rule much of the remaining older architecture for military and religious buildings is Islamic, with a clearly expressed structure usually in ornamented masonry or stucco surface ornamentation.

The modern history of Delhi is one of displacement, where intervention carries political premise into a realm of representation and symbolism. The assertive imposition of monumental forms, disconnected from the rich Mughal residue of architectural traditions and city building, marks a special page in the politically inspired transformation of the colonial landscape — a collision of cultural forces rather than interaction, where the narrative of imperial representation through ordering of space was deliberately disengaged from historical continuity.

THE MUGHAL CITY

It is said that Delhi was built five times over the millennium preceding the city of

CHANDNI CHOWK forms the main street running between the Red Fort in the east and Fatehpuri Masjid in the west. Jahan Area, a daughter of Shahjahan, laid down the planning framework in 1639. The Chowk was developed in four parts: the Urdu Bazaar with the Lal Mandir Jain Temple founded in 1656; the Kotwali incorporating the Sunehri Masjid built in 1721; the Asharfi Bazaar from the Kotwali to the Town Hall, also named the Faiz Bazaar after the canal that ran through the Chowk opening out to a pool in the centre of the octagonal square; and westward to the Fatehpuri Masjid. The Chandni Sarai to the north of the square was an extravagant lodging and gathering place for merchant travellers built by the daughter of Shajahan in 1739. By the mid-nineteenth century Chandni Chowk formed the main commercial thoroughfare in Delhi, lined with arcaded two-storey shops. Besides being the most opulent street in the city, it also formed a processional route. The remainder of Shahjahabad grew in a relatively organic way through the allocation of sites for *havelis*, gardens, temples, mosques, shrines and monuments dedicated to different faiths. Around these were clustered hundreds of smaller dwellings — the houses of tradesmen and artisans, along with apartments for servants and storerooms.

THE SPATIAL STRUCTURE OF DELHI has been shaped by a series of complex forces reflecting the accrued imprints of successive rulers, pre-Mughal history, the Raj and large-scale urban expansion in the post-colonial period. While there have been major shifts in the city framework and the National Capital Territory, the indigenous city still fulfils an important commercial role, and all major occupational activities are concentrated in the old bazaar areas such as Chandni Chowk, Paharganj and Naya Bazaar.

Shahjahanabad. Shah Jahan assumed the Mughal throne in 1628 and is best known for the erection of the Taj Mahal in Agra. Following this he moved his entire court to Delhi and founded the city of Shahjahanabad, to the north of older city remains. As the sovereign city of the Mughal empire during the seventeenth century, the urban design of Delhi was framed around *haveli* — the courtyard mansions and gardens belonging to princes and merchants. These walled complexes made up separate and well defined neighbourhoods to the west of the Qila Mubarak — the king's palace within the fort. Chandni Chowk bisected the city, running between the palace and the Ajmeri Gate, and the Jami'ah Masjid occupied a central place in the city to the south-west of the palace. The *haveli* comprised a complex arrangement of spaces, residential clusters and artisan activities in different quarters, as part of an extended "family" under the patronage of each patriarch, who had authority over an entire neighbourhood through land grants. Master masons or *mistri* traditionally fulfilled a role similar to master builders in Victorian England, where skilled craftsmen, masons and stoneworkers formulated details based on a common design vocabulary and customary use. Walls were punctuated by carved balconies — *jharokā*, and lattice-work screens — *jāli*. Streets were named after the prominent patriarchs, which extended their community identity. In 1803 the British laid siege to the city, displaced the Mughal Emperor Shah Alam II, and went on to occupy the old fort. After the British occupation in 1803 and during the reign of the last Mughal emperor, Bahader Shah, a new merchant and professional class emerged that constructed many of the smaller *havelis*, with caste- or trade-based streets and neighbourhoods or mohullas made up of narrow alleyways.

Jyoti Hosagrahar observes that the Archaeological Survey of India, carried

1 Hosagrahar, J, *Indigenous Modernities: Negotiating Architecture and Urbanism*, Routledge, London and New York, 2005, p9

out by the British in 1867, gave primacy to isolated monuments and stylistic traits. This obscured the complexities associated with the morphology of the city and its cultural transformation, whereas the British deliberately reshaped urban space through a Victorian preoccupation with social and spatial differentiation.[1] While the Mughal city survived relatively intact until the British siege of 1857 following the Sepoy Mutiny, new housing was injected into the evolving pattern of mercantile development, which gradually overwhelmed the old *haveli* cityscape. The previously self-contained neighbourhoods were loosely sub-divided into a fragmented arrangement of residential blocks. Much of the land and property was appropriated and subdivided by the British, and then redistributed to those who had been loyal during the insurgency. Much of the eastern city edge was turned into a Cantonment, and all buildings within 500 metres of the city walls were demolished,

A NUMBER OF PALACE STRUCTURES lie along the eastern edge overlooking the Yamuna River: the Mumtaz-Mahal, Rang-Mahal, Khas-Mahal, Muttamman-Burj, Diwan-i-Khas, the Hamman and Hira Mahal, located on a raised marble platform. The pavilions served different functions and although much damage was done during the military occupation, their previous decoration and gilding has been restored. Water from the Yamuna River was pumped via marble channels, ornamented pools and fountains through the various pavilions and into a fountain in the Rang-Mahal. It was known as the nahr-i-bihislot river of paradise. The Muthamman-Burj was the setting for a daily ceremony — darshan — where the emperor appeared daily in front of the people; a ceremony duplicated by King George V at the Coronation Durbar of 1911.

The Hayat-Bakhsh garden was made up of lawns divided by water channels. Two pavilions known as the Sanan and Bhadon stand in the garden, providing a delicate foreground to a series of barrack blocks, which were built by the British to house troops stationed within the city with little regard for historical values.

The Red Fort from Chandni Chowk

THE FATEHPURI MASJID was built in 1650 by Nawab Fatehpuri Begum, a wife of Shah Jahan. It terminates the western end of Chandni Chowk. It is entered through cusped arched gateways on the north, south and eastern sides. Single and double storey apartments were used as arcaded shops around the courtyard. It was sold to a private bank after 1857 but was later restored to the Muslim Community and became a venue for religious and political meetings. The Gododia Market or Kivana Merchants Spice Market established in the early twentieth century, adjoins the Fatehpuri Masjid and forms a mixed commercial and residential court with access from the Khaori Baoli Bazaar.

reducing the habitable area by around one-third. Loss of income meant that buildings fell into disrepair and were converted to form a new morphology of street-oriented commercial avenues comprising shops, workshops and warehouses. These retained the carved entrance gateways, but with truncated mansion blocks and courtyards to the rear. The evolving framework gave rise to a new mercantile class accompanied by the formation of guilds, speciality bazaars and professional services. Thus the older framework of buildings and spaces were subject to constant conversion and infill. They became progressively fragmented to accommodate large numbers of people, while the courtyards became shared open space. Consequently the old *haveli* cityscape gradually disappeared.

In the latter part of the nineteenth century, planned interventions in the old city by the British fundamentally changed its older morphology. Streets were widened, and the ruler's palace converted into a military garrison, becoming known as the Red Fort. Almost one-third of the city was demolished,

with mansions and mosques cleared. Massive clearances were necessary for the new railroad constructed on an east-west alignment in the 1870s, an arterial road, institutional buildings and municipal infrastructure. In the remainder of the old city, an increasingly wealthy merchant class began to regenerate some of the deteriorated or abandoned buildings but to a reduced size, introducing a new vocabulary of European architectural elements and decoration, with neo-Classical columned porticos, pediments, pilasters, wrought iron balconies and stained glass.

The reinterpretation of the robust urban structure reinforced a symbolic association between the older *haveli*, and an emerging and progressive social order. In the process it facilitated a transition from the feudal state to a new entrepreneurial class by the early twentieth century.

With the gradual transformation of the walled city, British civilians moved to a separate quarter — the "Civil Lines" — laid out along wide streets with one and two storey bungalows in a landscaped suburbia. This technically represented a more spacious

The Jami-Masjid

and healthy type of settlement, in contrast with the prevailing deteriorating and unhygienic conditions in the old city. Many Indian professionals employed by the British also moved to the Civil Lines, establishing a complex economic interdependency but also a widening social and cultural gulf with the indigenous city.

THE RED FORT

The chief architect of the Palace was Ustad Ahmad Lahori who worked directly for Sha Jahan. He had previously worked on the Taj Mahal, and introduced a design fusion of Islamic, Persian, Timurid and Hindu styles. It is linked to the western city by the remaining Lahori and Delhi Gates — both of which are aligned to the cities they face, and to Salingarh Fort to the north. By the time of the siege in 1857, the public part of the fort in the west had became much like the city outside. The British occupied the fort and cleared a number of Mughal buildings in order to build barrack blocks, which still remain. In 2004 the Indian Army, which had occupied the fort after independence, turned it over to the

Archaeological Survey of India.

The Lahori Gate facing Chandni Chowk serves as the principal and ceremonial gate. It is a three-storey structure flanked by towers, crowned by open pavilions and integrates a row of *Chhatris*.

The Naubat-Khama stands at the entrance to the palace area and formed the formal entrance to the Diwan-i-Am. Drums were played at propitious times, and only the most important visitors and processions were allowed to use it. Floral designs were carved into the red sandstone. After 1857 the building served as a residence for British officers, before its later restoration.

Two years after completion of the Palace, work began on the Jami-Masjid directly to the west. It was constructed from the same red sandstone as the fort, and raised on a high plinth with three wide flights of steps leading up to the north, south and main east gates. At courtyard level they are linked on three sides by pillared colonnades marked by domed pavilions at each corner, allowing views of the surrounding city. Although it serves as the congregational venue for Friday prayers, it was

also an important commercial centre with a daily market. The spaces around the mosque are still used for much the same purpose.

The Diwan-i-Am or "hall of public audience" is a central feature of the complex, open on three sides with *chajjas* straddling the outer walls. Although the structure is of red sandstone, it was originally overlain with shell plaster and polished ivory. The marble canopy, under which the emperor held court, is set against the east wall, decorated with inlay work by a Florentine jeweller who was also employed on the Taj Mahal. A number of decorative panels were removed by the British and only restored to their original position in 1903 at the insistence of the Viceroy, Lord Curzon.

NORTH DELHI AND THE CIVIL LINES

To the north of the Red Fort but within the walled city were the estates of the princes and courtiers, which were taken over by East India Company administrators after 1803. After 1857 the new railway alignment cleared a swathe through the Salimgarh Fort, severing the northern area and its

Delhi Railway Station

Maidens Hotel was the most stylish hotel in Delhi at the turn of the twentieth century, and built originally as a single storey structure. Edwin Lutyens and Herbert Baker stayed in the hotel on visits, while working on the architecture of New Delhi.

The Secretariat was designed by E Montague Thomas to accommodate government administrative functions prior to their re-location to New Delhi. Its central tower is flanked by two low blocks and domed end pavilions. The building now houses the Delhi State Assembly.

Kashmiri Gate entrance from the remainder of the Old City. The area was the centre of Britain's administration until the completion of New Delhi, and still houses early colonial residences and college buildings. St Stephens College built in 1891 now houses the Election Commission offices. With British settlement in North Delhi, Kashmiri Gate was a major link with the Old City, now reinvigorated by the adjoining rail interchange.

Delhi Railway Station was built in the 1870s, along with the new rail line, on land cleared by the British to the north of the Town Hall. Across the road were railway staff quarters. The crenellated towers and pointed arches had no precedent in Delhi, combining both Gothic and Mughal characteristics.

Further to the north the vast British military cantonment was constructed in 1828 and became the setting for the Durbars, where in 1911 the announcement was made to move the capital from Calcutta to Delhi. After 1857 the European community moved from the Old City to the Civil Lines while the military occupied the Red Fort. Prior to the completion of New Delhi, the northern area became the temporary capital and the area still personifies the spatial residential setting, government establishments and colonial architecture of some of the remaining buildings — Ludlow Castle, Maidens Hotel and the Old Secretariat

(designed by E Montague Thomas in 1912) that now houses the Delhi State Assembly. Older government buildings have now been taken over for institutional and educational uses, including Delhi University. The area remains a leafy, tranquil area with new and large houses sitting in spacious grounds amidst occasional Mughal remains and the faded remnants of colonial bungalows.

INTERVENTIONS IN PUBLIC SPACE

The concept of public space was at the centre of colonial planning, but its secular identity was associated with a formality related to orthogonal forms, visual corridors and symbols of order and authority, in contrast to the traditional notion of space for gathering and discourse. Thus public space was overlaid with a contested meaning, and government sponsored secular buildings superceded the traditional priority accorded to temples, mosques and madrassas.

The intricate web of spaces and pedestrian routes in the old city became increasingly narrow and privatised as public space gave way to private face-to-face interaction, and where territorial control was important. As in other Indian cities, the administration spent much time on surveys aimed at identifying individual holdings in the face of boundaries that had been created informally over

centuries. Constant adaptation and building extensions had produced a system where both private and community interests were inter-related, dictated by benevolence, custom and social status.

In 1848 a public health act was passed in Britain which placed great emphasis on government intervention to improve poor environmental conditions and slum housing. At the same time planning theorists proposed model cities with housing layouts that emphasised public health, and were taken up by enlightened industrialists in northern British cities, for example at Port Sunlight and Saltaire. For nineteenth century Europeans this related to scientific progress and enlightenment, and indirectly to the "civilizing mission" in their colonies. In a similar way to Napoleon III's restructuring of the old city of Paris (in part to improve sanitary conditions but also to ensure effective policing), public health reform in Delhi entailed large-scale eradication of the congested fabric both for sanitation and security in the name of essential welfare. The major clearance around the Red Fort that contained some of the grandest *haveli* and mosques, spared the Dariba gold and silver bazaar between the Jami Masjid and Chandni Chowk where it remains today. The clearance was also a punitive and politically inspired

CONSTRUCTION OF SHAHJAHANABAD, the old walled city of Delhi, began in 1638, supervised by an architecturally minded emperor. The Red Fort or Lal Qila was built on the banks of the Yamuna River, separated from the city itself by a moat. The city was polygonal in plan, and the palace within the fort consisted of various marble pavilions overlooking the river. The city itself contained the mansions or *havelis* of princes and senior courtiers, each set within walled compounds which were virtually self-contained in terms of each household's needs, with large courts and gardens. The main streets were lined with arcades and developed as specialist bazaars for independent merchants. Interspersed with these were mosques, temples and inns, and a canal brought in water from the northern suburbs to serve both the main bazaar, Chandni Chowk, and the palace. The number of mosques and temples testifies to both the wealth and religious commitment within the city, although there were gradual social changes.

FOLLOWING THE BRITISH SIEGE of the city in 1857, architectural styles took on more European features and decorations, seen today in the carved stone street doorways. An almost continuous building and redevelopment programme from that time, reinforced by refugees following Partition, made Old Delhi the most populous and congested city in India. Complicated infill development and intimate patterns of linkage and connection, carved out of the older built framework, form passageways that often open out into courtyards entered through the original doorways. At the same time much of the new housing growth in south and west Delhi dates from this period, but since then multi-occupation has led to an almost indecipherable interlocking of blocks, spaces and access routes. The old city is still broadly structured through its main routes, focussed on the old fourteen gates of which only the Delhi Gate to the southeast, Ajmeri Gate to the south-west, the Turkman Gate to the south, Kashmiri Gate to the north, and Nigambodh Gate to the north-east have escaped demolition.

cordon sanitaire aimed at nobles who had supported the Indian mutiny. The systematic process of demolition and reconstruction ensured that compensation was paid to each affected owner, and confiscated properties were auctioned so that the process effectively changed the old established social composition.

In the southern part of the city, the informal street and courtyard system was rationalised as far as possible under British occupation, influenced by a reforming zeal redolent of Victorian England. An informal system of negotiating property boundaries and construction work was largely replaced by new by-laws which regulated physical height, width and building projections, but also private encroachments of public space such as the traditional covered passage or *chatta*. New building work was made subject to municipal approval, and advance notification of events was required to enable street space to be used for religious rituals, pageants and celebratory processions.

This process of intervention over the rights of space and passage was, in practice, a matter of negotiation with the authorities, and while officially structures could be demolished, officialdom was generally placated by compensatory fines, some of them extortionate. Similarly street vendors and shops with extended street displays were subject to payment of rent to the municipality.

By the turn of the twentieth century, Delhi had two distinct and highly differentiated sides — imposed formal layouts through municipal interventions, and the traditional footprints of indigenous residential neighbourhoods. In practice, given the nature of colonisation, each was dependent on the other. Changes in the structure of society redefined the interpretation of public space through a gradual reconstitution of uses. New spatial forms and redefined spaces continued to be contested and mediated, with a plurality of appropriated functions and meanings

2 Hosagrahar, 2005, op. cit.
3 Hosagrahar, J, 'Negotiated
   Modernities: Symbolic Terrains
   of Housing in Delhi', in *Colonial
   Modernities*, Eds. Peter Scriver
   and Vikramaditya Prakash,
   Routledge, 2007

underlining the different cultural and economic standpoints.

In old Delhi, the channelling of water was seen as both a necessary utility and a landscape element. The narrow Faiz canal or *naheer* channelled water along the centre of Chandni Chowk and along the Faiz Bazaar from the fourteenth century Tughluq canal to the north, which historically supplied water to the fort, palaces and gardens in the city.[2] The Municipal Committee divided the city into twelve wards to best implement public health measures, road maintenance and installation of the complicated network of supply pipes, but this was expensive. Protests over taxes to pay for the measures led to delays, and priority was given to the Civil Lines and the cantonments. Even in 1931 only five per cent of people in the old city were served by the new water system. At the same time environmental controls redefined the city and assigned new values to it, centred around a cultural interpretation of health standards and regulatory responsibilities.

The spatial separation of European and indigenous populations was limited by a local administrative elite who moved from the walled city to the newer enclaves, while the older urban framework became gradually more overcrowded. An overriding urban design factor was the political agenda of modernisation to enhance the image of a benevolent empire, justified by municipal control and intervention, and coupled with an idealised vision of "order" linked to the health of the city. However new housing areas gradually came to assume similar characteristics of the old city, reflecting extended family and employment ties.[3]

By the end of the nineteenth century, new transport infrastructure and industrial expansion, together with agriculture reforms, contributed to the city's growth as a commercial centre. However clearances within the city and the 500 metres wide military zone around the outer walls constrained opportunities for planned development. There was thus a dual demand for a rationalised form of urban renewal within the city and a need for urban expansion.

At the time around one-third of residents lived in improvised settlements outside the city walls, with access through the Lahore Gate. In 1888 the gate was demolished and the city government overcame military obstacles to extend the city across the previous no-building zone. The "model" plan that was put into effect was the Lahore Gate Improvement Scheme, originally envisaged as a long commercial avenue. The Sadar Bazaar and Grand Parade was extended westwards, linking Chandni Chowk with a central square facilitating the development of a new business centre with adjoining residential uses. Land was divided into regular lots based on a set market price, providing an impetus to private development. The locational and logistical advantages of Delhi, as part of an emerging city building and railway network during the late nineteenth century, led to it becoming a major rail hub, distribution and commercial centre, linked to an extensive hinterland. This in turn attracted textile industry so that by 1911 it had a population of 230,000. Escalating land values reflected a shift from the older trading centre to Kishengunj in the

THE DELHI MUNICIPAL COMMITTEE, established in 1863, was charged with civic improvements. One of its first interventions was the construction of the Delhi Institute which later became the Town Hall. It was located adjacent to an octagonal central space on Chandni Chowk, in place of the Chandni Sarai, creating a prominent visual focus in a neo-Classical style. A "figure-ground" plan of interlocking spaces that emphasised sequential spatial experience was thus replaced by a formal building as a space occupier in an axial composition with the Victoria Clock Tower. This symbolically re-emphasised the city core, exerting a sense of civic dominance exemplified by the central statue of Queen Victoria, later replaced by one of Swami Shradhanand. In one symbolic piece of urban design, the authoritarian emphasis was re-focussed from the palace to the administrative centre, and the vibrancy of definition and multi-use replaced by an imposing space that subsequently served as a rallying ground for the independence movement.

west. However regulation was difficult, and a government commissioned report later led to the establishment of the Delhi Improvement Trust which aimed to co-ordinate land administration, and the means to enhance land management and value. A subsequent survey documented all buildings within the city limits as a baseline for future planning and a modernising landscape of planned communities.

THE IMPERIAL CITY: AN URBAN DESIGN OF POWER

At the turn of the twentieth century, a classical revival in Europe, propelled by the Ecole des Beaux-Arts in Paris, began to transform architectural approaches and transmit these with appropriate adaptations to colonial empires, including British India and French Indo-China. With the industrial revolution and the rewards of imperialism at their height, the new Baroque Classicism grew out of major public building programmes in British cities, and the requirement for an assertive but refined style was applied to a spate of new country houses. A timely urban design initiative in London was a new ceremonial route designed by Aston Webb between Buckingham Palace with its newly constructed classical façade, and Admiralty Arch at Trafalgar Square. Along with the Victoria Memorial, this heroic processional route reinforced the majesty of the imperial vision, with London and the monarch at the heart of empire.

The opportunity for a similar grandiose 'stage set' on which Indian representatives and British officials could enact the rituals and displays of power came in 1911 when, on a visit to celebrate his coronation, George V announced a transfer of the capital from Calcutta to Delhi. This was in part to escape the aftermath of Bengal partition in 1905, but perhaps also to exploit the Mughal historical associations with northern India,

SHAHJAHANABAD is the largest medieval city in India and is now a compact concentration of small manufacturing establishments, segregated by trade, and an enormous wholesale market that establishes a constant flow of products from workshops and showrooms to retail outlets by all means of transport. Interwoven with these are residential mohullas converted from the surviving *haveli*, layered in a three-dimensional interplay of rooms, stairways and platforms. A small number of *havelis* are still in single family occupation.

Shops that line the main bazaar streets form continual commercial frontages, with trading blocks having access to warehouse facilities off the main streets. Housing has assumed a spatial hierarchy with merchant's homes above shops along principal avenues, with more cramped accommodation off the secondary street system where continuous accretions of building additions and roof terraces have created increasingly dense quarters. Wholesale areas maintain a relationship with the traditional urbanism and manufacturing trades.

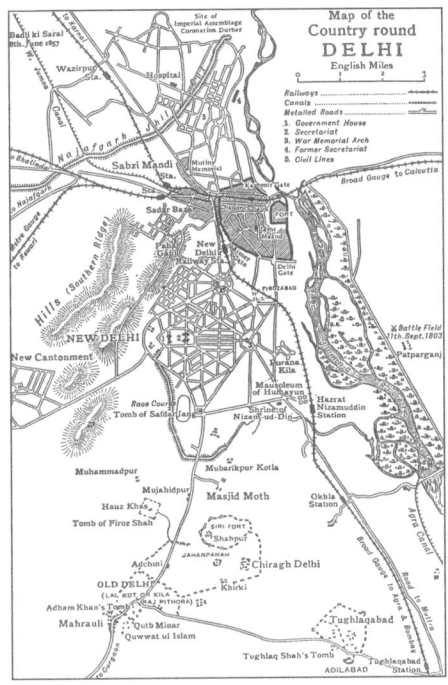

with a new Imperial administrative service housed among historical Mughal settlements, tombs and mosques. A town planning committee was set up, headed by George Swinton, Chairman of the London County Council, and an early decision was made to build what was effectively a new city on a south-west axis from the Ajmeri Gate.

The viceroy, Lord Hardinge, determined that whatever the available Indian models, the architecture should be essentially symbolic in its representation. Eventually Edwin Lutyens, a committed champion of the refined Beaux-Arts approach, was appointed as Chief Architect, assisted by Herbert Baker who had recently completed the Pretoria Union Building in South Africa. Both agreed that an Imperial capital should establish an "eternal" concept of British sovereignty that could only be interpreted through a neo-Classical approach while adapting its staid forms to the climate, together with the refined assimilation of compatible cultural references. The design approach was therefore more methodical than stylist.

A new capital created an unprecedented opportunity for an imperial urban design, and brought into conflict advocates of different architectural and planning persuasions. Those in favour of an Indo-Saracenic design with its artistic cultural traditions saw an opportunity for Britain to emulate and take forward the "grand style" laid down by Mughal rulers in Shahjahanabad as trustees of its ancient culture. Conversely, followers of the in-vogue Classicist-Baroque approach in Edwardian London urged a design approach that reconciled "East" and "West" in a more refined way through an "Oriental" classicism. From the outset it was considered politically expedient to have an "Indian styled city" although this came under criticism in some quarters for its failure to set an Imperial example that established the majesty of empire as well as its spirit. Leading spokesmen strongly advocated the design involvement of *mistri* — Indian craftsmen and master-masons working, according to tradition, under a master builder but within a modernising context. However while the *mistri* were eventually appointed in large numbers, they were only allowed to assist with minor work. Lutyens himself caustically dismissed India's architecture and deplored the notion of a hybrid Indo-Saracenic style. Baker on the other hand held that colonial architecture should "fire the imagination of the painters, sculptors and craftsmen of the Empire, that they may, interfusing their arts, together raise a permanent record of the history, learning and romance of India".[4]

The new imperial city — New Delhi — was inaugurated in 1931. Its sense of solidity betrayed the growing insecurity of British rule, although C Northcote Parkinson used it as an example in *Parkinson's Law* to substantiate his thesis that "perfection of planned layout is achieved only by

institutions on the point of collapse". It was five times as large as the old city, and planned on a grand scale by the Town Planning Committee with later amendments by Henry Vaughan Lanchester, who introduced a radial layout with major roads focussed on historic edifices. The main government buildings were positioned on axial vistas, providing an almost surreal contrast to the indigenous city, and with a spatial order that effectively reflected the hierarchical status of administrative officialdom. The focus

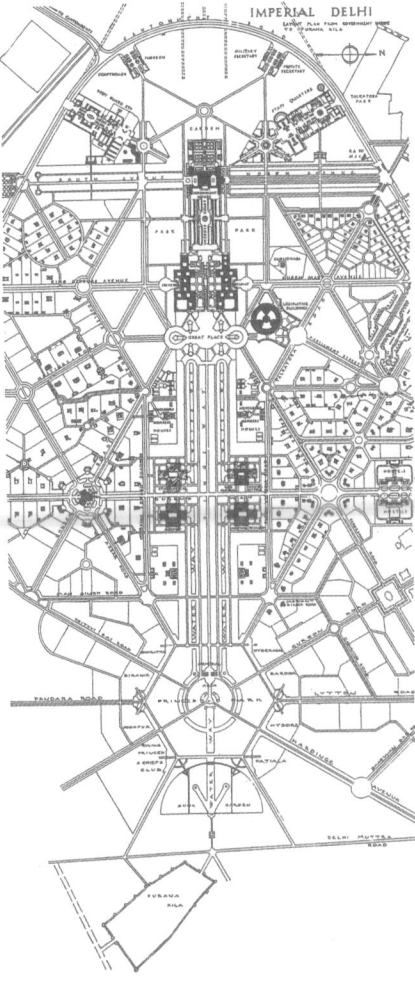

THE PLAN FOR NEW DELHI owes much to the garden city theories of Ebenezer Howard, prevalent in England at the time. While a newly planned appendage to the old city was considered more suitable than the more restricted opportunities available in North Delhi, the southern site was also advantageous in terms of land acquisition. A key planning and urban design issue was the opportunity for a coherent relationship between new and old areas. Conservation and improvement would be considered hand-in-hand with new infrastructure and open space, along with opportunities for both a physical and visual relationship between new government buildings and the Red Fort and Jami Masjid in the Old City. The plan as a whole was based on a series of wide intersecting avenues focussed on traffic circles, modified where necessary to accommodate pre-existing antiquities. These ideas evolved into a largely ceremonial Beaux Arts layout with references to both Christopher Wren's plan of 1666 for rebuilding the City of London, and L'Enfant's plan of 1902 for Washington. It was based on key vistas, with Government House on the western Raisina Hill and the main view corridor of King's Way, now the Rajpath, directed towards the north gate of the Purana Qila. The main north-south road, Queen's Way, now the Janpath, linked Connaught Place in the north to a circle in the south.

The overall plan, with its overscaled hexagonally inclined boulevard system focussed on traffic circles, established a framework around monumental buildings within self-contained sites. It now presents an uneasy combination of compositional grandeur and garden city chutzpah. The modern city reads as a series of isolated and generally low density developments, both institutional and commercial, incorporated on a largely ad hoc basis and internalised behind tree-lined and heavily-trafficked avenues. The expansive design has meant there is little pressure for physical intensification, so that even government bungalows sitting in large garden sites are still largely used for their original purpose. The dominating architectural landmarks of Imperial governance has bequeathed to New Delhi a duality of high expression and low urbanity that fail to resonate with what should be a strong capital identity.

Outside the Rajpath and Janpath, New Delhi is bereft of three-dimensional urban definition — post-independence public buildings and national institutions that mingle with new hotel towers are set well back from roads behind guarded gateways, high walls and fences, and separated by distances that determinedly discourage foot traffic.

THE DELHI TOWN PLANNING COMMITTEE specified Connaught Place as a monumental plaza, 300 metres in diameter, encircled and unified by three-storey colonnades of shops in seven sections together with a new rail terminus. Roadways entering the circus would be spanned by grand archways with a continuous upper cornice. This was not completed until 1934, although they are only two storeys in height, which failed to achieve a sense of coherent urban scale and cityscape. For a time this was filled with stylish shops. Today Connaught Place is the focus for eight major roads and several minor ones. The outer ring of Connaught Circus forms a gigantic roundabout, whole the inner Connaught Place, defined by Rajiv Chowk, forms a green open space with an underground shopping mall and an interchange Metro Station.

5 Irving, R.G., *Indian Summer –*
   Lutyens, Baker, and Imperial
   Delhi, Yale University Press,
   London and New Haven, 1981

6 Irving, 1981, op. cit.

7 Metcalf, T.R., *An Imperial*
   Vision: Indian Architecture and
   Britain's Raj, University of
   California Press, Berkely, 1989

8 Tillotson, G.H.R., *The Tradition*
   of Indian Architecture, Yale
   University Press, London and
   New Haven, 1989

9 Hosagrahar, 2007, op. cit., p151

was Government House (now Parliament House), terminating the western view along King's Way, symmetrically lined by the Secretariat buildings with War Memorial Arch at its eastern end. Government House and the Secretariat buildings were joined in composition at the crest of Raisina Hill, expressing the "unity of the viceroy with his Government.[5] Inadequate consideration of the gradient however reduced the intended visual prominence of Government House. A series of wide avenues intersected at prominent "places" — Connaught Place and Windsor Place in the north, and York Place in the south. These in turn were linked to subsidiary intersections, each designed as a prominent focal point. The north-south processional route — Queen's Way or *Janpath* — connected Connaught Place and a proposed railway station to King's Way or *Rajpath*. To the east was Prince's Park and the All India War Memorial — the present India Gate. A new Cantonment was built to the west of the new city.

Robert Grant Irving sets out the division of design between Lutyens and Baker — the former set out the complex master plan framework and worked on the Viceroy's House and the India War Memorial, while the latter designed the two Secretariats, and later the Council House for the Legislative Assembly.[6] Baker's Secretariat building combined two corresponding sets of elements: a prominent collection of columns, colonnades and domes, and the subtle grafting of certain appropriated features — the *chattris*, *jaalis* and *chajja* to differentiate from and extend the predominantly European design language.[7] It is Edwin Lutyens however who is most associated with the new capital, as a member of the Delhi Town Planning Commission in 1912. He shrewdly viewed classical architecture as representing a stable but evolutionary style reflecting its adaptability by different societies. Lutyens's design for the Viceroy's House in conjunction with the secretariat buildings, was part of an axial composition which included the ceremonial King's Way, was integrated with a symmetrically ordered Beaux Arts plan. In practice, the totality of the urban design is remarkably restrained, substituting rigorous control over abstract decorative devices, and subordinating a grandiloquent gesture for the more sober but enduring values of European classicism.

The twin approaches differed only in the extent they interpolated and fused traditional Indian features as inserts, within rationalised classical design compositions. Tillotson attributes Lutyens with achieving, through the dome of Viceroy's House, an elemental geometry with an original form that is "wholly classical and wholly Buddhist in spirit".[8] This was a legacy bequeathed to subsequent works in New Delhi, and marked the demise of the *mistri* tradition through lack of application in the modern design era.

URBAN CHANGES

By 1931 the urban population of Delhi was 440,000. The majority of new migrants moved to the remaining parts of the old city where population densities were thirty times higher than in New Delhi — the highest of any Indian city — underscoring the disparities between the two communities.[9] The accompanying rise in property values continued to make building extensions, subdivisions and infill difficult to regulate, and municipal strategies were in frequent conflict with customary practices and the ability to confound officialdom through recourse to legal procedures. Temporary open-sided structures — *barsati* — were frequently

converted and extended in an increasingly spontaneous way.

The Delhi Improvement Trust was established in 1936 to relieve overcrowding by zoning new development enclaves to facilitate redevelopment in the old city. Residential neighbourhoods to the south and west were laid out on land acquired from large agricultural estates and designated to different socio-economic groups and market sectors in relation to lot size and location. Sites were also allocated for commercial streets, markets and industrial areas.

One of larger clearance schemes involved the resumption of a dense city quarter between the Delhi and Ajmeri Gates, demolition of the old city wall, and planned

Labels visible in the illustration: MONGA R.K. GEMS · NATURAL PERFUME OILS · JRAL PERFUME O · EIR NATURAL PRODUCTS · EXPO INDIA · NATURAL PERFUME OILS

THE CITY'S ECONOMIC FUNCTIONING now forms a significant component of its physicality and its channels of access and communication. This reflects a combination of retail, wholesale and manufacturing activity. Product transfer continues without a break through the main streets and alleys, to and from markets, storerooms and outlets, via all available modes of transport. Human carriers, pushcarts, bullock carts, pedal carts and tuk tuks tenaciously weave through streams of

pedestrians with a reassuring level of give and take, and generate the city's most underlying and admirable characteristic. Change has been a constant factor that has erased much of the extraordinary collection of *havelis*, religious edifices and historical structures. The old city is itself a monument to the forces of historical growth and adaptation, and remains a symbol of urban robustness — the intangible and fragmented patina of history still remains visible in its morphology.

redevelopment for three to five storey houses, apartments and shops along the line of the old wall to achieve optimum densities. Design controls on front façades were enforced to achieve overall consistency in line with a European model of design, order and space. Similarly redevelopment of the Faiz Bazaar with standard lots and pre-designed street façades imposed a rational sense of order based on the normative ideals rooted in a foreign cultural context, in contrast to the more spontaneous and adaptive layouts of indigenous neighbourhoods. Modular design prototypes and a need to conform to by-laws, together with light and ventilation requirements, inevitably created undifferentiated localities.

This raises a perennial dichotomy associated with benevolent government programmes, and the ability to meet citizens' aspirations through a transforming agenda based on formal utilitarian practices. Visions of modernity must relate as far as possible to customary practices. Both social networks and overly controlled "model" environments inaugurated under the colonial agenda became compromised through cultural disjunction, speculation and affordability. Planning notions of decongestion were thwarted through continued waves of immigration, where "ideal" layouts mattered less than basic accommodation, social propinquity and economic interdependencies. Normative ideals surrounding the refashioning of space and society were, in practice, subject to question, modification and change by the communities themselves. However Improvement Trust projects and the evolving urban economic patterns at the time were largely in line with the overall spatial rationalisation and ambitions of New Delhi, with its bureaucratic order and sense of omnipotence. New Delhi was designed to represent imperial majesty and efficiency; it was devoid of the peripheral or marginal uses which the old city accommodated, and separated from it by

[10] King, A.D., *Colonial Urban Development: Culture, Social Power and Environment*, Routledge & Kegan Paul, London, 1976

planned intermediary uses.

After independence in 1947, the Delhi Development Authority took over from the Trust, and was charged with preparing a plan for the metropolitan area. Urban expansion through new estates continued to fill in the spatial and cultural vacuum between the old and new cities. Following the partition of India there was a considerable influx of population to Delhi, and ten years after independence the old walled city with ten per cent of Delhi's land area had 60 per cent of its total population, with ten times its gross density.[10] However the two were bound together in an ambiguous and propelling duality.

While the Development Act of 1957 was intended to guide development, the regularisation of non-conforming development areas and illegal subdivisions was difficult to control effectively, particularly in urban fringe areas. In addition resettlement estates to rehouse populations living in squatter areas were development with minimum services but have evolved to become vibrant communities housing diverse activities. A National Capital Region Planning Board was set up in 1985 and divided the city into zones to accommodate planned urban expansion, although many developments that continued to go forward were unauthorised. Up to 2001, the Master Plan for Delhi called for the acquisition of 20,000 hectares of land for residential and commercial uses, much of which has now been developed with extensions of municipal services and transport to the new communities. Delhi's concentration of political and administrative power, together with its role as a financial hub, has attracted a strata of the educated middle class, with a 2012 population of 16.8 million people.

Modern Delhi is therefore a tale of two cities, conjoined like Siamese Twins, but inhabiting markedly different urban realms and serving radically different purposes.

But the city is more about amalgam than overlap — the Old City and the colonial core of the Civil Lines to the north, which was once the centre of the European community, is now a tranquil university and residential area. The walled city remains as a planning anachronism — on one hand it forms a multiplicity of dilapidated buildings, conflicting uses and congestion, but on the other it represents a robust continuation of the old Mughal city with a condensed and sustainable blend of old residences and work opportunities. In contrast New Delhi is the centre of the political elite, the business core, and middle-class housing areas that have pushed city limits far to the south and west, encompassing previous small settlements and market centres. Among these are scattered monuments, remnants of ancient city walls and gateways, including UNESCO World Heritage sites. The inner zone is delineated by a radial highway and integrated commercial centres, foreign embassy enclaves, middle class housing and mixed use bazaar areas while the urban fringe contains a changeable mix of urban and rural functions with pockets of residential and business development. Much of the new commercial development has developed in close proximity to older cores, with the Noida commercial district on the city fringe linked by road and metro line to the inner city precincts.

PAKISTAN

Lahore

THE MUGHAL EMPIRE that began in 1524 is associated with a great flowering of architecture. The Badshahi Mosque was built by one of the last Mughal emperors, Aurganzeb, in the ancient walled city. It is a *tour de force* of urban design, both because of its immense size, and through its combination of red sandstone and white marble inlay.

The Alamgiri Gate to the Badshahi Masjid rises twenty-two steps above the Hazuri Bagh — the forecourt for the grand mosque — lined with cloisters, that acted as a stage set for the emperor and his entourage when they came to offer Friday prayers. Following the Sikh uprising in 1799 Ranjit Singh became emperor and built the marble pavilion in the Hazuri Bagh shown to the left of the drawing, utilising material removed from Mughal monuments. After the Anglo-Sikh wars, the British dismantled the outer wall of the old city and appropriated both Mughal and Sikh buildings for a variety of purposes. New public buildings took on an 'Anglo-Indian' or 'Saracenic' style which had a far-reaching influence on urban design.

THE ANCIENT GANDHARA CULTURE
of northwest Pakistan dates back to the fourth century BC. Its urban design represents the evolution of Graeco-Indian culture, founded around 300 BC by Alexander the Great, who built the Macedonian cities of Taxila and Pushkalavat. Gandhara later became a centre for Buddhism with a grand stupa built at Dharmarajika together with temples and monasteries, which came to characterise its architecture. Gandhara became a centre for Buddhist pilgrimage around AD 60, and incorporated Peshawar and the Lower Swat and Kabul valleys. From the fifth century up to the Arab conquest of Sind, the Hindu and Jain temple architecture became progressively refined, characterised by richly sculpted Buddhist-inspired stonework grafted on to the medieval architecture of northwest India and Kashmir.

Following the annexation of Sind Province by Arab forces in the eighth century, various new cities were planned, and the first Muslim citadel and Grand Mosque in Bhambore dates back to 727. The most predominant type of building from the Muslim Sultanate period is the mausoleum, built on a square plan form with a central dome. The re-conquest of India by the Mughals introduced Persian influences, which combined and interacted to produce tangible and long-lasting imprints on the Punjab. Evidence from tombs outside the pre-Mughal Old City suggest that Lahore was founded around the eleventh century and was relatively close to the fourteenth century Arabic trading routes through north India to China. Surviving buildings from this period indicate a common cultural and architectural identity with Iran and Afghanistan. The first Mughal emperor, Babur, invaded the Punjab in 1524, and early Mughal emperors used Lahore as a military base until Emperor Akbar moved his court to the city in 1584, from Fatehpur Sikri in the south, to better protect the empire. The Mughal succession in 1526, with its focus on India, was physically

View from the Naulakha Pavilion in the Shah Burj towards the Alamgiri Gate and the Badshahi Masjid.

expressed by a great flowering of the arts and a prodigious building programme, activated by Akbar, which conveyed imperial power as well as architectural grandeur. Military architecture, exemplified by the Mughal forts, became centres of government with their associated palaces and *havelis* of princes and courtiers. In 1739 Delhi was sacked by the Persians and the Punjab came under Afghan control until their defeat by the Sikhs, who had led uprisings from Amritsar. By 1799 Ranjit Singh was pronounced Emperor in Lahore. Following the Anglo-Sikh wars, the British annexed the Punjab in 1849 and established the Raj over India, with the Punjab as its most prosperous state.

In 1885 the Indian National Congress was formed, and the British adopted a 'divide and rule' policy in Bengal that, although eventually revoked, stoked calls for separation by the Muslim League. Its leaders, steeped in the Arab-Persian cultural tradition, began to resist the Hindu dominated Congress. Muhammad Ali Jinnah, who had previously endeavoured to bring about Hindu-Muslim unity, came to prominence after Congress refused to include the Muslim League in the formation of provincial governments. The "Lahore Resolution" in 1940 led directly to Partition and the establishment of a separate Muslim State — Pakistan — in August 1947.

THE MUGHAL CITY

Lahore Fort was built and destroyed several times until its fortification under Akbar in 1556 utilising Persian brick building traditions. Akbar constructed a well-protected and spatially ordered palace citadel in the north-west sector of the Old City, and at the same time reinforced the city wall fortifications and introduced thirteen gateways. In a similar way to Old

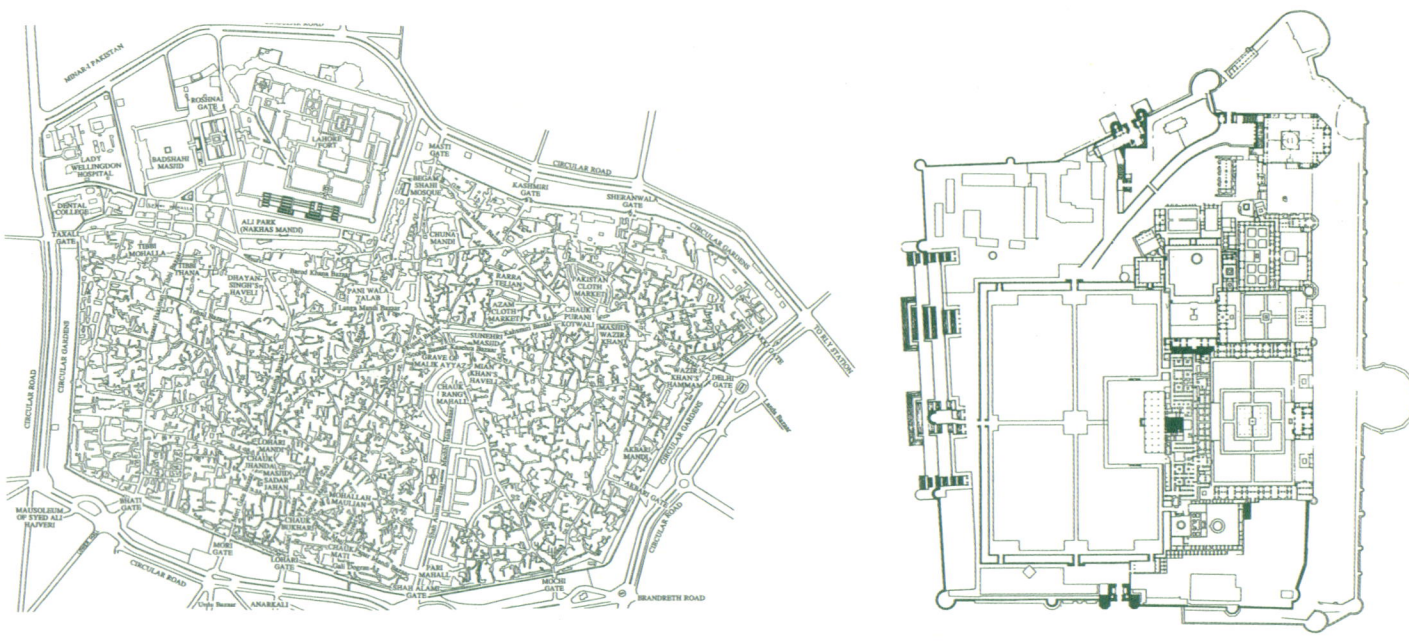

The Walled City of Lahore

Lahore Fort

Delhi, princes and court followers built large *havelis* which housed extended families and retainers. Prominent personages also sponsored religious buildings and monuments within the city, and some of the main avenues later became important market streets such as the Kashmiri and Chun Mandi Bazaars, lined with shops.

Akbar's grandson Shah Jahan, notable for building a capital in Delhi, remodelled the palace and constructed the extensive gardens of Shalimar to the east of the city. The two largest and most prominent mosques are the Badshahi Masjid built by Shah Jahan's son Aurangzeb to the west of the fort, and the Wazir Khan Mosque in the east of the city. The latter was founded in 1634 and frames an elaborate eastern forecourt opening to a large square — the *jilaukhana* — which formed an integral part of the old city's urban design and a focus for major internal routes and bazaars. Aurangzeb also constructed the Alangir Bund to stabilise the Ravi river bank outside the city walls, which was later remodelled

through a series of private gardens. Unlike the other major Mughal cities, which were developed along more cosmological Islamic lines, Lahore grew in a more piecemeal way, based on consolidation around major features, including *havelis* and bazaar streets.

Indigenous domestic architecture in the city evolved to accommodate both social and cultural traditions with climatic sensibilities in terms of massing, orientation and carefully articulated fenestration. Materials were generally bricks, stone and timber, and traditional design forms were manipulated into intricate patterned components with an expressive vocabulary of decoration, ornamentation and relief work that reflected enduring urban design values as well as craft traditions. Design was formalised through use of established forms and materials, and animated by vernacular devices incorporated by local craftsmen or *mistri* that included rooftop pavilions — *barsat,* and projecting bay windows — *jharoka*. This produced a spatial consistency that was alleviated by

practical differences and the spontaneity of decoration. Building frontages onto main streets were narrow but continuous, with shops open to the streets via a raised plinth — *tharra*, that provided a continuous frontage along the façade creating a threshold space for conducting business. Secondary systems of alleys, communal spaces and private courtyards created a relatively organic morphology. Within this, individual building volumes, projections and roof spaces varied according to the maximum span of wooden beams and the thickness of brick walls, which cooled the interiors. Additional ornamentation was applied through wooden lattice screens, incised panels and carved door frames.

Mughal Lahore spread well outside the city walls, with around 70 per cent of the population living in suburban neighbourhoods with distinct identities often associated with craft guilds or particular features that characterised the localities. The city framework of a dense urban core and satellite communities spreading outwards from the walled city — established by the Mughal emperors — provided a spatial setting for subsequent periods of rule.

During the reign of Emperor Aurangzeb in the late seventeenth century, war with the Marathas further south diverted attention from Lahore, which began to decline as a trading centre as the overland trading route was re-directed through Qandahar. The indigenous architectural tradition began to disintegrate with the end of the Mughal empire and the commensurate disintegration of architectural patronage, and for a time the wealthy provincial courts of the maharajahs became a focus of the arts. The accumulation of merchant wealth gradually transformed the process of urbanisation which in turn accelerated industrialisation, with guilds of craftsmen and artisans turning to small-scale manufacturing.

Transactions in land ownership and sub-division helped to shape not only physical form but also the population density and social characteristics of urban neighbourhoods or *mohallas*. While proprietary rights were recognised, the expansion of merchant activity throughout the eighteenth century resulted in negotiated division of properties, which introduced different caste and religious bodies. Neighbourhoods therefore became increasingly heterogeneous yet retained their continuity with the past through identifiable physical characteristics.

THE FORT AND BADSHAHI MOSQUE

The Badshahi Mosque and its large forecourt — the Hazuri Bagh or 'garden' built by the Mughal emperor Aurangzeb — are located in the northwest section of the Walled City to the west of the citadel and linked to it through the Alamgiri Gate oriented towards the mosque. The Roshnai Gate from the north is the only original gate within the Walled City. Its centrepiece, the marble Hazuri

Walled City

Decorative façade of the Rang Mahal High School

The tomb of Samadh of Ranjit Singh rises above the wall surrounding the Hazuri Bagh completed in 1848. The high fluted dome is influenced by Mughal architectural traditions.

Across the Hazuri Bagh is Hathi Pol, the Gateway that allowed the royal entourage to enter the citadel on elephants.

Baradari pavilion, was built by Ranjit Singh in 1881 with material removed from Mughal mausoleums, and was used for receptions and the functions of the Sikh state.

The Badshahi Mosque built on a raised platform above the city, rivals in similar size and form, the large Mughal mosques in Delhi and Agra, and was constructed on the site of a previous royal palace. The courtyard has sides measuring 170 metres with walls that integrate eighty cloisters, originally covered in brick, and later with red sandstone. It is reached via twenty-two steps up to the east portal on an axis with the Alamgiri gate and flanked by two curvilinear bastions. White marble is used on the mosque itself with three bulbous domes above the prayer chamber making an identifiable composition. During the Sikh wars, the guns on the minarets were used to bombard the adjoining fort structures. In the foreground is the tomb of Allama Muhammad Iqbal, Pakistan's national poet. To the north of the Hazui Ragh is the Samadh of Ranjit Singh constructed against the outer wall, built on the site of his funeral pyre, and completed in 1848. The fluted bulbous dome is more pronounced than those of the adjoining Badshahi Mosque.

THE WALLED CITY

The *andaroon shahar* or Walled City of Lahore forms the most ancient and concentrated realm of social and economic activity in the Punjab. It can be loosely divided between the two realms of public and private space. The public realm is dominated by a dynamic culture of transaction and congregation. Main thoroughfares that link the thirteen gateways and secondary alleyways are equally choked with the connective infrastructure of commerce and its necessary traffic of people and goods, propelled by motorised rickshaws, drawn by oxen and donkeys, or pulled by human effort. This is urban design delineated by the give and take of navigation, casually negotiated through informal politeness and priorities. The urgency of connection largely relates to the convoluted but intrinsic relationships between retail and wholesale operations. Public space is largely a world of industry, commerce and languid social intercourse, where the daily rhythm is structured by the call to prayers five times a day from the many mosques — notably Masjid Badshahi and Masjid Wazir Khan.

The Walled City is a place where the tangible footprints of physical occupation over a thousand years — from ancient Macedonia, to Mughal, Sikh and British colonial occupation — intermingle with the more elusive cultural residue of artists, musicians, poets and writers. Trade, military conquest and invasion represent a chronology of interventions that have been translated into a strata of monuments, urban forms and economic forces that continue to interact and bring about change. The old city framework embodies ancient fortifications, religious buildings, and princely havelis interwoven within bazaars and a secondary labyrinth of narrow residential streets. In terms of urban design, the three-dimensional mix of public and private spaces creates an informal but expressive urban environment where residents, trades and businesses interact. The medieval layout of narrow streets lined by buildings of four and five storeys has secured a legacy of changeable solids and voids where covered alleys provide a perpetually shaded system of movement defined by ground level shops and workshops, while rooftop terraces provide private social spaces for eating, sleeping and neighbourly exchange.

Excavations carried out in Lahore Fort place the history of the city back in the sixth century AD. The earliest written reference dates to 982 as the name of a territory whose capital was Mandahukur.[1] By the mid-twelfth century Lahore was one of the leading cities in South Asia with its nucleus in the current Walled City. Up to the sixteenth century

The Sonehri Masjid elevated above the Chowk Kashmiri Bazaar, whose shops contributed to its upkeep.

it survived periodic Mongol invasion and famine before its long period of prosperity and development under the Mughal dynasty from 1525. Akbar made the city the Mughal capital in 1584 and it consequently became the residence of nobles and scholars, with a mix of palaces, *havelis*, pleasure gardens and mosques. A large military force required expansion of the fortifications and the entire city was encircled with a nine-metre high brick wall, pierced by thirteen gates, which still retain their positions. The Roshnai Gate

leading to the Hazuri Bagh from the south, still has its original structure.

The Wazir Khan Masjid and Hammam (public baths) are located off the Delhi Gate Bazaar. The chowk defines the entrance gateway to the mosque, which served as the imperial place of worship before construction of the Badshahi Masjid. The highly decorated eastern entrance provides a transition to an elegant courtyard with cloisters to the north and south, decorated with glazed mosaic tiles, frescoes of floral patterns and calligraphy

The courtyard of the Wazir Khan Masjid looking south across the elaborate courtyard. The mosque was founded in 1634 and also served as a university.

from the Quran to create a sense of repose. Oriel windows and tapering finials are typical Mughal architectural features. The forerunner to the Wazir Khan Masjid in structure, plan form and decoration is the Begam Shahi Masjid built by Jahangir's mother in 1614 and situated by the east gate to the fort.

THE GATEWAYS

The gateways to the old Mughal City represented specific activities as points of identity. The Shah Burj Gate was the exclusive entrance used by royalty leading to Shah Burj, the Harem quarter. The Picture Wall covers an illustrated surface area of around 8,000 square metres, divided by panels with glazed tile mosaics of warriors, camels, horses and elephants. This decoration represents a distinctive departure from the glazed calligraphy and floral patterns found in Mughal architecture. Alamgiri Gate was built as a ceremonial entrance to the fort and faces the Badshahi Masjid, flanked by two curvilinear bastions. The Roshnai Gate between the Fort and Badshahi Mosque was traditionally frequented by courtiers and royal servants, and was known as the "gate of light". The Kashmiri Gate is an entry point to the Chuna Mandi area — traditionally an important Sikh part of the city. The Sherannata Gate gained its identity from the carved images of lions said to have been kept by Ranjit Singh. The Akbari Gate forms an entrance to the food and spice market founded by Emperor Akbar. The Delhi Gate is an important arched entrance to the old commercial area and the Landa Bazaar, and was widened by the British to accommodate troop movements. Mochi Gate is named after the traditional occupation of *mochis* or shoemaking. Taxali Gate takes its name from the *taxaal* or mint which occupied the area during Mughal times. Finally, the Shah Alami Gate — derives its name from the *haveli* of Mian Khan, at one time the highest house in the city, and destroyed by the British. The area

The Eastern Gateway to the Wazir Khan Mosque is flanked by projecting balconies and presents a glittering pattern of tile mosaic illustrating its strong Persian influence.

Delhi Gate Bazaar

now houses the largest wholesale bazaar in Lahore — the Rang Mahal.

During the Mughal dynasty, Lahore was one of three capitals on the sub-continent (the others being Delhi and Agra), although its position on the north-west frontier facilitated the incorporation of local traditions of construction and decoration. The Sikhs who ruled Lahore between 1768 and 1849 added a number of structures to the fort, but also dismantled others. The most prominent addition to the old city was the *samadh* or mausoleum of Ranjit Singh to the north of the Hazuri Bagh, typical of Sikh shrines and temples which sit at the centre of an open court. The British interfered little with the fort and old city, instead concentrating on the trappings of new city building and administration.

Under Akbar, Lahore was divided into 36 districts of which nine were in the Walled City. Within the walls the city expanded eastwards through a series of bazaars, and was completed by Shah Jahan. During the Mughal and Sikh periods the old city evolved clear ethnic and trading territories based on power groups, ethnic divisions and caste. The street system was based on a hierarchy of main bazaars or *guzars*, secondary neighbourhood streets or *mohallas*, and local streets and culs-de-sac or *galis*. Religious buildings comprised mosques, temples, shrines, and dharmasalas. *Havelis* of wealthy merchants could occupy 300 square metres of ground area, while some of the palaces covered up to two hectares. However only around 20 per cent of early recorded *havelis* still exist — the remainder were progressively sold in small land parcels or *katras* while others such as Wazir Khan's *haveli* were destroyed under the period of Sikh rule.

After the British annexed the Punjab in 1849 they demolished the walls, less for strategic reasons and more for the bricks, which were used in the construction of new buildings. The moat was converted into a park, known as Circular Gardens. A large reservoir was constructed by the military, and water was piped through the old city. The construction of the North Western Railway and the Lahore Railway Station established a new network of functional relationships and alignments, which have remained. The development of a civil secretariat to the south of the city, and a new cantonment to the southeast, effectively determined the future direction of urban growth.

Partition in 1947 led to destruction of parts of the Old City, particularly areas such as the Shah Alami bazaar identified with Hindus and Sikhs. They fled to India to be largely replaced by Muslim households, which reinforced the cultural and social characteristics of Pakistan society. Muslim refugees from India occupied empty Hindu and Sikh properties, and established new trading and workshop

2   Weiss, A.M., *Walls within Walls: Life Histories of Working Women in the Old City of Lahore*, Westview Press, Colorado, 1992
3   The Sustainable Development of Walled City of Lahore Project, 2009

Walled City

clinics which minimise outside visits. In this situation, the dense urban environment with its inherent overcrowding becomes a form of social control. A further aspect of social and physical demarcation is the difference between groups who are native to the old city and those who are descended from migrants at the time of Partition. Indigenous roots and family ties form a tight community of fraternities, guilds, ethnic and religious affiliations.[2]

From the 1970s the population has declined, reflecting changing cultural and lifestyle values and bringing about a shift to commercial and industrial activities as derelict premises are turned into shops, workshops and storage areas. The existing old city now covers around 250 hectares with a population density six times the average for Lahore as a whole. The main activities are shoe manufacturing, printing, jewellery, furniture making and milling operations. This reflects the growth of the central business district along commercial axes, while the Circular Road around the old city forms a physical separation between old and new commercial functions, with one portion of the road acting as a freight terminus. There are close links between the metropolitan commercial areas outside the Circular Road and the informal business transactions of the old bazaar streets in terms of manufacturing and storage, which generate a large amount of goods traffic by hand cart and horse, bullock or donkey cart. Around twenty-two clusters of wholesale and retail trades extend into the old residential fabric which tends to have a negative impact on building condition, and encroachment onto public space. Expanding commercial pressure is therefore turning the previous homogenous residential and commercial mix into a more functional assembly of separate uses with differentiated characteristics.

At the same time the inevitabilities of social and economic circumstances are

regimes. In 1952 the Lahore Improvement Trust was empowered to redevelop parts of the old city with the aim of resolving urban problems and making circulation more efficient. Plots were sold to private developers subject to only minimum regulations, so that certain new developments detracted from the scale and texture of the older morphology.

The extended family structure and traditional separation of activities between men and women associated with *purdah* — a practice that pertains in particular to working class women — impacts on both the social and physical sphere of the private domain, separate from the public realm of the city. While opportunities are available for women to earn income through home-based labour, there is little opportunity for mobility in the commercial and industrial environment of the Old City. This has ramifications for the relationship of *Kuchas* or 'secure' urban locales generally identified with one of the city gates, where there are concentrations of shops for household goods, schools and

Shalimar Gardens

Anarkali Bazaar

changing the underlying characteristics of the old city, through increased commercial growth and a notable decrease in residential population — from over 200,000 in 1974 to around 145,000 in 2012 — living within constantly adapted older structures. This has in large part been the result of lack of service infrastructure, in particular water, electricity and sewerage. Electrical supply from the main distribution system has been informally connected, resulting in exposed transformers and bundles of wires which give rise to somewhat hazardous conditions. These factors have brought with them commensurate threats to the urban heritage. The current conservation project dates from 1980 and is now funded by the World Bank in collaboration with the government. The overall objective is to preserve the walled city as a living community by re-establishing its

historic and environmental qualities. This entails physical conservation and restoration of environmental assets, while enhancing its social and economic functions.

From surveys carried out through the Lahore Project, around 22 per cent of structures are considered to have some architectural or historical merit, and many have been identified for conservation. The first of these areas comprises four neighbourhoods between Delhi Gate and Masti Gate along Chowk Kotwali — part of the old Mughal route between Delhi and Lahore Fort. This includes 57 streets and 812 houses, as well as groups of structures that represent major streetscapes.[3]

Strenuous efforts are being made by the Sustainable Development of Walled City Lahore Project to restore parts of the city and its notable monuments with assistance

from the Aga Khan Programme for Islamic Architecture, and the Pakistan Heritage Foundation. The overall planning intention is to exercise greater control over building use, modification and new construction in order to protect the cultural heritage as a living city. Projects underway by the Lahore Development Authority include new electricity distribution, water and sewage systems, and improved pedestrian connections, together with refurbishment of older properties, facilitating new uses for old buildings that harmonise with the historic character. Existing arteries will be designed to link together places of historic value. In all, 3,951 buildings are identified as warranting inclusion in the conservation programme.

Shalimar Gardens was constructed in 1642 by Shahjahan some five kilometres to the east of the citadel. It covers in excess of ten

4 Glover, W.J., *Making Lahore Modern : Constructing and Imagining a Colonial City*, University of Minnesota Press, Minnesota, 2008, p12

5 Vandal, P and Vandal, S, *The Raj, Lahore and Bhai Ram Singh*, Research and Publication Centre, National College of Arts, Lahore, 2006

hectares surrounded by walls which originally featured paintings. Gardens represented an integral aspect of Mughal city building, and Shalimar is particularly renowned for its internal use of water. This was supplied by the Shah Nahr or Imperial Canal. A system of aquaducts and hydraulic devices led to a series of water channels, waterfalls and fountains designed as a series of terraces, allowing a progression of experiences through gardens and water features. The upper level of Bagh-e-Farah Bakhsh was reserved for the royal court, overlooking a central lake. The central *baradari* is positioned above a marble waterfall which discharges water to a lake that contains 152 fountains.

SIKH INTERVENTION AND BRITISH ANNEXATION

During the eighteenth century Sikh forces began to gather strength and in 1780 Lahore was partitioned among three Sikh rulers. Amritsar became the Punjab's main religious commercial centre before Ranjit Singh re-established Lahore as the administrative capital of an independent state in 1799.[4] In 1812, Ranjit Singh added an outer layer of walls around the Old City, separated by a moat. Merchants continued to build large properties while the administration endowed Sikh and Hindu temples together with mosques, and allocated grants for building land, which consolidated important links between rulers and prominent citizens. At this stage many of the larger *haveli* compounds became crudely sub-divided and broken down into *mohallas* within the older development pattern and street boundaries. Urban administration was carried out under a city manager or *Kotwal*.

In 1846 The Illustrated London News published an item which said: 'If the Punjab were placed under the immediate domination of the British Crown … it might become a most valuable acquisition … for its mineral wealth and agricultural produce'.[5] Only three years later, after several fierce battles with the Sikh Army, it was annexed. At the time, Lahore was a walled city surrounded by the ruins of old settlements and tombs. In order to stabilise a volatile situation, the British demilitarised the fort, dismantled part of the fortifications and interspersed barrack blocks and godowns among the Mughal buildings and lawns, while utilising many of the older buildings, including mosques and tombs, for a variety of public and residential uses. The famous tomb of Anarkali, which had been used as a residence by a general in Ranjit Singh's army, was converted into a garrison church.

After the second Anglo-Sikh War the British annexed the Punjab in 1849, which then became part of British India. Lahore's importance increased at the expense of the older Sikh religious stronghold of Amritsar. In 1859 the British dismantled the outer wall of the Old City and filled in the moat to prevent political insurrection. In 1884 they also constructed the *Paniwala Tilab* or water tank to replace the system of individual wells. William Glover argues that the older city template established a spatial logic for continued development under the British administration. This became symbolically charged through the appropriation of both Mughal and Sikh buildings, including the adaptation of old tombs for colonial purposes.[6]

British officials effectively concentrated on two aspects of urban intervention: the first was an attempt to upgrade the old city which made local surveillance easier, although the tight urban layout, high development density and generally poor standards of infrastructure made incursions difficult; the second was the consolidation of the surrounding area through a type of suburban development aimed at shaping new local environments. The latter involved new forms of physical organisation, not unrelated to preconceived garden city planning theories that were current in Britain at the time. Encapsulating these situations was the utilitarian proposition that uniform, regular and orderly use of space were necessary factors in conceptualising and regulating civil society while keeping existing social structures intact. This was partly achieved by an Anglo-Mughal mix of brick-built architecture for new public and institutional purposes.

The indigenous city was seen by British officials as an illegible and degraded environment — albeit one that resounded with life, business and tumultuous movement — where the opaque sequence of streets and spaces represented the antithesis of an ordered society. It was termed "The City of Dreadful Night" in Rudyard Kipling's famous story. To come to terms with this required an empirical approach based on information

6 Glover, 2008, op. cit., p18
7 Glover, 2008, op. cit., p57

and survey. In 1891 a census was conducted, however even the normally accepted classifications and terminology with regard to places of residence failed to coincide with the prevailing complex spatial relationships, ownership patterns and social practices. Far from illuminating the indeterminate patterns of a durable assemblage of activities and people, the census rendered the city as static and undifferentiated. In such a situation intervention was limited, without the catalyst that existed in Delhi where large areas of the old city were effectively cleared to prevent the spread of political unrest after 1857. In Lahore urban interventions were relatively small in scale and limited to piecemeal environmental improvement works as "object lessons" in urban transformation.[7]

AN ANGLO–INDIAN URBAN DESIGN

While Mughal buildings have become synonymous with Islamic architecture, this covered only a short time frame in the history of Islam. The Anglo-Indian or 'Saracenic' style evolved through somewhat problematic considerations of cultural assimilation and representation in the official architecture of the British Raj. While its architecture reflected the European mainstream — which ranged from neo-Classical, Baroque and Victorian Gothic — the Saracenic style, after a faltering start, began to feature in the requirements of new public buildings such as law courts, colleges and railway stations. However in plan form and massing these generally remained within the European tradition. At best Indo-Saracenic details create a convincing and intriguingly integrated realm of design, marking an ambiguous but far-reaching influence on stylistic development that spread well beyond the Indian sub-continent. At a more prosaic level this was matched by a more practical range of architectural forms applied to low-cost military, warehouse and factory buildings by public works and army engineers.

A combination of pointed arches and stepped gable ends reflect a European Baroque intervention within a broadly Saracenic concept.

THE PUNJAB HIGH COURT was completed in 1889 to highlight the importance of the legal system to the imperial power. Built in brick masonry, it was among the first Anglo-Mughal buildings in the Punjab, harmonising with the neighbouring museum in its use of white marble and moulded brickwork. Its architect was J W Brassington, who had helped to initiate the development of Indo-Saracenic buildings in Madras. Two tall towers incorporate fluted portions, said to be modelled after the Kutub Minar in Delhi. The building displays the 'scales of justice' emblem in white marble.

8 Mumtaz, K.K., *Architecture in Pakistan*, Concept Media Pte Ltd, Singapore, 1985, p192-194
9 Vandal, 2006, op. cit.

The main building of Aitchison College combines grand planning by Swinton Jacob Mayo and elevations by Bai Ram Singh of the Mayo School of Art.

The term 'Islamic' tends to label Muslim architecture on the basis of religious and metaphysical concerns applied to the diverse Muslim world as a whole. It is in many cases inspired by the religious philosophy and ritual of Islam, although clearly much of the secular and materialist design is based primarily on function and contemporary culture. Islamic architecture, much like the term 'Saracenic', suggests a design entity that can be identified on the basis of certain typical characteristics. Kamil Khan Mumtaz suggests that architecture in Pakistan can be divided into several distinct layers: the first reflecting the political, social and economic values of a dominant elite; the second as an expression of an aspiring professional class; and the third as a reflection of vernacular building tradition. Underlying this is the integration of both the spiritual and material, where formal elements can vary through time and place, while the constants relate to the rituals of Islam.[8] Artistic symbolism and integration of calligraphy help to establish compositional unity but also a metaphoric calibration of material surfaces with the attributes of religious inspiration.

New urban forms acquired a rhetorical significance that evolved through a combination of two factors. Firstly an eclectic Indo-Saracenic style and formal arrangement of object buildings began to emerge across Indian cities. In Lahore this began through the design for Aitcheson College by Bhai Ram Singh and Swinton Jacob, which combined a sense of imperial grandeur and Indian iconography, with its elaborate brick detailing and interlacing of Moorish arches and red marble *jallis*. A second factor was the commercial growth in Lahore that gave rise to new art and design establishments, among which was the Mayo School of Art — one of four sanctioned by the government and administered from the South Kensington Museum in London with its charismatic Principals, John Lockwood Kipling and Bhai Ram Singh. These teachers and practitioners, influenced by the Arts and Crafts Movement in Britain, redirected design studies from their engineering foundations towards architectural drawing, aesthetic theory and ornamental design. This was based on analysis of indigenous building traditions, but also blended with European design discourse in an attempt to forge a new cultural identity. The symbolic value of grand colonial architecture was acknowledged as part of the debate over style, although most designs were carried out by engineers and geared more to industrial design, which matched the needs of the major building and infrastructure programme under the British. Architectural drawing was only gradually introduced into engineering studies. The Mayo School of Art is now the National College. It was one of four educational establishments for the promotion of arts and crafts, and its curriculum evolved to encompass carpentry, print making and building design. The administration block in brick masonry was designed by Khan Bahadur Ganga Ram in the Anglo-Mughal style, and provides a formal gateway to the sequence of small precincts used as exhibition spaces.

Bhai Ram Singh, one of the most influential designers from the Mayo School, was trained firstly as a carpenter, developing these skills into architectural designs that fused Indian and Western elements. In part

View across Lahore from the National College of Arts

this stemmed from the Jeypore Exhibition of 1882 and the Calcutta International Exhibition of 1883. The collaboration between Kipling and Ram Singh on the Mayo School of Arts in Lahore, on a prominent site carved out of the gardens of Wazir Khan, created a graceful and climatically suitable design of moulded ornamental bricks and terracotta, with ornamental embellishments and interior works by the students. The same vocabulary was used when extending the design some ten years later.

All buildings constructed during this period form part of a consistent stylistic composition with a simple overall design and rich detailing. In 1888 Ram Singh designed the Lahore museum abutting the Mayo School of Arts building on the Mall. Later projects included the Lahore General Post Office, Albert Victor Hospital, the boarding house of the Government College, and Khalsa College in Amritsar. The latter was completed in 1910 using a design vocabulary that was later applied to other works such as Punjab University and Queen Mary College in Lahore with their rhythmic proportions and brick texture that blended overall design integrity with fine detailing.[9]

The two educators, together with Ganga Ram who was technically an engineering graduate, were responsible for some of the most important institutional buildings in colonial Lahore — Ram oversaw construction of the High Court, Aitcheson College and the Anglican Cathedral, while Kipling and Singh collaborated on the Lahore Museum and Khalsa College in Amritsar. Ram and Singh also jointly worked on the Dayanand Anglo Vedic College in Lahore. Singh's design for the Arts Block, with its central *shikhara* tower form based on Hindu religious buildings, combined elements of Vedic tradition with the compositional attributes of Anglo-European civic design. In the process, architectural solutions were transformed into expressive urban design.

During the colonial period domestic design became subject to more objective layout requirements commencing with the introduction of Municipal Committees that regulated construction and attended to matters of public health and sanitation. These changes brought about more organised layout patterns with greater access to light and ventilation, coupled with a reorganisation of internal space for more specialised uses. Building elevations began to convey a status that reflected Western neo-Classical devices such as pilasters and decorative cornices. As new urban quarters began to be built in the civil station, the regularisation of layouts encouraged the Town Improvement Act of 1922 which established a framework for municipal improvement trusts. This produced new urban settlements based on a grid form of low-rise shophouses developed in the 1930s.

The notion that a well-ordered urban environment could foster social and cultural change was arguably nurtured in the nineteenth century industrial cities of Britain, and became part of a reforming agenda in Indian cities through exemplary work and instructive model environments geared to societal transformation, moral benefit, and physical modernisation. Systematic planning programmes formed a motive for various kinds of urban intervention within the cultural narrative of the city. Colonial-era "Western" buildings and Indo-Saracenic stylistic overtures essentially marked a process of historical change that reflected both cultural interfaces and negotiated arrangements between protagonists.

Inaugurated in 1861, the railway line had a major impact on Lahore both through its new connections across the subcontinent, and through the impetus given to new local streets and places related to the station. The straight rail alignment from Delhi uncompromisingly cut through the royal tomb complex at Shadara to the north of Lahore. By 1874 the city had become the workshop centre of the North Western Railways, which prompted the need for a College of Engineering. New "canal colonies" were constructed through the irrigation of previously unproductive land, encouraging population growth in these areas and stimulating the development of railway networks to transport products.

Prince Edward Hospital

ANARKALI'S TOMB has, since 1847 formed part of the Punjab Secretariat complex constructed in a largely Indo-Saracenic style by the first British Resident, Henry Lawrence. A member of the harem of the Mughul Emperor Akbar, her tomb was built by his son Jahangir as an octagonal structure over the sepulchre. In 1857 it was consecrated as St James' Church, and in 1891 was made the home of the Punjab Archives, documenting the history of the British Punjab. Anarkali marks the location of the earliest British building — the Civil Secretariat — which was constructed along with army barracks, until these were relocated to the new cantonment at Mian Mir. The Secretariat was originally known as Anarkali House, built on the site of a Mughal palace by Jean Baptiste Ventura, a French general in Ranjit Singh's army. It became the British Residency in 1847 when it was extended and the compound enclosed by a wall. It now functions as the office of the Chief Secretary of the Punjab within a landscape setting, surrounded by a series of single storey neo-Classical blocks housing various functions including archives.

The original Anglican Church was converted from the Tomb of Anarkali in the original civil station, and plans for the new Cathedral were drawn up by Oldrid Scott, and completed in 1885. Various towers were added at a later stage, and the building is still known as Kukkar Girja or Rooster Cathedral after the weathercock that topped the old lantern tower.

King Edward Medical University

As the civilian component of the city evolved, the major government buildings, railway stations and Secretariat formed activity nodes linked by paved tree-lined roads which became the new commercial arteries of the colonial city, such as the Lower Mall between Anarkali, which housed the British administration and the Fort, and the Upper Mall which linked the Cantonment with the Secretariat. The latter was lined with new institutional buildings — the Governor's House, Aitchison College and officer's residences — while Mayo Road linked the civil railway station with the Cantonment. Emperor Road, between the Governor's House and the Railway Station, became the most important ceremonial route, lined with important buildings of the Raj. In general street layouts and widths were dictated by the needs of services — water, drainage and carriage traffic.

In contrast, the surrounding villages were seen to be in need of sanitary reform and water supply regulations administered by district commissioners. Model village and township layouts, which included defined areas of agricultural plots irrigated by canals, subsequently gave rise to their name of "Canal Colonies". The Canal Colonies were initiated through construction of the Upper Bari Doab Canal in 1861, which transported water from the Ravi River over 160 kilometres to enable green cultivation of the densely populated cities of Lahore and Amritsar. This was followed by similar canals from the Jumna, Sutlej and Chenab for irrigation of previously desert areas. Commencing in 1905 a new canal system opened up large areas to the south-west of Lahore facilitating the creation of both fertile farmland and new settlements. New colony towns were laid out in a generally standard geometric form with wide straight streets and large sites for detached houses. Within their uniform design, separate areas were demarcated according to existing social hierarchies and relationships within orderly

THE LINEAR URBAN DESIGN

of the Upper Mall or Shahrah-e-Quaid-e-Azam effectively showcases a range of imperial buildings in an Anglo-Mughal style, but also commercial constructs that promote its vibrant character. It was built by the British in 1851 to link the civil station at Anakali and the Mian Mir Cantonment, with a direct connection to the Walled City. In the late nineteenth century it was remodelled under the direction of the Executive Engineer, Sir Ganga Ram. The Mall is embellished by a sequence of contrasting but complementary building compositions and styles. These can be grouped from west to east as: Government buildings, including the Civil Secretariat, Government College and the Town Hall around the old Anarkali area; the Anglo-Mughal institutional buildings, High Court and mercantile structures; the Charing Cross building group; and the imperial edifices, colleges, and residential facilities for British administrators set in large gardens. Interspersed between these are nineteenth century churches, cathedral, schools and the railway station. Kim's Gun (a canon) stands sentinel over the western part of the Upper Mall, made famous in Rudyard Kipling's novel. The local belief is that ownership of the gun denotes ownership of the Punjab.

The Town Hall was built to mark Queen Victoria's fiftieth Jubilee and completed in 1890 by Prince Albert Victor. Public buildings of this type were new to Lahore, and followed a pattern of planning buildings around a courtyard with verandas for climatic protection which incorporated elements from Moghul architecture. In the Town Hall this included square corner towers capped by a central dome and onion-shaped cupolas along with lancet arches from the Sultanate period. Its two-storey section incorporated a lancet arch alcove flanked by 'horse-shoe' arches.

A number of buildings fronting the Upper Mall were built by nineteenth century merchants with neo-Classical elevations but local details. Examples of these are the Dhoni Chand Building, Dawar Building, Jan Muhammad Building, Ganga Ram Building, Ahmad Mansions with its central clock tower, and Ghulam Rasool Building with its central cupola tower.

THE LAHORE MUSEUM, Auditorium and Library was designed by John Lockwood Kipling and Bai Ram Singh, and completed in 1890. The building is expressive of the Anglo-Mughal style in red brick with a white marble portico and frontal fountain. The composition of geometric elements, cupolas and corner towers surmounted by hemispherical domes is designed to complement the adjacent National College of Arts and Punjab University Hall.

THE ORIGINAL LAHORE MUSEUM, known as Tollinton Market, was constructed in 1864 as the Punjab Exhibition Building to house arts, fabrics, manuscripts and calligraphy. Its design rather than its scale follows the style of a colonial bungalow with a sloping roof, dormer windows and verandahs. It is capped by two square towers. The wooden structure is supported internally by a series of brick display areas. The building was remodelled as a market in the 1970s, with its previous display areas used as market stalls. It was fully restored in 2012 as an exhibition centre.

10 Glover, 2008, op. cit., p68

spatial settings. By methodically codifying and replicating standard spatial models, the intention was to improve material conditions and in the process instil an appreciation of ordered environment.

LAWRENCE AND MONTGOMERY HALLS

William Glover instances the dignified neo-Classical Lawrence and Montgomery Halls and the related municipal garden as the first projects to introduce a formal compositional townscape on the Upper Mall (the Shahrah-e-Quaid-e-Azam), although its spacious setting gives it the ambience of a country house, lying opposite the Provincial Governor's House. Its historical garden, the Bagh-e-Jinnah, was laid out in 1860 and covers some 112 acres. The neo-Classical design was purposely adopted to underscore British authority after the First War of Independence, and is named after two Lieutenant Governors of the Punjab. Lawrence Hall, fronting the Mall, was completed in 1862 and was designed for theatrical entertainment, primarily for the European community but served for a time as Lahore's town hall. Montgomery Hall, financed by Indian patrons and completed four years later, was more complex and contained various cultural uses for the wider community. The two halls were later linked together in an elegant ensemble through an elaborate connection that metaphorically underpinned the conjoining interests, and set within the equally genteel new landscape of Lawrence Gardens. These were tended by horticulturists from the Royal Botanical Gardens at Kew, which made for 'a prominent setting for the cultivation and display of Anglo-European gentility in the city'.[10] Urban design was therefore used as a means of conveying and expressing a collaborative milieu, even if social inclusiveness was somewhat superficial and restricted to the mercantile and princely elites. The halls have been refurbished and serve a new purpose as the Quaid-e-Azam Library.

Laurence and Montgomery Halls

THE GENERAL POST OFFICE

forms a distinctive landmark along the Upper Mall, built in 1905 at the corner of Church Road. The site itself necessitated a trapezoidal plan form, its elegant design and central pediment establishing a neo-Classical form, which plays on light and shade associated with the repetitive deep verandah pattern. Its Mughal references are introduced through octagonal corner towers capped by cupolas and a domed central tower. The building was extensively refurbished in the 1990s under the direction of the Heritage Foundation to incorporate its original features and a new wing, which encloses a courtyard.

THE CIVIL STATION

The British Military Cantonment or 'Civil Station' to the southeast of the old city and adjacent to the Bari Doab Canal at Mian Mir was 35 square kilometres in size — fourteen times the size of the Old City. Its layout underlined the essential urban differences between new and old. The location, urban design and architecture was based on established military strategy, in that a new and spacious setting, located some distance from the great body of the population, ensured both security and easy mobility for troop movements while at the same time reducing the defensive capacity of the older city. It was laid out on a broadly rectilinear north-south grid of roads based on both a spatial and social hierarchy. Main road connections enabled troop movements to by-pass the Old City, while east-west roads linked the Cantonment to the Civil Secretariat at Anarkali.

The Civil Station was effectively a new town which served the purposes of a colonial capital in the Punjab. It therefore had to serve an elusive mix of roles — administrative, military and commercial — but also had to ensure inclusivity between British and Indian residents while accommodating the hierarchical organisation of social groups that shaped the distinctive colonial landscape. The occasion of Queen Victoria's Jubilee brought together a substantial building programme of institutional building works throughout India, and generated a timely impetus to the nucleus of public buildings in the Civil Station, symbolic of a new and ideologically inspired purpose.

A park at the centre of the Civil Station provided a setting for the Anglican Church to the north and recreational areas to the south. Senior officers and both European and Native infantry were accommodated according to rank. The indigenous but overcrowded neighbourhood of Morang, located within the Civil Station, was long considered as a

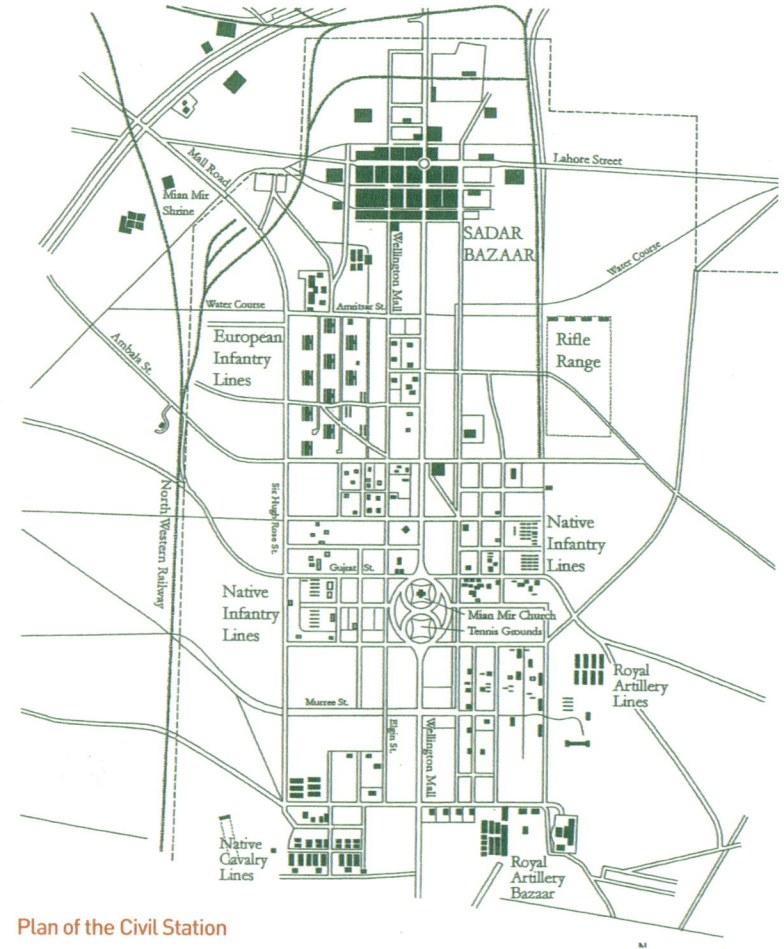

Plan of the Civil Station

target for removal, its saving grace being that it housed many of the domestic servants who worked in the station. However, piecemeal and rudimentary improvements to its drainage and infrastructure enabled it to withstand more direct intervention.

While the tradition of tight urban massing gave way to a spacious layout pattern, the initial buildings were simple with long barrack blocks, utilitarian public buildings, and bungalows for senior officers, all of which were standardised according to the Military Services Handbook. A shopping centre for Europeans was located at the centre of the Cantonment, and at the northern end was the Saddar Bazaar around which was arranged the housing for local support staff. On the eastern periphery were farms and stables. It now provides houses for the

military and senior civil servants, set within large compounds defined by avenues of tree planting.

MODEL TOWN

On the outskirts of Lahore, Model Town was based on a plan form that partly subscribed to the utopian "garden-city" theories of Ebenezer Howard, published in 1898 in response to the congestion and pollution found in British cities at the time, and supported by Patrick Geddes who acted as planning consultant to various municipalities. The town illustrates a generally successful attempt to set up a garden city on behalf of retired local civil servants and professionals, and represents the brainchild and perseverance of a lawyer, Dewan Khem Chand. During Geddes' visit to Lahore in 1917, he submitted a report which advocated the notion of new "suburban" development adapted to the natural and preserved features of sites.

The Cooperative Model Town Society, orchestrated largely by retired Indian government employees, translated Howard's ideas within a formal geometric layout with axial avenues focussed on a central park surrounded by a ring of community and institutional uses, and with sites around the fringe dedicated to fruit gardens, factory and service areas. The process of plan making illustrates a transplanting of urban design ideas to very different physical and cultural situations. The plan covered 800 hectares and the scheme was launched in 1921 by 200 founder members of the co-operative. It provided 1,264 plots divided into eight sectors, with the great park of 40 hectares at its centre. It fulfilled the aspirations of a burgeoning middle-class for a suburban idyll while retaining traditional domains within individual households.

This contrast with the Old City continued to underscore the dual identity of Lahore. Domestic design drew on local typologies built by the British in the Civil Lines, mainly in the form of detached bungalows with shaded verandahs, symbolic of the exclusivity and consumption of space normally projected and enjoyed by the British. As these became occupied by extended Indian families additional floors were added, adapting the new cultural model to traditional requirements and adding a significant dimension to Lahore's evolution into a modern city. The town today has largely lost its older urban design as newcomers have transformed the predominantly single storey structures, with their delicate interpretation of European form and stylish details, into a different spatial relationship of two- and three-storey modern houses which maximise plot coverage.

The Co-operative Model Town Society Office

The Lahore Railway Station designed by William Brunton was the first purpose-built British institutional building, designed along the lines of a medieval fortified castle.

1 Ashihara, Y, *The Hidden Order*, Kodansha International, Tokyo and New York, 1989, p135

EAST AND CENTRAL ASIA

The historical imprint of China on East, Central and Southeast Asian civilization and urban design is of quite fundamental significance. The earliest Shang dynasty emanated from the North China plain around 1122 BC, and evolved into a creative artistic culture and a skilled artisan class. This flowered into a sophisticated intellectual and philosophical age under the following Zhou period of rule over the next millennium. An important concern was to improve and order the workings of society, which stemmed from various schools of thought, the most predominant being Confucian tenets that embraced the cultivation of ethical conduct and behaviour.

A second tenet was Taoism founded by Lao-tzu, a figure to whom the Tao Te Ching is attributed, and which merged intellectual and philosophical principles with the attainment of unity, harmony and the complementarity of opposite states. These two schools of thought have persisted through the centuries, transmitting a core doctrine of values that were absorbed into an extended Chinese empire, emphasising imperial prestige, order, ritual and authoritarian bureaucracy, even through periods of political division and reunification, that exerted a powerful and spiritual momentum over art, architecture and city building.

Han dynasty rulers had established relations with Japan and subdued many of the bordering countries of Central Asia including Tibet and Vietnam, extending a sphere of influence almost to the borders of the Roman Empire. However it was during the T'ang dynasty that city development reached its zenith. Chang'an, the walled capital that is now Xian, had a population of two million — the largest city in the world — and was laid out on a grid plan with the imperial city and government quarters facing south. The conception of the city as a "whole" necessitated a monumental construction programme for which new building technologies were developed. The physical aspects of city layout, and the well orchestrated structure of government, established a framework for a tiered administrative and organisational hierarchy that extended to the provinces and prefectures, and to neighbouring protectorates that surrounded the "Middle Kingdom". New building techniques were taken to Japan by skilled craftsmen and used in the construction of temples in the Heijō and Heian capitals, Nara and Kyoto.[1] During this period urbanisation and new forms of architecture continued to emerge unabated until the fall of the dynasty in the tenth century.

The Song period was a time of cultural stability and expanding trade guilds. Maritime trade with other Asian settlements, which flourished particularly in southern China, was centred around Guangzhou. With the invention of the magnetic compass, maps were compiled and naval power built up.

The Mongol invasion in the thirteenth century under Genghis Khan formed part of a wider campaign to conquer large parts of northern and central Asia. While the Mongol empire was shortlived, it appropriated but streamlined the central bureaucracy, modernised the educational system and moved the capital to Beijing which was substantially rebuilt. During this period of prosperity, new land routes promoted relations with the West. A new walled capital was built under the succeeding Ming dynasty at Nanjing in 1368, but its relocation back to Beijing in the fifteenth century came to symbolise the monumental form of Ming city building. The most predominant form of intervention however was the initiation of large-scale naval expeditions — to develop sea routes to countries of South and Southeast Asia, to conduct diplomatic relations with many of its neighbouring countries, and to implement the tribute system. It was during this period that Western adventurers began to arrive in China, first the Portuguese (via Goa and Malacca), who arrived at Guangzhou in 1517, and were later handed a lease of nearby Macau.

The Manchu Qing dynasty consolidated rule over China in 1644. They reinvigorated the established political structure and embraced Confucian traditions. This was also a period of major emigration of Chinese to Southeast Asian cities, especially those undergoing rapid development as colonial cities under European dominance. In so doing they introduced Chinese cultural and design influences to these growing cities and in return, through the junk trade, introduced Western merchants into China's southern ports, in particular Canton. The imposition of trading restrictions on the part of China and the importation of opium by East India traders was the combined cause of the two Opium Wars that led to treaty settlements marking the end of China's isolationist policy. Concession areas for foreign powers together with the principle of extraterritoriality, established 'unequal' but international legal terms for Western rights in China which lasted for almost a century. The settlements included the ceding of Hong Kong to the British.

By the mid-nineteenth century large parts of East and Central Asia were dominated by Western interests, arguably introducing material progress at the cost of national autonomy and identity. By the early twentieth century nationalism was rapidly evolving in the wake of militant Western occupation and colonial regimes that were gradually transforming national economies but also having to confront new and complex ideological movements. In the meantime Japan was preserving its political independence through new modernisations grafted onto traditional cultural patterns that were to turn it into a dominating power in Asia.

After aligning itself with the Axis powers of Germany and Italy to contain Russia, Japan moved into China in 1937, and simultaneously into direct confrontation with the West. After 1941, Japan extended its reach into Southeast Asia and over the following few years controlled China, the Indonesian and Philippine archipelagos, Malaysia, Singapore, Vietnam, Thailand and Burma. In China a century of unequal treaties and internecine conflict drew to a close with the retreat of the Japanese but civil war continued to polarise the country, which culminated in the People's Republic of China being proclaimed by Mao Tse-tung in October 1949.

After the death of Mao, Deng Xiaoping advanced the Four Modernisations of agriculture, technology, industry and deference and in the 1990s broadened its diplomatic relations. Under a new Basic Law, Hong Kong reverted to China, becoming a Special Administrative Region in 1997. Macau, the oldest Western settlement in East Asia, similarly reverted in 1999. Thereafter China moved to rapprochement with other countries in East and Southeast Asia.

JAPAN

Whilst subject to ancient Chinese cultural influences, Japan was unified by its central location in the Inland Sea and its rich agricultural tradition. After AD 400, the Yamato rulers unified the country through their court in Nara, establishing a long standing imperial continuity of divine monarchs which traced its history to the Sun Goddess, Amaterasu. This gave rise to the *Shinto* pantheon of spirit gods with its emphasis on rituals which have survived to the present time, becoming absorbed in urban culture and design. Buddhism was imported from China in the sixth century AD, and over time various Sinic concepts were appropriated including the Chinese calendar. The Yamato capital was designed with a rectangular form similar to the Chinese capital Chang'an.

The Heian court based in Kyoto lasted

until 1185 and was largely taken up with cultural ritual and etiquette. However changing economic conditions led to a rise in feudalism which continued until the sixteenth century when Japan was reunified under Oda Nobunaga. His successor Toyotomo Hideyoshi conducted the first full-scale survey of Japan and centralised land records. Portuguese traders arrived in 1542, followed by Jesuit missionaries led by Francis Xavier, and the Spanish from their Asian base in Manila.

In 1600 Tokugawa Ieyasu became Shogun and ruled Japan from a fortress at Edo, the present Tokyo. The nobility or daimyo were divided into various categories on the basis of land holdings. Under Ieyasu the country was sealed off from Western traders apart from the Dutch whose maritime experience and lack of proselytising ambitions facilitated the establishment of the Dutch East India Company in Nagasaki Bay. The major cities of Edo, Heian and Osaka became cultural and intellectual hubs, and home to the most prominent religious shrines. By the eighteenth century Western scientific study, shipbuilding and military knowledge began to be assimilated, helping to affect the modernisation of Japan. The opening up of the country began in 1854 with the Treaty of Kanagawa under pressure from the United States and the persuasive influence of an American fleet in Tokyo Bay. In 1864 an allied fleet of American, British, Dutch and French ships effectively terminated the Tokugama shogunate and in 1868 Emperor Meiji restored the imperial court. The Meiji period saw modernisations to the country involving massive industrial development and investment in infrastructure.

In 1894 Japan moved to occupy Korea, Manchuria, and the Shandong Peninsula. The resulting Treaty of Shimonoseki with China ceded the Liaodong Peninsula and Taiwan to Japan although the latter was later ceded back to China. The peace treaty in 1905, following the Russo-Japanese War,

acknowledged Japan's military control over Korea which was formally annexed in 1910. The worldwide economic depression in the 1930s had a significant impact on Japan whose economy was highly dependent on international trade. To counter this Japan increased its military capacity and gradually consolidated its control over northern China, and in 1941 commenced war in the Pacific and a major movement into Southeast Asia. The Potsdam agreement in July 1945 set out zones of occupation in Asia, the demilitarization of Japan and the restriction of Japanese territory. Japan itself was occupied by the allied forces from 1945 to 1952. While imperialist intervention was reversed, the ramifications in the immediate post-war period were enormous.

Post-war Japan commenced a route to economic superpower status on the back of demilitarisation, technological innovation and political reform. The peace treaty of 1951 formally ratified the renouncement of Japan's territorial claims in China, Korea, Taiwan and Southeast Asia, and partial reparation agreements were later signed and official ties formed with the People's Republic of China, Burma, the Philippines and Indonesia. Centralised economic planning through the 1980s and 1990s accelerated both social change and economic growth, although the latter has faltered in recent years. However, cultural cohesion persists on the back of embedded traditions, social conventions and behavioural patterns stemming from societal hierarchies and a largely mono-racial state.

KOREA

Korea is the oldest state in East Asia, but for much of its existence came under the ideological influence of China. Beginning with the Siu period of reunification, its culture and language was heavily influenced by Chinese script and literature. From its close ties and cultural receptiveness evolved a long commercial and military interaction,

2 Eds. Dent, C.M. and Huang, D.W.F., *Northeast Asian Regionalism*, Routledge, Curzon, 2002, p65

with Korea adopting much of the central administrative apparatus of China and the Confucian examination system.

The early capital of the Kuguryo kingdom was in Pyongyang, and its territory extended to the Han River basin and the area around the present city of Seoul. The political unification of the peninsula came about at the end of the seventh century. The Koryo dynasty, from which the name *Korea* is derived, presided over an independent country until the late fourteenth century before falling victim to the Mongol invasion which made way for the Choson dynasty in 1392. This was subject to periodic Japanese invasion and occupation. In the late eighteenth century the first Western ships arrived on the Korean coast to demand trading rights and diplomatic representation, as foreign powers became further entrenched in treaty port expansion around the coast of China. The Meiji Restoration in Japan with its rapid modernisation programme, acted to open up Korea and remove all forms of Chinese influence. In 1910 Korea effectively became a colony of Japan, and remained under authoritarian Japanese rule until 1945.

With both Soviet and American occupation after 1945, Korea became the subject of a power play between North and South. The ensuing Korean War ended with a truce in 1953 which provided for a demilitarised neutral zone, and North Korea effected a treaty with the People's Republic of China. While North Korea has remained relatively isolated from the international community, South Korea's economic direction was set through a series of five-year plans which had a major impact on city design. From the 1980s its economic growth accelerated as one of the four 'Little Dragon' economies of Asia. However, reunification of the country between such disparate political and economic entities has proved impossible, and the notion of peaceful integration and even economic co-operation remains elusive.

The Greater East Asian Co-Prosperity Sphere imposed by Japan prior to World War II carried a brutal imprint of oppression that recast itself in Cold-War demarcations namely between North and South Korea, and between China and Taiwan. This still surfaces in security or sovereignty disputes over the Diaoyu Islands in the East China Sea, and North Korea's nuclear programme. These differences can arguably only be overcome through closer economic cooperation. China now holds hegemonic power in the region, and as relations between China and Taiwan have begun to thaw, Taiwan has been increasingly drawn into economic co-operation with the Mainland.[2] Interdependencies between primate cities within these countries will continue to have strong consequences for transnational networks, free trade areas, linked infrastructure and city development.

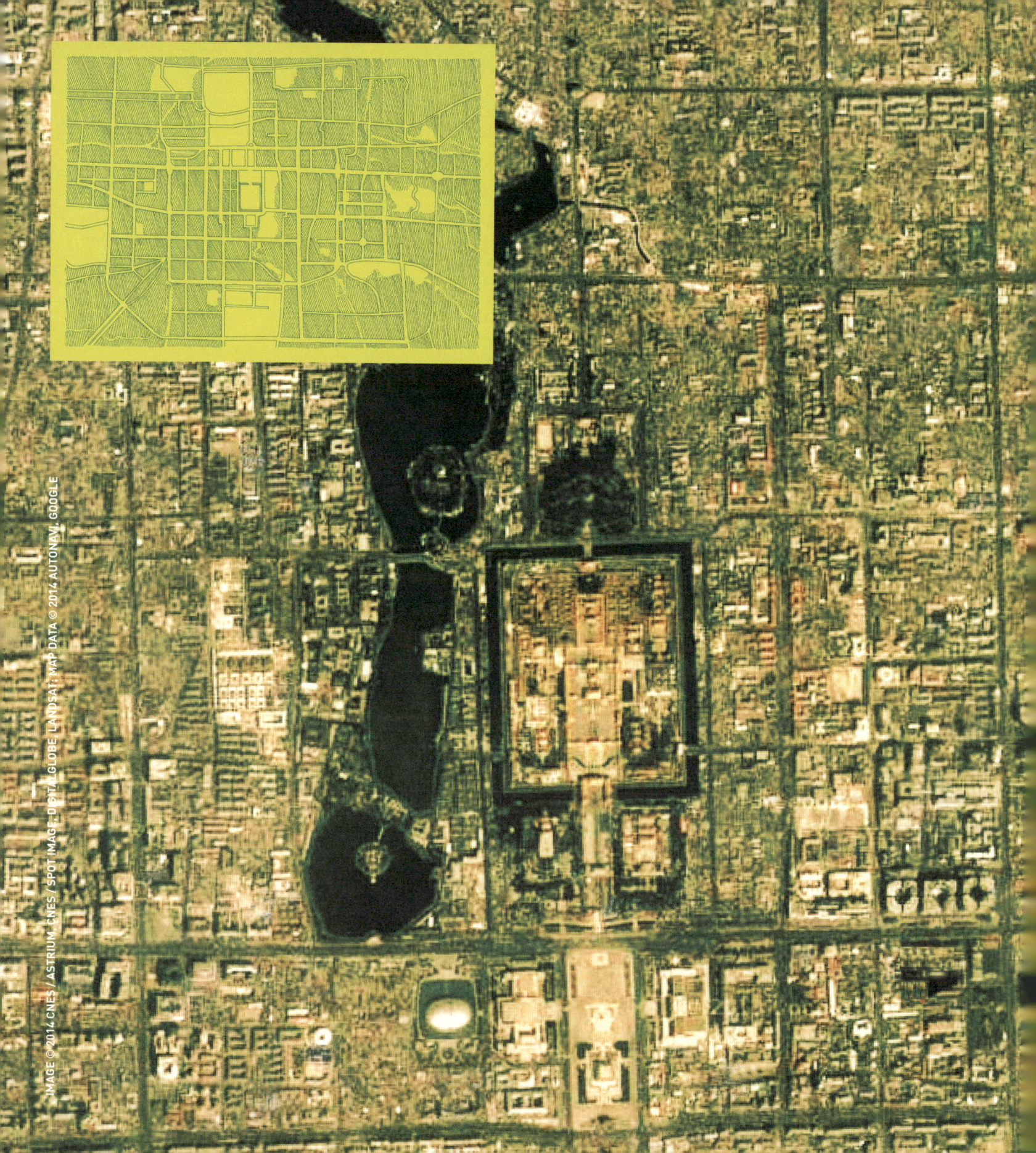

Beijing

THE URBAN FOOTPRINT OF BEIJING IN 2014 is 3,500 square kilometers with a population of 20 million. The overall population density of 4,900 per square kilometer can be broken down into 1 per cent for the Inner City, 3 per cent for the Outer Area, 53 per cent for the First Ring Suburbs and 43 per cent for the Second Ring Suburbs. Dispersion population growth outside the core, even beyond the Sixth Ring Road, has effectively contributed to a lower urban density than that in the 1950s at around 23,500 persons per square kilometer, similar to that of Manhattan.

1 Aldrich, M.A., *The Search for a Vanishing Beijing*, Hong Kong University Press, Hong Kong, 2006

2 Wu, L.Y., *Rehabilitating the Old City of Beijing*, University of British Columbia Press, Vancouver, 1999

IT IS RECORDED IN THE ZHOU LI — which sets out an intuitive set of ordered and symmetrical city layout principles — that during the Warring States Period between 475 and 221 BC, a new city was constructed on the site of the old City of Ji, which itself dated back 3,000 years. The city was divided geometrically by nine longitudinal and nine latitudinal lines, so the ordered pattern of streets was established at an early stage. Over the next 2,000 years it was of strategic importance in northern China, and was gradually laid out during the thirteenth century Yuan Dynasty when Kublai Khan established Dadu as the capital city, making it one of the world's oldest centrally planned cities. An imperial edict of 1285 stated that all inhabitants of the city who were in high positions and who wished to move into the Capital, would be given priority, and a maximum of eight *mu* of land would be allocated to each. If all the land was not taken up in this way, then common people were then allowed to construct houses and reside

there. Nobles and wealthy officials therefore maximised this development opportunity, building courtyard houses along a geometric layout of streets and passages that resembled a gigantic chessboard based on a south-north orientation — *Jing*, or an east-west orientation — *Wei*.

The Mongols conquered territories that included much of northern Asia, extending even to Baghdad and Damascus, thereby introduced Arabic and Persian influences to city construction and laying the basis for the culturally prolific Ming dynasty. From 1402 capital construction projects were designed according to auspicious cosmological influences, and to a large extent the city became a stage set for rituals relating to solar solstices and equinoxes. The 'almanac' system of siting important buildings was dependent on accurate astrological studies, although the most sophisticated mathematical calculations were introduced in the seventeenth century by Jesuits, who controlled the Imperial Observatory until 1838.[1]

PLANNING THE FEUDAL CAPITAL

Wu Liangyong has stated that planning of the city crystallized much of the urban design ideas from the Han and Tang dynasty city of Chang'an, the Northern Wei period city of Luoyang, and the Northern Song dynasty city of Kaifeng, including the evolution of palace complexes.[2] Beijing's spatial form was a highly regimented and symbolic personification of Confucian ideology with its complex and carefully orchestrated interplay between hierarchical forms of social organisation and power structures. It was laid out with the Imperial Palace at the geographic centre, the ancestral temple to the east, the sacrificial altars to the west, and the market centre to the north. The Ming layout included lines of government offices to the south around a central space — the 'Imperial Way', which later evolved into Tiananmen Square. Up to the Qing dynasty, spatial emphasis was achieved through the strategic location of gateways, palaces and temples within a gridded framework.

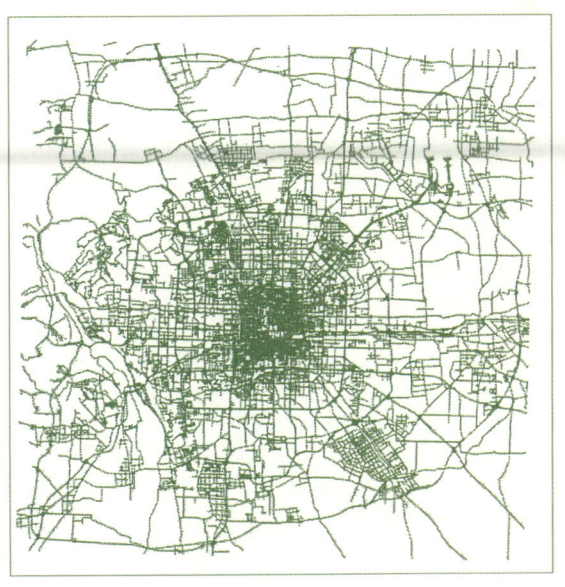

City growth, 1951–2014 (left); Street network of Beijing (right)

Source: Wang, Z, *A Comparison Study on Urban Morphology of Beijing and Shanghai*, Bachelor degree project thesis, Högskolan i Gävle, 2013

THE FORBIDDEN CITY

The Imperial Palace was constructed by the Ming Emperor Zhu Di over a 14-year period, commencing in 1406. It lies in the heart of the Old City and was the ruling seat of Government for Ming and Qing emperors, known as the Forbidden City. It was separated by high walls from the Imperial city itself. The palace buildings are arranged symmetrically along a north-south axis representing a central meridian line that positioned the imperial palace and its political order at the centre of the Middle Kingdom. The central axis was introduced as an architectural rule during the Han dynasty, acting to regularise city and palace layouts. This 7.5 kilometre "imperial road" runs from the Bell and Drum Towers in the north to the Yongding Gate in the south. The layout is associated with the five primary elements of *feng shui* — metal, wood, water, fire and earth. This is recorded in the Rites of Zhou, which set out elaborate rules for functional division of space into courts for living quarters, business and worship.

The Forbidden City complex is rectangular in shape, bounded by red walls with a gate tower on each side. Main buildings sit on raised terraces to emphasise the compositional effect, with careful proportionality between the building forms to achieve the optimum visual effect associated with the sequential revelation of space. The central opening of the outer triple gates was used only by the emperor and the right to proceed to the inner gate was conferred as a special privilege. The Wumen or Meridian Gate is the front entrance from the south, built in 1420 as the 'official' entrance; the Shenwumen or Gate of Divine Might is to the north; Donghuamen or Flower Gate is to the east; and Xihuamen or Flower Gate lies to the west. Tall watchtowers mark each corner. The Forbidden City is flanked by four temples — the Yue Tan, Temple of the Moon to the West; Ri Tan, Temple of the Sun to the East; Di Tan, Temple of the Earth to the North; and Tian Tan, Temple of Heaven to the South. The Gate of Heavenly Peace — the main entrance gate from Tiananmen Square — is regarded as the finest example of a towered gate in China, built by Emperor Shun Zhi in 1651 and where imperial proclamations were posted.

The southern outer court consists of three main ceremonial halls — the Hall of Supreme Harmony, the Hall of Complete Harmony and the Hall of Preserving Harmony. The main buildings of the northern court are the Hall of Celestial Purity, the Hall of Celestial and Terrestrial Union, and the Hall of Terrestrial Tranquility, flanked by Six West and Six East Palaces.

In 1925 the Forbidden City was converted into the Palace Museum, and large-scale repair and renovation has enabled a number of the halls to display artworks and paintings, dating back to the Shang and Zhou dynasties.

The Qiniandian or Hall of Prayer (for Good Harvest), with its circular hall and triple roof form, was renovated in 1751 as a site for sacrificial offerings to the gods, and later rebuilt after being struck by lighting. Its sophisticated round wooden structure and 28 column placements symbolise the heavenly sphere while its blue tiles represent the sky. The numerology related to rings of support columns represent the constellations and time periods of the lunar year.

The various city wards were defined by major thoroughfares, allowing the different residential districts to be virtually traffic-free.

The Northern City eventually adopted the name "Tartar City" during the Mongol dynasty and became home to Manchu mansions during the Qing dynasty. The Southern city became the Chinese City associated with commercial activities.

In 1403 during the last years of the Ming Dynasty the name Dadu was changed to Beijing. The city was consolidated and defined through massive city walls with the imperial "Forbidden City" positioned on a south-north line, forming an invisible 7.9 kilometre central axis from the Bell and Drum Towers in the north to the Qianmen Tower in the south, passing through the centre of the throne room. All construction related in a symmetrical way to this central axis, symbolising the hierarchical importance attached to imperial authority. In 1419 the city wall was adjusted to create the existing Inner City, with the Imperial City measuring 2,500 m by 2,700 m enclosing the Forbidden City. While the Imperial City housed prominent residences and gardens, the Forbidden City accommodated the Emperor, the Imperial Family and also functioned as the Centre of Government. The commanding scale of buildings and courtyards present a sequence of solids and voids which vary in size. The vast horizontal scale of the city is punctuated by man-made vertical components — notably Jingshan Hill

to the north of the palace, and a series of gate towers that have contributed to a controlled but powerful skyline.

The inner city or *Dong Jiao Min Xiang*, measures around forty square kilometres, and comprises large houses, palaces, and former foreign embassies. The smaller Hui Guan area to the south was laid out on a more irregular street pattern with small scale *siheyuan*, commercial buildings, theatres and visitor accommodation. Overall, Beijing's strong physical representations established its historical identity and regulated subsequent development up to the Qing dynasty when an outer city wall was constructed, effectively dividing the city into two areas. While the Qing dynasty was established by Manchurian nobles, people who belonged to the Han nationality were forcibly moved from the inner to the outer city, prompting the rapid growth of new housing, mainly in the form of courtyard dwellings. From then onwards, previously regulated street types — known as *xiaojie, dajie or hutongs* and based on width — became more diverse, and the number of urban passageways gradually grew to more than 2,000. The complementary interplay between the regular pattern of buildings and natural water elements embedded within the landscape framework, formed a regularised basis for the evolving city morphology. Many of the streams that flowed through the outer city area were later filled in and their names given to the new hutongs. Even today,

THE BUDDHIST PAGODAS originated in India, and served as holy reliquary sites. The site of the White Pagoda Temple or *Ba Ta Si* dates back to 1092, but in 1271 was reconstructed by Kublai Khan in the Tibetan style, although with strong Nepalese roots. Its height now dominates the local siheyuan. Small-scale incremental regeneration has retained the hutong fabric around the temple, rehabilitating the complex and refurbishing older buildings to create extended space for temple activities and a reinvigorated temple fair. Adjacent to the White Pagoda Temple was the hutong courtyard house of Zheng He, the admiral who, in 1402, embarked on four voyages with an imperial fleet of several hundred ships, travelling through Southeast Asia, across the Indian Ocean to the Red Sea. This led directly to a strong Chinese presence in Java, Malacca, Sri Lanka and even further afield. The crew included artisans and scholars, and they impressed local rulers with presents of silk, jade and other goods which underscored the power and wealth of China. The image of Zheng He can still be seen in the Chinese temples across Asian port cities.

THE TEMPLE OF HEAVEN complex lies to the south of the Forbidden City on the Imperial axis, and is four times its size. It is said to symbolise the meeting of heaven (the circle) and earth (the square). Ming emperors used the temple, built in 1420, as an altar where ritual prayers were offered for good harvests on auspicious dates. Diligence and respect were also shown by symbolic acts such as ploughing furrows of land or planting seedlings — activities still carried out by royalty in Thailand, Cambodia and Japan. Similar altars were located on the northern, eastern and western outskirts, indicating a combination of divine right and political might. In 1545 the Daxiangdian or Great Hall was constructed and later the temple was enclosed within the Outer City wall. The temple was re-built under the Manchu Qing dynasty, but was ransacked by Anglo-French forces in 1860 and again by the allied force sent to put down the Boxer Rebellion in 1900. After the founding of the People's Republic of China in 1949, the temple buildings were repaired and the complex opened to the public. As an altar for worshiping heaven, the overall planning and building shape is symbolic, relating to prevailing theories of positive and negative energy, and the relationship between heaven and earth.

The main temple buildings are situated at both ends of the axis linked by a raised walkway — at the northern end, the altar of Prayers for Grain; at the southern end, the Circular Mound Altar. Their circular timber structures surrounded by 4,000 cypress trees in a central urban situation, represent a legacy of exquisite architectural design symbolic of ancient rites, and a continuation of established philosophical theory, historically related to urban form.

The Circular Mound Altar reflects an ancient belief that the universe was round in shape. The terrace is paved with nine rings of stone slabs representing the positive yang energy of heaven and the nine divisions of the universe. The Huangqionyu or Imperial Vault of Heaven was used for storing spirit tablets for ceremonial use on the Circular Mound, built by the Qing Emperor Qianlong in 1752. Its circular form represents the celestial sphere, and is surrounded by an "echo wall" signalling an elusive communion between heaven and earth.

JINGSHAN PARK is situated on the central meridian of the city. The Bell and Drum Towers, which were erected in 1420 as wooden structures, lie at the northern end of the axis. They were used during the Ming dynasty as a means of broadcasting time in the morning and evening. Jingshan Hill — the tallest point in Beijing — was erected with fill excavated from construction of the moat around the Forbidden City in order to meet feng shui criteria. This dictated that the most auspicious outlook to the south must be protected against the north — not coincidentally, this was from where the sand-filled winds emanated as well as invading armies. Later groups of buildings were erected, including the Shouhuangmen Gate and Hall of Imperial Longevity, surrounded by flocks of crane and deer parks — the symbols of long life. The Qinanglou Tower was a place to pay homage to Confucius and cultivate diligent habits. The Vairochana Buddha that was placed in the Wanchunting Pavilion on the hill summit was destroyed during the Cultural Revolution.

Five pavilions on top of the hill contained bronze statues of Buddha representing the five regions. Only one — the Vairochana Buddha — survived the allied looting of 1900. The 23-hectare park was opened to the public in 1955 and now forms a composite cultural entity associated with the Palace Museum.

The Bell Tower rises above the entrance to a courtyard house.

The Zhong-Gulou area is centred on the Drum and Bell Towers, along the north-south axis. The two towers stand at each end of a small square, surrounded by siheyuan. Drum Tower Street has retained its traditional associations around the Guan Yue Temple. The temple however is now the government office of the Tibetan Autonomous Region.

South Cathedral constructed in 1650 and presided over by Matteo Ricci.

The ancient Ocean Observatory

THE YUANMINGYUAN GARDEN was an extensive imperial water garden created during the Qing dynasty on a 60-hectare site. It was constructed over a period of a hundred years by which time it occupied 500 hectares of which one-third was lakes. This formed part of a programme of garden and woodland creation in the western outskirts which became used for private villas. The building of Yuanmingyuan or Garden of Perfection and Brightness commenced in 1709 and became the largest imperial garden in China, famous for its exquisite buildings and cultural treasures, and for its harmonious garden design.

The destructive intervention of Anglo-French forces in 1860, under the Earl of Elgin, led to much of the complex being burned down and looted, leading to the Treaty of Peking which ceded Kowloon to Britain. Before restoration was complete, the Allied Forces again attacked the city and destroyed the remaining buildings, with the debris used for building materials. The Yuanmingyuan was listed as a protected monument and partially restored for educational use. The ruins of many major buildings, including eighteenth century reproductions of European Baroque palaces and those that fused Chinese and Western styles, such as the immense Ocean Observatory, originally sat within a group of fountains. Only the ruins remain as stark monuments. The twelve bronze animal heads that formed part of the Haiyantang garden, represented branches of the Chinese chronology system and were also famously looted, although a number have been retrieved and returned to China.

the present system of lakes and water features represent part of this ancient waterway system. During this period, five gardens were laid out — *Yuan Ming* or Royal Summer Palace, *Qing Yi* or Summer Palace, *Chan Chun*, *Jing Yi* and *Jing Ming*.

The walled Legation district in the early twentieth century enclosed an area along the east side of Tiananmen Square, to the south of Chang An Avenue, and represented a wholly foreign quarter. It originated as the Ming dynasty termination of the Grand Canal, when the neighbourhood became an entrepot and a gateway for tribute missions to the emperor. Gradually foreign missions were established, along with the mansions of court officials and Manchu princes. Following the British-Franco invasion in 1860, a Legation Quarter was set up within the city walls and occupied by Britain, France, Russia, America, Japan, Prussia, Italy and Portugal. Foreigners were allowed to walk along the walls rather than the unpaved streets. The Boxer uprising of 1900 channelled popular dissent against foreign intrusion, focusing on both disturbance to "earth dragons" and the activities of missionaries and Christian converts. Support of the Boxers from the Qing court led to an ineffective siege of the Legation Quarter. The Protocol of 1901, apart from stipulating onerous terms for reparations by China, consolidated foreign control over Beijing. Different countries rebuilt their embassies, commercial buildings and banks in various styles, much as the Concession Areas were built in the port cities. St Michael's Cathedral was built in the Legation Quarter in 1903, and although later vandalised, it opened again in 1980. After 1949 the Foreign Affairs Ministry closed the Western legations and the wall around them was later dismantled.

The urban environment therefore presents a palimpsest of physical transformations that reflect changing political ideology, but also how this has consistently reflected

Engraving - The British Legation, Peking, 1873

China's national identity and centralisation of power. Physical development and periods of reconstruction and urban expansion have repeatedly and symbolically underscored the city's identity.

TIANANMEN SQUARE

Tiananmen Square, in its historical, cultural and political representation, is unique in Asia, although adopted and refined from an earlier urban design model in Chang'an — the T'ang dynasty capital. It forms an integral part of an axial composition symbolically and functionally related to the Imperial Palace, and the hierarchical order of the state. The square took its original shape from the early Ming dynasty layout of the Imperial Way, lined by administrative offices, and during feudal times it was the site of state ceremonies, Imperial edicts and judicial functions.

After 1912 various alterations reduced the former tight spatial setting and opened it up as a public gathering space and political emblem. During the Socialist period the square was again extended to the east and west and, to celebrate the 10th anniversary of the People's Republic, it was re-planned with a widened Changan Street to accommodate parades. To better define the space and reinforce its focus, it was flanked on the west by the Great Hall of the People and on the east by the Museum of Chinese History and Revolution. A monument to the People's

Heroes was placed on the central axis with Tiananmen Gate as a northern focus and Zhengyangmen to the south. From the 1970s the ceremonial nature of the space became an arena of confrontation, as a place to launch the new economic reforms, but also as a place of symbolic state intervention, epitomised by the 4th June 1989 protests and crackdown. Positioned at the heart of the capital it continues to be a stage for national events, but has also became a central locale where embedded ideologies are challenged by new ideas.

SIHEYUAN HOUSING AND HUTONG LANES

Hutongs are narrow lanes around 9.3 metres in width that, according to Yuan dynasty city plans, mainly ran East-West, possibly to provide shelter from the northern winds, and provided access to local groups of dwellings. Within these small communities, the basic residential unit was the courtyard house — siheyuan — as well as temples and monasteries. Their orientation allowed main rooms to be located on the northern side of the courtyard facing south, with the courtyard accessed through a gateway on the southern wall. Siheyuan are timber-framed with brick walls and tiled roofs, and in imperial times were subject to design decoration and colour restrictions according to ownership status. Even in a semi-dilapidated state they embody a strong sense of community and interaction

3 Ness, A, *Beijing : The Changing Historical Conservation Scene*, Heritage Conservation Paper, October 2004

between long-term residents, with daily necessities available within walking distance.

The courtyard residences themselves formed the basic unit of the old city morphology, built and occupied by high-ranking Mandarins and merchants since the Yuan Dynasty. The older street system divided the city into regular urban quarters. The main streets running parallel to the central axis, are intersected by side and branch lanes, creating an ordered and regularised layout pattern. Residential courtyard houses lined the streets, with distinctive architectural devices that embellished and unified the composition,

such as *menlou* (entrance gates), *pailou* (archways), and *yingbi* (street walls).

While the city gradually grew in size, it was the Chinese Revolution in 1911 that presented an opportunity for improved east-west street connections. These intersected the central north-south axis and established a further catalyst to the development of new residential enclaves. The area of Beijing at that time exceeded 24 times the size of the old city and by the time the People's Republic of China was founded in 1949 it is estimated that 17 million square metres or around 17,000 courtyard dwellings existed within the 62

square kilometres of the Old City. There was a saying that the hutongs were so numerous in Beijing that those without names were beyond calculation — like the hairs on an ox. Andrew Ness has written that, after the founding of the People's Republic of China, there was a strong divergence of opinion over which form of development the capital should take. Different factions favoured either an entirely new administrative centre in the western suburbs or large-scale redevelopment of the old city, which symbolically represented destruction of the old to make way for the new.[3] The redevelopment option was agreed, but not commenced until the late 1970s when the investment impetus could no longer be resisted. As streets have become progressively widened to cater for motor vehicles rather than bicycles, new trunk roads constructed, and an accelerated programme of redevelopment introduced, the traditional low-density hutongs have come under constant threat of demolition.

During the Cultural Revolution the City Planning Office was closed down, and many of the single-storey siheyuan were taken over by central government and rented, often to several families in multi-occupation. From 1982, these were subject to large-scale redevelopment through a constitutional amendment that allowed the state to assume ownership of all urban land, with residents only having the right to claim land-use rights. The 1980s and early 1990s was a time of enormous pressure for urban change and planning mechanisms were insufficiently sophisticated to protect these irreplaceable heritage areas, even those in close proximity to the Forbidden City. While a large number of buildings associated with the imperial palace, temples, gardens and mansions were listed for protection, many of the courtyard residences were in a dilapidated state, lacking modern conveniences. This made the argument for demolition and redevelopment that much easier. In the mid-1980s however,

Elaborately carved gateway in Ouya Hutong, Xicheng District

4 Weng, L, *Hutongs of Beijing*, Beijing Arts and Photography Publishing House, Beijing, 1993
5 Ness, 2004, op. cit.
6 Alexander, A, de Azevedo, P, Yutaka, H and Dorje, L, *Beijing Hutong Conservation Study*, International Heritage Fund, 2004

the City Planning Commission introduced height controls and plot ratio limitations within the inner city, with no buildings exceeding the height of the Forbidden City.

The word *hutong* is said to be derived from the Mongol word for 'well', with canals supplying water from the western suburbs and linked to the Grand Canal where barges transported rice from southern China to the imperial granaries. With the disappearance of the physical street matrix, the associated nomenclature and symbolic representations also go. These date back to the Yuan and Ming dynasties and often related to: the shape and length of the passage, such as "Jia Bao" (narrow lane) or "Zhu Gan" (literally "bamboo pole" denoting a long narrow passage); cultural aspects such as city gates, wells, monuments or bridges which have tended to prevail long after the point of identity disappeared; the informal representation of urban occupations reflected in surviving names, such as Performing Music Hutong and Knitting Yarn Hutong; or auspicious sounding words as in Xi (happy); Fu (fortune) or Shou (longevity).[4]

The impetus for improved conservation mechanisms was in part caused by the redevelopment of 200 siheyuan houses covering six hectares in the Nanchizi area to the east of the Palace Museum, which accommodated around 1,000 households. These dated back to the Qing dynasty and had been occupied by high ranking officials. Although the dwellings were run down, they had maintained their traditional character and layout pattern. Thirty-one courtyard-type dwellings in relatively good condition were offered for public sale, and the remainder demolished to make way for new public housing. Only 300 households were able to remain in the area, the others relocated elsewhere. Prevailing height restrictions prevented large-scale development, but the unfortunate "rationalised traditional" result persuaded the government that no similar

renewal exercises should be carried out.[5] They were possibly also prompted by the experience of gentrification exercises in other cities that had both attracted considerable investment and successfully revitalised run-down urban neighbourhoods.

Throughout the 1990s a somewhat discreet process saw the acquisition of a number of the finest remaining siheyuan properties by a small group of individuals and companies, while others became occupied by former senior government officials or organisations. However around 4.5 million square metres of the older built-up area was demolished during 2002 and 2003 to make way for new commercial and residential complexes. It is now estimated that around 3,000 siheyuan still remain in the city, of which 539 have been placed under protection. In 2002 a master conservation plan prepared by the municipal government was approved, covering twenty-five historical areas in the inner city with five categories based on historical and cultural type, which included the hutong streetscape. This list was extended in 2004 to encompass fifteen additional historical areas of which five are situated in the inner city. Collectively these cover around 20 per cent of the Old City of Beijing or around 1,000 hectares, and are subject to conservation guidelines.

In 2004, the Beijing Municipal Administration quietly introduced legislation which "encouraged individuals and work units to acquire courtyard-style residences in historical and cultural preservation areas". Provisional Regulations formalised this situation, setting out principles under which overseas and domestic bodies, representing either individuals or corporations, can purchase siheyuan residences under strict legal conservation conditions laid down by the Beijing Heritage Conservation Plan. Buyers are permitted to re-sell or gift these properties, or pledge them as collateral against loans. The latter is somewhat ambiguous — the Provisional Regulations

mandate that district administrative bodies must provide buyers with documentary evidence that the properties form part of heritage protection areas, of which around 60 square kilometres remain. A conservation project based on social surveys jointly carried out by the International Heritage Fund and Tsinghua University, published in 2004, suggested a reform of the *Weigai* system under which residents of dilapidated buildings were re-housed and the sites upgraded.[6] It was recommended that this process should be limited and ensure: minimum relocation of residents; security of tenure; and specify target areas for conservation, infrastructure and living space improvement. However news reports continue to document the destruction of parts of the Dontangzi and Red Star Hutongs as a result of the Municipal Administration of State Land awarding land-use rights to development companies without the consent of families who had lived in the areas for several generations but had insufficient evidence of property ownership.

The remaining hutongs have, since 2008, become a tourist commodity, often explored by pedicab, particularly in and around Shichahai and the adjoining lakeside area.

THE SUMMER PALACE

The Summer Palace was created from pristine wooded hillsides to the west of the city, and has existed in some form from 1150 in the Jin dynasty. It combines the areas of Wanshouwan or Longevity Hill, and Kunming Lake, and was the largest imperial estate in China comprising five inter-connected gardens and three hills. During the Ming dynasty the gardens were owned by various wealthy families, and it became an imperial garden only in the Qing period. In 1749, under the emperor Qianlong, major re-building work was carried out and the West Lake enlarged and renamed Kunming Lake.

In 1860 the Anglo-French Forces invaded

Beijing and destroyed many of the buildings and gardens, and looted their treasures. Some twenty years later the Qingyiyuan Garden was restored and renamed Yiheyuan (Garden of Peace and Harmony), but this was again plundered by the Allied Forces in 1900 and the last of the temples destroyed. It was restored after the 1911 Revolution, and in 1924 it was turned into a public park, although many buildings became private residences. Its full restoration began only after 1949. The Palace is divided into four areas — the Court, Front-Hill, Rear-Lake and Front-Lake. The urban design, as in all imperial palaces, is focussed on a symmetrical arrangement along a central axis, bringing together Buddhist and Taoist cultural references.

The arrangement and disposition of buildings is the result of symbolic position and axial organisation, visual integration and elusive metaphysical criteria relating to heavenly influences and good fortune. For example the 17-Arch Long Bridge relates to ancient Chinese numerology, while the Pavilion of Buddhist Incense on Longevity Hill was originally built as a pagoda in a fortuitous position overlooking Kunming Lake. The pagoda was subsequently rebuilt as a pavilion, and again in 1891 after the destruction of the Summer Palace. Modelled on the Liuhe Tower in Hangzhou, it is inscribed with the words *Shiyan fengjiao* in reference to the good fortune resulting from observance of moral etiquette and social customs, and *Qixiangzhaohui* referring to favourable feng shui.

Poetic nomenclature is often encrypted in calligraphy such as *Huazhongyou* (literally 'Strolling through a Scroll Painting'), and describes the physical experience within a cluster of storied buildings, pavilions and platforms. *Zhichuntang* ('Harbinger of Spring Pavilion'), or *Deheyuan* ('Garden of Virtue and Harmony'), encapsulate both use and emotion as part of an urban design narrative.

BEIHAI PARK forms one of the three lake parks, together with Zhonghai and Nanhai, associated with the Forbidden City. It features a classical Chinese garden landscape of halls, altars and temples that date back to the tenth century Liao dynasty. The Qionghuadao Islet is surmounted by the White Dagoba, situated above the Yong'an Temple of Eternal Peace. The Yong'anqiao Bridge of Eternal Peace that links the Islet with the Round City is a three-arched carved stone bridge built in the early Yuan dynasty. The Yong'ansi Temple was built in 1651 and was first named the White Dagoba Temple where lama monks from Tibet would intone Buddhist scriptures. The Tibetan Dagoba is an iconic structure, and having been re-built twice after suffering earthquake damage, is also a reliquary stupa. It is said that the Qing Emperor Shunzhi gave permission for its construction to demonstrate the power of Buddhism as a means of national unification.

[7] *South China Morning Post*, January 30, 2012

The former Peking Railway Station built in 1900 served as the terminus for the Tianjin Line, before being replaced by Beijing Station to the east.

The Beijing Railway Station designed by Yang Tingbao and built in 1959 to commemorate the 10th anniversary of the People's Republic of China. It drew on the eclectic combination of traditional Chinese features and Soviet inspired Modernism.

PLANNING AFTER 1949: THE SOCIALIST PERIOD

In 1927 the Kuomintang relocated the capital back to Nanjing, and Beijing was renamed Beiping or City of Heavenly Peace. In the wake of the Boxer Protocol this acted to constrain development in the city, and urban growth was also effectively curtailed for some time after its restoration as the capital of the People's Republic of China in 1949.

The political significance of a national rebirth after 1949, with a new and revolutionary government superimposing itself on the old city, was impelling but lacked real vision. Ideological conflict and upheaval evolved physically into a state of benign neglect. Planning followed the Soviet inspired model, geared to reconstruction and industrialisation. Redevelopment to cater for urban growth placed inevitable pressure on the Old City and destroyed much of the historical single-storey fabric, while most of the remainder was poorly maintained. In 1950 architects and planners from Tsinghua University (Liang Sicheng and Chen Zhanxiang), made a new proposal to primarily focus administrative functions in the western suburbs between Gongzhufen and Yuetan in order to preserve the old city, with diplomatic activities in the east. The plan was rejected,

however Liang Sicheng gained a considerable reputation. It was reported in January 2012 that his former courtyard house in Dongcheng District had been torn down, despite being designated a cultural relic.[7]

A further plan was produced by the Beijing Urban Planning Committee in 1953, based on functional land-use zoning and street widening. It laid down a broad interventionist approach to the old city structure and the purposeful rejection of the traditional north-south urban axis. This involved a utilitarian interpretation of social planning to serve the state, particularly with regard to housing and industrial construction. However the lack of a firm planning strategy to guide redevelopment massively detracted from the traditional unity of the city. A series of master plans between 1957 and 1958 emphasised 'collective' neighbourhoods of up to 20,000 people. This evolved into the *danwei* system of virtually self-contained living and work

8 Wu, L.Y., *Rehabilitating The Old City of Beijing*, University of British Columbia Press, Vancouver, 1999

communities, which minimised commuting and helped focus city efforts on industrial development but at the expense of a drab and homogenous cityscape. This itself was aimed at unifying social behaviour and living patterns, redolent of the 'Great Leap Forward' years and the ensuing Cultural Revolution when ideology overtook the needs of urban development and translated into an assault on ancient city relics. Temples were frequently turned into other uses. The Temple of the Fire God in the Western City for example was turned into a Workers' Cultural Centre. The widening of Changan Street and expansion of Tiananmen Square in the 1950s, with its low-rise but monumental buildings such as the Great Hall of the People and the Museum of Revolution and History, were intended to symbolise the importance of the capital, but detracted from the sense of scale and points of focus associated with the cityscape. Planning followed the Soviet-inspired model, geared to reconstruction and industrialisation. Government attention focussed on how new architectural projects could best fit within the traditional cityscape — an approach known as *zhong er xin*. The Beijing Railway Station for example incorporated older imperial roofscape features in its design.

Under the First Five-Year Plan, housing had a lower priority than industrial development. During the Cultural Revolution there was little physical planning, although a programme of building new public facilities, including hospitals, was carried out in the city. Residential planning was highly influenced by Soviet inspired row house forms. Older siheyuan were converted to accommodate several families with many demolished to make way for apartment blocks of up to six storeys — a situation that worsened after the Tangshan earthquake. At the time, much of the housing located in the Old City was in the form of single-storey development, and a high percentage was dilapidated with little service infrastructure.

Up to the commencement of the Modernisations in the late 1970s, urban districts were demarcated by wide primary roads with piecemeal redevelopment leading to a largely concentric development pattern. As foreign investment grew during the 1980s and 1990s, stimulating economic momentum, enclaves were opened up for commercial and hotel development, high tech industry (in Zhongguancum Science Park), and new housing districts, accompanied by the completion of the Second, Third and Fourth Ring Roads. The massive rise in housing construction after 1974 had a major impact on the overall land use pattern through uncontrolled infill development, thus the strong horizontal physical and visual connections began to break down. In 1980, a new set of planning and policy guidelines was produced for construction works in the city, aimed at improving social and environmental conditions, but also to reinforce its role as the nation's cultural centre, reflecting Chinese history and unique urban design along with its recent revolutionary past. In 1985 the Municipal Urban Planning Commission promulgated the city's first regulations on height control for buildings within the inner city. The controversial redevelopment of Nanchizi to the east of the Palace Museum led to greater stress on heritage protection, and a conservation plan for the former Imperial City area was made public in 2003. While this restored the appearance of older sites, it also introduced a form of cosmetic gentrification.

In 1989 the Municipal Government stated that no more high-rise development should take place inside the Second Ring Road, and selected a number of derelict housing areas for renewal. They also set plot ratio limits and conservation criteria for the appearance of areas containing typical 'Old City' streetscapes. Under the more recent 1991-2010 plan, industrial, government and commercial development on the city periphery has eased pressure on the old core, and new residential suburbs have led to further decentralisation. The revitalisation programme in the core city has continued; firstly through greater local investment, increasing private ownership, and subsidised rentals for residents of redeveloped properties from work units, which has led to the establishment of housing cooperatives; and secondly through inducing willing residents to resettle in suburban locations, allowing further regeneration of the Old City. In this respect, the cost of new housing has been virtually covered by private investment, with preferential policies accorded to developers. Investment in infrastructure was given a substantial boost by the eight-year period of preparation for the 2008 Olympic Games, which consolidated Beijing's identity as an international city.

A NEW HOUSING MODEL

Wu Liangyong, director of the Institute of Architectural and Urban studies at Tsinghua University, illustrates the long history of the courtyard house as a prototype, dating back to the concept of residential quarters made up of groups of such houses or *li*.[8] These took the form of walled street blocks in the wards of Han dynasty cities, with alleys providing access to individual siheyuan. These later became known as *fangli* and grew into larger precincts, which retained their distinctive gate towers and entrance arches that evolved into the Beijing hutong.

The essential characteristics of the layout follow an integrated system dating from the thirteenth century Yuan dynasty. These include a hierarchy of thoroughfares, on a general grid pattern; mixed-use street blocks with a range of building types including shops and temples; and courtyard houses with a large number of plan variations. They are generally based on an organisational axis to which all the building components relate. The layout also establishes a clear distinction between private, public-private,

Ju'er Hutong housing, by Wu Liangyong

Moslem Quarter of food shops, demarcated by a pailou gateway

and communal space, with many layers of transition between them. The interplay between layers of 'enclosing' elements provides for countless architectural interpretations, while the courtyards themselves provide opportunities to integrate local plants, ponds and shade trees.

The Ju'er Hutong neighbourhood to the northeast of the Forbidden City dates from the thirteenth century Yuan dynasty, and still houses a number of old courtyard mansions that formed part of the Nan Luogu Xiang Preservation District. In 1987 a design team from Tsinghua University under Wu Liangyong conducted a survey of housing conditions and on this basis selected part of the area as a pilot renewal project inspired by traditional courtyard housing groups and their associated urban tissue.

One of the intentions of the pilot project was to create a low-rise housing prototype for developments of up to four storeys, that could be applied to other sensitive areas. This recognises both the cultural and practical values of the older cityscape, calling on the traditions of the siheyuan as well as aesthetic aspects. The project promoted a policy that required residents who returned to the renewed neighbourhood to purchase

their units, or have the option of moving elsewhere within the district. The concept was based on sustaining the intimate social interactions and human scale of the older area, together with both courtyard communal space and private spaces. This new housing type maximised the permissible plot ratio through new courtyard housing clusters in four separate phases, made up of two and three storey building forms to fit within the nine metre height limitation. Roof terraces and pitched roofs maximise the internal floor area, and basements provide additional living space per resident. Ultimately, this low-rise complex provides as much floorspace as a ten-storey apartment block.

A lesson learned from the success of this project is that design and technological innovation together with a strong community working closely with a development company and a local housing co-operative, can produce typological and compositional solutions beyond the macro management of planning institutions. Also the small-scale phasing of new development, together with conservation and rehabilitation, can create sensitive and successful regeneration. That said, renewal in a context of rapid economic growth and land leasing arrangements has had to deal

with escalating land prices, while balancing socialist market imperatives and affordability. This inevitably has an impact on housing space standards and aspirations, whereby housing reform mechanisms — put in place to finance affordable housing and subsidies for low-income groups — must also adapt to forces of change and equate need with social stability.

At the heart of the conservation issue is the conflict between modernisation and the preservation of historic single-storey housing within Beijing's core urban area. A second issue that resonates throughout development in Chinese cities is the rights of ownership to both property and land. Clearly rehabilitation within heritage areas brings considerable environmental as well as economic benefits. This can technically be combined with pockets of redevelopment that can collectively act to preserve some of the historic cityscape of siheyuan housing and hutong lanes.

Various planning and heritage reports emphasise the immense value of the historic city, and the ongoing need for sustainable urban regeneration. The latter requires strong Government support and planning co-ordination between municipalities to secure effective land-use control. Pilot

The area around the Xi Hai, Hou Hai and Qian Hai lakes incorporate preserved old mansions around their perimeter. It was regenerated in 2003 with a series of promenades and lakeside cafés.

The Yandai Xiejie historical residential and commercial area between Dianmen Wai Dajie and Shichahai Lake. The majority of the rehabilitated buildings are associated with lakeside restaurants, recreation and evening entertainment. The buildings still retain traditional features of carved windows and screens, but interior structures have been lost.

projects have shown that the logistics involved in combining rehabilitation with incremental redevelopment within the hutong framework can achieve reasonably high population densities. This however requires proper financing, infrastructure upgrading programmes, security of tenure, and compensation where necessary. The more transparent the process, the more likely residents will participate.

THE MODERN AND FUTURE CITY

Beijing is now the key city within a metropolitan mega-region which brings together Tianjin as part of a 150 kilometre regional development corridor to the southeast. Greater Beijing encompasses some 16,800 square kilometres. This is made up of the Old City, planned urban districts, and municipally administered rural areas.

Roads and rail lines connect Beijing with a supporting web of cities — Tangshan in the east with its coal and energy resources; the port city of Tanggo, and the historic resort towns of Chengde to the north-east and the coastal town of Beidaihe. These now form part of a regional urbanisation programme based on industrialisation, manufacturing, forestry, agriculture and tourism. Beijing's essential political, business and cultural role has, since the early 1980s, facilitated continued expansion through ring roads and transport arteries. This has enabled new development districts to be developed through a regional pattern of urbanisation that has combined satellite communities and commercial sub-centres. However, according to the Greater Beijing Plan, three new towns focussed around different forms of industrial development are planned — Shunyi, Yizhuang

and Tongzhou. Conservation zones have also been identified for ecological protection and water catchments.

The designation of Beijing as the Olympic host city for 2008 was a catalyst to the formulation of an integrated open space and conservation framework. The superimposition of an Olympic Master Plan involved not merely the Olympic Park but major improvements to city transport infrastructure, and communication facilities. At the same time co-ordinated regional policies accelerated development of the greater Beijing-Tianjin-Hebei corridor, orientating city development towards more administrative and tertiary growth associated with the expanding market economy. Since 1989 height controls have been imposed on the inner city, which has broadly preserved its visual sanctity with most new high-rise development outside the line of the old city wall — now the Second Ring Road, the first being the walls of the former Imperial City. The Olympic Plan — developed as an extension to the traditional north-south axis to the north of the Imperial Palace and broadly located between the Third and Forth Ring Roads — reinforces the vigorous geometry of the city plan and its history of placing the most important buildings along the central axis.

The modern city has retained its strong axiality, largely through the preservation of its historical north-south series of towers, temples and spaces, with the Forbidden City at its centre. The more contemporary east-west axis, along the monumental Chang'an Avenue alignment of some twenty-two kilometres, acts as the main functional bridge between new and existing areas. Tiananmen Square acts as a spatial fulcrum at their point of intersection, establishing a massive space at the core of what is now an international city, but also fulfilling the role of accommodating vessel for political signifiers including the Great Hall of the People, Chairman Mao's Mausoleum and the entry point to the Palace Museum. These axes, together with the Second, Third and Fourth Ring Roads, describe the compositional framework for urban growth from the early 1990s when there was a pronounced shift of commercial development to the east, but also to Financial Street in the west with a business environment set around green spaces and courtyards. Other commercial centres include Wangfujing Street, a traditional market area from the fifteenth century to the east of the Forbidden City, and Xidan Street.

Under the current heritage protection system, Beijing has 3,550 sites listed as cultural relics. Important buildings and monuments generally harmonise with their heterogeneous context and spatial setting, while serving as visible symbols of social stability and nationality identity. This has in turn put increasing urban pressure on the core city where building heights are controlled, roads

Liulichang literally means "glazed tile factory", dates back to the early Ming period when it produced tiles for the new palaces in Beijing. During the Qing dynasty it became an area of guesthouses for visitors and those sitting the imperial examinations. The street evolved as two parts – the eastern section became a centre for antique shops, and the west as a centre for scholarly books.

OLD FACTORY SPACE adjacent to Beijing's Third Ring Road — Factory 798 — was part of an amalgamated complex built in the 1950s with aid from East Germany. The factory complex comprised around forty industrial buildings, constructed of reinforced concrete and brick, with slanted glazed roofs. With the decline in industrial production, buildings were rented out and refurbished by artists and designers so that the present agglomeration of adopted and extended buildings form part of the Da Shanzi art complex — a mix of studios, exhibition spaces, bookshops and cafes. It also now houses a branch of the Central Academy of Fine Arts. While the long-term future of the complex is indeterminate, the ad hoc mix of adapted and new uses, and the colonising of outdoor spaces as display areas, suggests a benign relaxation of unnecessary controls in the face of a flourishing Chinese artistic resurrection and international market interest.

IMPOSED HEIGHT RESTRICTIONS in the commercial and shopping district to the east of the Palace Museum, have led to a range of hybrid forms through a mix of tradition and modernism. Streets are interspersed with pedestrian shopping and market precincts, which display an informal range of symbolic elements — gateways, tiled roofs, calligraphy and signage. These break down the street scale and create a sense of contrast and vibrancy.

are wide, and a considerable area is taken up by imperial parks and lake areas, including the Summer Palace, Yuanmingyuan Park and Forest Park to the north of the city. Height restrictions on the development of Finance Street (off Fuxingmen Avenue and along Pacific Bridge Street) are due to their close proximity to the seat of Central Government in Zhongwanhai. By contrast height restrictions have not been incurred in the Chaoyang Central Business District, and this has encouraged the development of statement-making buildings including the Yintai Centre, and China Central Place. The extravagant ambitions to underscore the cultural identity of the capital, tempts architects to two extremes — the exotic and understated, such as Paul Andreu's National Grand Theatre; and the curiously iconic and over-stated such as the OMA designed CCTV complex, which rises awkwardly 234 metres above its bland neighbours in the expanding office hub, as a structural grand gesture.

As with so many rapidly expanding Asian cities, Beijing has experienced a twenty year process of redevelopment, rather than the slower and more metabolic process of regeneration based on housing reform and socio-economic restructuring; one that might

best accord with social, economic and physical criteria at a grassroots level, and the interests of stakeholders. This is partly because of economic imperatives, but also through overly simplistic and more immediate solutions based on standardised and industrialised apartment block types. The physical transformation of Beijing cannot be considered separately from political factors and the swift, radical overhaul of both its policies and priorities. Housing development has been a major driver of urban form. In 1991 ninety per cent of the housing stock of 10.5 million square metres had been built since 1949. Some twenty-three years later, the total housing figure stands at 630 million square metres, mainly in the form of high-rise apartment buildings within new satellite communities on the urban fringe, while urban renewal has been largely based on ad hoc infill.

Urban design from the 1990s onwards, in the context of a socialist market economy, has largely involved a balancing of new residential, institutional and commercial office development with effective city management, particularly in terms of traffic planning and public transport. Pedestrian circulation, with respect to overall layout and road design, is a critical factor in new and rapidly expanding developments, particularly those planned at a gigantic scale with no overall urban design. In both Finance Street and the Central Business District there is little pedestrian connectivity between large clusters of commercial developments, although plans have been put forward to integrate these via a system of underpasses, similar to the system in Zhongwanhai. Delegation of administrative responsibility from Beijing Municipality to district governments has encountered planning problems in terms of co-ordinating different priorities — for example urban regeneration, commercial development and conservation of architectural heritage. Despite the introduction of a Development Control Plan for the central part of the city, the competing economic objectives of the four City Districts has led to varied but large-scale business

Wangfujing Food Street

Qianmen Street, to the south of Tiananmen Square, has been resurrected as a shopping avenue with period buildings borrowing features from the Qing dynasty.

centre developments, underscoring the difficulty of planning coordination and control without effective policy integration.

The city layout has evolved as a hierarchical arrangement of uses built around ritual processes or *lizhi* intended to reinforce the principles of an ordered feudal ruling system and the authority of the state. The occasional tensions between different administrative arms (in particular between the central state and the municipal level of city government), continue to have implications for the public realm, where societal, urban management and economic forces collide. Emerging civil society relies on a responsive planning and decision-making system. This is particularly pertinent to the on-going processes of urban renewal and the changing nature of semi-rural land at the urban fringe and surrounding suburban fabric. The absence of a unified

land market coupled with the frantic pace of investment and the widening boundaries of economic control, have perpetuated a range of demarcated development zones. At the same time, the process through which Beijing's local authorities relate to central and municipal government imperatives creates an ambiguous situation between control and autonomy. On one hand it reflects the historical persistence of intervention, while on the other it is responsive to social initiatives, entrepreneurship, and to the requirements of a growing number of non-government organisations. In this situation effective planning, transport and environmental issues become secondary to the urban transformation considered to be a necessary part of social modernisation in an expanding mega-region. The central urban design issue therefore remains one of reconciling emerging land use patterns and

trends with the means of expressing continuity of Chinese culture and identity.

In terms of urban design, the city currently lies somewhere between its historically persistent frame of reference, and a more spatially extensive monumentality — part symbolic and part programmatic. Its feudal planning objective was to create an imperial spatial setting and in the process, emphasise state control over its citizens. Its position today is to express the symbolism of the modern state and civil society, while conveying the continuity of Chinese history and culture. In line with other rapidly expanding Chinese cities, Beijing is embracing new conservation initiatives but without nostalgia. Like China itself, it looks determinedly and rationally to the future rather than the past.

Tokyo

JAPAN

ASAKUSA KANNON, named after the Buddhist Goddess of Mercy, gave rise to the Senso-ji Temple, the most important place of Buddhist worship in Tokyo. In 1621 a massive levee was constructed to prevent flooding of the temple from the Arakawa River. It has also traditionally been a place of entertainment, beginning with the relocation of the Yoshinara red light area to the urban suburbs of Asakusa in the sixteenth century. In 1842 the Kabuki theatrical centres and their animated entertainments and pleasures gardens were moved to areas such as Asakusa on the periphery of the city, away from the status-driven values of expanding civic and commercial quarters, and forming vibrant new attractions in close association with the remote temple environments and natural surroundings. These could be described as "shadow cities", representing an alternative urbanism at some distance from the increasing administrative controls of the city. Until World War II Asakusa was the largest entertainment and artistic district in Tokyo, acting as a centre of Bohemian pursuits — theatre, circuses, literature, sexual license — but with a strong sense of community. Eventually the entertainments were moved away from the temples to ensure a clear distinction between the sacred and profane.

1   Soja, E and Kanai, M,
    'The Urbanisation of the World',
    in *The Endless City*, Eds. Ricky
    Burdett and Deyan Sudjic,
    Phaidon, 2010

2   Nailo, A and Hozumi, K, *Edo,
    the City that Became Tokyo*,
    Kodansha International,
    Tokyo, 1982

MODERN TOKYO sits at the core of Asia's largest mega-urban region, with a population of 54.7 million people living in the Greater Tokyo Area including around 13 million in the metropolitan area.[1] Extended urbanisation, industrialisation and globalisation is contributing to a continuously evolving urban geography of the city region along the southern coast of Honshu to Osaka and beyond. Tokyo presents another dimension to the constant process of growth and change — from the eighteenth century through to its emergence as a post-war global city, yet culturally and socially still responsive to past influences.

The history of planning and urbanisation in Tokyo reflects its slow transformation from a water to a land-based city, where the palimpsest of overlays and superimpositions still bears the marks of the older structure. Its original name "Edo" means "mouth of the river", and its early planned configuration on the Musashino Plain was dictated by geomantic principles, but also by a series of waterways and canals that personified the role of water in Japanese 'place' design. Feudal Japan was beset by incessant militarism, which affected firm central leadership until its reunification under the Tokugawa Shogunate. It was transformed into a capital city by Tokugawa Ieyaso and became a market for everything from construction materials to fresh fish. By the seventeenth century Portuguese, Spanish and Dutch adventurers had begun to filter into the country, bringing with them new trading regimes, modern weapons and Catholic missionaries. Westerners were later banned from the country, with the exception of isolated trading expeditions. In 1720 the ban on Western study was lifted, and as a result the Japanese quickly learned Western science, including armaments and shipbuilding. Until the mid-nineteenth century the country was stable under a centralized bureaucracy, but relatively sealed off.

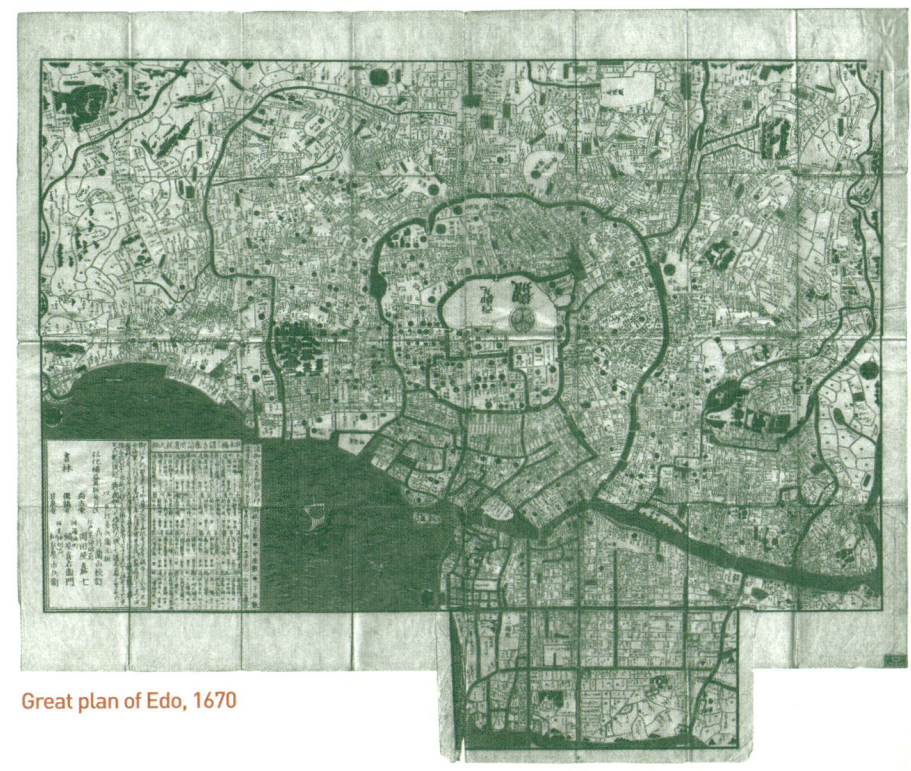

Great plan of Edo, 1670

When Japan emerged from isolation around 150 years later, virtually at the height of the industrial revolution in Europe, Edo was by far the largest city in the world and developed a dual identity built around the influences of *yamanote* (garden) associated with 'high ground' estates, and *shitamachi* (water) associated with the 'low city'. The most active spaces were associated with waterfronts, reflecting their transportation role for people and goods. Temples and shrines were built in association with waterside spaces because of its sacred connotations. However by the mid-nineteenth century, water channels began to be filled in, and industrial uses started to displace the traditional buildings. The development of a railroad up to the waterfront assisted this transition. Emerging commercial corridors

and gathering areas then began developing along the river and re-channelled canals. Piers and bridges became important public places for markets and performances, one of the first being the fishmarket at Nihonbashi Bridge — the symbolic centre of the city. The largest open space in Edo — Hirokoji — was created as a fire-break and became the setting for temporary theatres, street performers and tea-houses.

Tokugawa rule was based on a strict hierarchy of social classes: warriors (shi), farmers (nō), artisans (kō) and merchants (shō).[2] The city was divided, according to road and topographic alignments, into the 'High City' area served by upland ridge roads, and reclaimed areas on the alluvial lowlands for retainers, commoners and farmers. A spiral canal system was incorporated into

3   Hidenobu, J, 'Ethnic Tokyo',
    in *Process: Architecture 72*,
    Tokyo, 1987

Kaminari-mon (Thunder
Gate) of the Senso-ji Temple
flanked by the twin deities
— Fujin (god of wind) and
Raijin (god of thunder). A
4-metre high lantern is
strung from the gate with
the character for "thunder".

the older planning framework with five major roads radiating from the core at Nihonbashi, making it amenable to growth and development. A complex relationship of hills, plateaux and river valleys formed the essential city topography. The sprawling city, built around the Shogunate castle, expanded rapidly largely due to the doctrine of *sankin kōtai* whereby the noble families or *daimyō* lived in sprawling hillside estates in close proximity to the Shogun, with their followers housed in closely packed settlements nearby. This in turn supported a growing population of merchants and tradesmen, each occupying a specific urban quarter. Thus, the *daimyo* compounds formed a spatial contrast with the dense and congested development pattern in the *shitamachi,* which extended around the dense network of waterways and along the Sumida River — an area that housed the city's rice warehouses.

The waterfronts were a setting for the early Meiji kabuki theatre, tea-house and entertainment complexes that, in

combination, present the popular image of Edo. The Nihonbashi Bridge and its immediate public surrounds formed the spatial centre of the 'floating world' of Edo where festivals such as *Tenka Matsuri* were held, and official decrees from the Shogunate government were posted. Edobashi also developed as an amusement and entertainment area set around a public square. Ryōgoku on the eastern side of the Sumida River became the most famous popular entertainment centre in Japan. The *shitamachi* district evolved from a series of waterfront spaces or *sakariba* that became centres of activity and festivity. Barges carried cargo to the extensive city market wharves and godowns such as the Kanda Produce Market on the Kandagawa River, which played a pivotal role in the distribution of goods.

An important structuring element was the sacred temple places and precincts associated with Senso-ji in Asakusa and Zojo-ji in Shiba on the city fringe, outside the busy street

systems.[3] These took on a symbolic role as protectors of the city during the Tokogawa period, and could only be accessed by a hillside approach. Residential and amusement quarters grew up around the temples, which became landmarks for popular gatherings and entertainment, and helped to build strong local identities to these locations. The Pleasure Quarter was concentrated to the north-east of Nihonbashi. It was enclosed by a canal and divided into five blocks, entered by a single gate.

In this way the configuration of the modern city began to take shape, along with an urban infrastructure of streets, waste management, and water supply via wooden pipes and bamboo conduits. The ancient 'commoner' artisan areas of the 'low city' evolved into commercial districts made up of tenements and merchant's housing, with some prominent Western-style buildings along the main frontages and alleys providing space for 'backstreet' shops and other uses. Samurai estates with landscaped gardens were built in urban situations which, in a similar way to the private gardens of Suzhou in China, would later revert to public use and enjoyment, contributing to green elements in central city locations but also providing a model for later middle-class detached houses. Neighbourhood divisions explained the enduring presence of external spaces — gardens, shrines and narrow pedestrian passages — that existed in an otherwise tight amalgam of buildings. New building forms on small lots adjusted to imposed constraints and became interwoven within the historical fabric of the city. Each block of houses was separated by a street entered through a gate or *kido*, which was closed at night.

Edo therefore grew around a patterned framework rather than a uniform grid, allowing the city to extend and change in a relatively flexible way through a series of neighbourhoods that were open to adjustment. Suburban valley settlements

APPROACH TO THE GOKOKU-JI TEMPLE COMPLEX established by Shogun Tokugawa Tsunayoshi in 1681, and the burial place of Emperor Meiji. In Japanese urbanism, buildings tend to interact with nature, which helps the moulding of the city in conjunction with less defined spaces. A number of landmarks located within the historical urban structure remain in the congested modern city. Temples and Shrines became the site of ceremonies which played both a sacred and popularising role in the vitality of the city, and were often surrounded by amusement venues and tea-houses. Unlike Western cathedral cities, the temple was not an imposing and formal structure, but a site of veneration which was gently incorporated into the city fabric and accepted as part of daily life. This can also be observed in the sacred structures that cling to the earth or cluster in foothills, merging with wooded hillsides and forested landscapes rather than dominating the setting through conspicuous spires or other vertical edifices. In this sense they avoid vertical expressions of symbolic dominance and accentuate the horizontal plane. The one exception is the pagoda, which in China acquired a secular purpose related to feng shui and therefore became associated with prominent sites where their form is still thought to influence the fortuitous nature of the physical landscape. In Japan pagodas are still closely associated with temple complexes, and in older districts have been retained as prominent landmarks.

Hozo-mon Treasury Gate of the Senso-ji Temple, with its protective statues and giant lanterns, contains Chinese sutras from the fourteenth century.

Bell of Time — this informed the people of the time of day during the Edo era. Bells were sounded at nine places including Nihonbashi, Honkoku-cho, Senso-ji Temple and Uena. The present bell was recast in 1692, and is 2.12 metres in height. It is now struck by a priest at 6 am every morning.

'Sounding through clouds of flower ... it is the bell in Ueno or Asakusa'
— a haiku by Matsuo Bashō (1644-94)

CHIYODA-KU forms a concentration of Japan's political, economic and cultural functions, within an established urban structure. The vast area of the Imperial Palace creates a symbolic void rather than a focus — a forbidden and 'invisible' private space around which has grown a concentrated and intense matrix of government and commercial activity. These have been virtually implanted onto a feudal setting and 'Westernised' through European architectural styles during the Meiji period but are restricted in height to acknowledge the dignity of the emperor and state. It was only in the 1950s that buildings in the adjoining Maranouchi district were allowed to be built over 30-metre high. Regeneration has been focussed around the refurbished Marunouchi building, which dates from 1923.

were incorporated into the city as row-houses and tenements with little open space other than the back streets. These provided areas for communal cooking, makeshift services and shrines, creating a basis for community expression tied into the urban structure and patterns of land use. By the end of the Edo period the city covered eighty square kilometres with 1,719 individual districts.

After the Meireki fire of 1657, trigonometric surveying techniques introduced by the Dutch were employed, and the Great Map of Edo was produced in 1670 which remained in use until the mid-nineteenth century. Rebuilding work involved major reclamation projects and new bridge construction which extended the city area.

In 1853 around the time that foreign treaty port concessions were being developed along the coast of China, four American 'Black Ships' under Matthew Perry sailed into Tokyo Bay. This coincided with the disintegration of the Tokugawa Shogunate (established 250 years earlier) through increased feuding between traditionalists and modernizers. Perry returned the following year to conclude the Kanagawa Treaty, which progressively

opened the four ports of Nagasaki, Kanagawa, Niigata and Kobe to free trade. While this effectively ended Japan's isolationism, it also generated a wave of Japanese nationalism or *kukutai*. However in 1864 an allied force pressurised the emperor to capitulate to this Western presence, and led directly to the end of the Tokugawa Shogunate, and to the Meiji Restoration of 1868. The fifteenth Tokogawa shogun vacated Edo castle, and Edo was then renamed Tokyo with a Western trading settlement established in Yokohama. A new constitutional monarchy then set out to integrate Japan into the modern world, with the Emperor taking residence in the Imperial Palace. Western technology and planning were introduced to assist with urban industrialisation but also military expansion.

A significant intervention in Tokyo's morphology came with the redevelopment of the hilltop *daimyō* estates following the fall of the Shogunate. These comprised extensive walled sites, accessed from the meandering hill roads that connected the old upper city of Edo to the Shogun's castle. Over time, from the late nineteenth century, these prominent sites were given over to government

4 Taut, B, *Houses and People of Japan*, Sanseido Co. Ltd, Tokyo, 1958

THE RELATIONSHIP between an urban Shinto shrine and its local community is one of unification. Shinto is animist and polytheistic, conveying the belief that earth spirits inhabit all natural and living phenomena, but that they symbolise the harmonious relationship between man and the divine powers of nature. This can also be expressed in man-made forms. Spirit shrines are located throughout the city, and there is a relaxed co-existence with Buddhist temples. While the juxtaposition of the spiritual and the urban can be both idiosyncratic and innocuous, the presence of small but eminently respected and independent sacred places associated with features such as trees or stones within the city, adds what might be termed a 'fourth dimension' to the urban landscape. Bruno Taut has stated that "Shinto binds the imagination to reality, thus making it fertile"[4]

Shrines were historically located on hillsides around the urban periphery. As a result, temples and forms of settlement that grew up around them tended to occur in scattered locations where activity foci had emerged through historical forces and in response to physical constraints. The large 'floating' roofs of important temples are expressive but not overly conspicuous. These sacred landmarks establish an informal and grounded relationship between temple compound and ceremonial space, hence they have evolved into social gathering points. Routes to hillside shrines and temples have little directional clarity and are somewhat disconnected from the religious complex, emphasising the journey itself rather than the object. This fosters a natural and intimate relationship with the community, which reflects the non-proselytising tradition of Buddhism and Shintoism. One might say this implies a causal link between perceived divine forces on one hand and the more transient aspects of life on the other.

compounds and foreign embassies, although in recent years they have been developed into large contemporary mixed-use complexes, such as Roppongi Hills. Western architectural forms in Japanese cities were designed by both European and Japanese architects and largely indicative of how the West was seen as being far advanced in terms of technology and finance, with a long history of formal city building. The long avenue between the Kan'ei-ji Temple in Ueno and the Senso-ji Temple in Asakusa, along what is now Asakusa-dori, took on the character of an entertainment street in the late Meiji period with new cinemas and theatres built in a neo-Baroque Western style. In the process this downplayed many of the cultural qualities inherent in Japanese urban design, although Japanese garden composition had a significant impact in the West and traditional villa design embraced many of the simple design attributes of Modernism.

The importance of bridge crossings is exemplified by the location of the First National Bank, built alongside the Kaiunbashi Bridge in 1872, and the Central Post Office adjacent to the southern end of

The original Tsukiji Hongan-ji temple was founded in Asakusa in 1617. The current stone building, with its domes and lotus-shaped main entrance façade, was constructed in 1935 by the architect Chula Ito. It incorporates decorative motifs that reflect Hindu and Buddhist influences from other Asian countries.

Edobashi Bridge. These laid down a new pattern of urbanisation that linked Western urban planning with the contextual spatial characteristics of Tokyo, and forming the framework for its first business district. In 1889 the Tokyo City Improvement Ordinance established a basis for public works, open space and road widening construction, including the first electric streetcar system. Stone bridges also replaced the older wooden structures. After 1910 Western design and layouts began to underpin new urban development, signalling an epoch of tall buildings, initially located at major corner sites. This transformed established Japanese notions of the city and eventually led to more axial and symmetrical layouts.

In 1885, the Imperial Diet adopted a new government constitution, which was later regarded by many Chinese dissidents as a possible model for post-revolutionary reform in China, built around the dual political strands of nationalism and socialism. Japanese ambitions began to extend to other parts of eastern Asia, with a series of treaties that ceded Taiwan, Korea and the Liaodong peninsula of Manchuria in 1905. The end of the Meiji era came in 1912 with the death of the Emperor, and the succeeding Taisho era saw a forceful advancement of territorial ambitions. In 1914 Japan added Tsingtao in northern China to its Manchurian possessions. In these areas Japanese city building and reconstruction adopted Western influences, as well as its urban design and public works pre-occupations. New buildings

in occupied territories were adroitly designed in European neo-Classical styles — from Russian Baroque structures in Harbin and Dalian, to a continuation of the Bavarian styles originally built by the Germans in Tsingtao.

With a population of around one million by 1907, modernisation of the city included the Ginza neighbourhood and 'Londontown', both by British architects, and the development of new urban quarters and government compounds. Manufacturing industry also commenced around 1890, initially with Western support and supply of equipment. World War One diverted both Western investment and manpower, and larger Japanese companies and manufacturing concerns, such as Mitsui and Mitsubishi, began to dominate the city economy and compete with Western owned industries in China. City planning legislation was passed in 1919 when the population had reached 3.3 million, and was aimed at controlling a surge of new commercial and industrial development that was re-shaping the city and enveloping its urban traditions. This formed the basis of Japan's first city planning and land-use zoning procedures.

Edo's historic waterfront of merchant's houses, godowns and active pedestrian traffic extended to the Meiji period, but completely changed character when rebuilding took place after the 1923 Kantō earthquake. A further result of the earthquake and fire was the incorporation of new 'firebreak' spaces around the bridges. These spaces became the focus for public life and events, although high embankments for flood protection gradually severed the city from the water.[5] The Imperial Capital Reconstruction Project incorporated a more Western approach to zoning and building regulations, including the controversial resumption of properties for street widening and public open space. It was also necessary to house an expanding urban population, which involved redevelopment

5   Hidenobu, 1987, op. cit.
6   Waley, P, 'Tokyo: Patterns
    of Familiarity and Partitions
    of Difference', in Globalising
    Cities, Eds. Peter Marcuse and
    Ronald van Kempen, Blackwell,
    London, 2000

7   Sorensen, A, 'Subcentres and
    Satellite Cities: Tokyo's 20th
    Century Experience of Planned
    Polycentrism', in International
    Planning Studies 6 (1), 2001,
    p9-32

and significant increases in density. This created the basis for expanding the city to the west following a new rail line with suburban neighbourhoods built around the stations. In broad terms, residential uses were allocated in the 'High City' and commercial, industrial and residential uses in the 'Low City'. By this time new urban centres — notably at Shibuya, Shinjuku and Ikebukuro — had already started to develop around the railway hubs, in addition to the termini at Ueno, Shimbashi and Iidabashi. Similarly, satellite communities began to be developed in the surrounding countryside through land speculation by private railway companies.

The reconstruction process included a programme of parks and promenades which meant relocating some of the older pleasure quarters and docks (dating from the Edo period) to the Low City. The landscaped linear spaces and plazas refocused and reshaped the older established associations with mixed-use pleasure oriented environments. Tall industrial and commercial buildings rose around the bridge and road intersections. Built in stone and brick, and with designs that achieved a 'fit' with the localities in terms of scale and form, they introduced a new permanent identity to these rapidly changing locales.

The most prominent open plaza was associated with the Sukiyabashi Bridge, which was framed by new theatre buildings. At street interventions, buildings were set back to create corner plazas, helping to shape a consistent urban design pattern complemented by integral commercial and residential buildings. The latter reflected the latest international modernism with diagonally oriented designs focussed on plazas linked with iconic buildings. A further influence on spatial planning was the growth of city apartment complexes, which helped sustain urban densities. Low-rise terraces provided the morphological basis for building commercial streets with shops at ground level and small apartments above.

GROWTH OF THE METROPOLIS

The City Planning Law of 1940 allowed for the resumption of land for open space, and much of the land that was compulsorily purchased at this time was later turned into metropolitan parkland. The end of World War II, with its widespread city destruction, was marked in many Asian countries by autonomous nation building and a slow move towards modernisation through government housing and social service programmes. This was accompanied by new forms of economic production, with the benign hand of the State subtly directing private market forces and international trade, while introducing measures to improve productivity. In 1948 under the 'Yoshida Doctrine', Japan's strategic security was taken over by the United States, while Japan was able to concentrate on rebuilding and development with a resurrection of large business federations that forged massive manufacturing programmes. This fuelled several decades of growth and the development of an enterprise society with close ties between corporate business interests and government ministries — zaibatsu. Urban development was centrally administered through the Tokyo Metropolitan Government, with little autonomy given to local municipalities. Paul Waley contends that, while the post war alliance between industrial capital and the state led to significant land use change, it did not produce a new spatial order but an accentuation of pre-existing trends, notably the accommodation of higher order functions and the sprawl within the Kantō Plain to the east through urban expansion.[6] This shaped the growth pattern of Tokyo but also led to somewhat haphazard development patterns.

The 1958 National Capital Region Development Plan and accompanying Improvement Plan aimed to rationalise and regenerate the urban area by incorporating a 'green belt' with residential satellite settlements beyond. This failed to resolve the pressures of urban development so consequently mixed-use sub-centres such as Shinjuku, Shibuya and Ikebukuro began to be redeveloped with tall buildings through land readjustment projects, which reduced pressure on the central business district. Restructuring of urban space or minkatsu was generally accomplished by a relaxation of zoning, as well as deregulation, which incentivised private development initiatives while reducing manufacturing industry in inner city areas. The second and third improvement plans in 1968 and 1986 eliminated the green belt, and emphasised the reinforcement of multiple sub-centres (fukutoshin) within the Tokyo Metropolitan Region with the aim of achieving a multi-core city. This included a new Waterfront Sub-centre on land reclaimed from the bay, together with a bridge crossing. However since the 1990s, government policies have been substantially re-directed towards local plan making and the encouragement of new growth points in recognition of the sprawling and variegated city form that covers some 15,000 square kilometres of the Kanto Plain. This now comprises a mosaic of dispersed but dense satellite districts or 'urban villages' bound together by road and rail alignments.

The growth of large metropolitan regions and their constituent nodes of activity raises a question over the reconciliation of metropolitan growth with coherent urban form. André Sorensen has examined the evolution of sub-centres and satellite cities in Tokyo — a situation comparable to a number of megacity regions in Asia where spontaneous development through new transport systems has stimulated growth points at the intersection of radial links, demonstrating the inherent advantages embodied by these locations.[7] While the Capital Region Improvement Plan of 1958 designated a greenbelt around Tokyo as a cordon sanitaire, the second plan ten years later eliminated this in favour of a

Suburban Development Plan. This led to the promotion of a poly-nuclear structure for the Tokyo Metropolitan Region, including a ring of 'business core' growth areas linked by major public transport routes. Metropolitan growth is therefore structured, less by land use planning, and more by the consolidation of new employment centres and convenient accessibility, which promotes continued dispersed development. Within this framework, new growth points are encouraged rather than being restricted by greenbelt issues. The result has been high population and job growth over the past twenty-five years on the outer urban fringe, with a pattern of employment intensity related to sub-centres, but also employment growth in Central Tokyo associated with the Shinjuku, Shibuya and Ikebukuro business nodes. The metropolitan area of around 15,000 square kilometres, is therefore becoming progressively built up. The power of national agencies and bureaucracies is a factor in the central emphasis of government buildings, underscoring Edward Glaeser's argument that entrepreneurial talent clusters around political power.[8]

The Tokyo region remains the industrial heartland of Japan, but the last two decades have seen a significant move of manufacturing industry from inner city areas to outer wards, commensurate with continuing industrial restructuring and a major shift to office building in the eight central wards. High-rise public housing estates have been developed in the east and north-east parts of the city, with more prestige apartment complexes in the central wards. In the process, this has changed parts of the city from a fine grid of small-scale operators, retailers and residents, to a courser morphology of high-order functions.

As a result of this, from the 1980s there has been a significant reduction of population in the central city, but a commensurate increase in commercial development and employment density. Employment growth has also occurred within mixed-use sub-centres, establishing a polycentric pattern of development within the wider metropolitan area. However in neighbourhoods some distance away from railway stations or main highways, large tracts of single dwellings remain, many of the them timber framed. Agricultural activity within the metropolitan area still permeates the urbanised parts of inner prefectures such as Chiba, Kanagawa and Saitama, with complex interactions between urban and agricultural activities by part-time farmers. The persistent co-existence of these activities promotes environmental benefits in terms of both landscape preservation and urban design contrast, but raises issues of resource conflict and customary rights.

The Ginza area has been subject to several stages of redevelopment. It was originally laid out in 1612 by Tokogawa Ieyasu as a neighbourhood quarter of timber shophouses and residences for silversmiths or *gin-za*. A fire in 1872 destroyed virtually the entire area, and it was redesigned as a new Ginza Quarter with a regularised layout by a British architect Thomas Waters, containing around 1,000 Western-style brick buildings, arcades and tree-lined avenues. Some ten years later, the municipal government constructed a new railway link between Yokohama and Shinbashi, making the remodelled Ginza a main gateway into the city of Tokyo. The older buildings were destroyed in the Kanto earthquake, and the remaining residential development was converted to commercial uses. The area therefore continued to evolve and regenerate around high-end shopping and entertainment, but many of the larger and most prominent buildings were destroyed by allied air raids in 1945. This in turn triggered a colossal post-war escalation in land values, so that new development now represents cutting edge commercial architecture and cool imagery. The best known older landmark, dating from 1894, is the Waco building at the Ginza 4 — Chome Crossing.

Shinjuku was originally occupied by *daimyo* estates and forests, but developed largely through its strategic position in relation to the new western railway as part of post-war reconstruction. It now represents the world's largest transport interchange. The Shinjuku Corporation was set up in 1960 and a series of high-rise developments over the next forty years has made it the densest sub-centre of tall buildings in Tokyo.

CULTURAL AND SOCIAL DIMENSIONS OF INTERVENTION

Modern Tokyo is culturally a mix of old and new elements. The city is one of intangible microcosms and hidden but orderly pockets of activity and repose. At the same time, it is a global city with an urban cachet, reflecting distinct geographies of consumption and cultural production. Its eclectic spatial setting is underscored by ambitious architectural interpretations of post-modernism, aided and abetted by "flexible" zoning regulations. High investment in growth-centred infrastructure has not been necessarily matched by social infrastructure, although this is compensated by an enduring acceptance of tight living conditions and the prioritising of community values over individual ones. A primary example is personified by the *machizukuri* groups, which empower local communities and citizen's organisations in building and managing neighbouring facilities, legitimately orchestrating public awareness campaigns, and preparing local communities in disaster response scenarios.

Urban neighbourhoods combine tight-knit communities while exemplifying a significant amount of spontaneous change, partly because the zoning system allows and even encourages a wide range of interspersed uses. This is expressed in compact high-density cores with their vertical stacking of different

[8] Glaeser, E, *Triumph of the City*, Macmillan, London, 2011

uses, and the competitive array of signage that advertises the fact. City quarters are rarely overly haphazard however, managing to balance efficient use of space with minimum planning intervention. In part this system is held together by an enduring sense of consensus, civility and self-reliance within urban neighbourhoods that signifies this communal mentality and shapes streets and places through inherent politenesses. A high intensity of mixed-use incorporated within the grain of urban streets and places creates both urbanity and vitality.

Although much of Tokyo's physical legacy has been lost to a more homogenised present, its cultural continuity creates an elaboration of urban traditions. This is achieved by utilising contemporary technologies and challenging spatial compositions, which consequently establish new urban places with their own integral identity and values. A combination of feudal land ownership and spontaneous development patterns, dictated partly by the extensive system of waterways, created a framework of urban blocks where commercial development, in the form of two- and three-storey shophouses, fronted onto the wider streets and canals. A more fine-grained system of residences existed behind, among narrow access routes demarcated by gateways. Street blocks took on characteristics associated with specific guilds, shops and entertainment areas with distinctive patterns of urban identity and attachment. Because of changes in the way building standards were interpreted and administered in the 1990s, sporadic intensification through redevelopment of individual 'outer' commercial and residential structures have formed an *anko-gawa* configuration — a 'hard' protective band of taller buildings around the periphery and an inner 'soft' core of low-rise but densely packed residential uses. This creates a marked gradation in terms of both scale and character, between the modern and busy urban streets flanked

JAPANESE CHARACTERS, with their stylised pictorial representation, carry a symbolic connection with what they convey. The areal composition allows for some flexibility in organisation and direction, allowing them to be scythed into component parts and re-assembled in an abstract iconography of patterns and combinations. Street texts represent a graphic collage of script that is both descriptive and iconic. Shelton compares the urban syntax to the stylised pictorial representation of kanji which can be read as independent characters in both horizontal and vertical formats . In an urban sense this metaphor translates into a complex and additive texture of parts and symbols with little compositional geometry. This fractured intervention,

experienced as a maelstrom of empowered imagery over architectural substance, is at once both blatantly commodified and insistently overpowering in its purpose. These then become place markers in areas such as Shinjuku much as monuments and spaces define places in the Western city.

Some urban vocabularies are less tangible, and reflect a type of self-organisation on the part of the community, which in large part reflects embedded cultural processes. Aspects that might appear organic or even chaotic can, on closer inspection, form surprisingly ordered environments, stemming not from clear planning parameters but from an underlying sense of community over the rights of the individual.

DESIGNERS OF CONTEMPORARY FASHION EMPORIUMS deploy iconic architectural containers to create commercial impact and project the flagship identity of the global label. Expressive forms broadcast cutting edge brand images through eye-catching configurations, surface transparency and prominent nomenclature — aspects that were alien to traditional Japanese streets, but which exalt the high-end contemporary street aesthetic. Product display adopts a museum-like approach to presentation akin to exhibition showcasing, interspersed with the peripheral trappings of plasma screens and information display that underscore the glamour of international exclusivity. The interplay between urban design and high fashion, given the flamboyance of shopping and entertainment districts such as Shibuya and Harajuku, has inspired alternative up-market agglomerations in several districts that project an avant-garde presence, such as Ginza and Omotesando.

The Ginza district was part of the shitamachi or "low city" — originally housing artisans specialising in particular trades such as silversmithing. Its gridded morphology is the result of the alignment of canals during the Edo period, and the reconstruction of the area after the great fire of 1872. The three-storey Ginza "Brick Quarter" became a fashionable commercial centre in the wake of the Kanto earthquake. The area was gradually redeveloped at a higher density due to its proximity to Tokyo Station. Its main street, the Chuo Dori, is closed at weekends, providing a pedestrianised environment focussed around its intersection with Harumi Dori.

The street blocks of Ginza first gave rise to Tokyo's concentrated matrix of large department stores with brand names that are in some cases several centuries old, such as Mitsukoshi and Matsuzakaya. These cover almost entire street blocks, and have more recently become home to custom-designed stores for exclusive brands — Prada, Dior and Gucci. Development profiles conform with regulatory codes and the mix of uses are reflected in the animated building envelopes, illuminated super graphics and screens that broadcast a diverse range of commercial messaging — some overt and others subliminal. Such buildings as Wako and Sony vie with each other for icon recognition as meeting places and nodes of congregation.

THE USE OF PAPER LANTERNS and tall banners to announce performances and create a colourful atmosphere began in the Edo entertainment areas such as Ryōgoku, and continues to animate active places in Japanese cities. They form points of identity such as the heterogeneous cityscape of Kabuki-chō in Shinjuku, a 'fantasy' and entertainment quarter where a street montage of signage displays, flags and symbolic features establishes an emphasis on physical interventions over the actual setting. This vertical stacking of different and contrasting elements on various levels transforms building frontages in commercial districts into channels of information relating to the services provided in the buildings themselves.

9 Rowe, P.G., *East Asia Modern: Shaping the Contemporary City*, Reaktion Books, London, 2005

10 Waley, 2000, op. cit.

11 Hidenobu, J, *Tokyo: A Spatial Anthropology*, University of California Press, Berkely, 1995

by high-rise buildings, and the traditional neighbourhood matrix of narrow lanes and residential subdivisions in the central part of the block, which are rich in associative meanings. Thus the historical pattern of layout (*chō*) is preserved, along with the social fabric and associations (*chōkai*) that provide community services and organise local events such as festivals.[9]

A strong sense of social order, encoded in respect for the community, is able to absorb both urban change and ensure that the trajectories of globalisation are strictly controlled. However a general lack of widespread urban neglect and deprivation should not conceal a troubling stigmatisation. Waley describes poorer quarters inhabited by the 'outcast' community of *burakumin*. They make up the city's marginalised sector of day labourers and low-level migrant workers in the Sanya district and represent the underbelly of the city — a reminder that the overall frame of social order and consensus often has an unacknowledged price in terms of social exclusion.[10] It was the site of executions in the Edo period and the area, now marked by a street intersection, is called Namidabashi, or Bridge of Tears.

Hidenobu Jinnai has examined the spatial anthropology of contemporary Tokyo through patterns of land, culture and traditions that date from the Edo period. Back then, street blocks and building layouts were shaped by the flow of rivers, wetland agricultural holdings, social structures and religious practices.[11] An overriding aspect of this is the rich variety of forms evident within the older morphology itself. This is linked with a highly differentiated topography, differences

in neighbourhood patterns, and the interweaving of traditional and contemporary elements, which reflect periods of demolition and reconstruction following disastrous events during the twentieth century. The Edo landscape focussed on composition and harmony with the setting, and a co-existence with nature, while Shinto beliefs enshrined the distant view of Mount Fuji, long regarded as a sacred mountain. Planning layouts drew this into a symbolic dialogue with building composition — not through monumental spaces, but carefully crafted visual alignments that create interaction between urban space and the surrounding landscape. Residential Quarters were demarcated by tall wooden gates or *kido* with gatehouses, which created

THE SUBDIVISION OF COMMONERS' land into progressively smaller parcels and streets, established a hierarchy of front streets and tight spaces. The collection of signboards and nameplates inspired the beginnings of a "billboard" street language related to everyday life that has continued to the present, where constant channels of advertising and information assert an overriding syntax. This iconography of use is reflected across a wide organisational matrix of main streets, pedestrianised back streets (the result of Government orchestrated street reorganisation after the 1923 earthquake), and compact pocket-spaces defined by row houses or tenements that continue to exemplify the spatial character of the Meiji period and preserve a strong communal identity. In the Ginza area this produces an urban duality of grand boulevards and secondary alleys packed with small bars and restaurants.

12 Shelton, B, *Learning from the Japanese City*, Routledge, London and New York, 1999

13 Sorensen, A, *The Making of Urban Japan: Cities and Planning from Edo to the Twenty-First Century*, Routledge, London and New York, 2002, p333

THE DEVELOPMENT OF SHIBUYA STATION as the terminals for the Toyoko and Inokashira rail lines, together with three subway MTR lines, was the catalyst to the growth of the area. It developed rapidly as people moved from the central city to the western suburbs after the 1923 earthquake. The station plaza is framed by tall department stores defined by vertical concentrations of neon signs, pixelated screens and illuminated advertisements that burnish its image. The sloping streets of Bunkamura-dori and Dugensake-dori offer a mix of cafes, galleries, 'short-stay' hotels and music venues.

as something imposed through a centralised system, leading to resistance in the face of restrictions on private property rights.[13] Lack of development controls can in turn lead to sub-divisions, strains on infrastructure, and fire hazards.

The various autonomous components that can be found in Japanese city environments are therefore not interdependent or necessarily geared to aesthetic composition, but constitute parts that can be added or subtracted at will, reflecting human activities without negating the overall sense of 'place'. They might represent what Charles Jencks has termed 'enigmatic signifiers' based on a mosaic of subcultures, each with their own value system. While certain characteristics are rooted in tradition and culture, they might also have much in common with theories of a scientific or philosophical basis such as fractals. This reflects the notion of change and random phenomena whereby the sense of intrinsic uncertainty forms part of the transitional processes within an urban environment of imprecision. In some respects this perspective can be better understood within the conceptual framework of Shintoism and Buddhism where problem solving is both intuitive and holistic, and where time and space are inter-related.

Monuments in traditional Japanese urbanism have never taken on the composed formality associated with place-making in the West, where axial patterns of connection underlie the geometry of historical cities. In the latter context, major public buildings, churches and cathedrals are conceived as tall and prominent monuments in the cityscape, situated in formal settings in relation to civic spaces which in themselves became contrived points of focus. In contrast to this, traditional Japanese urbanism had a low-rise and somewhat uniform morphology with few protruding elements, the exceptions being castles belonging to the shogun, and walled hilltop *daimyo* compounds which

entrances to streets but could be closed at night, fulfilling a sense of physical unity, orientation and identity.

During the following Meiji period, Western building forms were layered onto the older layout, and *daimyo* estates were redeveloped to provide necessary sites for new public functions, reinforcing this intricate interaction between old and new. Further Western urban design ideas were introduced in the 1920s, along with a series of modern urban spaces including broad avenues and plazas, but also small back streets, intricate urban tissue and waterways that form the spatial basis of the present city. Jinnai has identified a strong correspondence in terms of the older pattern of irregular divisions and site boundaries, and contemporary city morphology. What might appear random is shown to be quite clearly referencing historical city alignments and spaces by which the city can be read.

Barrie Shelton, in exploring the diverse cultural strands in the Japanese city, stresses

that various social dimensions and rituals permeate the urban design language through an interventionist and additive process made up of different parts. This opens up a heterogeneous collage of physical expression. He also notes that Japanese urban design is essentially preoccupied with areal units of urban organisation, while Western design is more concerned with the 'line' as an ordering and compositional mechanism.[12] Tokyo, as with other Japanese cities, has frequently borrowed planning ideas from the West but this has not prevented urbanisation proceeding and adjusting according to its own cultural and organisational values. These have been influenced by land-use and ownership traditions, and the context of a century of destruction and reconstruction, which is embedded in the city psyche. It has enabled the city to respond to the indeterminacies of post-industrial change in a positive and pragmatic way. This is despite what has been termed "the weak relationship of planning and civil society", whereby planning is seen

14 Shelton, 1999, op. cit., p117
15 Hidenobu, 1995, op. cit.

16 Tsukamoto, Y, Kaijima, M and Kuroda, J, *Made in Tokyo*, Kajima Publishing Company, Tokyo, 2001

17 Maki, F, *Investigations in Collective Form*, School of Architecture, Washington University, St Louis, 1964

18 Kurokawa, K, *Rediscovering Japanese Space*, John Weatherhill, Tokyo, 1988

were constructed according to topographic constraints, unrelated to any formal urban composition.

While many older and important city waterways have been progressively filled in to make way for major road alignments (*odori*), place-names incorporating certain nomenclatures indicate their ghostly presence in the city — bridges (*bashi*), island (*jima*) and river (*gawa*) seem to permeate the urban vocabulary.[14] This emphasises the role that canals and rivers played during the Meiji period, where bridges became prominent urban design elements, emphasising concentrations of activity and public functions. One of the most well-known — *Nihonbashi* in Edo — was the subject of many early woodblock prints by Hiroshige.

Nodal points were also meeting areas associated with bridges and the related network of street connections between historic urban quarters in Tokyo. Similarly, people tended to gather at cross-roads or *tsuji* and these became prime sites for feature buildings. Hidenobu Jinnai has traced examples of such early buildings in Tokyo, which included the First National Bank built in 1872, the Central Post Office in 1874, the Yomiuri Shimbun Newspaper Office in 1908 and the Nomura Building in 1929.[15] When the waterways were reclaimed, these sites became prominent landmarks within the new road system, while the canal-side pedestrian environments were transformed into active and wide street edges alongside the emerging development corridors.

This introduces another aspect of contemporary Japanese urbanism — even as urban planning schemes become gradually skewed towards the grandiose — that of constant adaptation and superimposition. This leads to a framework of indeterminacy, even in situations where there is some underlying form and visual structure. The decentralised metropolis of Tokyo is also a city of dynamic expression where a vigorous

The Ameyoko market alongside and below the rail tracks at Ueno.

combination of technology and tradition contributes to an elaborate imagery. The many hybrid buildings form an intriguing response to these fluid development conditions, with functional combinations and spatial compositions that comprise a marriage of incompatibility. Yoshiharu Tsukamoto, Momoya Kaijima and Junzo Kuroda explain this as a complex and practical response to urban conditions and programmatic requirements. It has become known as '*dame*', literally 'no-good architecture' which reflects the reality of the city.[16] It also provides a means of cataloguing the chaotic spatial collages that have a hidden order through their interdependence, and is relevant to the wider Asian context that is experiencing cycles of construction and destruction.

Fumihiko Maki points to the ambiguous relationship between urban centre and urban fringe in the Japanese city, and the collage of characteristics representing a palimpsest of imprints that extend the relationship between building, mass and space.[17] The elements that normally establish underlying context such as the street or 'line' framework, tend instead to reflect more fragmented, disconnected and time-related associations — a lateral rather than linear process.

Kisho Kurokawa has noted that the concept of 'boundary' need not be a rigid demarcation but a transitional threshold, often between public and private areas, that reveals itself in a subtle, indirect way.[18] He uses a biological metaphor when referring to

THE VERNACULAR MARKET SPACE

is one of the most vital forms of place identity — generally integrated with low-rise, mixed-use and high-density areas. The relationship between building and street activity is fluid and impermanent, forming a contemporary manifestation of the old bazaars and festival spaces. Subterranean malls connect subways with stations, and include labyrinthine shopping environments, linked to the tall building complexes above, through tiers of retail malls that double as pedestrian corridors. Gaps in the fabric are regarded as opportunity spaces to be filled by spontaneous realms of activity. Some of the best examples are the café and market spaces associated with urban rail corridors such as Ameyoko and Shinbashi.

Located beneath the elevated structure of the main north-south railway tracks between Yūrakuchō and Shinbashi, there are a large number of restaurants. These date back to the American 'Occupation', when the badly damaged area was used for temporary activities including cafés, sake stalls and street markets. Some of the cafes are makeshift stalls in the warren of spaces below the railway; others are sophisticated restaurants with an inviting exterior opening out onto narrow pavements either side.

[19] Hidenobu, J, 'Ethnic Tokyo', in *Process: Architecture 72*, Tokyo, 1987

the Japanese city — a 'rhizome' comprising "an interwoven complex of heterogeneous parts which is centre-less yet dynamic, forever changing, and able to propagate itself". There is something here of the unpredictable cosmos — complex, chaotic, self-organising, and characterised by intrinsic uncertainty.

The aerial image of the city possibly stems from the traditional perception of urban geography as a realm of 'areas' rather than streets. A larger neighbourhood or *machi* might contain a number of smaller and generally irregular areas or *chome* within which individual units are located. These do not occur as part of any unifying sequence, but a patchwork of relatively autonomous plots that might accord with historical sub-divisions. It explains the elusive address system, which reflects the intricate identification with street block patterns at various scales. This also serves to break down ill-defined neighbourhoods into identifiable entities which has helped transform cities into a narrative of urban villages. Streets within these areas are connective but have no clear hierarchy and do not necessarily identify any particular 'street space' through a consistent visual language, therefore identity is based mainly on familiarity and experience, divorced from perceptible tissue. The traditional narrow *roji* in older Tokyo neighbourhoods separate low-rise dwellings into condensed, intimate quarters. These have, in effect, become semi-private communal spaces. Interfacing façades incorporate sliding screens to ensure privacy, and in the process establish a consistent yet variable aesthetic. The wider primary routes or *tori* that are more heavily traversed, are commonly integrated with retail stores and market functions. Historically *kido* gates symbolised entry to a *machi*, and only special areas were delineated by walls, such as the Yoshiwara area of ancient Edo.

Shophouse structures in many parts of Asia, with their multifarious design references, establish a traditional relationship with

THE DUALITY OF TALL AND MODERN STREET FRONTAGES with a maze of narrow streets and adaptable premises behind, generates a framework of vitality, change and indeterminacy. This, establishes a tension between rationalised urbanism and liberating expression — new and old are inextricably interlinked, and vernacular elements still permeate the post-industrial fabric as an urban mosaic, with no systematic street vocabulary or symbolic centre. Hidenobu Jinnai states that the city is comparable with the board game sugoroku made up of autonomous neighbourhoods with little subordination to the whole.[19]

the pavement threshold or a continuous semi-public pedestrian realm embedded in systems of colonnaded walkways. However, Japanese urbanism tends to embody a more inconspicuous and informal morphology of small streets, independent of major boulevards and elevated highways. Product displays rarely extend into the public realm of the street, so that there is a more immediate interface between building and street functions. In some situations arcaded structures extend over the pavement, but are often constructed independently from the buildings themselves. In a similar way arcades are sometimes superimposed on narrow pedestrian spines, acting as self-supporting entities. These might be commissioned by local trade organisations to provide climatic protection and facilitate pedestrianisation.

Connective arcades form a matrix of pedestrian channels associated with the Senso-ji Temple.

20 Hagiwara, S, 'The Alley as a Spiritual Axis for the Community: The Hikifune Project, Tokyo', in *Public Places in Asia Pacific Cities: Current Issues and Strategies*, Ed. Pu Miao, Kluwer Academic Publishers, Dordrecht, 2001

TSUKUDAJIMA lies at the mouth of the Sumida River. It means 'island of cultivated rice fields' and was settled in the seventeenth century by fishermen brought by Tokugawa Ieyasu from Settsu Province. The areas of Tsukishima and neighbouring Tsukuda escaped both earthquake and fire, and represent tightly packed street blocks and narrow alleys. Most of the houses are constructed of wood with traditional features, and their thresholds are carefully demarcated by arrangements of plants, bamboo and cycle storage areas. A number of older houses have added balconies that extend almost across the alleys while some ground floor premises are used for local services.

PUBLIC SPACE AS EVENT SPACE

The definition of 'public domain' is ambiguous in connotation. In Asian cities formed through colonial plan making, the notion of public space is based on both access by the community, and accentuation in terms of appearance and architectural definition, taking its cue from the Western concept. In the Japanese city, public space is often conceptually utilitarian in nature, devoid of aesthetic considerations but adaptive to urban functions and meanings, so that fresh discoveries are always possible. Tanya Hidaka and Mamoru Tanaka point out that prior to the Meiji period there was no Japanese word for privacy, so the concept of "public" space has historically been bound up with public event more than physical boundary. This is personified by the transparency of thin screen walls, which break down the boundaries between "public" and "private". Undifferentiated space allows it to be determined by a variety of users at different times.

Tenement houses constructed in urban blocks during the Edo period resulted in large stores oriented towards the main streets, while a mix of workshops and residences, that might be only 1.2 metres in width, lined the narrow streets to the rear. Narrow lanes have always served the role of pedestrian passageways between neighbourhoods but have also become public spaces for gathering and passive recreation, with animated forms of community vitality. In many cases these continue to serve as communal areas where "public" and "private" domains can be constantly re-defined and re-asserted in relation to a range of activities. However land readjustment projects or *Kukaku-Seiri* aimed at improving public facilities and road widening have opened up some older areas for redevelopment through public-private partnerships. These have exploited land values and modified the patterns of connection, but retained the idea of the traditional street system.[20]

Dense commercial concentrations integrate 'through block' connections and passages that have not been subject to historical realignment, and these facilitate different modes of use. Complementing these at high level are elevated cross-street connections which create an active web of commercial avenues and intersecting axes that pass through and around multi-storey atria.

HARMONY AND IMPERMANENCE

Buddhism was introduced to Japan by religious followers who had studied in China, and manifested itself in masterful artistry, architecture and landscape. The Buddhist notion of impermanence points to an intrinsic interconnectedness based on transitory processes rather than finite elements. There is therefore little notion of permanency relating to the layered 'culture' of the city, and this serves as a strong impetus towards renewal and change, together with an ambiguous attitude towards building heritage. The traditional notion of architecture as something of a finite intervention in the West, contrasts with the idea of transience deeply embedded in certain Asian cultures, but particularly in Japan. To a large extent this reflects the predominance of available materials. In the West, stone and brick combat the extremes of climate and can endure for centuries, allowing for the idea of building as permanent monument. By contrast in Japan the predominant medium of building was wood, which is more at one with nature, but must accede to the ravages of time. Japan, in line with Buddhist and Shinto beliefs, has absorbed these aspects of cultural traditions, such as the ritual rebuilding of the Ise Shrine every twenty years since the eighth century — a process that expresses the timeless cycle of decay and rebirth.

A number of Buddhist societies have absorbed traditions of impermanence in their urban fabric, but in its cultural conjoining with Shintoism (a seemingly intuitive 'animist' religion that existed long before the introduction of Buddhism into the Japan from China in the sixth century), Japan has evolved a unique blend of intellectual beliefs, collective consciousness and rituals, which underlie the way the city is viewed and used. A fundamental aspect of this is that opposite states are not mutually exclusive — discontinuities are physically real as well as perceptual, and identifiable places, which the user has directly experienced, are often divorced from defining built fabric. This rationale introduces a more abstract concept of 'place', one that need not be associated with physical solidity.

Arata Isozaki has used the elusive term *ma* to reflect the personal yet non-intrusive experience of space, which is conceptually in line with the self-effacing nature of traditional society and forms part of a well-functioning community. In the 1960s

The Nezu-jinja shrine was rebuilt by Japan's fifth Shogun, Tokugawa Tsunayoshi in 1706. A series of red torri gates line the route to small shrines including the Inari fox shrine.

THE TOKUGAWA SHOGUN GRAVEYARD at Kan'ei-ji is situated on the Yamaka Plateau. The local districts of Yamaka, Nezu and Sendagi are known collectively as Yamesen. Having survived the Kantō earthquake, the area comprises a grid of narrow streets with intermittent wooden houses, graveyards and Tokyo's highest concentration of temples, dating back to the mid-seventeenth century. The area is close to Tokyo University, founded in 1870 on land from the feudal clans.

The Hie-jinja shrine was transplanted on Sotobori-dori in the seventeenth century in order to deflect evil from Edo Castle, and is regarded as having a strong protective influence.

21 Nitschke, G, 'From Metabolism to Metamorphism – Notes towards a Philosophy of Change in Man-made Creation', in *Architectural Design*, May 1967

22 Ashihara, Y, *The Hidden Order: Tokyo through the Twentieth Century*, Kodansha International, Tokyo and New York, 1989

Gunter Nitschke explored the Japanese sense of place *ma* related to space in the city. He concluded that a 'place' tends to be defined by certain types of activity. This is independent of compositional elements, which spatially define a particular urban setting in the way that Europe's set-piece streets and squares create a formal organisation of space.[21] The Metabolist movement devised a dynamic symbol that expressed the notion of movement, change and flexibility, borrowed and adapted from the *I Ching* symbol of complementary elements. This reflects the basic principle of dualism — the universe was seen as being shaped by two opposing but complementary forces, *yin* and *yang*, and any form of development must try to establish an effective balance between these two forces, which applies in an abstract as well as a concrete sense. This 'tension' is best observed in garden design and the placement of important elements, which metaphorically overlaps into the city culture.

Cosmic harmony is produced through *yin* and *yang* dimensions of humanity so that, on reaching culmination an intuitive sense of balance is achieved where no dimension dominates. The asymmetrical urban design form of Tokyo represents a shift away from the Western emphasis on "whole" form to which the parts subscribe, to a situation where the proliferation of the parts allows constant and spontaneous change and adaptability in accordance with function and practicality. Yoshinobu Ashihara indirectly acknowledges this, in raising the notion of a "hidden order" inherent in the character of the Japanese city.[22] This situation is reflected in a somewhat flexible system of planning and pragmatic application of building controls. The result is a more ambiguous development framework than in Western cities where a greater regularity of form and building outline is encouraged. Urban planning therefore relates more to short-term solutions rather than long-term strategies.

Toyokawa Inari is a combined temple and shrine on the fringe of Motoakasaka and the Detached Palace. It is dedicated to the Toyokawa Dakini Shinten (one of many Buddhist masters) who protected the ancient Buddhist doctrines enshrined by the founder Kangan Giin. Inari is a fox deity and the messenger to Ebisu, the god of commerce.

Much of Tokyo has regenerated itself from the Tokugawa period, overcoming earthquakes, fire, volcanic activity and bomb damage. This is reflected in the short life span of most buildings, and the notion of architecture as something transient rather than permanent. Standardisation of building lots is almost impossible, so that intervention creates the semblance of an organic urbanism, redolent of expedient disorder and somewhat adventurous addition. While certain older and notable pieces of Japanese architecture are imbued with a delicate refinement, much traditional building is asymmetrical. It represents an architecture of parts, assembled with an intimate reticence of detail and texture that relates to actual use, and softened by the seasons to absorb the impact of natural forces.

Land assembly is generally carried out by *jiageya* — land speculators who assemble parcels of low-rise buildings in older communities, so that as owners sell their assets, those renting property also have to leave. The Roppongi Hills development is first and foremost an object lesson in land assembly, involving some 600 owners occupying around eleven hectares of land on or around an old *daimyo* estate. The scheme (produced by the Mori Building Company) was established through a pooling arrangement of amalgamated small sites — a solution that has maximised redevelopment value, primarily for integrated commercial office, hotel, residential and entertainment uses in three urban segments with the *daimyo* garden preserved. The Roppongi Tower is the largest commercial building in Japan and a Tokyo landmark. Further examples of comprehensive redevelopment involving transfer of property rights are Tokyo Midtown and Tokyo Station City; both represent large-scale commercial developments.

Tokyo itself has been substantially rebuilt a number of times after undergoing such disasters. In 1657 a fire destroyed most of the city and killed a quarter of its population. Reconstruction with firebreaks, embankments and watchtowers changed the face of the city. Up to 1868 the city was subject to 97 serious conflagrations. Earthquakes in 1854 and 1855 were followed by flooding and cholera epidemics. The 1923 Kanto earthquake affected around 44 per cent of the city and 60 per cent of its housing, while the allied bombing of Tokyo in 1945 killed hundreds of thousands. The process of rebuilding — in response to disaster rather than economic impetus — has therefore tended to predominate over refurbishment, acceding to the indeterminate whims of climate and catastrophe, but with a mix of revitalisation and respect for tradition. This needs to be planned for however. Much of the 'low' area of Tokyo lies below sea level, and is therefore vulnerable to flooding from rising sea levels. In addition some urban neighbourhoods still have a preponderance of wooden housing, vulnerable to the impact of earthquake and fire.

New waterfront development began to emerge in the 1970s along the Sumida River and spread to the Tokyo Bay area. Bridges were constructed for road traffic and expressways aligned with the river. High-rise development then began to replace the older defunct port buildings and factories, along with new promenade space, while many of the warehouses were converted to galleries, cafes and lofts, much the same as in Western dockland developments. Past reclamation proposals for Tokyo Bay include Kenzo Tange's plan of 1960 and Kisho Kurokawa's 1987 proposal for a new island in the bay area. In 1987 the Tokyo

Metropolitan Government announced plans for a new waterfront quarter on 450 hectares of reclaimed land along the Odaiba shoreline, although this was later scaled back to become a residential and renovation area, and a catalyst for further riverside initiatives.

Post-war reconstruction in the context of an increasingly buoyant economy introduced modern earthquake-proof building in Japan, but with an acceptance of ingrained urban traditions. A visitor to Hiroshima in 1970, a mere quarter century after the atomic tomb had utterly devasted the city, would have been astonished, not by the massive rebuilding programme, but that the new city had all the operational hallmarks of an old-established urbanism — an intimate and active street framework layered onto a regenerated infrastructure. At the same time, historical components are not necessarily discarded, and tend to be reintroduced into contemporary designs where they comfortably co-exist with modern functions.

HAMA-RIKYU GARDEN was a tidal pond in the Edo period that depended on the intake of seawater from Edo Bay. In 1654 the brother of the 4th Tokugama Shogun — Matsudaira Tsunashige — reclaimed the land and built a residence and garden. It was completed by the 11th Tokugawa Shogun, Ienari. After the Meiji Restoration the garden became a palace for the Imperial family. In 1945 the garden was given to the City of Tokyo and opened to the public under the Cultural Properties Protection Law of Japan.

Across the street is the Shiodome complex — formerly a railway terminal and the site of Shinbashi Station. Its name translates as 'restraining the tide', and together with Hama-rikyu Garden was filled in during the seventeenth century. Today the complex comprises thirteen high-rise commercial, hotel and residential towers.

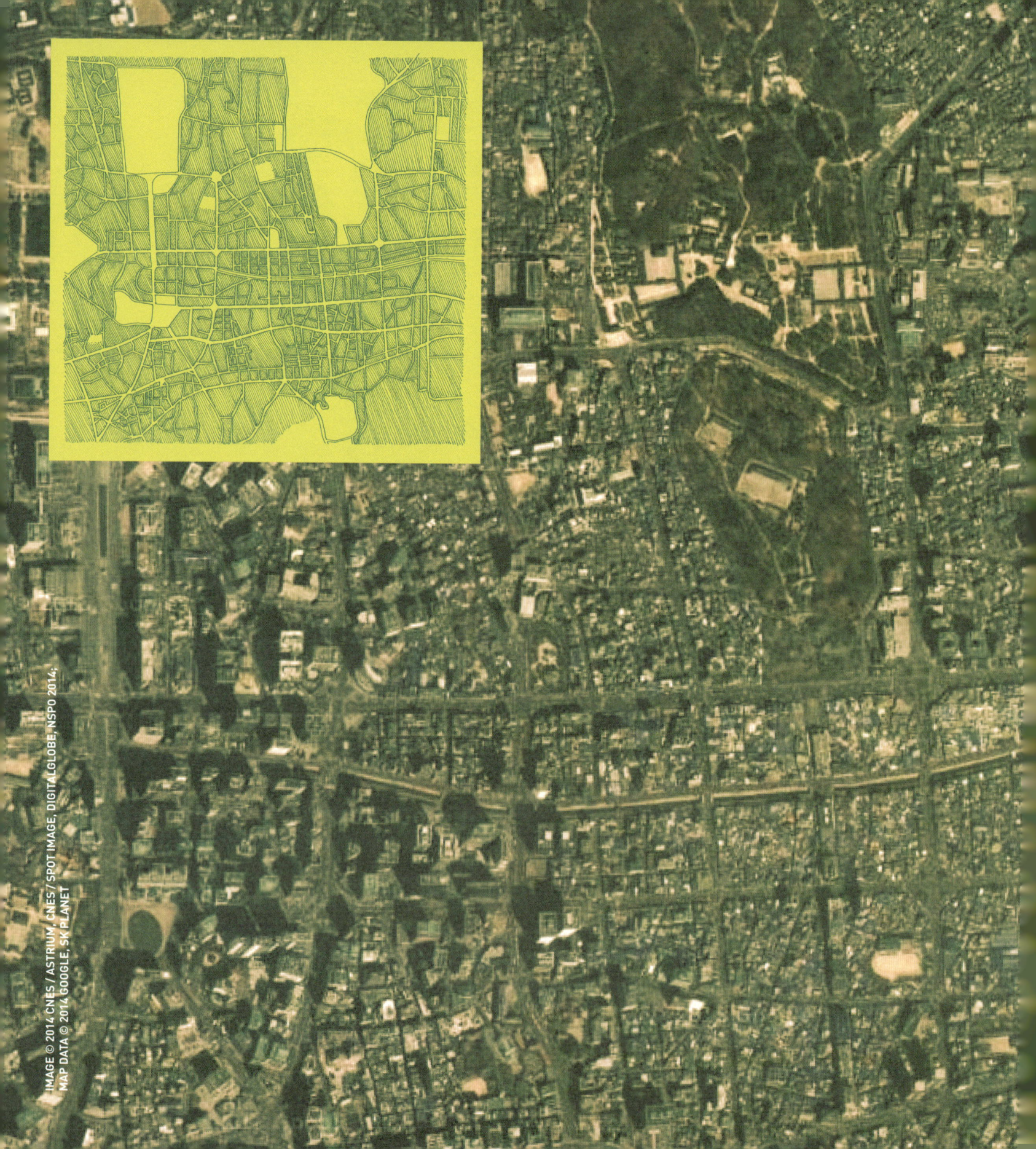

Seoul

KOREA

CHEONGGYUECHEON RIVER SPRING, a sculpture of a spiral shell rising upward, by Cousje Van Bruggen and Claes Oldenburg, conjures up the vitality of the Cheonggyecheon River. The urban 'recovery' of the watercourse, which restored an ancient stream bed, has required a contemporary form of intervention. The river was reinforced with stone embankments to provide flood protection in the eighteenth century, and during the Japanese occupation was straightened, and then entirely paved over in the 1950s with an elevated highway constructed above it. The regeneration of the river based on the slow movement of water and pedestrians through a 5.8-kilometre stretch of the central city has refocused its linear urban design, welding together diverse development sectors, and generating a visual and recreational focus. In the process it has recalibrated the urban ecology of Seoul, opening up an enervating sequence of channels, landscape embankments, murals and water features that engage a wide gamut of users.

THE NAME 'KOREA' is derived from the ancient kingdom of Koryo. Hanyang, the city in the Han River Basin that became Seoul, evolved through a series of distinct stages — beginning in 1394 when the capital was relocated from Kaesŏng, during the Chosŏn or Yi dynasty founded by Yi Seong-gye. This makes it one of the oldest capitals in Asia. Only 20 per cent of the country is flat — the remainder comprises mountain ranges that date from the pre-Cambrian period. The city is said to be shaped by *hyongsedo* geomantic principles, facing south from Pugaksan Mountain, with the Blue Dragon (Naksan Mountain) to the east, and the White Tiger (Inwangsan Mountain) to the west. Four great gates faced each of the Cardinal directions. Emperor Yi T'aejo ordered the construction of Gyeongbokgung Palace, south of Pugaksan Mountain, and thereafter the city developed through construction of other palaces, temple compounds, government buildings and residences for ranking officials within the fortified capital. The royal ancestral shrine or *Jongmyo* was constructed to the east of the Kyongbokgung Palace, and *Sajik*, the altar of the guardian deities, to the west.

The central city is demarcated by *Pugak-san* (North Peak Mountain), and *Nam-san* (South Mountain) and planned according to *feng shui* principles, which placed particular importance on the position of hill forms. City fortifications began during the reign of Taejo in 1396, and walls connected the four mountains that surrounded the city with nine gates, five of which are still standing. Its length was divided into 97 sections for assignment among the various provinces in proportion to the number of conscripted workers they provided. It is said that the sections were based on the characters from a Chinese Classic, *Ch'onjamun*, such as *chi*—earth, and *ch'on*—heaven. Royalty and nobles lived to the north of Chong-no, the east-west axial thoroughfare that divided the city, with

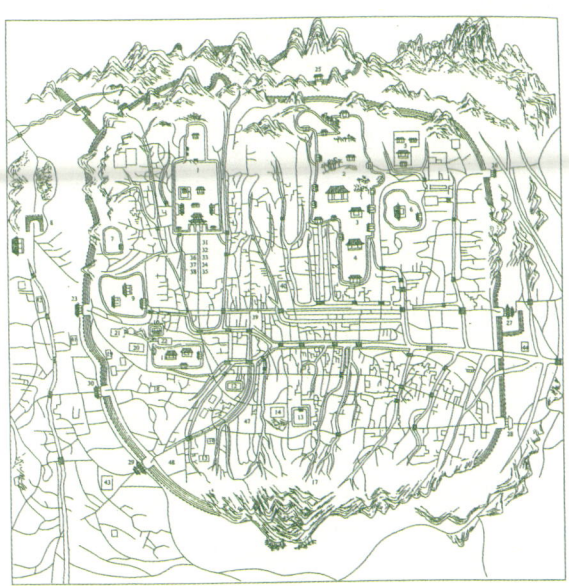

Map of Seoul, 1900

THE FOUR MAJOR GATES within the old city wall were named *in* (perfect virtue), *ui* (justice), *ye* (civility) and *ji* (wisdom). This was part of the Suwon Hwaseong Fortress, built using a combination of Joseon techniques of fortification, and Western experience adopted from Qing dynasty China. The Sung'yemun or South Gate was the main entrance to the city during the Xi dynasty. The Longdaemum (Great East Gate) was originally built in 1398 and reconstructed in 1868. This is distinguished from other gates by an onsong or crescent shaped revetment enclosing the courtyard.

The gate of the Toksu Palace faces City Hall Plaza. It was built as a villa in the fifteenth century. Two neo-Classical Western buildings within the compound house the National Museum of Modern Art.

THE NATIONAL MUSEUM is located in the Gyeongbokgung Palace grounds. Behind the Queen's residence is a terraced garden — the Garden of Amisan for immortals, containing four hexagonal chimneys. The various decorations have symbolic meanings. The phoenix symbolises the green, the bat symbolises fortune, and the plum and chrysanthemum symbolise virtue. Various symbols signify longevity — the crane, deer, herb of eternal youth, pine tree, bamboo and stone. The terraced garden symbolises a mountain and the pots symbolise a lake.

the merchant and artisan class to the south. Social hierarchy therefore, was reflected in the physical division and regulation of land, which was initially distributed according to social class, but then incrementally sub-divided further, establishing a complicated configuration of private sites and physical layouts.

Seoul is officially *Sǒul T'ǔkpyǒl-si*, the Special City; Pusan being the other. It encompasses around 614 square kilometres north of the Han River which flows west to the Yellow Sea. Administratively the city is divided into seventeen wards or *ku*, which are sub-divided into several precincts or *dong* and still further divided into *pan* or 'village' neighbourhoods made up of narrow alleys, which constitutes the address systems outside the downtown area.

In terms of cultural heritage, the most tangible are the remaining four palace structures, constructed at different stages during the Yi dynasty: Gyeongbokgung with its 'Hall of Diligent Government' in the north; Ch'angdokgung and Ch'angkyongwon in the east; and Deoksugung in the south, with the Taehanmum Gate facing the Central Business District. The guardian deities of the city, together with the main city gates, defined the main activity nodes and demarcated the alignment of access paths. The heart of the old city was Gyeongbokgung Palace. The Kungjong-jon, or Hall of Government, commanded an unobstructed view to Namdaemum — the Great South Gate.

The cityscape represents layers of political, social and cultural transformation with the co-existence of Korean, Japanese and Westerns features. Urban cultural heritage includes historical sites but also everyday rituals. Most registered cultural properties are in the old walled city area — palaces, public buildings and *Yangban-chon* houses reassembled from Chosǒn dynasty originals. Buddhist temples and associated symbolism represent interventions into the ways of

1 Bae, C.H. and Richardson, H.W., *Regional and Urban Policy and Planning on the Korean Peninsula*, Edward Elgar Publishing, Cheltenham, Camberley, and Northampton, 2011

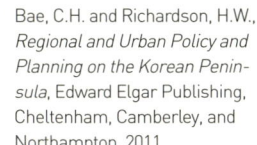

THREE YEARS AFTER THE JOSEON DYNASTY was founded by Yi Seong-gye, the main royal palace — Gyeongbokgung "The Palace Greatly Blessed" — was completed with Mount Pugak-san and Mount Nam-san as a backcloth, adhering to geomantic principles. The areas northwest of the palace included a former aristocratic quarter in the Yi dynasty, known as *udae* (as opposed to araet dae where poor residents lived). Fronting the main Gwanghwamun Gate was the Yukjogeori Street of Six Ministries, today's Sejongno, which is home to Seoul's major government offices. Along the central axis was the nucleus of the palace — the throne hall, reception hall and the King's residence. Much of the building was razed during the Japanese occupation between 1392 and 1398. Changdeokgung was rebuilt as the main palace. Gyeongbokgung was largely reconstructed in 1867 by Taiwon'gun, covering 69 hectares and following the layout of old Chinese cities. The palace was largely dismantled during the Japanese occupation and in 2010 the Gwanghwamum Gate was restored to its original form.

the Confucian Yi court, which attempted to extinguish Buddhism. However city temples abound. The centrally located Chongye-sa Temple forms the main Buddhist hub, off An'guk-dong. Bong'ŭnsa Temple is the oldest in the capital dating to the Silla dynasty of AD 794, and was moved to its present site in 1562. Korean cultural identity and social cohesion reflect strongly-rooted connections with both Japanese and Chinese traditional traits, with a syntax similarly derived from the vocabulary and grammatical structure of these countries.[1]

Until the late nineteenth century Korea was politically dependent on China, and its capital had been planned on *hyongsedo* geomantic principles in the fourteenth century, with a similar organisation to ancient Chinese cities. Traditional architecture and urban design was heavily influenced by Chinese styles — temples were painted in primary colours called *tanchong* using

KOREAN RELIGION relates strongly to both urbanism and symbolism, spanning an eclectic range of spiritual beliefs that cross convenience boundaries, according to personal circumstances. These include: Taoism, Buddhism and Christianity, but also Shamonism rituals and Animist beliefs related to the spirits of land, river and harvest. An important source of veneration is Tan'gun — the mythical "general of the heavens" and founder of Korean civilisation. Buddhism became the institutionalised religion of Korea in the fourth century AD. During the Koryŏ dynasty temples became the great centres of learning until the Yi dynasty, while Buddhism was encouraged by the Japanese occupiers as a means of cultural assimilation. A statue of Buddha looks out over the Bongeunsa Temple and further towards the Samseong Business District and World Trade Centre.

A FORESTED HILLSIDE PARK in the Gangnam area of southern Seoul forms the royal burial grounds of Seolleung and Jeongneung. Seolleung is the tomb of King Seongjong (the 9th monarch of the Joseon dynasty) and Queen Jeonghyeon. Under the reign of Seolleung the main statute of State Administration was completed, and many advances made in national culture. Jeongneung, the tomb of King Jungjong, is located in a second area. The stone statues, some of which represent military officials, are symbolic of strong sovereign power during the Joseon dynasty 1457-1494.

special motifs and symbols that had specific meaning. Four Chosŏn dynasty palaces survive, Changdokkung being the best preserved, constructed in 1405 and continuously enlarged or re-built after fire or coups, and served as a royal residence until 1989. Many of the buildings were destroyed during the first Japanese invasion under Hideyoshi in 1592 and later in 1597, after failed negotiations with Ming emissaries from China. This was followed by Manchu invasions in 1621 and 1637. After their retreat Korea remained secluded to the outside world until the late nineteenth century.

THE COLONIAL CITY

Christianity entered Korea via the sixteenth century invasion by Christian-Japanese troops. Catholism was imported from converted Chinese adherents, but many thousands of Catholic converts were persecuted and put to death in the nineteenth century. Both Catholic and Protestant missionaries contributed to the later independence movement. A number of other minor religions sought to fuse different native beliefs, most of these blending the ethics of Confucianism, Buddhist theocracy and Taoist philosophy.

The early nineteenth century was a period of unrest at a time when Western incursions in neighbouring China and Japan were at their height. The country was partially opened to foreign trade and commerce, and Westerners who arrived in the nineteenth century were permitted to settle and establish legations in Chong-dong, inside the western wall to the north of Toksu Palace. The British Embassy and the adjoining Italianate Anglican Cathedral dating from 1898 are still in active use. The Myungdong cathedral, over 70 metres in height, was the first tall building and changed the city skyline. However, repression of Western teaching and Catholicism deepened after the Taiping rebellion in China, and foreigners were excluded from the peninsula after 1864. Both Russian and American attempts to open the country to trade failed, but in 1875 three ports were opened for trade with Japan leading to a gradual rise in Japanese influence. Following the Tonghak uprising in 1894, Japan commenced military occupation in 1905 and was given control of Korea's foreign relations and administration, which led to the annexation of Korea in August 1910 with the fall of the dynasty. At the time Seoul still housed legations from England, France,

America, Russia and Germany.

Japanese intervention effectively suppressed Korean identity through the "Japanisation" of language and culture, during which Seoul lost much of its historic fabric but absorbed a more ordered morphology. This reflected infrastructural and institutional developments already underway in Japan, linked with a modernising agenda based on urbanisation. Japan renamed the city Kyungsung, and commenced a systematic building programme of street widening, railroads and ports, facilitating agricultural and industrial development to fulfil Japan's domestic needs. Extensive land surveys were carried out which facilitated the expropriation of land and re-organisation into new building lots as a base for city expansion, but they were devoid of an overriding urban design framework. The fine-grained system of narrow streets and alleys were rationalised to form a large-scale orthogonal grid system adjusted to the constraints imposed by topography, and over time this was extended to sub-districts. In the inner city this has established an interplay of broad main road alignments, and a more meandering pattern of local streets. Urban development took place along the valley areas creating a dense

[2] Hae, U.R., 'Seoul : Removing the Reminders of Colonialism' in *The Disappearing Asian City*, Ed. William S Logan, Oxford University Press, Oxford, 2002

pattern of streets in the central area. Japanese residential areas were located at the northern foot of Nam-san mountain outside the old city wall, while western residencies were clustered around the Duksoo Palace. Korean properties were demolished to make way for widened streets and civic spaces, and the city wall was dismantled in order to extend the tram system. The Japanese commercial district developed along Namdaemunro with the main Korean commercial area along Jong Road where the concentration of businesses evolved into the present Central Business District.[2]

The intrusion of politics in heritage preservation is illustrated in the history of the Capital building, constructed by the Japanese in 1926 as the headquarters of the occupying government. This was intended to be part of a Baroque plan with symbolic buildings at key intersections. Its location was deliberately chosen to sever the strong positive geomantic influence of the site and the spiritual axis of the city. This neo-Renaissance building, erected in front of the Gyeongbokgung Palace, therefore established a new symbolic order. It remained for some years as a symbolic reminder of colonial rule. After 1945 it become the headquarters of the American military government and later the home of the Korean Legislative Congress. It was damaged by North Korean troops and then partially reconstructed in 1961. Following the removal of government offices to the new administrative capital of Kwach'ŏn, the building became the national museum in the compound of Gyeongbokgung Palace, but was demolished in 1995 to reinstate the *feng shui* integrity of the palace compound. Original structures that were pulled down in 1926 to make way for the Capital building have now been reconstructed.

The Japanese introduced a 'Western'

order to the city plan which reflected the infrastructural and institutional developments already underway in Japan. Between 1910 and 1945, a course urban grid was superimposed on the prevailing fine-grained network of streets, which led to an expansion of the urban core. The city was enlarged four-fold between 1936 and 1944, with the development of a major residential and commercial area — Yongsan. The first modern planning legislation was introduced in 1934, and this produced a conjunction of a large-scale orthogonal grid comprising major boulevards and a more fine grained hybrid grid of secondary road channels and alleyways dictated by the local topography. However this imposed colonial urbanism, which transformed the city, was also equated with cultural alienation.

THE POST-COLONIAL CITY

Liberation in 1945 generated ideological conflict. U.S. forces moved into the south under the Potsdam Accord, and the Republic of Korea was established in 1948 with Seoul as the capital. Almost concurrently, the Democratic People's Republic of Korea was established in the North with Pyongyang as the capital. The North then launched a full-scale invasion, which ended in a

MARKETS form an important component of the overall city retail system. Jongno Avenue running east-west, was a trading centre for merchants and still retains its vibrant character. The Great South Gate Market Namdaemun Sijang and East Gate Market Tongdaemun Sijang are two of the largest markets in Asia. The former traditionally functioned as a centre for food and rice storage, and today has more than 10,000 shops. The underlying morphology can be divided into several types:

- The street markets, the largest of which is Namdaemun Sijang. This follows a matrix of narrow streets and alleys where open street carts establish a dynamic connection with shops alongside;
- A labyrinth of underground arcades such as Namdaemum, Hoehyeon and Euljiro, and Myeongdong which create a connective tissue of retail alignments, up to one kilometre in length; and
- A north-south corridor of wide arcaded sections — Seun, Daerim, Sampung and Shinsong.

The mixed-use Insadong-gil development links the Bukchon Hanok area with the Namdaemun market streets.

The Myeong-dong area comprises a matrix of narrow streets southeast from City Hall Plaza. The main thoroughfare ends at Myeong-dong Cathedral. This is a congested mixed-use quarter, with bars and cafes on different levels interspersed with shops, and is constantly adapting to new uses.

ceasefire agreement in 1953. A series of military regimes followed until 1987 when new political reforms were introduced. The devastation of much historic city fabric during World War II and the Korean War, including the destruction of around 250,000 buildings, provided something of a 'blank canvas' for new urban infrastructure.

After the Korean War and a long period of stagnation, Seoul began a massive reconstruction process under the military-led government of Park Chung-Hee that led to revitalising land reforms and large-scale urbanisation as a reaction against the bland Japanese interventions. This began in the 1960s under the Second Five-Year Economic Plan, with the establishment of high density housing, industrial facilities and centres of higher education. Ten major cultural buildings were constructed, including the

National Museum, which was designed along the lines of ancient Korean architecture. Many projects from this time were ironically, funded by Japanese loans, as a result of normalising relations. Sae'oon Sang'ga, a monumental mixed-use project comprising four blocks linked by elevated decks, was built virtually at the same time, scything through the dense fabric of the older urban landscape along a firebreak instigated by the earlier Japanese government. A large version of this — the Yoida mega-structure plan — was intended to link the City Hall district with the National Assembly district, but was superceded by a more conventional urban design featuring lines of residential towers. These now dominate the area to the south of the Han River.

The Seoul Metropolitan Area of some 11,745 square kilometres has around 49

per cent of the national population of 24.5 million. However, there are thirty-nine cities in South Korea with a population in excess of 250,000 and there has been significant job decentralisation followed by some out-migration from the primate city. Rapid urbanisation from 1960 was made possible by economic transformation in the direction of export-oriented industrialisation. The government embarked on a series of five-year plans, with a new city master plan being adopted in 1966. New development from the 1970s took the form of planned suburbs some 15 to 25 kilometres from the core, and the relocation of heavy industry to designated sites south of the Han River. Around one million people live in five new towns outside an imposed green-belt, which in itself intensified land costs within the inner city. As a result an urban renewal process began

3   Ha, S.K., 'Seoul as a World City: The Challenge of Balanced Development', in *Planning Asian Cities*, Eds. Stephen Hamnet and Dean Forbes, Routledge, London and New York, 2011

4   Bae and Richardson, 2011, op. cit.

Gyeongdong Sijiang — an Oriental market selling dried herbal medicine and which interfaces with a traditional cooked food market.

in the 1990s, replacing low-rise streets with high-rise estates, although inflated land prices and housing shortages have led to the growth of informal settlements.

The population explosion that has transformed Seoul from a city of two million in 1960 to eleven million in 2012, echoes its economic transformation, and instigated a range of new urban typologies including business quarters and *Tanji* — modern residential complexes. In order to control growth of the Metropolitan Region, the Capital Region Management and Planning Law enacted in 1982, and the Capital Region Plan of 1984, broke down the region into zones with different development and planning criteria attached to each, based on growth control and environmental preservation criteria. In addition, some government offices have been relocated to other cities. In 1994, a degree of deregulation of land-use policy within the Capital Region allowed zoning categories to be simplified into those covering restricted density restricted growth, and deferred development.[3] The city population density is around 16,500 persons per square kilometre, although net migration peaked in 1975 reflecting decentralisation to new satellite towns.[4]

In 2003, plans were made to relocate the administrative capital — including more than 200 government bodies — to Chungcheong Province, allowing Seoul to develop as the commercial hub, although this proposal was later modified. More qualitative objectives were set out by the Metropolitan Government in 2006. These aimed to balance the new agglomeration economy of concentrated financial and producer service functions (associated with 'Global City' stature), with a 'state-centred' model more redolent of primate functions.

Over the past decade, the city image has been strengthened through an urban design emphasis on place-making, cultural activities and new growth scenarios based on 'green' technologies, renewable energy initiatives and upgrading of ecosystems along the Han and Cheonggyecheon River corridors. Namsan Mountain defines the southern part of the centre, its lower slopes developed with hotels and cultural facilities, and offering a recreational amenity as a municipal park, reached by cable car. Namsangol Garden was designed to evoke the original mountain terrain and natural flow of water, and contains five relocated Hanok houses. It is also pierced by three road tunnels linking the northern and southern parts of the city. *It aewŏn* extends along the southern part of Nam-san. The area housed Japanese troops during the occupation, and was later the site of the 8th US Army headquarters. The Korea Housing Corporation built Western-style housing in the area, much of it occupied by foreigners. It now forms a strip of bars, and clubs, or small café-bar rooms.

In terms of commerce and high-tech industry Seoul is an advanced city, capable of assuming a 'gateway' role in North-east Asia through its investment in advanced transportation infrastructure — high-speed rail connections, Incheon International airport, and major regional development. A continuing challenge for Seoul is the relationship between the Metropolitan Region and the rest of the country, which needs more forceful strategic planning and economic integration, and ultimately dealing with the question of North Korea. The modern urban framework has evolved through a century of traumatic events,

shaped in a more contemporary form by the political division between North and South Korea, which is demarcated in physical terms by the De-militarized Zone. This has created a societal duality of patriotic attachment and justifiable paranoia, which is nurtured by unpredictability and the difficulty of rationalising a fully coherent spatial strategy for Korea as a whole.

THE CHEONGGYECHEON RIVER: REGENERATION THROUGH MULTIPLE INTERVENTION

Water in the city serves several significant urban functions — from drainage to transport. Chief among these is the environmental benefits it gives to urban living, along with its ecological functions as new urban habitats.

The urban recovery of the Cheonggyecheon River required a special type of intervention, both restoring and transforming an ancient watercourse along a central spine, where the stream hydrology formed part of the overall drainage system. Early settlement patterns reflected the variable water levels along the stream course and flood plain, while development was framed by the four main hills that still encapsulate the urban topography.

In the eighteenth century the river was reinforced with stone embankments to provide flood protection, and during the Japanese occupation its alignment was straightened and lined by light-weight stilted housing and factory structures. Further engineering works to mitigate flooding formed steep channels, which broke down its connection with the city and its upstream section was decked over. It therefore became disassociated from any transformative role in the urban development that followed massive population growth through the influx of refugees from the North at the end of the Korean War in 1949, and in the restoration of Seoul as the capital after the Japanese occupation.

Similar to various Chinese cities, where water courses and moats around walled settlements were filled in to form roads, the Cheonggyecheon River was entirely paved over between 1956 and 1970, and an elevated highway constructed above it to expedite traffic movement from the city approaches. By 2003 this was carrying some 170,000 vehicles per day. The two greatest obstacles to restoring the river's presence were therefore: removal of the highway and commensurate re-programming of traffic movement; and

compensation for the small businesses that lined the road corridor. Its demolition in 2003 and subsequent restoration in 2005, reinvigorated the economy and created a confident spirit of betterment — literally a 'Korean Wave' surfing on the back of urban amenity and a networked lifestyle. It also provided an opportunity to provide unobstructed access to new recreational amenities.

The overall transformation is as much an exercise in deconstruction as in restoration. It opened up previous imposed layers that represented high-speed mobility, and replaced them with a new ecology relating to the slow movement of water and pedestrians along a 5.8-kilometre stretch through dense urban fabric.[5] The route comprises three identifiable sections ranging from natural stream to urban enclosure, with diversified channel sections to induce variety and enliven the landscape setting. But the project itself also has a multi-dimensional impact that ranges from the ecological and climatic, to the economic and cultural. Three major organisations were involved: the Restoration Project; the Citizen's Committee which mediated between the Metropolitan Government and local interests;

5 Ed. Busquets, J, *Deconstruction / Construction : The Cheonggyecheon Restoration Project in Seoul*, Harvard University Press, Cambridge, Massachusetts, 2011

and the Restoration Research Corps. Apart from its complicated construction, the project had to deal with traffic planning, restoration of historic bridges and connections with adjacent areas. At the same time, investment was directed at urban renewal for gentrification and development of new residential and commercial uses. A significant factor in its public acceptance was the speed of construction over a two-year period. The resulting environmental transformation matched the re-shaping of other urban forms, and in the process created a symbolic icon to underscore the image of a positively changing city.

The Cheonggyecheon intervention has acted as a restorative agent, resurrecting the city's ancient *feng shui* significance. In this sense it has recalibrated the urban design focus of Central Seoul, creating a visual and recreational facility that has welded together the northern Gangbok and southern Gangnam sectors of the city. This is made more tangible through the intimate spatial dialogue with local shopping areas, markets, and commercial environments, that, in themselves, represent a cultural link between contemporary and past urban places.

The impact of linear space is heightened at street level by the insertion of plazas, which have restored a sense of place and activity. In reducing the area given over to highways, the issue of movement has increased use of public transport, with surface motor traffic redirected from the business cores alongside the river.

This urban design intervention is linear in nature, extending the organisational capability of design to knit together diverse streetscapes and channels of continuity — bridges, pedestrian corridors and footpaths. These create a connective matrix while offering places of solitude and detachment from the city. They also expand the spatial realm and social diversity of Seoul's inner districts. The east-west river corridor is intended to intersect with four north-south axes. Each conveys different urban design characteristics, including a historic avenue which integrates Gwanglowamun Plaza with Changkyung Palace, reinforcing the geomantic link that was broken by the Japanese–built Yulkok Road. These axial strategies form part of the 'Urban Renaissance Masterplan' for the city (prepared in 2007), which also proposed restoration of parts of the old city wall. In

the process, it has recovered the historical morphology and urban ecology of the city, including elements such as reconstructed stilt houses in the Cheonggyecheon Museum. The ancient Gwangtonggyo Bridge, whose ruins were found during excavation, was restored to its original position. Remnants of industrial archaeology and former infrastructure sculpturally evoke their former powerful presence and re-contextualise the setting as a series of venues for cultural events, concerts and poetry readings.

The variety of individual design components offers a giddy combination of urban elements that cumulatively choreograph an urbanism of movement and intersection — bridges, viaducts, stepping stones, ramps, stairs, service structures, passive seating and active promenades — set around the satisfying flow of moving water as part of an integrated but varying composition at various scales. This includes a 50-metre long 'Wall of Hope' mural in glazed ceramic tiles. All of this provokes different interpretations and associations of use that enable an informed reading of the city. In appropriate keeping with the wired up modern city, the river environment

signifies an ambiguous relationship between cityspace and cyberspace... from natural landscape elements to the elaborate technical mechanisms that purify and pump water around the system, as well as interactive information systems and LED lighting fixtures. An intriguing aspect of the revitalised Cheonggyecheon is its ingenious combination of re-engaged archaeology, flood control, visual and recreational amenity, and complex hydrology. Water is pumped from the Han River to create a constant and even water flow that in future might utilise clean effluent from treatment plants. Its elevation, three to five metres below street level, relates to a complex subterranean infrastructure of storm drains, outfalls and buried pipes. A 50-metre deep storm sewer tunnel maintains the water volume needed to feed urban streams with a constant water flow, creating a 'water-recycled' hierarchy.

The river now acts to reduce the heat-island effect of the surrounding built-up area, thereby constituting a breezeway. Over 2,000 street trees were planted alongside the channel, and nine fountains installed along its length. The environmentally restorative design itself opens up a varying ecosystem of channels, landscaped embankments and water features that engage different users. This creates a rich series of habitats that supports a diversity of new life, including giant carp that swim upstream from the Han River, as well as many bird, insect and plant species. Its western termination connects with a 280-acre forest preserve.

The project is also pertinent for the way it has brought together diverse public, professional and government bodies through a deft process of political handling, to ensure both its rapid implementation and its effectiveness.

The business centres of Asian cities offer numerous examples of elevated public realms that interface with private passages and concourses and respond to increased urban

IN 1795 KING JEONGIO, the 22nd monarch of the Joseon dynasty, commissioned the compilation of a volume of drawings by the most talented court painters, these depict the royal procession from Changdeokgung Palace and crossing Gwangtonggyo Bridge to Hwaseong. It has great historical value, providing an insight into the formalities and customs of the time.

densities. The Cheonggyecheon linear public space frames a different dimension, crossed by twenty-seven bridges at street level. It creates a more intimate relationship with the city than skywalks, while satisfying the need for multi-level inter-relationships that the contemporary morphology demands — it is independent of the city but connects the most vital parts of it. It is therefore integral to the urban experience.

THE BUKCHON HANOK COMMUNITY

Bukchon Hanok Maeul historically served as a village for aristocratic households dating back 600 years to the Joseon dynasty. It is now a preserved neighbourhood with an ongoing programme of restoration and new infill buildings. Tiled roofs and elegant walls define the identity of the area set among narrow and sloping streets.

Bukchon lies north of the Cheonggyecheon — the royal palace. The area integrates indigenous styles from the late nineteenth century, situated in meandering narrow streets, and set apart from the modern thoroughfares. The *hanok* courtyard housing associated with Bukchon has been subject to preservation and restoration since 1990. These large family compounds formed dense networks where courtyards could only be accessed from narrow passages through large formal gateways. Hence there is a strict hierarchy of space but at a relatively informal level, which creates opportunities for active use. In recent years artisans have revived some of the traditional crafts particularly in the Insa-dong area, and many of the old properties have been preserved. The area is divided into ten localities, where nineteenth century Hanok houses merge with shops that were modified and restored in the 1970s. The main commercial street, Samcheongdung-gil, provides a mix of galleries, cafes, and traditional workshops.

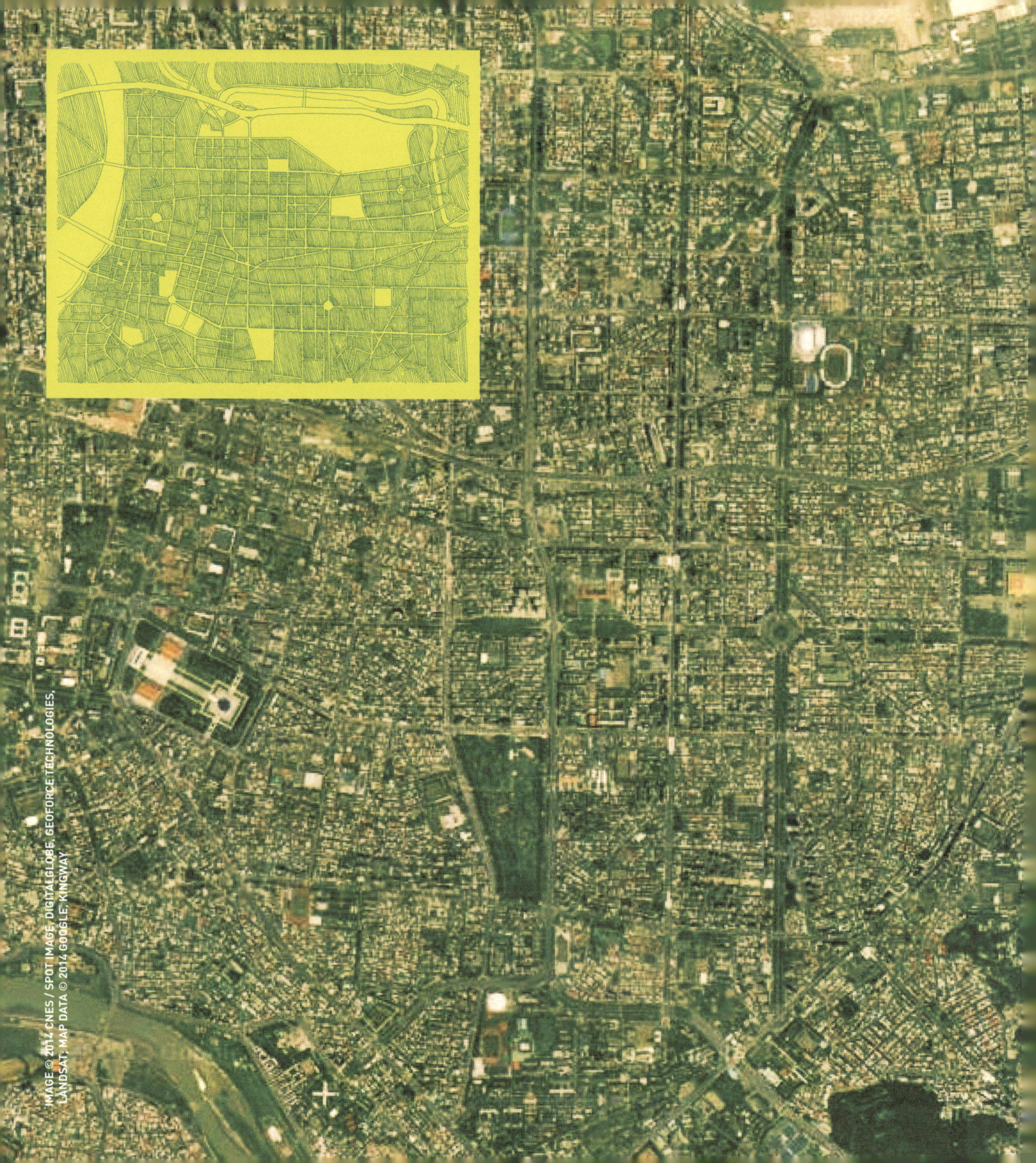

Taipei

TAIWAN

THE DADAOCHENG AREA is one of the oldest in Taipei, associated with the Danshuei River. It evolved as a market settlement and became built up in the mid-nineteenth century as new urban immigrants established merchants guilds and commercial establishments. Dinhua Street is the most historic in the city, and contains a large number of restored shophouses within its matrix of narrow streets. During the Qing dynasty, Western trading companies were established in the area, and later neo-Baroque façades and Art-Deco details were added to older buildings. During the Japanese colonial era, the area became a centre for tea processing and its mix of nationalities introduced a mix of cultural and religious institutions. Street upgrading has been carried out by the City Government Urban Regeneration Office, whereby owners of run-down property can apply to transfer their development rights to other sites. This has proved successful in bringing about street upgrading.

TAIPEI MUNICIPALITY is located in a basin surrounded by mountains and covers around 270 square kilometres, dominating national political and economic development. The city of Taipei lies at the heart of Taiwan's urbanisation, reflected in both its historical evolution, and its tenuous economic and political restructuring after 1949, with particular regard to unfolding events across the Taiwan Straits in China. Political changes over the past century have impacted on the identity of the city and on development of its metro area. In addition, a sequence of interventionist forces have delineated ideological aspects of urban design through its cultural and political symbolism.

Migration to the fertile Taipei basin dates back to the seventeenth century through immigration from China's coastal provinces during the fall of the Ming dynasty. Port settlements began to emerge along the Danshuei River during the Qing dynasty, facilitating the export of agricultural products, including oolong tea. At the time Taiwan, in a similar way to neighbouring Fujian Province, was an established trading community orchestrated through guild structures.

While the Portuguese sailed along the coast of *Formosa* before settling in Macau in the mid-sixteenth century, it was the Spanish who constructed Fort San Domingo in the Danshuei area in 1628 and vied with the Dutch East India Company for regional supremacy. After the early foreign settlers were driven out around 1660, the Qing Empire ruled the island and from 1709 there was systematic immigration of Chinese to the Taipei Basin with the first developments in the Dadaocheng area along the river.

Increase in trade with the Mainland's port cities led to the growth of Mangka around the north of the Danshuei river, which formed the first large port settlement. Amoy across the Straits was officially opened as a Treaty Port in 1843 and Foochow in

THE BOPILIAO HISTORIC AREA forms part of the Tamsui district and has been subject to a restoration plan since 2004. Its older buildings, architectural style and materials date from 1799 and housed rice, printing, tea, and herbal shops, a temple and public baths. With input from conservation groups and residents, the Bopiliao area is significant to both the urban regeneration process and for education purposes. It now houses a heritage and cultural education centre, galleries and exhibition areas, together with spaces for creative industries which have triggered environmental improvements in the surrounding area. The conservation strategy has been to maximise the re-use of original building materials including red brick, stone and timber, and to re-connect the historic buildings with the surrounding urban context. The technical building methods have employed a fusion of new and old, such as traditional bamboo-mud wall construction, timber window and stone carving, with some new materials imported from the original source in Fuzhou.

1 Ching, C.H., 'The Development of Economic Structure: Producer Services and Growth Restraints', in *Globalizing Taipei: The Political Economy of Spatial Development*, Ed. Reginald Kwok, Routledge, London and New York, 2005

The renovated East Gate was the entry point for the Japanese invading army in 1895. Its elaborate roof form was added during renovation in the 1960s, and provides a central landmark in the area.

1844 under the Treaty of Nanking. Western powers, capitalising on the faltering Qing dynasty, later re-focussed the treaty through the Convention of Peking, allowing further port cities to be opened up for trade. These included the Baliben port of Mangka. This grew during the nineteenth century as a distribution centre in the area around the first commercial port at Dadaocheng. However, the latter quickly surpassed the former to become the main commercial port settlement in the Taipei basin. The river port areas functioned primarily as trans-shipment centres for rice, tea and camphorwood to markets in mainland China.

In 1875 Taipei became a prefectural city — the last walled city of the Qing dynasty, after its completion in 1884. Construction of the Taipei city wall, with its five principal gateways, began in 1882 and formed the basis for a future concentration of development in the western part of the city. The first governor of the new province, Liu Mingchuan, constructed a new administrative compound with the walls between Mengjia and Dadaocheng. It was planned according to strict *feng shui* principles with the Yuanshan Mountains to the north and the Hsindian River to the south. The city was designated a provincial capital in 1891, leading to rapid development of rail infrastructure to the east and north, and the amalgamation of Taipei, Dadaocheng and Mangka as a port and industrial city.

Following the Japanese invasion in 1895, the imposed "Taiwan House Regulation", based on a European Baroque style, was applied to new urban street blocks and prominent buildings, and over the next thirty years most Qing dynasty buildings were destroyed to eradicate their symbolic status. The city walls were dismantled between 1901 and 1908, and urban development was focussed on the Zhongshan area.

MILITARY INTERVENTION

The Treaty of Shimonoseki in 1885, following the Sino-Japanese War, effectively ceded Taiwan to Japan. In similar fashion to the occupation of Seoul, Japan began a reorientation towards Japanese cultural norms, investing heavily in new infrastructure and industrial development. Railway planning began in 1898, linking Taipei with annexed cities to the south-west and Keelung to the north. This accelerated the urbanisation process, which in turn stimulated economic growth, fuelling the needs of the Japanese empire.

In 1905 the first city plan was implemented for a designated population of 150,000 within a gridiron structure, which replaced the more informal streetscape. This reinforced the development core of the western city around the new railway station. Older Chinese buildings within the walled city were destroyed including ancient temples, and a major Shinto shrine erected. Taipei was divided into 52 neighbourhoods, effectively separating the Japanese and local populations. In line with Japanese public building design in Mainland cities such as Dalian, European neo-Classical designs were used, which supplanted Chinese identity with something altogether more ambiguous.

During the 50-year period of Japanese occupation, Taipei experienced rapid growth through Japanese government personnel, military families and other immigrants. The modern planning system was introduced through the Urban Planning Ordinance of Taiwan in 1936, which laid down a regulatory, control and enforcement system together with standards for infrastructure provision.[1] Demolition of the city walls facilitated the integration of wide roads and

The red brick Administration Office building with its elaborate central watchtower was constructed in 1919 by the Japanese in a European style on the site of the Ch'ing Defence Ministry. The grand entrance portico was added during post-war refurbishment and the building now serves as the Presidential Office.

THE GOVERNMENT HAS PLAYED A KEY ROLE in shaping the structure of public retail markets in terms of both civic buildings and the designation of streets for stall trading. The first of these amenities was built in Ximending by the Japanese colonial government and there are now 53 public markets in the city. These have in most cases been re-built or refurbished as centres of activity, and incorporate community centres, facilities for the elderly, and libraries, thereby playing an important role in urban neighbourhoods and complementing the modern retail chained industry. The Red House is a two-storey octagonal and cruciform structure in red brick designed by Kindu Jyuru, and built in 1908 during the early Japanese colonial period to replace a wooden marketplace outside the West Gate. Ximending was the main Japanese residential quarter and the Red House became a Japanese market for high quality Western goods with an upper floor restaurant. It was first known as the Xinqi Street Market and is the only one of its kind remaining. The original market sold flowers, books and medicine and dry goods. After World War II it served as a storytelling hall and then as a theatre. In 1997 it was designated as a historical landmark and now serves as an arts venue that defines one side of a market square. It therefore serves as a window to changing ideological trends and Taiwan culture.

improved infrastructure, together with the consolidation of various districts within a planning area of 800 square kilometres. Japanese planning imposed an ordered street grid lined by tenements of six to eight storeys. Where these remain, they form layered strata of activities, given over to street markets in the evening, and punctuated by an elaborate assortment of booths and food stalls. The Taipei Metropolitan Urban Plan of 1932 covered the area between the Danshuei River to the west and Songshan in the east, with the new Songshan airport to the north and Taipei Imperial University in the south.

At the height of the occupation, one-third of the population was Japanese, most of whom lived in the old city. Japanese rule in Taiwan paralleled their intermittent involvement in China, and its development programme included a city expansion plan to the east, industrial development, and expansive boulevards together with new highway infrastructure that connected with surrounding mining and agricultural

townships. The introduction of Western industrial technology underscored the primate city role of Taipei, but this came to a sudden end when Taiwan was restored to China in 1945 after World War II.

AUTHORITARIAN INTERVENTION

With Taiwan's return to China, the departure of Japanese residents, and subsequent retreat in 1949 of the Kuomintang under the leadership of Chiang Kai-shek from Mainland China to Taiwan, around two million political refugees fled to the country. Attempts to bring about political reform were rebuffed by the Kuomintang who introduced martial law. During this period, planning was used to reinforce authoritarian rule over Taiwan, reflecting the ambition of the Kuomintang to form a buttress against the Communist government in China. Urban development from the 1950s combined land reform with a shifting economy based initially on agricultural exports and then light manufacturing of textiles and electronic goods in the 1960s. Development was extended to the eastern suburbs, commensurate with growth in export-based manufacturing. Under the elusive but protective arm of America, who provided the only source of economic aid, this reinforced the move to self-sufficiency, and economic growth shifted to secondary and tertiary industries. Taiwan adopted an export-oriented industrialisation and manufacturing model, with special zones set up in Taipei prefecture along with major regional infrastructure for electronics, petrochemical production and ship construction.

In the 1960s and 1970s, small and medium manufacturing enterprises in the form of numerous satellite factory communities, forged links with production chain networks that concentrated in specialised products co-ordinated by trading companies.

Until comparatively modern times, strategic planning policies tended to reflect

TEMPLES, WHETHER BUDDHIST, TAOIST OR CONFUCIANIST, have played an important role as centres of population concentration. They are insinuated in both the urban and social fabric of urban places as atmospheric focal points, but generally with strict adherence to a formalised layout, although their landmark status is not necessarily dominant. In some cases, religious icons were brought by new immigrant communities, and urban neighbourhoods built around them. Traditional customs, together with a profound belief in the power of iconic deities to improve earthly quality and ward against disaster, accounts for large-scale participation in spiritual activity within and around temples and shrines. Religion therefore interfaces with superstition, ancestor worship and celebratory rituals where divine intervention must be met by an offering on the part of the petitioner. Both the Longshan Temple and nearby Qingshan Temple contain shrines in honour of deities who were thought to intervene in staving off disasters and pestilence.

economic and political developments in Taiwan itself. Industrialisation initiatives shaped the export-led growth of Taipei Prefecture during the 1970s, with global economic links consolidating the role of service industry. Taipei grew rapidly in size, with a number of satellite cities planned to house new immigrant populations. New public buildings erected in a Chinese 'Classicist' style, made a public point of demonstrating Taiwan's commitment to heritage protection and modernisation, which was seemingly at odds with Mainland China at this time. Such projects included the Grand Hotel, which replaced the Japanese-built Shinto Shrine, and the Sun Yat-sen Memorial Hall.

Following the city's designation as a special municipality, the first Comprehensive Development Plan was formulated in 1979 and its boundary expanded to incorporate several outer districts. A year later, the Secondary City Centre Plan proposed a new Financial District in Xinyi while the 1983 Taipei City Land Use Plan imposed land use zoning and plot ratio control over the entire city.

The government-directed transition to high-technology industries in the 1980s and the commensurate investment in cheap production facilities in Southern China were key factors in the development of new industrial technopoles in the 1990s. Rapid urbanisation blended with 'clean' industrial development in places such as the Taipei-Hsinchu corridor, which specialises in microelectronics and computer manufacturing. Industrial realignment led to a growth in producer service industries to support investment in the Mainland, stimulating regeneration within the city-region itself and its connective imperatives with other emerging global cities.

Economic restructuring in the 1980s in the face of forceful political functions and the opening up of China for foreign investment, began to shift towards value-added

Taiwan National Museum

production through Science Park development — particularly the Taipei-Hsinchu research and development growth corridor, together with its outsourcing factories. The Hsinchu science-based industrial park created in the 1980s is located some 70 kilometres from Taipei City and provided high-end residential development to attract talented personnel. Its proximity to the city enabled management and marketing functions to be located in the Central Business District, while specialised producer services and cultural industries located in the city could provide services to industrialists in the park. By 1987 the Taipei

Metropolitan Area had a population of 2.6 million with a number of core development areas, in particular the business district core extending to the north and east. A well-educated labour force provided a plentiful supply of talent for the developing service sector. This helped to reinforce the primate role of the city, shifting the development balance away from the older districts in the west towards a new commercial landscape within the economic core of Zhongzheng, Zhongshan, Songshan and Da'an with a mix of residential and commercial uses. The major east-west axis has the Presidential Office

THE ZHONGZHENG AREA is the former seat of the Qing dynasty and Japanese administration with its core circumscribed by the line of the old city wall, which demarcated a new highway alignment at the turn of the twentieth century. Modern monuments have been built in a Chinese style, while the older civic buildings are characterised by Western architectural styles, some of which were undoubtedly based on Asian colonial forebears, and continue to fulfil civic functions. The area integrates parks and amenities that also constitute political spaces. The Sōtokufu (Colonial Administration Building) was built by the Japanese in 1919 and personified its subjugating visualisation of the city. Its footprint inscribes the word Ni for 'Nihon' on the large site as a visual axis with the Governor General's residence. After 1949, the Sōtokufu became the Zongtongfu or presidential palace, and the centre for nationalistic ritual devoid of its Japanese connotations.

Building at the western end, and the Xinyi, Government and Business District to the east.

Industrial capital also began to invest in Mainland coastal cities, leading to regional economic networking. Production was outsourced in even greater volumes from the early 1990s. Consequently Taipei experienced a phase of strategic economic restructuring whereby the knowledge-intensive sector began to spatially reorganise the physicality of the city. With the Taipei Metropolitan Area accounting for over forty percent of Taiwan's economy, high value businesses and corporate headquarters have tended to gravitate towards the central city. With the support of community planning institutions, this has created the impetus to introduce new business areas in the east and regenerate older areas in the west. Political tensions at the time focused on the insular arguments of maintaining national independence, both economically and politically, rather than the importance of investing in China in the context of intensified global competition and the opening up of less developed economies in Asia. However, prohibition policies could not realistically stand in the way of rapid growth and development in China. From the mid-1990s, Taipei began forming an economic development and production region with Southern China, and Taiwanese hi-tech firms began relocating to the Yangtze Delta

growth corridor. The Taipei Metropolitan area expanded to include Hsinchu County, which was consolidated through new high-speed rail connections. Investment in transport and service infrastructure began to re-shape the city into a polycentric form. This paralleled the transition to high-tech manufacturing and the launch of the first Science Park development at Hsinchu to the north-east along the Keelong River, which has driven modern economic and commercial growth. New satellite centres were created either from redundant government land or reclamation from the Keeling River. These were focussed on knowledge-based industry, such as the Neihu Science and Technology Park, the Nanking Software Park and the Beitou Knowledge Park for bio-tech development. The Neihu Science and Technology Park, with its cluster of over 2,000 IT corporations along the new Zhongshan expressway, evolved from a light industrial development area. It is only minutes away from the city centre, which satisfies consumer demand for new commercial services. Also, it is linked by freeways to other science parks in northern Taiwan, and internationally with manufacturing sites in the Pearl and Yangtze River Deltas. Its consolidation has been at the expense of other non-technological land uses, which are restricted through an exclusion list. Therefore, apart from coffee shops there is little animation of the ground plane normally associated with mixed-use developments. Development has spread to two adjoining districts in Da Zhi and Nei Hu and plans are afoot to join together all technology zones under one administration.

URBAN REGENERATION

For administrative purposes the city is divided into *chu* districts of around 150,000 people, and further sub-divided into *li* and *lin* areas, which reflect different levels of administrative function and community representation. Taipei is not the most ideal setting for a

[2] Selya, R.M., *Taipei*, John Wiley and Sons, New Jersey, 1995, p153

WANHUA is the oldest settlement area in Taipei, through its association with the Danshuei River. Its original name was "Manka", dating to the time before the arrival of the Han Chinese in the eighteenth century. The Dalongtang and Wanhua neighbourhoods within Datong District traditionally made up the largest market settlements. The Dadaocheng area was urbanised in the mid-nineteenth century with new immigrant communities representative of established merchant guilds. Commercial establishments were centred around Dinhua Street close to Danshuei Wharf. It grew into the

region's most important market centre during the nineteenth and early twentieth century. The area around the Bao'an Temple and the Confucius Temple, to the north of Dinhua Street, is currently being regenerated. This will open up the historic Bopiliao area with its blocks of arcaded imperial Qing Dynasty streets and houses dating back 200 years, which were associated with the timber processing industry and the nearby wharf. This reconstructed area will eventually form a connection with the Longshan Temple and the Herb Lane (Qingcao Xiang) dried medicinal plant area, which date from 1738.

primate city. The city and low-lying basin area suffer from ground subsidence, and in 1971 the national government imposed a ban on the pumping of ground water.[2] However there are still large subsidence zones related to geological conditions. Flooding hazards occur through heavy rainfall as spillover flows to the centre of the basin, although 320 kilometres of storm drains have been built in the old city area. New land for urban development is limited — up to sixty percent of the city topography is unsuitable because of slopes, leading to high land values. While hill ranges need to be preserved for water catchment and to prevent erosion, many of the lower hill slopes have been used for housing and industry at the expense of agriculture. Housing must compete with other urban needs for land, and sites are generally fragmented. Urban renewal is therefore carried out to generate higher density development.

An Environmental Improvement Plan in 1995 extended urban regeneration efforts to

local community level. As a result, the City 'Green Framework' Plan has adopted an integrated landscape and recreation strategy for the city and the Historic Area Plan for Dadaocheng takes an energetic approach to heritage conservation. The formation of protection zones has not only restricted development in mountain forestry areas and along the river systems that flow through the city (the Tamsui, Hsintien, Dahan and Keelong), but also encouraged an urban parkland programme to enhance local amenities.

The Ximending urban renewal initiative in the late 1990s helped revitalise the traditional centre of Taipei and established a catalyst for upgrading the surrounding area, including reconstruction of the capital core and expansion of its economic activities, along with central government agencies.

The Department of Urban Development, which includes the Urban Regeneration Office, is shaping a rejuvenated vision for the city that encompasses the Taipei basin as a

whole. This entails the revitalisation of old waterways and transformation of the piers into leisure spaces so that the water margins are transformed for ecological tourism. The aim is to extend this into the mountain areas that surround the city. The east-west axis of development includes cultural parks, sports parks and civic boulevards as part of a "green net". The pressure of balancing new and old is an important factor. Within the Dadaocheng and Wanhua areas there are many early and unique street systems and narrow lanes, and Dinhua Street is subject to a constant programme of upgrading and reconstruction. Dadaocheng is one of the oldest areas in Taipei. Its name stems from 'grain drying field', when a trading business was developed along the Danshui river in around 1853. The Danshui valley then opened as an international port, and when Taiwan became a province in 1885, Dadaocheng became its largest city. In 1920 it was brought under the control of Taipei City.

Taipei city government has undertaken

three urban regeneration projects. Dinhua Street is now the most historic avenue in the city, integrating a range of neo-Classical, Baroque and Art Deco architectural details along with Chinese Hakka characteristics. The street accommodates rows of colonnaded shops, which became the centre of medical products, and many of these are more than a hundred years old. Towards the end of the Qing dynasty, a "foreign" street was constructed for the establishment of Western trading companies. During the Japanese colonial era, the area was named Harbour Town, which became the centre for tea processing. The area therefore evolved with a mix of nationalities, epitomized by the old Xia Cheung Huang temple, the Chi Shing temple (first constructed in 1853), and the Padaocheng Prebyterian Church.

Much of the street upgrading work has been orchestrated by the City Government Urban Regeneration Office of the Department of Urban Development. Owners of run-down property can apply to the office to transfer their development rights to another site with architects acting as brokers. While this has not been without problems, it is a creative strategy that has been fruitful as a proactive street upgrading process. Linked to this, a Community Empowerment Policy was inaugurated in 1995 that aims to inspire a "Creative City", and requires community planners to operate under the Department of Urban Development. Communities are invited to produce "vision maps" for local neighbourhoods, and a large number of urban improvement projects have been completed throughout Taipei.

COMMUNITY PLANNING

The failure of much post-war planning up to the 1990s can be attributed to the marginalisation of regulatory control and the indeterminacy of funding from the central government as a means of maintaining authoritarian control over Taiwan's

development model. Since the 1960s a laissez-faire growth model has permitted major rural immigration to Taipei, effectively doubling its population within one decade. While ten percent of land was reserved for public uses, only a fraction of this was built on. The development emphasis (up to the 1980s) was mostly related to road infrastructure with very low allocation of public open space compared to other Asian cities.

Li-Ling Huang identifies two critical factors that changed this situation around in the late 1980s: first, the weakening of the central state in the face of economic change; and second, social transformation. The latter generated a demand for democratization following the lifting of Martial Law in 1987, culminating in the Taipei mayoral election of 1994 followed by a presidential election in 1996.[3] Social mobilisation was commensurate with political re-structuring and the emergence of autonomous Non-Government Organisations.

In turn, this opened up the urban

3   Huang, L.L., in Conference
    on Community Planning
    'Public Engagement in the
    Planning Process', Organized
    by the Hong Kong Institute of
    Planners, September 28, 2012

planning process to new ideas for improving the physical environment. In 1996 the Urban Development Bureau established the Neighbourhood Plan programme, which was open to civic groups and community organisations. This consequently revitalised the city government's own procedures in delivering physical space and social identity provisions. Between 1996 and 2001, from a total of 200 proposals, thirty-five had been constructed, mainly in the form of recreational and pedestrianisation facilities. The introduction of a 'Community Planner System' provided a formula for consultants and academics to work with communities, with local offices providing services to neighbourhoods of around 12,000 citizens. While this does not resolve all community needs, it has gradually become more refined, focussing on specific neighbourhood issues, and identifying opportunities with direct community benefits.

From 2001, city residents have been encouraged to actively implement sustainable renovation and improvement projects, including ecological and landscape works to upgrade older neighbourhoods. Regeneration exercises include a revival of Confucian cultural landmarks, and the restoration and adaptive re-use of old warehouses for arts, exhibition and performance activities. Government-orchestrated urban renewal activities extend to the temporary use of public property that has fallen into disuse, for utilisation by private organisations.

Urban regeneration of Taipei's oldest districts — Datong and Wanhua, and the Guisui Street area renewal — is undertaken through a community planning and training project, assisted by an Asian Community Planning Resource Centre (established in 2001), and a Community Planning Fieldwork School. These organisations facilitate dialogue and mutual education with other Asian cities. Community Planning Service Centres are established in various administrative

THE DINHUA STREET area represents a commercial core of dried goods and traditional medicine shops with the Xiahai Temple of the City God at its heart, which houses the original Manka icon. The temple, built in 1859, is said to be responsible for the historic good fortune of the local community and contains a Martyrs' Hall in memory of those who died in 1853 protecting the city god at a time of civil conflict.

THE RELATIONSHIP OF TEMPLE BUILDINGS AND SPACES

revolves around enclosure, axiality and sequence so that gateways, main hall, rear hall, side halls and drum or bell towers are located in a consistent and symmetrical way. The normal orientation is towards the south following ancient geomantic criteria. The Taoist temple in Taiwan is generally highly decorated, as typified by the Qingshan Temple — the roof form is stylised with an upturned ridge and a symbolic orientation. The most common decorations are the dragon and phoenix, and the gods of longevity, happiness and prosperity. The highest roof tops the main hall but the decorated main gate also symbolises the temple status. In terms of its detailed architectural decoration, the raised beam construction technique incorporates an intricate system of brackets and supports that showcase magnificent wood carving and inlay work, adding to the status of temples.

The Longshan Temple is one of the most revered in Taiwan, renowned for its woodcarvings and 'stone dragon' columns. In the nineteenth century the temple became the centre of commercial and military affairs, with its deity Guanyin protecting the city from disaster.

4 Huang, L and Kwok, R, 'Taipei's Metropolitan Development: Dynamics of Cross-Strait Political Economy, Globalisation and National Identity' in *Planning Asian Cities : Risks and Resilience*, Eds. Stephen Hamnet and Dean Forbes, Routledge, London and New York, 2011

The Baoan Gong Temple

THE CHIANG KAI-SHEK MEMORIAL HALL AND CULTURAL CENTRE form a prominent though not entirely compatible set of uses within a large plaza. The composition marries the twin national concert hall and theatre structures, and is built in a flamboyant Ming dynasty style, with the 76-metre high memorial edifice crowned by a blue tile roof.

districts with ten participating universities and colleges who 'adopt' communities and encourage students to become involved in community action centres. These are free to choose their own working themes, including preparation of upgrading proposals, analysis of neighbourhood issues, and environmental matters.

Examples of greening and renovation projects that have benefited from the Community Planner System include: the Jiqing neighbourhood walkway (traffic-segregated pedestrian system); regeneration of the Ningxia Night Market within a connective system of new urban spaces in Dadaocheng; restoration of Qingguang pedestrian areas, linking the traditional market with local commercial corridors, streets and parks, and strengthening the bond between residents and businesses; a pedestrian system in the old Mengia district linking night markets, cultural destinations and temples; and the Yongkang renovation project within the Xinyi District.

In all these cases, community development associations, consultants and academics contributed to neighbourhood rebuilding processes, emphasising cultural and historical characteristics with enhanced urban frameworks.

TAIPEI CITY DEVELOPMENT

Taipei City now covers an area of 272 square kilometres. Its average population density of 9,611 persons per square kilometre is the highest of all Asian cities. Almost half of its total area is given over to the Yangmingshan National Park, farmland and other protected areas. The spatial framework follows a SW-NE axis for city development, which links the CKS International Airport in Taoyuan and the seaport in Keelung by road and rail networks. The Taoyuan Aviation City covers more than 6,000 hectares. This positions Taipei as a trans-shipment and distribution hub in relation to Mainland China. In effect, the strength of economic links with China is a key aspect of Taiwan's global strategy

and national identity.[4] The metropolitan area itself encompasses eight major hubs, including both old and new centres and six peripheral ones in surrounding areas outside the outer circulation system. The plan utilises transit-oriented land use development as part of the metropolitan transportation framework to avoid urban sprawl, and links Taipei City, Taipei County and Taoyuan County. A further urban design initiative is a series of themed intersecting 'axes' that cross the city — including the Taipei Riverfront Axis, the Historical Axis and the Artistic Axis. This 'green' emphasis, which extends to wetland construction and cleaning up polluted water courses, also recognises the massive growth in tourism, mainly from China. Urban space has itself become a contested entity, as political monuments, such as the Chiang Kai Shek Memorial Hall, have become iconic places of tourist visitation.

New transport connections have consolidated development in Taipei City,

Taipei Prefecture, Keelung City and Taoyuan Prefecture, with different quarters evolving varying socio-economic characteristics and land prices. Thus the high-end development market associated with the Municipality has formed an inter-dependent relationship with the industrial oriented Prefecture. The core Municipality includes twelve urban districts: the inner zone covers various wards of Keelung City and other townships within the Prefecture at a density of around 10,000 people per square kilometre; and the outer zone within the mega-region includes various satellite centres. The latter have transformed previously agricultural land within Taipei and Taoyuna Prefectures and are populated at around half the core density, but have experienced massive increases in housing stock. The outer urban boundary is some sixty kilometres from the city core. As the urbanised region has expanded, economic restructuring is leading to increased investment within the inner and outer zones. This has been commensurate with increases in foreign workers from Mainland China and Southeast Asia in response to the 'open door' policy after 1992 and its integration within the global economy. High-speed rail systems continue to shape regional development configurations, shortening travel times between major cities, and strengthening production networks.

While new city parks satisfy the need for an improved overall city environment and a better city image, their implementation has come through resumption of poor housing areas. Unlike Hong Kong and Singapore, the government has never embarked on a major public housing programme to alleviate conditions of the urban poor and reduce the cost of its labour force. From the 1990s, housing demand has largely been met by the private sector — public housing construction ceased in 2000 — with the result that home ownership levels have reached the 80 per cent mark, but at a cost of some social

THE NIGHT MARKETS in Taipei, such as Hua Xi Market, represent an institutionalised version of the established market culture of individual street vendors and traders, blending an informal leisure experience with cooked food and goods outlets, as well as daily necessities. They cater for both locals and visitors and are located either in pedestrian precincts or narrow streets that can be closed to traffic in the evening. While shops generally line the street, the central 'territorial' division of stalls creates a symbiotic relationship between permanent and temporary uses. The markets add a sense of vibrancy to the older urban street matrix, helping to reclaim congenial street life back from traffic dominated arteries.

inequality and a high degree of sharing and overcrowding.

THE XINYI PLANNING DISTRICT

A strategic component in Taipei's pursuit of global city status is the state-led development of Xinyi District — the focus of the Xinyi International Centre Rezoning Plan completed in 1995, and envisaged as Taipei's financial and logistics hub in terms of its relations with the Asia Pacific Area. The stated objective was to establish the district as the 'window of Taiwan's internationalisation'. The former military base was first developed as a government quarter in the 1990s, and the district occupies an area of 11 square kilometres. It now forms the financial as well as the political centre of Taipei, with housing for 40,000 people.

The relocation of the Taipei City Council and Municipal Government offices to the area in 1994 has attracted local and some multi-national companies. It has since grown as a post-industrial multi-function area (rather than as a centre for producer services) containing large-scale shopping, entertainment and high-end residential uses, and with major buildings including Taipei 101 and the World Trade Centre linked by a skywalk system. With the City Hall located in the west of the City and the Presidential Office in the east, the plan symbolically expresses the separation of city and state. The wide street grid is laid out to accommodate a range of disparate uses — Public Assembly Hall and Cultural Park, City Hall, Sun Yat-sen Memorial Hall, the World Trade Centre, and the Taipei Financial Centre (Taipei 101) which spatially dominates the district. This has produced a contrast in urban form between large-scale street blocks and the surrounding fine-grained streetscape, hence the experiential quality is one of contrast and separateness, rather than cohesive expression and streetscape. To counter this, large-scale outdoor events are hosted to emphasise a

The Spiderman image signifies not only the dexterity of the comic book hero in scaling tall buildings, but the Warner Village multiplex, which has assisted the international image-making promotion of the Xinyi District.

citizen friendly environment, suggesting that while the Xinyi district projects a global identity, its spatial stature of activities is largely domestic.

The plan for Xinyi involved a strategy of land consolidation with urban design guidelines to control the phasing and form of development. Different arms of the government held large land parcels with large business groups owning the majority of private land, leading to escalating prices during the implementation process. High-income condominium developments initially diluted the impact of its role as an integrated business complex, and subsidies were used to reactivate commercial development. This has provided a catalyst for growth up to the present time, wherein the promotion of Xinyi as a new urban place is also a means of attracting new users.

5 Hsu, J.Y., 'The Evolution of Economic Base : From Industrial City, Post-Industrial City to Interface City', in *Globalising Taipei : The Political Economy of Spatial Development*, Ed. Reginald Kwok, Routledge, London and New York, 2005

Taipei 101 was, until recent times, the world's tallest building at 508 metres, and underscores the symbolic association between ultra-tall buildings and the modernising Asian city, signifying its fraternity with 'world city' builders. It is, in every sense, a city landmark, comparable to the Petronas Towers in Kuala Lumpur, the International Finance Centre in Hong Kong, and the Jin Mao Tower in Shanghai. Its design defers to the reincarnation of traditional references, without sacrificing a strong post-modern identity. Its analogy with a Chinese lantern seems appropriate as both a physical likeness and a symbolic beacon.

CHANGES IN URBAN FORM

Major urban changes since the 1960s have collectively acted to realign global growth as part of an urban restructuring process, focussed on the growing requirements of the expanding service economy, but with a resigned acknowledgment that future economic trajectories are likely to form part of China's global trade agenda. Taipei has only been Taiwan's primate city since the turn of the twentieth century, when industrialisation created urbanisation of the northern coastal cities. Around forty percent of Taiwan's industrial and commercial activities are now located in Taipei's metropolitan region. However, a high-speed rail connection connects the capital with Taichung and Kaohsiung in the south and this reconfiguration of the State serves to integrate these cities within a transnational production framework with Taipei as the globalising hub and centre of political power.[5] Globalisation has brought with it a commensurate reduction in state intervention and ideological politics, and a generally relaxed approach to civil society, which has contributed to urban change. Taipei's economy is still dependent on a large manufacturing sector. This comprises small and medium-size enterprises engaged in high-tech products and specialising in the

production of components for multi-national corporations — part of an expanding trans-border production network with China. This tends to be at the cost of a weak international position, but with increased global ties within the Asia-Pacific region. The return of the KMT Government in 2008 encouraged a policy of Cross-Strait co-operation, signified by an Economic Co-operation Framework Agreement in 2010, while the Greater Taipei Plan has acted to co-ordinate and guide new development within the metropolitan region. In the process this has compelled the government to join with private sector forces to precipitate changes in urban form — something that Saskia Sassen has termed "different levels of both agglomeration and dispersal".

The politics of national identity in relation to China continues to impose limitations on the development of wider economic networks. While cross-Strait investment from Taiwan has intensified the economic inter-relationship, this brings into question Taiwan's own programme of industrial restructuring in the face of China's claim of sovereignty over the island. This in turn tends to impact on transnational investment, which impedes the growth of Taipei as a hub location in the Asia-Pacific region when compared with Hong Kong and Singapore. This is exacerbated by internal political differences, and a strained relationship between Taipei City and central government. However, political devolution continues to bring other benefits to the city, assisting a well-established process of community planning that is actively regenerating older run-down areas and facilitating new social capital. The complex China-Taiwan relationship hovers over the political economy of Taipei, with the imperatives of economic cooperation and mutuality maintaining a delicate stability and diluting the ever present tension — both China and Taiwan are members of the World Trade Organisation.

THE XIMENDING AREA along the river to the north of Wanhua was laid out with wide boulevards, theatres and restaurants as a leisure and recreation area. The area is focussed on the Ximen Plaza which housed the West Gate of the walled city. The bold definition of the plaza outlined by walls adorned with giant messaging devices, evokes a strong place identity. The local street grid was constructed by the Japanese after demolition of the city walls. Wuchang Street and Emei Street are pedestrianised at weekends and form a Japanese inspired fashion and manga hub.

IN ORDER TO FACILITATE
the redevelopment of former industrial
estates into high-end retail development and
shopping malls, strict land use controls have
been relaxed and a greater emphasis on
community planning has been encouraged.
This focuses on improved urban design,
open space provision and environmental
improvement. In terms of urban design,
a central tenet has been to consolidate
street character and increase pedestrian
accessibility, which is evident in the Ximen
mall with its connective system of people
movement. In this context multi-use activities
are used to create variety and a sense of
activity, and in the process reinforce continuity
of commercial and recreational activities.

Museum of Contemporary Art

Macau

SPECIAL ADMINISTRATIVE REGION OF CHINA

**SEVERAL CENTURIES OF
PORTUGUESE OCCUPATION**
merged with predominantly
Cantonese traditions have
created a collective cultural
identity and pluralism in
Macau. This is unified by the
physical setting of streets and
places defined by Portuguese
urban design influences, and
reinforced through centuries of
collective collaboration. At the
same time it has also produced
a civilizing spiritual interface
and coexistence between
religious allegiances and
their expressive role as both
prominent architectural set
pieces, and as part of the social
fabric. Old established religious
festivals continue to play a
ceremonial role in the public
realm of the city.

A PORTUGUESE CITY ON THE TOE OF CHINA

Macau operated as a port long before the Portuguese arrived in 1577. Traders from Fujian Province settled in the area in the thirteenth century, and it became a thriving centre of trade built around its inner harbour. The first Portuguese national to arrive in China was Jorge Alvares on a mission that came about almost by chance. The Viceroy of Goa, Afonso de Albuquerque happened to be in Malacca in 1511 when several large Chinese junks arrived in the port. The captains agreed to escort Alvares to the Chinese coast in a chartered vessel, which eventually anchored off Castle Peak, in what later came to be Hong Kong's New Territories. From this base a new trading route was established between Canton and Lisbon via Malacca.

By this time many overseas Chinese communities in Southeast Asia were trading with each other and with China through the Indies, the Philippines, Indo-China and Malacca. However China was in the throes of dismantling its massive naval force, partly because of the colossal cost and partly through a conservative international outlook. With its negligible sea defences, China's long coastline was vulnerable to attack, and as foreign commerce had been declared illegal, the next Portuguese expedition avoided the Pearl River and established a trading base off the Chekiang coast on the Yangtze delta. The development of Liampo became the first Western settlement in China, and led to the development of new trade routes with Japan and Malacca. Several years later the settlement was destroyed on orders from the Provincial Governor, and in 1553 the anchorage was moved to a more sheltered position to the west of the Pearl River delta, and two years later to a narrow peninsula fronting an inner harbour along the Pearl estuary to the north. It is alleged that the Portuguese were allowed to settle in the area

THE A-MA TEMPLE dedicated to Tin Hau, Goddess of the Sea, is sometimes known as the Temple of Barra as it incorporates the steep and rocky lower terraces of Barra Hill into its scattered layout of buildings and shrines that have become a mecca for Mainland visitors. Tin Hau temples date back to around the twelfth century in South China, and might have had their origins in animist water spirits associated with the sea before assuming celestial status granted by imperial appellation in 1684. The temple, constructed in the late fifteenth century Ming dynasty at A-Ma-Gau, inadvertently gave Macau its popular name, on the arrival of the Portuguese in the 'gau' or local bay. A large boulder carries the image of the Fujian junk said to have carried the deity to Macau. The temple has been renovated and rebuilt over the years, and has played a prominent role in extending the influence of Tin Hau to many other Chinese communities.

1   Fok, K.C., 'The Existence of
    Macau: A Chinese Perspective',
    in *Macau on the Threshold of
    the Third Millennium*, Institute
    Ricci de Macau, Macau, 2001

2   Boxer, C.R., *The Portuguese
    Seaborne Empire 1415-1832*,
    The Calouste Gulbenkian
    Foundation, Lisbon, 1997

3   Anderson, P, 'Portugal and the
    End of Ultra-Colonialism', in
    New Left Review 15, 1962

as a practical means of protecting Canton, further up-river.

Permission to settle in the area was documented at the time, but the vagaries associated with its precise status and constant Portuguese claims to sovereignty rights was to be debated and challenged for more than 300 years, before being ratified by the Treaty of Tientsin in 1887 following the Taiping insurrection. Indeed what has been termed the 'Macau Formula' was almost continually shaped by a combination of pragmatism and tolerance on the part of China to equate trading advantages with security. The Portuguese were, for the most part, compliant in furthering their own economic interests in the face of a broad spectrum of different regimes, over a period spanning 442 years.[1] This long period of uninterrupted contact between East and West represents the most consistent example of cultural interchange between Europe and Asia.

The acquisition of Macau provided the Portuguese with both a physical base, and an unprecedented economic opportunity. With its large and durable trading vessels called *carracks*, made from Indian teak and located in Goa and Cochin, Portugal had precisely the right carrying vehicle for trade with China. Most importantly, this was at precisely the time when Japanese ships were excluded from entry to Chinese ports, and when Chinese ships were forbidden from leaving them. Fukienese shipbuilders and carpenters adapted their local design and construction methods to the larger Portuguese ships, creating a significant shipbuilding industry on the South China coast.[2] Thus, in a similar way to Britain's tenacious merchant adventurers that were to open up the treaty ports in China some 300 years later, the facilitation of trading connections was the work of buccaneering individuals rather than governments, even though colonial possessions in other parts of Asia depended on trading returns to finance their administration and operations.

In 1573 around two kilometres to the north-east of the settlement, a customs barrier was erected which facilitated a levy on goods going either in or out of Macau. Labourers were allowed into the city during the day but had to leave every evening. Farming was carried out largely by the Cantonese, and if the Chinese authorities so wished, food supplies could be cut off by simply closing the barrier gate. Shortly after this, trade fairs were arranged in Canton twice yearly, which encouraged the more formal organisation of foreign trade and assured a rigorous imposition of customs taxes. China could therefore control Macau's China trade through Canton, while effectively excluding the Portuguese from the remainder of the country.

The fact that a Portuguese presence was tolerated at the behest of China for their mutual benefit, physically demarcated by the Barrier Gate, reflects the particular characteristics of the Portuguese ventures in Asia, where the imperial relationship was based only on the control of product exchange rather than exploitation of raw materials and use of colonial 'possessions' as consumer markets.[3] While this prevented the development of a more ambitious trading regime, it was also reflective of its ideological and ecumenical agenda. The emergence of Macau — with its dual function as a gateway into China and as Ming China's window onto the world — signalled a relaxation of certain restrictions combined with a degree of open-mindedness. This offered a creative way to supplement China's vassal-state trading system and marked a turning point in the history of China and Europe.

Austin Coates has given an account of the seasonal shifts in trade: the Portuguese fleet arriving in late Spring for the annual trip to Nagasaki with goods for trade that included European bric-à-brac, cotton from India and spices from the Indies; the loading

Saint Lawrence Church is probably the richest and most beautiful church in Macau, not only because of its decoration, but also because of the objects inside. The original church was made in wood and was built in 1560, but the existing one dates from the first part of the nineteenth century.

4 Coates, A, *A Macau Narrative*, Heinemann Educational Books (Asia) Ltd, Hong Kong, 1978

The Guia fortress was built between 1622 and 1638 and symbolically represents Macau's military, missionary and maritime past. It contains a chapel established by Clarist nuns depicting both Western and Chinese representations. The Guia Lighthouse, built in 1865, was the first to be built on the Chinese coast.

of Chinese silk for sale in Japan; the summer trade fair in Canton; the return of the fleet from Nagasaki in the autumn with silver off-loaded for exchange on the Canton market; the loading of Chinese goods for voyages to the Philippines, India and Europe; and the export of Japanese silver and copper together with silk and pearls from China, via Macau to Malacca.[4] The link between the Catholic crusading zeal and trade exploration was established early — by 1586, Macau was known as the 'City of the Name of God'. Merchants and their sea captains had, by law, to transport priests — 'The preachers take the Gospel and the merchants take the preachers'.[5] During the late Ming and early Qing dynasties, missionaries from different European religious orders, such as the Jesuits, Dominicans, Augustinians and Franciscans, entered China through Macau, engaging in missionary work and bringing with them a certain cultural influence.

By the late sixteenth century the lower slopes fronting the outer harbour, against the backcloth of the Monte, Guia and Penha hills, had become well developed. The Praia Grande alongside the bay was filled with houses and trading establishments, the towers of

churches acting as vertical landmarks, and the Jesuit seminary and St Paul's Church dominating the composition. The construction of St Paul's was in timber but with a formal stone façade added later, comprising niches and carved figures. It was to be the façade alone that later withstood the fire of 1835.

Portuguese ascendancy was halted abruptly by the union of Portugal and Spain in 1580, which resulted in the administration of Portugal's overseas 'possessions' by Spain. After the defeat of the Spanish Armada in 1588, Philip II of Spain closed Spanish and Portuguese ports to the British and, several years later, to the Dutch. This resulted in a loss of trading ties with Manila, and led to consolidated avenues of trade with the Malabar ports and the Malay-Indonesian archipelago, and a new silk trade with South America. With the establishment in 1602 of the Dutch East India Company, the Dutch took effective control of the most valuable trading routes. The appearance of a Dutch fleet in Macau was the catalyst for the construction of fortifications, which began in 1606. These included the Barra fort which overlooked the inner harbour, and

the Guia and Penha forts which commanded the outer harbour.[6] The Monte fortress was the principal military facility in Macau. The northwest and southwest walls, facing the Mainland, do not have battlements, suggesting that the fortress was designed only to fend off attacks from the sea. The protective walls were built in chunambo — a mix of mud and crushed oyster shells — and stretched from the fortress to Guia Hill. The events of June 1622 have long entered Macau folklore. The Dutch advanced on the Monte fortress, which was manned mainly by Jesuit priests. They were defeated by a combination of the "hand of god", St Iago, and an accurate strike on the Dutch powder magazine — an event commemorated annually with thanksgiving. In a more material sense, the episode immediately led to the stationing of a permanent military force, the construction of a city wall across the northern boundary, and elevated city status within the Portuguese Asian 'possessions'. Today the Fortress still has the old cannons, which were made by the Bocarro foundry.

By this time, Macau had become the largest of Portugal's remaining scattered settlements. It was at this low point that a pledge of loyalty from the people of Macau was sent to the new king of Portugal, João IV, and it became the city's future motto — 'City of the Name of God — None Other More Loyal'. Macau was the base for the Jesuit mission in China and other parts of East Asia, therefore Jesuit priests entering into China service would first come to the city, where they would be trained at St Paul's College in the Chinese language together with other areas of Chinese knowledge, including philosophy and comparative religion. They also brought in the first movable-type printing press to be used on Chinese soil, and published the first paper in a foreign language. Macau was thus the training ground for the Jesuit's mission in China and other parts of Asia. St Paul's College was the

5 Berhe, J, 'Macau : A Multi-Community Society', in *Macau on the Threshold of the Third Millennium*, Institute Ricci de Macau, Macau, 2001
6 Coates, 1978, op. cit.

THE LEAL SENADO is built in a neo-Classical style and represents the centre of Macau. The name is derived from the term "Loyal Senate", which was bestowed by the Portuguese King in 1654. It lies on the Av de Almeida Ribeiro, adjacent to Senate Square, and houses the Institute for Civic and Municipal Affairs. Its presence is a token of the governing body's loyalty to Portugal during the sixty years of Spanish rule in the 1600s. Built in 1784, it has been closely linked with the municipal affairs of Macau over several centuries. It features classical Portuguese architecture and an art gallery, a black wood-panelled library styled after the Mafra Convent in Portugal, and an open courtyard lined with blue and while ceramic tiles.

THE GROUP OF BUILDINGS AND SPACES ASSOCIATED WITH CAMOES SQUARE AND CASA GARDEN has a long history and some very well known historical connections. The Camoes Museum was originally built as a large private house. Its role as a museum ended when the authorities reorganized the museum collections, and in 1989 the building was purchased by the Orient Foundation with the intention of complete restoration and refurbishment as their headquarters. It adjoins one of the most beautiful garden areas of Macau, including Camoes Grotto, which houses a bust of Portugal's national poet — Louis de Camoes. Leased for a number of years to the East India Company it used to be a British enclave until the founding of Hong Kong. It adjoins the English Church and the Protestant Cemetery, where many British seafarers and traders are buried, as well as the artist George Chinnery. It was used by Lord McArtney as a base during his overtures to China — a vain attempt to present his credentials to the Chinese Emperor and open China's doors to British political contact and trade.

largest seminary in the Far East at the time, and acclaimed as the first Western-style university in the region.

The commercial resurrection of Macau came through the growth of European trade with China during the eighteenth century. Foreign traders were not allowed to take up permanent residence in Canton, therefore they needed to establish residence in the near vicinity. In Macau they were able to do this when the Church was opened to European merchants, creating a new focus for foreign relations with China. In 1757 the Portuguese officially gave foreigners permission to live in Macau, and the East India Company rented premises in the city around Camoes Square. With the merchants came Protestant missionaries. One of those, Robert Morrison, compiled the first English-Chinese dictionary and was the first person to translate the Bible into Chinese. He founded the small chapel next to the Protestant Cemetery. It is this factor above any other, that positions Macau in the context of the treaty ports that were to eventually emanate from this relationship. It was not, either literally or figuratively,

plain sailing, but provided a stepping stone for the British (via the East India Company), and later France and the United States, to extend their influence in southern China, and enabled British interests to predominate in Macau under a benign Portuguese regime.

In 1808 however, even this well orchestrated arrangement was turned on its head when British troops from India effectively occupied the city, and were only withdrawn following threats from the Chinese authorities. At this time the technically prohibited trade in opium was in a somewhat hesitant state. After 1821, when the East India Company's monopoly was abolished and the Guangdong authorities started to clamp down heavily on private traders, British and American opium merchants avoided Macau entirely. Partly as a result of this, Macau avoided too great an association with the trade in the eyes of China. However, the success of British 'gunboat diplomacy' in China prompted the Portuguese government to appoint a new Governor, Socio Maria Ferreira do Amaral and declare Macau a free port. The Governor of Kwantung, Hsu Kwang-tsin put a price on Amaral's head, and as a result of Amaral's assassination the Portuguese sent warships to Macau. The new Governor, Isidoro Francisco Guimaraes, was pragmatic in commercial terms, and introduced licensed gambling to the enclave, thus forming the basis for Macau's key industry at quite an early stage. He also negotiated a Sino-Portuguese treaty acknowledging Portuguese sovereignty over Macau in 1862.

For almost three centuries, until the colonisation of Hong Kong in 1842, Macau's strategic location at the mouth of the Pearl River meant that it retained a unique position in the South China Sea, serving as the hub in a complex network of maritime trade that brought tremendous wealth and a constant flow of people into the enclave. With the ceding of Hong Kong, and the

[7] Flores, J. M., 'The Portuguese Chromosome: Reflections on the Formation of Macao's Identity in the Sixteenth and Seventeenth Centuries', in *Macau in the Threshold of the Third Millennium*, Institute Ricci de Macau, Macau, 2003, p39-55
[8] Flores, 2003, op. cit., p51

OPPOSITE THE MAIN ENTRANCE TO THE CHURCH IS THE DOM PEDRO V THEATRE — the first Lyric Theatre in the East. It was built in 1860 to commemorate the Portuguese monarch and renovated several times in a neo-Classical style. The colonnade, arcade and main entrance were added to the main building in 1873. Named after King Dom Pedro V, the theatre was built with funds from the local Portuguese community and became a focal point for celebrations and ceremonies. It presents occasional theatrical performances, especially during the Macau International Music Festival.

The building that houses the Robert Ho Tung Library was constructed around 1894. This originally belonged to D. Caroline Cunha. It was later bought by Sir Robert Ho Tung in 1918 to be used as a villa, and after his death the building was presented to the Macau Government to be used as a public library, which was opened in 1958. A library extension was conceived by Macau's Cultural Institute — a creative example of place-making within a restricted heritage site. The mansion's three-storey frontage remains unchanged, and the new extension accords with the height limit of the older building's roofline. An enclosed garden offers an area for quiet contemplation. Adjoining the library on Seminario Street is St Joseph's Seminary dating from 1758 which conforms to a typical Jesuit missionary style. It traditionally trained priests for missions in China and other parts of Asia.

opening of the treaty ports to foreign residents in 1842, the majority of Macau merchants (including many Portuguese) left the enclave for the more robust trading environment of the nearby city of Hong Kong. Shortly after, both the French and American diplomatic missions signed treaties with the Chinese Imperial Commissioner in the Temple of Guang Yin garden in Wangxia. The issue of sovereignty was finally resolved through a Sino-Portuguese treaty, signed in Tientsin in 1887, allowing Portugal to join other European nations under a protocol of activity and commerce on a similar basis to Hong Kong.

THE URBAN STRUCTURE

Jorge Manuel Flores has drawn comparisons between Macau's central urban design and Portuguese urban prototypes such as the city hall, the Misericórdia or House of Mercy, parish churches and seminaries, which remain from the early city layout.[7] The Municipal Council or *senada da câmora* was set up in the late sixteenth century based on that of

St Agostinho Square is the setting for a series of prominent buildings from the eighteenth and nineteenth centuries. The baroque-styled church dedicated to Saint Augustine was constructed in 1814 on the site of an even earlier chapel built in 1586, and forms the starting point of the annual Snhor dos Passos Procession.

FOR MANY YEARS WHAT IS NOW SENATE SQUARE was dominated by traffic and on-street parking linked to Avenida Almeida Ribeiro. In 1994 it was closed to traffic and paved with the black and white sets, traditionally found in Portuguese coastal towns — the pattern suggests a wave motion. Today it is a pedestrian plaza, a meeting place and a focus of local and tourist activity. A programme of improvement also encompassed the harmonious cluster of surrounding buildings, including the General Post Office and the Holy House of Mercy. The "Ritz" building was one of the first older buildings around the Largo and Avenue Almeida Ribeiro to be updated and restored with a retained façade, and is used by the Macau Tourist Office. Five new floors were squeezed into the space of the original three levels. The original central courtyard is echoed in the new internal arrangement, respecting the complexity of the three-dimensional 'cubist' grid. The regeneration of Senate Square was the catalyst to further rehabilitation projects in other historic locations — St Augustine's Square, Cathedral Square, Barra Square and Lilau Square in the old city (completed in 1999, 2004, 2006 and 2009 respectively), together with St Francisco Square in Coloane and Taipa Market Square. During the UNESCO World Heritage classification process the city square and streetscapes were cited as being rich representations of the historic city. The atmosphere and character of Senate Square continues into S. Domingo Square and the Baroque church of the same name built in the seventeenth century.

THE CENTRE OF ALTRUISM in Macau, the Holy House of Mercy, was founded in 1569 by the first bishop of Macau, Dom Belchoiro Carneiro. The House worked with the local community and provided charitable assistance. It was also a home for orphans and the poor and facilitated a number of other charitable institutions such as hospitals, nurseries, old people homes, a leper's institution, refugee camps and a cancer hospital. It was also known as the "Cheque Paid Church" — workers were originally paid their salaries inside the House.

9 Wang, W.J., 'Macao Historical Urban Fabric: Study of Patio and Beco as Catalyst Buildings', in *World Architecture 234*, December 2009, p112-115

previous Portuguese settlements, and became the central instrument of local government.[8] Public spaces — often in the form of squares associated with prominent churches and defined by related building groups — also reflect the Mediterranean city from mediaeval times, in that both formal and informal open space evolved through centuries of urban adaptation. Such spaces do not, as a rule, form components of historical city fabric in China, but in Europe they have long acted as neural networks accommodating places of event, celebration, markets and meetings.

Flores draws on specific urban design references, such as the churches and religious monuments that form neighbourhood reference points and contribute to both physical and spiritual identity. The irregular alignment of the old city wall followed the natural terrain, rather than the tight geometric pattern of older Chinese cities constructed according to geomantic principles. Furthermore the idea of *rossios* or 'common lands' was introduced. Yet Macau also assimilated urban characteristics from the more unstructured port cities of southern China, reflecting its informal commercial expansion and lack of coherent planning structure.

Macau's historical urban framework can best be understood as an almost medieval network of urban plazas, public buildings, sacred places, monuments and city walls. A hierarchy of circulation routes shape the city's physical character. Wang Weijen has ranked these as boulevard (Avenida), road (Estrada), street (Rua), slope street (Calcada), ramp (Rampa), alley (Travessa), lane (Beco), and cul-de-sac (Patio).[9] These establish a connective system that defines the older neighbourhoods.

European and Mediterranean archetypes brought to Asia were adapted to the more rigorous and tropical climates of India, Ceylon, Malaysia, the Philippines and Indonesia, where building materials,

The atmosphere and character of Senate Square continues into S. Domingo Square where the Baroque style church of S. Domingo forms a prominent face onto the public plaza. It was founded in 1587 by Dominican priests from Mexico. In 1822 the first Portuguese newspaper in China was published from this building.

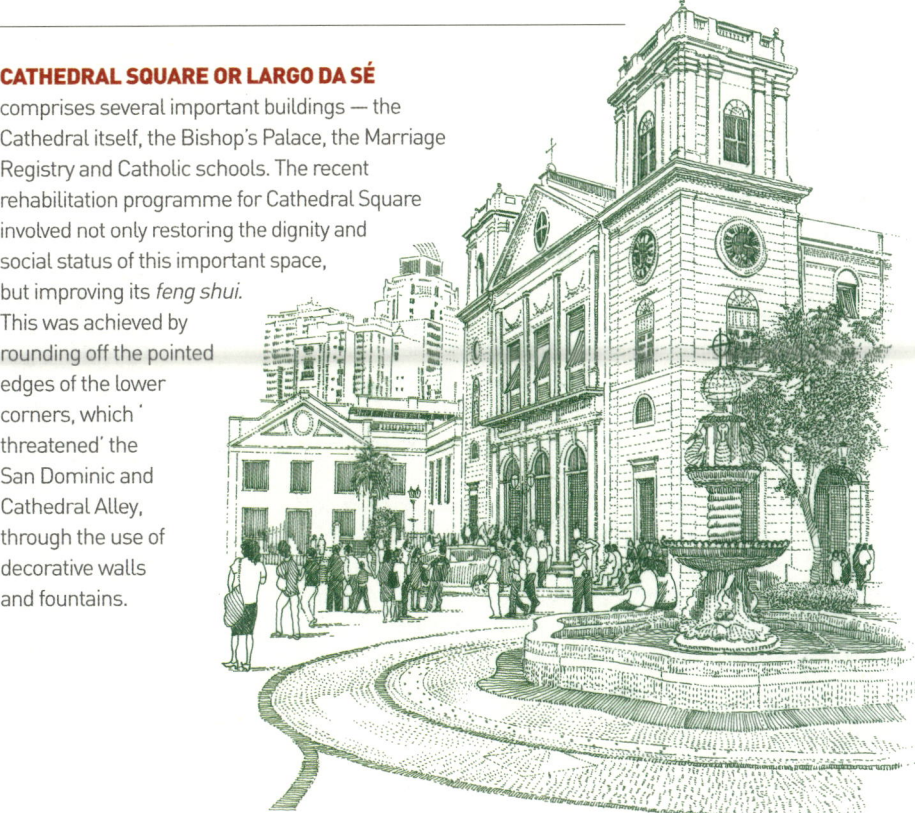

CATHEDRAL SQUARE OR LARGO DA SÉ

comprises several important buildings — the Cathedral itself, the Bishop's Palace, the Marriage Registry and Catholic schools. The recent rehabilitation programme for Cathedral Square involved not only restoring the dignity and social status of this important space, but improving its *feng shui*. This was achieved by rounding off the pointed edges of the lower corners, which 'threatened' the San Dominic and Cathedral Alley, through the use of decorative walls and fountains.

THE POST OFFICE BUILDING ON AV DE ALMEIDA RIBEIRO was opened in 1931, and was designed by Eduardo Henrique Lima Soares. It is now regarded as one of the main elements of the Largo (main square). The building was refurbished in 1989 to update its functions with the main public counters snaking between a multitude of internal structural columns with serpentine lighting. It acts as a local landmark, defining the entrance to the square on the opposite side of the Ritz building.

THE HISTORIC CENTRE OF MACAU is a living reminder of the city's original settlement, encompassing architectural heritage interwoven with modern buildings within the original urban fabric that includes streetscape, urban squares, historical buildings and piazzas. The architectural heritage, predominantly European in nature, stands in the midst of traditional Chinese architecture, providing contrast and continuity with the port. It is the oldest, and the most complete array of European architectural legacy standing intact on Chinese territory. The Portuguese themselves imported an interesting blend of southern European styles made up of classical features, colonnades and grand public façades, but the styles that evolved became increasingly hybridised with Chinese features and details characterising some of the original shophouse fabric. The Rua de S. Domingo, Rua Pedro Nolasco da Silva, Rua de Tercena and Rua das Estalagens represent the core of the traditional Chinese Bazaar area. The area also represents a scenario of constant economic change from curio and antique shops to new stores serving the massive numbers of visitors from the Mainland.

10 Marreiros, C, *Culture of Metropolis in Macau: An International Symposium on Cultural Heritage Strategies for the 21st Century*, Cultural Institute of the Macau, Macau, 2001

ornamental appendages and building skills created a framework for different design interpretation. Infused into this ensemble in Macau are Chinese features together with enigmatic ingredients dictated by *feng shui* considerations that both enrich and localise architectural identity — so-called 'Luso-Chinese' architecture.

The urban structure up until the twentieth century was limited to the lower western part of the peninsula between the Inner Harbour and the Praia. In the heart of the old city was the Chinese Bazaar, surrounded by regular city blocks. The area known as the Christian City was the residential area of Portuguese, while the Chinese City was known as Wangxia, meaning 'looking back to Xiamen' and reflecting the Fujian roots of most Chinese immigrants.

At the beginning of the twentieth century, the city started to extend northwards outside the walled boundary, comprising street block layouts of two-storey houses. The street architecture of the Chinese City followed simple principles of layout and composition, which related to houses, temples and other structures, giving a pleasing appearance of urban cohesion. Spaces were embedded within the building framework in terms of courts rather than large external public spaces. The Portuguese quarter contained the symbolic civic, ecclesiastical and military buildings, with an urban fabric patterned by a sequence of public spaces. While the streets themselves were quite narrow, the irregular structure correlated well with the prevailing topography. The urban framework therefore takes on a more informal feel that spontaneously relates to the grouping of landmark buildings. Many of the buildings embody a European style from the outside, but a more Chinese layout internally, based on central courtyards and axial room arrangements, and with embellishments that borrow from diverse cultural influences and localised craft traditions. Builders used their intuitive knowledge and experience to construct decorative façades, window and cornice details in line with the compositional quality and main disposition of the buildings. In this way the evolving urban design language is both rich in texture and unique in its composition and execution, establishing a vivid sequence of elements that frame the cityscape.

A number of factors have influenced both the urban structure and urban design patterns in Macau. The train of events initiated by the Government led progressively to a programme of upgrading in the 1960s, identifying individual buildings in terms of their stylistic attributes. This was extended in the 1970s using a more vigorous approach which classified "both individual buildings, both Portuguese and Chinese, and also groups of *conjuntos* (structures) and *percursos* (itineraries) in an integrated way".[10] In this sense, defined spaces such as squares, streets, central places and their component parts,

THE MANDARIN'S HOUSE is situated at the corner of Rua da Barra and Antonio da Silva Lane. It was built in around 1881 and covers 4,000 square metres. The traditional Chinese compound features a mix of Chinese and Western detailing and is the former residence of Zheng Wenrui and his son Zheng Guanying, who published a number of books that are considered Chinese classics. It was here that Zheng completed 'Warnings to a Prosperous Age' in 1893 — a seminal text in which he advocated radical institutional and economic reforms for the modernisation of China. The Cultural Institute of Macau bought the house in 2001 and have since renovated it. Experts in traditional Lingnan–style architecture from Guangzhou ensured strict adherence to the historical style over its eight-year renovation period.

were treated as composite elements whose character was to be preserved.

In 1982 the Instituto Cultural de Macau was created, incorporating a special Cultural and Preservation Department that established the logistical framework for preservation of monuments, groups of structures, specific sites and zones of protection. This was followed in 1984 by legal regulations which governed sale and purchase of classified sites and protected areas, along with tax incentives to promote investment in preservation. Control plans also set out parameters for building massing and visual protection, and a preservation fund was set up for contributions from the public and private sector to facilitate preservation. The Orient Foundation has since purchased various buildings, including the old Camôes Museum and old residential buildings along the Avenida de Conselheiro Ferreira de Almeida, which now house the Cultural Institute's facilities, including its archives and library. Various other buildings such as museums, have been subject to rehabilitation, and around 14 per cent of the Macau peninsula now falls within a zone of protection.

THE EVOLVING CITY

Much of Macau's post-war urban history up until the mid-1990s involves the slow transformation of the peninsula through incremental redevelopment, including new housing estates on Taipa, a university, and an airport. Despite a fear that Macau would become economically marginalized after the political transition of 20th December 1999, its economy and even its culture remain steadfastly planted between China and the West. This is perpetuated in cultural and educational programmes, and synchronized in a unique way by its historic architectural legacy that establishes a rich dialogue with the city.

Prior to the handover, increasing attention was given by the departing administration

Along the picturesque Rua do Padre Antonio and Rua da Barra is the old Lilau District, marking the earliest Portuguese settlement. It houses a sequence of old buildings and a fountain, whose water, according to tradition, makes the one who drinks it return to Macau. It is known locally as the 'Old Lady's Well'. The surrounding buildings have been converted to small apartments and studios.

THE RUA DA FELICIDADE runs parallel with the Avenida de Almeida Ribeiro. It is known locally as Happiness Street. It was a former red light area and was, in the past, the centre of Macau nightlife. The old shophouses have been restored to their turn-of-the century appearance with carved red lacquer façades and shutters. It is now a pedestrian street housing a range of teahouses, delicatessens and cafes. Its range of blinds, signages, balustrades and entrance doors reproduce the street character of the late eighteenth century.

to the city's precarious historic fabric and unique urban identity. Partly to overcome regulatory shortcomings and better assimilate development, new heritage legislation was drafted in 1992. A central aspect of this was a more focused conservation approach. This was coupled with the rehabilitation of historical urban spaces through the diversion of traffic and linked pedestrian routes as part of a cultural tourism circuit. Strategies included the preservation of iconic or symbolic relics such as St Paul's, to more provisional façade renovation and repairs. Up to 1999 this formed a belated but determined attempt to stamp the Portuguese cultural legacy on the city, and was accompanied by a spate of artistic festivals, new museums, arts institutions, and public monuments. Thus an interesting duality emerged whereby a programme of cultural preservation was developed at the same time as new and seemingly incompatible casino concessions were attracting massive foreign capital. This extended the city's profile as a leisure and entertainment hub at virtually the same time as UNESCO was granting World Heritage status for its historic centre. This came to fruition in 2005 and Macau became the 31st

THE MOORISH BARRACKS were built to house a 200-member regiment from Goa, the then Portuguese colony in India. They were completed in 1874 and located on Barra Hill, facing the inner harbour. Originally designed by an Italian architect in a neo-Classical style with Moorish touches, the Barracks feature pointed arches and mosaic-like ornamentation that reflect, to some extent, the Saracenic architecture of northern India. They now house the Macau Maritime Administration. The 2005 renovation was undertaken by Macau-based architects Rui Leão and Carlotta Bruni. The built interventions, which are difficult to see from the front, create connective layers of stairs and ramps that provide improved linkage between the various levels, which now meet at the new central entrance pavilion. This orchestrates a dialogue between past and present functions.

11 Duarte, J.I., 'Macao: Economic
Transformation in a Series
of Snapshots', in *World
Architecture 234*, December
2009

The Military Club on the Avenida da Praia Grande was constructed in 1872 on the initiative of a group of Portuguese military officers, and still serves as a recreation club.

this is the reclamation zone which effectively joins together the former islands of Taipa and Coloane, and the development of Hengqin Island to the west (part of the Zhuhai Special Economic Zone) for a new Macau University Campus and bridge crossing.

A significant interventionist initiative was the Praia Grande Bay Rehabilitation Plan, which proposed two large lakes along the south-west peninsula, effectively separating the old city from new harbourfront development. To the east, reclamation facilitated an orthogonal layout linked back into the city, but in the process this lost the visual connection between the Guia Hills and the sea.

A series of Portuguese architects have persevered with the rejuvenation of historic monuments, and the integration of new and old development — a continual mix of Portuguese and Chinese cultural characteristics that include cobbled squares, Western churches, historical public buildings and narrow streets. Over the past decade this has progressed hand-in-hand with the expansion of large-scale infrastructure, and mammoth construction projects for the themed entertainment industry — a startling and contrasting juxtaposition of typologies, that provokes an improbable dialogue between the traditional and transplanted urban textures.

INCUBATION OF CULTURAL COHESION

Several centuries of Portuguese occupation, together with an inherent infusion of Cantonese culture perpetually drip-fed over the years, along with frequent demographic fluctuations, produced a society that went beyond the simple co-existence of very different entities. The term Macanese refers to those born in Macau of at least one Portuguese parent — the *Filhos de Terra*, or sons of the earth. Macanese married both Chinese and Europeans, creating a truly multi-cultural ethnicity with global

site in China to be granted this status. A city of 550,000 people at a density of 1,800 inhabitants per square hectare, now plays host to two million visitors every month. This has translated into vigorous economic growth of some 15 per cent per annum from 2001 through private investment, particularly for tourism-related development.[11] It has been accompanied by the import of large numbers of foreign workers granted the right of abode. It has also had a significant impact on urban space as new growth has re-oriented the traditional development axis and traffic flows, adding pressure on urban services and infrastructure.

At a strategic level Macau is situated as a node in the 2020 Development Plan for the Pearl River Delta, in terms of new highway, bridge and rail networks, including the implementation of a 29-kilometre long bridge project joining together Macau, Hong Kong and Zhuhai. An Urban Concept Plan in 2008, consisting of five action plans, aimed to diversify the city's economic structure; foster the co-existence of traditional and contemporary cultures; and realise a green and sustainable city. A substantial facet of

12 Cheng, C.M.B., *Macau – A Cultural Janus*, Hong Kong University Press, Hong Kong, 1999, p83

13 Cheng, 1999, op. cit.

14 Cheng, C.M.B.,'Macau: The Forming of Friendship', in *China Perspective 34*, March/April 2001

connections. Collective cultural identity is therefore elusive, but relates to aspects of heritage and religion, together with shared memories, experience and a common sense of destiny. It is perhaps best expressed through the statue of the Macanese poet Jose dos Santos Ferreira which was erected in a new garden on Avenida da Amizade in 1999.

The "Portuguese chromosome" — a phrase used by Jorge Manuel Flores to explain the cultural identity and pluralism of Macau — has in many ways remained undiluted by its dynamic synchronisation of different cultures. This unifies the city in a physical sense, but also produces a spiritual interface and coexistence between church and temple; Catholic seminary and Confucian ritual; European theatre and Buddhist festival; magnificent edifice and city mall; historical fabric and modern make-believe caricature. The dual identity has been described as a "Cultural Janus" in the sense that the contrasting cultures look in opposite directions but have been reinforced over the centuries through conflict and compromise.[12] These factors have underscored its interactive identity and outdistanced the territory's colonial foundations. Macau played an initial role as a bridgehead for advancing Christianity in China, but this was countered by initiatives in the late Ming dynasty to assimilate and standardise somewhat mythical deities and indigenous places of worship, thereby balancing cultural identity with social and religious allegiances. Thus a balance of ideologies emerged that coalesced within the social fabric of the territory, assimilating rather than segregating belief structures.

The tolerance and acceptance of both Christianity and Buddhism owe much to the underlying Taoist philosophical value system that permeates Chinese society, and allows for a receptive inclusion of diverse religions and spiritual factors relating to the human condition. This fusion of disparate and sometimes conflicting beliefs, might be best compared with the range of deities found in different Buddhist temples which suggest what Christina Cheng has called "situational need rather than permanent religious affiliation".[13] The improbable but symbolic triumvirate of unifying and civilising forces in Macau can therefore be ascribed to Tin Hau, the Goddess of the Sea — exemplified by the oldest temple in Macau, the Ma Cho Kau temple; Kuan Yin the Goddess of Mercy; and the Virgin Mary.[14] Perhaps the virgin trio, with their codified spiritual and cultural belief systems, help to foster a unified foundation of tolerance through deification — a Lusitanian symbolism synchronized with the more elusive moral dimensions of intercession and intervention. In late nineteenth century China, religious deities had become ambiguously associated with political order, whereas in Macau religious allegiances came to represent unified or civilizing doctrines that have forged a relatively harmonious tradition of tolerance.

Macau Special Administrative Region Government Office

1 Osborne, M, *Southeast Asia: an Illustrated Introductory History*, Allen and Unwin, Sydney, 1990

HISTORICAL DEVELOPMENT

The main land mass of Southeast Asia is penetrated by the Mekong River through the countries of Indochina, namely Cambodia, Laos and Vietnam; the Irrawaddy through Myammar; and the Chao Phraya through Thailand. The extent of the region, stretching across 35 degrees of latitude and 50 degrees of longitude, and the climatic extremes related to this, creates a highly variable geographic character, agricultural pattern and settlement. To the south, the Malaysian Peninsula extends some 1,500 kilometres to Singapore, and further to the east integrates the vastly different geographic and cultural entities of the East Malayan States — Sabah and Sarawak. The Indonesia archipelago is even more diverse, from underpopulated Sumatra through Java, which accommodates 60 per cent of Indonesia's population, extending to the Celebes, Kalimantan, Sulawesi and Irian Jaya. To the north of Brunei, the Philippine archipelago comprises the three island groups of Mindanao, Visayan and Luzon, which have a history dominated by several centuries of Spanish rule.

The concept of a Southeast geographical region is broadly bound together through its anthropological and cultural similarities arising from common traditions and a broad linguistic unity reinforced by historical trading links. While Chinese and Indian religious concepts and political motivations had significant influence over architecture and city building, the ancient settlement forms and individual temple complexes have a clear individuality. Hinduism was absorbed in many of the expanding settlements, possibly through the influence of Brahim scholars who were adept at statecraft.[1]

Empires and national boundaries gradually evolved and changed through neighbouring alliances and dependencies. The new Mongol dynasty in China in the thirteenth century recalibrated established political boundaries to the south and indirectly brought about regional turbulence through invasion and disruption of trading regimes.

Angkor became a dominating power between the tenth and fourteenth centuries through its expertise at hydraulic engineering. This facilitated an agricultural economy able to support a substantial population, signified by its great temples — the result of underlying religious ideals and technological skills rather than trade. The collapse of Cambodian economic power came about through the ambitions of lesser states, and the rise of other regional powers, notably Thailand.

However the fundamental elements of Thai architecture were absorbed from the Angkorian culture. Chinese historical influence over Vietnam in terms of societal and political development reflected Vietnam's role as a tributary state, but the country rose to become one of the leading states during the "classical" period up to the end of the fifteenth century.

The Malay peninsula is located at the convergence of major sea routes linking it with China and India. It has been continually exposed to cultural interventions and these are evident in urban design, religious monuments and architecture. The northeast monsoon facilitated the arrival of Chinese, Japanese, Thai and Bugis ships during the early part of each year, with Indian and Arab vessels arriving with the southwest monsoon in June. Islam was introduced to the archipelago in the thirteenth century, and the Malay language evolved from Sanskrit. However, the Chinese had frequented the Malay peninsula since the T'ang Dynasty through their trading relationships with Persia and Arabia. The Kingdom of Malacca dates back to the beginning of the fifteenth century, when it became a dependency of the Chinese Empire and a key port in the Chinese junk trade. The Bugis migrated from the Celebes in the seventeenth century and with their great navigational skills established a powerful position in the Malay states.

SOUTHEAST ASIA

2 Evers, H.D. and Korff, R, *Southeast Asian Urbanism: The Meaning and Power of Social Space*, St Martin's Press, New York, 2000, p31

The urban history of what became known as the Straits Settlements is closely associated with Western intervention along the Malay archipelago, primarily in Penang, Malacca and Singapore. The first Western settlement was Malacca, established as a fort by the Portuguese Affonse de Albuquerque in 1511, the year after the seizure of Goa. His goal was to take control of the seaborne trade routes in Southeast Asia. From this base he opened up trade with the Siamese court at Ayutthaya, and the spice trade with the Moloccas. In 1641 the Dutch, reaching out from their main Asian base at Batavia (modern Jakarta), conquered the Portuguese and ruled Malacca until being displaced by the British in 1795. The acquisition of Singapore in 1819 brought together three important port cities under separate state influences — Selangor and Negri Sembilan under Melaka; Kedah and Perak under Penang; and Johor, Kelantan, Pahang and Trengganu under Singapore.

INTERVENTION FROM THE WEST

While there is a long tradition of urbanism in Southeast Asia, the growth of large cities came about through western intervention. The first major colonial city, Manila, was founded by the Spanish in 1571; Batavia, present-day Jakarta, by the Dutch in 1750; Bangkok by Rama I in 1782; and Singapore by the British in 1819. Added to this is that early city formation attracted large numbers of ethic groups from other parts of Asia, some even orchestrated by the colonising powers. While the major cities began life as small trading townships; sacred settlements such as Ayutthaya, Luang Prabang, Pagan or Mandalay; or palace and religious compounds such as Batavia, Bangkok and Yogyakarta, the ties between city and country were commercial rather than cultural. In their current state the primate cities are also capitals, far exceeding other national cities in terms of population, and commanding the prime location for national administration,

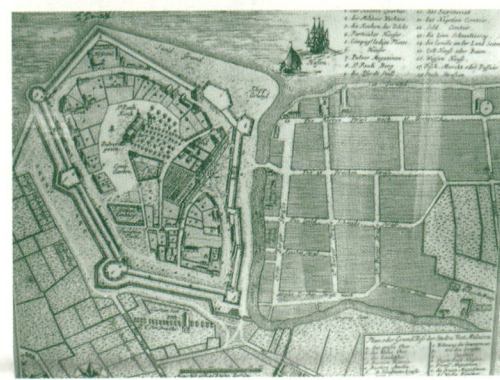

Malacca Fort (left);
Batavia, 1750 (below)

business investment, industrial production and port development, with economic control over a large hinterland. An important conclusion can be drawn from this — that the courts of rulers, be they kings, sultans or governors, have long contributed to the growth of cities that were central to the development of national states. Their national dominance by elite groups markedly inhibits the growth of secondary cities to anything like the same level. They also contain by far the largest concentrations of temporary settlements and informal economic sectors.

The hierarchical model of urban development evolved through the growth of entrepôt cities as nodes relating to trading routes. Inland provincial cities formed interdependent parts of this network, occasionally leading to conflict over patterns of trade, access to resources and territorial control in relation to the process of state formation. Until the priorities of colonial powers changed from control of trade to control of production and cultivation of commercial crops, most island states and cities remained relatively independent.[2]

Angkor Wat

The production of such things as spices and coffee in Java, tea in Ceylon, timber in Burma and rubber in Malaysia created colonial plantation economies, creating a dual structure of colonial administration and commercial control that came to signify new and consolidating patterns of urbanism.

Scattered coastal communities in the Philippines formed part of longstanding trading relationships with China and Japan before the Spanish arrival in the late sixteenth century. As in all Spanish and Portuguese settlements, the strong link between church and state, and the domination of authoritarian Christian regimes on peasant societies, was profound. The Philippines, between 1571 and 1898, became the only Asian country with a Christian majority, opening it up to continued Western influence.

Colonial intervention, facilitated on the back of longstanding Asian trading routes and entrepôt centres, shaped new political boundaries through force or diplomatic channels. British colonialism also saw substantial native population movements — for example by 1900 Indian immigration made up half the population of Burma, which was itself administrated from Calcutta. In many ways this contributed to new political leanings, escalation of land values, and in some cases determined religious affiliations, creating the basis for new societal frameworks. This was translated into highly active regimes of urban planning and city building.

Early urbanisation of the Malay Peninsula, in particular Malacca and George Town in Penang, was a result of the entrepôt trade through an expanding international mercantile network. The intensification of industrialisation in Europe saw increased demand for raw materials such as tin, and later rubber and oil palm products, which reinforced the nineteenth century colonial ambitions of the British.

The "Straits Settlements" were administered from Penang, and while control was later moved to Singapore, Penang enjoyed strategic significance when the Settlements were granted "Crown Colony" status in 1867. The Malay States of Perak and Selangor were brought under the British "Residential System" in 1874, Negri Sembilan followed in 1885, and Pahang in 1887, forming the Federation of Malay States administered from Kuala Lumpur.

In 1874 agreements were drawn up between the British Colonial Office and the various States, whose influence began to spread well beyond the Straits Settlements which had already became a Crown Colony. In 1896 the Federation of Malay States was created with a new capital at Kuala Lumpur. In 1909, Britain's treaty with Siam gave them control over the northern states which became protectorates, and finally a similar protectorate over the southern state of Johor created British Malaya. Colonisation was secured through a combination of British rule and local royalty, which maintained a workable balance in the face of growing nationalism and the erosion of traditional culture. From 1910 revenue from the tin and rubber industries was used to facilitate an improved national infrastructure and communications network.

Up to the mid-nineteenth century after European arrivals, Southeast Asia remained divided and there was little real resistance to Western expansionist ambitions. However in the main, European powers were more concerned with acquiring control over sea routes than in urbanisation. As a result

certain cities such as Malacca, Penang, Manila, and Batavia, together with Macau in relation to China, evolved as defensible garrison bases as well as entrepôts. In the Philippines, the Spanish imposed strong civilian authority, together with a powerful ecclesiastical structure and a Dominican-run educational system. This mass indoctrination was reinforced through the division of land into vast ecclesiastical and private estates. These have since been passed on through family dynasties, and have continued to hold back the country's economic and political development to the present day, despite being the first Westernised country in Asia to embody an advanced legal and administrative framework.

The northern Mainland States that became known as Indo-China, experienced long periods of disunity and invasion. In Thailand, Ayutthaya opened up to all the dominant foreign trading powers, developing both commercial and military ties. After destructive periods of war and occupation by the Burmese, the Chakri dynasty was established in 1782 under the rule of Rama I, who began to modernise the country. His successors concluded the first treaties with the English East India Company in 1822, and Thailand was the first Asian country to conclude a most-favoured nation agreement with the United States in 1833.

The period of intense Western colonial activity in Southeast Asia had an undoubted impact on economic, political and cultural history, but its nature was varied and the long-term repercussions of intervention uneven. In some situations it has had far-reaching significance in the alignment of borders and boundaries, and the implanting of organisational systems that overlapped into city building, while never entirely supplanting indigenous values. The period of major city building only commenced in the mid-nineteenth century. Colonial intervention was consolidated over most

parts of Southeast Asia, alongside the growth of primate port cities and gradual control over local economies through trading houses, shipping, insurance companies, and banks. That the colonising powers used force where necessary is undeniable, but the urban history of colonial settlements, often written from an imperial viewpoint, has sustained a myth that foreign powers overcame considerable obstacles to open up backward areas with little or no settlement.

The volatile geo-political interplay of Lao, Burmese, Cambodian, Vietnamese and Siamese forces resulted in frequently shifting territorial boundaries and an elusive convergence of cultural itineraries, often underscored by the appropriation of sacred Buddhist artifacts. Thailand was the only country to keep its sovereignty owing to a strong degree of political dexterity and compromise, with an increasingly nationalistic outlook but one which prudently appointed Western advisers to oversee aspects of modernisation. Similarly with Western activity in nineteenth century Chinese treaty ports, Thailand was subject to both economic and political intrusion and conversion which opened up the country to foreign enterprise. Its independent identity was to a large extent the result of Britain and France wishing to avoid a common frontier between their 'possessions', and Thailand therefore served as a buffer state.

The French, who had a strong base in China after the Opium Wars, appropriated Cochin-China in southern Vietnam around the Mekong Delta, and from this base established protectorates over central and northern Vietnam, Laos and Cambodia. In 1887 the French Indochinese Union was created, with a privy council but only limited political participation by national representatives, a monopoly over finance and trade, and a strong policy of cultural assimilation with French education and culture. At this point Cambodia formed an effective buffer between Vietnam and Thailand, and subsequent French control acted to reinforce this role.

POLITICAL CHANGE FROM 1900

In the Philippines, the Spanish-American War of 1898 was followed by the occupation of Manila by the United States. This resulted in the establishment of civilian rule in 1901 under an American governor-general, William Howard Taft who attempted to lay down a framework for social and economic reform. This included the redistribution of some of the expropriated land belonging to the Catholic Church, and integration of the country within the American tariff system.

During the 1930s the economic downturn in the West had a massive impact on Asian export industries for both rubber and tin, but also agricultural crops. In the Dutch East Indies, the spice trade with Europe helped the Dutch government to consolidate control over much of Indonesia, except for the Portuguese outpost of Timor. Many low-paid workers in Asia lost their jobs, adding to both economic inequality and political uncertainty. Japanese success in the Russo-Japanese war of 1905 and the Chinese Revolution of 1911 also established important precedents for revolutionary change. The Japanese invasion of Southeast Asia impacted the region in almost every way, but the most telling was the transformation of societal relationships, and the demolition of the myth of Western invincibility.

In the period between the two World Wars colonial expansion established boundaries that, with only limited changes, have prevailed to modern times. However this was a time of covert change, when economic expansion and export production were transforming the region, and new political movements began the drive towards independent states. In the post-World War Two situation, well-established resistance to foreign rule was redirected towards a search for new national identities. New ideologies

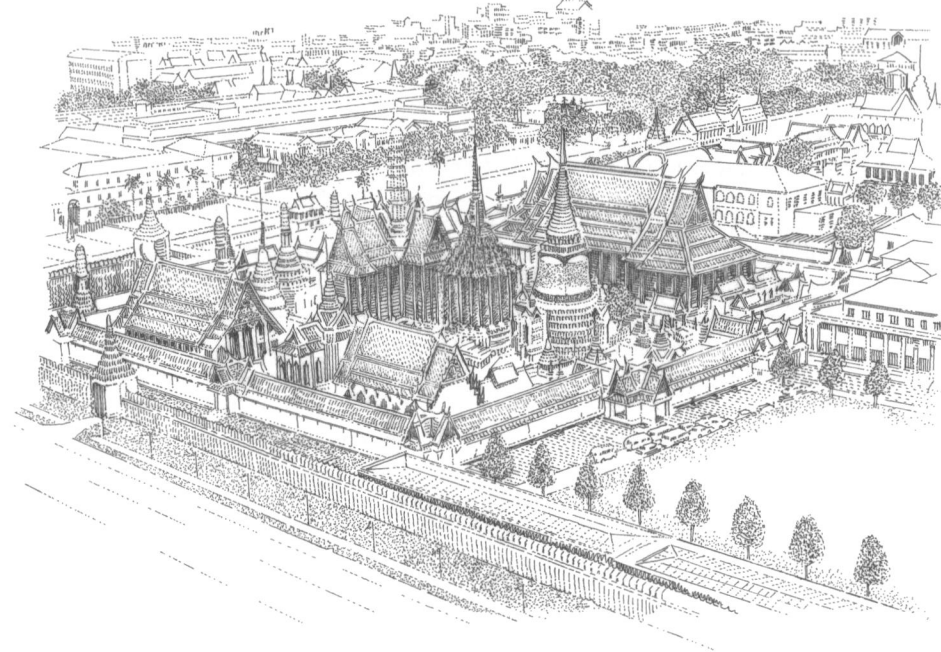

sprang from Western political theories of democracy, but also from Socialism and Communism, as a springboard to change. Awareness of social and economic disadvantage slowly translated into latent nationalism that, particularly in Vietnam but additionally in Malaya, Indonesia and in China, became steeped in socialist ideology. In Malaya with its large Chinese population, radical influences spread from Communist China in the 1950s.

Britain's strategy under its new socialist government in London, was to establish a Union of Malaysian States as part of a continued imperialist programme of social improvements in order to re-establish allegiance. This was partly intended to generate hard currency from the Malaysian rubber industry in the face of Britain's near bankrupt situation after World War II. The contradictions inherent in this policy were largely regarded as an entrenchment of the older imperial order, and indirectly helped to generate the foundation of a new Malay political movement which emanated in a

Malaysian Federation in 1948.

The existence of Buddhist and Islamic movements produced a strong sense of community and belief that easily evolved into nationalist policies, and religious buildings gave an affirmation of identity to political gatherings. The resulting independence movements had essentially two outcomes — the protracted wars in Vietnam and Indonesia against the repressive regimes of the French and Dutch; and the more gradual but occasionally problematic transfer of power elsewhere.

In 1955 Tunku Abdul Rahman built a rapprochement between the Malay and Muslim organisations: the Malaysian Chinese Association and the Malayan Indian Congress; with Britain taking responsibility for the medium-term defence of the new Malaysian confederation of Malaya, Singapore, Sarawak and Sabah. Merdeka was announced in 1957 and the Federation of Malaysia was inaugurated in 1963, to include the East Malayan states of Sabah and Sarawak, with Kuala Lumpur as the Federal Capital.

Following Malaysian independence, the government took pains to maintain ethnic stability which had broken down after years of guerrilla warfare. They introduced a series of interventionist plans to unify the nation through "positive discrimination". These are written into *Wawasan 2020*, the national development vision that has set ambitious development targets such as the Klang Valley "Super Corridor" to attract global high-tech and communications infrastructure. Land ownership has been formalised from previous rights, which had been simply acquired by historic occupation. This has essentially allowed State acquisition of land for public or related purposes considered beneficial to economic development.

Tensions in Indo-China erupted into major hostilities. The Second Indochina War between 1965 and 1975 spilled over from Vietnam into Laos and Cambodia, and following the establishment of the Socialist Republic of Vietnam in 1976, Communist affiliations fluctuated between Hanoi, Vientiane and Phnom Penh. As ties with China decreased following Deng Xiao-ping's modernisations, those between Vietnam and the Soviet Union increased. The collapse of Soviet power created the first opportunities for normalisation with the West, and the lifting of trade and direct investment embargoes in 1994 paved the way for modernisation programmes.

Changing priorities in the post-colonial period within newly independent states have posed both housekeeping and economic problems. Housing and education in the face of rapid population growth, ethnic rivalries and immigration trajectories initially created problems of planning and land use organisation, quite apart from affordability. However, the increasingly connective regional framework effectively repositions the major cities in relation to the agglomeration economy and its attraction for manufacturing development as well as the service sector.

American and European companies have continued to control large parts of commerce, agriculture and natural resources, but in large Southeast Asian cities that have a low per capita income and a large informal economic sector, such as Manila, Bangkok and Jakarta, an important economic sector is urban subsistence production.

Regional co-operation is high on the agenda, with wealthier countries emphasising investment in neighbouring countries, often in the form of industrial townships, resort development and infrastructure projects. The birth of ASEAN in 1967 has increasingly motivated practical means of co-operation, and the resolution of regional disputes has led to the convergence of strategic interests with those of China, by far the largest economic force in Asia. An expanded ASEAN and the importance of trade between the West and Pacific Rim countries are actively reinforced by multi-national investment, ushering in a new era of urban growth. As a result, the countries of Southeast Asia are being increasingly drawn into the global economic system through APEC at the same time as they have increasingly gained control over their own economic destinies. Economic competition between primate cities, as much as between countries, continues to impact on patterns of urbanisation reflecting economic and social transformation. In any event, the spatial impact of change is profound.

Takbat Devo Procession, Uthai Thani, Thailand

THAILAND

Bangkok

BANGKOK EXEMPLIFIES the urban design dilemma facing the rapidly developing Asian city in accommodating social and spatial change, and highlighting the need to reconcile issues of both tradition and modernity. A force for conservation in the city is a continued reverence for spaces and buildings identified with the Chakri dynasty through the royal court and its extensive cultural and memory associations, in particular the urbanism of Rattanakosin as representing the historical continuity of authority combining an architecture of both history and power-monarchy. The palace, marked by gilded roofs and Buddhist stupas, embraces a place of both visitation and ritual in the city.

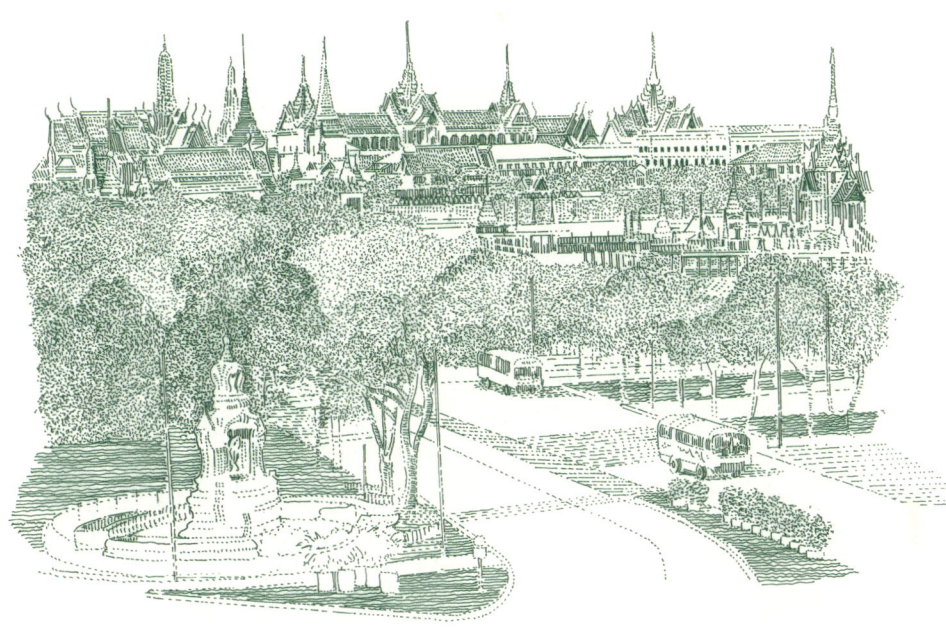

UNTIL THE JAPANESE INVASION DURING WORLD WAR II, Bangkok had an ambivalent relationship to other parts of Siam, which only formally changed its name to Thailand in 1949. Prior to this, the city had evolved as a royal edifice surrounded by elite groups of bureaucrats and retainers, and a large trading community of Chinese merchants, living and operating within a quilted pattern of individual temple complexes, gardens and rice fields.

HISTORICAL INTERVENTIONS

The ancient Thai capital of Ayutthaya was, in the early seventeenth century, both a prosperous port and a political centre. It housed a large number of Asian ethnic groups engaged in both trade and production — Burmese, Malay, Tamil, Chinese, Shan, Mon, Khmer, Lao and Vietnamese. The resulting ethnic neighbourhoods led to hybrid patterns of architectural interaction that later helped to frame the distinctive Thai building style. The Dutch East India Company set up operations there in 1604 as part of an ambitious trading gambit, exporting Siamese commodities to Japan in exchange for Japanese bullion, which could be used for the purchase of Chinese silk and Indian textiles. Its officers dealt directly with the Thai court as unofficial diplomatic representatives, and were assimilated into court rank. The company enacted a naval blockade in 1663 to gain concessions, and company officials shared responsibility for social order as administrators, establishing cross-cultural interactions between Asian and European communities. A treaty in 1664 established "extraterritorial rights" for Dutch employees. In 1685 this was extended to French subjects, including Catholic missionaries, and the treaty effectively allowed foreign communities to administer their own settlements. The two-storey company lodge on the Chao Phraya River, built in a European style, signalled the gateway to the city from the river. In

general foreigners interacted with local society rather than being fully integrated, but initial settlements expanded to include local populations who were employed across the company as carpenters, sailors and coolies, virtually under diplomatic immunity. However most foreigners were expelled after a change of royal patronage in the 1680s, and the city was only opened up to Western merchants after 1830.

The Chinese horticultural and trading community in Bangkok dates from the seventeenth century when they occupied the waterfront area in Rattanakosin. They were relocated to the Sampeng area to the south when the palace and associated buildings were constructed. In many ways ethnic integration has produced an urban fabric containing a mix of Thai and Chinese elements — some of the brick houses date back to the late eighteenth century with some building groups built under royal decree. The older high density Sampeng Quarter has continued to thrive as a commercial area, virtually since the founding of Bangkok. It has been subject to some restoration, but its character persists through established trading

THE BUDDHIST TEMPLE OR PALACE offers a collection of features which form a consistent design language. The most prominent features comprise: the Chedi — a tapering tower enshrining important reliquaries; the Prasat — a sanctuary or religious edifice derived from Khmer temple architecture; the Prang — a tall richly carved stone spire; the Mongkut — an assemblage of decorative tiers topped by a pointed finial; the That — a tall tapering tower; and the Chofa — a graceful finial that decorates the end of the roof ridge on temples and prayer halls.

The Erawan shrine at the junction of Ploenchit Road and Rajdamri Road was established only in the 1950s, but establishes a persistent value to its location.

and living patterns. The smaller Pahurat area contains the city's Indian business community.

Bangkok was built along similar lines to the old capital located on the low-lying Chao Phraya delta, and traditionally constructed around a system of waterways which shaped the development form of the city. It was given the abbreviated title 'Krung Thep' by King Rama I in 1782 when it became the new capital, meaning 'City of Angels' but also indicating its Indic and Buddhist traditions.

The historic rationale of the Thai primate city is borne out by the hierarchical ranking of subordinate settlements, surrounding and protecting the capital. Beyond these was a series of partly independent states. These were controlled through a system of patronage and sophisticated ministries, both of which sustained the centralised power structure of the court. In turn this led to a further accumulation of vassal states and migration of large numbers of people to the

capital, and extensions of the canal network to facilitate the movement of military troops and goods.

The older city name of Bangkok — "Bang" means 'water settlement' — reflected the long established system of canals. This rural and predominantly water-based environment penetrated the city itself through a labyrinth of waterways, which was gradually transformed through new street layouts, imposing an urban pattern on a city that had no prior urban traditions. A further factor was the historic role of the royal city as both the actual and symbolic centre of power in the country. Because of this inalienable authority, it represented and dictated the rate and type of growth in the country.

In the seventeenth century a new transport channel was created to shorten the route from the southern part of the river to Ayutthaya — the ancient capital to the north of Bangkok. The first royal city was established by King Taksin on the Thonburi side of the river in 1768 after the fall of Ayutthaya to the Burmese. It was relocated under the new Chakri dynasty fourteen years later, and the grand palace constructed in the Rattanakosin area adjoining the river surrounded by fortifications. The city was defined by two canals — the inner Khlong Lod and the outer Khlong Ong Ang. At this time many of the structures known as *phae* literally floated or were built on stilts along the river edge. The only permanent sites above the flood plains in the gradually urbanising city and around the palace, were given over to long-established temples or *wat*, such as the royal temple of Chana Songkram.

The traditional connection between the royal family and Buddhism dates back to the Sukhothai period when the king's patronage and financial contributions to temple construction enabled the expansion of Buddhism. The relics associated with them made these quarters — marked by gilded roofs and tall stupas — sacred places that

1 Askew, M, *Bangkok: Place, Practice and Representation*, Routledge, London and New York, 2002

have a ritualistic place in the city fabric. The royal barge processions and festival rituals, past the temples along the Chao Phraya River to the old palace, still serve to embellish the importance of religious identity, demonstrating loyalty, respect and continuity.

Urban design remains aligned, in a tangible way, with Bangkok's symbolic historical role as a royal capital — palace and temple landmarks establish a dominant presence along the riverscape, but increasingly compete with other spatial imperatives. According to Mark Askew, the new capital of Krung Thep, founded in 1782, "was heir to a tradition which fixed the royal city as a symbolic and structural locus of political power, social hierarchy and religious legitimacy".[1] The old city wall was marked by tall city gates such as Pratu Phi (Spirit Gate), and forteen *pom* or watchtowers named after animals or Hindu gods such as Phra Kan the God of Death, to dissuade enemy attacks. Only two still exist — Pom Mahakan and Pom Phrasumane, with the remainder demolished in order to widen streets.

The signifiers of the royal palace continue to embody the symbolic characteristics of the Hindu-Buddhist sacred city — a city space designed for ceremony, which underscores its auspicious setting. The palace therefore becomes not merely a defining focus of ritual and authority, but a symbol of Thai history and identity, with a ruling dynasty and a governing elite that brought about favourable trading alliances some two centuries earlier. Bangkok's role as an international port city with the embellishments of international commerce — the riverside trading houses and godowns — are not only 'modern age', but their interspersion among a mosaic of water villages along the Khlongs and Chao Phraya River, surrounded by wetland agriculture, has traditionally provided another dimension to the city.

The functional and spatial character of the city has been shaped by the interaction

Religious symbolism marks the identity of settlements along the Chao Phraya River.

of natural and institutional factors. However it was overlaid by a powerful yet elusive strata of religious beliefs and their associated symbolism, which evolved from the water-related and agriculturally-associated communities. These are marked by *wats* and, informed by the spiritual depth of Thai Buddhism, gave identity and focus to the Khlong settlements. Many villages evolved as craft centres. These were often associated with the temples that then grew into urbanised neighbourhoods given over to certain trades, and inhabited by different ethnic groups including Chinese, Khmer, Vietnamese, Lao and Thai Muslims from Southeast Asia. Many of these developed as craftsmen's villages or *Ban* — Ban Moh was Potter's Village, now the goldsmiths quarter; Ban Baht was the Alms Bowl Makers Village; and Ban Pok Mai Fai was the Fireworks Village. These older neighbourhoods are still discernible by their locational characteristics adjacent to temples, waterways and bridges. They became linked by roads and land infill, while trading quarters attracted new immigrants and instigated more solid and permanent shophouse groups within the old city walls, which corresponded with Khlong Ong Ang.

As the area to the east of the Chao Phraya River became more urbanised, Thonburi scarcely changed through the twentieth century, with a waterside landscape of small houses, large agricultural holdings and gardens served by a floating service infrastructure of supply and passenger boats. These water-related imperatives created a form of plantation economy, but came to establish the future commercial character of the city. Waterways were historically left largely unbridged to deter invaders, but by 1900 there were more than 2,000 bridges. Some of them were modelled on Dutch drawbridges such as Khlong Laud drawbridge, rebuilt for the Rattanakosin Bicentennial celebrations in 1982, or Chinese "camel hump" bridges to facilitate the passage of boats. The system of bridges and road connections, which commenced in 1926, has essentially determined the city's modern spatial pattern.

While agriculture had a long subsistence tradition, occupational change arose in relation to the commodified production of rice and export crops, which evolved into a system of urban market outlets, street bazaars and trading sub-systems associated with temple compounds, and floating markets associated with city canals. Rama V began to lay out the city through wide boulevards and bridges, including Rajdamnoen Avenue, modelled on the Champs Elysée. These acted as the accessways and settings for new palaces, with neo-Classical and Baroque styles borrowed from Europe, such as the Ananta-Samakhan Throne Hall situated on

2 Van Beek, S, *Bangkok: Then and Now*, AB Publications, 1999

Riverscape along the Chao Phraya River

the Royal Plaza. In the 1890s the Hualampong Railway Station was built, modelled on grand European precedents. This created a city of astonishing contrast but important infrastructure at a time when Thailand was opening trade ties with the West.

From the royal complex of Rattanakosin Island, roads branched out like spokes of a wheel. The first, Phra Ahit Road was lined by palaces; the second, Charoenkrung (which later became New Road), evolved into Bangkok's Chinatown and housed a tight matrix of shophouse streets which still remains. Sampeng Lane became a commercial street within a wider district given over to theatres and houses of pleasure; and New Road, built in 1863, became the centre of colonial-style residential and mercantile buildings forming elite foreign neighbourhood quarters. Silom Road drew its name from the windmills made from bamboo and fabric that drew water to irrigate the adjoining fields, examples of which can still be seen along the Gulf of Thailand. The third spoke — Bamrungmuang Road — was later extended to become Sukhumvit Road. The final spoke was Radomnoen Avenue — the Royal Walk towards a royal residence in Dusit Park.[2]

With nineteenth century Western cultural intervention, together with the introduction of modernised forms of industrialisation, came new architectural styles even within the royal palace, such as the Chakkri and Anantha Samakhom throne halls. Boulevards and plazas for prominent statuary mimicked those in European cities, fashioning a revitalised capital city based on global symbolism. New shophouse construction followed road and bridge building, while palace development stimulated inner city growth for commercial and residential development, following urban models from Penang, Singapore, and Calcutta — then the capital of British India. The ancient monopoly of land by the nobility gradually gave way to a commodified system of land use, with ownership patterns reflected in new land titles. The Western commercial district grew around Silom Road with offices and rice mills, while banks were established to cater for trading businesses in the 1880s. Malcolm Falkus notes that Danish merchants help to introduce electricity and towngas, and British and Danish merchants jointly formed the first railway company, to run from Bangkok to Paknam.[3]

By the mid-nineteenth century, Bangkok was a major centre for the junk trade with China, Indo-China and Singapore. The Chinese quarter therefore grew along the river edge to the south of Rattanak from where it imported goods from the hinterland. In this way the expanding economy became tied into an international trading system, that accelerated physical expansion of the city and its transport infrastructure. This helped to reinforce the power and patronage of the royal court, which maintained its investments in urban land and buildings. The Chakri dynasty consolidated commercial links with China, and the growth of new steamship routes stimulated the migration of Chinese businessmen and merchants who established plantations and factories, and craftsmen who constructed shophouses and temples. The new exchange economy and the gradual transfer of financial administration to the emerging private sector saw the expansion of the Chinese quarter, and the rapid emergence of new development forms.

Unlike colonial cities of the same period, or the foreign concession areas in China, Bangkok had no clearly defined European quarters, although nine land grants were made to foreign concerns between 1893 and 1911. The city developed some of the characteristics of colonialism under an indigenous elite. The development of its port between 1851 and 1910, under the reign of later monarchs, was heavily influenced by Western trading powers in Asia, who also established consulates to represent their trading interests. The most significant factor in its international development was the Bowring Treaty of 1855 with Britain. This effectively removed former import and export constraints, abolishing the rural monopoly on trade and the taxes associated with it, and allowing foreign businessmen the right to live in the city with consular protection — almost exactly the type of extraterritoriality that had been the subject of 'unequal treaties' in China. Similar treaties with the United States and European powers were to follow. Around the 1900s, there were ten consular courts in Bangkok, each operating a different legal

3 Falkus, M, 'Bangkok in the Nineteenth and Twentieth Centuries: the Dynamics and Limits of Port Primacy', in *Gateways of Asia. Port Cities of Asia in the 13th -20th Century*, Ed. Frank Broeze, Routledge, London, 1997

4 Falkus, 1997, op. cit.
5 Asian Coalition for Architecture and Urbanism, *Re-engaging Urban Canal*, Sam-Dee Printing Co Ltd, 2009

system. A large number of Western advisers were seconded to aid the Thai government in reorganisation and modernisation, particularly in terms of commercial and infrastructure development. This introduced Bangkok to the trade routes with India and the East Indies, and with Europe, which began to flourish with the introduction of new steamship routes and the opening of the Suez Canal. By the 1920s there were regular steamship routes to Hong Kong, Singapore and Swatow through the Straits Steamship Company and the China Navigation Company.[4] The first steam railway was built between Hualampong Station and Paknam on the Gulf of Thailand in 1893, and electric trams were introduced in 1903.

Floating Market on the Bang Noi Canal

THE ROLE OF WATER

The river has remained the focus of communication and activity, and until well into the twentieth century more than 80 per cent of the population were engaged in water-related agriculture. Port-related use along the Chao Phraya River, some thirty kilometres from the Gulf of Thailand, fuelled the growth of a large immigrant community of workers, particularly from China, who were to have a significant impact on commercial and mercantile business. Chinese settlements dominated the waterfront, establishing its largest community in the Sampheng 'Chinatown' area. Along the banks of the river, the wharves, warehouses, dry docks and slipways of Western trading companies were developed together with rice and saw mills, customs house, banks, and legation quarters for Russia, Portugal, the United States, France and Britain. City development broadly followed a linear pattern of uses along the river, extending along new canal systems which were later filled in to form New Road, Silom, Sathorn and Suriwong Roads, and becoming the basis of Bangkok's emerging business precinct. In the early twentieth century, the low-rise Oriental Hotel, the East

Asia Company offices and the Hong Kong Shanghai Bank built in 1890, were the tallest buildings along the river outside the royal palace.

Bangkok's historical canal structure was constructed in the late eighteenth century, and connected to the Chao Phraya and other major rivers, which flow through Thailand's central plain. While many of the older canals have been progressively filled in, some parts remain as working channels.

The San Saeb Canal dates from 1837, and its 72 kilometre length has formed an artery through Bangkok for two hundred years, connecting urban communities through a collective social and working space. It was originally constructed to transport goods to eastern provinces and later attracted a range of Chinese, Muslim, Vietnamese and Laotian ethnic settlements along its banks, along with a collection of temples and mosques. It effectively cuts through the heart of the city between Bangkapi and Bangkhanak.[5] Khlong Padum Krung Kasem, built in 1857, was

known as 'Canal Encircling the City'.

Under the Bowring Treaty of 1855 which allowed free trading rights for foreign concerns in Bangkok, the original military purpose was re-directed to trade and irrigation commensurate with the increase in agricultural production for export. Building codes were introduced for construction along the waterways to minimise projections. In 1903 three lock gates were built in order to maintain water level at low tide, and the first bridge at Chatermlok was built in 1908. In the city, old land parcels along the canal edge have been transformed through the development of tall blocks, but the suburban zones still maintain their ethnic identity.

While the canal linked older communities to river markets, shaped initially by the waterway system, socio-spatial changes have reoriented this relationship, from water, with boat piers as the main transportation nodes, to road and expressway channels. The Mahakan District in the east is located around the intersection of several canals,

housing ethnic communities in close proximity to important historical buildings, including the Golden Mount. The Bobe District in the heart of old Bangkok was the traditional wholesale textile centre and has retained its role as a modern garment trading area. Khlongs were often named after the particular trades they served, such as Khlong Rong Mai (Silk Factory Canal) and Khlong Ong Ang (Water Jar Canal). The Phratunam area to the west has become almost entirely redeveloped, housing some of the largest shopping plazas in the city, while the San Saeb Canal boat route runs parallel to Petchaburi Road with its flows of heavy traffic. The Asoke District to the west has developed within a major mixed-use business and residential area along Sukhumvit and New Petchaburi roads, and is developing around the sky train link to Suvarnabhumi.

Bangkok still has more than 100 kilometres of canals traversing the city. The floating markets continue to reflect the interface between land-based and water-based lifestyles that developed in response to a combination of factors, including both the high water table and the river and canal-side communities served by water-borne transport. This relates to the city's historic structure as much as it suggests a future role for the inner city Khlongs, some of which have resurrected their previous use as transport channels.

TWENTIETH CENTURY INTERVENTION IN THE CITY

The development of Bangkok as an administrative centre brought about various changes in the city morphology through the establishment of new transport infrastructure and public buildings. Institutional and administrative buildings together with foreign consulates adopted European styles ranging from traditional Thai to neo-Classical and Jurgendstil architecture. Between 1900 and 1936 the built up area expanded more than three times over, with both its form and direction dictated by the fine grained pattern of canals. This largely explains the complexity and lack of coherence within sub-districts, and the overlap between ordered development along major street corridors geared to a predominantly service economy, and the relatively informal uses behind, with their appealing interaction between the urban and rural. In 1940 Radomnoen Road, the axial street lined with many royal buildings, was revitalised to present a commercial focus with hotels, stores and theatres, and showcasing the democracy monument as a central feature. At the same time the royal palace was converted to a parliament building. The accompanying transformation of Bangkok from a sacred city to a national capital effectively consolidated its primate status, and formed the basis of massive population growth throughout the twentieth century, and the expression of Thailand's modernisation. Ceremonial and cultural rituals associated with religious complexes and streets, now share these spaces with a broader political and commercial imagery.

The mystique of the Chakri dynasty, and its associated aristocratic domination of administrative and commercial power, was substantially reduced by a military coup in 1932. New state enterprises did not bring about any fundamental socio-economic change or wealth redistribution, but in the years after the Japanese occupation during World War II, various key agents have acted to shape the Thai economy and the socio-spatial form of Bangkok. The post-war economic structure of Thailand continued to be focused in Bangkok, with American aid

6 Askew, 2002, op. cit.

directed towards repairing the city's utility and service infrastructure, including the new port of Khlong Toei some eight kilometres downstream. American support was also geared to establishing a bastion against growing unrest in neighbouring Vietnam, Laos and Cambodia.

Post-war change has been about reconciling increasing numbers of migrants with the inevitabilities of economic growth and socio-cultural change, while also managing a city through engineering and planning procedures. A series of national development plans from 1961 onwards followed a Western economic model of boosting manufacturing and export capacity. This, along with new transport infrastructure, reinforced the primacy of Bangkok and its immediate hinterland. These programmes helped to consolidate Bangkok's economic and demographic dominance and led to a rapid growth of the trading and banking sector, but also an expansion of state involvement in economic affairs. A 30-year strategic plan for Greater Bangkok was produced in 1960, but there existed many organisational and bureaucratic constraints to comprehensive urban planning, and government expenditure was mainly directed towards energy and transport infrastructure. By this stage, the city's built-up area had risen to around 90 square kilometres including new development in Thonburi.[6] Investment in manufacturing, particularly in the municipality of Bangkok, led to a major programme of joint venture industrial development between government and the private sector. This generated a massive increase in low-income migrants although there was no expansion in housing supply, and this in turn led to the growth of large temporary settlements. The percentage of migrants in the inner core has decreased in recent years, commensurate with the attractions of growth in construction and associated employment opportunities in the peri-urban region.

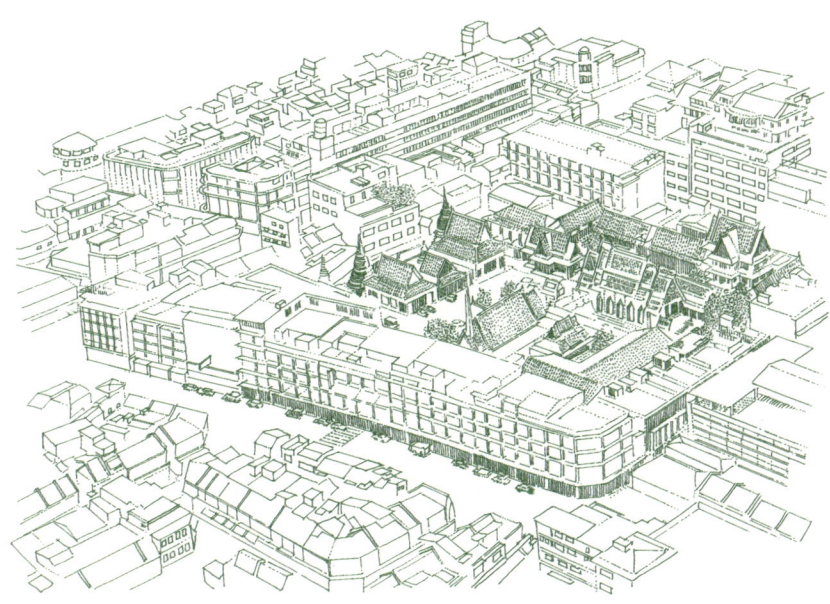

Sacred places insinuate themselves through the city, imbuing places with a spiritual force around which new patterns of usage occur. Thus urban design often represents an interaction between material fact and myth, embedded etiquette and informality.

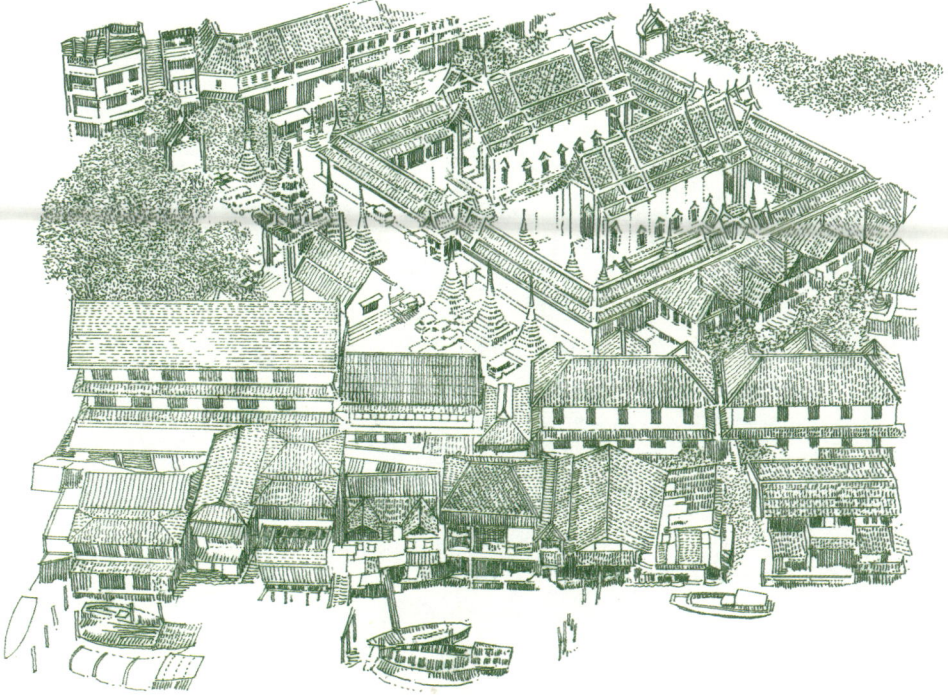

7   Sutiprapa, J et al, 'Bangkok: Globalising City of Angels', in *Mega-Urban Regions in Pacific Asia*, NUS Press, Singapore, 2008, p105

8   Askew, 2002, op. cit.

A major characteristic of the city is a mix of uses in many of the inner districts, with offices, shopping and industry forming an undifferentiated series of developments following the alignment of the major roads, and has led to densification of the urban core through redevelopment. Urban neighbourhoods have few identifiable characteristics but are interspersed with temple compounds and shrines, burnished by the colourful realms of street trading. Like other modernising cities with rising wealth, the commercial centre with its commodified malls and high-rise typology is an increasingly dominant paradigm. However just off the main highways such as Sukhumvit Road is a separate and parallel world of two-storey houses and gardens, linked by narrow streets or *soi* sometimes housing local market traders. These low density areas have gradually filled up with low cost housing for new arrivals in the city and small-scale

industry amidst the compounds of older families, as many wealthier middle-class residents have left the inner city for suburban environs.

The Fourth National Social and Economic Development Plan in 1977 focussed not just on redirecting growth from Bangkok to other provincial centres, but also on preservation of the Rattanakosin area of Bangkok and other ancient cities including Sukhothai. Later plans have attempted to reconcile the need for balanced socio-economic development and environmental management in the face of the dislocated impacts of growth. Reclamation of wetlands has led to a rising water table, and pumping of underground water sources has brought about serious ground subsidence and flooding. As a result, the densest development along the perimeter of city blocks tends to abut major highways.

In the 1980s, a series of land use controls and preservation measures was introduced

to protect the older Rattanakosin area, and the integrity of the Grand Palace, Wat Phra Chetuphon, Wat Mahathat and Wat Chana Sungkhram. The outer area, up to the Khlong Ong Ang was subject to certain development controls intended to protect sensitive view-sheds and older shophouse streets, and regulate building heights. This was later extended to the historic part of Thonburi. Overall, this has helped to preserve the older morphology.

The Bangkok Metropolitan Administration was set up in 1972 along with a National Housing Authority, however up to the 1990s urban settlement patterns were being transformed through the controlling influences of the urban land market. In some ways this represented the archetypal consequence of rapid economic growth without the necessary planning and environmental controls. Modernisation of the city during this period drove new road and expressway programmes, which in turn opened up development areas in the wider Metropolitan Region for foreign direct investment. Main development corridors have grown along roads serving the old international airport at Don Muang, and along the southeast corridor to Chonburi and Klong Toei Port. A system of ring roads has been superimposed on the radial roads forming a framework of expressways which service manufacturing and heavy industrial sites. However in the wider urban region, ribbon development has been largely wasteful of land. The aviation complex at Suvarnabhumi Airport to the east of the city incorporates developing business zones and is projected to generate population growth of almost 700,000.[7]

Continued unregulated private land subdivision, urban expansion and redevelopment of sites along major road corridors for commercial and condominium development has led to fragmented development patterns with interspersed

Mix of uses create informal commercial corridors along street edges.

Informal street markets sell products brought in daily from the countryside.

pockets of under-utilised land, as well as serious traffic congestion. The latter has been only slightly alleviated since 2003 by a skytrain system that forms an intrusive but efficient form of connection through the central city, following the primary road system. The 20 kilometre Metropolitan Rapid Transit Authority Subway became operational in 2004 linking inner city nodes and catering for a ridership of 40,000 people per hour.

While its longstanding independence has enabled the country to evolve and maintain many informal cultural patterns, it has also constrained development of urban management systems in the face of long traditions of royal authority and private land ownership dating back to its historical water-based agricultural economy. Land has been urbanised according to the geography of agricultural holdings, which were historically served by the Khlongs, therefore connective road frameworks were slow in evolving.

NEW URBAN DIRECTIONS

The Bangkok Metropolitan Administration (BMA) Area has a population in excess of 50 per cent of the total national urban population — the highest of any capital city. It covers around one-third of the Bangkok Metropolitan Region, which includes five other provinces around the Gulf of Thailand — Samut Prakan, Samut Sakhon, Nakhon Pathom, Pathum Thani and Nonthaburi. The BMA population of some 10.3 million people is more than thirty times the size of the second city, Korat. Urbanisation therefore takes on many meanings in relation to patterns of change, although the city's social and economic transformation is nevertheless shaped to a large extent by its historical cultural values and the meaning ascribed to these. The complexity of spatial and socio-cultural change in the city can be attributed to a range of characteristics and their interconnected relationship between transactional and local forces — investment flows, land utilisation, tourism and other factors — which establish a "construct of interacting agents and institutions".[8] The emerging pattern of urbanisation within the city therefore represents a co-existence of different activities largely influenced by

the private sector within a flexible planning framework, including a large informal and temporary sector. Small scale industrial operations within the inner city and urban fringe intersect with new business estates. Temporary housing and squatter areas make up around 15 per cent of all housing stock, some of which can be found in scattered clusters within the urban area, often in juxtaposition with new residential and hotel towers. Government master plans with flexible land-use classifications are difficult to implement in the face of low-income communities in rural occupations who would prefer to sell their land for development, while traditional *Ban* neighbourhoods are threatened by resumption for infrastructure works.

Meanwhile, a combination of subsidies, housing, and sites-and-services projects has tended to progressively concentrate public housing provision for low-income groups around the urban fringe. This has extended the boundaries of the metropolitan area, creating a regional pattern of new development and industrial zones stretching

Emerald Buddha Temple displaying several features of temple architecture – the central Mongkut tower and the Chofa sky tassels on the ridge-ends of the temple roof.

but exotic and diverse urban design. These elements are bound together by an ecology of adaptation and flexibility, where informal micro-manufacturing businesses flourish alongside street vendors and give identity to inner districts. It represents a landscape of fragility in the face of the global juggernaut of twenty-first century capitalism, where new environments of consumption form a contrast with areas of urban deprivation, but also something of a release valve. An unbalanced wealth gap together with unco-ordinated interventions in the urban development process, and a keen frustration with unpopular drivers of change, can make the city a theatre of contest and confrontation. This became evident in the social unrest on the streets of the city in 2010 and that have re-occurred in 2014, as an indirect result of the perceived culture of cronyism between business and government.

The overriding planning characteristic of Bangkok is its concentric rings of district development, of which the inner-most and oldest districts are the most distinctive and diverse, with the palace precinct at Rattanakosin at its core. The transformation of the river city districts of Phranakhon, Pomprap and Samphanthawong are framed by old canal systems. Each reflects the interdependencies between their distinctive historical socio-spatial characteristics, ecological interfaces, and contemporary forces of change. The result tends to be a patchwork of uses and places with new and specialised functions established around *wats* and markets. Commercial towers have developed along the main road avenues and Khlongs, with more informal commercial and residential settlements clustered behind along narrow lanes and secondary canals. This introduces a multi-layered facet of the inner city, where different uses co-exist and overlap.

Mark Askew describes the transformation in the economic and spatial character of the market area in the Banglamphu district of

north to Ayutthaya and south along the coast to Rayong.

The city embodies a strong cultural and even a spiritual identity, where the tangible built heritage has become a somewhat cosmetic commodity, fashioned into icons that ostensibly promote Thai culture, but also oriented to the economics of tourism and visitation. But, as in other cities with strong spiritual undertones that resonate in their design, there is the notion of *Moradok* — an active consciousness for the values of heritage. This thought process takes root in professional and voluntary agencies, and after a while becomes a fashionable trend, even if cultural and environmental preservation sometimes has a commercial side to it. Thai culture has become an instantly recognisable blend of aggregated images, many of them associated with architecture and ornamentation. Stylistic references and motifs are replicated with apparent nonchalance — the iconic and expressive Thai roof form is

evident even on commercial buildings, and in some cases traditional carved wood details are reproduced in concrete. This encapsulates continuity with the past as well as projecting an urban identity. The raked gable profiles, floating above the Khlongs and ricefields, projects a reassuring heritage of palace and temple. Its most simple form — the small pavilion or *sala* — has become a symbolic urban signature, attached to otherwise bland pieces of contemporary architecture to broadcast their hospitable Thai associations. The design of temple complexes follows a transition from the secular activities and rituals at ground level to the vertical spiritual passage demonstrated by the temple roofs, wats and stupas that point to a high ideal.

In its scattered precincts and *soi* lanes, Bangkok has evolved a hybrid identity that spans from cultural heritage to red light district, from shophouse clusters to backpacker quarters and ethnic guest house concentrations, all of which form a dispersed

9   Askew, 2002, op. cit., p120
10 Webster, D and Maneepong,
    C, 'Bangkok: New Risks, Old
    Resilience', in *Planning Asian
    Cities: Risks and Resilience*,
    Eds. Stephen Hamnet and
    Dean Forbes, Routledge,
    London and New York, 2011

Bangkok over a period of fifty years. In the 1960s Chinese gold merchants expanded their business into the well-visited area from nearby Sampheng, alongside clothes shops and informal food vendors. The latter was the result of increased urban migration, establishing a strong link between the city and the countryside.[9] The building of a large department store in the 1980s attracted new clientele but in the process displaced many fresh-market traders. However this simultaneously led to the expansion of the informal street-based sector with the local street matrix becoming the centre of small businesses, generating a livelihood for people from the surrounding area. In recent years this has extended to serving the local needs of a 'backpacker' market for foreign travellers in the Khaosan Road guesthouse precinct. Social and economic change has inevitably re-shaped the community structure and intensified the pressure on land for redevelopment, leading many older residents to relocate elsewhere.

Planning interventions in response to growth trends in the 1980s and 1990s largely involved decentralisation initiatives for industries to locate outside the Bangkok Metropolitan Administration area, mainly to the Eastern Seaboard to accompany new port development. In addition, ambitious proposals have been prepared for several new and expanded townships around Bangkok, with separation from the Metro Area emphasised by a Green Belt.

A 1996 City Plan for Bangkok was prepared by an MIT team working in consultation with city planning agencies. The strategy is centred around the need for planning intervention to promote the knowledge-based service economy of the city, expanding its specialised commercial and financial roles. In so doing, the goal is to promote higher education and space for service providers through the purposeful provision of mixed use areas for relatively small scale and environmentally

clean uses. The Bangkok Plan also proposed an outer "intelligent" arterial highway, which would carry a fibre optic network intended to incentivise new businesses to locate around the urbanising city fringe. Multi-nodal centres are proposed around the river core in relation to major rail terminals with interchange facilities for inter-nodal connections, while perimeter locations are identified for metropolitan sub-centres with mass transit and highway connections.

Environmental improvement plans for the city include upgrading of slum housing areas alongside the Khlongs, creating new serviced housing enclaves while restoring water edges for open space and recreational purposes. The latter could form part of an extensive greenway system, incorporating a continuous esplanade along the Chao Phraya River aimed at installing flood prevention mechanisms. The plan also seeks to introduce measures to protect the important city monuments from tour-related traffic and uncontrolled activities, which act to despoil the setting, thereby re-emphasising the historic pattern of development. In combination, these initiatives could, if implemented in concert, circumscribe continued growth within a series of central quarters, and be served by

more coordinated pattern of transport and infrastructure.

Political instability and risks, such as the catastrophic floods that inundated large parts of the city in 2011, have destabilised economic performance. Studies have been undertaken on the Metropolitan Region regarding future threats to the city from climate change, including flood-sensitive land-use zoning and less harvesting of ground water, which will increase its resilience.[10]

In the wake of the 1997 financial crisis, economic planning has focussed on the development of amenity services centred around its historic culture, hospitality industry and quality of its natural environment, while acknowledging the need for a competitive high-end manufacturing economy. Industrial development has therefore extended through the Bangkok Metropolitan Region, particularly in Chonburi on the eastern seaboard and Ayutthaya, well outside the city itself, while the urban core has increased in terms of commercial importance. The city's concentration of government activity and places of high cultural value induces a high sense of attraction,and over 120 countries now have embassies or consulates in the city.

The landing stages associated with Ta Tiang and Ta Prachan, alongside the Grand Palace, generate local trading use of the traditional market square, defined by groups of shophouses.

Yangon

MYANMAR

LOOKING NORTH FROM SULE PAGODA WHARF along Pansodan Street, the Myanmar Port Authority Building with its landmark corner tower reflects the importance of the pre-war port of Rangoon as one of the largest in the British Empire. Built in 1928 it was designed by Thomas Oliphant Foster, who also designed the New Law Court Building on Sule Pagoda Road, replacing a previous 1865 building. To the west is the Division Court Building constructed in 1900. It was built in stages to accommodate its original tenant — the Currency Department — and is one of the oldest masonry structures in the city, featuring distinctive octagonal corner domes. One wing of the building was destroyed by bombs in World War II. In the distance is the Art Deco pagoda-style entrance to the Myanmar Economic Bank, formerly the Chartered Bank of India, Australia and China, completed in 1941.

1 Pearn, B.R., *A History of Rangoon*, American Baptist Mission Press, Rangoon and Burma, 1939, p50

The twelfth century Ananda Temple in Pagan continues as a centre of Buddhist worship.

THE BURMESE PEOPLE originated in the eastern Himalayas, settling in Myanmar and merging with the older Mon culture. The borders of Burma (now Myanmar) with Assam in India, Yunnan Province in China, and Thailand have been continuously re-drawn over several centuries of military opportunism and the exigencies of colonial land mapping. The ancient built tradition incorporates a realm of religious structures — pagodas, stupas and monasteries, around which acts of devotion and festivity accentuate the importance of display and ritual within the physicality of the urban realm. The twelfth century Ananda temple in the ancient city of Pagan is considered the design apogee of the country's architectural heritage. This structure is representative of the remaining two thousand religious forms in the ancient city that stretch along the alluvial plains beside the Irrawaddy River, spread out through a fan of rivers and streams that flow to the Bay of Bengal and form the country's 'rice bowl'. Intricate tiered roofs on temples and pagodas along with bulbous stupas that evolved from the design of burial mounds, establish a cosmic landscape of edifices, which convey a lineage of spirituality and veneration. The royal palaces themselves were designed and embellished to exemplify the god-like state of the court, with much of the space given over to monastery buildings and places of meditation.

The range and diversity of ethnic communities have indirectly shaped continual discourses on national identity and self-determination. The Pagan period began with the first king, Aniruddhadeva, defeating the Mon Kingdom of Lower Burma and bringing scholars and monks to Pagan in the mid-tenth century, where their teaching led to the development of a cultural and religious centre. Buddhism, Hinduism and Brahmanism combined in forming a remarkably tolerant society personified by

its range of religious monuments. This was brought to an end in 1287 by the Mongol invasion from the north under Kublai Khan, after which Burma devolved into smaller states followed by prolonged periods of disintegration and reunification. In the early sixteenth century the Portuguese established the earliest Western trading post at Martaban, and were able to control the sea routes across the Bay of Bengal, which attracted traders from Britain, Holland and Italy. War between neighbouring states was rife, until the powerful Konbaung dynasty was formed in 1752 at Shinebo.

Rangoon's history essentially relates to two factors: its historical association with the Shwedagon Pagoda, and its role as a port on the Andaman Sea through the easily navigable Irrawaddy. Until the mid-eighteenth century the Mon-Burman settlement of Dagon, set around the Shwedagon Hill on the southernmost spur of the Bago hill chain, was a centre of religious life. Its growth into a city was brought about by King Alaungpaya who re-established power over the Mon rebellion and made the city his headquarters in 1755. The city was christened "Yangon" (Rangoon) meaning "the end of strife". It was restricted to a small area between the ancient Sule Pagoda and the river, and surrounded by a teak stockade, which became known as the "Fort". The southernmost of the east-

west streets was named the Kaladan or "the street of the foreigners" as this was where the first Western traders gathered.[1] Outside the stockade three wooden wharfs ran to the river, so that in reality the settlement was a small island. Early stockade houses had to be built on piles, and drains were necessary to carry off water during the spring tides. Mineral baths in the form of a 'tank' were built to the north of the Shwedagon where the European inhabitants bathed. All the buildings were constructed of teak apart from the brick Customs House, later replaced by the Law Courts.

British trade with Burma dates from 1617 through a mission by the British East India Company from their Indian base in Masulipatam. Within thirty years the Company had begun trading with Burma from the port of Syriam to the south of Rangoon, and with reduced customs duties for company ships, trade was generally regarded as mutually beneficial. In 1753 the company assumed control of the island of Negrain to further their interests in competition with French and American traders, but sensing the British threat, the Burmese King took back the island and retained it until the early nineteenth century. The Burmese Kingdom at that time held power over a territory that extended from the Andaman Sea and Malay Peninsula in

2 Thant, M.U., *The Making of Modern Burma*, Cambridge University Press, Cambridge, 2001, p23

3 Blackburn, T.P., *The British Humiliation of Burma*, Orchid Press, Bangkok, 2000, p93

Shwedagon Pagoda

the south to Bengal in the west, with smaller principalities being expected to pay tribute to the Court of Ava. The mercantile community of Chinese, American and European traders was generally divided among ethnic lines. Merchants utilised business profits to develop a ship-building and refitting industry based on the abundance of locally available teak. Most of the ships became part of the East India Company's fleet and in 1767 a grant was made to the Company for a factory at the river edge. In 1783 the capital was moved to Amarapura, and built with a mix of brick and stucco that was clearly influenced by Indian Mughal traditions.

By the mid-eighteenth century Burma was engaged in its own imperial expansion, sacking the Siamese capital Ayutthaya in 1767 and several years later annexing Arakan along the Bay of Bengal. Captives of Arakan and Manipur were brought back to populate the new capital of Amarapura. The 'Immortal City' had a dominating influence over a hierarchy of smaller satellite towns, and housed the most important Buddhist schools and monasteries which provided educated leaders in the King's service.

By 1810 Burma was sending missions to the Mughal court in India to propose an alliance against the British. They reasoned that as Eastern Bengal had belonged to Arakan, now controlled by Burma, then they had the right of possession. In 1810 a fire

destroyed most of Rangoon with considerable loss of life, and after 1814 the port trade virtually collapsed. The French and English competed for influence with the Burmese Court, and relations between the Burmese Government and British India remained strained amid rumours of invasion. By 1819 the Burmese army advanced west to Assam, and commenced a series of forays that would lead directly into conflict with British trading interests in the region.

The British East India Company had long tried to establish trading ties with Burma from their base in Calcutta, and refugees from Arakan into British protectorates provided political motivation for a military incursion. This led to the First Anglo-Burmese War of 1824-6 when Rangoon was briefly occupied by the British and left the Burmese Kingdom in a near bankrupt state with a substantial imposed indemnity. The departure of the Company's troops led to serious damage in the town and the small pagodas surrounding the Shwedagon. Much of the infrastructure also fell into disrepair, but from 1832 there was increased military activity in Rangoon that restored the importance of the city through new building work and street improvement. The regenerated city form was reoriented away from the river with the Shwedagon Hill as its citadel, while Custom House Wharf continued to be the central business focus of the mercantile community.

The second war of 1852, which proved to be the longest and most expensive in British imperial history, was largely provoked by the British following complaints by foreign traders about taxes on shipping through the port of Rangoon.[2] The defeat of the Burmese river fleet by a British armada, and the capture of Rangoon, led to the Treaty of Yandabo in 1826 under which the Burmese court ceded a number of provinces. However the administration of Rangoon reverted to the Burmese Government. The Secretary of State for India was supported in his desire to annex Upper Burma to the Bombay Burma Trading Corporation — a company of British merchants in dispute with Burma over extraction of timber.[3] Ultimatums to the Burmese Government were deliberately designed to be unacceptable through violating national customs and religious traditions, and in 1852 British forces seized the main cities and Lord Dalhousie, the Indian Governor-General, declared the occupied territory 'a new province of British Burma' which involved the ceding of Arakan and Tennasserim provinces together with Pegu. The hill states were permitted to remain largely autonomous although officially subject to the same direct role as Lower Burma.

The forward-looking reign of the new ruler, King Mindon, in the wake of the loss to the British, led to a refashioning of state procedure and a new capital at Mandalay. Scholars were sent to England, France and Italy, and the administration itself was centralised with clear lines of authority and new financial policies to raise income through increasing trade links with China and the sale of natural resources. This encouraged further British commercial expansion under the country's nominal sovereignty, commensurate with protection of their strategic interests. A treaty of 1862 to promote trade between Upper Burma and the British Empire facilitated inclusive access to the country's markets.

Rangoon was virtually rebuilt in 1852

4 Falconer, J et al, *Myanmar Style: Art, Architecture and Design of Burma*, Thames and Hudson, London, 1998
5 Pearn, 1939, op. cit., p183

The octagonal Sule Pagoda is a city landmark at the junction of Sule Pagoda Road and Mahabandoola Road. The pagoda marks the centrifugal point of the city plan prepared in the 1850s. It dates back 2,000 years and was originally known on Kyaik Athok, alluding to the relic of Gautama Buddha said to be enshrined there.

focused on the older settlement of Dagon around the Shwedagon Hill. It subsequently became the predominant city in colonial Burma, and its administrative centre. Development was in a grid form, overseen by a new Department of Public Works and built by the Bengal Corps of Engineers. Funding for land formation and flood control was raised by selling private lots.[4] Military intervention and the consolidation of British power after 1852 had a marked impact on urban planning and design, which was infused with new and hybrid architectural vocabularies. These acted to absorb and unify local indigenous traditions and ornamentation with architectural forms that had been tested and refined in places as far apart as Calcutta and Singapore, and which themselves had been influenced by European Baroque and Edwardian styles.

Because so much building had been cleared, it was possible to design a new port city to meet modern requirements. Plans for laying out Dalhousie Park were made in 1856, although the most valuable urban space was the *maidan* which served as both a parade ground and a race course. While education received some government subsidy, most schools were operated by religious bodies with sites granted by government. Dr William Montgomerie, who had twenty years' experience with the Singapore Town Committee, submitted initial planning proposals. Similar to Singapore, the planned city was to be developed along the river frontage, with a Strand some "160 feet in depth" to be kept clear of buildings. Streets "60 feet in width and 200 feet distance from one another would be placed at right angles to the Strand, and running north-south would be cool and always have one shaded side".[5] Land at the back of Strand was to be allocated for mercantile purposes, and divided into lots 40 feet wide and 150 feet deep. Enclosed conduits were proposed along the centre of each street, to carry water from the river at high tide up to reservoirs near the Sule Pagoda which fed a sewage system. Rows of mango and tamarind trees were to be planted down the centre of streets to give shade.

By the 1860s the plan form had to be extended to the west, although the eastern area developed more slowly, with most sites used for mills and timber-yards. Commerce expanded after the Commercial Treaty of 1862 with the Burmese King, and Rangoon became the principal port of British Burma. The majority of commercial establishments were run by British concerns, but the city also housed German, French and Dutch companies along with Muslim and Hindu merchants.

Opposite the Sule Pagoda is the building that housed the first department store in Myanmar known as Myanmar Aswe, built in 1905. After 1945 it served various government uses including the Ministry of Hotels and Tourism between 1992 and 2005.

Shipping was orchestrated initially through the British India Steam Navigation Company and the Calcutta and Burmah Steam Navigation Company.

The symmetrical chess-board plan was refined somewhat by Lieutenant Fraser from the Bengal Engineers, with a bund along the river supported by a single line of piles. Fraser also adjusted the number of lateral roads, and proposed a canal with sluice gates to retain water at high tide, although this idea was later abandoned. Streets were named after military and political leaders, merchants and physical landmarks. The plan however lacked radial roads or a satisfactory link with the regional road system, although the river was for many years the principal means of transport.

British India directed that infrastructure costs would be borne by Government, while the auction price of land would go into the Treasury, and a monthly municipal tax was instigated to meet the needs of the city administration. As land was owned by the government, no former land rights were recognised, but previous occupants were granted new or equivalent sites at a minimum price. The allotment of sites proceeded rapidly, including a number of free grants to religious bodies including churches, a temple, a mosque and synagogue.

In 1866 a palace rebellion proved a turning point for the Burmese regime, at a time when Upper Burma was strategically important to the British in terms of their China policy following the Treaty of Tientsin in 1858. Commercial treaties in 1862 and 1867 effectively secured British control over Upper Burma and its economy. By this time large British trading firms such as Burmah Oil and the Bombay Trading Corporation had established themselves in Rangoon. Accompanying this were cultural, economic and intellectual changes within Burma that led to a political coup d'état and the massacre of potential successors. This endeavour was intended to set in motion a series of reforms to preserve the country's independence, while accommodating British interests together with the modernisation of national infrastructure. The latter in itself led to greater integration of the economy with global markets, coinciding with the opening of the Suez Canal in 1869, and increasing the demand for tropical products and foreign visitation. The Irrawaddy Flotilla Company with a fleet of paddle-steamers established a network of river routes for both trade and passengers.

Most of the offices were sited between the Sule Pagoda and the river. The British Secretariat was completed in 1867 on the Strand and after 1917 it became the Postmaster General's office. Other major buildings included the Law Courts, Customs House, the Roman Catholic Cathedral on Fytche Square, the Baptist Mission Church, the American Church and the Holy Trinity Church. In 1873 a General Hospital was built on Commissioner Road. Cultural uses ranged from the Assembly Rooms to a Museum and the Rangoon Literary Society with a large lending library.

By 1881, 44 per cent of the population of 140,000 were Indian, so there were regular sailings between Rangoon and Madras. Hence, a significant amount of accommodation including early shophouse terraces were built by Indian merchants. However a large number of temporary immigrants were agricultural labourers from the Coramandel coast and Orissa which necessitated cheaper rental accommodation and caused severe overcrowding.

The commercial community in Rangoon supported intervention in Upper Burma. At a town hall meeting in 1884 attended by Europeans, Chinese and Indians, a resolution

6 Pearn, 1939, op. cit., p251
7 Thant, 2001, op. cit., p208
8 Woodman, D, *The Making of Burma*, The Cresset Press, London, 1962, p245

Merchant Road houses a number of old banks. On the left is the former Mercantile Bank of India, which awaits renovation, and on the right is the recently renovated premises of Oppenheim & Company, now occupied by the Innwa Bank.

calling for its annexation was passed. Burmese elders of the Municipal Committee took a more prudent and discreet line. The Chambers of Commerce in Britain were circularised by the Rangoon Chamber with a requirement to bring pressure on the imperial government to interfere in Upper Burma, and this eventually led to the Third Anglo-Burmese War of 1885.[6] As British commercial expansion became more assertive, voices increasingly called for annexation of Upper Burma to consolidate trading conditions, counteract rising French power in other parts of Indo-China, and to prevent any foreign influence damaging British interests in Burma and China. This was the broad context for British military intervention in 1885. In March 1886 the entire country was put under British administration as part of their rule over India with a Lieutenant-Governor based in Rangoon.

Within fifteen years of annexation, exports had tripled and imports doubled. Commercial and industrial undertakings included rice, timber and oil production, and the growth in wealth was reflected in new shops, banks, hotels and shipping offices. The Hong Kong and Shanghai Bank opened in Shafraz Road in 1888. Commerce remained largely in foreign hands through Chambers of Commerce. Race meetings were held on the *maidan*, under the rules of the Calcutta Turf Club.

By 1901 the population had grown to 248,000, and new rules to prevent overcrowding prescribed a "minimum floor space of 24 square feet per person". The enforcement of a land revenue system, based on a division of state and non-state land, led to a surge in civil litigation over ownership claims. This resulted in the growing commercialisation of land and a commensurate loss of control by the traditional ruling lineages and hereditary office-holders. The impact on social and economic organisation was substantial as increasing amounts of land became privatised, leading to the rise of a strong commercial and landlord class. When all the land in central Rangoon had been sold, a policy of short-term leasing was introduced which disincentivised investment in suitable buildings and services, and generally contributed to unhealthy conditions, although sewage and water supply systems were introduced in the late nineteenth century.

The British army garrison in Upper Burma numbered around 7,000 with over 10,000 military police, along with some Burmese administrators and a British Indian bureaucracy.[7] The king and his family were sent into exile in India on 1st January 1886, and this succeeded in truncating the long established social order. At the same time it undermined the traditional moral power of the Buddhist hierarchy with its strong literary and educational function. What proved to be a short-sighted proclamation was issued, which read "By Command of the Queen Empress, it is hereby notified that the territories formerly governed by King Theebaw will no longer be under his rule, but have become part of Her Majesty's Dominions, and will during Her Majesty's pleasure, be administered by such officers as the Viceroy and Governor-General of India may from time to time appoint". The crown jewels, reliquaries and other valuable regalia belonging to the court were looted and much of it dispatched to England. Gold ancestral images were melted down.[8]

Reintegration of Burma was fashioned through British policy-makers in Calcutta and Rangoon, with a bureaucracy largely imported from British India. This transformed the ceremonial symbols of state towards a more expedient government rationale that imposed its authority on traditionally minded Burmese society. Fixed frontiers with Assam, Tibet and China were negotiated which included a range of rural frontier communities that came under Rangoon's authority.

The strategic location of Rangoon as a port for agricultural exports and maritime trade made it the prominent place for a capital. Major investment in transport infrastructure was made to meet the needs of the military,

9   Charney, M.W., *A History of Modern Burma*, Cambridge University Press, Cambridge, 2009, p8-11
10 Charney, 2009, op. cit., p19

Pavement dining on Mahabandoola Street. The clock tower of the High Court building, in Queen Anne neo-Gothic style, peers over the ensemble. The imposing dimensions of the complex, constructed between 1905 and 1911, extend to Pansodan Street in the East.

physically and socially, with growth in the export economy of the south attracting rural migrants from the north. A programme of dyke construction in Rangoon created new arable land out of swamps, but while export crops provided necessary revenue, the costs of cultivation were high. The situation also led to problems with regard to land rights through the activities of Indian moneylenders, notably the Chettiers, who acquired land in the case of default.[9]

PLANNING THE CITY

The British laid out the city in a grid form, superimposed on the indigenous layout. A wave of permanent buildings went up during the 1880s and 1890s, replacing the older flimsy construction to cater for government, institutional and commercial uses as the city grew in importance and attracted more wealth. New buildings included a Secretariat complex, Dufferin Hospital, Court buildings and Government House. The British also built prisons, including the largest in the empire at Insein. A steam tramway was built in 1884 and replaced by a trolley bus system some thirty years later. The entire main line railway system was transferred to Burma Railways in 1896. Escalation in urban land prices around the turn of the century led to land speculation in the core city area, but short-term leases under colonial land policy disincentivised investment by urban residents and many were evicted.[10] In 1908 the non-military parts of the Shwedagon Pagoda were transferred by the Government to the Pagoda Trustees and were thereby brought within the Municipal jurisdiction. Because of the city's location on a peninsula — bounded on the east by the Pazundaung Creek and on the south and west by the Hlaing River — urban expansion was only possible in a northerly direction. However this was not possible because this area accommodated Government House, the Pagoda precincts and public amenities such as gardens, parkland and museum grounds.

and in 1889 a railway system was built to link Rangoon with Mandalay which already had a population of around 180,000. This was a time when the Indian Raj was at its height, attenuated by new state structures but where colonial institutions in most cases replaced older social traditions. In a similar way the legacy of a contrived homogenous identity in Burma ignored ingrained ethnic diversity, which would later prove a major obstacle to nationalism and lead to long periods of military rule. The Village Act, with its controlling and authoritarian agenda based on enforced foreign practices, created an alien bureaucracy, while a series of intrusive censuses caused multiple confusions in terms of categorising ethnic groups.

The three Anglo-Burmese wars during the course of the nineteenth century saw Burma spiral from heights of the independent Konbaung Dynasty to a duality of north and south, and finally to colonial rule, which orchestrated its representation to the outside world and acted to shape post-colonial events. Colonial intervention with its economic momentum reconfigured the country both

THE STRAND HOTEL, situated between 38th Street and Seikkan Thar Street, was built in 1901 by the Sarkies Brothers — owners of the Raffles Hotel in Singapore and the E&O Hotel in Penang. The neighbouring hotel annex is now the Australian Embassy. The hotel has been renovated several times: in 1927, 1939 and 1949, and was given a final face-lift in 1993. Further west is the building originally occupied by the Bombay Burma Trading Corporation.

STRAND ROAD was the first street to be developed for trade because of its strategic position alongside the Yangon River. To the right is the building originally constructed by Bulloch Brothers & Co in 1908. It was purchased by the State in 1936 and converted into the Central Post Office. To the left is a four-storey building, originally built to house a shipping company — J&F Graham, in 1898. After independence it became the British Embassy, and also contains the British Council library. To the far left is the Port Authority Building.

LOWER PANSODAN STREET
(formerly Phayre Street) is made up of an amalgam of heritage buildings in the form of offices, banks and institutional buildings. The Lokanat Gallery Building (formerly Sofaer's Building) sits at the junction of Pansodan Street and Merchant Road. Built in 1906 in a neo-Classical Italianate style, it housed legal and financial offices, but also shops and galleries. It was designed by Isaac Sofaer, a member of the early Jewish community in Rangoon. The building is now partially occupied by the Internal Revenue Department. Next to this is the Inland Waterways Department Building, formerly the Irrawaddy Flotila Company Building built in 1933 with a colonnaded frontage, from where it operated the largest fleet of Inland Steamers in the world. Further to the south is the Myanmar Agricultural Development Bank and the Port Authority Building.

Therefore the town form developed inversely to other Asian cities, which had a built-up core area. Rangoon's geographic centre was sparsely built but with commercial and industrial development along the river and creek.

Outer suburban development was hampered by difficulties in adopting the existing plan, and by lack of communications. It was not until the first motor vehicles began to arrive in the city, and in 1913 the electric tramway, that new areas of reclamation created conditions for a more co-ordinated pattern of development and road construction. This in turn facilitated the implementation of suburban housing and institutions, helping to alleviate conditions in the central city.

New public buildings and spaces were constructed at the same time. A Zoological Garden was established within the Victoria Memorial Park and opened by the Prince of Wales in 1906. The High Court and other Government buildings were built in 1915 and the Agri-Horticultural Gardens moved to adjoin the Zoological Gardens in 1923. The city economy was seriously affected by World War I, and the rice trade suffered through the closing of German, Austrian

and Dutch commercial companies. However, Scott Market was completed in 1926 and the Strand Wharf in 1931. A new City Hall and Council Chamber, incorporating Burmese architectural features, was opened by the British Governor of Burma on a new road — Corporation Street — in 1936.

Consulting architects, some with experience in Colonial India, were appointed to design the most important Government buildings, and realise a grand vision, drawing on monumental designs from Delhi, Bombay, Calcutta and Madras. For many of the buildings, steel frames and decorative elements were shipped from Britain. Plans for other structures had to be approved by the Government and after 1928 an Architectural Advisory Committee was appointed to control the standard of architecture on the most important streets.

In 1920 all urban development and land acquisition rights were placed in the new Rangoon Development Trust which carried out reclamation and road building. The latter opened up new suburban areas for wealthy European, Chinese and Indian settlers, causing deep resentment among Burmese. The result was the 1935 Government of

[11] Charney, 2009, op. cit., p23

Burma Act which included a new constitution for the country and established a structure of government that was put into force in 1937. Many future Burmese nationalist leaders emerged from Rangoon University, including U Nu a future prime minister and Ko Ang San, a leading figure in bringing about Burmese independence.

Increasing confrontation with the government over discriminatory procedures incited younger and more radical members to take up an anti-imperialist cause. In the vanguard of unrest came a new political awareness that was channelled into nationalist movements following the Government of India Act of 1919 that excluded Burma. This led to an extension of the Act, which involved a degree of self-rule under new constitutional reforms. Consequently, this raised the question of ethnic divisions within the country, such as the Shan states that enjoyed some autonomy, and the societal and racial divisions more related to Rangoon in particular.

Colonial Rangoon in the 1930s, with its modernisations and international links to the West and to other Asian cities, became a melting pot of intellectual and political ideas related to a new self-awareness. This was built around associations supported by the Burmese press, but with their foundation built on Western organisational models that defied the realities of a highly divided society with diverse motivations and expectations. In 1937 Myanmar achieved a measure of self-government separate from British India, but became subject to internal struggles between political factions, which made it unstable. The global Depression of the 1930s had a significant impact on the Burmese economy and led to the Hsaya San Rebellion which, while ruthlessly put down by the British, encouraged the growth of a dormant nationalist movement.

By 1937, less than one-third of the city population was indigenous, with most coming from Upper Burma, and a majority of the entire population being from South Asia.[11] The result was a city that developed as an administrative and commercial complex but where the dominance of foreign interests largely excluded all but the most privileged and westernised Burmese. Hindustani was the main language as the country was governed as part of British India. Indian immigrants brought with them industrial skills, but also

THE CENTRAL OPEN SPACE centred around the Sule Pagoda and City Hall to the north of Mahabandoola Garden (formerly Fytche Square) is the civic heart of Yangon. City Hall was constructed between 1925 and 1940, designed by Sithu U Tin, blending a palatial European form with Burmese architectural features which include tiered pyatthat roof forms and traditional decoration inspired by the ancient capital Pagan.

[12] Eds. Hlaing, K.Y., Taylor, R.H., and Than, T.M.M., *Myanmar: Beyond Politics to Societal Imperatives*, Institute of Southeast Asian Studies, Singapore, 2005, p19
[13] Woodman, 1962, op. cit., p538
[14] Charney, 2009, op. cit., p97

filled middle-ranking government posts, while the Chinese dominated local trading activities and became some of the largest landowners and influential citizens. Burmese dominated the outer neighbourhoods, mainly engaged in agricultural activities.

Ethnic tensions were palpable although a small but increasingly conspicuous body of Western-educated Burmese entered commerce and even the colonial administration. This educated body became gradually more concerned with vernacular and cultural issues, and the still deeply held values of Buddhism that had declined under colonial rule. In 1937 Myanmar separated from British India and was subject to growing internal struggles between different political parties.

World War II forced Britain to seek solidarity with its colonies, but an anti-war campaign in Burma forced a suspension of civil liberties. Japanese militarism unleashed on Southeast Asia was at first encouraged by latent nationalist movements whose leaders initially regarded the Japanese as mentors, and admired their domestic industrial modernisations.[12] Before the eventual Japanese invasion in mid-1942, which succeeded in driving the remaining British-Indian forces from the country, British teams demolished most of Rangoon's economic infrastructure.

Japan declared Myanmar independent, but as in other Japanese colonies it was unable to maintain popular support. The war devastated the country both physically and economically. Many of the buildings in Rangoon were destroyed, and much of the city became overwhelmed by ramshackle accommodation as impoverished citizens returned. Reconstruction was put in the hands of the Civil Affairs Service and widely interpreted as a means to rebuild British interests in the face of nationalist opinion that continued to view Western influence as damaging. With the final steps in place for Indian independence, an

Anglo-Burmese Agreement in January 1947 promised independence and talks were held to determine the status of the Shan and other 'Frontier' states. For various reasons, including the assassination of Aung San and other members of the Executive Council, the immediate post-war period left a leadership vacuum, largely through the lack of a common ideology, and so failed to achieve solidarity.

In 1941 the British, and the Chinese Nationalist Government, agreed on an acceptable boundary. However in January 1947, prior to independence, China laid down claims to the northern Kachin states that had previously been under British control — this area was the gateway to Tibet, which they occupied in 1951 as a 'military district of China'. The matter was only resolved under a Joint Commission in 1961 on the 13th anniversary of Burmese independence, which established a properly demarcated boundary for the first time in its history.[13]

After the transfer of power in January 1948, political infighting devolved into armed rebellion and civil war. The new government, while remaining neutral, was under pressure to match its socialist economy with the US Government's Cold War strategy in the region while having to deal with the aftermath of Japanese occupation, a devastated economy and political fragmentation. Collectively these combined to set a course for military intervention and a "caretaker" government between 1958 and 1960. One of its first initiatives was to move 170,000 squatters from Rangoon to three satellite towns with designated lots for each family, electricity, piped water and construction supplies. This enabled a clean-up operation along with infrastructure improvements to the city itself, with thousands of people participating in what became known as "sweat campaigns".[14] The return of civilian government and the promotion of Buddhist nationalism witnessed street demonstrations. With much of the

country hostile to the government, a military coup headed by a Revolutionary Council was launched in March 1962 at a time of armed conflict between Communist and anti-Communist forces in much of Indo-China, and border disputes with China in the midst of the Cultural Revolution.

The stated intention was to establish a workable political infrastructure within a single-party system, and in so doing underscore the role of the army as the self-appointed pillar of the post-colonial state. Gradual control over all forms of media, plus military supervision of educational institutions imposed a clear separation of politics and religion. This was accompanied by a Marxist restructuring of state institutions including the economy, through nationalisation of banks, factories and all private businesses. With controls over all aspects of state affairs came the eradication of any influences that might instigate a fundamental reshaping of the country. In 1979 Burma began to withdraw from various international organisations (apart from the United Nations) as well as bilateral relations with friendly states.

The transition to one-party civilian rule under the Burma Socialist Programme Party brought with it a programme of economic misdirection and exploitation so that in 1988, with further economic deterioration, the government collapsed and the army established itself through the State Law and Order Restoration Council. On 27th May 1989 — a date fixed by astrologers — the name Burma was changed to Myanmar, with a commensurate city name change from Rangoon to Yangon. The name *Myanmar* is said to embrace all ethnic groups, including the hill tribes.

Aung San Suu Kyi came to be viewed as the leader of the pro-Democracy movement. This represented a unifying force, but also led to a further entrenchment of military control and her house arrest until 1995 following the annulment of election results in 1990. Up until 2012 the military regime was plagued by rivalry, infighting and extensive corruption alongside abject poverty. While many Western countries and Japan introduced trade sanctions against Myanmar, the country's admittance to ASEAN opened the door to co-operation from China, India and Russia, which included the supply of military hardware, as part of individual geopolitical strategies.

Throughout this period Rangoon remained as the centre of government, but also as a theatre of protest. Investment in the city was largely limited to tourist infrastructure built in the 1990s. This was accompanied by enforced resettlement of several hundred thousand people into new towns and in 2005 it was announced that a new capital would be built at Nay Pyi Taw in Central Myanmar, some 600 kilometres north of Rangoon, facilitating a centralisation of authority. A peaceful "Saffron Revolution" of monks in 2007 was brutally suppressed, and the inundation of Cyclone Nargis in 2008 further devastated the country while the military blocked outside aid.

A long-established constant is the struggle to deal with ethnic divisions on one hand, and to reconcile civilian groups and authoritarian controls on the other; so that national unity through political solidarity has failed at every turn. Resentment at foreign domination has been insufficient to translate into nationalism without an overriding ideology, and military self-interest has continually thwarted the legitimacy of democracy movements. A further factor is the physical geography of the country. Myanmar's 673,500 square kilometres are almost entirely encircled by the Western Hills along the border of India and Bangladesh, while its northern and eastern borders with China, Laos and Thailand are similarly flanked by the high Tibetan range. The spatial divisions stemming from this have generated long-standing differences between tribal areas,

and the Burmese in the delta region.

Notwithstanding constant expressions of concern, Western countries have maintained a discreet interest in economic opportunities and a significant number of non-government organisations have developed a recent presence in the country. Since 1989 China has supported Myanmar politically, and economic co-operation through cross-border trade has been supported by the construction of new road links and infrastructure development, with China professing interest in access to the Andaman Sea and the Bay of Bengal, which could act to destabilize bilateral relations with India. Similarly Thailand, which shares a long border with Myanmar, houses a large number of refugees and through ASEAN, follows a cautious approach to political dialogue.

Multi-party elections took place in late 2010 with the government party Union Solidarity and Development Party winning the majority of seats, and a new government established in 2011. In April 2012 Aung San Suu Kyi's National League for Democracy party won an overwhelming majority of the 45 seats up for election. The events of 2012 have brought a partial return to democratic functions and the recognition of the potent significance of Aung San Suu Kyi after receiving her 1991 Nobel Peace Prize in Oslo. This personifies a belated gesture of acknowledgement that a malfunctioning economy and an anomalous durability of military rule must ultimately be resolved by charting a way forward based on national reconciliation and popular consent. In Yangon a lack of urban planning, ineffective road

The Boyyoke Aung San Market is a focus for visitor activity, comprising a series of interconnected arcades, colonnaded streets and pedestrian precincts.

infrastructure and traffic management act to curb both urban growth and progressive city development. The Hlaing Thar Yar Industrial Zone on the outskirts of the city employs 58,000 people but is beset by power shortages reflecting the fact that two-thirds of national supply comes from hydropower. The World Bank is currently advising Myanmar on an electricity law.

Revenues from the exploitation of rich natural gas reserves could in theory provide a basis for a form of market socialism and state efficiency, similar to that which has propelled China towards modernisation as well as entry to the global marketplace on the back of a state-controlled system — but one which allocated special governance arrangements to specific regions. To exploit Myanmar's economic potential and diversify its economy, the government must ensure a stable political situation and build up basic infrastructure in order to reassure foreign investors. China is currently investing in Kyaukpyu as an international deep-sea port gateway and oil

15 Courtauld, C, *Myanmar: Burma in Style*, Odyssey Books, ACT, Fyshwick, 2013

16 Association of Myanmar's Architects, *Thirty Heritage Buildings of Yangon*, Serindia, Chicago, 2012

and gas terminal on the northwest coast of Myanmar. In 2011, China Railway Engineering and the Myanmar Ministry of Railways agreed to build an 868-kilometre passenger and cargo rail link between Kyaukpyu and Kunming in Yunnan Province — the shortest trade route between India and China. A further 900-kilometre long expressway is being built from Ruili, a Chinese border city, through Mandalay to the port. However whereas China's modernisations over the past twenty-five years could fall back on its relatively unified societal traditions, Myanmar must first assimilate a coalition of support from disparate and mistrustful divisions within the country. There must also be an overriding rationale for this. This should stem from the satisfaction of mutual interests in order to reconfigure the country, but must ensure that the constellation of surrounding and self-interested Asian states act to assist rather than exploit this process in a spirit of peaceful coexistence.

THE URBAN DESIGN FRAMEWORK

The city's urban design is focussed along a series of wide east-west boulevards — Anawrahta Road, Maha Bandoola Road, Merchant Road and Strand Road. These form junctions with major north-south roads, and the formed grids are further sub-divided by fifty-two narrow streets. The most prominent nineteenth century government edifies, institutional buildings, trading houses and prominent residential structures defined a grand sequence of colonial-era landmarks along the major road channels while the secondary street system primarily provided residential and shop-house terraces. While many of the older buildings have weathered and commercial buildings have been largely repurposed, the urban streetscapes are among the finest in Asia, integrated within a simple but robust morphology of building types and spaces.

The evolving street matrix contains a range

The High Court was designed by James Ransome, Consulting Architect to the Government of India, which explains its uncompromising grandeur of Empire. The massive clock tower required extensive pile foundations of hardwood thitya logs. Since the capital relocated to Nay Pyi Tau, the building is no longer occupied.

Shophouses along Sule Pagoda Road display both Chinese and Indian characteristics through a rhythm of arched openings, decorated pilasters and neo-Classical corbels.

Typical street architecture in the Chinese quarter of Yangon.

The narrow north-south streets to the west of Sule Pagoda Road provide opportunities for informal uses to spill out from the ground floors onto the street, together with outdoor markets.

of buildings from 1852 to the mid-twentieth century that provides a three-dimensional history of modern Yangon, from trading houses and administrative buildings sitting on prominent sites that contribute a high level of legibility to the cityscape, to the extensive shophouse terraces that represent predominantly imported architectural forms. Many of the old trading establishments have changed their use over the years, while the removal of many institutional buildings to the new capital at Nay Pyi Taw have left a number of older colonial edifices such as the Secretariat and High Court in search of new identities. The colonial core represents the city's nineteenth century role as a busy port settlement, imbued with the building legacy of the European trading firms in existence at the time. Many of the housing terraces and shophouse streets were built by Indian settlers and Chinese immigrants, in styles that reflect a combination of neo-Classical and indigenous architecture, with a range of flamboyant decorative devices.

Some new buildings incorporate the woodworking skills of local craftsmen and materials to create a modern counterpoint to the cultural traditions of indigenous architecture. The Burmese design legacy of both religious and secular buildings has bequeathed a diversity of forms that are both symbolic and climatically practical with respect to the overall environment and harmony of place.

Public buildings were generally designed by consulting architects from Calcutta or Bombay, but display a more refined High Victorian tone than the flamboyant Indic-Saracenic style that became refined through its 'pattern-book' approach in Indian cities. Because of the shortage of locally available building materials apart from timber, steel frames and wrought iron fitments were frequently shipped from England. A further

challenge was the foundation of buildings which had to originally sit on water-logged reclamations. The Secretariat was built on sunken *pyinkado* logs, while the Custom House with its high tower was constructed on a reinforced cement raft.[15]

In the face of increasing building decay, many state-owned buildings are now empty and vulnerable to redevelopment, while a large number of residential terraces are in poor condition. Since the change in political climate there is a forceful new development agenda, challenging the sanctity of the compact street grid. In 2012 the Yangon Heritage Trust was established with the aim of preserving the city's heritage buildings and establishing appropriate new uses to extend their life. Back in 1996, the Yangon City Development Committee had compiled 189 heritage buildings, covering institutional, commercial and religious buildings, together with privately owned structures.[16]

The approach to the Shwedagon from the surrounding area is marked by a transition from the commercial to the sacred.

THE SHWEDAGON

Religious architecture in Myanmar stems from the continuous tradition of Buddhism ingrained within the country. Acts of devotion, festivals and visitation to sites of religious significance are reflected in ornate design forms that incorporate a consistent range of elements. Stupas, pagodas, temples and monasteries are often found within the same sites. Stupas are located at the centre of square compounds or terraces, surrounded by smaller shrines to facilitate offerings. Temples and monasteries are crowned by a tiered roof form, the *pyat-that*, constructed over the Buddha image. The *pyat-that* associated with old-established palaces where it towered above the throne room, typifies the close link between ancient royalty and Buddhism, and is intended to replicate the verticality of Mount Meru at the heart of the Buddhist cosmos. Myanmar's rich woodcarving tradition forms an essential part of the architectural landscape in Rangoon.

The site of one of Asia's oldest and most sacred monuments on top of Singuttara hill was formed some 2,000 years ago and the main pagoda rises some 100 metres above this. It is said to contain relics of the Buddha Gotama. Donations by the ancient royal dynasties facilitated its continual enlargement.

There are four approaches to the Shwedagon from the cardinal directions, and eight planetary posts around the base are associated with days of the week. Above the base are the plinth and three terraces. Pavilions and *zeidis* or golden pagodas amalgamate around the base of the central stupa.

The hill approaches form continuations of the surrounding streets, with the main southern staircase being the traditional entry point for visitors from the river. Shwedagon Pagoda Road is lined with other pagodas, monasteries, resthouses and stalls selling symbolic offerings and images.

As a profoundly Buddhist country, the Shwedagon has both a cultural role as a sacred place and centre of pilgrimage, and a symbolic role as an important national landmark. Its collection of Buddhist architecture reaches into and sanctifies the city itself, bringing its history into the present and giving it focus.

Four types of pagoda exist — the major ones containing personal relics of the Buddha; those that enshrine the Dhamma or Buddhist teaching; those containing utensils of the Buddha; and those that enshrine images. Yangon's history is associated with the Shwedagon Pagoda on Singuttara Hill, which fulfils the first criterion. Its main approach from the south — Shwedagon Pagoda Road — is lined with monasteries or *kyaung*, and resthouses or *zayats*. The Shwedagon represents a secular and timeless religious focus, with a spatial grouping akin to an urban setting of different buildings experienced as a sacred place. Religious constructions and marble terraces cater for worship, ceremony and informal occupation brought together through spiritual experience and a single stream of clockwise pedestrian rotation from devotees. The golden Pagoda is re-gilded with gold leaf in stages every

[17] Moore, E. Mayer, H. and Pe U.W., *Shwedagon: Golden Pagoda of Myanmar*, Thames and Hudson, London, 1999, p172

ten years with the golden *hti* at its peak. The entire ensemble of pavilions, halls and pagodas shines over the city as a symbolic emblem of myth, legend and spiritual devotion, that has been continually enlarged over the centuries. The main stupa encases earlier ones, and was raised to its present height of ninety-nine metres in the eighteenth century. It has survived the ravages of both war and military occupation by the British who added barracks, an artillery station and military fortifications.

The bell-shaped form of the main stupa is said to be derived from the Thuparama Pagoda in Sri Lanka, but with a more elongated profile giving it greater prominence. Four devotional halls or *tazaung* mark each face aligned with the staircase approaches. Between these are sixty-four shrines or *stupas* and behind these sixty-four *zeidi-yan* spread around the entire base.

The covered stairway approaches reveal a sequence of platforms and stalls selling images and offerings, magnifying the sense of arrival before the full extent of the stupa ensemble is revealed. Eight cardinal positions corresponding with planetary points are located around the base, reflecting the astrological calendar.

The arrangement of shrines and buildings has no symmetry or obvious chronological grouping, apart from the northern sector where shrines are linked to the older part of the platform. Similarly directional alignment of devotional halls is of little concern. Many people visit one of the planetary shrines associated with the day of the week on which they were born. The key components are the images of Buddha and spirit figures visited by devotees with offerings — gifts from individuals, government bodies, or commercial organisations. The latter are also permitted to build pavilions on the platform. One of the "Noble Truths" of Buddhism is the five aggregates of body, sensation, conception, volition and consciousness which

create the need to find solice in prayer.[17] The anthropomorphic connection creates a spiritual link between urban functions and perceived cosmic influences of time and space associated with auspicious qualities. These beliefs are typical of the Theravadan Buddhism practised in Myanmar where human action necessarily relates to universal harmony. This is reflected in the strong moral authority of the monastic community.

The eastern approach to the Shwedagon pagoda platform. Two 10-metre high mythical lions or chinthe flank the eastern stairway approach.

Phnom Penh

THE PSAR THMEI OR 'GRAND MARKET' in Phnom Penh formed part of the French colonial urban planning framework for the city designed by Ernest Hêbrard, which included the improvement of urban infrastructure and public institutions. The monumental market building was intended as a focus for growth in the western part of the city. It continues to form an iconic landmark in the central square of the busiest section of Phnom Penh, and is now surrounded by makeshift market structures that extend its internal function. Its simple but aesthetically ingenuous design provides natural ventilation, and screen walls filter out the bright sunlight.

1 Osborne, M, *Phnom Penh: A Cultural and Literary History*, Signal Books, Oxford, 2008
2 Osborne, 2008, op. cit.

A SEQUENCE OF POLITICAL INTERVENTIONS

Phnom Penh's strategic location on the Mekong Delta lies at the foot of the Tonle Sap — a waterway that serves a balancing function during the summer monsoons. The control of drainage through engineered water channels or *prek* is reflected in ancient Khmer city planning, although this was used mainly for the creation of land for palaces and religious compounds. Archaeological evidence suggests a large settlement in the vicinity of the present Phnom Penh, well before Angkor was founded in the twelfth century. Its growth as a strategic trading centre at the confluence of the Mekong and Tonle Sap rivers has been attributed to the emerging commercial trade between the Cambodian court and China, before Angkor was abandoned around 1431.

By the fifteenth century Phnom Penh had developed into a prosperous commercial settlement based on trading links with China along the Mekong River, and its strategic location in relation to Vietnam, Thailand and Laos. Milton Osborne suggests that its older name — *Chatomok*, which can be translated as 'Four Faces' — might be associated with the four-faced carvings of the Bayon temple at Angkor, bringing to mind the title of Han Suyin's book set in the 1960s in Siem Reap.[1]

The low *Phnom* or 'hill' with its ancient stupa and temple has been a place of veneration since the Cambodian court left Angkor around 1440, and the historic city spread out from there. During the sixteenth century the city became known to Portuguese explorers from Goa and Malacca.

This dates from when Afonse de Albuquerque (who conquered Malacca in 1511) consolidated control over sea routes in Southeast Asia, including trade with Ayutthaya, the ancient Thai capital. The Iberian connection appears to have commenced around 1550 through Dominican missionaries who prepared the first published map of Cambodia but conspicuously failed in lengthy attempts to convert the predominantly Buddhist population. They did however open the way for Portuguese traders and the first acquisitive Spanish visitors from their Asian base in Manila, reinforced by military strength. Despite access to the royal court, their belligerence marked the decline of both Iberian adventurism and Western religious endeavours, although a small but robust Catholic community was established in Phnom Penh that lasted for three hundred years. In 1643 the Cambodian ruler came under the influence of Malays and embraced Islam. The Dutch, who had taken Malacca from the Portuguese in 1641, established a short-lived trading post in Phnom Penh and built a church, the Eglise Hoalong by the Tonle Sap, that survived until the Pol Pot regime in the 1970s.[2]

The Dutch departure in the 1670s marked the end of European involvement in Cambodia for some time. Vietnam usurped part of its territory, including what is now Ho Chi Minh City, blocking access to the sea at the north of the Mekong, and in the process discouraging further sea-borne expeditions from European powers until 1859 when it fell under French control. In the meantime however, further intervention from neighbouring Thailand saw Ankor itself come under Thai control. In 1834 Thai forces razed Phnom Penh and retreated, having looted its treasures. This left the Vietnamese to assert control over Cambodia and many of its cultural institutions, only for control to revert to Thailand several years later under a predominantly Siamese court.

In 1853 the new monarch, abetted by French missionaries,

The ancient temple on the Phnom

To the west and far south are the wider boulevards and narrower side streets of old villas dating from the late nineteenth century, although many of the two-storey colonial structures have been replaced or converted.

The French Administration Quarter included the centrally located and restored Post Office (built in 1910) together with other buildings along the Avenue Daun Penh. These now include the National Library, the National Archives and the Hotel le Royal. The starkly imposing American Embassy is now located on the Circle Sportif — the old French sports centre.

entreated Napoleon III to offer "protection" and in 1855 a French force was sent to Vietnam and seized Saigon in 1861. After the death of the Cambodian King in 1860, with different factions fighting for the succession, Catholic missions were destroyed. This became a reason for French intervention and Prince Norodom opened the door for a protectorate to be established in 1863 that granted the French special trading rights. Norodom was crowned king in 1864 and the following year moved the capital from Udong to Phnom Penh, commencing construction of the royal palace compound two years later. Norodom also encouraged Chinese to settle in the city, and these new settlers went on to build streets of shophouses. They were later joined by Malay and Indian traders. Phnom Penh proved to be a better trading centre than Udong, and enabled the French to control marine traffic. New palace buildings gradually replaced older ones, including a gift to Norodom by the French Empress Eugénie of a delicately prefabricated cast iron palace, which still stands in the palace compound. The preliminary structure of the colonial city morphology, defined by the Tonle Sap, Sihanouk Boulevard to the south and Monivong Boulevard to the west, was established by King Ponhea Yat, and the main street or Quai Norodom, by King Norodom I.

Relations between the French and Norodom were at first cordial, but in 1884 they demanded that Cambodia pay for the protectorate and facilitate a predominant role for the French at court, reinforcing this by 'gunboat diplomacy'. Although the king acquiesced, this led to a general uprising, but this failed to halt the French-led development of Phnom Penh.

Under the direction of a new *Résident Supérieur* Hyn de Verénville, the French plan of the 1890s was laid out to the west of the Tonle Sap around the *Phnom* which is still the highest point in the city. In order to create a secure earthen base to the height of the

3   Chapman, W, 'Too Little, Too Late? Urban Planning and Conservation in Phnom Penh', in *The Disappearing Asian City*, Ed. William S Logan, Oxford University Press, Oxford, 2002

A centrepiece of the Grand Palace — Empress Eugénie's prefabricated palace constructed of cast iron was originally used to mark the opening of the Suez Canal in 1869 and was presented as a gift to King Norodom I.

Remnant of the French Baroque townscape

river levee, a sequence of land reclamations and embankments were constructed through dredging of alluvial deposits from the river and a system of canals to collect run-off. This created the basis for a matrix of streets laid out according to a grid of piles around 3.5 metres apart, which in turn dictated the width of new shophouse frontages. The Chinese city grew around this development framework to the north of the palace and this still dictates the layout pattern of the older trading core. The French Quarter to the north was laid out more spatially with wide avenues and classically styled villas, and encircled by a canal which was later filled in to become the Avenue de la Gare. The grid form was devised by French planner Daniel Fabre. Various public buildings were constructed around a central square including the central post office and administrative headquarters — later the Hotel le Royal. It was decreed that no building should be located on the bank of the Tonle Sap, which led to the present corniche along Sisowath Quay, named

after Norodom's brother and successor, and facilitating a wide vista to the front of the palace. Fabre also regenerated the Phnom hill through the construction of a grand stair with Ankorian details.

The earliest French buildings were of a relatively simple construction, being primarily for government use. However in the 1880s King Norodom allowed customs duties to help pay for new administrative accommodation and city improvements including street drains, and foreign residents were allowed to purchase land.[3] This led directly to a more extravagant style of urban design.

One of Norodom's final acts was to inaugurate the Temple of the Emerald Buddha (the 'Silver Pagoda') in 1903. French diplomatic activity ensured a further forty years of colonial rule which saw the transformation of Phnom Penh's built fabric, and was generally supported by the royal court. While the king remained a symbolic figurehead to his subjects, French officials participated in traditional court ceremonies.

In common with other colonial regimes of the time, the French regarded their role as a *mission civilatrice* towards a people who had somehow fallen from the ancient greatness of Angkor civilisation.

The *Service d'Urbanisme de L'Indochine* was established in 1921, and Ernest Hēbrard, the French architect and urbanist set out a plan for Phnom Penh that was, at least in part, a strategy for the improvement of urban infrastructure, and the installation of utility services, public institutions and low-cost housing. Hēbrard's expansion plan divided the city into districts based on pre-existing ethnic neighbourhoods, and on predominant uses. The plan was also related to the new railway system, with the Avenue de la Gare effectively dividing up the city and its diverse population groups, but linked through a commercial district to the new railway station. The plan provided for urban neighbourhoods for ethnic Cambodian, Chinese, and Vietnamese (who were introduced by the French to act as junior

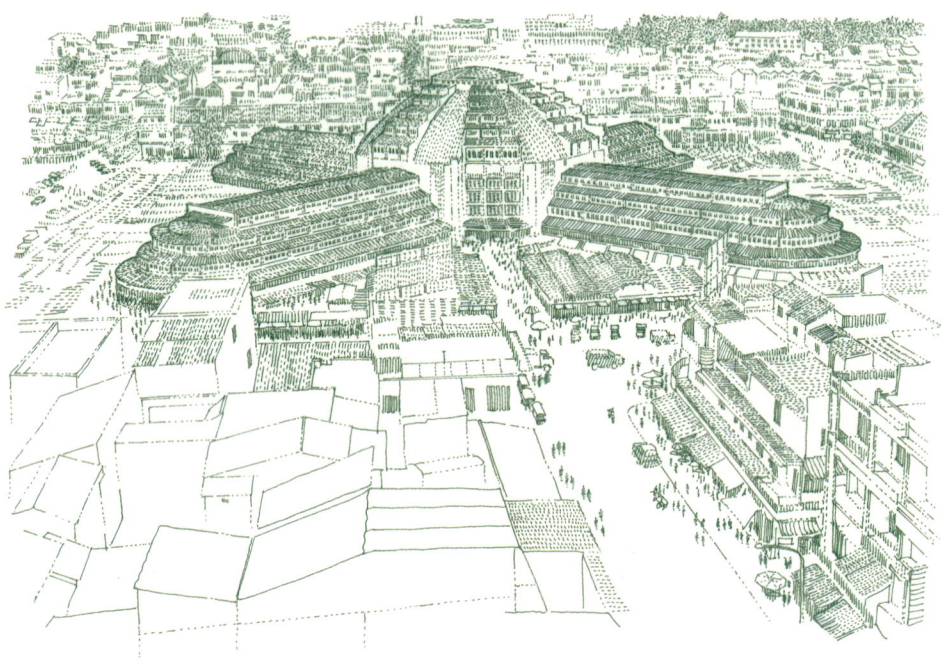

THE PSAR THMEI OR GRAND MARKET was completed in 1937, designed by French architects Jean Desbois and Louis Chauchon. This is a truly urban building with four large bays that reach out and draw in the marketers. The form reflects its purpose — to effectively divide streams of business around different types of produce and product. The Art Deco concept, in reinforced concrete, is surmounted by a large cupola some 45 metres in height supported by piled columns. It forms an iconic landmark in the central square of the busiest section of the city, and is now surrounded by makeshift market structures that extend its internal function.

administrators), as well as a consolidated European Quarter and port buildings enclosed by a ring road. Future development across Tonle Sap by means of a bridge to the eastern Chruoy Changvar Peninsula ultimately housed a large Islamic population, linked by a network of new streets and thoroughfares.

The programme of public works, including a general hospital and an Ophthalmological Institute, was curtailed by the Japanese occupation in the 1940s, and did not resume until Cambodia's independence in the late 1950s. At this point, work began on new sub-divisions to the south and west, through a system of reclamation defined by dykes equipped with large pumping stations.

The Second World War, as in several colonial empires, created its own intervention in the period between pre-war governmental arrangements and the sobering aftermath. In the interim, perceptions on both sides changed and the myth of invincibility that had hovered around Western powers

underwent a subtle re-evaluation. There could be no return to complete normality. The French, like the British in India, were rocked by the loss of manpower and a bankrupt economy at home. The coronation of Norodom Sihanouk in 1941 coincided with large-scale Japanese activity throughout Indo-China, while occupied France survived uncomfortably through the Vichy regime. In practice, French authority was gradually eroded by the controlling Japanese presence, while the popularity of Sihanouk was reinforced, particularly in the countryside. In March 1945 the Japanese mounted a *coup de force*, overturning the French administration and promoting the establishment of independent states in Cambodia, Vietnam and Laos. The later return of control to France did little to dilute nationalist sentiment and there were increasingly forceful calls for independence. This effectively fused the embryonic movements that were later to wreak revolutionary havoc within the country — those who, like leading Vietnamese revolutionaries, had studied in France and were fighting the French in Vietnam, survived as a clandestine guerrilla force, later to evolve into the Cambodian Communist Party.

Full independence was achieved in November 1953 and shortly afterwards Sihanouk abdicated the throne in favour of his father in order to more directly engage in political life, forming a new Socialist Movement — the *Sangkum Reastr Niyum*. This was aimed at reconciling all factions under one organisation, backed up by security forces as a precaution against dissent. Superficially Sihanouk was strong enough to combat challenges to his authority. While Chinese and Vietnamese made up around two-thirds of the population (which in 1960 had risen to 409,000), neighbouring Vietnam was in violent conflict and China provided a bedrock of support for the Cambodian regime. However, with only a restricted elite admitted to the upper tiers of administration

4   Osborne, 2008, op. cit.

and members of the extended royal family holding important positions in government, corruption was endemic. The banking industry was largely presided over by the French, who also controlled much of the rubber import and export trade; Chinese residents controlled much of the business and professional life; the Vietnamese were active in minor commercial enterprises; and a small Indian community of chettiers mainly acted as money lenders.

Up to 1970, the systems of government evolved an elusive duality through an established affinity between the French and Sihanouk's court, so that the Cambodian ruling and political hierarchy complemented rather than controlled the French domination of urban and cultural development. Much of the elite institutional bodies were headed by the French, who additionally oversaw the semi-official news agency, the *Agence Khmère de Press*, which was suitably deferential to Sihanouk. Up until 1963 when United States aid was broken off, there also existed a core of Americans who oversaw various aid agencies.

These separate forces, together with the wealth of the business community, contributed to rapid city growth. The identity of Khmer culture, distinct from that of Vietnamese, Chinese and Siamese during the early twentieth century is elusive. Artistic forms, including those as diverse as architecture and dance, had drawn on neighbouring influences, and vice versa. In this sense, intervention might be better described as assimilation — a credible reflection of decades, if not centuries, of cultural interface and mutual influence. It happened to be a Frenchman, Henri Mouhot, who introduced the Angkor ruins to a Western audience in 1860, and French efforts played a considerable part in its reconstruction. In this respect, one uniquely interventionist role was to retrieve the past for the benefit of the Cambodian present. This was accompanied by a rise in nationalist

The old European Quarter — originally laid out as a series of villas with steep roofs, shuttered windows and wrought ironwork — has been largely redeveloped or transformed through temporary appendages, all surrounding the French Embassy compound.

sentiment among the intelligentsia and various quasi-governmental organisations helped to promote the preservation of Khmer culture. As in China during the 1930s when a number of Chinese architects acquired their training in America, many Cambodian urban designers were trained in France during the growth of the modern movement, and attempted to put these ideas into practice within a culturally abstract Khmer context — for example buildings such as the National Theatre, the University of Phnom Penh, the Royal University and the Independence Monument.[4]

New architectural forms failed to ignite a programme of regeneration in a climate of progressive economic decline during the 1960s, and many of the modern monuments were later destroyed or fell into disrepair. Commensurate with this came governmental decline, rising insurgencies and lack of control over border regions, reflecting this power and decision-making vacuum. The coup against Sihanouk and the establishment of the Khmer Republic was marked by apathy in Phnom Penh. However

the possibly inadvertent result was to elevate the aspirations of the Communist Party and generate support for this from the fervent Communist leadership in neighbouring China and Vietnam. They were joined by an aggrieved Sihanouk himself, who was bent on revenge against those who had deposed him.

Through a combination of circumstances, an already chaotic regional situation deteriorated even further. War engulfed Vietnam, and the Cultural Revolution in China coupled with an American bombing campaign against the Khmer Rouge, and endemic corruption through the trading of armaments, led to vast numbers of refugees arriving in Phnom Penh from the surrounding rural areas. This led to an intensification of existing urban land use, and multi-occupation of the older subdivisions and shophouses of up to five storeys accessed from lanes to the rear, while shops occupied the street frontages.

In April 1975 Khmer Rouge forces (made up predominantly of young soldiers on the outer margins of society) entered Phnom Penh, indoctrinated with ideological

5   Osborne, 2008, op. cit.

Temple Gateway

Decorative Gateway at the Grand Palace

propaganda that targeted the self-indulgent habits of the privileged urban regime. In part this also represented a deep, if somewhat disjointed view of imperialist intervention. Thus commenced a tyrannical programme of unprecedented viciousness and extermination in the "killing fields". One of the first and most unlikely events was the inexplicable evacuation of the city itself — virtually all the intellectual and cultural elite were either killed or sent to the countryside. Over the next five years the essential fabric of Phnom Penh was destroyed or dismantled in a 'cultural revolution' paralleling China's regime that aimed to obliterate both its history and cultural artefacts. This was followed by destruction of Western buildings, such as the cathedral and churches, and massive vandalism of houses, offices and monuments including the sacking of the national library, the Ecole Francaise, the French Embassy, and the Romanesque Cathedral (built in 1897 as a sign of respect for Vietnamese Catholics). Buildings seen as distinctly Cambodian, such as the Palace and National Museum were not damaged, although a large number of institutional buildings were emptied and used for more mundane purposes. This possibly reflected an ill-defined but underlying ideal of an unsullied and independent empire that harked back to the ancient Khmer civilisation — exemplified by a flag with a central feature of an Angkor temple.

During this period, Cambodia experienced the extremes of urban intervention that, from historical evidence, are seemingly destined to occur periodically — an intervention not as a force for constructive or idealistic change, but rather for destabilization and destruction. The city population was reduced to administrators and military personnel.

THE MODERN CITY

The return of Sihanouk from exile in Beijing, to seemingly preside over the deconstruction and decay of Phnom Penh, culminated

in Vietnamese forces 'liberating' the city in January 1979 as Sihanouk and several hundred Chinese advisers were evacuated back to Beijing. The Vietnamese invasion, with Cambodia ravaged and on the brink of famine, was in part political rather than merely liberating. Supported by the Soviet Union, the Cambodian puppet regime orchestrated through the People's Republic of Kampuchea was largely intended to bolster Vietnamese interests in Indochina in competition with those of China. The 'skeleton' population of around 30,000 were joined by returnees, who first had to undergo selection procedures and "re-education" at one of the many holding centres around the city periphery. Vietnam sent both administrators and professionals to provide basic state organisation and restore services.

The majority of street buildings and institutional complexes had received no maintenance and were in a forlorn state. The city's service infrastructure had almost completely collapsed. Certain main streets were opened up but large urban quarters remained unoccupied or were filled with squatters. Buddhist monks returned to the city and slowly revived the old-established temple culture, but one that was arguably circumscribed by the prevailing political situation. Milton Osborne observes that after 1984 a fragile normality was achieved through the gradual assimilation of a returning Chinese dominated merchant class.[5] With the impending rapprochement between China and the Soviet Union, and with persuasive support from members of ASEAN, the Vietnamese withdrew from Cambodia in 1989.

The re-establishment of private property rights and the ensuing private land market, together with reconstruction orchestrated by the United Nations, have enabled the city to slowly regain most of its functions, but with a newly urbanised population and with few social or cultural links to the past. The recognition of private property rights was a substantial step towards developing a coherent form of land-use control, encapsulated in the Land Law of 1993. This was extended two years later through national planning regulations, which have helped rationalise a form of development control at a time when neighbouring countries were beginning to invest again in Cambodian enterprises. The differentiated city quarters have since dissolved their inherent characteristics, with the older boulevards becoming principal traffic arteries, and old colonial buildings converted to a variety of uses (including accommodation for senior military personnel), hemmed in by areas of redevelopment at increasingly higher densities. Large pockets of urban land are held in well-connected private hands, while there is little overall development control and inadequate city infrastructure. However the city represents an urbanism of adaptation and opportunity, where industrial investment and tourism are generating a momentum towards modernisation and with some evidence of historical reconstruction. The Bureau of Metropolitan Affairs has initiated various city improvement projects such as open space and parkland associated with the palace precinct, major boulevards and around the Independence Monument.

In 1993 the United Nations took on a transitional administrative role through United Nations Transitional Authority in Cambodia, which presided over the first ever election, marred by the reluctance of the Prime Minster Hun Sen to give up power. The fragile political situation remains beleaguered by the tenuous strands that link military muscle with a somewhat compromised monarchy. Phnom Penh is one of the poorest capitals in Asia and foreign aid is crucial in maintaining economic benefits to the wider population. The transition of power within the royal family — passed on from Sihanouk to his son Sihanomi following his abdication in 2004 — provides a superficial sense of

established order without power, while control effectively resides in the authoritarian corridors of the Cambodian People's Party.

The palace buildings facing the Tonle Sap date from the 1860s. While they command the most prominent site in Phnom Penh, the Palace compound is less a centre of royal mystique and intrigue than a tourist attraction that seems isolated and detached in relation to other cultural traditions which previously filtered down from court culture to inform and dramatise the wider city quarters. A high tier of officialdom tends to operate with impunity, and continues to have an influential stake in city development. Closely linked with this is the hierarchy of limitless 'connections' or *guangxi* that oils the wheels of business.

Until the conflagration brought about through the Khmer Rouge in the 1970s, the city identity was associated with its

royal palace and related structures, and to its French colonial layout. Recent urban expansion in the 1990s to the north and south of the centre has embraced some of the former outer suburbs. Both the destruction of Western 'imperialist' symbolism (including Catholic churches), and the massive build up of population from the 1980s have led to large-scale redevelopment which has reduced the colonial character of the city.

Modern Phnom Penh is an ambiguous mix of French colonial planning and re-building from the 1990s. The city quarters broadly follow different functional areas — the government and administrative area in the north first established by the French in the 1860s; and the commercial and banking district to the south comprising predominantly twentieth century buildings. The Chinese shophouse district is near the commercial core to the west of Sisowath Quay

PHNOM PENH has embraced six major religious establishments, each founded by the royal family and each signified by a temple and associated communal and educational buildings together with funerary monuments. The wats, stupas and steep roofs designated sacred places as well as urban landmarks. The design of the Phnom Penh Museum was carried out by George Groslier and completed in 1920 using traditional Cambodian architectural references, and the open courtyard is one of the most beautiful and tranquil places in the modern city. In 1996 this was modernised with the help of Australian aid. Together with the royal palace, the spires and 'floating' roofs continue to dominate the surrounding low-rise cityscape seen from the Foreign Correspondents Club.

and comprises a tight matrix of five and six storey street blocks of housing and hotels with apartments above shops, stores and cafes at ground level. The original brick and timber structures of the Chinese Quarter, dating from the 1870s, have not so much been preserved as exorbitantly refurbished and extruded upwards in a maelstrom of canopies and terraces, both ornamental in stucco work and visually chaotic.

In the central city, the Grand Palace and National Museum dominate the eastern sector adjacent to the Men Ground — the established site for royal cremations. Directly opposite is the UNESCO headquarters, converted from an old French villa. To the south of the palace was the quarter for Cambodian nobility during the colonial period, and the area has retained its exclusive associations with the political and power elite. To the north of the palace compound, Sisowath Quay comprises a collection of three and four storey terraces and adjoining shophouse streets regenerated into a vibrant matrix of cafes, restaurants and small hotels (including the Foreign Correspondents Club) together with local traders and food vendors occupying

the pavement areas. Many of the shophouses have been converted or reconstructed on an incremental basis from the port-related uses (for example chandlers and trading houses) founded by the Bordeaux merchants during the colonial era.

A project by the Atelier Parisien d'Urbanisme in conjunction with the Ministry of Culture in 1997 produced a set of urban design guidelines according to a typological analysis. Although this is a well-intentioned document, it has not provided the means of protecting older buildings and linking them within a wider regeneration and economic development framework.

Intervention of such extremes, experienced over 50 years, has bequeathed an urban residue of relief in the form of tangible threads of normality, but tinged with caution and hesitancy. This has generated a more subtle type of conflict between the resilient spirit of the population at large and the endemic corruption that holds back development of the urban economy. Newly wealthy neighbours — Vietnam, Thailand and in particular China — have injected both investment and reinforcement of ethnic participation in commercial activities in Phnom Penh. Some older buildings have been restored, but it is difficult to completely or quickly resurrect a fully regenerative urbanism from the debris of so much devastation and abandonment. The city is therefore much like an orphan with opportunistic parents rather than an embryo, with an inherited genetic structure that simply requires nurturing. While a spate of non-government organisations have underlined a potential shift in the balance of economic power, it is the street consolidation and infill that now creates the essential identity of the city — notably its densely packed but low-rise inner urban framework which now characterises the activity core.

Cambodia's growth rate has averaged four per cent per annum since 1990, but

6 Asian Development Bank,
   *Income for the Poor
   through Community-based
   Environmental Improvements
   in Phnom Penh*, September
   2002

rapid urbanisation, poor infrastructure and inadequate pollution control has contributed to over 15 per cent of Phnom Penh's population living in precarious conditions in neighbourhood communities or *Sangkats*. Grants awarded by the Asian Development Bank through the Japan Fund for Poverty Reduction have focussed on community-based self-help mechanisms to improve living and working conditions in several congested *Sangkats* in the south of the city. These measures are aimed at upgrading and rehabilitating the community infrastructure with completed facilities being maintained by the community itself. This includes community-based waste management practices, which range from collection and recycling to composting and transportation. Microcredit facilities provide loans for group investment in income-generating projects, encouraging a sense of ownership. Local residents are involved at various stages, beginning with the definition of precise needs, as well as planning and implementation.[6]

The area between Tonle Sap and Norodom Boulevard — the traditional Chinese Quarter — comprises a tight matrix of residential street terraces focussed on the old market square or Psar Chaa.

Old French Villas facing the Tonle Sap, now converted to commercial uses and UNESCO offices.

Hanoi

VIETNAM

IN THE SEVENTEENTH AND EIGHTEENTH CENTURIES Hoàn Kiếm Lake was used for naval manoeuvres and in 1739 the Khanh Thuy Palace was built on a small island in the lake. The Ngoc Son Temple was built in 1843 on the site of the old palace, and extensively renovated in 1805. It was christened Temple de Jade by the French, and is now reached by an elegant footbridge. The Hoan Kiem Lake itself represents a central recreational focus in the city, framed by residential and commercial structures that reflect the strict zoning of uses introduced under French colonial urbanisation, which projected city planning as a force for cultural progress as well as economic development.

1 Ed. Nguyen, K.C., *Preserving Hanoi's Architectural and Landscape Heritage*, Ministry of Construction Research Institute on Architecture, Construction Publishing House, Hanoi, 1999

The Quan Chuong Gate to the Old City — the only one to survive out of sixteen gate towers along the ancient ramparts. It was constructed in 1749 and restored at the beginning of the Nguyen Dynasty in 1817.

THE TERM 'VIETNAM' applies to the present unified country that formed the three component regions of French Indochina — Tonkin, Annam and Cochin-China. The present city of Hanoi was established in the fifth century under Chinese rule and transformed into the capital in the eleventh century under the name of Thang Long (Ascending Dragon). The city was virtually encircled by three rivers, with a central Royal City (IIoang Thanh) sitting within a citadel surrounded by defensive ramparts, and a separate Merchant City (Kinh Thanh) for the remainder of the population. These distinctions were marked by architectural differentiation in terms of massing, colour and decoration. A number of religious buildings were built during the eleventh and twelfth centuries that remain and form historical landmarks — the Quan Thanh Temple, Voi Phuc Temple, the One Pillar Pagoda the Văn Miêu (Temple of Literature), and Ly Quoc Su Temple. As the high-ranking mandarin city evolved according to dynastic changes, the commoner's city expanded through growing business activities, and its legacy is represented by the Thirty-six street market quarter. This dates back to 1461 when Hanoi was divided into guilds, and the area developed as both a communal housing and crafts quarter, identified with specific streets, trades and religious buildings.

The city was enlarged in the fifteenth century, and under the later Le-Trin Dynasty in the eighteenth century foreign trade grew rapidly through the English and Dutch who established trading posts. This in turn led to the expansion of the old merchant city to the east of the citadel, which was rebuilt in 1805. In 1831 the city was rechristened Hanoi, or "City in a bed of the river", but seventeen years later the palaces were destroyed and all valuables moved to a new capital, Hue.[1]

The city environment represents a multi-layered legacy of intervention, firstly through the impact of two millennia of feudal Chinese cultural predominance; then by French colonial planning from 1873 to 1954; and finally an exhaustive socialist flourish by the Soviet Union between 1955 and 1990; not withstanding American military intervention during the Vietnam War. These significant influences are amalgamated surprisingly well into a fragmented cultural and politically charged landscape that includes temples and pagodas, but also iconic remnants of French cultural domination — albeit one that assimilated certain traditional features — which characterise public buildings and private housing. Throughout this long period, Vietnam has retained both its language and identity. The city's urban design is therefore

2 Karnow, S, *Vietnam – A History*,
Penguin Books, London and
New York, 1997

Taoist places of worship
or "den" (introduced by
the Chinese) marked
the beginning of temple
construction. Temples
dedicated to Confucius are
named according to their
location. One of the best
examples is the Temple
of Literature, or Van Miêu
Quôc Tu Giam.

The entry gate to the Quan So Pagoda on Quan Su
Street, which was built in the fifteenth century and is the
headquarters of Buddhism in Vietnam.

the result of an accumulation of political and cultural heritage, symbolic of the post-modern city. More recently this has been subject to the regenerative infiltrations associated with growing economic and social pressures.

Vietnamese history since the tenth century has been based on the evolution of the dominant ethnic group the *Kinh Viet* within the geographic region that lies to the South-west of China, including Laos and Cambodia. While the eleventh century citadel that eventually became Hanoi was symbolic of an emerging Vietnamese identity, the establishment of rudimentary political boundaries have been influenced by many centuries of Chinese rule. This translated into an almost overwhelming cultural imprint through the introduction of Confucian practices, which evolved into Taoist and Buddhist institutions and even a Chinese

oriented society. It also had an impact on urban design, introducing hierarchical and regularised layouts through *phong thuy,* a cosmic symbolism attached to the orchestration of city space, in a similar way to Chinese cities.

While Vietnam had occasionally been visited by Western traders, the first European to establish a settlement was Antonio Da Faria, a Portuguese explorer who in 1535 established a harbour to the south of what is now Danang, calling it Cochin-China — based on the Chinese characters for Vietnam and China. At the time, a civil war between the northern Trinh and the southern Nguyen made east-west trade almost impossible. A catalyst to closer Western ties came from the Catholic Church, which made a deep imprint on the Country from the seventeenth century onwards, and provided a measure of freedom

from the oppressive *mandarinate*. Similar to the Chinese reaction against the arrival of foreign powers, the Vietnamese rulers feared a proselytising religion based on individual conversion and 'salvation', as this conflicted fundamentally with a Confucian respect for authority and there was the difficulty of countenancing a clear division between the temporal and the spiritual. The Confucian influence also prioritised rural agricultural production over urban commerce, slowing the city's growth. The Jesuit influence was extended through French religious leaders who formed the Society of Foreign Missions, and in the same year a group of bankers established the East India Company, ostensibly to promote trading relations. A commercial firm in Rouen, actually paid for the transportation of missionaries in exchange for their commercial services.[2]

THE CITY INCORPORATES A REALM OF RELIGIOUS STRUCTURES as an integral part of its historic fabric. The inner city districts evolved from villages and guild quarters, which each includes a communal house (*dinh*) and temple (*dên*). Many of these remain, presenting both a physical and spiritual landscape contained within the street fabric. The communal house evolved from the spiritual needs and customs of each gild or community, as places of worship, ceremonial performance and gathering. The deity might represent the village founder or a god, so the building sometimes had the combined attributes of temple and ancestral hall. Thus their design was formally inter-twined with cultural traditions, agricultural cycles, and land development issues. It was also where urban affairs and concerns were discussed. The active participation and contribution of all members of the community in building and decorative embellishment acted to strengthen the sense of joint identity and destiny. This depicts the entry gate to the Ngu Giap Communal House on Hang Cot Street in the old city.

Like temples and pagodas, the location, orientation and disposition of building components were subject to geomantic principles, having a highly visible and symbolic profile. The entrance gate, which historically demarcated the formal access to a building via an internal courtyard, remains as a sculptural and decorative element in the contemporary streetscape. Stylised script and symbolic characters on the outer street wall and gateway express such terms as longevity, prosperity and happiness. The outer wall and decorated entrance therefore relates both physically and spiritually to the public realm, orchestrating a spatial buffer between the street, the court and the central place of ceremony. As the guilds themselves have evolved from traditional craft villages and urban enclaves, so the communal house and its identifiable street presence acts to consolidate the heritage and cultural ties between craft traditions and new or emerging urban street functions. Their role serves more than that of historic monument — their active presence in the community relates equally to continuing societal traditions. Vertical inscriptions of text adjoining the opening give an account of the locality and the building construction.

[3] Logan, W, 'Hanoi townscape: symbolic imagery in Vietnam's capital', in *Cultural Identity and Urban Change in Southeast Asia: Interpretative Essays*, Eds. Marc Askew and William S. Logan, Deakin University Press, Geelong, 1994

THE OLD MERCHANT CITY

The old merchant city is known as the "Thirty-six streets and guilds quarter". The guilds date back to the twelfth century, and constituted discrete areas where people involved in the same crafts lived and worked in activities such as pottery manufacture, paper making and dyeing. The merchant city was consolidated during the fifteenth century. The streets became marketplaces for specialized crafts, demarcated by temples, pagodas and communal houses, and surrounded by agricultural villages, lakes, rivers and canals. The Vietnamese word for street pho is said to derive from the Chinese character meaning "wharf". The names of streets still indicate the merchandise traditionally made and sold within each guild area, although the current product range now varies widely. Foreign traders, including Chinese merchants, established themselves on certain streets. The shophouses are still run by artisans and traders, centred along Hang Chieu Street, which is demarcated by one remaining gate tower.

The underlying fabric of the Old City accommodates 21,920 households and 84,000 residents in an area of less than 100 hectares. A preservation plan for the area was issued by Government in 1995, and development control plans for the protection and preservation of the area later set out urban design criteria for renovation in terms of height, façade treatment and materials. However the older fabric has been increasingly threatened through poor and unauthorized renovation work. In 2009 civic authorities announced they were seeking approval to move one-third of residents in the Ancient Quarter to high-rise estates in Viet Hung on the city's outskirts. Market reforms have indirectly associated the Thirty-Six Streets quarter as an attraction to tourists and visitors, although it continues to suffer from inadequate infrastructure, uncontrolled traffic penetration, chaotic construction

NOTABLE STREETS adopting the names of traditional craft guilds include Hang Bac (Silversmith Street), Hang Bo (Basket Street), Hang Dao (Silk Street), Hang Luoc (Comb Street) and Hang Ca (Fish Street). Until the mid-nineteenth century, buildings in the old city had to adhere to the royal 'Annamite Code' which forbade consumers from erecting buildings in a solid construction of over one storey, and also prohibited excessive decoration.[3]

4 Balderstone, S and Logan, W, 'Vietnamese Dwellings: Tradition, Resilience, and Change', in *Asia's old dwellings Tradition, Resilience, and Change*, Ed. Ronald G Knapp, Oxford University Press, New York, 2003, p135-157

THE TRADITIONAL HOUSE DESIGN in the old city, with wood panelling along the street frontage and sloping roofs parallel to the street, began to change in the early twentieth century to encompass balconies, cornices, arched and rectangular window openings, balustrades and decorative embellishments including pilasters. Redevelopment gradually took place within street blocks through sub-division, leading to the typical "tube houses" — similar to the barrel houses of Canton — perpendicular to the street with narrow shophouse façades constructed in the early twentieth century. The average width varies between two and four metres but with a depth of up to sixty metres. Doorways or open entrances lead directly to lateral passages that provide access to a sequence of communal spaces and courtyards. The latter maximise natural light and usually contain a well or stand-pipe, and in some cases an open staircase to upper levels. Private domestic spaces, which might be occupied by several families, also open off these passages. While the lateral wall line is solid, light and ventilation are introduced through the tall first floor window openings. This configuration of uses encourages a high level of domestic interaction, which increases with building density. Washing of clothes, cooking and eating is done in the courts and on the pavement, which is regarded as part of the private territory associated with the shophouse. This becomes a neighbourly gathering place particularly at certain times. Courtyards technically allow for natural ventilation and light, although many of these have now been filled in to provide additional living accommodation. This together with the redevelopment of the older two-storey street front 'trading' section into units of up to six storeys, has given the old city a much greater physical and population density.

A WIDESPREAD DESIGN TOOL employed in traditional timber framed Kinh Viet dwellings is a gian module which divides the structure into spans based on the available lengths of timber for beams. Similarly, early shophouses had a consistent regularity of form and spacing. According to wealth and social standing these could encompass between one and five gian (although they might have different overall depths and height), and a basic unit of measurement, a thuoc, that is now standardised at 0.40 metres.[4] Other aspects of design were influenced by Chinese geomantic traditions — phong thuy or feng shui which determined the forces of orientation, screening and landscape. Continuing renewal and redevelopment has instigated a longing for tradition, particularly among the 'one-gian tube houses' — a variation on the bamboo barrel houses found in Guangzhou, possibly reflecting the traditional Chinese influence in Vietnamese culture. These are made of local brick or concrete with stucco work, timber floors, roof framing, window shutters and doors. In the old city the terraced units share party walls, with the front space acting as a shop, and a series of two-storey units extending behind, divided by open courts, and protected by pergolas. This provides for a compact matrix of uses at a high physical density, and maximises the street frontage.

5 Karnow, 1997, op. cit.
6 Karnow, 1997, op. cit.

7 Luan, T.D., 'Hanoi : Balancing
   Market and Ideology', in *Culture
   and the City in East Asia*,
   Clarendon Press, Oxford, 1997,
   p174

and poor housing conditions that threaten to overwhelm its cultural heritage and traditional streetscape.

THE COLONIAL PERIOD 1861-1954

In response to the imprisonment of a French missionary, Dominique Lefebvre, a French force under Napoleon III was sent to attack three Vietnamese ports and in July 1861 claimed the city of Saigon for France. The Vietnamese ruler had no option but to cede three southern provinces of Cochin-China and open up several ports around the Mekong delta for trade with France. One of the early French governors of Cochin-China, Admiral La Grandieve, extended control over Cambodia and in 1867 unilaterally occupied the remaining provinces that were not already in French hands.[5]

Following French military intervention in 1873 under the Philastre Agreement, a new commercial and residential quarter in Hanoi was laid out by the colonial authorities to adjoin the Red River, and this was gradually extended to the west. The broad avenues, 20 to 30 metres wide and lined with stuccoed villas and street planting, not only evoke French town planning of the period, but were similar to those occuring in the French Concession Area in Shanghai built in the same period. The emerging urban design was orchestrated by French architects, planners and engineers, and apart from new military installations, a new road matrix was laid out along the axis of Rue Paul Bert (now Trang Tien Street) that linked the French Quarter of Hoan Kiem and the citadel. An enthusiasm for comprehensive renewal led to the destruction of anything that stood in its way — for example in the eastern sector a new French government complex was built on the site of an old religious precinct, and a new Governor General's residence necessitated demolition of the ancient Mieu Hoi Dong Pagoda.[6]

As France itself gradually became a republican battleground and nationalist sentiments gained credence, there was a feeling that it had, like other empire-building countries, a 'divine and civilising mission'. New voyages of exploration confirmed the abundance of wealth in South-west China flowing through Vietnam to the Gulf of Tonkin. In 1883 France concluded a treaty which gave them unconditional control over Tonkin in the north, and Annan in the centre. In 1885 — virtually at the same time as the Treaty of Shimonoseki was forcing a fractured China to make considerable indemnity payments and concessions to the occupying powers — France, Britain, Germany and Russia received permission to build or extend new rail connections, including those between Hanoi and Kunming in China. Also in a similar manner to the sacking of the Summer Palace in Peking, in 1885 French troops burned the Vietnamese imperial library — a massive act

of colonial vandalism. They then brought together the separate and culturally diverse Kingdoms of Laos and Cambodia within the Federation of 1893.

From this time Hanoi became the central city of the Union Indochinoise Francaise, which led to a large-scale reconstruction programme. The Kinh Thien palace within the citadel, which dated back to the eleventh century, was demolished and the old city expanded with wide boulevards bordered by brick buildings, linking it with the French Concession to the south. Tran Hung Dao served as the southern limit to the new quarter. Older water courses were rationalised and the central Hoàn Kiếm Lake was reconfigured with wide landscaped promenades. A series of public buildings and monuments were erected, and a more spacious urban quarter replaced the citadel. At the same time, the traditional craft markets extending along the streets were relocated into four covered markets, of which the Dong Xuan market remains. The alignment of the citadel walls are now 'engraved' into the city fabric by the streets of Phan Dinh Phung, Phung Hung, Hung Vuong and Tran Phu. Three historic areas have been conserved within the citadel — Doan Mon (gate of Kinh Palace), Bac Mon (Northern Gate) and the Hau Lau palace. To the west of the citadel, the Ba Dinh quarter, together with the colonial administrative buildings and villas, have been transformed into the political, diplomatic and cultural centre of Hanoi. The old French (Hoan Keim) Quarter is now the economic and commercial heart of the city.

The defeat of Russian forces by the

Japanese at the Battle of Shenyang in 1905 stirred up wide Chinese and Vietnamese patriotic sentiment, and many leading political and revolutionary figures, including Sun Yat-sen, began to regard Japan as a leading Asian example of nationalism and socialism. Under French occupation, political reform became secondary to business interests, and this turned a significant number of educated and influential Vietnamese into revolutionaries. The most prominent was Ho Chi Minh who applied to the Colonial Secretariat for admittance to a Government School. He assimilated the philosophical ideas of Voltaire on self-determination, which matched his increasingly Socialist leanings — a potent mix of patriotism and Communism. After years of exile in the Soviet Union and other parts of Asia he slipped back unnoticed into Vietnam in early 1941 where he and others formed the Vietnam Independence League, or Vietminh.

After 1945, the Viet Minh took control of Hanoi and declared Vietnamese independence. However the following year

Hanoi was recaptured by a united force of French, British and Chinese, bringing about more than thirty years of armed conflict. French involvement ended with the battle of Dien Bien Phu in 1954, and Vietnam was divided along the 17th parallel. In 1975 Hanoi became the capital of the Socialist Republic of Vietnam and forged a new economic and cultural allegiance with the Soviet Union, hence becoming even further entrenched when other forms of economic aid from the West dried up. During this period, Socialist icons in the form of administrative and military buildings, memorials and Ho Chi Minh's Mausoleum were imposed on key symbolic sites around Ba Dinh Square, creating a sterile assembly of monuments, while large areas of prefabricated social housing were built in outlying areas. New plans for Hanoi were drawn up by Soviet planners in 1973, which exceeded the previous French master plans only in the extent of their controlling ambitions and defiance of cultural and financial reality. In practice few of the planning proposals were implemented,

and overcrowding in the inner city caused building conditions to deteriorate. Since 1990, when the Soviet Union withdrew from Vietnam, the country has gradually developed a more liberal ideology of economic reform — *Doi Moi* — based on a multi-sectoral urban market economy and privatisation of state-owned enterprises.[7] This has opened up Vietnam to more international economic influences, and the fabric of Hanoi, Saigon and other cities continues to undergo transformation through private investment and development. Technically, state legislation has been in place since 1984 to protect historic buildings, and a number of prominent French colonial structures have been restored by funds from the French Government and are now utilised for major Government uses and embassies.

THE POLITICS OF DESIGN

Gwendolyn Wright has explored the politics of design in French colonial urbanism and traces its distinctive locales in Indochina. A revealing aspect of this was a policy that sought to address the types of urban problems familiar in late nineteenth century France, while attempting to assimilate cultural differences, as a model for metropolitan cities.[8] At the time young French architects and urban designers such as Tony Garnier, Henri Prost and Ernest Hébrard were moving away from the classical aesthetic tradition to a more contextual and urbanized approach that related to new economic, social and industrial development. This 'new order' was exemplified by Garnier's design for a *Cité Industrielle*, and Hébrard's proposals for a *Centre Mondial*, both of them theoretical studies which projected the city as a force for cultural progress, and artistic as well as economic development. From this, and the opening of the Parisian *Ecole Coloniale*, stemmed ideas for the integration of oriental references into new architectural projects. Urban designers therefore embarked on an experimental mission, which in theory protected indigenous traditions but acknowledged the cultural predominance of the mother country along with its embedded but hotly debated 'civilising mission'. This type of intervention by stealth tended to imply a gradual transformation of indigenous systems and traditional cultural forms, where French cultural emblems predominated. Hanoi and Saigon were the beneficiaries of lavish public buildings, including opera houses, even before the installation of proper city infrastructure. Borrowing from colonial precedents in North Africa, the idea of "dual cities" was introduced. Alongside the forms of existing cities and within carefully delineated zoning plans, expansive *villes nouvelle* were constructed which extolled the virtues of modern Western urbanism. These aspects, in combination, set out a controlling but problematic role for French colonial urbanism.

Wright states that after 1874 free land concessions were given to Europeans providing that they built on them within three years. Spacious boulevards were laid out as a miniature version of Haussmann's Paris model but without its grand compositional elements, and named after notable French luminaries.[9] The governor-general's palace in Saigon was broadly based on Versailles, and an international architectural competition was held for the Notre Dame Cathedral in 1875. The Hôtel de Ville was based on the baroque original in Paris that had been destroyed by the Communards. In practice the main rail lines were little used for many years, but provided opportunities for grand stations in Hanoi and Saigon.

The assimilation of the culturally disparate parts of Indochina within the French empire took some time, and reflected shifts in "protectorate" policy and priorities. In 1879, the launch of the "Third Republic" in France signalled a move to civilian government, which was marked by a burst of urban extravagance and artifice that extended to colonial undertakings. In Hanoi a cathedral was built in 1888 on the site of the demolished Bao Thein pagoda. The Hanoi opera house was constructed within a few years of Garnier's Paris Opera, and completed in 1911. At the same time political instability and constant changes of government in Indochina created a vacuum which tended to be countered by new tranches of city building, superimposed on the older and poorly populated citadel towns.

From 1888, Hanoi was transformed through new layouts and the reconstruction of Rue Paul Bert into a fashionable avenue similar to Rue Catinet in Saigon, lined with flowering trees. Moats around the citadel in Hanoi were filled in to form roads, in a similar way to the canals in Phnom Penh and those in Bangkok.

In 1900 the capital of the Indochinese Federation was moved to Hanoi — the new Council Building was the first to be built as a hybrid of indigenous architectural motifs, cultural prototypes and modern construction, and this was later extended to other public buildings. The enormous but sparsely decorated Lycée Sarraut was situated on a direct axis with the new neo-Classical palace for the Governor-general in Hanoi, suggesting a clear hierarchy of ties between government goals and educational priorities. The new *Ecole Française d'Extrême-Orient*, was founded in 1899 to carry out research on historic monuments and provide specialised archaeological services. This later helped to preserve a number of Buddhist pagodas and palace monuments in Hanoi, and to supervise the recording and part-restoration of the temple cities at Angkor Wat in Cambodia.

In 1920 a new technical council was established, and Ernest Hébrard was appointed as its head. Hébrard was the most notable architect of the period. Schooled in Beaux-Arts urban design traditions, he perceived his influential role as that of an urbanist, possibly in the same mold as Ildefons Cerda in Barcelona. As an experienced urban designer he had already drawn up guidelines and design codes for Thessalonika and Athens, and swiftly immersed himself in the Indochinese urban cultural habitat, seeking to discern its historical underpinnings, climatic responsiveness and stylistic forms. This established a somewhat self-conscious basis for amalgamating indigenous architectural characteristics with design innovations associated with French modernism, together with the means to resolve contemporary problems such as traffic planning. It arguably illustrated a greater degree of sensibility than the flamboyant Indic–Saracenic designs devised by British architects in Indian cities, or the Moorish style Government Office Complex and Post Office in Kuala Lumpur, in terms of juggling mixed references from various countries and traditions. However at an urban level, Hébrard did not fully grasp the many political and social nuances enveloping Vietnam beyond the purely aesthetic.

In 1921 Hébrard drew up plans for

8 Wright, G, *The Politics of Design in French Colonial Urbanism*, University of Chicago Press, Chicago, 1991
9 Wright, 1991, op. cit., p177
10 Luan, 1997, op. cit., p174

Vietnam's main cities, and in Hanoi introduced a strict zoning of uses, including the *plan d'amenagement et d'extension* which set out broad building parameters for axial streets and boulevards, and compartmentalised zoning — although this was only partially implemented. The plan evolved as a series of town houses that combined characteristics of Hanoi's terraced shophouses with French garden villas. The majority of residents were middle-class Vietnamese. The resultant cultural layering, through an amalgam of styles within a well-defined and robust urban framework, was later overseen by Louis-Gorges Pineau in 1943. Its blend of the neo-Classical and Art Deco into a supposed style *indochinois*, with characteristic large shaded terraces, overhanging eaves and high shuttered doorways, provide evocative examples of climatic design. Eventually this led to a master plan and a series of public buildings that broke with the past and introduced new ideas based on international modernism. The result is an exotic blend of grand planning with carefully zoned residential, commercial and industrial land uses. In so doing it possibly revealed an adaptive approach to architectural design, much as the Beaux-Arts movement in Europe blended classical details with the opulence of the baroque to form a new artistic ornamentalism.

Meanwhile economic growth — through massive increase in rice production and rubber plantations — began to transform Vietnamese cities, introducing new European commercial, shipping and banking districts, set well apart from concentrations of factories, processing areas and go-downs. However the majority of public works went into projects that benefitted colonial investments outside the cities such as roads and hydraulic irrigation systems. Hébrard's approach to urbanism, which demanded full artistic control, was out of step with the political and economic realities, and largely unfavourable to the interests of private investment priorities. While French and Vietnamese establishments existed together in the commercial quarters of Hanoi and Saigon, European and native residential districts were planned in separate but not entirely segregated ways. However, like Indian cities under the British, segregation was effectively introduced through specific land allocations, together with the introduction of different layout and sanitary standards which reinforced separateness rather than regulated it — the archetype of intervention through imposed colonial city space.

Hébrard's preoccupation with urban design as a cultural component of French colonialism became directed towards proposals for a new government district in Hanoi. This projected a strong axial plan that placed ministry buildings in a parkland setting, with the governor's palace at the head. Three commercial boulevards were intended to traverse the former citadel and terminate at colonial monuments, but changes in political direction curtailed most of the grandiose projects apart from the Ministry of Finance, completed in 1927. Other significant architectural works that best represent Hébrard's ambitions to fashion a harmonious urbanism based on the assimilation of cultural characteristics, were the Institute Pasteur in Hanoi — now the Microbiology Institute, and the National History Museum.

CONTEMPORARY FORCES OF CHANGE

Following independence a new master plan was prepared by Soviet planners. During the socialist period after 1955 and for almost thirty years thereafter, most city planning followed the intrusive ideology of the state, and was given over to public buildings and flamboyant examples of socialist architecture, including regimented rows of medium-rise public housing blocks typified by the Nguyen Cong Tu area south of Hanoi. The *microrayon* or self-contained communal quarters that housed up to 60,000 people were not dissimilar in form and content to the *danwei* that formed the controlled neighbourhoods of Chinese cities during the Maoist period.

At the Sixth Communist Party Congress in 1986, Vietnam adopted reforms based on a multi-sectoral urban market economy or *Doimoi*. This represented a shift from a centrally planned economy to a market economy under certain regulatory conditions, and a broad opening up to the outside world.[10] As the capital city this has led to rapid economic growth in new businesses, services and manufacturing in Hanoi, and privatisation of state-owned enterprises. A post-modernist upgrading has been taking place since the early 1990s which has involved the privatisation of land and an outburst of speculative building activities within and

[11] Casault, A, 'Endangered Street Life: Building Frontages and Street Activities in Hanoi', in *Public Places in Asia Pacific Cities*, Ed. Pu Miao, Kluwer Academic Publishers, Dordrecht, 2001

[12] Logan, W.S., 'The Golden Hanoi and Heritage Protection in Vietnam's Capital : Containing Cultural Globalisation', in *The Disappearing Asian City*, Oxford University Press, Oxford, 2002

of building frontage, development intensity and the capacity for street front activities.[11]

Outside the old merchant city, there is still a substantial amount of two storey indigenous and French Colonial street architecture in the form of shophouse and row house terraces. In residential areas such as Hai Ba Trung to the south of the Hoan Kiem "central" commercial district, there are more established villa-type residences on large sites, and smaller row houses built originally on individual plots for middle-class French and Vietnamese government workers. In both areas there is a significant amount of redevelopment with predominantly low-rise housing being replaced by infill blocks with a more high-rise profile — prescribed by the amalgamation of lots — to meet the design requirements of offices and hotels. Thus the pattern of small lots is gradually coalescing, although the active street frontage is generally maintained. Continuous commercial frontage and colonisation of pavement areas for public display and domestic activities still provides a matrix of local utility establishments. As residential densities are increased and conditions upgraded through redevelopment, the residential component becomes more divorced from the street, while ground level retail space becomes more valuable and open to more up-scale activities.

William Logan points out that the lack of strong central planning opened the door for more 'spontaneous' planning activities by individuals outside the formal control system. This resulted from land reform and the growth of private enterprises in the 1980s, which led to greatly increased levels of household investment. While the 2010 Hanoi Master Plan represents continued centralisation of planning control, in practice the process is quite decentralised but within "broadly understood parameters" that represent a long history of contestation over planning and heritage issues.[12]

around suburban Hanoi. The current city plan aims to extend urban growth to the south, and along the north edge of the Red River, with consolidation of the Ba Dinh quarter as the political centre. This is transforming the landscape of the city, as older buildings are replaced by high rise residential, commercial and hotel developments in central locations. Meanwhile the urban fringe forms a pastiche of closely-packed two to four storey housing blocks whose designs can only reflect a prodigious reaction to the years of austerity, but interspersed with semi-rural paddy fields and farm houses.

In a similar way to Chinese city growth, a combination of urban migration, the withdrawal of the state from housing provision, and decentralisation of planning and economic control are together creating a new realm of urbanisation which does not exclude adaptive re-use of older structures and heritage buildings, along with *phong thuy* — a continued respect for the integral urban

components of Buddhist shrines, temples, and communal houses, but with equal regard for the residue of Catholicism and its built artefacts. The remaining iconic religious buildings — notably Buddhist temples and pagodas, together with distinctive 'communal' houses — reflects the mix of strong Chinese influence with localised construction techniques, although these commonly represent the end result of re-building and restoration to very similar styles.

In older residential streets, two-storey structures built in the colonial period are typically set back from the street by a front yard, with a symmetrical arrangement of façade elements, balconies which extend along the entire frontage, and internal courtyards. Along certain streets these layout characteristics have proved useful for their conversion to cafes and restaurants with climatically comfortable sitting-out areas, secluded terraces and outward street spaces. In the process, this retains the configuration

STREET ACTIVITIES themselves can be divided into: permanent shops, fixed pitches, temporary or mobile uses. Mobile vendors continually patrol the street selling food, fruit, vegetables and tea. Hawkers sell household goods from bicycles or cooked food from pushcarts. Fixed pitch stalls act as street cafes and are often temporary in nature but occupy a permanent position under shaded awnings or trees where they need not interfere with other busy street activities.

THE PHILIPPINES

Manila

THE PLAZA MAYOR OR TOWN PLAZA was introduced as a distinctive urban design feature by Spanish city builders. It was often associated with the forecourt of a church and as an organisational feature around which the principal streets were formed. These spaces continue to provide a setting for everyday life in the city, as both a meeting place and market place. Quiapo Church on Recto Avenue is home to the Black Nazarene, brought from Mexico in the seventeenth century. The church was rebuilt in 1935 on the site of earlier models dating back to 1586. In front of the church is Plaza Miranda, which acts as a stage for activities, and a locus for local market streets which sell herbs, flowers, shoes, tailoring services and tin manufacture. Public markets are places where people conduct business with regular patrons in a social as well as a trading sense. As a predominantly Catholic country, almost all shopping malls have spaces which can be converted to venues for celebrating holy mass at prescribed times of day.

METRO MANILA is located on the west coast floodplain of Luzon facing Manila Bay, and bounded on the east by the Sierra Madre volcanic hills. It has a population in excess of 12 million and covers an area of around 636 square kilometres. If the six surrounding provinces of Pampanga, Laguna, Cavite, Batangas, Rizal and Bulacan are included, the urban region contains one quarter of the total Philippine population and generates around 30 per cent of the nation's GDP. While the country extends 1810 kilometres from north to south, representing the world's second largest archipelago with 7,107 islands, the two largest islands, Luzon and Mindanao, contain two-thirds of the population. Despite its size, the land area is only 300,000 square kilometres.

Metro Manila has developed in three stages: firstly as the Spanish city of Intramuros which gradually grew to incorporate twelve surrounding settlements; secondly after the introduction of American rule in 1898 when the various townships were incorporated into the city of Manila which continued to expand through the growth of manufacturing industry; and thirdly after independence in 1946.

By the mid-sixteenth century the area around the Pasig River was the largest coastal settlement in Luzon and home to a prominent Muslim community in the Namayan area. While the Philippines had established trading connections, particularly with Chinese merchants, there is scant evidence of complex urban settlements or socio-political integration prior to the Spanish occupation. Manila's indigenous people were the Tagalog who lived and traded around the Pasig delta, and prior to the Spanish arrival were a mainly Muslim community ruled by Sultans. By 1565, the major influence was through the Islamic city of Brunei, with emergent Muslim settlements along the Luzon and Mindanao coasts, where the *barangay* or indigenous local communities formed tenuous

associations throughout the archipelago, rather than urban concentrations. These depended on the agricultural practice of *swidden* which necessitated a cyclical rotation of basic crops, so that settlements had no "social surplus" and were therefore both impermanent and decentralised.

The island chain was first visited by Ferdinand Magellan in 1521, while searching for a westward route across the Pacific, during which time he became the first navigator to encircle the globe. However it was not until the expedition of Miguel López de Legazpi in a voyage from Mexico to the Philippines, that the islands were claimed for Spain. It marked the beginning of 333 years of Spanish rule and 117 Spanish governors general.

The first Spanish base was Cebu where the City of Santisimo Nombre de Jesus was founded in 1565, but food supply shortages forced them to withdraw before finally finding a secure anchorage in Manila Bay at the mouth of the Pasig River in April 1571. The Spanish were able to obtain a major foothold in the northern Philippines, as the diverse collection of small Sultanates lacked any centralised organisation. Some forty years later in 1597, the Spanish narrowly avoided naval defeat by the Dutch who destroyed the Spanish fleet in Manila Bay, but attacks gradually ceased after 1662 when Holland became more preoccupied by the Spice Trade with the Moluccas and their lucrative trading links with Japan.

A telling part of the colonisation process was the introduction of the *encomienda* — allocation of large land holdings to Spanish followers and prominent citizens which served as both a means of ordering land ownership and development, while generating an intensification of agriculture and food production. Everything outside the City of Manila, including planning, was left to clerics who maintained Spanish hegemony and gradually accumulated vast tracts of land. Catholicism found a receptive context in the

KAART van de FILIPPYNSE, CELEBES, en MOLUKSE-EILANDEN.

(Above) The printed image through a process called Xylography or woodcut, followed by a more conventional printing process in 1604, fabricated by Christian converts. One of the most elaborate books of the eighteenth century is Flora de Filipinas by Fr Manuel Blanco, in four volumes. It is said that the name "Manila" is derived from the Ixora Manila identified in this early book. Blanco was responsible for laying out the tropical garden at San Agustin. (Below, right) Intramuros Manila, 1650

close pattern of kinship, and the innocent superstitions previously focussed towards the benevolent spirits of animism were easily re-directed to divine intervention from the repertoire of Christian saints. The widespread acceptance of a single sovereign deity and the subjugation and tribute payments that accompanied this, evolved under Spanish rule as an almost supernatural experience where religious icons, guardian deities and key buildings came to be associated with legendary powers bestowed with invincibility — something that has since been handed down through religious festivals, morality plays, processions and pilgrimages.

The development of a city plan in accordance with Hispanic Law was a symbolic act which gave notice of Spain's long-term intentions. The Spanish complex took the form of a walled city — Intramuros — that was laid out in a formal plan with separate quarters for Spanish and other ethnic groups, including the indigenous Filipinos. It grew to incorporate twelve surrounding settlements. Defensive moats and turreted walls made of volcanic tufa helped the city overcome periodic attacks from various

Japanese and Dutch and Portuguese fleets in the seventeenth century, but also forced a prolonged insularism. Only members of the Castilian gentry were privileged to live in the walled city. Three gates faced the river, two faced the bay, and a further two connected the walled city to outlying ethnic quarters. These areas were made up of native *mestizo* communities, and Chinese in the Christian Chinese commercial districts of Binondo and Tondo across the Pasig River, along with small Armenian and Japanese settlements. The large Chinese community outside the city walls was vital to the economy, importing porcelain, silks and furnishings from China for other parts of Asia, and re-exporting merchandise to Mexico through the galleon trade. This provided the main source of Manila's early wealth and power.

The built components of the old city, around the four kilometre perimeter, survive in the form of walls and reconstructed buildings, flanked by Bonifacio Drive and Roxas Boulevard. The substantially re-built houses in the existing area of Intramuros provide an indication of the older stone and brick structures, with elaborate iron

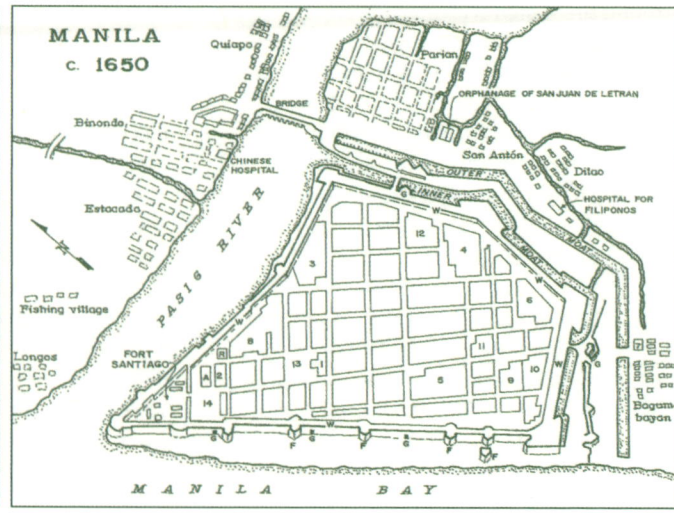

grillwork, impressive entrances, balconies and courtyards.

DEVELOPMENT OF THE CITY

The development of Manila as a primate city, following its Hispanic foundation, took on a distinctive pattern of urbanism. The formation of the new colonial capital adhered to pre-established organising principles applied by the Spanish to their South American colonial cities. The urbanisation process under which the Philippines was colonised by the Spanish *conquistadores*, differed from any other part of Asia. While the Portuguese, Dutch and British, prior to the nineteenth century, were primarily concerned with commercial endeavours, Spanish imperialism had been honed in the Americas through territorial expansion, economic exploitation and cultural transformation as part of an expanding empire. They were thus able to draw on considerable city-building experience in a situation where urbanisation was seen as a means of exerting political and religious control over the population.

THE PLAZA SAN LUIS is a cultural complex built in the seventeenth century Spanish style and houses the Casa Manila museum, constructed with adobe volcanic tuff originally quarried in Makati and Bulacan. Its façade was reproduced from a house at Calle Jaboneros in San Nicolas. Traditionally in this area the first floor of houses was rented to shopkeepers, and extended over the pavements to shade pedestrians and protect the stability of living quarters during earthquakes.

INTRAMUROS is a place of history and imagination. The oldest Western colonised city in Asia, it suffered periodic conflagration from earthquake, fire and military conflict. Its built structures were therefore almost constantly re-built and its streets and spaces reconfigured. It is now, despite ongoing efforts to restore individual buildings and fortifications, a skeleton but with some of its body parts still living and breathing. Its demise came in February 1945, when fires lit by retreating Japanese troops were met by bombardment from Americans under General McArthur, who had vowed to retake the city and succeeded in largely demolishing it.

From 1945 until the 1960s Intramuros was abandoned as its various religious orders rebuilt churches elsewhere — some to Quezon City, others to Quiapo and Pasay City, while the University of Santo Tomas moved to the Sampaloc district. Only San Agustin Church and Manila Cathedral were repaired or rebuilt. In many instances the stone was used for new constructions, and it was only in 1979 that the Intramuros Administration was established with a plan for re-zoning the area and rebuilding certain features such as the Parian Gate. The Administration has since built Casa Manila (a house museum), carried out restoration of Fort Santiago, and regenerated Plaza Roma, Plaza Sampalucan and Puerto St Lucia.

INTRAMUROS was laid out according to the codified urbanisation ordinances of 1573, which consisted of a street grid with open plazas which both offset major public buildings, and served as places for congregation. The walled city enclave of 0.6 square kilometres never changed in size. The principal streets were associated with the Plaza Mayor flanked on the south by the Cathedral, on the west by the Palacio del Gobernador or Governor's residence, and on the east by the Ayuntamiento or city hall which became the Government Centre during the American administration. The Calle Real connected this space with a network of principal and secondary streets that divided the city into sixty-four blocks within four barrios: San Antonio facing the river, San Carlos facing the bay, San Luis and San Gabriel. The Calle Real del Palacio continued northwards across the Puente de España to connect with the northern districts of Binondo, San Nicolas and Tondo. As Manila was a coastal city, the Plaza Mayor was constructed close to the Pasig River, although later reclamation extended the land area further to the west. Land was set aside for Augustine missionaries and for a royal hospital. Although Intramuros evolved into a centre for religious activities, it was also a centre for fiestas, processions, open-air theatres, and bull-fights. The processions live on in the commemorations of the Black Nazarene in Quiapo, the Virgen de Lourdes in Quezon City, and the Virgin de los Remedios in Malate.

From this imperial outpost the Spanish acquired territorial gains in neighbouring countries, and as a result of its European supremacy over Portugal as part of a Crown Union from 1580, the latter's territorial gains in Asia became prey to other colonial powers. After the Dutch occupied the Portuguese port of Malacca in 1641, Manila was to grow into the most important Iberian city in Asia, and was gradually transformed into a political and religious centre. However it was also an entrepôt, forming a basis for the trans-Pacific galleon trade between China and the New World through the newly discovered Eastern Passage. Beginning in 1565 the galleon trade between the coast of Mexico and the Philippines became so great, that the body of water was known as the "Spanish Lake". A significant aspect of this was acceleration of Sino-Filipino–Hispanic commercial trade flows, with Chinese luxury goods in silk, porcelain and perfume transhipped through Manila to Hispanic America. It was later regulated to prevent market saturation. The galleon trade itself led to a rapid rise in population. This provided little incentive to develop local resources, but instead introduced large numbers of Chinese merchants to participate in the direct junk trade with China, which discouraged the development of local production. Out of a population in excess of 40,000 in 1620, there were almost as many Chinese as Filipinos, and more Japanese than Spaniards, with a cosmopolitan collection of transient labourers, craftsmen, traders and mariners from different parts of Asia.

The "ideal" colonial city form itself, evolved from the planning and layout of more than 200 colonial cities in the America *conquista* such as Mexico City founded by Hernando Cortes. The Spanish laid out cities in accordance with the Laws of the Indies or *Ordinanzas* of 1573, which established the basis for governing Spanish colonial settlements. The parameters, orchestrated through Philip II, were uniquely designed to guide the siting of buildings and spaces. Prior to this there was communal ownership of land, but this was replaced under the Spanish by the *encomienda* system where enormous tracts were awarded to the military and Catholic orders, which altered the course of urbanisation and economic life up to the present time. Settlements were classified according to the capital city or *ciudad*, smaller cities or *ciudades* and townships or *cabeceras*.

In 1513 a royal order directed the following: "The places chosen for settlement [should] ... be healthy and not swampy, good for unloading goods [if ports]; if inland to be on a river [near to]... good water and air, and close to arable land ... In view of these things necessary, for settlements, and seeking the best site in these terms for the town,

1 Reed, R.R., *Colonial Manila – The Context of Hispanic Urbanisation and Process of Morphogenesis*, University of California Press, Berkeley, 1978, p39
2 Reed, 1978, op. cit., p40

then divide the plots for houses, these to be according to the status of the persons, and from the beginning it should be according to a definite arrangement; for the manner of setting up the lots will determine the pattern of the town, both in the position of the plaza and the church and in the pattern of streets, for towns being newly founded may be established according to plan without difficulty. If not started with form, they will never attain it".[1]

Robert R Reed has speculated that the major feature of such cities — the rigid grid design and the orderly arrangement of both public and private buildings — may have been derived from the Roman scholar Vitruvius. These ideas came to the fore in the works of Leone Battista Alberti, the sixteenth century Renaissance designer, whose 'ideal city' doctrines of urban theory set out in *Ten Books on Architecture* were in vogue at the time and used in the planning of Italian cities. In terms of urban design this implied a monumental plaza, a grid layout, small squares of various functions, planned prospects and wide thoroughfares.[2]

While the master plan for Intramuros in Manila was not entirely based on the *Ordinanzas*, the integrated layout and overall morphology is nevertheless quite consistent with its fundamental precepts. Accordingly the layout was apportioned to the Spaniards in sixty-four equal city blocks, divided into the barrios of San Antonio, San Gabriel, San Luis, and San Carlos, and was laid out with well-arranged streets and squares. Streets were laid out so that one side was always shaded. A further square was located in relation to the fort and royal buildings. The extravagant blueprint for Intramuros was formulated by Legazpi, and successive governors constructed the cathedral, eighteen churches, convents, schools, a hospital, a university and a printing press where the first book in Spanish, *Doctrina Cristiana* was printed.

San Agustin church and monastery, completed in 1607 under the supervision of Fr. Antonio Herrera, has five interconnected baroque chapels, and houses the largest ecclesiastical museum in the Philippines. It is the oldest stone building in Manila, and is one of four Baroque Churches in the Philippines to be designated as a World Heritage Site by UNESCO, in 1993.

The Zaguan was the area where horse-drawn carriages deposited church-goers. Benches were provided for the coachmen.

Religious buildings, palaces and barracks were laid out on a regular pattern of street blocks. The main street was Calle Real where stone Chinese lions provide an ambiguous gateway to San Agustin Church, built on the site of the first church of Intramuros dating from 1606. This houses the remains of the first conquistadores, including Legazpi, early governors and archbishops.

Intramuros can be literally translated as "within walls". The first fortifications were carried out in 1574 to stave off an attack by the Chinese Limahong, but the first stone walls were constructed some twenty years later. The earliest map of Manila by Ignacio Munoz in 1670 shows fortifications largely in place, although these were constantly repaired and reinforced until 1872. In the early seventeenth century, to combat threats of invasion from the Dutch, a moat was constructed along the eastern edge of the city and later extended around the southern edge of the citadel.

A physical mark of Spanish urban design was the integration of the town plaza as a setting for activities, and in some cases this has become the one retained fixture in urban development, and a basic facet of Filipino culture and everyday life. Plazas were identified as the central growth point in city building and typically created the basis for the formation of principal streets. The prevailing link between Church and State was underscored by the location of the Cathedral and Town Hall. These were both defining and dominating elements associated with the central space, hence religious and political gatherings established the plaza as a gathering place around which commercial streets developed. These can be readily observed in the church plazas of Bimondo, Quiapo and Tondo. The *Plaza Mayor* or primary town square was originally used for bullfights until its transformation into a tree-shaded space.

Revitalisation of Fort Santiago began in

The church of Santo Seng Kong on the major Tondo thoroughfare, Juan Luna, faces a market plaza and acts as a transport focus for jeepneys and pedicabs, which serve the wider street community.

the 1960s around Manila Cathedral. This represents a Romanesque structure that encapsulates the city's turbulent history, continually reconstructed six times since 1581 because of invasion, earthquakes, typhoon and fire. The square fronting the cathedral was originally used as a military parade ground and is now named Plaza Roma to reciprocate the naming of Piazza Manila in Rome, after the first Filipino cardinal to be ordained.

The first buildings were constructed with readily available local materials, but a fire in 1583 led to the large-scale reconstruction of the city in stone (from quarries in Makati) and brick. A major earthquake in 1645 led to

the beginning of a mix of Spanish-Mexican buildings along with local indigenous traditions to create an *arquitectura mestiza* consisting of a lower storey of mortar and stone, and an upper storey of wood.[3] Early domestic architecture followed designs from other Spanish colonies, but wooden structures with clay roof tiles were vulnerable to earthquakes, and after 1886 galvanised iron roofing was introduced from England. The first stone building works in the capital were the cathedral, and an integrated defensive system of protective fortifications at the mouth of the Pasig River, therefore by 1650 Intramuros was surrounded by permanent stone bulwarks two metres

3   Javellana, R.B., *In and Around Intramuros*, Jesuit Communications Foundation, Quezon City, 2003
4   Zaragoza, R.M., *Old Manila*, Oxford University Press, Oxford, New York, 1990

thick, with three city gates and a ten metre wide moat. Thousands of local men were mobilised for this work under the direction of Spanish engineers, and special taxes levied. The galleon trade generated huge profits, manifested by the imposing public buildings, churches and private substantial two-storey houses which established an enduring and monumental imprint. These grand structures helped reinforce the city's material and symbolic authoritarian role as a colonial metropolis and military stronghold in Southeast Asia. Government buildings were built of hewn stone or bricks, with colonnaded courtyards, grand staircases and large reception rooms.

Intramuros was a city of churches and religious monuments belonging to various denominations, for example San Ignacio Church of the Jesuits, and Santo Domingo Church of the Dominions. Architecture was strongly influenced by a Spanish-Mexican baroque style which was also reflected in the elaborate interiors. Tree-lined promenades followed the contours of Manila Bay, and the evening *paseo* became a feature of daily life that has continued to the present day. At the same time the country area around the city was divided up into large private estates for the Spanish Manilenos, who constructed palatial mansions. This private division of land prevailed until the twentieth century, and had a significant impact on later patterns of urban expansion.[4]

The city morphology gradually became structured into distinctive quarters for both local and ethnic groups. These greatly exceeded the number of Spanish settlers and were mainly divided into Filipino, Chinese and Japanese sectors — in part to minimise local unrest and to circumscribe commercial activity, but also to preserve the integrity of Intramuros as an enclave for the Spanish elite. The fusion of Spanish, Mexican, Chinese and Filipino design influences produced a unique identity that had much to do with its

Manila Metropolitan Cathedral rises above the old city mall and moat, now a golf course, seen from Bonifacio Drive.

THE UNIVERSITY OF SANTO TOMAS was founded by the third Archibishop of Manila, Miguel de Benarides in 1611 — first named the Colegio de Nuestra Sênora Rosario. It was elevated to the rank of a university by Pope Innocent X in 1645, designated a Royal University in 1785 by Charles III of Spain, and a Pontifical University in 1902 by Pope Leo XIII. It was originally located in Intramuros but was relocated in 1927 to its present site on España Street, although only the stone portal — the Arch of the Centuries — was transferred to the new campus. The reconstruction of the University of Santo Tomas Gateway entrance used stones from the original University Building in Intramuros, destroyed by American bombardment in 1945.

THE MAIN BUILDING was designed by Fr Roque Ruaño and inaugurated in 1927. It was prefabricated in forty separate parts, two centimetres apart, allowing for structural movement in the event of an earthquake. A statue of Saint Thomas Aquinas crowns the Archway at the España approach to the University. In front of the Main Building is a bronze statue of the founder of the University, Fr Miquel de Benarides, the third Archbishop of Manila, cast in Paris in 1889 and originally sited in Intramuros.

attraction and growth as a trading hub and religious centre. The Japanese trade between Nagasaki and Manila, and the supply of exotic goods for transhipment to the Americas, introduced a large Japanese community in Dilao, to the east of Intramuros. It attracted a large number of Japanese Catholics who, at the time, were being persecuted in their homeland, but after 1639 when the flow of immigrants ceased, this distinctive quarter was gradually subsumed within the growing suburban development.

By the turn of the seventeenth century there were 20,000 Chinese residents in Manila as traders, artisans, craftsmen and labourers, and as farmers they also provided much of the food for the city. They were a key factor in the growth of the commercial entrepôt and the overall urbanisation programme — despite suffering periodic setbacks and even massacres at the hands of the Spanish and Japanese. The policy of ethnic segregation assigned most Chinese to a site in Parian adjoining Intramuros, but frequent fires in the dense and narrow streets led to the destruction of the area and its incorporation as a firebreak around the Spanish city. In order to facilitate the assimilation of Chinese and *mestizos* into the Catholic Church, a new settlement in Binondo to the west of the Pasig River was later granted under the authority of the Dominican friars.

As the suburban *arrabales* grew into urbanised communities, the local Filipino population was conscripted to work as labourers and farmers, and became increasingly absorbed into both the Hispanic political culture, and the missionary contingents of Augustinians, Franciscans, Jesuits, and Dominicans. Through the period of Spanish occupation, churches and related institutions were designed with imposing architecture, forming nodal elements around Intramuros in suburban parishes and in new urban settlements throughout the country.

The Plaza Santa Cruz is surrounded by old banking houses including the oldest savings bank in Manila, Monte de Piedad, founded in 1842. The plaza is dominated by the Santa Cruz Church.

These replicated the characteristic attributes of the *Ordianzas* but they were also marked by distinctive ethnic configurations. Of these, the pre-Hispanic settlements of Binondo, Santa Cruz and the Chinese district of Quiapo were the most important, broadly developed on large land holdings purchased by the Jesuits and leased out mainly to the Filipino, Chinese and *mestizo* populations. Other and more distant *arrabales* such as Ermita, Malate, Makati and San Miguel gradually evolved as market settlements. In total, the acquisition and structure of land organisation helped to configure the metropolitan primacy of the city as a whole, along with its diverse communities and complex societies. While the Spanish attempted to emulate the expansionist regimes of the British and Dutch trading companies, they had little success.

During the Seven Years War the British bombarded Intramuros and occupied it between 1762 and 1764, demonstrating to the Spanish a need to improve defences — which they did by enlarging the moat and adding parapets to the walls, and demolished six settlements outside the walls towards the end of the nineteenth century. Political and economic reforms gradually allowed a degree of local participation in government in the face of a growing nationalist movement, and led to the foundation of the first Philippine Republic.

INTERVENTION AND THE CITY

The Philippines represents the first example of systematic territorial gain and intervention by a Western power, during a period when other forms of colonial expansion in Southeast Asia were concerned less with urbanisation programmes, and more with facilitating an economic role to the cities. As a result, the cultural, political and environmental functions of most imperial regimes was somewhat limited until the nineteenth century, when a new phase of colonial imperialism and urbanisation emerged. When the galleon trade stopped in 1815, the port was opened to foreign vessels, and the character of the city changed as it expanded. This was to fashion new systems of settlement, which introduced an ordered urban growth of emergent dependencies. These were tied into extensive transportation and maritime networks that developed with the opening of the Suez Canal in 1869 and the subsequent growth in world trade and steamship travel. In 1880 a severe earthquake damaged Intramuros destroying the palace, and a decision was made to transfer the palace function to Malacanan, further to the east in the San Miquel district, where it remains as the residence of Philippine presidents. The first rail line between Manila and Dagopan was built in 1892 with British financing, in order to connect Manila with the agricultural heartland of Luzon. More main lines to the north and south were later constructed, along with a programme of major road development overseen by the American regime. While Intramuros remained as a civic, religious and educational hub, economic growth was largely propelled by American and English trading companies situated in the Chinese community of Binondo.

By the end of the nineteenth century, Manila had become an international trading and manufacturing centre, but the Spanish presence in Asia had by that time been depleted by the Portuguese, Dutch and British colonial aspirations. With the Treaty of Paris in 1898, which ended the Spanish-American war, the Philippines, Guam and Puerto Rico were ceded to the United States, beginning a term of American rule that lasted until the Japanese invasion of 1942. This signalled a significant change in emphasis towards wider city building, urban infrastructure and commercial aspects.

Under American civil rule the Bureau of Public Buildings was established in Intramuros. The first American Governor General, William Howard Taft, invited Daniel Burnham, the architect of the Chicago World's Fair, to prepare a City Plan for Manila. Most of the planning proposals were never implemented, but the rebuilding of government accommodation outside Intramuros, preservation of the old city, and an imposed system of parks and boulevards increased its status, creating a destination for increasing numbers of migrant workers and leading to the growth of outlying districts such as Pasay and Ermita. Burnham's plan led to the reclamation of the old city moat, which remains as a Municipal Golf Course. The large bay front from Luneta Park to Cevite was constructed along what is now Roxas Boulevard — in reality a formalisation of the old esplanade. The harbour was modernised in 1910, electric trams were introduced, and in the 1930s regular air services were established between Manila and the west coast of the United States. Trade relations were liberalised, with the Philippines becoming an important source of agricultural products, although inward investment mainly benefitted the landed gentry who controlled large estates, including tobacco and sugar plantations. American investment in banking, transport and communications propelled economic growth.

In 1935 the Philippines was designated a Commonwealth but World War II prevented its immediate path to independence until 1946, making it the first colonised country in Asia to be free of Western rule. The Japanese left behind a razed city with a small residue of monuments and public buildings. Only the San Agustin Church was left intact in Intramuros, and in 1993 was designated a UNESCO World Heritage site. The more benevolent American occupation left a legacy of English education and contemporary Western culture. The Pacific War devastated parts of the Philippines, and displaced people began to move into the cities in large numbers. Despite Japanese occupation between 1942 and 1945, the pre-World War II population of around one million, increased in the post-war period to 2.5 million by 1960.

In response to the spiralling cost of land and traffic congestion, industrial uses began to establish in the adjacent municipalities of Pandacon, San Juan and Mandaluyong, with commensurate growth in population. However the spatial pattern of urban growth in Metro Manila has been notable only for its lack of overall land-use planning and co-ordination. While city plans have been prepared, they have at best been only partly adopted, and urban development initiatives have been largely left in private hands. Thus parts of the city resemble an indeterminate amalgam of uses that have grown indiscriminately, and much of the older urban neighbourhoods evoke a temporary quality, quite apart from the persistence of large slum areas. An exception to this laissez-faire pattern is Quezon City, conceived as a new Capital City and symbolizing post-war aspirations for a new national identity. However much of the new development was built for state employees and suburban subdivisions for the middle class.

The lingering economic polarisation within the country has confounded post-independence planning. A major reason for the lack of coherent and rational planning headway, or an effective regulatory system in Manila is the perennial problem of land ownership. Hence new development directions have been the result of interventions by private capital with prominent families having accumulated large tracts of land going back to the Spanish occupation. Through a complicit blend of state intervention and private holdings, large-scale commercial and residential projects — such as Fort Bonifacio — have usurped attempts to generate a more publicly inspired urbanism. The largest and, in commercial

Commercial avenue alongside the Redemptionist Church at Paranaque.

terms most successful is Makati, carried out by the Ayala Corporation in the 1960s. The riverene community of today's Makati, historically enjoyed a lucrative trade with Chinese merchants, and the Franciscans built their first mission outside Intramuros there in 1578. Modern Makati was first established as a series of luxury residential developments in Forbes Park and then as a finance centre with a critical mass of foreign business houses, banks and hotels, orchestrated through strict zoning and development parameters. Ayala Avenue is the principal street, reflecting an internationalism that scarcely extends outside Makati itself, but which is the centre for Manila's business and service industry. The alignment of the avenue was, in the 1930s, the runway of the international airport. Behind the tall and anonymous frontages are the secure gated residential communities of a guarded elite, representing pockets of affluence in a city that has otherwise been perennially under-funded in terms of public benefits.

Steady economic growth from 2008 has gradually fuelled foreign investment and a construction boom that is transforming the city skyline. Older areas such as the Eastwood industrial zone have been metamorphosed into new business districts, catering for the fast growing outsourcing sector which employs more than 600,000 people. On the Fort Bonifacio site, the 'High Street' project built by Ayala Land will house the Philippine Stock Exchange and new hotels and high-rise commercial and residential developments by 2017. A new 100-hectare 'Entertainment City' complex of casinos is being constructed on Manila Bay.

Manila exemplifies an embedded dichotomy in relation to post-colonial urbanisation. The relationship between the material and built forms of the city is poorly synchronised with its social, cultural and economic systems, and creates constraints to effective modernisation. The spatial concentration of private capital and land ownership manifests itself in massive inequalities with regard to wealth, housing and opportunity. State intervention has been based on a problematic and ambiguous approach to achieving an international identity in tune with most of Asia's primate cities. The Urban Development and Housing Act of 1992 required developers of residential subdivisions to devote 20 per cent of their total area to low-cost housing. The creation of the Metro Manila Development Authority in 1995 acknowledged the need for a single umbrella organisation to co-ordinate planning, transportation and housing in the light of deteriorating conditions. The Authority prepared a Physical Framework Plan up to 2006, but there is a chronic management problem in terms of traffic, air pollution, waste disposal, and provision of urban services and utilities. The plan has therefore largely failed to progressively re-shape exclusionary planning and development trajectories, despite professed ideals. The inability to implement plans, along with weak land administration, has led to dispersed and ad hoc patterns of urban development with markedly different physical and socio-economic characteristics. A Special Economic Enterprise Development Zone on the old military sites at Subic Bay and Clark Air Force Base is part of a programme to decentralise industrial development from the inner city, and where new residential development can be constructed along with export processing zones.

INTERVENTION IN THE SETTLEMENT PROCESS

Centralised planning at a metro-level came through the declaration of martial law in 1972, and with it a further swelling of the population, and a worsening of physical conditions. In the early 1970s a government sponsored programme of eviction and resettlement succeeded only in freeing up land for private development, while squatters turned to other city sites. However at a political level, this introduced a modernist vision for a new society linked to a spirit of nationalism. This led to the centralisation of institutional control over planning and development programmes, including a new Ministry of Housing, the Metro Manila Commission (in 1975), and the Ministry for Human Settlements (in 1978).

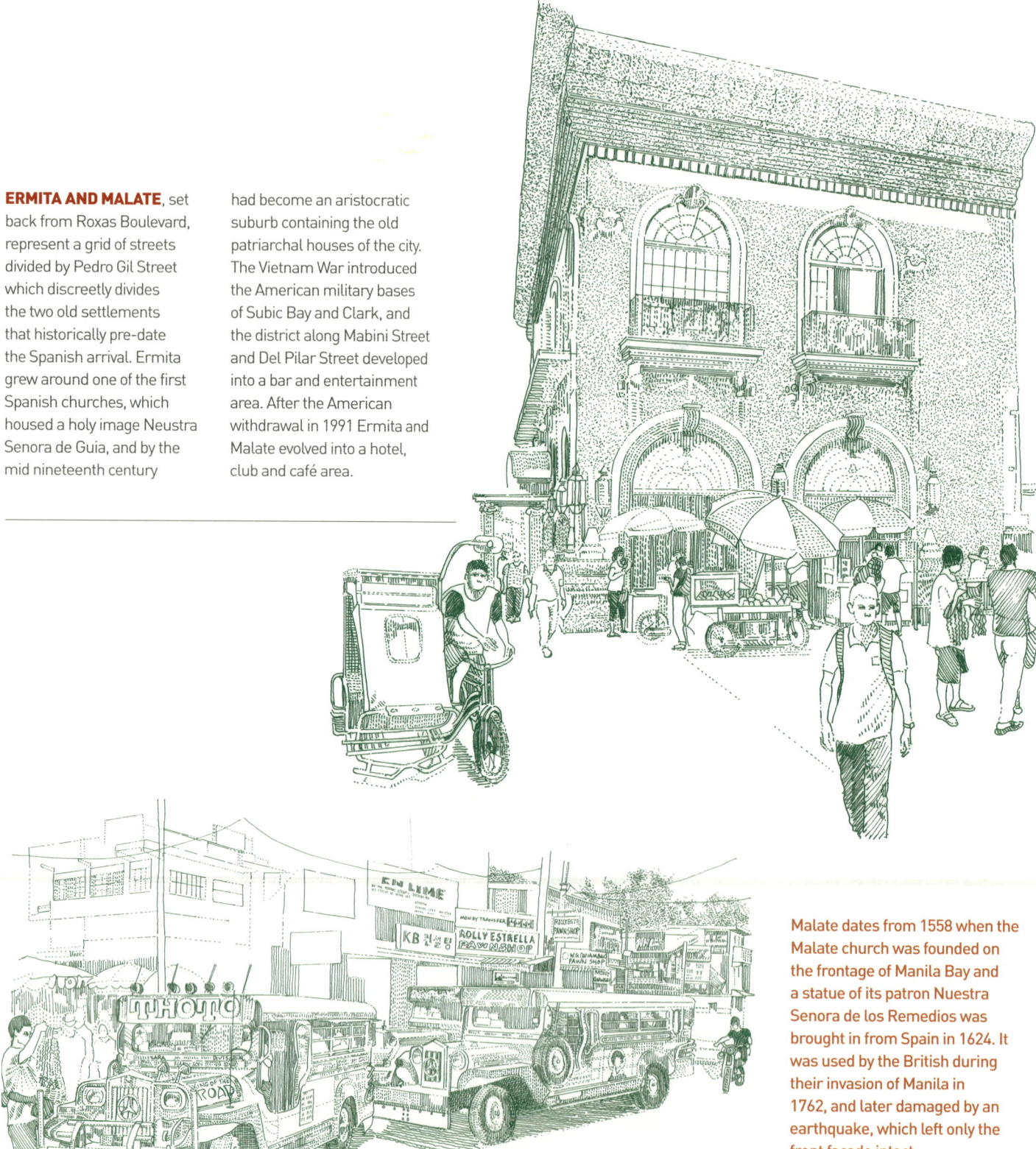

ERMITA AND MALATE, set back from Roxas Boulevard, represent a grid of streets divided by Pedro Gil Street which discreetly divides the two old settlements that historically pre-date the Spanish arrival. Ermita grew around one of the first Spanish churches, which housed a holy image Neustra Senora de Guia, and by the mid nineteenth century had become an aristocratic suburb containing the old patriarchal houses of the city. The Vietnam War introduced the American military bases of Subic Bay and Clark, and the district along Mabini Street and Del Pilar Street developed into a bar and entertainment area. After the American withdrawal in 1991 Ermita and Malate evolved into a hotel, club and café area.

Malate dates from 1558 when the Malate church was founded on the frontage of Manila Bay and a statue of its patron Nuestra Senora de los Remedios was brought in from Spain in 1624. It was used by the British during their invasion of Manila in 1762, and later damaged by an earthquake, which left only the front façade intact.

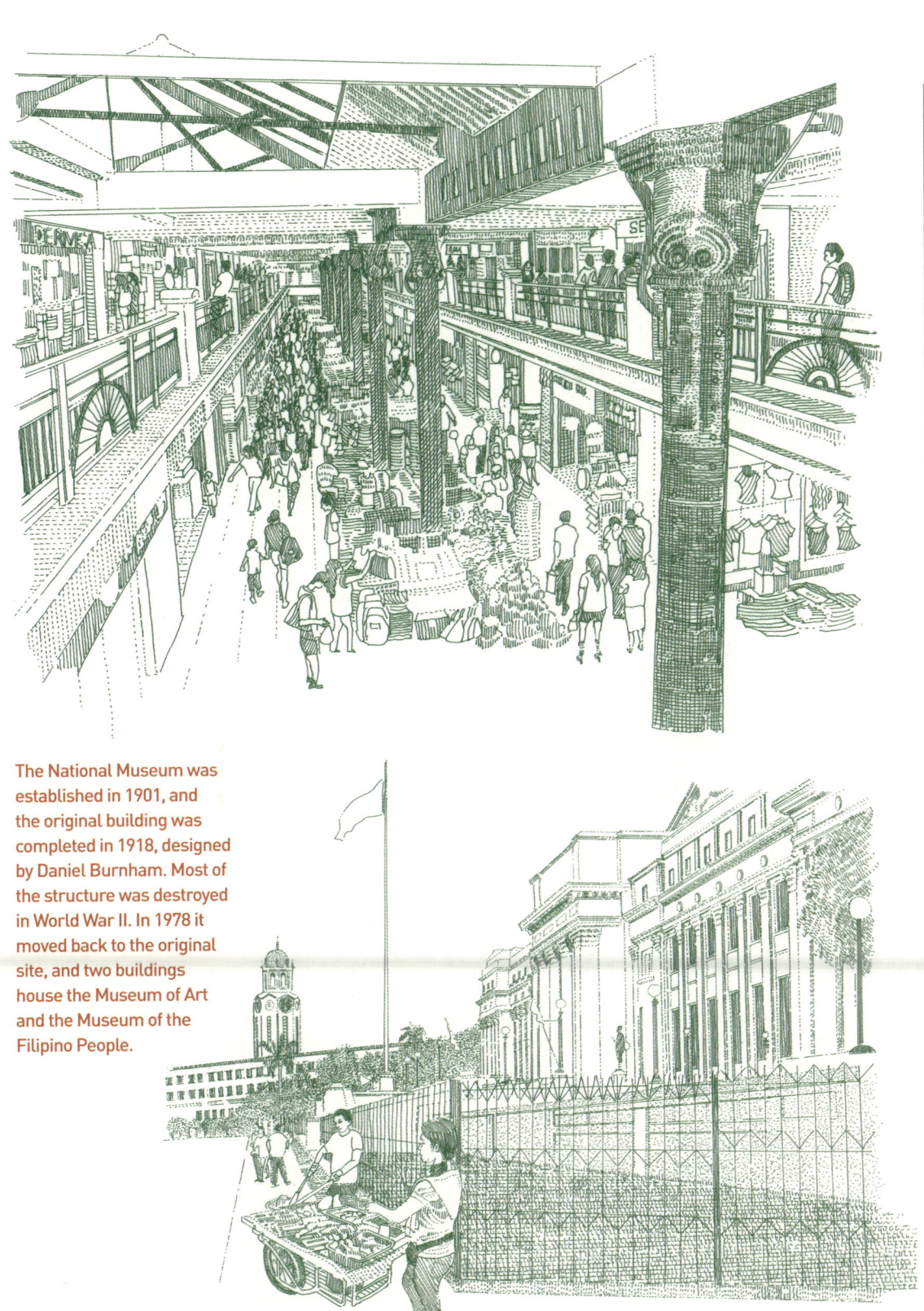

The National Museum was established in 1901, and the original building was completed in 1918, designed by Daniel Burnham. Most of the structure was destroyed in World War II. In 1978 it moved back to the original site, and two buildings house the Museum of Art and the Museum of the Filipino People.

THE TUTUBAN CENTRE to the north of Binondo is a former railway station, converted into a shopping complex in 1993. The old station was inaugurated in 1891, and served as the hub of rail transport in Luzon until the 1960s. The first railway line linked Manila with Dagupan City in Pangasinan Province, and was built by the British-owned Manila Railway Company Ltd, after bidding for this at an auction in Madrid. The company was renamed Philippine National Railways in 1964. Its neo-Classical design is the only such structure in the Philippines and is a city landmark. The cast iron columns are topped by Corinthian capitals. The main building is connected by sky bridges to the Divisoria market. This faces Bonifacio Plaza, named after Andres Bonifacio who founded the Katipunan — the first revolutionary movement for independence. This part of Manila is undergoing extensive urban regeneration, retaining its historic significance.

5 Pinches, M.D., 'Modernisation and the quest for Modernity: Architectural Form, Squatter Settlements and the New Society in Manila', in *Cultural Identity and Urban Change in Southeast Asia: Interpretative Essays*, Eds. Mark Askew and William S Logan, Deakin University Press, Geelong, 1994, p13-42

6 Pinches, 1994, op. cit.

The ambitious and idealistic plans were tacitly supported by the World Bank, and initially involved a sweeping programme of reform covering housing, environment, education and the promotion of employment opportunities through entrepreneurship. Squatter settlements were regarded as unsightly, and it is estimated that between 1973 and 1980 around 400,000 families were evicted, although parallel initiatives also led to prototypes for approved *bayanihan*, or mutual help housing projects.[5] The 1981 Plan for Metro Manila zoned large areas of the city for residential, commercial, industrial and agricultural uses, and was geared to more effective urban management. It was a visionary plan of modernisation, but one that was overly directed to prestigious public buildings, showcase architecture and beautification programmes. Large-scale upgrading and 'sites and services' projects were successfully implemented at the Tondo Foreshore and Tatalon, in part because of the security of land tenure and the ability to construct permanent dwellings under recognised market conditions. Michael Pinches gives several reasons why these upgrading programmes ultimately failed: first because it became apparent by the mid-1980s that they could not recover the full costs of implementation as laid down by the World Bank; second because of the continued influx of poor immigrants into the city that overwhelmed available resources; and third because the state-supported acquisition of city land went against the interests of private land owners and powerful financial interests.[6] A probable further factor remains a lack of will, in situations where poorer families form part of political constituencies.

Around 150,000 migrants arrive in Manila each year, and the continued proliferation of squatter settlements and inadequate infrastructure, particularly in the Tondo and Pasay districts, is a lingering testimony to the inability to orchestrate social, land and

The district of Tondo abuts the northern harbour piers. Its foreshore area has a density of around 2,000 people per hectare, in a densely packed squatter area. It was selected as the first urban renewal and upgrading project in the city.

housing policy. The resulting imbalance, together with a privately controlled real estate market, makes housing unobtainable for a large proportion of the population, partly because land is scarce. Thus, squatter settlements grew incrementally around the inner urban periphery, along the foreshore, river estuaries and World War II bomb sites that had not been restored, forming an urbanism of exclusion. These settlements, which contain 700,000 households or 31 per cent of the city population, have evolved a strong collective and economic identity of their own, with extensive interpersonal, co-operative and mutual help relationships, which accommodate extended patterns of kinship and help social integration.[7] Settlement forms mark localised spatial configurations, with complex systems of construction, open space and walkways, along with an informal provision of water supply, electricity and waste disposal. They form urban regimes of impermanence and vulnerability, but also embody resourcefulness, improvisation, and flexibility to extend and adapt.

Squatter settlements, however, reflect a special process of intervention — that of stakeholder action and self-help in response to an urbanisation process that is unable to reconcile the operational needs of an expanding labour market with the ability of the state to provide acceptable accommodation. This has led to a sophisticated but informal construction and real estate sector attuned to ambiguity

7 Santiago, A.M., 'Case Study of Land Management in Metro Manila', in *Megacity Management in the Asian and Pacific Region Vol 1*, Eds. Jeffry Stubbs and Giles Clarke, Asian Development Bank, Manila and Philippines, 1996

8 Roberts, B, 'Manila : Metropolitan Vulnerability, Local Resilience', in *Planning Asian Cities – Risks and Resilience*, Eds. Stephen Hamnet and Dean Forbes, Routledge, London and New York, 2011

surrounding the legality of land titles in many low income areas.

In some situations rents are paid to legal landowners, while construction itself is usually carried out by operatives from the construction industry with materials purchased from suppliers —suggesting that the settlements form part of an integral economic system. One aspect of this is that the houses themselves reflect the traditional rural domestic *barong-barong* architecture, and take on the characteristics of a village in the city. In some cases these *barangay* communities gradually absorb the symbolic trappings of modernisation through the incorporation of permanent building materials and equipment. It can therefore be argued that self-help and social integration are the means by which the urban poor can increase their status within the city, assisted in their upwardly mobile route through state intervention.

A further aspect of urban resilience — a natural form of intervention — is that of risk from different types of catastrophic events and their consequences in terms of chain reactions, with only limited capacity to deal with disaster.[8] Natural risks in and around Manila include: typhoons, tropical cyclones, associated flooding and subsidence because of the low-lying urban area, and vulnerability to earthquakes as a result of its location on two fault lines which make it one of the highest 'at risk' cities in Asia. A Disaster Risk Management Plan was prepared for the metropolitan area in 2007, to promote co-ordination measures, map likely impact areas, and orchestrate local communities to share responsibilities for safeguarding their own localities.

THE LEGACY OF INTRAMUROS

In 1945 the old city lay in ruins — the result of American bombing during its recapture of Manila. Since then efforts have been made to restore parts of Intramuros, including Fort

Santiago. Its central location and large site of around 88 hectares have at times put it under considerable pressure for redevelopment, but San Agustin Church has remained a focal point for visitors and ceremonial events, reflecting the importance of tourism to the national economy. Intramuros is now one of fifteen urban districts and in 1979 the Intramuros Administration was created through a presidential decree to restore, as far as possible, the old city and house the Spanish collection of the National Archives. It is empowered to regulate re-building initiatives and ensure that the architecture conforms with the Spanish tradition. However until the 1990s — despite the National Historical Institute emphasising restoration of cultural sites and the importance of the area as a symbol of the city's heritage — there were only limited preservation initiatives, partly because of the absence of a comprehensive plan. To date, six out of eight principal gates have been

restored together with various fortifications.

The main focus of activity is Fort Santiago and General Luna Street, in which Manila Cathedral and San Agustin Church are located together with a reconstructed section — Casa Manila. The Corte Real tourist centre is privately sponsored, and since the introduction of the Intramuros Administration efforts have been made to improve local amenities. It has issued policy and design guidelines which direct restoration efforts towards achieving architectural conformity with the nineteenth century architecture, through a long-term re-building programme. The Administration has reconstructed parts of Fort Santiago along with a public park, and has encouraged private site owners to replicate buildings from the Spanish colonial period as a 'living museum'. As a model for this, a block of typical houses was constructed. The programme poses an obvious problem of equating creative reconstruction and

reinvention of historical character with social and economic regeneration. There is also an important educational component in terms of a dynamic working model for conservation practice and adaptive re-use, and balancing this with the sensitive use of sophisticated building technology to meet the practicalities of life in the wider city. In particular the prime location of Intramuros and its proximity to Manila's business centre puts it under pressure from development interests. A number of historical plazas— such as the Plaza Santa Cruz; Plaza Ka Hernández in Tondo, the most densely populated district in Manila; and the Plaza San Lorenzo Piaz associated with Binondo Church — have been drastically curtailed in size to accommodate new road areas.

While Manila has enormous diversity, with various areas being revitalised for cultural, recreational and commercial activities, its main priority is coping with population pressures. An unflinching Catholicism, the legacy of Spanish occupation, collides somewhat awkwardly with the lingering secular sub-culture of Americana. The ingenious transformation of the US military jeep to the ubiquitous Jeepney metaphorically corresponds with the changing nature of the cityscape from 1945, and its cultural and economic relationship with the United States. Post-war Manila has become a city of sprawl and outlying districts, from the new business and commercial centres of Makati, San Juan and Quezon City, to the older and frenetic Binondo, Santa Cruz, Quiapo and Tondo, where street and market patterns tend to focus on historic church plazas.

Intramuros remains something of an anomaly — a valuable and identifiable landmark of the city, central to its very formation, but one confronted and surrounded by urban problem areas. The walled enclave itself must be viewed as an invaluable resource that must function as both a historic symbol and viable urban place.

FORT SANTIAGO which occupies a triangular site at the mouth of the Pasig River was named in honour of Spain's patron saint, the Apostle James, who is said to have brought Christianity to Spain. It was built along with military barracks in 1714 and restored in 1982. The stone relief carving on the entrance gate shows San Tiago Matamoro slaying the Moors. The fort was constructed on the site of a previous wooden palisade. Work commenced in 1590 under a military engineer, Leonardo Turriano and was completed three years later with two kilometres of stone fortifications and gateways. The bastion of Santa Barbara was built to protect the river entrance. Baluarte de Santa Barbara was named after the patron saint of artillerymen, built in 1592 to protect the entrance to the Pasig River, it provided quarters for the artillerymen and the house of the commandment. It housed the US Army headquarters in 1994, and was used as a prison during the Japanese occupation.

BINONDO AND TONDO date back to pre-Hispanic times. The former was granted to Chinese settlers in the eighteenth century at the height of the Manila-Acapulco galleon trade, and became the nineteenth century commercial hub of Manila. It grew into Manila's Chinatown, and in turn became the city's wealthiest urban district. It is now characterised by a maze of narrow streets with cramped shophouses and small business establishments built during the early twentieth century in a neo-Classical / Art Deco style. These are interspersed with old colonial houses and banks, redolent of the nineteenth century resplendence of the district.

Plaza Calderon de la Barca or 'Plaza Binondo' is part of the Chinese parish. Binondo Church is a post-war reconstruction of an early Dominican edifice built in 1614 as a shrine to Nuestra Senora del Rosario. The western façade and octagonal bell tower belong to the original building, which was destroyed in World War II. Nearby is the Divisoria, a centre for traders and wholesale merchants. Binondo also had its own Chinese theatre — the Teatro Quinol Chino.

INDONESIA

Jakarta

THE BUILDING THAT NOW HOUSES THE MINISTRY OF FINANCE was constructed between 1809 and 1828 in the Empire Style. It was originally the state palace of the governor general of the Dutch East Indies. Herman Daendels chose Weltevreden as the seat of government. It was originally a military compound around a central space used for exercises. It developed as a central city square, Waterlooplein, with a monument at its centre commemorating Napoleon's defeat. The square became the main public space in Weltevreden and is now known as Taman Fatahilla. A new military parade ground was located on the western bank of the Ciliwung River — later named "Koningsplein" and now Medan Merdeka or National Monument Square. The original South Wing was the Societeit Concordia, an Officer's Club and now the Hotel Borobudor, and the North Wing was the High Court. After independence this became the seat of the Mahkamah Agung — Indonesia's Supreme Court.

1 Jayapal, M, *Old Jakarta*, Oxford University Press, Oxford, 1993

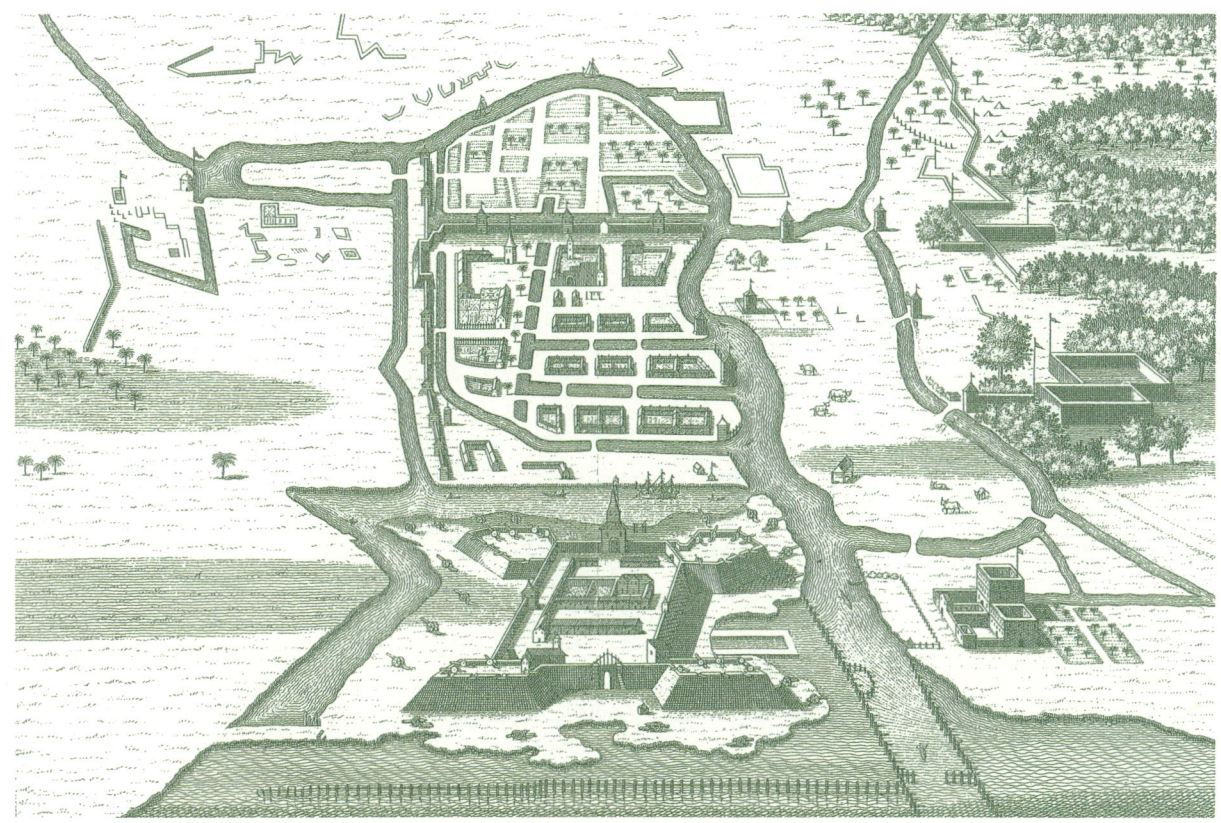

Batavia in 1629, from Antoine François Prévost, Histoire Générale des Voyages, Paris, 1746-61.

BATAVIA – A TRADING COMPANY INTERVENTION

Around the second century AD a number of sophisticated civilisations came to the fore in southern Asia, built on a thriving trading regime between coastal communities and a strong Indian cultural influence, which took root in Buddhist and Hindu temples, incorporating indigenous adaptations and interpretations. The maritime Kingdom of Srivijaya based at Palembang established ports along the Malacca and Sunda straits from the late seventh century. Subsequently, successive Hindu-Javanese rulers controlled trade throughout the archipelago, including major routes to southern India. From here Muslim traders from Arabia, who already controlled overland routes between Europe and China, began to establish Islamic settlements along the coastal communities. The important port of Malacca that had long been a vassal of China, reverted to Islam in 1436 and its rapid growth brought the Javanese port towns within its ambit. Local political alliances quickly facilitated the spread of Islam through Java and the Spice Islands. The conquest of Malacca by the Portuguese in 1511 was part of a wider plan to undermine Islamic influence and to dominate maritime trade in the Indian Ocean, inspired by "Gospel, Gold and Glory for the king".

By the end of the sixteenth century, the Netherlands was the major commercial centre in Northern Europe, and in 1602 a group of merchants formed the United Dutch East India Company — the Vereenigde Oostandische Compagnice (VOC) — to secure control of the spice trade, if necessary by military force. It was licensed to establish colonies and requisition the military for defence purposes.[1]

The West Java port town that later grew into Jakarta, the capital city of Indonesia, was established by the Dutch in 1619 in a protected bay. It was able to serve both

2 Blussé, L, 'On the Waterfront: Life and Labour around the Batavian Roadshed', in *Asian Port Cities 1600-1800: Local and Foreign Cultural Interactions*, Ed. Haneda Masashi, NUS Press, Singapore, 2009, p120

3 Blussé, 2009, op. cit.

THE MUSEUM BAHARI (on the right) dates from the Dutch East India Company period in 1652, and was originally used as a godown for spices, coffee and Indian cloth. The outer wall of the museum, parallel to Jl Pasar Ikan, was part of Batavia's city wall. The 12-metre high nineteenth century lookout tower, the Uitkijk, was constructed by the Dutch on the site of the Jayakarta customs house in 1839. The adjacent lower tower functions as the administration office of the harbour, and both exist as part of the Maritime Museum complex.

mercantile and strategic objectives and had the capacity to contain more than 1,000 vessels. It formed a vital part of a maritime network that extended to Nagasaki, the Coromandel coast, Ceylon, Malacca and Thailand. The town was christened Batavia by the Dutch garrison, in honour of Dutch national forebears — the Batavians. Ports on the Straits acted as independent entrepôts and provisioning harbours, and facilitated the growth of powerful ruling jurisdictions through control of trading routes. The port of Sunda Kalapa gained prominence in the early sixteenth century — through Muslim traders who avoided Portuguese controlled Malacca — and was later renamed Jaya Karta or 'Prosperous'. It was to become the centre of a struggle for trading rights between European nations, and a symbol of Dutch colonial policy as the hub city in the Indonesian archipelago. The city plan compiled by the Dutch was intended to accommodate around 500,000 people, close to the old harbour of

Sunda Kelapa, including significant numbers of Portuguese, Malay and Chinese who had established trading links with Java. This gradually transformed the settlement into the largest commercial entrepôt in the archipelago, although it was isolated from other urban centres such as Jojakarta and Surabaya, and distinct from inland areas under aristocratic control. However the location of such a strategically important settlement, in a low-lying area bisected by several rivers, meant that the city was always prone to floods.

Batavia was not merely a new trading city but was established as a fortified military stronghold to protect western Java from both the Portuguese, who at the time controlled the expanding shipping routes connected to other Asian ports and the Indian Mughal Empire; and the Spanish who occupied Manila. It therefore functioned as both a trading port and military base (as opposed to a capital city), with massive wharves for ship building and repair. Bricks were brought from Holland and Coromandel stone from India — as ballast in the holds of the 'East Indiamen' — to build the castle and public buildings, while the arches of the city gates were prefabricated in Europe.[2] Jayakarta's fort contained all

The original shape of the harbour at Sunda Kalapa is now obscured, and much of the harbourfront is occupied by informal structures, wooden piers and fishing boats.

the important VOC buildings, and to the south-west were the wharf buildings and warehouses that now make up the Museum Batavi, or maritime museum. This is close to the 1817 wharf where port workers still load and off-load goods from wooden Buginese *pinisi* boats that sail throughout the archipelago. The Ciliwung River was canalised to facilitate transport from the interior, while Chinese junks were able to enter the canals to unload merchandise from East Asia — in volumes that for many years was equal to that transported by the entire VOC fleet.

The city was different from earlier colonial settlements in one important respect — it was effectively founded by the Dutch East India Company, which had a monopoly over Asian trade in the Indonesian Archipelago. A characteristic feature of the walled town was that it included quarters for local and other ethnic groups who subscribed to the trading and military functions. The company granted tracts of land in the surrounding districts where various Indonesian communities constructed their own *kampung*s. In Batavia and other Dutch colonial settlements, the company replicated types of municipal construction works they were familiar with in Holland, such as canal systems lined

with terraces, town halls and hospitals, as well as churches and other institutions in the Calvinistic tradition of opulent civic architecture.[3]

As well as trading, the large Chinese community contributed skilled labour for agriculture and port operations. The shophouses were an amalgam of Dutch architecture and Chinese features. The rapid influx of Chinese helped to open up new agricultural estates, until 1740 when riots over reduced sugar quotas led to the creation of a special suburb outside the city walls. Jakarta's Chinatown thereafter grew around Glodok, where the purchase of business licenses contributed in large part to government revenue. As in other Straits cities, new arrivals were integrated within the economy via compatriot organisations connected with cities in China such as Foochow, Amoy and Canton.

The remainder of non-European society was largely made up of Javanese, Malays,

SUNDA KELAPA dates back to its fourteenth century role as a Hindu spice trading port and harbour. The harbour was situated on both sides of the Ciliwung River, and was originally known as Kelapa (Coconut) Harbour. The traditional Bugis schooners, the panisi, traded with Malacca, Macassar and Tanjungpura, and still play a part in commercial links with cities through the archipelago.

4   Jayapal, 1993, op. cit., p13

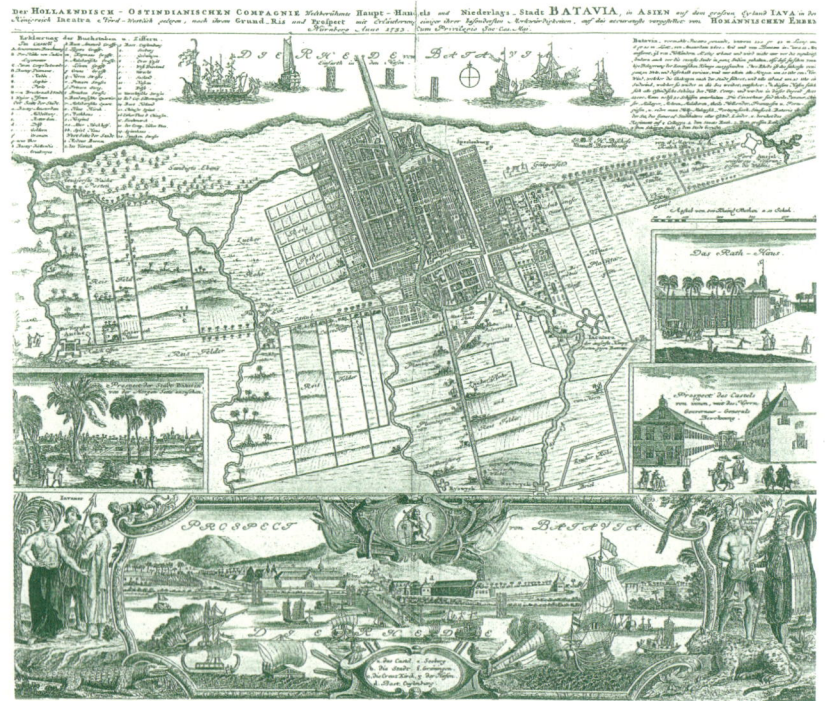

Map of Batavia in 1655, published by Homann Heirs, Nuremberg, 1733

The Dutch drew up building regulations which enforced the use of brick, and street houses were built with a front 'stoop'.

Buginese, Balinese and Mardijkers from early Portuguese settlements. Kampungs took on the characteristics of different ethnic groups, which nominally survive in modern Jakarta neighbourhoods such as Kampung Bugis, Kampung Bandan and Kampung Bali.

THE COLONIAL CITY

A combination of volcanic activity from the neighbouring Mount Salak and an outbreak of malaria in the early eighteenth century, caused a marked decline in the city's fortunes, accompanied by the bankruptcy of the VOC. The Company charter was terminated in 1800 after the Dutch defeat by the French in Europe — an event that effectively ceded Malacca and other Dutch possessions to the British. After a brief period of British rule, Batavia was restored to the Dutch in 1814 in order to counterbalance French influence in Asia. With a shift in colonial priorities in the Straits Settlements, Batavia gradually turned into a centre of colonial administration and the capital city of the Dutch East Indies. Canals were constructed of limestone coral and ran through the middle of roads. These served as water transport routes, with lighters coming from the harbour, while the roads were flanked by shade trees.

Herman Daendels (as Governor–General of Java from 1808), and Stamford Raffles (as an "interim" British lieutenant-governor between 1811 and 1816) promoted direct rule, organising the East Indies into districts, divisions and villages. Raffles attempted to introduce the system of land tenure that prevailed in India, whereby tenant farmers rented land from the government, but had the liberty of cultivating what they wanted, however this was largely thwarted by the complex Javanese land tenancy system.[4]

In 1829, the Dutch administration introduced a "Cultivation System" of fiscal administration through a tax on land, which facilitated highly efficient plantation agriculture on the back of forced labour —

in effect cultivating export crops at the expense of their own needs. This major intervention led to massive trading profits for the Dutch, much of which was ploughed back into new roads, waterways and railways. In turn this led to a massive population increase on Java, but initially failed to stimulate an urban economy, forestalling the establishment of townships. However military campaigns against indigenous rulers through the course of the nineteenth century eventually unified the entire archipelago under Dutch rule.

After 1869 the opening of the Suez Canal, combined with Dutch political consolidation and commensurate expansion of private investment, encouraged a wave of European immigration and new public works including churches and a city hall. The city walls were demolished and new public squares built in the heart of the city — the Waterlooplein in Weltevreden and the Konigsplein. The working core of the city was around Koningsplein with residential areas to the north and Waterlooplein to the east. In a similar way to the Padang in the Straits Settlements or the Maidan in colonial India, these became spaces for both recreation and ceremonial activities. Waterlooplein, now Lapangan Banteng, was surrounded by the Governor-General's residence (now the Finance Department), Government offices and the Concordia Club (now the site of the Hotel Borobodur).

The economic success of the 'Liberal System' in the 1870s resulted in a massive expansion of European trading houses and banks. Batavia extended southwards following a steam tram system (inaugurated in 1881) along the Molenvliet, around what are now the urban neighbourhoods of Medan Merdeka and Lapangan Banteng. With continual silting up of the river mouth, loading and unloading of large ships required a fleet of lighters and the look-out post at Pasar Ikan — the Uitkijk — would fly a blue flag to indicate accessibility of the canal. Rivalry with

THE MOLENVLIET CANAL

along what is now Jalan Gajah Mada was built in 1648, and by the mid-eighteenth century was the most fashionable avenue in Batavia, lined with mansions built by Dutch merchants. During the course of the twentieth century, the buildings along the canal were gradually redeveloped. The Bank Tabungan Negara, originally the Postsparrabank, was built by J Van Gendt in 1930 in a Dutch vernacular style, and for a time functioned as a museum. It now sits in the midst of a busy road thoroughfare.

The drawbridge across the Ciliwung River was built in 1628 to connect the Dutch and English forts. It was known originally as Jembatan Pasar Ayam — the Chicken Market Bridge. The name Jembatan Kota Intan came from the fort which had four bastions, one at each corner.

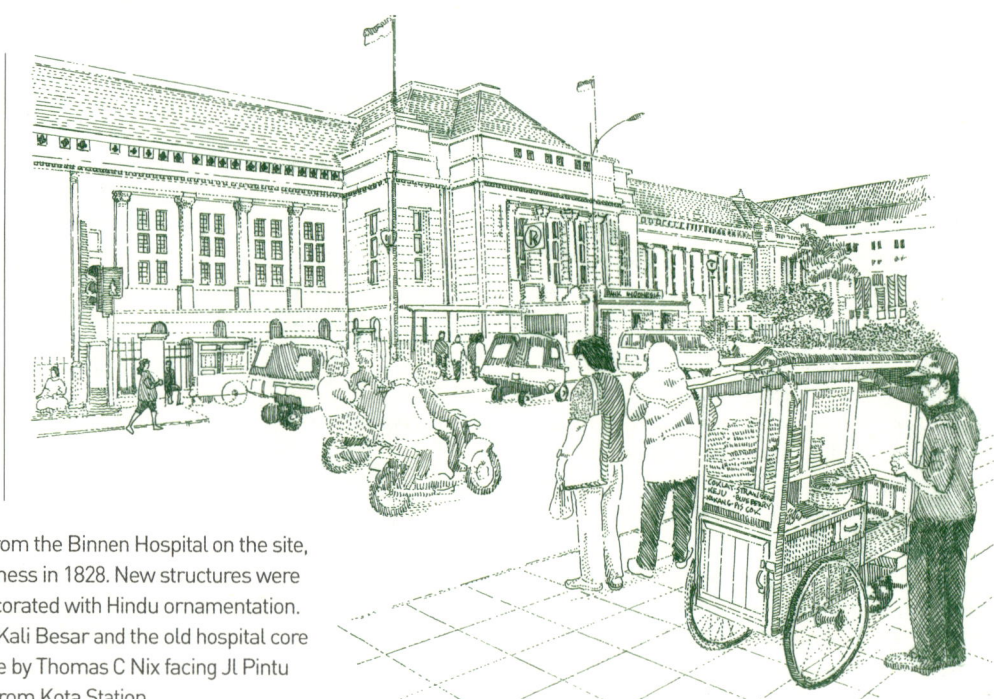

THE BANK INDONESIA BUILDING evolved from the Binnen Hospital on the site, with the De Jarasche Bank commencing business in 1828. New structures were added in 1912, one in a neo-Classical style decorated with Hindu ornamentation. In 1922 the bank built a new west wing facing Kali Besar and the old hospital core was demolished. Further additions were made by Thomas C Nix facing Jl Pintu Besar Utara — the main street leading north from Kota Station.

The Wayang Museum, formerly the Stedelijk Musuem, is a conversion of two Dutch town houses built in 1912 on the site of the Old Reformed Dutch Church. Inside is the tomb of Jan Pieterszoon Coen, the founder of Batavia. Behind the Museum is a collection of older houses along the canal.

Singapore made it necessary to improve port facilities, and Tanjung Priok's deep harbour was completed in 1886. This was located some 15 kilometres to the east of the Batavia Roads, allowing visitors to travel into the town by train. At the same time the Molenvliet Canal opened up the hinterland to industrial development such as sawmills. The European quarter of Weltevreden grew around Koningsplein, focussed on the new centre of Government. Building design developed in a colonial empire style of white-painted colonnaded forms with consistent elevations of tall windows and decorated doorways overlooking landscaped gardens in close proximity to clubs, which acted as the focus of social life. Fashionable new residential areas extended to Kramat, Salemba, Parapatan and Pegangsaam, and a French quarter developed in Rijswijk.

The public squares in Weltevreden became foci for civic and private structures, both unified and distinctive in character, in a neo-Classical style and with an orderly distribution of urban functions. This was extended in 1918 by the development of a largely European suburb in Menteng laid out as a garden city expansion to the city. This mode of development produced one of

The Masjid Jami Kebon Jerub was the first mosque to be built in the Glodok area in 1786. It was designed in a Chinese style, and houses a tomb from the prominent Chinese Chai family.

the most prestigious neighbourhoods in the post-colonial period as the city changed and evolved around it. Wealthy Chinese bought up many of the private estates during the nineteenth century, together with large sites in the business quarter. In the process they founded new settlements in Pasar Baru and Pasar Senen.

The turn of the twentieth century saw momentous change in Indonesia with the roots of political change taking place in the city, notwithstanding national political struggles elsewhere. By 1900 the population was 116,000 which grew through immigration to 435,000 by 1930, thereby reshaping the city through infill and consolidation of the earlier I-shaped plan form.

The new suburbs of Gondangdia and Menteng, built along contemporary Dutch models, were developed on former kampungs, while the impetus for new development involved a gradual loss of agricultural land. As roadways became asphalted, commercial offices and public buildings began to change the character of the central and northern districts, underscoring the significant difference between the Westernized city and the poorer kampungs on the city outskirts.

In 1901 the so-called 'Ethical Policy'

propelled government intervention to improve health and education facilities, and open up more political regeneration. This was seen partly as a means of extending the 'benefits' of Western culture and education while encouraging a sense of national ideology through a modern educated elite. This process represented the first stirring of Indonesian nationalism, which began in the higher educational establishments of Batavia between 1908 and 1940. With economic growth came a new Indonesian assertiveness that refused to equate modernisation with Westernisation. As the Western community became increasingly bourgeois and reactionary, the spread of Islam stemming from increased Arab migration also infiltrated into society. Meanwhile, the Chinese began to identify with growing nationalist movements in China at a time when its 'treaty' ports were dominated by Western powers.

By 1930 Batavia housed the largest European enclave in Southeast Asia. However this was at the expense of almost entirely separate governance systems for indigenous and other non-European communities, including the Chinese who controlled a large part of economic production and at one stage owned 40 per cent of all private

DURING THE EIGHTEENTH CENTURY the wealthiest Europeans began to build country mansions, the most fashionable avenue being along the Molenvliet Canal on Jalan Gajah Mada/Hayam Wuruk. The canal was originally built in 1648 to float timber downriver to the harbour shipyards. By the mid-eighteenth century, mansion development along the Jacatra Way extended to Weltevreden in the South. The only surviving example is the two-storey house built by Reinier de Kleck, a member of the Council of the Indies and governor general in 1740. It is set in a large garden, and between 1926 and 1979 was used to house the National Archives.

5   Silver, C, *Planning the Megacity: Jakarta in the Twentieth Century*, Routledge, London and New York, 2008, p45

6   Freek, C, *Under Construction: The Politics of Urban Space and Housing During the Decolonisation of Indonesia, 1930-1960*, KITLV Press, Leiden, 2010

land holdings.[5] Kampungs continued to accommodate poorer members of the community, and the Municipal Council acquired a number of large estates with the intention of laying out new 'model' low-income communities with proper service infrastructure. However a lack of sufficient subsidies by the colonial government, together with escalating land prices, effectively served to exclude traditional kampong dwellers and encourage the implementation of newly laid-out areas as Dutch suburbs or 'Gondangdia'. At the same time the growth of a Dutch-educated urban elite and a neglect of the urban masses began to generate tentative steps towards Indonesian nationalism, the first major political parties, and later a pan-Islamic movement.

By the mid-1930s the city population had grown to around 500,000 through immigration and annexation of the adjacent municipality. The development of a deep water port at Tanjing Priok helped the city gain ascendancy over Surabaya and assist in the political integration of the Indonesian archipelago. At the same time improved rail connections facilitated accessibility to the export crop producing areas.

REVOLUTIONARY CHANGE AND POST-COLONIAL GROWTH

Dutch complacency in the face of Japanese threats, led firstly to uncertainty and later upheaval in the wake of Japanese occupation in 1942.

The change in name from Batavia to Jakarta was undertaken by the occupying Japanese power on the first anniversary of Pearl Harbour. With its onset, European street names were replaced by Indonesian or Japanese ones. While Indonesians were initially encouraged to anticipate independence, Japan was primarily concerned with the wider Pacific War, and instead the country was merged within a

"Co-Prosperity Sphere" of Japanese interests and protectorates in Asia. Although there was a prolonged slump in trade, the urban population increased during the occupation despite the hardships.

The archipelago was divided into three separate regions and every attempt was made to turn Jakarta into a Japanese city, but with the minimum of available resources. Jakarta was divided into a complicated network of administrative units called *tonarigumi* to establish assistance and defence duties. The Japanese recognised that overtures to the Javanese Muslim population was a means to gain support, but nationalist leaders in the country chose to campaign for Indonesian liberation with the egalitarian spirit of revolution.

With the surrender of Japan to the Allies in 1945, the Indonesian declaration of independence led to a protracted period of recalcitrance on the part of the Dutch. Calls for "Merdeka" in 1945 by the Republican Cabinet were initially quelled by British troops, who arrived in October to receive the Japanese surrender. From 1946 the Dutch again tightened their hold on the city and reoccupied administrative buildings. In January 1948 the United Nations intervened to bring about agreement between the Dutch and the Republic. With opposition mounting to Dutch forces, coupled with the suspension of United States aid to the Netherlands, sovereignty was agreed between all parties in December 1949. A new government of the Republic of Indonesia was appointed in August 1950 on the fifth anniversary of the *merdeka* proclamation, and this had a significant bearing on urban administration.

The process of decolonisation, and the revolutionary chaos under the Sukarno era that followed, might be considered the reason for both the disarray of land registration and the problems that have ensued. These relate to the informal and insecure land tenure systems, and through this the development

of squatter settlements, which have been afforded a degree of protection because of their sheer size.[6] The acute housing shortage that arose then, is still chronic in the modern city. During the immediate post-war period of activity, much of Jakarta became a no-man's land of abandoned kampongs and burned out housing areas. With inflows of refugees entering the city together with Chinese migrants, and the release of around 45,000 European prisoners-of-war, Jakarta had an estimated shortage of 70,000 units in 1948. Informal requisition of housing was accompanied by legal protection of temporary occupants under the Rent Tribunal Ordinance, and the Housing Allocation Bureau.

A Town Planning Ordinance in 1948 provided a legal and administrative framework for housing and urban design. The new Jalan Thamrin served to shift the development emphasis further south to Kebayoran Baru (only eight kilometres from the city centre), where new government and institutional buildings would better reflect a modernising image than the older colonial quarters. Much of the finance came from foreign loans, but most urban decision-making was divided between different bodies. It was based on the principle of zoning for different categories of housing —Kampungs, small houses and villas — and was inspired by garden city models in Europe, although its surrounding greenbelt later gave way to development. The project was carried out under the aegis of the Central Foundation for Reconstruction and provided 7,500 housing units. Land was annexed from local farmers and formed part of a major land resumption process, which effectively doubled Jakarta's land area in 1950, facilitating southern expansion of the city over the next twenty years. Building work was carried out by the government, with subcontractors employed to assemble standard house types. While the houses were intended for low-income families, middle-income groups and civil servants settled in the area, and many of the small houses were eventually rebuilt.

At the same time, between 1950 and 1965 the city's development was highlighted by a series of symbolic landmarks, among them the National Monument comprising a tall obelisk with a gilded flame at the centre of the Lapangan Merdeka — Independence Square. It was intended to be highly visible across the flat city landscape, while its base contains a museum of Indonesia history. A new city mayor was appointed to orchestrate Sukarno's grand gestures for sports complexes, mosques and commercial centres. New infrastructure and architectural centrepieces were harnessed to create a new built identity for the city, which underscored the role of Jakarta as the nation's capital.

An Outline Plan for the city was formulated in 1957, produced by the Public Works Department as a model for other Indonesian cities, but was never executed. Instead it provided an early indication of difficulties associated with vested political interests and conflicts between national, regional and municipal levels of administration. This was in contrast to colonial planning in other cities, where policy makers were granted a high degree of authority and urban plans made cities broadly intelligible. A shortage of low-income housing commensurate with the rate of urban growth has remained a chronic problem since the 1950s and has constantly underlain social tensions in the city. It has also left new housing provision largely in the hands of real-estate developers and large corporations.

A key premise of a United Nations sponsored plan for Jakarta in 1957, was that government spending should be directed at the provision of infrastructure and services, and that housing should be provided by the private sector in three broad locations or 'growth poles' — Bogor to the south, Tangerang in the west and Bekasi to the east.

This provided the basis for a metropolitan strategy, although the rate of migration consistently over-ran population projections. In addition, presidential intervention in the urban planning process (in order to showcase monumental projects as symbols of national status) hindered the achievement of unified urban design and necessitated both clearance and displacement. President Sukarno, a civil engineer by training, even contemplated building an entirely new city in Kalimantan. Other major projects such as the Pulo Mas plan for large-scale public housing was almost completely compromised in its implementation.

The city boundaries were extended to encompass an area three times that of the old municipality to accommodate massive growth in population, partly generated by the relocation of the Republican Government from Yogyakarta. By 1965 the population was almost four million, but contained a wide range of distinct ethnic groups — often referred to as Jakarta's *gado-gado* culture.

A gradual process of nationalisation put large parts of the economy, including banks and utilities, into State hands. Housing became a critical issue, the main emphasis being to accommodate government employees and business leaders, tied together through a web of connections. The majority of immigrants shared existing housing, often in older areas devoid of sewage and electricity services, leading to illegal occupation of land and the growth of squatter settlements, the most densely populated areas being in the inner city. Growth and decay existed side-by-side, and land that was required for planning purposes or threatened public safety was simply resumed and cleared. Policies for high-rise housing encountered social resistance as well as resource constraints, although multi-storey commercial development began to permeate the core business areas.

The Municipal Council served as a conduit for channelling the interests and grievances of

Kampung groups, but its power was reduced, commensurate with more authoritarian involvement in city affairs by the President and increasing emphasis on national identity. In 1967 Sukarno was relieved of his office, and General Suharto was confirmed as President with Ali Sadikin as Governor of Jakarta. This was at a time of economic growth, which fuelled foreign investment and an ensuing construction boom, or *pembangunan*. Private construction focussed on offices, shopping centres, hotels and luxury housing.

A plan for the Greater Jakarta region was promulgated in 1965 and adopted in 1967. It proposed that the urban districts of Tangerang, Depok, Serpong and Bekasi should continue to consolidate as growth poles. This was reinforced in the 1980 Jabotabek Metropolitan Development Plan which proposed planning emphasis on a concentric ring of 'self-sufficient and multi-functional new towns divided by green swathes which would also act as water catchments'. These would be served by a road- and rail-based east-west corridor between Bekasi and Tangerang in combination with the north-south corridor linking the city with Bogor.

Management of population growth continued to present a problem however, highlighted by expanding squatter settlements alongside rail alignments and the city's canals. Around 70 per cent of Jakarta's population were Kampung dwellers. The only cost-effective means of affordable improvement was to upgrade the physical environment rather than provide for fully serviced housing, utilising World Bank loans for essential services such as lined drains, water hydrants, toilet blocks and laundry facilities.

While the 1985 structure plan emphasised the provision of a comprehensive public transport system, the eventual spatial plan adopted a road based policy with a radial toll road model, paving the way for waves of uncoordinated urban expansion from the late 1970s onwards. This grew

[7] Douglas, M, 'Globalisation, Mega-projects and the Environment : Urban Form and Water in Jakarta', in *Environment and Urbanisation Asia* 1(1), SAGE Publications, New York, 2010, p45-65

The National Museum on Medan Merdeka was opened in 1868 by the Batavian Society for Arts and Sciences founded in 1778, and has been a driving force in preserving Indonesia's archaeological and fine art collections. It was designed in the style of a Roman villa. The bronze elephant was presented by the King of Thailand in 1871.

The Kantor Pos Pasar Baru was built between 1912 and 1929, designed by J F Hoytema in an Art Deco style. It was built as the Hoofdbureau van de Post en Telefoondienst, and since 1963 has served as Jakarta's Post Office Building.

around its low-income service sector, which had been sustained by large-scale rural-urban migration. Therefore core and suburban centres were surrounded by slum developments along rail alignments, rivers and coastline. The Jabotabek plan therefore proposed an extensive Kampung Improvement Programme with reconstruction of temporary areas as permanent urban settlements.

Indonesia's participation in OPEC from 1973 signalled an opportunity to implement urban development programmes through oil revenue. As improved transportation enhanced access to the city, development grew around export-oriented industries. This in turn led to the rise of a suburban middle-class within new townships in the Jabodetabek mega-urban region, mirroring the period of intensive growth and expansion during the 1980s and 1990s, up to the Asian financial crisis in 1997. Urban space has generally been structured by class differences, which overlap with consumption patterns. This is evident from the 100-plus shopping malls and the parallel construction of gated suburban communities — the predominant form of urban expansion in Jabotabek since the mid-1980s.[7] Jakarta's shift from mono-centric city to sprawling multi-core metropolis with problems of planning co-ordination and individual rates of expansion, has exacerbated environmental problems. Consequently, population movement within the mega-urban region has seen reduction in densities across the city core, and a commensurate increase in the surrounding districts.

A programme of toll roads connect strategic nodes within Jakarta's polycentric framework, and a system of priority bus lanes came into force in 2004, which has largely failed to alleviate traffic conditions as ridership volumes are too low, and it does not form part of the current spatial plan for the city. In May 2013 it was announced that two consortia of Japanese and Indonesia

firms will commence building the first six-kilometre section of a new Mass Rapid Transit system from the southern part of the city to the centre to be completed in 2017. This will eventually stretch over 110 kilometres within the metropolitan area with both elevated and underground sections.

REVITALISATION AND RESTRUCTURING THE CITY

A continuous process of land conversion and redevelopment in the inner city has produced an intensified pattern of land use and an increase in residential density, but at the social cost of displacing some low-cost housing neighbourhoods.

Preservation and rehabilitation of historic environments has been carried out since the 1980s. The first project was in the Kota quarter of North Jakarta which included: the conversion of the Dutch *stadhuis* — the city hall built in 1710 in Fatahillah Square, now the Jakarta History Museum; the Bank of Indonesia; the adjacent Justice building;

buildings around the harbour of Batavia at Sunda Kelapa; and the Chinatown Kali Besar area of Glodok. The Seni Rupa Fine Arts Museum on the east side of the Faahillah Square occupies the former Supreme Court building completed in 1879. However buildings not officially classified as historic structures remain unprotected. Initial plans for the Kota area focussed attention on heritage protection. Restoration proposals were drawn up in 1992 for an integrated scheme of reconstructed buildings including Kali Besar, Sunda Kelapa and Pasar Ikan, intended to encourage the growth of heritage tourism by revitalising part of old Jakarta.

This has been superceded by a large-scale project — the North Jakarta Revitalisation and Waterfront Reclamation Project. This comprised 28 square kilometres of reclamation from the Bay of Jakarta for residential and commercial development, which commenced in 1996 despite the risk of flooding. The project was divided among several large development companies, and

A NUMBER OF OLD BATAVIAN HOUSES are still located alongside the Kali Besar Canal in Kuta. The brick townhouse which forms part of the terrace was built for the Governor General Van Imhoff in 1730. It acted as the Navy Academy from 1743-55, and then a government guest house until 1808, and is a mix of European and Chinese influences. Its red brick façade give it the name of "Toko Merah" or Red Shop.

The neo-Classical Chartered Bank of India Building on the Corner of Kali Besar Barat was constructed in 1910 by EHGH Cuypers, with a landmark corner dome and a ground level arcade.

8 Silver, 2008, op. cit., p142
9 Silver, 2008, op. cit., p159

The Gedung Kesenian, formerly the Stadsschouwburg was built in 1821 in the Empire style as a theatre, established initially by the British. It was occupied by the military during the Japanese occupation and re-opened as a theatre in 1987.

some historic warehouse buildings have been converted for a variety of uses. In addition some of the most significant nineteenth century buildings around Merdeka Square in central Jakarta have also been restored for public uses. The Presidential Palace on Jalan Medan Merdeka is converted from two nineteenth-century villas. The oldest, Istana Negara, was a merchant's villa and later the governor's residence. The Istana Merdeka was added in 1879.

KAMPUNG IMPROVEMENT

The Indonesian Kampung can generally be defined as an indigenous collection of native dwellings. In an urban sense it is more associated with its depressing transformation from semi-rural enclaves adjacent to agricultural holdings, to overcrowded squatter communities. Kampungs in Jakarta have therefore become permanent fixtures but with mainly impermanent structures, subject to the forces of growth and change, and lacking in proper infrastructure.

A Kampung improvement programme was introduced in 1969 in order to provide a better standard of accommodation in the face of deteriorating conditions caused by massive rural-urban migration. Prior to this there

had been no investment in infrastructure. A 'sites and services' upgrading on a partial self-help basis, for Kampungs with high population densities, was considered a low-cost alternative to a new housing programme. It was designed to facilitate participation by residents in undertaking basic infrastructure improvements in essential drainage, water, sanitary facilities and paved accessways. The programme created some sense of ownership among residents, and was extended through World Bank funding between 1974 and 1981, covering all Jakarta's Kampungs over an area of 5,400 hectares, which varied widely in need. A traditional practice known as *gotong royong* or mutual self-help assisted the implementation process — it stresses the collective importance of community over the individual.[8] It is aided by a system of conciliation or *mufakat* which underscores the spirit of co-operation. However over the long-term, the improvement programme has been poorly sustained due to: an ill-conceived policy to encourage the private sector to provide low-income housing; and the high cost of land which has encouraged Kampung removal. This has eliminated affordable housing in inner-city locations and driven the growth of peri-urban settlements.

Redevelopment has also contributed to continued out-migration from the urban core to the periphery.

The older Kampungs continue to survive as urban neighbourhoods within the city framework, and form strong communities. Permeability is maximised through a matrix of pedestrian routes, which provide access not just to housing clusters but pocket industries, such as *becak*–driving, recycling businesses and street-based occupations such as hawking. Maintenance continues to be a problem and canals, together with the Ciliwung River which should represent a means to integrate attractive landscaped connectors through the city, are seriously polluted — an issue that can only be corrected through a piped water supply and sewage system. Kampungs continue to present a 'parallel universe' within the city — high density but poor housing accommodating the majority of the population, juxtaposed with modern precincts built by international capital and elite residential areas such as Menteng, where high walls and security apparatus convey a sense of exclusion. As in other modernising Asian cities, attempts in Jakarta to restrict or clear street vendors and purveyors of small services by creating new centralised markets and official supply chains, inevitably reduce essential earning capacity of the poorest sectors and increase their economic vulnerability.

THE METROPOLITAN REGION

The Jakarta metropolitan region now comprises the core city which covers 650 square kilometres, together with a further three districts — Bekasi, Tangerang and Bokor, each of which has a core urban component. They are collectively termed Jabotabek, and encompass 6,200 square kilometres with a population of around 26 million. The city region is subject to three critical and long-standing problems in the face of continually intensifying urban development: first, the combined urban pressures from in-migration of people; second, traffic congestion from inadequate spatial planning and lack of public transport investment; and third, the increasing vulnerability to flooding from thirteen rivers which flow across the alluvial plain and constantly replenish it with silt.

The modern Jakarta Metropolitan Region has its roots in the Sukarno presidency of the mid-1960s, when abundant oil revenue facilitated a concentration of investment in new development through state-owned enterprises. The main development emphasis was a north-south corridor alignment to Bandung. As a result the population increased rapidly until 1980 with accelerated growth outside DKI Jakarta. During this period, foreign investment in the tiger economies of Hong Kong, Singapore, Taiwan and South Korea began to seek out more cost-effective locations for manufacturing industry, from which Jakarta benefitted. This led to major employment in the city region, which attracted massive in-migration. Development of Jakarta City was largely determined by globalised financial and business trends, which superceded the manufacturing industries of the 1970s. Centres such as Mega Kuningan have replaced the traditional low-rise street network, with high-rise commercial and residential developments, transforming them from busy mixed-use neighbourhoods into exclusive self-contained clusters.

This accelerated development pattern was characterised by classic "desakota" conditions of low-density housing and industry within a network of Kampungs and agricultural holdings. These supported rice production, garden produce and plantation products, and were fed by canals within the floodplain. The holdings became progressively subdivided and infilled, creating a mix of urban and rural uses. A combination of poor land regulation, fragmented land administration and abuse of development permits, established a basis

for uncoordinated growth patterns with poor access and services. In the 1990s, large-scale subdivision projects defined peripheral areas of the city, with major development interests acquiring substantial tracts of land, which became subject to speculation. Between 1980 and 1994, approximately 66,000 hectares around Jakarta were converted from agriculture to urban use.[9] This process made the preparation of coordinated land use plans

difficult, and led to the growth of suburban retail centres and industrial estates which often violated environmental regulations concerning development in the floodplain.

The Jabotabek Metropolitan Development Plan in 1993 identified five zoned areas based on environmental constraints and opportunities, with large-scale development proposed on land elevated above the flood plain on an east-west axis. This was further

[10] Mannas, S.G.M. and Kumalasari, R, 'Jakarta-Dynamics of Change and Liveability' in *Mega Urban Regions in Pacific Asia*, Eds. Jones GW and Douglas M, NUS Press, Singapore, 2008

[11] Rakodi, C and Firman, T, *Planning for an Extended Metropolitan Region in Asia: Jakarta, Indonesia Case Study*, prepared by Revisiting Urban Planning: Global Report on Human Settlements, 2009

[12] Rakodi and Firman, 2009, op. cit., p11

[13] Douglas, 2010, op. cit.

underscored and extended under the plan review some ten years later, based on an integrated urban infrastructure programme. The zones, from north to south, identified: areas where urban expansion should be avoided; areas for limited urban expansion and agricultural intensification; major urban development on land above the coastal plain with good drainage; limited urban development on steep slopes; and upland conservation and recreation associated with forested land. A number of privately sponsored 'new town' projects, which mainly act as dormitory suburbs on the eastern and western edge of Jakarta — such as Pura Jaya City, Bintaro Jaya and Bekasi New Town — began to proliferate in the 1990s. They each cover around 1,000 hectares, with 'gated' developments targeted at middle-class families and built mainly on 'greenfield' sites with associated industrial and commercial uses. Low-cost housing enclaves were built in more remote locations.

Within the downtown area, Merdeka Square became the focus of a commercial spine extending southward along Jalan Thanrin and Jalan Sudivman, accompanied by a new central business district in the 'Golden Triangle' which was developed on the site of densely populated urban Kampungs. These absorbed large areas of open space, with over half the city's public parks converted to other functions.

The Asian financial crisis of 1997 exposed the bubble economy that had been building up since the 1980s through investment in urban mega-projects. It had serious consequences for Jakarta, precisely because urban economic activities associated with land and property came from overseas loans and national banks, so that non-performing loans led to the collapse of development schemes. Work was halted on all road construction projects, although these were reactivated again in 2002. A significant amount of land was then acquired by the city, and a welcome political

trajectory towards democratic government created an energised basis for increased foreign investment, but with a perceptible shift towards service industry.

Since 2002, neo-liberal reform has accelerated both economic and export growth with foreign direct investment in 2012 reaching record highs. The population of the Jakarta Metropolitan Region has increased from around two million in the 1960s to around 25 million in 2012, with accompanying realms of consumption that reflect new urban wealth. However an ineffective approach to land registration and urban management still persists which, along with a lack of enforcement mechanisms, makes co-ordinated urban spatial planning difficult to implement. Disorder and lack of public consultation during the plan-making process creates deepening problems of disparity and separation within civil society, which are hard to rectify.

As a result of these problems, lack of effective land management overlaps with issues of environment, as unplanned settlement expands across vulnerable surfaces, blocks water channels and extracts groundwater. Settlement over the region's aquifer, together with deforestation and siting of development on hillsides, has reduced water catchments. Meanwhile up to 90 per cent of wetland in North Jakarta has been converted to other uses, so that its impervious structure causes routine flooding.[10] This raises the central question of sustainability within a vulnerable metropolitan region where a "guided" land policy aimed at deflecting growth away from environmentally fragile and susceptible areas, is not backed up by planning controls, zoning and enforcement procedures. Furthermore it reflects problems stemming from intensified global production and investment trends, which are transforming long-standing economies to cities of global consumption. In Jakarta this is accompanied by a layering of mega-

projects over previously low-rise cityscapes, privatisation of public spaces and institutions, and ever-increasing infrastructure works to accommodate flows of goods, with governments acting as the facilitator. This in turn initiates the construction of symbolic projects such as exhibition and convention facilities, which raise the global profile of the city but in many cases are difficult to assimilate, both spatially and environmentally.

In terms of evaluating the success or otherwise of planning and development policies, Rakodi and Firman believe the significant factors to be the structural problems and inefficiencies of the public sector with regard to planning and land administration.[11] Inadequate investment in infrastructure in the region has been accompanied by disjointed administrative arrangements. This is exacerbated by a poorly regulated banking sector and over-extension of many private development companies. A current proposal to decentralise the government of the metropolitan region requires local governments to be given a greater share of revenues to better plan for wider needs. This underlines the difficulties stemming from official land titles where property rights are weakly defined. Land development permits must technically be issued in accordance with development plans, and landowners can only sell to holders of permits. The latter have become major land speculation tools and inadvertently contribute to uneven forms of land development, with sprawl and congestion at the urban edges rather than planned communities.[12]

The Jabotabek experience is a cautionary one, illustrating an unpreparedness for untrammelled urban growth and global economic intervention. Furthermore, planning has not been sufficiently matched by circumspect land management, development regulation and environmental protection at a local level. As a result the region has

14 Salim, W and Firman, T,
'Covering the Jakarta City –
Region History, Challenges,
Risks and Strategies', in
*Planning Asian Cities: Risks
and Resilience*, Eds. Stephen
Hamnet and Dean Forbes,
Routledge, London and
New York, 2011

experienced extremes of urbanisation: first, the construction of major built development in a relatively ad hoc manner that reflects an informal system of land acquisition and assembly, and where intensified construction, deforestation and depletion of ground water has degraded the vulnerable ecology; and second, the increase in temporary settlements and lack of adequate infrastructure in the city.[13] While anti-poverty programmes have been introduced, Jakarta still has an estimated 400,000 people living below the established income threshold.[14] Over-development and subsequent erosion in water catchment areas have increased the frequency of flooding. This is exacerbated by the difficulties of land clearance, a lack of stormwater run-off nullahs, and dilapidated drainage systems, which now lead to periodic water inundation within the city area itself.

Political reforms since 1999 have encouraged a significant increase in foreign direct investment. In response to some of the prevailing problems, the 2010 Spatial Structure Plan has prioritised environmental objectives including: improved infrastructure and water supply; the cleaning of major rivers to form scenic corridors; and additions to the system of flood canals. The plan divides DKI Jakarta into different zones with multiple business centres: the Northern Zone comprises the new development area along the North coast in Jakarta Bay to include residential, commercial and tourist facilities; the Central Zone which encompasses high density commercial and residential development; and lower densities in the South to preserve the water catchments.

The city's economy has soared between 2000 and 2013 with GDP growth averaging around 5.2 per cent with massive foreign investments, and the residential market is fuelled by strong employment growth. The McKinsey Global Institute forecasts that Indonesia is on track to become the seventh largest global economy by 2030. However

its democratic credentials and improvement in governance has created a market for investment property at one end of the spectrum, while its inadequate infrastructure, pollution and wealth gap act to keep Jakarta in the bottom quarter of the Global Liveability Index.

While Indonesia contains the world's largest Muslim population, it is abundantly diverse owing to the eclectic values of local customs, cultural traditions, ancient Hindu rites and Buddhist practices, which provide for elaborate architectural interpretations and symbolic ceremonies. Jakarta is both a microcosm of indigenous Indonesian culture but also a dense urban conurbation in an overwhelmingly rural country. The intrinsic characteristics of a port city remain in its cosmopolitan population of ethnic groupings, harbourside activities and informal urban quarters, which contrast, somewhat awkwardly, with the essential facets of the modern city. The urbanised capital city is the seat of national government but it also has a provincial level government *Daerch Khusus*

PHYSICAL EVIDENCE of Jakarta's historical pattern of intervention exists only in the remnants of canal alignments, and in isolated pockets which illustrate the eighteenth and nineteenth century architecture and civic layout. The Taman Fatahilla town square area of Old Batavia has been restored, and the surrounding Dutch colonial buildings have been converted into museums. The Jakarta City Museum with its tall central cupola was formerly the Stadhuis or City Hall completed in 1710 under the direction of the Chief Carpenter of the VOC.

[15] Salim and Firman, 2011, op. cit.

Reference of a kind – A symbolic windmill as hotel signage acts to resurrect the historical Dutch connection to the city on Jalan Hayam Wuruk

Conservation of a kind. The biggest and most highly ornamented Chinese residence in Glodok was owned by Khouw Kim An, the last Chinese mayor of Batavia. Its prominent location on Jalan Gajah Mada appeared to preclude intensification of development on the site. The solution was to deck over the building supported by large structural columns, and construct a hotel above.

Ibukota Jakarta. Parts of this fall under two other provincial jurisdictions, creating problems of effective urban management.[15] The nature of society continues to shift and evolve through ethnic and demographic changes, with different subcultures holding different positions in the city economy but welded together in the twenty-first century by forceful economic growth, a consciousness of nationhood and rising levels of education. However Jakarta persists as a city of contrast. Rising levels of foreign investment have catapulted the city to become a centre for international commerce, yet the physical division of the city into pockets of affluence amidst deep-seated problem areas is akin to the modern highways that scythe through the city but where the traffic on them fails to move forward for much of the time.

The political transition at a national level has translated into more sustainable values for Jakarta at a planning level, with a somewhat greater focus on social inclusiveness and a more participatory process attuned to local rather than central government priorities. This has been gradually introduced in some of the rapidly urbanising peripheral townships. For example in Depok, which lies within the Jobotabek urban growth corridor, stakeholder forums made up of various civic groups have provided necessary input to local plans, which deal with economic and social as well as planning issues. This is a step towards engendering a more responsive and sustainable megacity and enables it to face ongoing planning challenges.

Gereja Cathedral was designed by the Dutch architect, Pater Antonius Dijkmans in a neo-Gothic style, then popular in Europe. It was at one time the tallest building in Batavia, and now dominates the adjoining Lapangan Banteng. It sits in juxtaposition with the Masjid Istiqlal built on the ruins of the old Dutch fort.

Early twentieth century offices built along Pintu Besar Utara in a Dutch vernacular style.

Singapore

TEMPLE STREET IN SINGAPORE'S CHINATOWN, facing South Bridge Road. The shophouse street, as a generic type, originated in Southern China and was brought to the city by Chinese immigrants in the nineteenth and early twentieth centuries, with urban design and street making traditions that dated back to the Song dynasty. This reflected a building form where family accommodation, rooms for rent, and business premises were closely related. In Singapore the shophouse style evolved to combine a blend of Chinese, Malay and European references and embellishments in their façades, carved doorways, stucco details, motifs and glazed tilework. Later and more eclectic models reflected British colonial influences such as fluted pilasters, Palladian fanlights, full-length shuttered windows, and upper storeys that projected over the pavement creating the colonnaded "five foot ways" that became a characteristic of the city.

1 Brendon, P, *The Decline and Fall of the British Empire 1781-1997*, Jonathan Cape, London, 2007, p416

HISTORICAL INTERVENTIONIST INFLUENCES

In 1824 a treaty between the British and Dutch partitioned the Malay Peninsula from Indonesia, ending a protracted battle for naval supremacy in the Indian Ocean. The treaty resulted in the British taking possession of Singapore, a strategically located deep-water harbour, adding to their previous capture of Penang in 1786 and Malacca in 1795. Fort Canning dates back to fourteenth century Temasek, said to have been founded by ancient Javanese nobility. It became known as Bukit Larangan, the ancestral home of Iskandar Shah — last of the Malay sultans before the British arrival in 1801. The East Indies, later the Indonesian archipelago of Java and Sumatra, came under Dutch rule. The formation of the Straits Settlement in 1826, and the amalgamation by Britain of its 'possessions' in Penang, Malacca and Singapore, heralded a new era of trade and development. In these cities the Chinese were welcomed as cheap labour and service providers, but also for their trading links and investment potential.

Stanford Raffles arrived in Singapore from India in 1819 ostensibly to establish a trading settlement under the auspices of the East India Company. However the island strategically guarded the Malacca Strait, which comprised the main sea route between the Indian Ocean and the South China Sea. Raffles drew up an agreement with the indigenous Malay rulers — the *Temengong* — allowing the newcomers to rule the territory in return for British protection. With the ceding of Hong Kong and the Chinese treaty ports to the British some eighteen years later under the Treaty of Nanking, Britain had in its control the two most defensible naval bases in Asia. Raffles famously stated, "Our object is not territory but trade; a great commercial emporium and a fulcrum where we may extend our influence politically as circumstances may hereafter require".[1]

A number of forces shaped the emerging city form, with its mix of colonial and indigenous immigrant influences. The early eighteenth century land use pattern made up of occupational and ethnic enclaves — the Chinese and Malay kampungs in the Beach Road area and the Indian community in the Serangoon neighbourhood — was reinforced through official colonial policy. Raffles and his successor John Crawford prepared the first plan for the island in 1823 which formalised the prevailing land use patterns, with priority allocation of land given to merchants and artisans.

Under the 1823 Plan, the lower Singapore River was seen as the centrepiece of the new settlement. The northern embankment was designated for use by the government and the area to the south for use by merchants. The 'fill' from the creation of the first Commercial Square was used to form South Boat Quay for godowns, trading and shipping offices. The square was later transformed into the present Raffles Place. With the advent of steam ships and the opening of the Suez Canal in 1869 (which reduced travel time to Europe), increased trading patterns brought requirements for new reclamation, bridge building and commercial structures. However the older river profile remained until the early 1980s with *bumboats* and lighters still plying a trade along a riverscape dominated by shophouses. Boat Quay was designated as a Conservation Area in 1989 — the first step in a rejuvenation programme along the Singapore River with new and upgraded quayside developments, including the current ambitious development of Marina City.

Although boundaries have altered somewhat over the years, the Chinese, Indian and Muslim enclaves have remained substantially unchanged.

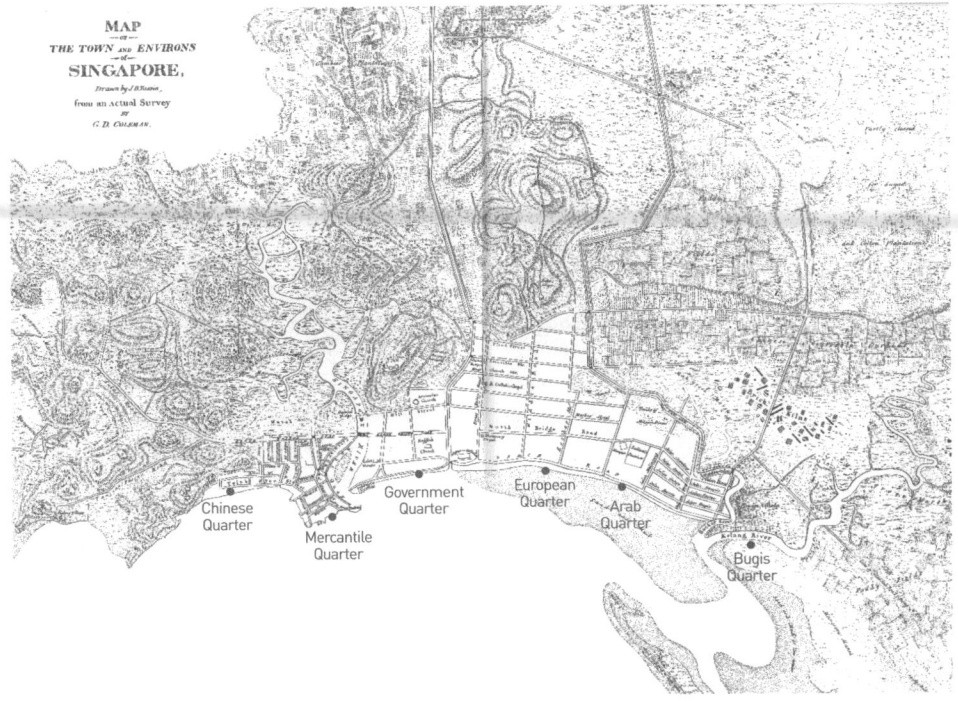

CHINATOWN

South of the Singapore River, an area was laid out for the Chinese community under the Raffles Plan of 1824, although much of the land at the time was owned by the East India Company. It was traditionally referred to as Niu Che Shiu for its reliance on the use of bullock carts to transport water. New Bridge Road was constructed in 1841 and land titles were issued in 1843 for newly formed streets which were subsequently sub-divided by the owners. Between 1857 and 1890 the area developed rapidly through a massive increase in Chinese immigrants, so that much of the new accommodation was in the form of cramped lodging houses. The majority of existing shophouse terraces were built in increasingly refined and decorative styles between 1890 and 1941, most of the uses being local shops,

clan associations and residential development. By the 1980s many of the structures were neglected, and became subject to an upgrading exercise carried out by the Urban Renewal Authority which overlaid a new commercial framework onto the restored fabric, reducing its authenticity but upgrading its role as a visitor destination, with a host of emblematic references to the Chinese community.

Chinatown covers 23 hectares and around 12,000 buildings. It is subdivided into four main areas: Tolok Ayer — the arrival point for nineteenth century Chinese immigrants, marked by old established trading companies, old shophouses and the Thian Hock Keng Temple; Kreta Ayer — an older street market area integrating the Sri Mariamman Temple and the Jamae Mosque; and the Bukit Pasoh and Tanjong Pagar residential areas. The

conserved landscape of this active enclave establishes, not merely a heritage area but a material repository of ethnic tradition and enterprise, and a cultural framework for the continuation of trades such as herbalists and calligraphers. Chinatown is a living community with its own range of services, trades and lifestyles. However regeneration means economic upgrading and gentrification, leading inevitably to attrition of some small businesses rooted in the community in the face of a more sanitised version, albeit one embedded in cultural heritage. A number of east-west streets lie between New Bridge Road and South Bridge Road — including Cross Street, Mosque Street, Sago Street, Smith Street and Pagoda Street — forming a matrix of three-storey shophouse terraces.

TRENGGANU STREET lies at the heart of Chinatown and its three storey buildings create a unified and compositional character. Narrow pedestrian connections demarcate bazaar areas, with market stalls and open shop fronts at ground level, and living quarters and commercial outlets above. Various design devices have been used in the upgrading process, including louvred shutters, balcony elements, old lighting features and lanterns that attempt to authenticate the character and atmosphere that prevailed in the early twentieth century.

Temple Street in Chinatown, facing towards People's Park

The plan took into account existing areas of settlement but imposed an idealistic grid over much of the area within topographic constraints, subdividing land into private lots, government uses and public spaces including the Padang. This introduced a regularity of layout assisted by a specification of certain development and construction parameters, and a Land Registry was established to consolidate the land sale process.

Chinese merchants, like in Hong Kong some twenty years later, were responsible for most of the first commercial construction in Singapore. The British East India Company took charge of delicate negotiations over land agreements and purchase with the local sultan, prior to Britain's permanent possession of the island. Colonial intervention followed the strict sectoral divisions honed by the British in their other 'possessions' — the European town, including Fort Canning between the government area and the Rochore River, was technically separated from the Chinese, Arab and other non-European town quarters, all of which could provide services to British officials and the business community. The local Malay settlements were located on the northern fringes. However affluent Asian merchants were actively encouraged to establish residential

and trading establishments throughout the area alongside Europeans, well outside the designated 'Chinatown' area just inland of the Singapore River and South Boat Quay. This effectively helped to establish the formative urban framework of the city. Many of the artisans and much of the building materials of timber and tiles came from Georgetown in Penang, which was by that time the most flourishing settlement along the Straits. A fire that destroyed many of the original wooden structures paved the way for more permanent construction, including shophouse districts based primarily on Chinese 'row house' building traditions, with commercial space located on the ground floor.

Two other policy interventions helped to substantiate the urban design approach: the first was the sale of building land by auction, allowing long-term investment in permanent building; the second was the imposition of a Town Planning Ordinance and Building Regulations that provided both specified layout criteria and a practical means of ensuring building safety. Raffles directed the first building committee to specify that: "all houses constructed of brick or tile should have a uniform type of front, each having a verandah of a certain depth, open at all times as a continuous and covered passage

THE ASSEMBLAGE OF BUILDINGS IN VICTORIA STREET that make up Chijmes, originally functioned as a Catholic convent and orphanage. Caldwell House, one of the oldest buildings in Singapore, dates back to the 1840s when it was the residence for a French order of nuns. Abandoned children were left in their care at the gateway on Bras Basah Road. The Convent was later extended and the Chapel, designed by Charles Benedict Nain, was based on a French Gothic style. It was tendered in 1990 with the proviso that the conversion should respect the architecture and former uses. Certain conservation parameters were set out which married cultural heritage with economic principles and this principle underscores much of the city's conservation programme. The resurrected architecture plays on its once cloistered and contemplative spaces. These now provide a secluded focus for dining and shopping while celebrating its illusory religious symbolism as part of a new commercial landmark. Restoration of the heritage structures was carried out by French conservation experts. The new recreational and restaurant complex received a UNESCO Heritage Award in 2002.

THE NAGORE DURGHA SHRINE, administered by the Jamae Mosque, is built in a similar style with square minarets joined by a decorative balustrade, an elaborate frieze and ground level colonnades. It was completed in 1830 making it one of the oldest buildings in the city, built to commemorate a holy prophet from South India. In its restored form, the design evokes the simple but unpretentious characteristics of its ancient roots. Both the mosque and shrine share similarities with the Sri Poyyatha Vinayagar Moorthi Temple in Malacca, with its old-established Chulia community. It is now an Indian-Muslim Heritage Centre.

THE JAMAE MOSQUE was constructed in 1835 for Muslims from the Coromandel Coast in India, replacing an earlier mosque on South Bridge Road. The Chulias had traded within the Straits Settlements from the time of the Dutch East India Company and eventually settled in Singapore, in what is now Chulia Street near the Singapore River. The distinctive towered entrance gate with its miniature domes and tiered niches, are references to the Muslim architecture of southern India, and forms the predominant feature on South Bridge Road at its junction with Mosque Street.

on each side of the street". Terraces were therefore linked and made more publicly amenable by means of covered colonnades — the 'five-foot ways' that helped evolve a stylistic and climatically suitable typology applied to vernacular building form. This was extended to other cities on the Malayan peninsular, and can still be experienced in the older parts of Singapore. New land owners subdivided linear lots into deep but narrow-fronted sites, where widths of dwellings were determined by the length of locally available timber beams and joints. An open court acted as both a skywell to introduce daylight to the dark interior, and a means of ventilation. It was also frequently used as a washing area, with a drainage channel introduced along the dividing lane at the rear.

British designers and surveyors helped to introduce aesthetic as well as building standards in the design of public buildings, and in the early years a sequence of able administrators assisted development. The city's first architect was George Drumgoole Coleman who brought to Singapore his experience of building Batavia (now Jakarta), and became Superintendent of Public Works in 1833. Coleman refined the town plan in 1833, oversaw major infrastructure works and designed a number of important public buildings, including the first Government House and the mansion that later became Parliament House. The site of the first Government House became known as Government Hill, but in 1857 the house was demolished to make way for a fort named after John Canning — first Viceroy of India. Some fifty years later the fort was renamed and became a military complex, and was used as command headquarters for the Japanese during its military occupation, later becoming a War Museum.

Coleman also introduced a Palladian style of architecture resurrected from the Italian Renaissance, that had gained popularity in England for public buildings and country houses. The use of Classical orders had by that time become widely used on East India Company buildings in other parts of Asia. However, Coleman incorporated the use of Classical orders and proportion, with decorative devices and climatic controls related to both the local context and prevalent Malay design forms. This produced a tropical architecture of elegance and identity, assisted by craftsmen well versed in local materials. Variants of this approach were applied to churches, commercial and public buildings, including the rebuilding of early timber structures. Convict labour from India was used extensively until 1873 on both infrastructure and building construction, with supervision by army officers who occupied a dual role as Superintendents of Public Works and Overseers of Convicts.

In this way neo-Palladian influences were adapted from Anglo-Indian designs emanating from the sub-continent. These were themselves adapted from the public building traditions of Victorian city building in Britain with its integral institutions and partly reflected the fact that until 1867 (when it became a Crown Colony), Singapore was under the control of the Indian colonial authority. The Padang, located in the heart of the civic district, has been retained as a central open city space since 1820, and the Singapore Cricket Club dating back to 1852 still forms its spatial focus. The injection of a classical language into the urban design vocabulary physically transformed the rapidly growing Straits settlements, and over time created a veritable pattern book of design references that demonstrated both skilful invention and sensibility in catering to tropical conditions — including roof overhangs, shuttered openings and wide verandahs.

A further intervention that resulted from European adventurism in China, was the massive influx of Chinese labour in the wake of the opium wars, and the consequent relaxation of emigration laws in 1859. Singapore was a direct beneficiary of this, and it required the passage of the Chinese Immigrants Ordinance in 1877 to stem the exploitive import of indentured labour, which was not formally abolished until 1914.

Following the transfer of rule from India to the British Colonial Office in 1867, Singapore began to attract large numbers of immigrants from both Europe and colonial administrations including India. This lead to city expansion to the west and the reclamation of Telok Ayer Bay along with the Tanjong Pagar Docks. In 1887 the Municipal Ordinance for the urban area was placed under government control, which introduced a more systematic approach to building approvals and overall urban design. Various public buildings, including the Town Hall and the Victoria Hall, were built around the Padang which remains an open focal point and recreation area within the city.

Within a hundred years Singapore had become the fifth largest port in the world. It supported a business community of half a million people and performed a strategic function, commanding commercial trading routes to China, Japan and the East Indies, and housing the headquarters of the British military forces. It had also become one of the most diverse in terms of its population, with Chinese, Indians, Malays, Javanese and Arabic traders among many others engaged in the important entrepôt trade with the Malay Peninsula, the Philippines, Siam and Borneo.

Most of the historic residential and shophouse terraces were built during the first decades of the twentieth century, combining an increasingly hybrid and ornate appearance with a blend of Chinese, Malay and Classical references in their applied decoration and motifs. In the process this created what might be termed an indigenous Straits style that can be found throughout all the settlements, reflecting the new wealth of merchants and the cultural eclecticism of the Chinese,

2   Lee, H.Y., 'The Singapore
    Shophouse : An Anglo-Chinese
    Urban Vernacular', in *Asia's Old
    Dwellings: Tradition, Resilience
    and Change*, Ed. Ronald G.
    Knapp, Oxford University Press,
    Oxford, 2003

Babanonya and Peranakan communities. New statutory requirements for the erection of buildings were enacted in 1884, which meant that developers or contractors had to commission Chinese architectural practitioners to design terraced housing and shophouse enclaves. Two of the best known were government draughtsmen who became private architects — Tan Seng Chong and Yeo Hock Siang, together with Moh Wee Teck who designed the terraces on Emerald Hill[2]. The almost accidental result of this lack of architectural refinement was the generation of a hybrid architecture. This comprised mixed Western and Chinese fenestration features together with free-spirited accentuation of Chinese-style embellishments, such as stucco details and glazed tilework depicting auspicious decorative patterns — motifs that reflected Malay-Islamic artistic traditions and Portuguese references from Malacca. As the style became more refined and structures grew larger in the 1920s at a time of soaring commodity prices, wealthy owners began to incorporate more formal neo-Classical elements such as fluted pilasters, Palladian fanlights, and 'Venetian' arch-lintel combinations with façades painted in different pastel colours.

The two and three storey terraces continued to be the mainstay of urban development, along with the consolidation of 'ethnic' quarters and new suburban growth trajectories around new railway alignments, port and military areas. In 1926 the Architects Ordinance was introduced, and the first town planning body was established in 1927. The formation of the Singapore Improvement Trust in 1927 helped to speed up slum clearance operations.

Similar to many young Chinese modernist architects of the 1920s and 1930s who studied primarily in America, the first architectural students in Singapore studied in London. Returning as qualified architects, they brought with them new and more

The Central Fire Station built in 1919 was originally designed for horse-drawn fire wagons. Designed in a flamboyant style based on an Edwardian classical trend popular in Britain at the time, it is topped by two prominent cupolas and a central tower. It is now a gazetted monument and has been adapted to form the Civil Defence Heritage Gallery, although part of the building still functions as a fire station.

KAMPUNG GELAM

The origins of Kampung Gelam lie in the allocation of around 23 hectares of land to Sultan Hussein Shah in 1823, which included a long frontage on Beach Road designated in the Raffles Plan. It derived its name from the Gelam trees that grew around the area of the Rocher Canal. The Arab, Javanese and Bugis origins can be discerned from some of the street names — Arab Street, Baghdad Street, Muscat Street and Kandahar Street. Much of the land and initial street formation was carried out by convict labour. In 1822 the area was designated for Bugis traders, Arabs, Javanese, Boyanese and other Muslim merchants. The original Masjid Sultan was completed in 1824, and rebuilt exactly one century later with its onion shaped dome designed by Swan and Maclaren — architects of some of Singapore's prominent neo-Classical buildings. Its domes and minarets establish a strong visual identity to the area, which is laid out as a street-trading backcloth to the Mosque, approached from Bussorah Street through terraces of restored shophouses that now house cafés.

The area houses an Arabic School, which is one of a small number of Islamic centres in Singapore. The two-storey structures along Pehang Street typify the early period, with a lack of ornamentation and two small windows on the upper floors. Kandahar Street typifies the late shophouse period with elaborate ornamentation. The two and three-storey shophouses display various styles prevalent at different periods — Early, Transitional, Late and Art Deco. The area was accorded conservation status in 1989, and most of the structures have been restored.

THE MASJID SULTAN forms the most prominent feature in Kampung Gelam. The current building in 1924 replaced the earlier 1826 mosque, which was named after Sultan Hussain Shah who allowed the British to establish Singapore Island as a settlement under the treaty of 1819. It is built in the Saracenic style which evolved via British architects in colonial India, and

situated on Muscat Street at the head of an axial approach from Bussorah Street.

Adjacent to the Mosque is the historic seat of Malay royalty — Istana Kampung Gelam. The simple two-storey structure was built by Sultan Hussein's son in 1840, and his descendants finally moved in 1999, allowing the house to be restored and converted into the Malay Heritage Centre.

THE SRI SRINIVASA TEMPLE is the oldest Hindu temple in Singapore dating back to the administration of the East India Company in 1827 when a site was dedicated for a temple to Perumal — a Hindu Deity. The entrance tower was substantially rebuilt in the 1960s. Like other South Indian temples, its major feature is a five-tiered gateway tower or gopurani, similar to the six-tiered entrance to the Sri Mariamman Temple in Chinatown with its tiers of sculpted deities. Its height and form create a dominant feature on South Bridge Road, accentuating the threshold function of the tower between the busy public street and the more meditative realm of the temple compound. It is associated with the annual Thaipusam Festival, and as a celebratory focus for other important Hindu festivals: Purattasi Sani, Navarathiri and Vaikunda Ekathesi. These temples traditionally played an important role in assimilating new Hindu arrivals into the community.

LITTLE INDIA

After the founding of Singapore in 1819 there was a convergence of people from many parts of Asia. Southern Indian immigrants settled in an area straddling Telok Ayer and the South bank of the Singapore River. Many were milk traders, while others were lightermen in the Telok Ayer basin, transporting cargo to and from the merchant ships and godowns.

The streets that make up "Little India", centred around the major north-south streets of Serangoon Road and Jalan Besar, evolved from the role of the nineteenth century Indian population in cattle-related activities that were prevalent in the Serangoon area. Settlers from South India first appeared in large numbers from the 1880s and the area began to develop as the main Indian settlement in Singapore. European mansions gradually gave way to commercial and residential terraces. These were mostly built in the period up to the 1920s, incorporating the eclectic baroque fenestration that incorporates richly decorated bas reliefs, patterned tiles with exotic motifs and pilasters topped by Corinthian or Composite capitals. This helps to ensure that no two streets are precisely the same. Certain streets such as Roberts Lane were built as two-storey shophouses with cantilevered upper floors. Little India is conspicuously "branded" as Indian-themed retailing, but there is also a "back of house" quarter of support services, where money lenders and letter writers conduct their activities. A combination of renovated shophouses around the junction of Kapor Road and Powell Road establish venues for both trading and café establishments.

Rapid urban growth in the early twentieth century coincided with the draining of Kampung Kapoor between Serangoon Road and Jalan Besar. East-west roads were built in various styles. A number of streets in the area have names associated with World War I such as Somme Road and Flanders Square. The highly decorated terraces of Petain Road, named after the Marshal of France, are unified by the consistency and repetition of pilasters and classical orders, ceramic floral tiles and terracotta flooring along the colonnaded frontages.

The area to the north of Bukit Timah Road is broadly defined by a series of east-west streets linking Serangoon Road, which bisects the area from north to south, with Jalan Besar to the east and Race Course Road to the west. It gained its original identity from the Tekka Market, which was first constructed in 1915 and named after the bamboo growers on the banks of the Rochor Canal.

THE ELABORATE PLASTER MOULDINGS, decorated pilasters and oval-shaped window openings festooned with decorated bas reliefs creates a consistent frontage of nine shophouses on Syed Alwi Road. It is said that the prevailing colour pattern reflects the finely woven Kebaya garments worn in olden times by the Nonya families, while the glazed tile work of flower decoration is reminiscent of sarong designs.

Like other quarters Little India houses a mix of religious establishments, but the major Hindu Temples are Shree Lakshmi Narayan, Sri Veeramakaliamman on Bellios Road and the large Sri Srinivasa Perumal Temple to the north of Kitchener Road. The tight street framework is made up mainly of two-storey shophouses which vary in depth, creating a morphology of cross-streets without a rigid grid. While short terraces have identical characteristics bearing the mark of a single original builder — for example along Powell Road and Desker Road — others embody a definite stamp of individuality through style and ornamentation. Older commercial shophouse streets embody the 'five foot' colonnaded walkways, but others were constructed primarily as residential streets, set back from the roadways.

austere Bauhaus and Art Deco trends, which translated into a rationalised urban shophouse style based on reinforced concrete construction with minimal ornamentation. British firms such as Swan and Maclaren, and Keys & Dowdeswell introduced a neo-Classical undertone to both private and public commissions in the early twentieth century. Other public buildings were designed by British architects such as Ronald MacPherson who worked for the Public Works Department. However declining economic forces, followed by the Japanese occupation, signalled a more sober approach to urban design.

The Old Supreme Court building was completed in 1939 in a late neo-Classical style, on the site of the Grand Hotel de L'Europe. Its most notable feature is a tympanum with sculptural reliefs by Rodolfo Nolli of classical Greek and Roman figures, including the Goddess Justicia. Various bas reliefs depict scenes from colonial Singapore, including the signing of the 1819 treaty by Sir Stamford Raffles. The dome is said to resemble St Paul's Cathedral. The neighbouring City Hall constructed in 1929, housed the city's municipal functions, and later served as the Prime Minister's Office.

The buildings have been recently converted into a National Art Gallery.

The Japanese invasion from the Johore Strait in 1942 was a death blow to imperial prestige. As the Second World War came to an end, the old type of colonial rule and administration in Malaya, Burma and Singapore gave way to urgent political adjustments. While Japanese intimidation and disdain for foreign and local populations alike had been loathed, the myth of Western invincibility with its relative aloofness and antagonism towards any form of opposition, had been fatally compromised. Hastily reassembled colonial administrations came to be challenged by a locally educated gentry, led by figures who commanded local allegiance.

MODERNISATION AND THE CITY

Post-war reconstruction has involved significant conservation objectives and massive building and public housing programmes. Singapore's urban character has not come about simply through the dynamic contrast between new and old, but in the juxtaposition of tall building and low-rise street frontage set within a tropical landscape. The post-colonial urbanisation of Singapore began in 1965 when the

'Singaporean Amendment' resulted in the island being ejected from the Federation of Malaysian States. The relatively sudden transition from a colonial to an independent state, accompanied by the commensurate rise of Asian nationalism in the immediate post-World War II period, compressed the time needed to adjust to a new culture of governance with competing priorities. That has indirectly left an imprint on urban design and has meant, not merely a need to overcome the residue of destruction inherited from the war, but the problems stemming from its relatively impoverished economy and hugely diverse social mix. It became necessary to hastily put together a plan for economic and industrial development, which focussed on the city's generally well-educated labour force. Since that time, Singapore's cityscape has reflected the priority given to economic development, with special zones designated for business, industrial and government uses. By the late 1960s many shophouse areas had evolved into four and five storey structures, and new public housing programmes tended to redefine part of the city, with a commensurate loss of older fabric. Street related functions began to be replaced by point blocks, and large commercial complexes on 'island' sites.

Singapore's original footprint was around 523 square kilometres and as late as 1968 it was a compact city covering only 648 square kilometres, with two-thirds of its population living and working in shophouses. From the 1970s the government set about refashioning the city space, establishing a template for regeneration. This reflected a programmed shift from manufacturing to higher-value added and high tech industries, attracting multinational corporations. The city's financial district took shape in the early 1970s, extending from the old mercantile centre at Raffles Place along Shenton Way and Anson Road. Under the 1991 Concept Plan, the Economic Development Board and

THE SINGAPORE RIVER has been at the heart of the city's development since 1819. It has undergone several stages of reconstruction from its role as the commercial lifeline of the emerging nineteenth century entrepôt to its present day role as a refurbished landscape of leisure. It is also the central setting for many public buildings that delineated the colonial area and shophouses that represented the working areas alongside. The river effectively demarcated separation between the European Town and the mercantile activities and houses of immigrant populations who forged a living from the river as lightermen, coolies and hawkers. The Singapore River has always represented the traditional central artery through the city, originally accommodating a series of working quaysides and the site of major public buildings. A substantial clean-up of the river in the 1980s signalled a transition to recreation and leisure uses, with regenerated shophouses, new activity nodes such as Boat Quay and Clarke Quay, and a conservation and conversion programme for older public buildings.

Bronze sculpture of children leaping into the Singapore River of Life. The river also signified death for many, through pirate activity, fatal construction accidents associated with bridge building, opium dens that once lined the river, and drowning accidents. During the Japanese occupation, decapitated heads were displayed along the Read Bridge.

THE RIVER is spanned by a series of bridges. The Cavenagh Bridge (built in 1869) is the oldest bridge across the river, with a steel structure fabricated in Scotland and assembled by convict labour. It was named after Major-General William Orfeur Cavenagh — the last Governor of Singapore before it became a Crown Colony. Its rigid frame limited the passage of boats at high tide. New bridges were necessary to meet the needs of motorised vehicles, and it is now limited to pedestrian traffic. The bronze sculptural figures evoke the memory of more recreational pastimes along the Singapore River. Two other bridges were constructed in the late nineteenth century — the Ord Bridge named after the first Governor in 1886, and the Read Bridge that now links the entertainment centres of Clarke Quay and Riverside Point.

Clarke Quay, with its umbrella structures, lies on the north bank of the Singapore River linked to Riverside Point by the Read Bridge.

3 Lee, 2003, op. cit.
4 Kong, C.H., 'From Port City
   to City State : Forces Shaping
   Singapore's Built Environment',
   in *Culture and the City in East
   Asia*, Clarendon Press, Oxford,
   1997, p225

the Urban Redevelopment Authority (URA) were made responsible for transforming the Republic, both economically and spatially. By 1994 Singapore's area of urban influence had spread to neighbouring Johor and the Riau Islands, later formalised as the Indonesia-Malaysia-Singapore Growth Triangle.[3]

In the two decades following independence, Singapore embarked on a redevelopment drive to eradicate slums and rural Kampung, and to re-house the population. Turning a corner towards a more conservation-oriented approach evolved from the search for a multi-cultural identity on the back of relentless economic development and as a bulwark against the onset of entirely Western values encouraged by the homogenising and fragmenting forces of globalisation. Various architectural and planning bodies mobilized support for greater protection of built heritage. This resulted in a large scale conservation drive to protect Singapore's architectural and cultural legacy, which began in the late 1980s, commensurate with other public housing and industrial initiatives. The clean-up of the Singapore and Kallang rivers marked a shift in environmental upgrading. It took place between 1977 and 1987 and resulted in the relocation of 26,000 families and 2,800 boatyards and polluting trades.[4] At the same time it was linked to the provision of potable water. Collectively this established an image of environmental responsibility, while reinforcing the image of the Singapore River as a symbolic centrepiece of its regenerated urban design.

Regeneration of the urban area is the responsibility of the URA, Singapore's planning agency established in 1974, that has the powers to acquire private land and property through resumption. In 1986 the URA commenced a programme of conservation and restoration of selected shophouse areas, and their adaptive re-use as residences, restaurants, shops and boutique hotels — an intervention that not only directed a trend away from demolition, but one that re-ignited public enthusiasm for street rejuvenation, built heritage, and local identity in the physical landscape. It has led to the designation of 44 conservation areas.

Master Plans are prepared under the auspices of the Ministry of National Development and its Planning Department, and are subject to periodic revision. The URA has effectively transformed the Central Planning Area for commercial and hotel development to meet economic goals. However intervention through conservation in the city is not merely given to preserving the past, but to underscore the cultural identity of its multi-ethnic Asian society. This has entailed enhancement of historic districts including Chinatown, allocated to the Chinese community under the 1828 plan, and the Civic and Cultural District. The 1990 Planning Act formalised this role, and extended "conservation area" status to ten areas including Little India, and Boat Quay and Clarke Quay along the Singapore River. The following year, the number of designated areas was doubled to include the original site of the East India Company; and the city's

THE ACTIVE WATERFRONT EDGE ON BOAT QUAY
overlooks the old Parliament House, which was constructed originally as a residence for a Scottish merchant in 1826 to a neo-Classical design. As its use did not conform with the town plan laid down by Stamford Raffles in 1822, it was later re-zoned for government use, housing the Supreme Court up to 1939, and later the Legislative Assembly and then Singapore's Parliament Building after Independence in 1965. It was restored in 1999 to form a centre for the visual arts, with ground floor restaurants providing a focus of activity along the lower Singapore River. It sits in close juxtaposition with the Empress Place Building named, along with its public square, after Queen Victoria, Empress of India.

EMERALD HILL ROAD OFF ORCHARD ROAD HOUSES an old-established residential area of two and three-storey terraced houses that provide a mix of both Western and Chinese architectural features, stylistic embellishments and motifs relating to Malaysian artistic representations of the time. The curvilinear terraces were built by thirty-one individual owners between 1901 and 1925 on a former nutmeg plantation leased by William Cuppage, the Postmaster General, in 1845. The 13-hectare property was later purchased by Chinese owners and subsequently subdivided into plots of different sizes. While some of the earliest houses were later redeveloped, the neighbourhood which comprised Singapore's first area conservation scheme, is notable for its consistency of elevational treatment, building heights and deep plan forms, with some short terraces having individual or shared forecourts with Chinese gateways, and others set back from the street through semi-private terraces. This sense of likeness tempered by difference has led to a harmonious rather than repetitive housing enclave, where details are refined rather than being overly eclectic. The setting is enhanced by both the overall topographic framework and the extent to which renovation and restoration has successfully reinforced the authenticity of materials, doors and window openings.

Muslim area set around the Sultan Mosque. A heritage trail takes in a number of revitalised historical areas and monuments.

Heritage has become a significant place making component, with more than 7,000 buildings, monuments and examples of local vernacular architecture conserved. This has in some cases involved conservation of the façade only, together with a re-fitted structure behind. However the process is assisted by restoration guidelines for pilasters, window shutters, ornamentation and improvement of the five-foot ways. Certain concessions are granted to building owners, geared to improvement of an entire locality or street front, with the retention of established trades where possible, and with the interests

of tourist consumption and marketability strongly in mind.

Achieving a balanced synergy between past and present is inevitably linked with "destination" tourism and the superimposition of thematic approaches and activity clusters. To some extent this involves the reworking of the past into the present through new narratives and itineraries. The URA imposes stringent guidelines for restoration and refurbishment, although prevailing market forces tend to inscribe a commodified imprint reflecting visitor attractions which include street performances. In this process history is re-packaged for the mass consumption of tourism, and heritage becomes a commodity

to be marketed. And yet the streets, unlike redevelopment areas of other cities, have not been emptied of life even if their meaning has been recalibrated. Community and diversity has not been lost but somewhat reconstituted. Historical neighbourhoods are not overwhelmed and made banal by looming precipices of tall buildings, but offset each other in a dynamic juxtaposition.

THE GREEN CITY

Singapore's current area of 714 square kilometres is heavily built up, although the city state has for many years adopted the mantle of a 'green city'. This does not mean that it is ahead of its time — only that 'green' now has a somewhat different connotation from the 1960s and 70s when Government commitments were geared to large-scale land acquisition which often involved the encroachment on 'unproductive' wooded and coastal areas. However by the 1970s Singapore had embarked on a garden-city campaign and a gradual shift towards environmental concerns, clean-up operations and urban landscape. The transformation of the Singapore and Kallang rivers at the heart of the city, reinforced the value of environmental conservation and reforestation. This was emphasised in the *Green Plan* published by the Ministry of Environment in 1992. In terms of urban planting and maintenance the city is almost unrivalled, and in 2010 it set out exemplary legislation on energy efficiency in building construction. The latest Concept Plan, published in 2011, proposes a broad emphasis on leisure and recreational facilities with parkland networks and nature reserves, and the opening up of reservoirs and inland waterways for water-based activities, further enhancing the 'green' identity of the city.

However this neither hides nor altogether compensates for the city's primary road system that scythes through the urban area in the form of four and five lane streams of fast-flowing traffic, dominating the urban

5   Koh, T and Lin, J, *The Land Reclamation Case: Thoughts and Reflections*, Singapore *Year Book of International Law*, NUS Press, Singapore, 2006

Stanford Raffles was responsible for a decree which stated that "Each house should have a verandah of a certain depth open at all times as a continued and covered passage on each side of the street". The incorporation of three metre wide colonnaded walkways is still a legal requirement.

experience. It has two consequences for its workability as a coherent centre — first, it rigidly circumscribes and 'contains' individual neighbourhoods which then tend to be branded neatly into shopping or ethnic districts so that the totality of experience is similarly contained; and second, traffic is then allowed to filter in a seemingly unrestricted way into the secondary and local systems which tend to be choked with both moving and parked vehicles. This might be compensated along Orchard Road by the wide boulevards and landscaped edges, but in general has a considerable impact on overall pedestrian movement at ground level. Discouragement of private vehicle use by various means seems to have been less than successful, despite a road pricing scheme introduced in the 1970s. It would be tempting to experiment with complete pedestrianisation and greening of South and North Bridge Roads, with at-grade pedestrian friendly crossings across the east-west road corridors. This could be complemented by a greater degree of traffic calming within individual enclaves and could, in effect, act to stitch together the various city quarters in a connected way, and make them more accessible on foot.

Sustainable growth patterns are facilitated through integrated planning and continued exploitation of limited resources. This has given rise to an increasingly high-rise spatial form geared to the achievement of 'Green Mark' standards introduced in 2005. Recent initiatives include an underground plan for subterranean cavern development, water collection and purification technology, and a deep tunnel sewage system in order to free up valuable surface area. The city's 'green credentials' have been extended at Marina Bay through sophisticated water desalination and treatment technologies.

Singapore, like Hong Kong, has a long history of reclaiming land from the sea, which has enabled it to increase its land area from 580 to 714 square kilometres since the 1960s, and accounts for 26 per cent of total land area with plans for an additional 100 square kilometres over the next thirty years.[5] Most reclaimed land has been used for transportation projects including Changi Airport, together with public housing estates, port facilities and commercial development, although one of the largest projects involved the integration of a small archipelago to the south-west with Jurong Island as a centre for the petroleum industry. The use of landfill from previous hill forms, has engendered a virtually flat landscape, and in recent years all reclamation has been carried out with dredged sand.

Three successive tranches of reclamation around the mouth of the Singapore and Kallang Rivers have been formed as a series of bayfronts. Marina North, adjacent to Beach Road, accommodates an International Convention and Exhibition Centre and two major commercial and shopping developments — Suntec City and Millenia Singapore. The Marina Bay waterfront houses Esplanade Theatres on the Bay — a cultural complex of concert hall, theatres and outdoor performance areas with a technically proficient roofscape, known locally at the 'durian'. Marina South is an amalgam of the Sands Complex along with commercial facilities linked by an esplanade and retail arcade, with a "double-helix" pedestrian bridge across the mouth of the bay. Towards the new seafront is the 54-hectare "Gardens by the Bay" development made up of inter-connected botanical attractions and biome structures showcasing indigenous plant life.

THE CULTURAL LANDSCAPE

Newly wealthy Asian states tend to anchor their emerging identities by harnessing cultural resources as a bulwark to counteract the homogenising forces of globalisation. A further means to buttress city identity is through heritage policies that use resources to exert symbolic value within the modernising and changing urban environment, in addition to serving as assets that underpin the growing tourism economy. Singapore has increasingly

ORCHARD ROAD is the major east-west shopping and entertainment spine to the west of the built up downtown area associated with Stanford Road and Raffles Avenue. Its wide boulevards, broken down horizontally by tree planting, external displays and the threshold space associated with many of the commercial buildings, can therefore accommodate large crowds and provide a green setting for promenading flaneurs. Of the many hotels in the area, one of the oldest is the Goodwood Park on Scotts Road, constructed originally as the Teutonia Club to cater for the German community in 1900. It was subsequently used as a base for Japanese officers during the occupation and as a War Crimes Tribunal Centre before being converted to a hotel in 1947.

Orchard Road takes its name from the fruit growing valley. It evolved through the twentieth century as an east-west road corridor linking the downtown commercial core and Fort Canning with the suburban development of row houses around Emerald Hill Road, Cairnhill Road and Tanglin Road to the west. From the 1960s, Orchard Road became the primary shopping and hotel avenue, reinforced by the opening of the MTR system in the 1970s. Its one-way traffic system facilitates a modest road width and the sectional layering of tree avenues, wide pavements and forecourts that create a diverse realm of spatial relationships, and a casual interface with adjoining renovated heritage districts.

In 2005 the Urban Redevelopment Authority (URA) announced enhancement initiatives for Orchard Road involving both buildings and interlinked spaces for exhibitions, performances and events. This has in turn incentivised redevelopment of older buildings with new surface typologies, floating canopies and protrusions such as Orchard Central and ION Orchard sitting above the Orchard MTR Station. These intersect with the public realm by breaking down orthodox distinctions between internal and external conditions, thereby extending the shopping environment into a more totalising social, visual and entertainment experience. Textured and transparent skins are transformed after dark through LED installations and multimedia façades. Thus the street becomes the subject of changing conceptions of space, movement and interface, geared to hyper-real expression but commodified identity. The effect is the contemporary equivalent of the traditional Asian street, layered with different activities, complexities and places, at the same time as brand stores themselves become increasingly ubiquitous.

branded its unique history and culture as part of a 'destination' agenda. Urban design strategies are instrumental in cementing the characteristics of a modern city and overcoming the constraints of a compact 700 square kilometre territory. In fifty years Singapore has been transformed from a low-rise city bent on post-war reconstruction, to a state of post-industrial global significance. Historical landscapes are often permeated with both real and mythical associations, and in Asia this extends to colonial structures that might be preserved and reinvested with new functions and meanings. In this sense the relationship between "history" and "heritage" is itself an unstable concept, as values of interpretation are open to debate on such issues as social acceptance, purpose and cultural ambiguity. For example, Singapore's Supreme Court built in 1939, and the older version which was adapted to become the House of Assembly, reflect colonial symbols of power in the same way that Hong Kong's current Legislative Council Building was created from the old Supreme Court, and will shortly again revert to its original function as the Court of Final Appeal.

6 A make believe 'ideal' town setting portrayed in the film of that name that was in reality a setting for a TV soap opera, where the central character was the innocent protagonist

THE VICTORIA THEATRE was originally built as a town hall in 1862, and completed in the Italian Renaissance style. It gradually became a venue for theatrical performances, and with the completion of the Victoria Concert Hall in 1903 the two buildings, in different but compatible styles, combined to form a cultural landmark. The statue of Raffles was dismantled during the Japanese occupation but reinstated in 1946, and was relocated from the esplanade in 1991.

Singapore is a secular state with all religions represented, reflecting a commitment to multi-culturalism — 42.5 per cent Buddhist; 8.5 per cent Taoist; 14.6 per cent Christian; and 4.0 per cent Hindu, with the remainder adhering to other religious beliefs or having no religion. Around 20 per cent of the population are foreigners as a result of a pro-immigration policy. Planning standards for the provision of religious building are set accordingly. To date twenty religious buildings including mosques, temples, churches, cathedrals and synagogues have been declared national monuments. They are incorporated into tourist promotional literature, along with religious festivals associated with ethnic districts such as Chinatown, Little India and Kampung Gelam. In turn tourists add value to these districts, establishing an ambiguous mingling of sacred place and cultural centrepiece.

The city's cultural landscape is underscored by differences of language, the social customs of different ethnic and socio-economic groups, the pantheon of deities, and the flows of immigration and emigration. This reflects a chronicle of historical narratives and vernacular influences, layered with meaning, that combine to inscribe a varied but ordered character on the city. Upgraded shophouse streets purposely resurrect the characteristics of old native quarters, while temples and religious festivals are proudly broadcast as tourist spectacles. Narrative gestures in the urban landscape can contain overt or subtle connotations of ethnic identity and culture associated with both authentic street environments with strong public use, or "back streets" of disorder and impermanence. However underlying the use of space in Singapore is a nuanced but tangible ideology that attempts to ensure that all development conforms to an orderly norm.

The development of Singapore as a "distinctive" and "unique" place, and the "cultural capital of Asia" is made clear in a Government "Renaissance City" report but there is a certain ambiguity between the real and the synthetic, and an occasionally unsettling correspondence to the fabricated 'reality' of the Truman Show.[6] There is little distinction between urban and rural, cosmopolitan and retro, authentic and slightly make believe. Spatial privileging tends to evoke specialist enclaves related to culture, entertainment, ecology or recreation. These are spatially demarcated and architecturally branded to symbolize iconic event spaces whether these are civic or ethnic quarters. At the same time it has to be said that these work well, and their profile is both positive and purposeful.

A challenging aspect of this process is the relationship between old and new buildings — the first to underscore historical identity and to attract visitors, the second to integrate more rationalised establishments. In the compact matrix of Chinatown, these have been brought together in programmes for Capital Square and China Square — a combination of restored shophouse streets and modern commercial development integrated by pedestrian connections that create different spatial experiences. The adjoining Far East Square encompasses a glass canopied structure which hovers over adjoining street blocks. Internal uses that encompass exhibition, restaurant and performance spaces are compatible rather than competitive with the adapted older buildings.

KAMPUNG BUGIS adjacent to the Rochor River was in place before the British arrival, and represented an old established and multi-ethnic neighbourhood of Bugis, Chinese, Indian and Malay traders. From the 1920s, Bugis Street evolved as a 'red light' and night time entertainment district, but only after midnight — during the day and early evening its shophouse mosaic of uses functioned in different ways. From early in the morning street hawkers sold food, and the shops opened later until around 6pm. In the evening the area was transformed into a bazaar and outdoor café area, and after midnight it changed its emphasis towards the feng-liuban

— those in search of more adult entertainment from its colonies of prostitutes and transvestites. Thus the tightly-knit area functioned on a somewhat chaotic but interactive 24-hour basis that had evolved over many years.

Planning intervention came in the form of a master plan in the 1990s for the wider Kaltang area, involving major redevelopment around the Kallang Basin and river, but with certain conservation and environmental improvement initiatives. The compensation and rehabilitation strategy entailed the regeneration of Bugis Street and its environs. It included something of a cosmetic reinvention of Bugis Street, intended to make physical improvements while retaining the old ambience of variety, street colour and spontaneity. The questionable solution was to reconstruct Bugis Street in an identical form to the old shophouses, but protected by an all-weather glazed canopy across the street from the original location and under the auspices of a private management company. Unsurprisingly, the well-intentioned intervention, while accommodating some of the original vendors and restaurant operators along with an induced array of uses, has failed to emulate its previous

street-oriented vibrancy. An informal alchemy of operation and flexible sub-divisions of use has been replaced by mechanistic ones that govern its operations and marginalise the previous 'alternative' cultural associations. In this way a resilient multi-use environment, subject to constant economic and social adaptation, has become a commodified festival marketplace with activities that are artificially programmed rather than naturally flamboyant, and where a previously intimate community of ownerships and tenancies, inter-related through common social as well as business interests, has been corporatised. With the relocation of long-time residents and commercial operators, historical continuity and informality is overwhelmed by an altogether different relationship, where business activities are carefully regulated under a formula that sets organisational parameters for the conduct of operations.

This type of orchestrated urban reinvention with the aim of 'renewing' the city and re-calibrating its historical culture on the basis of a commodified business model is not limited to Singapore. It has infiltrated the financial underpinning of other modernising cities where authenticity is being replaced by a state orchestrated and commercially sponsored version of the real thing. There is a central dichotomy, in that as cities become wealthier and land values escalate, the top-down interventionist role of government in community and economic matters increases. While more "bottom up" planning is now carried out with public participation, development forces also need to be controlled and directed, not merely liberated, and the overall emphasis must be on reconciling regeneration of the city with the social and cultural continuity of its established quarters, and the values of its citizenry.

7 Goh, R.B.H., *Contours of Culture: Space and Social Difference in Singapore*, Hong Kong University Press, Hong Kong, 2005

8 Kong, L and Yeoh, B.S.A., *The Politic of Landscapes in Singapore*, Syracuse University Press, New York, 2003

9 Kong and Yeoh, 2003, op. cit., p203

Thian Hock Keng Temple

Telok Ayer Market

BEFORE LAND WAS RECLAIMED to establish Collyer Quay and Shenton Way, Telok Ayer Street stood on the original shoreline, and became the historic receptacle of many religious buildings and clan associations. Telok means 'bay' and Ayer means 'water' in Malay, and Telok Ayer was a bay where horses and bullocks came to drink. Chinese junks landed immigrants in the area, so it grew as a Chinese enclave. Thian Hock Keng and Fuk Tak Chi became the most important temples in the area, but there were also smaller ones. The Hokkien community was the largest ethnic group among the immigrants — the remaining were Cantonese, Hakka.

The Telok Ayer Market replaced an earlier version which had to make way for reclamation. The new market was constructed in 1894 on Raffles Quay, utilising pre-fabricated cast iron parts from a Glasgow foundry, which were assembled on site. It was dismantled in 1986 to facilitate construction of the Mass Transit System and re-assembled in 1991 as the Lau Pa Sat Festival Market — a 24-hour food centre.

Telok Ayer Street is the site of some of the oldest religious institutions. The Thian Hock Keng Temple was built in 1842 on the site of an ancient shrine. Chinese immigrants from Fujian who came by sea would immediately go to the temple to give thanks for a safe journey. It contains calligraphy presented by the last Qing dynasty emperor in 1907. In 1998 craftsmen from China were brought in to remove and repair the decayed components using traditional methods of joinery. It received a UNESCO Heritage Conservation Award in 2001. Today Telok Ayer forms a 'museum' street attesting to the ethnic heritage and diversity of the city.

Singapore's commercial mandate has unified its ambitions and made it essential to be receptive to both global economic and cultural trends. In this sense its national identity is characterised by constant revisions of planning goals coupled with a transforming zeal to facilitate social progress. But a further aspect is the adoption of the Singaporean urban model as an influential paradigm in other parts of Asia, such as Suzhou. This has socio-economic, cultural and spatial inferences based on the perception of what embodies Singapore's successful urban design and management formula. A simple replication of these factors, even with careful design, management and operational controls, does not however necessarily propagate the workable economic and successful societal models that have succeeded in Singapore.[7]

Lily Kong and Brenda Yeoh have studied the rapidly evolving context for change in Singapore since 1965, arguing that the various ideological positions of the State, aimed at maintaining economic development, have shaped the urban landscape and continue to legitimise it.[8] They identify various "landscapes" that function as places of local meaning — for example places of worship, performance, heritage and housing that have been directed towards "nation-state" building through reconstruction. This might be said to contrast with Hong Kong since the 'handover' to China in 1997, where the imprecise definition of "Special Administrative Region", far removed from independent statehood, has floundered on unclear political responsibilities and ideologies with respect to the identity and consciousness of "place" and "nation". Kong and Yeoh offer evidence of the duplicity of the urban landscape in its "endorsement and reinforcement, but also divergence from, state ideologies".[9] This is partly about deconstructing older traditions and affinities, and replacing them with a new pragmatic social contractedness that facilitates communities to better serve the needs of the state while also allowing for multiple interpretations.

THE CIVIC CORE

What is now the civic and cultural heart of Singapore was the historic seat of the British colonial government. In this area of only 105 hectares, many landmark buildings were constructed after 1819 — military, religious and administrative, although some have been redeveloped. In 1988 the Urban Redevelopment Authority introduced a Civic District Master Plan to revitalise the area including regeneration, improved walkways and landscape, along with a lighting plan launched in 1995 to illuminate historic landmarks at night.

The Central City is defined on maps as comprising separate quarters — Orchard Road, Marina Bay and City Centre. Orchard Road represents the east-west high-end shopping street extending from Fort Canning to Tanglin Road, off which are situated hotels and small residential enclaves including Emerald Hill. Marina Bay continues to be developed on new reclamation to the east of Nicoll Highway, Raffles Quay and Shenton Way, primarily for hotel, commercial and recreation uses. Finally, the City Centre extends from Lavender Street and Crawford Street in the north, to the Ayer Rajah Expressway in the South. The latter area contains the older ethnic neighbourhoods that evolved from early settlements along the Singapore River.

Singapore deliberately set out to create a 'Civic District' as a cultural focus, through a series of refurbished landmark buildings adjacent to the Singapore River and Fort Canning — including the Art Museum, St Andrews Cathedral, Raffles Hotel, the old

General Post Office (now the Fullerton Hotel), the Victoria Theatre and Concert Hall, as well as the restored shophouses of Boat Quay. In this way social, religious, political and cultural history are amalgamated in a symbolic display of colonial history roughly corresponding to the ethnic partitioning inherent in the nineteenth century plan. This reinforces historical monumentalism but in a re-packaged representation of the new city image.

The Downtown Core comprises four zones — the Central Business District, City Hall, Marina Centre and Bugis, each of which has a different type of public space at its core. The City Hall focus is the Padang — a large recreation space surrounded by public buildings which acts as a setting for major city celebrations. The Marina Centre is marked by an interconnected series of retail spaces and malls, with green spaces constructed in association with MTR Stations. Bugis forms a precinct of reconstructed shophouses within a commercial realm of food courts, shopping and entertainment facilities. The new Marina Bay area combines a number of flagship projects including Singapore's first integrated resort and casino, hotel, convention and exhibition facilities, together with a new financial centre.

One objective of urban design in the Downtown Core is to promote walking through multi-faceted connections between transit stations, 'interceptor' car parks and all main destination points, including colonnaded walkways, galleria, skywalks and underground links. Underground pedestrian routes connect MTR Station Concourses to commercial and recreational systems in an integrated way, creating a variety of circulation conditions linked to an extensive retail framework. Vertical zoning of functions allows for different 'layers' of uses, appropriate to each level. These are constructed by private developers according to design parameters set by government, and linked by multi-layered circulation routes.

PUBLIC HOUSING STRATEGY

A large proportion of Singapore's built environment is in the form of public housing estates orchestrated through the Housing Development Board. Like Hong Kong, new town and housing policies have been interlinked since the early 1970s, aiming to relieve massive overcrowding in the more central urban areas. In the process this has transformed both the built and social environment within multi-ethnic integrated communities while establishing a stable basis for labour supply and general upward mobility, which have helped Singapore's subsequent competitiveness in the global marketplace. More than 80 per cent of the population live in affordable public housing, of which almost 90 per cent own their own home with a vested interest in community infrastructure.

Government intervention has, since 1965, played a significant role in reshaping the largely ethnic neighbourhoods — namely the Chinese, Indian and Malay quarters. Chinese, who make up around 76 per cent of the population, tended to dominate the central core area in the post-independence period, during Singapore's transition from an entrepôt to a labour intensive manufacturing and trading economy. A 1991 Strategic Economic Plan set the goal of redirecting growth towards the development of an International Business Hub with higher value-added activities to compete with other metropolitan areas in Asia.[10]

While new luxury condominium housing contributes to the fabric of the city itself, overall housing distribution is spread among 16 new towns from Jurong in the west, to Tampines in the east and Woodlands in the north, with population sizes varying between 150,000 and 350,000. Since the mid-1980s residents were decanted from older blocks of small units, and both physical restructuring and upgrading carried out with an emphasis on large flats. In the process this has

10 Van Grunsven, L, 'Singapore: The Changing Residential Landscape in a Winner City', in *Globalising Cities – A New Spatial Order*, Eds. Peter Marcuse and Ronald van Kempen, Blackwell, London, 2000

11 Van Grunsven, 2000, op. cit., p119

12 Kong, L and Yeoh, B.S.A., 'Housing the People, Building a Nation', in *The Politics of Landscapes in Singapore*, Syracuse University Press, New York, 2003

13 Liu, T.K., 'Urban Design Begins with Master Planning', presented at Urban Design as Public Policy conference organised by the Hong Kong Institute of Urban Design, March 31, 2012

facilitated urban renewal in central locations, but also conservation and preservation of older shophouse structures in a number of historic areas. The Planning Act was amended in 1989, providing for the establishment of a Conservation Authority. Similarly by mid-1993, all the old Kampungs had been demolished and their residents rehoused in new towns, furthering the homogenisation of the shophouse landscape.

Through relocation policies it was partially intended to develop ethnically mixed enclaves in the new towns in order to accelerate a problem-free transition towards a modern urban-industrial society. In response to this there was a spontaneous regrouping of ethnic households in particular locations through flat re-sales. This was combated by Government with new sets of allocation rules aimed at limiting the proportion of flats each ethnic group is allowed to occupy.[11] This insistent but charitable justification of a balanced social and ethnic mix is counteracted to some extent by the rise in 'gated' communities, just as it is in other modernising Asian cities. This relates to the dynamics of class and ethnic structure in the face of economic change, exacerbating spatial and socio-economic divisions.

The ideological roots of "home ownership" extend to the creation of community spirit, and through this a sense of nation building and economic growth based on development and construction. An important aspect of public housing is its integration as part of a wider infrastructure that includes factory sites within the new towns, and the provision of transport networks. It has also helped to realise the vision of a modern and highly managed city, where controls are even introduced to ensure a balanced racial mix in public housing estates. In 1989 selective upgrading of older estates was initiated through a process of decanting residents to modern blocks while older ones are redeveloped — part of a continuous improvement programme that also raises

the value of residential investment and encourages a sense of stakeholding. In 1995, a new scheme was launched to convert leases of public housing to strata titles. This permitted upgrading to condominium-type estates, in line with "the aspiration of a more affluent society", although one which reflects high average densities, signified by improved patterns of design and layout.[12]

Something that sets Singapore apart from other Asian cities in terms of its planning has been its long-range Strategic Concept approach. On the one hand this guides public investment to meet national development objectives, while on the other developing workable urban design solutions to prevailing opportunity areas through co-ordinated and collaborative governance. Over forty years Singapore has averaged more than eight per cent annual growth and now enjoys one of the highest GDP rates through a combination of free-market capitalism and state-led industrialisation. It invests in its own human capital and attracts foreign talent through its sophisticated institutions,

rule of law and good infrastructure. While Singapore and Hong Kong share an efficient administration and good overall urban management, the latter has developed a 'policy silo' mentality, while the former has a single tier of government which purposely facilitates co-ordination, collaboration and trade-offs between government ministries and institutions. This allows planning and development objectives to be reconciled at a strategic level, and facilitates a focussed approach to housing, urban regionalisation and sustainable environment. In this way the impact of a diversified globalised economy is translated into local place making initiatives, with the active engagement of the community. The Economic Review Committee established in 2003 set out innovation, creativity, development of cultural capital and responsiveness to change, amongst other policies, as being essential drivers of growth. This continues to focus on ordered development, urban identity and environmental quality.[13]

Double Helix Bridge, Marina Bay

MALAYSIA
Kuala Lumpur

THE SULTAN ABDUL SAMAD BUILDING was designed to accommodate the British Colonial Secretariat at the end of the nineteenth century. The architectural form of this, and that of other important public buildings, was designed by British colonial engineers, drawing on styles which emanated from the Saracenic architecture of India. While it has no Islamic design precedents, its fusion of influences has come to represent an identifiable style now associated with the city. It extends 122 metres in length and incorporates a 43.6-metre high clock tower, which dominates the eastern edge of Dataran Merdeka Square. The existing copper domes establish the building's Islamic pretentions in a hybrid Indic-Moorish style. The smaller towers in white cement were placed to balance the dominance of the clock tower, and the building is constructed in coloured brickwork interspersed with white stone. It has undergone several renovations, including rear extensions for offices. It now houses the federal and high courts.

1 Evers, H.D. and Korff, R,
*Southeast Asian Urbanisam:
The Meaning and Power of
Social Space*, St Martin's Press,
New York, 2000

KUALA LUMPUR, in contrast to the older settlements of Malacca and Penang, is a modern city. Its foundation in the mid-nineteenth century stemmed from a landing point on the Gombak river estuary, where tin miners could obtain supplies. Its name roughly translates in Malay as "Muddy Estuary", and it largely remained a temporary mining settlement until 1874 when Frank Swethenham, the British resident of Selangor, moved his administration to the growing town. With its establishment as the State capital, the old streets were widened and permanent buildings erected in brick and stone. In 1896 it became the capital of the Federated Malay States of Selangor, Negeri Sembilan, Pahang and Perak. The multi-ethnic community settled in various parts of the settlement after 1896. Market Square became the commercial centre dominated by Chinese settlers and extended to the Chinatown area. To the north along Java Street (Jalan Tun Perak) were the Malay community, with the Indian *Chettiars* or money-lenders nearby. East of the Padang was the centre of British administration.

At the time, the main commercial activity on the Malay Peninsula (apart from rubber plantations) was mining around the Kuala Lumpur and Khang Valley area, and the settlement grew haphazardly around the estuaries of the Klang and Gombak rivers in the mid-nineteenth century.

The first settlers were Sumatran Malays and Chinese tin miners, but British intervention after 1873 led to the British Resident Commissioner being relocated from Malacca to Kuala Lumpur, establishing the beginning of its planning administration in 1880. This was further reinforced in 1895 when it became the chief city in the newly formed Federation of Malay States, primarily because of its strategic location and links with the other Straits cities. The British laid out the city plan and its infrastructural components, and in the 1890s and early

twentieth century British architects such as A.B. Hubback and A.C. Norman developed a Moorish or 'Mahometan' design style for public buildings. This comprised a hybrid of design properties that transcend both cultural and functional boundaries, and for which there was no previous local parallel.[1]

Certain architectural forms evolved from both creative interaction and intervention. The former Selangor State Secretariat building completed between 1894 and 1897 came about through the experience of the State Engineer, C.E. Spooner in the colonial administration. He pursued a 'Mahometan' style based on the Saracenic architecture of India as being in keeping with a tropical environment. The architect was A.C. Norman although the actual design was carried out by the Chief Draughtsman, R.A.J. Bidwell. This lyrical and disciplined fusion of

Jalan Petaling — part of the shophouse street in the old Chinese quarter, now revitalised as a street bazaar complete with Chinese-style gateways, giant screens and a lightweight roof which stands proud of the adjoining building structures.

THE OLD CHINESE QUARTER in Kuala Lumpur was centred around Market Square, and extended along the High Street, now known as Jalan Tun HS Lee. The Chinese community provided for its citizens through benevolent societies, temple organisations and clan houses. The largest and most ornate shophouses were built along Jalan Cheng Lok close to the business centre, which still serve their original operations. Jalan Tun H S Lee was one of the earliest Chinese shophouse streets dating back to the 1880s, and built in brick and plaster. Many of the shophouses along this street and Jalan Sultan are several feet below the height of the road, which has been built up to accommodate layers of underground services. The shophouses, interspersed with new block types, continue to play a role in the retail structure of the old city.

THE OLDER HEART OF KUALA LUMPUR lies to the west of the Gombak and Klang rivers and formed the centre of British colonial rule set around the Padang, now known as Dataran Merdeka and used for National Day celebrations and other public events. The ornamented fountain in the corner of Merdeka Square, overlooking the National Textile Museum, was ordered from England and assembled in 1897 by the Sanitary Board. The square was previously known as the Parade Ground or Padang, built by the British in 1884 as a venue for social activities and cricket. Merdeka Square was named after the Independence Day celebrations in August 1957. On the western side of Merdeka Square is the old Selangor Club designed in a half-timbered style by A C Norman, and to the north the small church of St Mary's built by the same architect in 1894.

Islamic forms with neo-Classical elements, strangely reminiscent of the Brighton pavilion, subscribes to no historic Islamic precedent. It remains a monumentally iconic building characteristic of Kuala Lumpur's identity, precisely because its expansive form responds to its dominating position in relation to the spatial context rather than the obvious functional demands of the intended bureaucratic users. In this sense, some forms of colonial inspired intervention demonstrate their capacity to take on new meanings and come to represent an archetypal local identity.

A C Norman went on to design further buildings including the General Post Office (now the Court of Appeal Building) completed in 1907, which features a similar interplay of borrowed elements. An arched walkway was added later to connect with the Sultan Abdul Samad Building. The latter includes a multi-storey arched loggia — a Palladian device applied on the main expressive façades but in an Islamic style. The open galleries and colonnades create an appropriate climatic solution that looks outwards in a social sense, rather than towards the shaded courtyards as in traditional Islamic architecture.[2]

The old township was centred around a large central market. With the relocation of this to a nearby site, the vacated plot became known as Old Market Square or Medan Pasar. Design guidelines were prepared by the Public Works Department for shophouses, which established an overall symmetry to the surrounding terraces.

Shophouse structures in Kuala Lumpur were adapted from building types in Southern China, and were typically built in terraces with common party walls. They can be divided into three styles according to age, and are found within the old city. The two-storey utilitarian style dates from the 1880s, with a width dictated by single wooden beams. The ground floor had a central doorway and a first floor with two or three shuttered windows, occasionally with fanlights. Steep roof lines

2 Abel, C, *Architecture and Identity*, Architectural Press, Oxford, 2000, p157

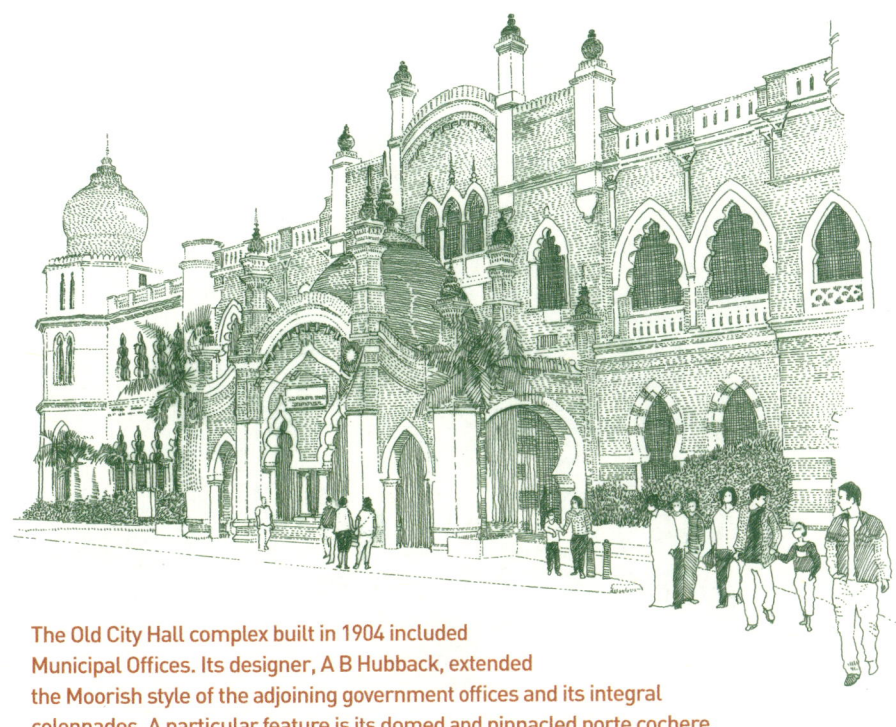

The Old City Hall complex built in 1904 included Municipal Offices. Its designer, A B Hubback, extended the Moorish style of the adjoining government offices and its integral colonnades. A particular feature is its domed and pinnacled porte cochere.

The Old High Court Building was completed in 1915 by the same architect. A two-storey loggia integrates Islamic arches of different kinds. Its expressive façade of open galleries and colonnades facing the river creates an appropriate climatic solution. The towers initially housed private tiffin rooms. The building was substantially reconstructed after a fire in 1992 and now houses Magistrates Courts.

THE MALAYAN RAILWAYS HEADQUARTERS BUILDING seen from the Railway Station, designed by A B Hubbock and completed in 1917. It represents a fine example of Moorish architecture reflecting Ottoman and Mughal influences dating back to the thirteenth century, blended with a High Victorian Gothic architecture — a frequently used style imported from Britain. The ground floor is adorned with 97 frontal arches, which form colonnades around the building. The first floor has 94 large arched windows and 40 circular arches of smaller size. The second floor has 171 arches. The building is capped by five Ottoman domes.

A TERRACE OF NEO-CLASSICAL SHOPHOUSES at 11-19 Jalan TAR constructed in 1915. Numbers 1-9 were built later in the same style by the developer and philanthropist Loke Yew. Large pilasters support decorative pediments, and the terrace is unified by its continuous cornice treatment and colonnade. Across the street the isolated front façade of two neo-Classical shophouses is waiting to be rehabilitated with the redevelopment of the adjoining site. The façade contains fluted pilasters with Corinthian capitals and an elegant Venetian window on the second floor. Seen from behind, the silhouette provides an inkling of the former vertical arrangement of floors.

often included raised or 'jack roofs' for ventilation purposes. The more ornate neo-Classical shophouses were mainly built to the north of Jalan Cheng Lock from 1900 to the 1930s. These were usually three storeys high and incorporated Western design and decorative elements with increasingly elaborate façade elements reflecting Palladian and Baroque influences such as ornately decorated windows, decorative plaster work and open balustrades. Art Deco façades from the 1930s and 40s were characterised by simple geometrically structured features with banding elements and sculptural motifs.

Later shophouse terraces were required to integrate covered "verandah-ways" or "five foot ways". As urbanisation continued, utilities were laid in the streets creating level differences between the roads and verandah-ways.

The "five-foot ways" or *kaki lima* — a characteristic of the older street pattern — form a streetscape of classical arches, effectively segregated from traffic and sheltered from sun and heavy rain. These elements, which characterise the old Chinese quarter of the city, are also used as an "overspill" extension of the adjoining shops. At the same time this provides a physical separation between the noise of the trading street and the residential floors above. As utility services are generally laid under the adjoining street channels, road surfacing can, over time, become higher than the older *kaki lima*. These people-oriented streets, which support multiple functions, are subject to change owing to a combination of factors: over-provision of road building in response to massive growth of private vehicle ownership during the mid-1980s, making many streets hostile to pedestrians; simplistic land use zoning which has tended to sterilise the street activities and frontages, with the introduction

The Lee Rubber Building, built by Lee Kong Chian and designed by A O Coltman in the 1930s, establishes a distinctive Art Deco corner at the junction of Jalan Tun HS Lee and Jalan Hang Lekir. The Lee Foundation was later set up to advance culture and education in the Chinese Community.

PEDESTRIAN MARKET precinct linking Jalan Masjid India with Jalan Tuanku Abdul Rahman, lined with stalls, tailors and barber shops. It is terminated by the neo-Classical Coliseum Cinema, built in 1921 as part of a larger property development scheme. It now acts as a landmark corner on Jalan TAR. Until the 1940s it put on performances of Malay opera performed by travelling troupes. The wide upper level verandahs have now been filled in. As recently as twenty years ago a characteristic of the building was its hand painted film billboards. The adjoining two-storey Coliseum Café built in Art Deco style incorporates the original terrazzo of the five-foot way alongside Jalan TAR. The nearby Odeon cinema, also Art Deco in style and built in 1936, conveys early innovations in arts, drama, comedy and music through decorative mosaic panels set into the façade. Every Saturday evening the street is closed to traffic and temporary market stalls are erected. The area around the Masjid India is known as "Little India" because of its history of Indian retail and wholesale establishments. Jalan Masjid India is lined with both Indian and Malay shops, filled with street hawkers, food stalls and vendors of medical products and herbal concoctions. Jalan Melayu contains some of the earliest Malay shophouses that were used as spice factories. Today these are occupied by Indian wholesalers and restaurants. Jalan Masjid India and Lorong TAR, prior to the 1960s, formed the centre of the city's red-light district known as Belakang Mati — Dead End.

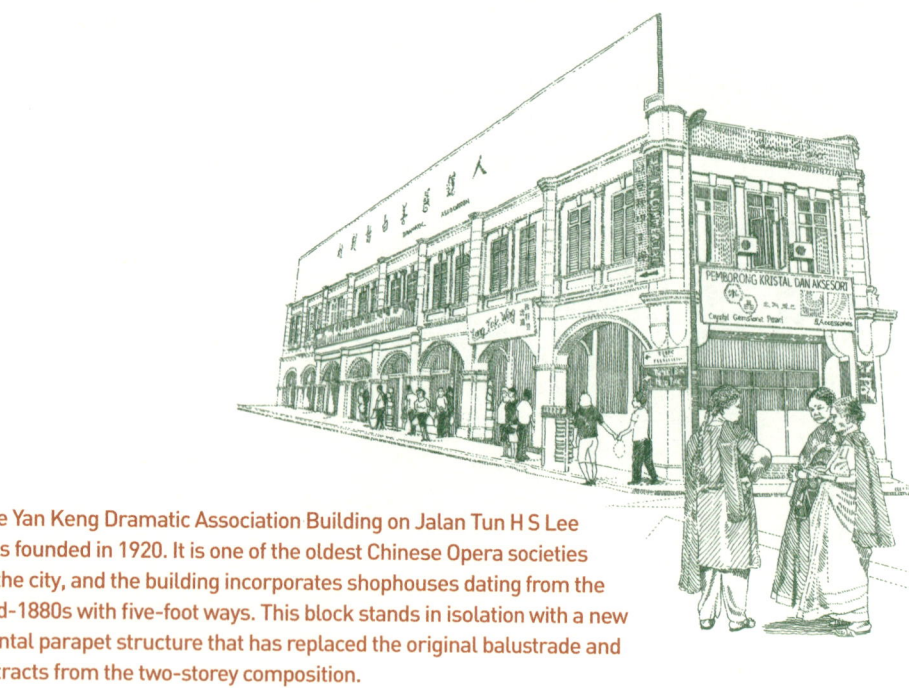

3 Evers and Korff, 2000, op. cit., p55

The Yan Keng Dramatic Association Building on Jalan Tun H S Lee was founded in 1920. It is one of the oldest Chinese Opera societies in the city, and the building incorporates shophouses dating from the mid-1880s with five-foot ways. This block stands in isolation with a new frontal parapet structure that has replaced the original balustrade and detracts from the two-storey composition.

of large and internalised shopping complexes; and lack of visionary urban design parameters associated with the urban context.

During the 1930s, European architectural firms and Western trained local architects introduced new aspects of modernism and art nouveau to public buildings and commercial structures, and the use of Art Deco in new cinema and entertainment buildings. Residential styles evolved according to available new Western technologies, with the adaptive use of local forms and materials. Hybrid forms and stylistic innovations were introduced from other parts of the East Asian Empire and from the burgeoning treaty ports in China. By the 1940s multi-storey 'mansion blocks' were being developed, producing shops at street level with apartments above, while the introduction of reinforced concrete created opportunities to cantilever upper floors over the pavement, sadly negating the need for colonnades along the 'five-foot way' alignments.

Clearly city development policies cannot be unduly separated from the influences governing national development that relate to cultural identity, economic growth, and social issues. The post-war years after the end of Japanese occupation reinforced the adoption of European modernist principles to

meet urban housing shortfalls. This approach epitomised the rapid building programme throughout the Malay Straits assisted by Western-trained architects. The colonial Public Works Department produced standard plans for public housing blocks, which were influenced by similar programmes in Britain, and began to introduce a more straight-laced and standardised urban design language.

In this unstable situation Kuala Lumpur comprised a partly segregated but overlapping mosaic of ethnic groups — Chinese, Indians and Malaysians, with colonial government housing in the western hills. The rapid increase in population resulted in the expansion of Kampungs within the city, which served as squatter settlements and estimated in 1954 to house around 140,000 people. Resettlement policies involved different housing solutions — Chinese and Indians in inner urban apartment buildings and Malays in housing associated with agricultural settlements on the urban fringe.

Lingering animosity between Malay and Chinese, mainly arising from a disparity in wealth between the two communities, came to the fore in 1969 with an outbreak of civil conflict. This fuelled the elections in which the majority of seats in the Malaysian Parliament and the State Assembly of

Selangor were won by the predominantly Chinese DAP political party. As a result of this the Government established the First Outline Progressive Plan and a new Economic Policy. Under this, an Urban Development Authority (UDA) was established in 1971 to restructure the urban growth pattern, develop new settlement patterns and orchestrate economic opportunities 'restructuring society through urban development'. The combined effect of these two interventionist initiatives, in terms of their operational objectives, has been described as 'socio-economic engineering'.

The 1976 Town and Country Planning Act in Malaysia established structure plans and local plans as the main instruments for regulating urban development, with particular regard to safeguarding floodplains and other ecologically sensitive areas. Plans now set out the type and intensity of land use and have to be approved by local authorities, and drafts have to be exhibited before formal hearings which allows for public comments. The town planning system requires the preparation of a local plan which sets out guidelines, and this is then gazetted as a legal document. This skews development towards physical rather than economic, social and environmental factors.

The expansion of the post independence civil service was concentrated in Kuala Lumpur. Industrialisation and increasingly efficient agricultural production have also acted to transform the urbanisation process through rural-urban migration. This has in turn led to a rapidly expanding population based on new patterns of land ownership. These have cut across ethnic lines and shaped both the social and spatial structure of the expanding.[3]

The emphasis on physical planning accelerated new and largely unsynchronised urban growth trajectories for new suburban housing development orchestrated largely by private developers, such as the Bukit Tunku and Bangar Hills neighbourhoods.

JALAN TUANKU ABDUL RAHMAN still contains family–run pre-war businesses. The main route through the old city was originally named Batu Road as it led to the tin mining area. By the 1930s, the agricultural estates in this area were replaced by commercial developments owned by ethnically diverse groups for retail, restaurant, hotel and cinema uses. A number of the older buildings exist, designed in early utilitarian, neo-Classical, and Art Deco styles and built between 1910 and the 1940s. The Malay communities of Kampung Rawa and Kampung Java were located to the north and east, and comprised Bugis and Javanese immigrants. A block of neo-Classical shophouses on the corner of Jalan Dang Wangi and Jalan TAR represent a sample of the street matrix architecture of the 1920s Chinatown. Many of the older services and retailers have remained in the block.

A SEQUENCE OF SHOPHOUSES in Jalan Lebuh Ampang forms a diverse street frontage as an intermediate terrace between tall commercial frontages to main streets. The Lebuh Ampang area was originally a Chettiar street — a caste of money-lenders from Southern India who were also based in Malacca, and a strong financial source in the early development of the city. The buildings comprise a full range of shophouse models. neo-Classical styles incorporate elaborate carvings and decorations, while others are more utilitarian with wooden fanlights and butterfly grills for ventilation. Stylised peacock decoration relates to Muruga — the Hindu deity of the Chettier cast.

The Government Printing Office was completed in 1899. Its cast iron columns allowed for an unimpeded interior space to house the large printing presses. The exterior features of bay windows, Flemish gables, triangular pediments and brick pilasters form a highly decorative assemblage, extended by roof canopies that were added in the 1940s. The building houses the Kuala Lumpur Memorial Library.

4 Lim, J.C.S., 'Post-Independence Kuala Lumpur: Heritage and the New City Image', in *Cultural Identity and Urban Change in Southeast Asia: Interpretative Essays*, Deakin University Press, Geelong, 1994

THE MASJID JAMEK was built in 1909 at the corner of Sungai Gumbak and Sungai Kelang, and is the traditional Muslim assembly point in the city. It was designed by A B Hubbock, the designer of the old railway station, in red brick and marble and its onion domes mirror some of the nearby older government buildings. It was built on the site of the first Malay cemetery and its inspiration was the Saracenic architecture of Northern India with its characteristic minarets and onion domes. Cupolas and minarets project from the arched colonnades. It remains as the oldest surviving mosque in the city.

Government efforts were meanwhile focussed on the Central City with major ring road and highway construction in the 1980s and 1990s linking the city with the airport, Port Klang, Petaling Jaya and Shah Alam, the new capital of Selangor. In the early 1990s, high-rise condominiums became the focus of private development in the inner suburbs with little overall planning or environmental co-ordination, and fuelled by investors from other wealthy parts of Southeast Asia. This has expanded the city area to around 240 square kilometres with a density of approximately 7,000 persons per square kilometre.

In 1991 a New Development Policy for the reorganisation of the Kuala Lumpur city region was drawn up. Since then the city has witnessed considerable mega-developments, including the Petronas Towers, which has propelled the transformation of Kuala Lumpur to global city status. The business district has experienced large-scale regeneration in the commercial 'golden triangle' which is served by a new monorail system. Since 2009 and a change of government, there has been renewed redevelopment of the central part of the city, particularly focussed on Kampung Baru — a

traditional settlement area. At the same time a new federal capital has taken shape at Putrajaya, some 40 kilometres to the south of the city. This is symbolic of the country's global aspirations but also its religious culture, accommodating a new royal palace, federal government offices, public buildings and commercial precincts distributed along a 4.2 kilometre spine framed by new parklands and wetlands. However its low overall density suggests a city more akin to Canberrra than to Kuala Lumpur, which raises questions over its fundamental sustainable objectives. Another new city, Cyberjaya, focussed on high technology industry and with a projected population of 250,000, is planned to the west. The new regional north-south development axis re-focuses the established east-west pattern of urbanisation linking Kuala Lumpur with the Klang Valley, and with a metropolitan population of six million. A new regional economic development strategy announced in 2010 seeks to consolidate and extend growth through global investment to form a polycentric metropolitan area with new container facilities at Port Kelang, and a new International Airport some 80 kilometres south of the city. The regional development momentum has facilitated restructuring of the old urban core through central planning, with major high-rise development in the city centre, and revitalization of shophouse streets in the older quarters.

In the city itself a likely consequence of the new growth pattern will be continued densification of the core area to reinforce multinational investment. The UDA has steered its redevelopment policy towards the replacement of the older shophouse enclaves while re-zoning these traditional mixed-use areas for commercial use, thereby forcing residents to seek alternative housing in suburban locations. Politically inspired intervention has effectively dispensed with much of the old colonial fabric and social texture, including many of its heritage

buildings in the name of a 'progressive' economic policy. This policy, that denuded the city centre of its original tightly knit character, was turned around in the mid-1980s with a new conservation movement *Badan Warisan Malaysia* — an intervention on the part of senior professional subscribers that spread to other cities in Malaysia. The organisation was established as a limited company in order to raise funds and acquire heritage properties. Through a combination of private donations, media campaigns, and the production of pamphlets on architectural heritage, a number of older buildings have been conserved, including the Central Market and the Former Peninsula Hotel — now occupied by the Malaysian Institute of Architects. The *Badan* also undertook to renovate and maintain heritage buildings and to bring these into the public domain. Equally importantly, this initiative established the credibility of a conservation approach along with a balance of mixed uses and a high residential density in the city.[4]

The current City Plan places optimistic emphasis on co-ordinated transport and land-use proposals. These are centred around improved public transport and concentrations of development associated with station-related nodes such as the mixed-use central station hub and its high-speed rail connections to Putrajaya and the new international airport.

A FORMER TOWNHOUSE known as Loke Hall, designed by A K Moosdeen in 1903. It was later converted to the Empire Hotel and then became the Peninsula Hotel. The building was in a dilapidated state until 1973 when it was converted and occupied by the Malaysian Institute of Architects for use as a Building Centre and Secretariat. The annex to the right, originally part of a terrace, is designed with Dutch gable ends, and encompasses an ornate wrought iron terrace.

Short pedestrian precincts off Jalan Petaling in Chinatown intersect with the main streets and generate a character based on informal and temporary elements — hanging lanterns, signage, hawker installations — which emphasise channels of display. Market uses add variety to the wider street matrix and attract different types of users.

Malacca

MALACCA served as a major port which formed part of a Muslim trading network until the city was taken by Portuguese forces in 1511. Along with other Portuguese settlements and Spanish Manila, this marked the beginning of European urbanisation in Asia. Malacca fell to the Dutch in 1641, who constructed the Stadhuys (the municipal town hall) between 1645 and 1660 within the fortress area. This was built on a hillside terrace and consists of four storeys covering 5000 square metres. It served as the Governor's residence in the eighteenth century and was the Dutch Administrative Centre until 1824. This use was continued by the British, who adapted various other Dutch buildings for government purposes, and the building became the State Governing Centre until 1979. Its colour was changed from white to red in the 1820s and was known as the 'Red Building'. It has been renovated a number of times, but the essential built construction by the Dutch has been maintained.

The city's collection of historic buildings gained UNESCO World Heritage status in 2007.

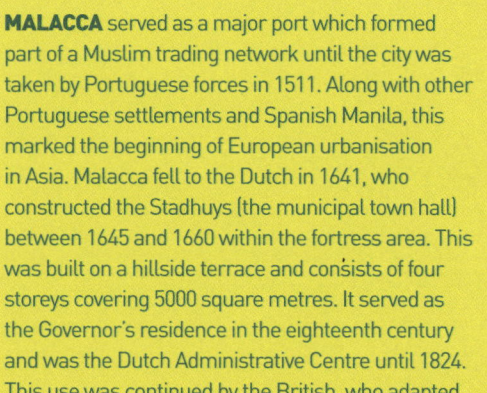

SITUATED ON THE NARROW STRAITS separating the Malay Peninsula from Eastern Sumatra, Malacca was established in the fourteenth century by Iskanda Sha. It acted as a principal port destination from the Indian Ocean and China, and for the Muslim trading network with the ports of West Java and Sumatra. Its cultural heritage is therefore rooted in Malaysia's Muslim history with people indigenous to the region. The Sultan's walled palace was located on St Paul's Hill with merchants' quarters along the lower slopes, and the city prospered through taxes and levies on goods.

By the early sixteenth century, Malacca had a strong mercantile community and developed as a trading society through the junk trade with Java. Under the Sultanate, Indian Muslims from Tamil India and Gujarat were the leading merchants. The business district and bazaar developed along the waterfront, while its strategic position on the archipelago brought together diverse trading interests from Arabia, Gujarat, Bengal and Java. Strong Muslim influences led to the adoption of the Islamic religion which spread to coastal settlements on the Malay Peninsula, Java and Sumatra. However investment in infrastructure and building was minimal, indicating that the port populations were relatively transient, shifting in line with the periodic re-alignment of trading routes.

Strategic alliances secured a continuation of the Sultanate and successive Sultans of Malacca erected mosques and palaces on St Paul's Hill, until the city fell to the Portuguese who replaced them with more defensive and ecclesiastical structures. It was there that the Dutch constructed their administrative offices, and where the British later expanded the growing urban centre to accommodate trading establishments, which signalled Malacca's strategic role within the Straits Settlements.

The first Portuguese fleet reached Malacca in September 1509 through an expedition

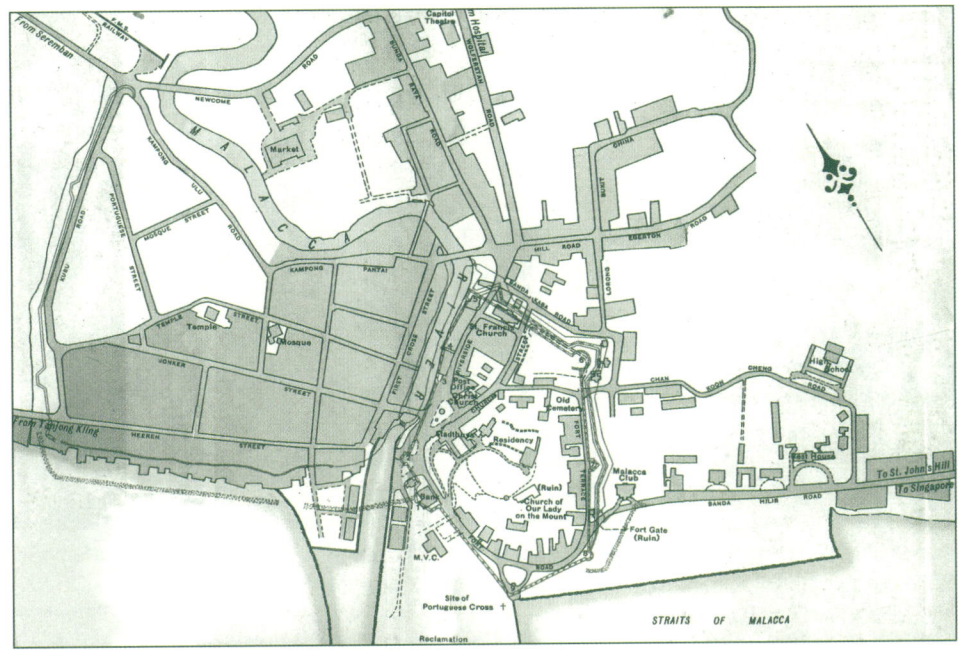

Malacca showing position of old fortifications

led by Diogo Lopes de Sequeira and aimed at opening up the spice trade in the Indian Ocean. However trade negotiations with the Sultan failed. The Portuguese returned two years later under Afonso de Albuquerque, and through an escalation of hostilities took the city in August 1511. Albuquerque retained the older town structure but, using slave labour, fortified St Paul's Hill through the Fortress *A Famosa* with the church *Nossa Senhora da Anunciada* alongside. This marked the beginning of European urbanisation in Malacca and its construction as a walled city. It also underlined the necessity of deploying military power to sustain trading flows, which were carried out through large war-boats.

Within the encircling walls of the fort were administrative buildings, official residences, a city hall, churches, convents, hospitals and a Jesuit college. Banda Hilir Road to the south of the fort was named by the Portuguese as indicating its "downstream" location in

relation to the Porta de Santiago, and was the centre of the Eurasian community. Four hundred years after the Portuguese arrival in Malacca, their descendants continue to speak the medieval dialect of *Christao*, once spoken in the southern ports of Portugal. Malacca's surviving *Rua Direita* or Straight Street was constructed to link with the main town square around which were the houses of the Governor and wealthy merchants. However under Portuguese rule, Muslim clerics also arrived from Mecca and Cairo, so that Mosques continued to be constructed.

Portuguese intervention, in a similar way to the Spanish in the Philippines, introduced a robust collection of classical architectural details such as stone columns and pediments so that the town took on the form of a hill city, and was acknowledged as such by Royal Charter in 1552. Following the arrival of Francis Xavier in 1545, a church was built on the hilltop — the *Anunciada* — the ruins

THE ETHNIC MIX AND HISTORICAL MEANING OF MALACCA is represented in the accumulated physical forms related to sacred spaces on Jalan Tukang Emas. The economic roots of the area can be observed in 'Goldsmith Street', named by the Dutch. The British, who might have perceived its expanding range of Chinese business interests renamed the local streets as Jalan Tukang Besi, Jalan Tukang Emas and Jalan Tokong — respectively Blacksmith Street, Goldsmith Street and Temple Street. The street fabric contains a number of distinctive religious buildings dating back to the sixteenth century when the street was populated by Indian keling merchants.

In the foreground of the drawing is the Sri Poyyatha Vinayagar Moorthi Hindu Temple — the oldest in Malaysia, and dedicated to Ganesha. The Straits-born Tamil-speaking Hindus came to be known as the Chitty, and it was they who constructed the temple in 1781, now run by the Chattiar community. The simple architecture of the entrance tower is complemented by Dutch detailing, vaulted domes and roof tiling.

The three-tier pyramidal roof of the Masjid Kampung Keling is Sumatran in origin with strong Hindu influences, expressive of inherent cosmological practices, while the minaret, initially constructed in wood, has long been the tallest structure in the area. Its architecture blends British and Portuguese details, with glazed tiles and symmetrical arches in the main prayer hall. To the north is the seventeenth century Cheng Hoon Teng (Green Cloud) Temple, built in 1646 with materials brought from China. It was originally the official seat of the representative appointed by the community to liaise between the social needs of local society and European colonisers. The temple has, over several centuries, been of fundamental importance to the Straits Chinese population. Nearby are the Tanel Methodist Church built in 1908 and the Kampung Hulu Mosque — the oldest in Malaysia, built in 1748.

St Peter's Church is the oldest surviving Roman Catholic Church in Malaysia, combining eastern and western styles. One of its bells was cast in Goa in 1608.

SERI MELAKA was the office and official residence for the Dutch Government in the seventeenth century on St Paul's Hill, which was earlier known as Bukit Melaka. It was the old palace site of the Melaka Sultanate before the Portuguese conquest. Seri Melaka functioned as the Governor's residence during the British period and beyond, until a new office was built at Ayer Keroh. The building was known as the Rajah's house. On 31 Aug 1957 the name was changed to Seri Melaka and has since served several Malay Governors. In 1996 it was gazetted as a heritage building and now forms part of the Melaka Museum.

ST PAUL'S CHURCH was originally a small chapel built by a Portuguese captain Duarlo Coelho in 1521 and called Nosa Senhora — Our Lady of the Hill. It was handed over to the 'Society of Jesus' in 1548 and a second storey added in 1556, and renamed 'Annunciation'. A tower was added in 1590. When the Dutch took over, the name was changed to St Paul's, which the Dutch used for 112 years until Christ Church was completed in 1753. They turned the church precinct into a burial ground for the nobility, hence the tombstones bear both Latin and Portuguese inscriptions. St Paul's lost its tower when the British took over, but they added the lighthouse at the front. The British did not use it as a church but for storage of gunpowder. They also erected a tall flagpole and renamed the site Flagstaff Hill. The church ruins were gazetted in 1977.

The Spanish-born Jesuit missionary St Francis Xavier was a visitor from 1543-1552, and his body was interned at St Paul's for nine months before being returned to Goa. A statue of St Francis was erected in 1952. The statue was sculpted in Rome and erected by the Malacca Historical Society in 1954 to commemorate the 400th anniversary of his arrival.

of which still stand on the summit. By the end of the sixteenth century the Portuguese settlements of Malacca, Goa and Macau were rivalled as centres of Catholicism in Asia only by Manila. Both Malacca and Manila had something else in common — a global trading reach to the Americas, and through this a strengthened relationship between East and West. As a result, more European countries began to look to the east of the Cape of Good Hope as an area of potential trading influence.

By the beginning of the seventeenth century Dutch trading companies merged to form the United East India Company, and began a series of blockades on Malacca from their main Asian base in Batavia. After a long siege of the city, Malacca fell to the Dutch in 1641 and following this, the fort structures were repaired and refocused, and the bastions re-christened.

The Stadthuys was built in 1645 and new administrative buildings constructed around the base of the hill. New roads were laid out and building design followed strict codes over form and materials introduced from Holland. This gave rise to an overall uniformity of scale and texture, with urban designs incorporating climatically friendly solutions through wide overhangs and deep verandahs.

The Dutch Reformed Church quickly destroyed all Catholic symbols, apart from the hill-top church which was re-christened St Paul's, and a new church was completed in 1763 next to the Stadthuys — Christ Church. The expanding township was built around these existing landmark structures. In time the pattern of trade changed with the port serving traders from Arabia, India and Java. Wars in Europe between neighbouring countries temporarily reduced the Dutch trading influence in the Malay Archipelago, and the occupation of the Netherlands by France in 1795 paved the way for "temporary" occupation of Malacca by the British, who nine years earlier had acquired nearby

THE CENTRAL SQUARE in Malacca, bounded by Riverside and Church Street, forms the historic focus of the town at the foot of St Paul's Hill. Its buildings reflect the history of Malacca from the sixteenth century. The Sultanate constructed mosques and palaces on the hill slopes, the Portuguese their fortress and churches, the Dutch their administration offices, and the British their trading houses and banks. Successive foreign regimes brought new allegiances, maritime connections and organisational networks, which encouraged urban growth alongside the river and around the hill. British occupation saw the addition of the Queen Victoria Memorial Fountain overlooked by surrounding government buildings. Plaques in the Square celebrate the Diamond Jubilee of Queen Victoria in 1897, and the visit of the Marquis of Dalhousie, Governor General of British India in 1850. By the end of the nineteenth century Riverside — now Jalan Merdeka and Jalan Lansamana — was the premier commercial and trading street with premises housing the principal merchants, and prominent department stores selling European goods.

The current form of the square began to take shape after the successful Dutch siege of the city. The established network of local streets remained but the overall urban design increasingly acquired the restrained characteristics associated with Dutch Calvanism. Street names were changed and planning controls introduced over building lines, architectural form and materials, which established a strong sense of uniformity Afonso de Albuquerque conquered Melaka in 1511 and started construction of the fortress in 1512, fending off attacks from the armies of the Sultan of Melaka and Acheh for over a century. Slave labour was used to construct the fort with walls three metres wide using parts from demolished palaces, royal mausoleums and mosques. The Portuguese fortress A Famosa and the church Anunciada, were the first in an Eastern city to be built in a European style, with streets, squares and public buildings along the lines of Western city building. A Famosa enclosed the entire European settlement, two palaces, the Portuguese Council of State and five churches. The Dutch contributed a moat around the fortress, with protective ramparts. This included a vocabulary of building elements such as pedimented arches and classical columns. A significant aspect of Portuguese intervention was their import of crops and animals from the Americas, leading to new forms of cultivation. The fort was almost obliterated by the British, under the Resident William Farquhar, but Sir Stamford Raffles intervened. The remnants, including the main gateway Porta de Santiago, were gazetted as a historical monument in 1977.

Penang with its protected harbour. A decision was made to transfer the Malaccan trading base to Penang, and in 1807 the garrison was withdrawn and demolition commenced on the fort. Only the intervention of Stamford Raffles, at the time a senior member of the British East India Company, saved many of the city structures but not the fort, which only remains as a single gateway — the *Porta de Santiago*.

In 1824 the British exchanged Benkulu in Sumatra for Malacca, allowing the Dutch to consolidate their hold on the Indonesian Archipelago, while Britain was able to include Malacca as part of the burgeoning Straits Settlements and so effect complete control over trade in the region. Little investment was made in the city, although it continued to serve as an administrative centre through adaptation of older Dutch public buildings set around the Queen Victoria Memorial Fountain.

British rule brought only minor changes to the spatial framework — existing Dutch buildings were adapted for government and administration purposes. Reclamation along

the foreshore was carried out in the early twentieth century, with a new esplanade to the east of St Paul's Hill which formed a focus for British ceremonial rituals. It was adapted in the 1930s to form a large public space — the *padang*. Until the new shoreline was created through reclamation, Fort Road — along which there are now a series of museums converted from old Dutch buildings — formed an esplanade set against the older Portuguese ruins on the hillside. The area around the hill remained as the civic centre, with the Residency at the top.

The French were responsible for the largest structure built during this period — the Church of St Francis Xavier, built to celebrate the 300th anniversary of his arrival in Malacca, on the site of the monastery of São Domingos founded by the Portuguese.

By the turn of the twentieth century rubber plantations brought new wealth to Malacca, which introduced a new phase of commercial building for banks and rubber companies. Exports began to focus again on direct European trade rather than transhipments through Singapore.

Following the Japanese Occupation between 1942 and 1945, and the new Federation of Malay States, *Merdeka* was proclaimed on the Padang in 1956. The administrative centre remained on St Paul's Hill, but the seat of government was later moved to Ayer Keroh and Malacca's townscape in the vicinity of its historic core became reconfigured through new commercial development. Conservation legislation was put into effect in 1988 for the historic centre, and it was declared a Historic City by the Federal government ten years later.

Malacca's UNESCO World Heritage status, shared with Penang, has increased its attraction to visitors. However this needs to convey a message of both cultural conservation and controlled revitalisation. A large sign in the historic centre announces the new heritage designation to visiting tourists, but it is clear that the older fabric cannot suitably contain the accompanying commercial demands. This is seemingly reflected in a lack of adequate planning control over new development and a mix of renovations and conversions, some of which

are extremely well designed while others are inappropriate. While there exists a legal framework for heritage protection, planning and development controls are insufficiently responsive, with little monitoring of building conversion works, some of which compromise authenticity. There is no evident form of traffic management, which leaves the older streets with narrow pavements vulnerable to constant vehicular intrusion. Recent and ill-considered reclamation has severed the historical link between the town and the sea, and has brought with it new development, out of scale and keeping with the old city and disfiguring the waterfront with unsympathetic commercial uses. It has also had damaging effects on its ecology and the marine environment in the Tranquerah and the Banda Hilir area. Much of the intangible heritage associated with the waterfront cocoa and palm plantations, housing compounds, the official residence of the Dutch Governor, and the religious missions and convents of the nineteenth century have disappeared, and older communities moved to the periphery of the city.

Chinese temple on Heeren Street (Jalan Tun Tan Cheng Lok)

BLACKSMITH STREET (JALAN TUKANG BESI)

Tukang Emas and Temple Street (Jalan Tukang) form a linked spine through the old town dating from the fifteenth century, joining together old established communities with trades, temples and opium dens. Under the Dutch they were dominated by Indian goldsmiths, but the present mixed use fabric encompasses a legacy of constant adjustment to changing events. Blacksmiths were operated by Chinese in the nineteenth century to cater for bullock carts.

The Cheng Hoon Teng 'Green Cloud' Temple is the oldest in Malaysia, supposedly built by an immigrant fleeing the Manchurian invasion of China in 1645. It is dedicated to three deities, and contains an inscription commemorating the visit of an imperial envoy in 1406. The altar is dedicated to the Goddess of the Sea, reflecting the seafaring nature of the old community. The temple also functioned as a Chinese Magistrate's Court and administered local affairs.

HEEREN STREET (JALAN TUN TAN CHENG LOK)

The seafront area to the west of Malacca served as a residential enclave for wealthy merchants dating back to the Sultanate, many of them Hindu natives from the Coramandel Coast. However the first street construction was carried out by the Dutch, who formed *Heeren Street* or "Gentleman's Street" along the coastline of Campon Chelin, which housed the town's Dutch merchant class. Few of these brick and timber structures remain, but the essential morphology based on a long narrow plan form and central court was the result of taxes imposed according to the width of building frontage.

The transition to a predominantly Chinese community stems from the local-born *Peranakan China*, or baba nyonya, who gradually acquired control of the growing Straits trade and took over many of the Dutch merchant houses. By the end of the nineteenth century Heeren Street was almost exclusively Chinese with individual two-storey houses richly adorned with traditional wall decorations, exquisite tiling and ornamentation, but often bearing the imprint of Western influence and Victorian furniture. The pivotal role played by Straits Chinese in economic and commercial development is reflected in the renovated and upgraded condition of hotels, antique shops and a heritage centre. Others have suffered destructive conversion, and have occasionally been given over to the breeding of swiftlets for suppliers of bird's nest soup.

JONKER STREET (JALAN HANG JEBAT)

Banda Malacca grew as a dense settlement during the Portuguese period, linked to the town core by a bridge across the Malacca River. In time it became the town's main thoroughfare, and was named Jonker Street by the Dutch, linked by a drawbridge to facilitate a tax on ships entering the river. The Dutch introduced building regulations aimed

A temporary 'gateway' off Jalan Hang Jebat forms a boisterous intervention that underscores the tourist and visitor focus of 'Jonker Walk' associated with UNECSO World Heritage designation, thereby repackaging the older fabric for mass consumption.

at ensuring permanent construction with prescribed materials and standard sizes for brick and tiles.

The street had a traditionally mixed population, and the transition to British rule saw the majority of properties taken over by Chinese merchants and transformed by more flamboyant frontages. Houses were redefined as shophouses with a variety of commercial uses at ground level, and inhabited by Hokkien, Hainanese and Cantonese clan associations. Jonker Street contains a wide mix of trades within its deep terraces including apothecaries, acupuncture clinics and coffin makers, interspersed with antique shops, and tourist bric a brac. The Thian Teck Kong temple still exists on the street, dedicated to *Xian Shi Yeh*. Other early twentieth century uses include a theatre, a Malay opera company, a Eurasian club and some of Malacca's most exclusive shops. Many of the older Straits Chinese families suffered casualties or were otherwise depleted during the Japanese occupation, and the economic base gradually changed to provision shops and service trades. While a number of shops have been preserved and their internal fittings renovated, others have been degraded by structural decay or conversions that misrepresent the UNESCO sanctioned fabric.

THE CROSS STREETS

The main east-west streets are connected by a series of "cross streets" that acquired their names as Citizen's Streets during the Dutch occupation. The streets were accorded first, second and third designation according to their distance from the Malacca River. First Citizen Street was occupied by Chinese merchants and furniture dealers. They could receive and transport goods from the waterway, and had storehouses immediately to the rear of the shophouses for sago and tapioca. Offices for the new plantation industries lined the street during the British period, and in 1924 the Straits Steamship Company opened an office there. An Indian trade in cotton textiles dates back to the Malacca Sultanate, but by the 1920s a demand for investment capital in the expanding rubber trade led to a new money lending industry by the Chettier Tamils from South India. Descendants of the first Chettier continue to operate from the ground floor of townhouses built in the early twentieth century when the area became known as Kampung Keling.

The Chinese ascendancy over the Muslim community in Malacca came with the arrival of Europeans, and the attempts by Portugal to establish a trading relationship with China.

FOLLOWING THE DUTCH SIEGE of the city, Jonker Street and Heeren Street acquired the name 'Dutch Village', and all residents had to rebuild old attap houses with clay brick construction and Portuguese roofing tiles. The transition to British rule in 1825 and the growth in Chinese clan associations changed the nature of the street. Clan houses or huay kuan represented Hokkien, Hakka, Cantonese and Hainanese communities, all of whom had different types of skills and kinship patterns. The Thian Teck Kong temple built in 1884 and dedicated to Xian Shi Yeh still serves the local community. The street later became a centre for the city's Eurasian community and the location of exclusive stores and showrooms. Damage wrought by the Japanese occupation and the abandonment of properties by Chinese made way for more utilitarian uses, but much of the traditional fabric was preserved. The 'Jonker Walk', introduced in 2000 has depleted much of the old residential and commercial community, replaced by tourist shops and a weekend night market.

UPGRADED WALKWAYS along the Malacca River and Quayside frame St Francis Xavier's Church from Jalan K G Pantai. The Malacca River was the setting for port works under the Sultanate during the fifteenth and sixteenth centuries, and are located at the narrowest point of the Straits and offering the advantage of changing monsoon winds. Four harbourmasters were responsible for the welfare of foreign traders, and at its peak 200 ships docked in the river, serving traders from Arabia, Persia, India, China, Ryuku, the Philippines and Thailand.

Through Chinese masons and carpenters, the Chinese made an active contribution to the building of Malacca under the Dutch. In the Second Cross Street area, which began to be known as Kampung China, the shophouses incorporated both indigenous elements and Dutch features such as gemel windows. The roofscape became embellished with expressive gable ends symbolic of celestial influences, while temples were inserted within the street fabric. Despite losing its population to Singapore after 1828, the Chinese quarter expanded through immigration from China.

Third and Fourth Cross Streets interconnect with the major north-south thoroughfares and were laid out under the Portuguese and Dutch administrations with shallow plots for small traders. From the mid-eighteenth century these streets began to form an expansion area to Kampung China. The area still houses traditional trades such as goldsmiths and silversmiths, Chinese cultural institutions including the Chinese Literary Association, and the Leong San Thong which was established in 1895 with a ceremonial hall that is still used by members. However during the Dutch and British occupation most poor immigrants in the 1800s lived in "Coolie Lines". Kampung Kuli took its Malacca name from the old established Coolie trade. Some of terraced houses on this street date back to the

seventeenth century, when width, height and positioning of fenestration were regulated. Verandahs face the street and internal airwells provide light and ventilation.

Kampung Pantai, on the northern edge of the old town, was the commercial retail centre. During the eighteenth century it was known as Main Fisherman's Street as many of its Malay residents were seamen. During the next century the Chinese community expanded to encompass the area, changing its mercantile character to the trading of wholesale food goods unloaded as cargo into the backs of godowns lining the river. Gradual reconstruction transformed the street frontage from the 1930s. The street façade now represents an eclectic mix of commercial interventions reflecting shifting economic patterns. Sections of the street morphology date back 500 years to the *Tranqueira* — the defensive palisade constructed by the Portuguese. When this was reconfigured by the Dutch, the streets were widened and the town grew outside the old limits. Kubu Road, which marks the limit of the old town, is derived from the Malay word for stockade, given to it by the British. Tranquerah Road follows the line of the defensive wall, paid for by the local merchants to link the town with Kampung Pantai and other areas along the coast.

BY THE LATE EIGHTEENTH CENTURY a number of properties had been transferred from Dutch to Chinese merchant ownership. The new owners employed Chinese artisans and craftsmen to regenerate the older two and three storey properties, with layers of more flamboyant intervention. A typical Peranakan house on Heeren Street blends Chinese with European Baroque, Dutch features and Palladian references. Modifications transformed the austere Dutch terraces with Chinese motifs representing the new cultural uses. Houses exuded variety through painting and ornamentation. Their the narrow width suited the refined social conventions of the Baba Nonya representing the Straits Chinese descendants of the first immigrants from China, while the central courtyard formed a suitable space for an altar. By the early twentieth century, more European influences began to be introduced, reflecting increased British influence in education, civic and social affairs. Decorative devices included Victorian and Art Nouveau floor and wall tiles that still form an evocative frontage on many of the houses, while Western furniture and paintings were combined with traditional Chinese interiors. Some of the older houses have been converted to small hotels that have resurrected and conserved these fittings.

IMAGE © 2014 CNES / ASTRIUM, DIGITALGLOBE; MAP DATA © 2014 GOOGLE

George Town

PENANG • MALAYSIA

THE GRID OF STREETS that forms the heart of George Town was laid out in the late eighteenth century, and reflected the ethnic make-up of the population with streets allocated to different groups on the basis of ethnicity and kinship. After the granting of British colonial status the urban design therefore evolved through overlapping domains but with an increasing European influence, coinciding with new building ordinances which had a significant impact on urban layouts. The George Town Dispensary designed by Swan and McLaren in 1923 is at the junction of China Street Ghaut and Beach Street. The Customs Building in the background fronting Weld Quay forms part of an ensemble of trading and commercial buildings built in the early twentieth century. The Malayan Railway Building, Wisma Kastam, was originally built as administrative offices for the Railway in 1907. Passengers bought train tickets and then boarded a Railway Ferry Steamer to Butterworth where the trains are still stationed. The distinctive clocktower formed a symbolic landmark associated with both arrival and departure.

THE ENGLISH EAST INDIA COMPANY

was incorporated by royal charter in 1600 with the intention of exploiting the East Indian spice trade. Within 150 years it virtually became an imperial power in its own right, before the British Parliament created a government controlled body and took away the Company's monopoly in 1813, after which it functioned as a government agency until 1873. Penang therefore became an example of 'colony creation' under the auspices of the East India Company rather than a conquered territory.

It is said that the first Westerner to visit Penang was Captain James Lancaster in 1593. By 1613, the network of English trading posts extended from Surat on the Coramandel coast of India through Southeast Asia to Japan. In 1623 the English East India Company concentrated its operations on the Indian sub-continent where it competed aggressively against the Dutch. At the end of the seventeenth century, the company's interest in the Malay Peninsula was aroused by the production of tin as a commodity, and they began to seek a base on the eastern edge of the Bay of Bengal, both as part of a new trading network with China, and as a strategic move to control emerging east-west trading routes. The Company was reliant to a great extent on independent merchant captains operating out of Madras or Bengal, who by this time were leading the thriving opium trade with China.

By the late eighteenth century the Company needed a base in the Straits which could be used to replenish its ships during long voyages carrying tea and opium between India and China. In 1785 the Sultan of Kedah allowed the company to establish a settlement on the island of Penang in exchange for trading rights and the East India Company representative Francis Light claimed Penang and its existing population of several thousand people as a British settlement. In 1786, it was named 'Prince of Wales Island' to

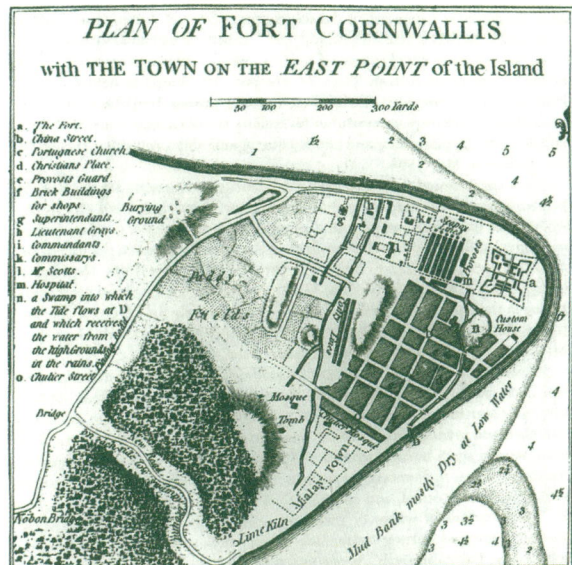

Fort Cornwallis, Penang, 1798

The original Government House, built in 1804 by convict labour, now stands in the grounds of the Convent Light Street, in its original condition. After the death of Penang's founder Francis Light it was leased to the East India Company and housed the Governor's Office and Council Chambers.

honour the Prince Regent, and was envisaged as a free port in Southeast Asia with the intention of linking it with the Indian export trade from Madras, Bengal and Bombay. The British, who arrived from India, brought with them *sepoys* and merchants, contributing to the wide ethnic mix that still prevails. This marks a break between previous European trading ideals and the new era of commercial transformation that was given even greater emphasis in Singapore after 1819.[1]

In practice Penang flourished only briefly as an entrepôt for the China trade. The settlement quickly attracted indigenous Malay, Chinese and Indians from Kedah, and the simplicity of the early settlement had much to do with the Company's insistence that it be self-supporting, with a need to raise revenue from land. The artisan and retail trade was in the hands of the Chinese, but Penang developed into a centre for local trade with the Indonesia archipelago and Bengal, rather than international trading links. In 1800 the colony was enlarged through the cessation of land by the Sultan of Kedah to form a buffer with the mainland, and named Province Wellesley after the Governor–General of India. The British seizure of Malacca and a subsequent invasion of Java made the colony a strategic holding with a new fort and shipyards. However the neutralization of French and Dutch naval threats after 1807, and Britain's command of the Indian Ocean, together with the better placed commercial base in Singapore after 1819, led to Penang's decline as a trading centre. After 1832 Singapore replaced Penang as the capital of the Straits Settlements, but in

THE PADANG, which now forms a green link between Fort Cornwallis and City Hall, was originally used for military functions while the adjoining Esplanade became the focus for waterfront flaneurs. The Town Hall on Jalan Padang Kota Lama was built in 1883 as more of a social than administrative facility, having a ballroom and library as well as an assembly hall. The adjacent and more extravagant City Hall was built in 1906. Other buildings along the edge of the Padang were primarily for sports and recreation, and were destroyed during the Second World War.

The Victoria Clocktower completed in 1902 in King Edward Place commemorates Queen Victoria's Diamond Jubilee — its height of 60 feet corresponds to the years of her reign.

[1] McPherson, K, 'Penang 1786-1832: A Province Unfulfilled', in *Gateways of Asia – Port Cities in the 13th – 20th Centuries*, Ed. Frank Broeze, Kegan Paul International, London, 1997

the late nineteenth century it grew as a sub-regional entrepôt and port, servicing colonial Malaysia. Tin became an important item of regional trade, followed by rubber in the early twentieth century.

George Town is situated on the north-eastern point of Penang Island. As part of Malaysia but one of the oldest 'European' fresh water anchorages and settlements in Asia, George Town holds a special place in Malaysian cultural history through its foreign influences and connections along early Chinese trading routes. Its strategic location attracted settlers from Southeast Asia — southern China, Java, Sumatra, the Celebes, Thailand, Burma and Malaya, but also from further-flung places such as Arabia and Armenia, together with adventurers from Portugal, Holland and Britain. Indian Muslims and Hindu spice traders from the Malabar coast were some of the first settlers. Muslims formed marriages with local inhabitants establishing the *Jawi Peranakan* or Straits-Muslim community. Similarly the offspring of Malay and Chinese marriages produced the *Baba Nonya* or Straits-born community. These people are virtually unique to Penang, with a set of beliefs that mixes Taoist philosophy with Confucianism and Buddhism, and a characteristic dialect that combines Hokkien Chinese, English and Northern Malay. It is said that the Chinese community was divided between the *lao keh* (the Baba Nonya who adopted the local Malay culture), and the *sin keh* who eventually returned to China. Indian merchants included Gujaratis, Bengalis and Parsees. They consolidated the strong East and North India trading connections, and after the arrival of businessmen from the East India Company, Sikhs were brought in as a rudimentary police force. New cultural identities developed with linguistic trajectories that combined strands from these many origins, including small European and Eurasian communities, and early kampung settlements, which were

IN THE NINETEENTH CENTURY WELD QUAY was one of the most vibrant waterfronts in Asia. Land reclamation culminated in the building of Swettenham Pier in 1904, which turned Penang into a transhipment centre, now catering for large passenger boats. Its old role is being revived, and abandoned old buildings are being converted into hotels. The "clan jetties" off Weld Quay represent old Chinese villages which extended over the water on stilts, and in the nineteenth century fuelled Penang's maritime trade. Of these, six are associated with the Lim, Chew, Tan, Yeoh, Lee and Koay clans, and reflect the old established cultural identity of the island, although the Koay jetty was redeveloped in 2005. The jetties incorporate local temples, timber homesteads, places for Peranakan and Chinese opera performances, as well as moorings for fishing boats and supply vessels, offering a complete contrast to the eastern waterfront edge of the city.

developed largely along ethnic lines. The Portuguese Eurasian community gathered in Penang after the Phya Tak massacre of Catholics in 1810 and established a settlement in Pulau Tikus, now known as *Kampong Serani*, or Eurasian Village. The first Armenian Jews came to Penang in 1802 from the Caucasian Mountains. Their trading role played a major part in the growth of Penang, and prominent families include the Sarkies brothers who established the Eastern and Oriental Hotel in George Town, and Raffles Hotel in Singapore. Several streets are named after Armenian families, such as Aratoon Road.

The urban geography of George Town therefore evolved around a compact assembly of kampongs, merchant enterprises and trading guilds, interspersed with mosques and temples, and grew rapidly through immigration and indentured labour. With the Treaty of Nanking in 1842 opening up a number of Chinese ports for trade with Britain, Penang began to operate as a free port, being a transit point for the transhipment of opium from India to China. It went on to develop a considerable spice trade from European plantations and processing facilities on the island which, together with the tin mines, attracted Hokkien Chinese labourers from Fujian and Canton. The Taiping rebellion in 1853 was followed by further waves of immigrants

At the junction of Church Street and King Street is a collection of clan associations and temples — Wu Ti Meow is the temple of the Toi San association. The Ng See Kah Meow clan association in the foreground incorporates a two-storey house. Toi San Nin Yong Hui Kwon and Wu Ti Meow Temple is dedicated to Kwan Kong, the patron deity of the Toi San Cantonese Association. The calligraphy was written by Leong Ting Fen, tutor to Pu Yi — the last emperor of China. The buildings are constructed in a Cantonese style with distinctive "horse head" gables.

BEACH STREET extended along the coast from Fort Cornwallis to Chulia Street, before new reclamation in the 1880s. It evolved as part of the port, and became the centre for European trading houses, banks, Chinese commercial shophouses and Chettiar moneylenders. Different names were given to various sections of the street signifying this diversity. The northern end of Beach Street represents the financial district with a range of European commercial, shipping and insurance company buildings constructed in the late nineteenth and early twentieth centuries.

Offices were generally constructed on upper floors with shops and stores on the ground floor. The central section of the street housed Chinese wholesalers, and the southern section was predominantly shops, trading establishments and clan temples. The two nineteenth century banking giants in the Straits were the Hong Kong & Shanghai Banking Corporation, and the Standard Chartered Bank which in 1875 occupied a site on Beach Street. The latter was redeveloped in the 1930s, and the building renovated in 1992 to its current Italianate classical design.

from China, introducing extended clan relationships, including triad "brotherhoods" who controlled different trading, plantation and mining sectors.

The replacement of sailing ships by steamships and the opening of the Suez Canal in 1869 increased the importance of George Town's harbour, which had to build long wharves to cater for a massive increase in world demand for tin and rubber. The entrepôt trade through Penang attracted immigrants from neighbouring Kedah to the east and Thailand to the north, along with Chinese from the mining communities of Taiping and Ipoh in Perak. After the First World War the development of mining and plantations also attracted increasing numbers

of Japanese traders. The elaborate shophouse terraces and suburban mansions still bear witness to the burgeoning urban economic status of the city during this period.

Continuing urbanisation reflected the localised identity of ethnicity and kinship. Particular streets were broadly associated with different communities and sub-sets of these, each with identifiable religious buildings, sacred places, clan houses and chambers of commerce that established an astonishing variety of imported urban forms from both East and West, leading to an intertwining of styles. This reflected similar habits within the wider population, with partnerships between etic groups. Therefore while urban space might have been contested,

over the years it laid down a unique cultural legacy.

The initial grid of streets was laid out in the late eighteenth century — Light Street (Lebuh Light), Pitt Street (Jalan Masjid Kapitan Keling), Chulia Street (Lebuh Chulia) and Beach Street (Lebuh Pantai). While specific locations were allocated to Chinese, Indian Muslims, Eurasians and Malays, there was no formal segregation. By the early nineteenth century the town was extended by Armenian Street and Acheen Street. As the town layout spread over the next century, the inner area of George Town was intensely developed with shophouses, although these were largely redeveloped or revitalised with new frontages during the early twentieth

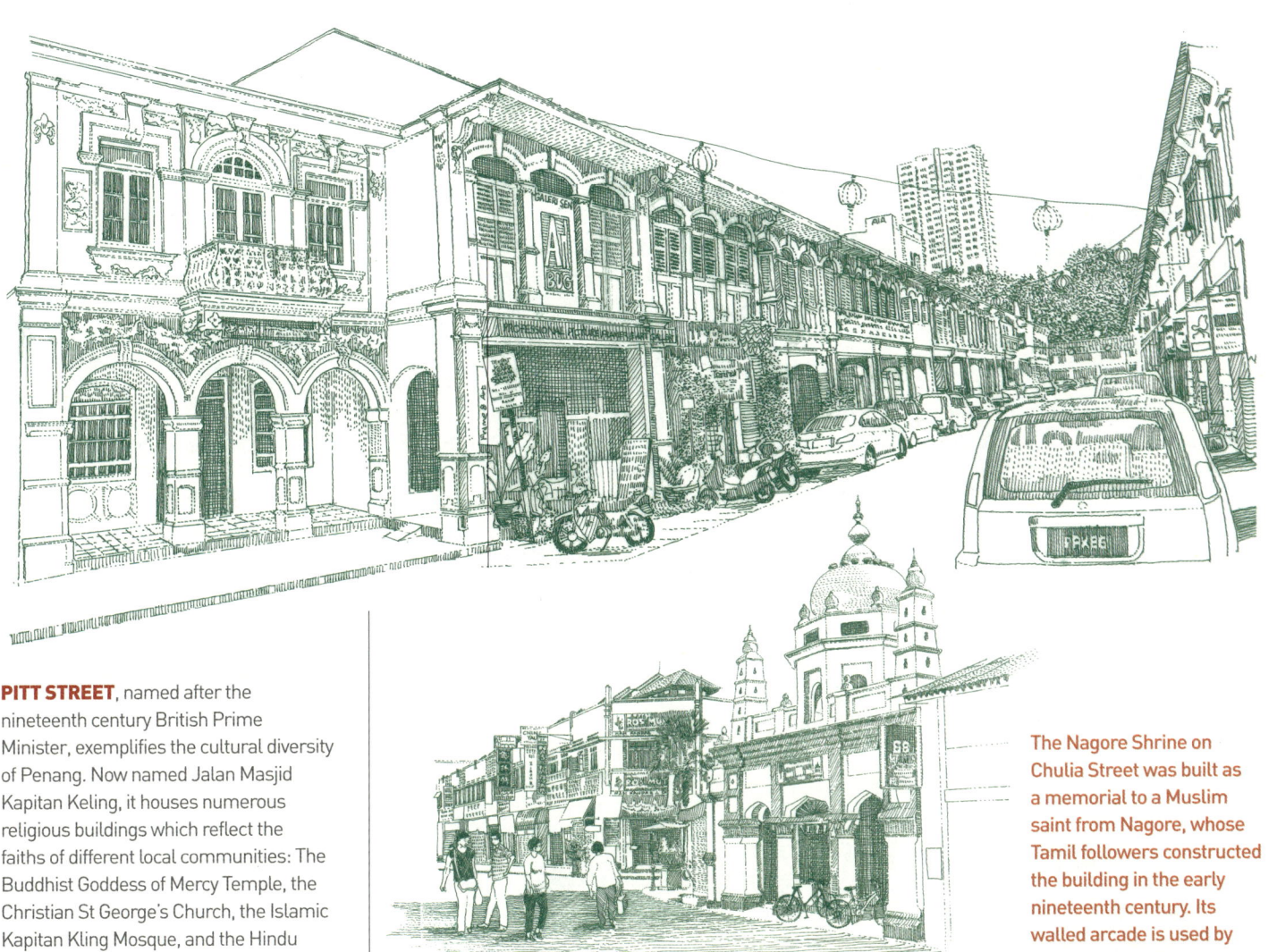

PITT STREET, named after the nineteenth century British Prime Minister, exemplifies the cultural diversity of Penang. Now named Jalan Masjid Kapitan Keling, it houses numerous religious buildings which reflect the faiths of different local communities: The Buddhist Goddess of Mercy Temple, the Christian St George's Church, the Islamic Kapitan Kling Mosque, and the Hindu Mahamariamman Temple.

The Nagore Shrine on Chulia Street was built as a memorial to a Muslim saint from Nagore, whose Tamil followers constructed the building in the early nineteenth century. Its walled arcade is used by makers of Muslim garments.

century, when new residential terraces and extensive suburbs were built, and Weld Quay was reclaimed.

The shophouse typology dominates the historic core of George Town, and underscores the urban design of its compact street system and mercantile community. The shophouse widths vary between 4.5 and 6.0 metres and establish a rhythm of overall consistency and likeness, but with an underlying pattern of variety and difference established through fenestration elements, plaster decorations and carved framing elements and columns. The Penang shophouse personifies its inherited cultural and ethnic mix with its combination of Chinese, European, Malay and Indian construction and decorative elements. These are interwoven with neighourhoods that are still identified with Chinese and Hindu temples, mosques and churches, and where street names conjure up the specialised trading activities of the nineteenth century.

The early architectural typology evolved through the advent of masonry construction and imported Chinese and Indian artisans. Many of the early nineteenth century brick and terracotta tile shophouse structures, which established the neighbourhood patterns and the trading framework of George Town, still exist. These retain an iconography of Anglo-Indian details, Chinese decorative devices and examples of South Indian architectural references evident in the local mosques and shrines. Cantonese and Hokkien craftsmen helped to promote stylistic renovations while establishing building traditions stemming from the mix of influences and cultures. This formed the basis of an informal "Straits Eclectic" architecture that combined a vernacular of ceramic and stucco decoration with classical Palladian façade elements. Other devices included louvred window openings, Georgian-style fanlights, and hip-and-gable roofs, which at best combined to form elegant and climatically appropriate styles. During the early twentieth century, owners built taller shophouses, which increased the potential for further embellishment such as structural pilasters and ceramic decorations.

Lebuh King

LEBUH ACHEH, to the south of the grid of streets laid out by Francis Light, housed early Arab settlers. It was originally called Malay Lane after the original Malay Kampong in the area. The settlement reflected the longstanding trading ties with Aceh in Sumatra, the centre of the spice trade, which was dominated by Arab and Indian Muslim traders. Islam spread rapidly through the archipelago in the eighteenth century, and one of the most influential traders, Tengku Syed Hussian Al-Aidid, settled in Penang in 1792, founding the mosque on Acheen Street. The mosque with its octagonal profile and distinctive minaret together with early half-timbered shophouses that accommodated Muslim families as part of an urban compound still survive as an example of nineteenth century Indo-Malay architecture. The street is also known as Pak Cheok Kay or Stone Worker's Street, after the Chinese stoneworkers who carved elaborate gravestones for the nearby cemetery.

The relationship of Lebuh Acheh Street with Lebuh Armenian reflects an intersection of cultures. The Armenian community, whose members included the Sarkies family, founders of the Eastern and Oriental Hotel, originally settled in the area. Many later emigrated to Singapore and the area was taken over by the prominent Straits Chinese clans. The result is a mingling of religious buildings, including St Gregory's Church built in 1822, the old Hokkien Tua Pek Kong Temple to the left and the modern, highly decorated Yap temple on the right. The Tua Pak Kong Temple dedicated to the God of Prosperity has a narrow access portal through a line of shophouses, concealing the inner temple which housed the Khian Teik secret society in the nineteenth century. The elaborate Leung San Tong Khoo Kongsi on Lebuh Acheh was designed for the dual function of ancestral temple and stage set for Chinese opera.

LEBUH KING HOUSES a number of old Hakka, Hokkien and Cantonese Clan buildings and temples. Its Tamil name is the 'Street of Boatmen' emphasising its link with port-related trades associated with the quays. In the foreground is the Lee Sih Chong Soo Association representing Hokkien descendants of Lao Tzu, and incorporating a small temple.

2   Jenkins, G, *Contested Space – Cultural Heritage and Identity Reconstructions*, Transaction Publishers, New Jersey, 1997, p46

3   Jenkins, 1997, op. cit., p47

4   Fels, P.T., 'Conserving the Shophouse City', presented at The Penang Story International Conference organised by the Penang Heritage Trust, April 18-21, 2002

5   Jenkins, 1997, op. cit., p54

NORTHAM ROAD lay to the west of the nineteenth century town limits, demarcated by the Protestant cemetery, resting place of many of the settlement's founders and members of the East India Company. Bungalow development created an elite residential suburb and over time, mansions along with extensive grounds belonging to some of Asia's wealthiest facilities, were built overlooking North Beach. As houses became increasingly ostentatious, the tree-lined road became known as European Road or Ang Mo Lor. These included Woodville belonging to Kim Lean Teng, a tea planter, who built a mansion in 1925 designed by the architect Charles Miller with a dome inspired by the HSBC bank building on Beach Road. Many of the houses were abandoned during the Depression of the 1930s and only a few remain, some of the old sites being redeveloped for high-rise blocks along what is now a busy traffic corridor.

Gwynn Jenkins's account of George Town's urban history suggests a periodic succession of design influences: from building techniques developed by master craftsmen where traditional forms addressing established cultural values and climatic considerations were constantly adapted, to the introduction of new forms redolent of Western precedents.[2] The rich urban design tapestry was reflected in a range of building materials, from locally available timber and brick, to the locally quarried granite used for foundations and for 'edging' along the five-foot ways. Terracotta tiles on the floors, lime plaster on the walls and unglazed roof tiles allowed moisture to evaporate which acted as a coolant, while local bricks used for houses and temples were supplemented by those shipped from Malacca after the destruction of the Portuguese and Dutch fortifications.[3] Louvred shutters for doors and windows began to be elaborately carved along with balustrades, contributing to an often sophisticated fusion of elements and cultural overlaps, with builders and craftsmen combining a range of indigenous trace elements and decorative devices.

A mix of design interventions and cultural adaptations came to represent the tangible character of George Town itself, with the gradual evolution of an authentic Indo-Malay style, which was adapted by other ethnic groups and reflected the use of more permanent materials. Two of the most evocative building types were the Indo-Malay houses with their integrative Asian appendages, and the Anglo-Indian bungalows built by the British and Straits Muslims.

The predominant urban form was the emergence of the shophouse streets that evolved in concert with those in Singapore and Malacca, and served a variety of purposes. These were usually built of brick, either back-to-back, or divided by a narrow lane. In combination, the grid matrix of terraces formed a highly workable living and working environment with a strong and identifiable sense of community. Roofs and façades of each house were independent, so they could be fashioned in slightly different ways while conforming to the framework of the ensemble as a whole. The characteristic two and three storey frontage was defined along

its street edge by a *kaki-lima* or continuous open colonnade, regulated under a Buildings Ordinance of 1887, while open courtyards were situated at the rear, which served the various purposes of natural ventilation, rainwater collection and cooling.[4]

While the first shophouses were relatively narrow in depth, later Chinese models incorporated internal courtyards which helped ventilate the interiors, and were orchestrated to exploit the *feng shui* flow of *chi*. Party walls rise above the roof pitch with shaped gables expressive of the five natural *Wu Xing* elements: square for earth (Tu); pointed for five (Huo); curved for water (shui); straight for wood (Mu); and round for metal (Jin).

The interplay of cultures also fuelled a mix of local and European influences after the granting of colonial status. Jenkins states that encaustic floor tiles produced in England replaced local terracotta tiles; British foundries produced cast iron filigree work and catalogues for overseas markets; and glass was used for the first time to replace louvres.[5] Urban housing began to take on elements of British, Indian and Chinese design in both form and façade, notably the introduction of the tripartite shuttered openings defined by decorative pilasters and arched fanlights. These features were introduced into Singapore's shophouse architecture at virtually the same time. Mansions were built by wealthy merchants in an eclectic late Victorian style incorporating neo-Classical details and ornamental devices from a multitude of cultural sources. Cast-iron columns, stained glass, carved timberwork and European ceramic tiles combined to form distinctive façades behind which were arranged the more traditional layout and hierarchical arrangements of the household. Equally extravagant details and embellishments then found their way into the late shophouse style with their painted friezes, mouldings and classical pilasters.

Bangkok Lane is situated next to the Thai Temple with a large stupa that rises above the local houses. It comprises forty semi-detached villas built in 1928 and designed by Chew Eng Eam, one of the earliest Western-trained architects in Penang.

ESTABLISHED TRADING NETWORKS together with British links with Burma and Penang encouraged southern immigration of Burmese in the late nineteenth century to work on plantations. Siamese from southern Thailand also settled in Penang after the invasion of Kedah. The two cultures shared many characteristics, and there are various Burmese and Thai Buddhist temples such as the Thai Wat Chayamangkalaram and Burmese Dhammikarama in Burmah Lane.

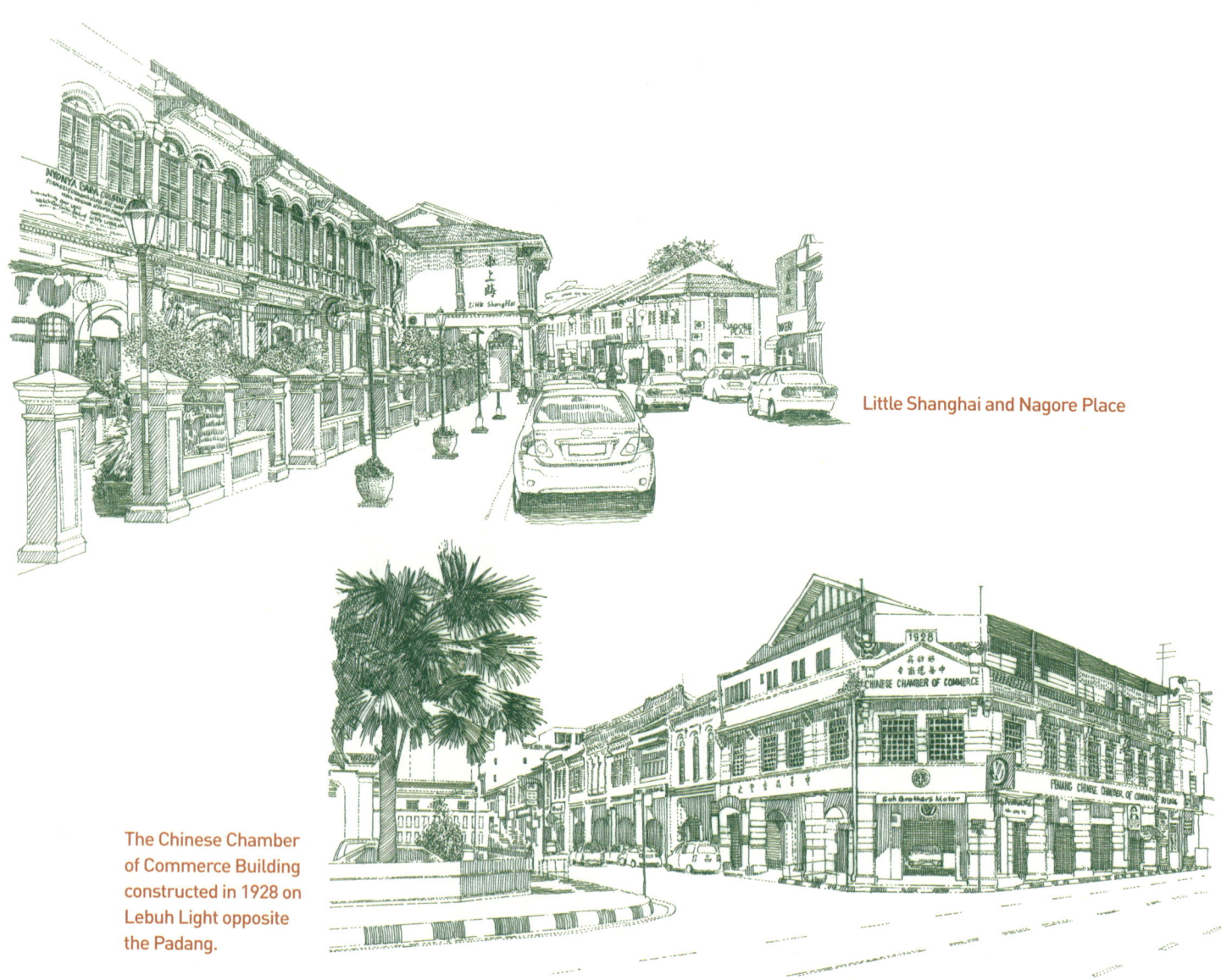

Little Shanghai and Nagore Place

The Chinese Chamber of Commerce Building constructed in 1928 on Lebuh Light opposite the Padang.

Around the turn of the twentieth century, outbreaks of cholera and malaria (largely the result of tight urban massing and overcrowding) led to the introduction of new building and health public ordinances inspired by the British precedents, which had an impact on urban layouts. Wider streets improved access to shophouses allowing better drainage and waste disposal, but also involved the setback of some street terraces which fractured the continuity of the colonnaded frontages.

In George Town, a significant catalyst to change was the relocation of the old port to the Bulk Cargo Terminal in Prai in the face of containerisation. This caused a re-orientation of the associated business and banking sector, related activities and reciprocal trades. However in 1987 in the midst of a buoyant ASEAN economy, draft design guidelines for conservation areas in the inner part of George Town were compiled, along with a Draft Structure Plan which proposed a historical and cultural enclave to include Muslim communities, the Hindu *Chettiar* community, and Chinese temples.

Legal instruments relating to conservation were originally based on the British system of planning and building control, but have been superceded by various Acts, including the National Heritage Act of 2005. This demonstrates a holistic approach to protection, preservation and funding (although with some uncertainties over acquisition), which has had an ongoing impact on development and historic sites in Penang and Malacca.

After Malaysia's independence, the withdrawal of Penang's free-port status marked a steady decline in industrial growth and economic policy. While there has been a marked increase in foreign investment, this has not kept pace with the Klang Valley, or Johor Baru with its proximity to Singapore. However Penang is now the hub of an

Indonesia-Malaysia-Thailand growth triangle, which is inducing higher land values and consequent pressures for urban renewal and ambitious transport planning. Since 1991 there has been a determined conservation agenda, which includes an inventory of heritage buildings. A five-storey limit is now mandatory for new development within the six designated conservation zones. A catalyst for this came in 1998 with the nomination of George Town for UNESCO World Heritage inscription, covering a defined area including the old British colonial administrative quarter. In 2007 the historic centre of Malacca was added to form a joint nomination for historic cities along the Straits of Malacca. This combined George Town's cultural and built heritage with Malacca's Malay past, which represented the beginning of the Malay Sultanate, and its historical interface with foreign powers on the Malay peninsula, and the city where Malay independence was first announced. UNESCO had by this stage recognised that its criteria should move away from a definition of 'heritage' merely as aesthetic authenticity, to an approach that endorsed the notion of an inclusive Malaysia. Their policy also emphasised a clear motivation to introduce social and cultural incentives for preservation, as well as more tangible values. This required that the cities should exhibit an important interface through developments in planning and the architecture of shophouses, townhouses and religious buildings, and that these should reflect the cultural tradition and fusion of styles within an urban ensemble.

The Penang Heritage Trust initiated the Education in Conservation Programme in 1996, in collaboration with the State Education Department to: raise conservation awareness; promote the need for conservation legislation; and design corporate-sponsored Heritage Trails within the inner city. It also has a consultative role in both state and local government processes, and conducts local and international networking.

The Blue Mansion on Leith Street, built by a wealthy Hakka trader and Chinese patriot Cheong Fatt Tze, dates from the late nineteenth century. Its elaborate craftsmanship and porcelain hardwork took seven years to complete. The restored historic house exemplifies the traditional style of Chinese mansion, but with louvred windows which denote Romanesque influence, along with Art Nouveau stained glass panels. The Victorian cast ironwork that defines the central courtyard were manufactured in Scotland.

THE CHUNG KENG KWEE TEMPLE, AND THE ADJOINING PERANAKAN MANSION AND ANCESTRAL HALL built in 1893, form an historic ensemble in Church Street. Chung Keng Kwee led the Hai San secret society in Penang until its prohibition, and in return for his donations to war relief in China he was appointed Mandarin of Second Rank. The Straits Eclectic mansion has a five-foot way along the façade and several sizable courtyards, the largest of which has a central balcony supported by Victorian cast iron columns.

THE KAPITAN KELING MOSQUE was founded in 1801 by Muslim troops from the East India Company, and both building materials and contractors were brought from India. Such a large space was granted to the Muslim community that the Government had to later buy back the majority of land in order to provide local amenities, including the Campbell Street market. The original single storey structure was later enlarged and made more elaborate, and shophouses constructed along the adjoining streets. In the early part of the twentieth century, the Municipal Commission carried out an extensive programme of urban renewal creating new terraced development around the mosque. The mosque has undergone various renovations and extensions including a large Mughal dome, turrets, and a minaret designed by Henry Neubronner. The original buildings, walls and the old minaret have been preserved.

The Hokkien Goddess of Mercy Temple with its ornately decorated copings and ridges is dedicated to Kuan Yin (Goddess of Mercy) and Ma Chor Poh or Tin Hau (Goddess of the Sea), safeguard of sailors. Its adjoining streets cater to the needs of visitors and are lined by mobile stalls selling flowers, joss sticks and cooked food, infusing them with the temple aura. Fortune telling through arcade sticks is a feature of the temple.

Urban revitalisation is thereby achieved through a combination of government and community efforts, which encompass planning, development and cultural issues. A characteristic of George Town is that certain streets are lined with *Ottu Kedai* or lean-to stalls that operate throughout the day-time and evening, flanking the shaded side walls and providing an active counterpart to the adjoining shophouse activities. These have become ingrained within the living fabric of the city, creating both a tangible and an intangible heritage. They also provide social spaces where people meet for breakfast or lunch. Uses change throughout the day and evening — with bicycle hawkers selling Indian delicacies and stall holdings evolving into cooked food establishments in the evening — regenerating the street life.

A fundamental factor in this is that Penang's historic cityscape reveals an underlying dynamic of intervention and change that evolved without a designated planning framework. Ethnically diverse communities became established among sequences of eclectic buildings whose architecture represents a combination of stylistic development, adaptation and invention. While ethnic Chinese make up around 80 per cent of the population of Penang, George Town is also inhabited by traditional inner city communities with different but overlapping domains. Many of the Hindus of the Little India quarter live in Chinese owned shophouses, yet in other areas Muslims and Chinese might rent from Hindu owners, so that cultural affiliations are extended into living and commercial patterns, although security of tenure is not always predictable. Spaces for example are designated for religious and cultural festivals such as the Chinese *Tua Pek Kong* procession, the Hindu *Thaipusan* festival, and the Muslim *Pasar Ramadan*, each situated alongside intricate patterns of trade operations associated with street markets and hawker stalls.

THE MAHAMARIAMMAN TEMPLE on Lebuh Queen was built in 1833 on land granted by the East India Company and is named after the Hindu goddess Mariamman. A statue of the goddess is paraded around the local street during the annual Navarithri Festival, establishing a traditional link between spirituality and 'place'. The temple features a grand entry gate to the street incorporating thirty-eight statues of gods and goddesses. The temple was originally built in 1833 and renovated in 1978. It primarily serves the local community of Hindu shopkeepers who have historical links to Madras.

REFERENCES

References are acknowledged within each of the chapters. I would however like to highlight a number of them that I have drawn on during my programme of research, for their illumination of urban design issues and distinctive insights within particular contexts.

In terms of overall history, Milton Meyers's two-volume *Asia: A Concise History* was a useful and comprehensive reference source. On the socio-cultural side, a number of references provide compelling details on both historical events and cultural relations associated with specific cities. Some of the most incisive of these that I have read with pleasure are: Gwynn Jenkins's *Contested Space: Cultural Heritage and Identity Reconstructions* in relation to the historic streetscapes of Penang, which provides admirable insight into the correlation between cultural identity, ethnicity and patterns of activity; Christina Miu Bing Cheng's *Macau – A Cultural Janus*; Jinnai Hidenobu's *Ethnic Tokyo – A Spatial Anthropology*; Brenda Yeoh's *Contesting Space: Power Relations and the Urban Built Environment in Colonial Singapore*; Jyoti Hosagrahar's *Indigenous Modernities – Negotiating Architecture and Urbanism* in relation to nineteenth century Delhi; *The Politics of Landscapes in Singapore* by Lily Kong and Brenda Yeoh; Donald M Seekins' *State and Society in Modern Rangoon*; Marc Askew's *Bangkok: Place, Practice and Representation*; Tribhuvan Prakash Issar's *Goa Dourada*; Robert Reed's *Colonial Manila*; and Wu Liangyong's *Rehabilitating the Old City of Beijing*.

On the subject of colonial ideology and the shaping of urban environments, several references provide a comprehensive overview of particular situations and contexts, notably: Anthony King's *Colonial Urban Development: Culture, Social Power and Environment;* Robert Home's *Of Planting and Planning*; Bill Ashcroft's *On Post-Colonial Futures: Transformation of Colonial Culture*; Thomas Metcalf's *An Imperial Vision – Indian Architecture and Britain's Raj*; Gwendolyn Wright's *The Politics of Design in French Colonial Urbanism*; and William Glover's *Making Lahore Modern: Construction and Imaging a Colonial City*.

A number of references provide a comprehensive and thoughtful overview of Asian urbanism from a regional perspective. These include: Hans-Dieter Evers and Rudiger Korff's *Southeast Asian Urbanism: The Meaning and Power of Social Space*; *The City in South Asia* by James Heitzman; *Culture and the City in East Asia* edited by Won Bae Kim et al; Peter Rimmer and Howard Dick's *The City in Southeast Asia: Patterns, Processes and Policy*; William Logan's *The Disappearing Asian City*; *Transforming Asian City* edited by Nihal Perera and Wing-Shing Tang; and Terry McGee's *The Southeast Asian City*.

In terms of the spatial transformation processes resulting from globalisation, the most enlightening and comprehensive references are: *Mega-Urban Regions in Pacific Asia* by Gavin Jones and Mike Douglass; *The Mega-Urban Regions of Southeast Asia* edited by Terry McGee and Ira Robinson; and Christopher Silver's *Planning the Megacity*.

Care has been taken to trace and acknowledge all sources, but in some instances this has not been possible. Where omissions have occurred, the author will be pleased to correct them in future editions.

ACKNOWLEDGEMENTS

In working on this book, and during my travels associated with it, I have been the fortunate recipient of help and advice from many sources.

Much of the basic research was carried out at the University of Hong Kong library with its remarkable and extensive resources including archives, and I would like to thank the very helpful and efficient staff. I would similarly like to credit the staff of the library at the School of Oriental and African Studies at University College London, for their kind assistance.

I would like to thank Bernardus Djonoputro, Secretary General of the Indonesian Association of Urban and Regional Planners for his hospitality and help in discussing planning in Jakarta, and for his introduction to various professional planners, including Henri Candi Sianturi and Dhani Muttaqin who guided me around the older Lapangan Banteng, Sunda Kelapa, Kuta, Glodop and Hayam Wuruk areas. Thanks must also go to Nadia Rinandi and Ria Febrian from the Architectural Documentation Centre.

Brian Pai, Secretary General of the Taiwan Institute of Urban Planning was most helpful in arranging meetings with the Department of Urban Development in Taipei, and I would like to extend my thanks to Mr Xu Yan-xing, head of the Urban Redevelopment Department of the Taipei Metropolitan Government.

I received enormous help and support from the Consulate General of Pakistan in Hong Kong. I would particularly like to thank the Consul (P) Mr Ali Nawaz Malik for doing so much to organize my visit to Lahore, where Mr Ehsaan Ullah Shahzaad, the Protocol Officer from the Ministry of Information in Lahore, guided me so effectively to meetings and places. I would also like to thank: Mr Orya Maqboul Jan Abbasi, Secretary of Archives, Government of the Punjab; Mr Muhammad Afzal Khan; Mr Rustam Khan, Assistant Director of the Department of Archaeology and Museums from the directorate General of Archaeology, Government of the Punjab; Muhammad Ali Tirmizi from the National College of Arts; and Azhar Syed, Chairman of the Lahore Chapter of the Institute of Architects.

I would especially like to thank my long-time friends and colleagues at URBIS, Alexander Duggie, Alan Macdonald, Sion Edwards, Craig Doubleday, Tim Osborne and Iris Hoi for their support. In particular I would like to thank my long-time secretary and personal assistant Lily Tam for her invaluable help in typing and co-ordinating manuscript drafts and final contents, and to Ho Fong for her insightful graphic advice and assistance.

My great thanks and appreciation go to Mary Chan from MCCM Creations for nurturing the book along from its embryonic idea to the final product, and to Wing Chan, Catherine Tai, Kaliz Lee and Chip Yip for the many hours of work on the graphic design and layout of the book.

Finally my gratitude to the many people I met along the way in a variety of situations.

THE URBAN DESIGN OF INTERVENTION

— Imposed and Adaptive Places in Asian Cities

Peter Cookson Smith

Published by MCCM Creations 2014
www.mccmcreations.com
http://mccm.wordpress.com
info@mccmcreations.com

English editing	Anna Koor
Editorial assistant	Chan Wing Wa
Cover design	Catherine Tai
Design and artwork	Catherine Tai, Kaliz Lee, Chip Yip

ISBN 978-988-13114-2-9